THE OXFORD IBSEN

Volume I

EARLY PLAYS

THE OXFORD
IBSEN
Volume I

EARLY PLAYS

Edited and translated by

JAMES WALTER McFARLANE

and

GRAHAM ORTON

London

OXFORD UNIVERSITY PRESS

NEW YORK TORONTO

1970

Oxford University Press, Ely House, London W1

GLASGOW NEW YORK TORONTO MELBOURNE WELLINGTON
CAPE TOWN SALISBURY IBADAN NAIROBI DAR ES SALAAM LUSAKA ADDIS ABABA
BOMBAY CALCUTTA MADRAS KARACHI LAHORE DACCA
KUALA LUMPUR SINGAPORE HONG KONG TOKYO

PRINTED IN GREAT BRITAIN

CONTENTS

PREFACE

As in all the other volumes of this edition, the translations here are based on the Norwegian text as printed in the Centenary Edition (*Hundreårsutgave*, 21 vols., 1928–57), edited by Francis Bull, Halvdan Koht, and Didrik Arup Seip, and on those draft manuscripts in Ibsen's own hand which have survived. In terms of bulk, there is not a great deal of this part of the material which is absolutely new to English readers, though up to now it has been rather scattered. *Lady Inger* was translated into English by Charles Archer and published as early as 1890 in *Ibsen's Prose Dramas*, edited by William Archer in five volumes; *The Feast at Solhoug*, translated by William Archer and Mary Morison, was included in the Collected Works edition of 1906 ff.; Anders Orbeck's *Early Plays by Henrik Ibsen* (New York, 1921) included *Catiline*, *The Warrior's Barrow* [here called *The Burial Mound*] and *Olaf Liljekrans*; and Theodore Jorgensen's *In the Mountain Wilderness and other works by Henrik Ibsen* (Northfield, Minn., 1957) contains both *Norma* and *St. John's Night*.

Where there are divergences between the first published edition (or acting version) of a play and the second, the *first* has been taken as the substantive text in the following pages. Previous translations have tended to work from the *second* editions. This means in particular that the earlier versions of *Catiline*, *The Burial Mound*, *Lady Inger*, and *The Feast at Solhoug* are given here in English for the first time. In addition, of course, the second version of *The Burial Mound* is given in its entirety. The fragments of 'The Grouse in Justedal', of 'The Mountain Bird', and of the second opera libretto of *Olaf Liljekrans* are new to English readers, as are also the essays on 'Professor Welhaven on Paludan-Müller's mythological poems' and on 'The Heroic Ballad and its Significance for Literature'.

Much of the more fascinating material in Appendix IV dealing with the part Ibsen played in the Bergen Theatre between 1851 and 1857 has been derived from a study of the theatre's manuscript production books: the Regie-Bog 1852–4, the Regie-Bog 1855–6, and the Regie-Bog 1857, all now in the University Library of Bergen. For making this and all the other very rich manuscript material available for their scrutiny, the editors are extremely grateful to the librarians of the Universities of Oslo and Bergen, and to their colleagues and staff; and although it is doubtless invidious to single out any one individual from among the many who have helped here with advice and expert assistance, they would nevertheless like to record a special debt of gratitude to Miss Solveig Tunold, head of the manuscript division of the University Library, Oslo. They would also like to express their appreciation of the help they have received from the librarians and staffs of the Universities of Newcastle upon Tyne, Durham, and East Anglia, and of University College, London.

The division of responsibilities between the two editors is as follows: Graham Orton translated *Catiline*, *Lady Inger*, and *The Feast at Solhoug*; James McFarlane translated *The Burial Mound*, *Norma*, and *Olaf Liljekrans* and its associated fragments; and, in collaboration with Kathleen McFarlane, *St. John's Night*; Appendices I, VI, and VII are Orton's work; and the Introduction and Appendices II, III, IV, V, and VIII are McFarlane's, who also exercised general editorial control.

J. W. McF.   G. O.
UNIVERSITY OF EAST ANGLIA   UNIVERSITY OF DURHAM
NORWICH

It is with the deepest regret that I must record the untimely death, whilst the book was in proof form, of Graham Orton, co-editor both of this volume and of the already published Volume IV, and my close and valued friend for many years.

J. W. McF.
January 1970

INTRODUCTION

The merit of Ibsen's earliest plays lies not in what they are but in what they presage. He is greatly disappointed who comes to them in the expectation of finding unregarded masterpieces of world literature; even the hope of discovering a body of intrinsically significant though apprentice work is only partially and uncertainly fulfilled. The essential fascination of these plays is that which is born of our own hindsight, of the impulse to identify in embryo those qualities that in time made Ibsen uniquely great. There are, here and there, rewarding glimpses of things prophetic of the disciplined power, the bleak poetry, the psychological penetration of works then unwritten; there is pleasure and indeed insight to be gained from observing the first stirrings of that stupendous talent which eventually erupted into *Peer Gynt* and *Ghosts* and *Hedda Gabler*. In this one takes a cue from Ibsen himself who, a quarter of a century after completing his first play *Catiline*, recognized in it much of what his subsequent work had been about: 'the clash of ability and aspiration, of will and possibility, at once the tragedy and the comedy of mankind and of the individual.' Nevertheless by any standards, let alone when measured against the towering stature of his later dramas, the achievement of these early works was modest indeed, and very uneven. All was promise.

As things primarily of historical rather than of intrinsic worth, they betray a great deal about the pressures to which their author was subject in these years of early manhood: the social inducements, the cultural constraints, the obligations and duties, the impositions and the embargoes that were active in shaping his life and career. They document the early stages of a protracted and difficult and at times painful process of spiritual and artistic emancipation. They help to define the nature of a kind of intellectual bondage from which it took him long years to break free. Summarily expressed, the two things that mainly held him fettered were the Norwegian Myth and the *pièce bien faite*. His allegiance to the one, his ambivalent disdain for the other were mutually reinforcing, a push–pull effect. Consolidated, they not only determined the essential features of his dramatic endeavour in these early years but also left traces on the whole of his later work.

In 1850, the year in which Ibsen made his debut as a dramatic author, Norway was a country wholly preoccupied with finding, or more accurately reasserting, its identity. And in seeking to define what it felt it was and hoped to be, its eyes were ever and again drawn to its own distant past and to what at one time it had impressively been. The Norwegian Myth, the sense of vanished glory and of what had constituted it, was the chief sustaining factor in a people freshly conscious of its destiny and of the promise that lay in its new social and political and cultural opportunities, in its role as a re-emergent (rather than simply emergent) nation.

For four centuries following the Treaty of Kalmar in 1397 Norway had—or, equally significantly, believed it had—been deliberately held in social and intellectual subjugation to Denmark. A popular phrase spoke of the 'four hundred year night', an image within which is contained the notion that the once heroic impulses of the people—impulses powerfully expressed in its ancient myths and legend—had been merely slumbering. Now, with the removal of the 'Danish yoke' and with the challenge of a new political freedom and a new constitution, the nineteenth century offered an extension of spiritual horizons and a new destiny. Norwegian culture was conceived as having been a continuing but latent and quiescent thing; it lived on, persistently, in the remote valleys of this distant part of Europe. What matter if in certain urban centres it had been overlaid by the metropolitan culture of Copenhagen? The people, the 'folk', had surely remained inviolate. No opportunity was to be neglected of re-creating a sense of proud nationhood, of proving to the world and to oneself that the new Norway was no whit inferior to the Viking old, that the embers of artistic and intellectual talent within the people could once again be fanned into bright flame wherewith to forge a nation that would be a shining example to the world.

By mid-century, Norway had entered upon a period of second-generation nationalism. The extreme Danophobia of the years immediately following the new constitution of 1814 had in some measure diminished; nevertheless the problem persisted of how best to create and foster a distinctively Norwegian culture in a land where Danish traditions were so deeply entrenched, where Danish language still contaminated the work of government, of the church, of the professions, and of the theatre. It was a problem not by any means restricted to politics and public life. It invaded all aspects of living; and in particular no artist or writer could expect to be exempt from its demands.

There was thus a firmly defined framework of reference within which Ibsen as a young dramatist was expected to work; and for long years he found himself exposed to forces and pressures of a very distinctive and peculiarly localized kind. This was something to which Ibsen was always especially sensitive: 'The locale has a great influence on the forms within which the imagination creates', he declared many years later in explanation of why there was so much reminiscent of Germany, of 'Knackwurst und Bier', about his later play *The League of Youth*. The cultural climate in which he wrote these early plays was one of intense patriotic aspiration, of chauvinistic endeavour. To express pride in one's nationhood, and to put one's abilities at the service of 'the people' was obligatory on all who played any kind of public role.

In all this, the Bergen Theatre occupied a unique place. Itself established in 1850, the same year that saw the publication of Ibsen's first drama *Catiline*, it was intended to serve as the focal point of specifically Norwegian theatrical enterprise in a land where after nearly forty years of political separation from Denmark, the theatre in all its branches still remained almost entirely dominated by Danes. This 'new' theatre—'new', alas, only in its corporate existence, however, for it had to make do with an old and inadequate building—was to serve as the instrument for revivifying and rejuvenating the innate creative spirit of drama that had for so long lain dormant in Norway.

When therefore Ibsen, as a young man of twenty-three, was engaged in 1851 by the most single-mindedly nationalistic theatre in the land to assist it 'as dramatic author', the normal expectations that he would serve the national myth were immeasurably reinforced. Commonly assumed as it was that the role of the modern poet, like that of his skaldic predecessor, was to serve as the mouthpiece of the people, making articulate what lay closest to the hearts and minds of the 'folk', how much more assertive this obligation was in this special context of Bergen. Ibsen soon showed himself to be in no doubt where his duty lay. The Prologue (see pp. 608–10) he wrote for the fund-raising festival evening in Christiania was a clear articulation of this sense of duty; and in it he fulsomely expressed what he felt was the poet's mission: to proclaim the nationhood of the people, to affirm its glorious past, to praise the noble simplicity of its way of life, to extol the glories of its tongue. The Prologue speaks of that heroic society long ago when the warrior's sword was an instrument of great eloquence, carving powerful images upon the features of his enemies; and of the age when the skald, in whom this same heroic spirit found gentler personification, transposed these selfsame things into a minor key. But then, Ibsen reminded his hearers, a sleep fell upon the land; the voice of the skald was silenced and 'a hush fell on all things, as on the barren strand when the shipwreck's splinters are rocked back and forth by the waves, rolling soundlessly upon the white sand'. At length the people broke their bonds, and art once more began to fulfil its rightful role as a sounding board for the vibrant strings of the people's soul, echoing the vanished splendour of the past and of the rich new life that only now was beginning to assert itself.

It is a view of life and art conveniently defined by the term 'national romanticism': romantic both by its insistence on pastoral ideals—the notion of the sturdy little people of natural piety which Ibsen was to castigate so fiercely in *Brand*—and by its essential reliance on the past, its indifference to new ideals, to any new social or moral engineering, or to any sense of radical innovation. And strongly emphasized within it all is the notion of the stage as a moral institution, as an agency with which to warn and flatter and encourage and exhort, as a formative influence in the creation (or re-creation) of a people and of a nation. Literature in these years for Ibsen was chauvinistically didactic in much the same way as it was for his Swiss contemporary Gottfried Keller who said that just as beautiful portraits were held up before a pregnant woman that her child should be influenced for the better, so on the national level the artist had to present to the ever-pregnant 'people' an enhanced and idealized portrait of what it might in time grow to be. The theatre was to have the same 'moral' purpose—part personal, part political—that Schiller had urged before the end of the previous century: 'Had we but a national theatre,' he had written in 1783, 'we would become a nation.' A measure of oblique flattery of the people was obligatory. The poet was expected to tell of the strong and simple pieties of the people, its pagan courage, the poetic vigour of its language, the virility of its native Northern culture in contrast to the effete sophistication of Southern lands. Popular delight in folk super-stition and the inhabitants of the Nordic supernatural world—trolls and nisses and hulders and hill-people and goblins—was clearly some-thing that called for literary exploitation. Inevitably, the ancient saga and the medieval ballad, the folk song and folk tale, history and legend were all energetically explored in the search for inspirational material. The result was a literature nationalistic in sentiment, romantic in its preoccupation with the past, folksy in its outlook, pastoral in its values, and yet for all that heroic in its aspirations.

Upon this basic groundwork of pre-empted loyalty and of conflict between skaldic duty and individual talent were superimposed other factors that both complicated and yet also in some respects unexpectedly reinforced the prevailing chauvinistic pressures. Dominant among these is the practical experience of his work in the Bergen Theatre between 1851 and 1857. For a young and ambitious author to be invited at the age of twenty-three to join this exciting new enterprise was on the face of it a stroke of amazing good fortune; even today it is difficult to believe that the effect on his career was other than wholly beneficial. At the moment of his appointment, he was the author of two plays, one of which had been published but not performed, the other performed but not published. How impressive this was in its day may be judged from the fact that no Norwegian play had been published at all during the previous seven years. The job that Ole Bull in his impetuous way offered him in Bergen must have seemed heaven-sent. The post not merely encouraged him to write for the theatre—it positively required him. In addition it offered enviable opportunities for having his work staged. He could in a most immediate and direct fashion familiarize himself with all practical aspects of dramatic production and gain valuable experience of the peculiarities and potentialities of the medium. He could build up an unrivalled knowledge of those plays from many different countries that formed the popular European repertoire of the day. Such things brought real and immediate benefit. But it was not all gain. What should not be underestimated is that for long years these things helped to coerce him along paths that ran counter to his natural bent, sadly delaying the moment when he finally realized where his true dramatic talent lay. How?

The Bergen theatre had been launched on a wave of patriotic fervour: at last the theatre in Norway was to have a truly Norwegian home. One almost insuperable obstacle stood, however, in the way of full triumph: there was in Norway no existing corpus of native drama adequate to sustain in performance the nationalistic aspirations of the people. There was admittedly a considerable repertoire of Danish drama, much of it based on impeccably Nordic themes; but this, alas, was the work of a nation from whose cultural hegemony the Norwegians were desperately trying to free themselves. Such plays were of course included in the theatre's programme; but they were neither numerous enough to prevail, nor Norwegian enough to give

entire satisfaction. A glance at the annual lists of plays performed in
Bergen in these years (see pp. 669–72) shows the extent to which even
the nationalistically motivated Bergen theatre was forced to rely on
the French *pièce bien faite* and on German and Danish imitations of it.
(Relatively very few English plays were put on in these years in
Bergen.) It is names like Scribe, Mélesville, Dumanoir, Bayard, and
Ancelot which preponderate. There is no Racine, no Corneille, no
Molière, no Goethe or Schiller, no Kleist or Grillparzer or Hebbel, and
no English works of any prime significance except one Shakespeare—
As You Like It.

Ibsen was under no illusions when it came to judging the quality
of the plays he was asked to produce. As early as April 1851, while
still in Christiania, he was prepared to make disparaging remarks
about the Scribean style of drama. In a dramatic notice of a German
play by Gutzkow, he commented that a surfeit of plays from France
and Copenhagen had left the Christiania public unable to stomach this
different German fare: 'When, year in and year out, one has grown
accustomed as our theatre-goers have to Scribe and Co.'s sugar-candy
dramas, well spiced with suitable quantities of various poetry substitutes, it is only natural that the more solid German fare must strike
even the ostrich stomach of our public as somewhat indigestible.' And
the following month, commenting on a performance of a play by
Duvert and Lauzanne, he remarked on the public's complaint that
nothing but warmed-up dishes were being served up: 'Something new
must be found. . . . We ourselves produce nothing, nor do the Danes.
Scribe has become stale.' He rejects what he thinks of as the alien morals
of the French plays that dominated the theatre of his day, morals that
were wounding to the ethical and aesthetic sensibilities of many a
patriotic citizen, cloying morals that spoiled the appetite for 'det
Nationale', truly 'national qualities'. He cites *L'homme blasé* as an
instructive example of what a play should *not* be like. But in rejecting
French drama, he is nevertheless wary of advocating a straight adoption of the German mode. German drama was to French, he claimed,
as a *tableau vivant* is to a painting, i.e. a stylized form of reality instead
of illusion. The essentially undifferentiated reality of the German
mode is unacceptable because it fails to acknowledge the necessary
economy of dramatic expression, the need for some minimum measure
of abstraction; on the other hand, French drama tended towards
extreme abstraction, to simplistic blacks and whites, to a denial of the
subtleties and complexities of reality.

How, then, is the genuinely 'national' author to pick his way among these hazards? Not by tricking out his plays with superficially national things, like folk dances, 'funny' dialect, strange oaths, rhyming contests, and the like; merely naturalistic copying, like the *tableau vivant*, was inadmissible. There must be some measure of abstraction, some attempt to capture, symbolically perhaps, those less easily definable qualities that echo the spirit of the people, 'those undertones which ring out to us from mountain and valley, from meadow and shore, and above all from our own inner souls'.

For the six years or so that he was in Bergen, the plays of the Paris 'drama industry' tended to represent 'the theatre' for Ibsen. Apart from his brief study trip to Denmark and Germany in 1852, and his previous eighteen months in Christiania (where the fare offered was very little different in kind from what his own theatre was to offer), the repertoire of the Bergen theatre represented practically his whole familiarity with living theatre. Not that this experience of the *pièce bien faite* was wholly without positive value for him. Inevitably these plays must have taught him something about the composition of a logical and consistent dramatic statement, about the fundamental syntax of the theatre. More important than these considerations, however, was the polarity these plays induced in his own dramatic philosophy. At one end of the axis were to be found the realistic, contemporary, prose plays of Scribe and Co.: superficial, ephemeral, contrived, contemptible. At the other was the more deliberate artistry of the Danish 'national' plays: measured, distanced, stylized, lofty. These two categories presented themselves almost as an Either/Or of dramatic composition; and in rejecting the one, he gave himself so much more completely to the other. It also appeared to exclude compromise: realistic prose dialogue, even of the mannered Scribean kind, seemed to be inimical to serious art; modernity, the exploration of contemporary themes, seemed indivisibly linked with superficiality. Serious drama apparently demanded some rather obvious kind of distancing: displacement into history or legend or myth; an archaic or otherwise heightened idiom; the medium of verse. The one thing that these two modes could apparently share, however, was a conventionally contrived dramatic structure. It is the application of Scribean *structuring* techniques to nationalistic themes and motifs that produces the unfortunate synthesis characteristic of Ibsen's work in these years.

Of the early plays in this volume, *Catiline*—the first—stands in some measure apart from the others, and also to some extent apart from the above generalizations. Written in the backwater of a provincial coastal town in the dark Northern winter of 1848–9 before Ibsen came to live in the capital city of Christiania, it is based on a concept of drama derived very largely from his matriculation syllabus, when his familiarity with the theatre proper was minimal. Although its setting is remote in time, although it is cast in verse, it is as yet free of the obtrusive nationalism that was very shortly to overwhelm his work.

It might be thought of as representing its author's own brief Sturm und Drang. Like Goethe's Egmont, Catiline is possessed of that irrational demonic driving force that spurs him on to great and daring deeds, but within which are contained the seeds of his own destruction. Like Schiller's earliest and turbulent drama of 1781, *Die Räuber*, this first play of Ibsen's might equally well have borne the motto 'In tyrannos' on its title page. Here is the Ibsenist version of the 'Kraftkerl', the charismatic figure who by personal magnetism and the imperious sweep of his vision leads the fight against petty-minded self-seeking and the corrupt and corrupting ways of society. Here, too, is something of the Schillerian notion of the 'sublime criminal', the man who though himself guilty of monstrous crimes nevertheless stands like a giant of fearful rectitude among his fellows, an object of admiration and fear together, loved and hated at one and the same time.

The drama was the product of two quite improbably matched stimuli: the widespread revolutionary fervour of the turbulent year of 1848; and the presence on the list of Latin set-books for the current matriculation examination of Sallust's *Catiline* and of Cicero's speeches. Ibsen's later preface to the 1875 edition of his *Catiline* dwells on these two matters. The February revolution, the uprisings in Hungary, the war over Schleswig were all aspects of the general unrest that deeply affected the young twenty-year-old. In the course of the year he wrote poems of passionate homage to the Magyars, composed a series of rousing patriotic sonnets to King Oscar urging him to take action in support of the Danes, and inspired by the news from abroad he startled and shocked the locals of Grimstad by the (to them) outrageous though sometimes unintentionally comic antics and outbursts to which these events provoked him.

Predictably, scholarship was quick to concern itself with the question of how far Ibsen had departed, in his portraiture of Catiline, from historical accuracy—or at least from what was at that time conventionally accepted as the historically accurate picture. One of the very earliest critical studies of Ibsen, that by Vasenius in 1879, attempted to measure the discrepancy between what history had made of Catiline and what Ibsen had seen in him. As the latter himself pointed out in a note to the first edition of 1850, there was in fact precious little in common: 'The factual background of the present drama is too familiar for it not to be immediately obvious how far it differs from historical truth, and also that history has only to be utilized to a limited extent, so that it must be considered primarily as a vehicle for the underlying idea of the play.' In line both with Lessing's firm declaration of nearly a century earlier, and with Hermann Hettner's more recent exhortation, Ibsen in his capacity as dramatist had made himself 'master over history'; and in aiming instead at the kind of truth that a purely imaginative reconstruction gives, Ibsen was perhaps trying to do for Catiline very much what Schiller had earlier done for Wallenstein, and for much the same reasons: to compensate for the fact that so many of the contemporary or near-contemporary reports were the work of opponents and detractors, whose accounts were therefore suspect. Although Ibsen 'lapped up'—to use his own phrase—Sallust and Cicero, he was greatly concerned not to take over uncritically their estimate of Catiline. He particularly mistrusted the testimony of Cicero; and in scornfully categorizing him as 'the indefatigable spokesman of the majority', Ibsen associates him with the role he was later to assign to the contemptible Aslaksen in *An Enemy of the People*, whose attachment to 'the compact majority' is one of the more nauseating manifestations of life as it is lived in a small-minded community. Catiline on the other hand—a Stockmann-like figure as the man who stands alone—is given a character in strong contrast to that which his detractors had created for him, and one which (as Vasenius points out) is much more in line with the one that more recent historical research has established.

The 'idea' was thus the sustaining force in the play, not conventional historical accuracy. The two chief historical sources, of whom Ibsen is thus openly suspicious, portray Catiline as a dissolute and corrupt and repulsive character; yet the suspicion remains that he must clearly have had great natural authority to be able to exert such unquestioned command over his followers. Not that Ibsen has created a wholly idealized character, and many of the warts are there: the crimes against the individual and society, the seduction of the innocent, sacrilege, bribery, arson. But by giving his attention to the *extraordinary* qualities in Catiline's make-up, to the destructive elements that made of him one of the influential figures in the development of history, Ibsen concentrates on what was for him the 'idea'; and in diverging thus from the usually accepted interpretation reveals more clearly than he would otherwise have done those things that were uppermost in his own mind. Equally, by fundamentally altering the original characters of Fulvia, Aurelia, and Curius, he was at pains to emphasize a pattern that continued to absorb him throughout most of his later career: the pattern of the man juxtaposed between two women who—here, as in innumerable guises in the later plays—represent Ibsen's conception of the two basic kinds of Woman: the terrible and the gentle. So insistent does this become in the play—and by extension, presumably, for Ibsen—that the struggle in the play between the two women for possession of the man becomes sheerly allegorical, with the women becoming unambiguously allegorical forces of Good and Evil.

Already in *Catiline* one becomes aware of two features that showed themselves to be remarkably persistent in its author's later career—though there were periods, notably in the 1850s, when they tended to become overlaid by other somewhat contingent considerations. The first of these was a deep-seated revolutionary cast of mind, an attitude to social change that in later life led him to declare—explicitly in his letters to some of his correspondents, and obliquely but powerfully in certain of his dramas—his readiness to support a revolutionary cause. One remembers, for example, his letter to Georg Brandes of 17 February 1871: 'The state must go! That revolution I shall join. Undermine the concept of state, set up free choice and spiritual kinship as the one decisive factor for union, and that is the beginning of a liberty that is worth something. Changing the forms of government is nothing more than tinkering by degrees, a little more or a little less—rotten, all of it. Yes, my friend, the main thing is not to allow oneself to be terrified by the venerableness of the establishment.'

The other was the conviction that, superimposed upon contemporary society's innate resistance to change, there was additionally a peculiarly Norwegian kind of social inertia that derived from the country's general geographical remoteness and from its consequent lack of social awareness. Ibsen himself has confessed that built into the drama there is a sense that although great things may have been happening in 1848 in the wider world, only the faintest ripples of this reached the remote and infuriatingly smug community in which he found himself living. Furthermore the very straitened economic circumstances in which he lived threatened to dull even his own sympathetic responses. This was a point he made in 1870 in a letter to Peter Hansen, in which he explained that *Catiline* had been written in a little provincial town where he was not in a position to give vent to everything that was fermenting in him, except by playing mad practical jokes that drew upon him the wrath of all the respectable citizens who were completely remote from the world that occupied him in his isolation. Five years later he returned with even greater emphasis to this same point when he phrased the preface to the second edition of the play: 'The long and the short of it was that, while big things were happening in the tumultuous world outside, I found myself at loggerheads with the small community in which I lived, cramped as I was by private circumstance and by conditions in general.' This is of course not unlike the circumstances that finally broke Captain Alving, as his wife was in time to realize: 'There was this lively happy boy . . . having to eat his heart out here in this little provincial town; pleasures of a kind it had to offer, but no real joy; no chance of any proper vocation. . . .' Whilst much the same considerations are at the root of Ellida Wangel's anguish as she feels herself deprived of contact with the open sea and all the promise of great and distant things it seemed to symbolize.

Catiline was written in time doubly hoarded: from the few leisure hours that remained over from his working week in the chemist's shop he first had to find time for matriculation study; and from these hours he then had to steal yet a further few—mostly night hours—to write this first youthful drama. The inner compulsion that drove him to it found an immediate correlative in Catiline's opening words: 'I must! I must! Deep down within my soul a voice commands, and I will do its bidding.' And it is here perhaps that the deeper identity between Ibsen and his subject matter is to be sought: in the sense of conflict it explores between on the one hand a calling, a mission, the author's conviction of his own innate ability or potential, and on the other an awareness of the constricting forces of society, the straitened economic circumstances, the long and tedious hours of work. The fate that he feared was expressed more directly in a poem of these years, which he also wrote in Grimstad—'By the Sea'—which puts the question whether, like the wave that beats in vain against the cliffs and falls back to be absorbed into the undifferentiated sea, he might not also submit to a similar defeat and be lost in oblivion.

Already before Ibsen left Grimstad there were clear indications that he had taken a decision to put his authorship at the service of popular nationalistic sentiment. This showed most immediately in his poetry. Lyric poems whose structure was immediately reminiscent of certain well-known folk songs and whose themes were based on popular legend began to displace the more subjective and confessional kind of poetry he had inclined to earlier. In the winter of 1849–50 he began work on a prose narrative with the title of 'The Prisoner of Akershuus', a piece which Ibsen himself described as 'a nationalistic Novelle'. He completed the first act of a drama he referred to at the time as 'Olaf T.'—almost certainly 'Olaf Trygvason'—which would have indicated a highly nationalistic theme taken from Norwegian history; and he drafted a one-act drama provisionally entitled 'The Normans', which was the play that later in revised form became *The Burial Mound*.

Thereupon to move, a few months later, from the relative isolation of Grimstad to the infectious atmosphere of Christiania was to become exposed to a much more virulent form of cultural nationalism than he had ever encountered tucked away in that little provincial coastal town. There was the heady atmosphere of life in the capital city; there was the exhilaration of the new student environment; there were journalistic enterprises to join; and there was the theatre. The shift from the markedly individualistic character of *Catiline*—derivative in many of its aspects though it was—to the tired conventionality of *The Burial Mound* gives some measure of the extent to which he fell victim to current enthusiasms. This second play of his marks an almost complete surrender to the received ideas of the day: determinedly nationalistic, as though to defy anyone to repeat the criticism made of his first play that 'because it was not national and relevant' it did not deserve much recognition; safely Oehlenschläger-like in language and style to ensure its appeal to a theatre management that had proved so unreceptive to *Catiline* and its Roman motifs; popularly Viking in its subject matter with its blond and blue-eyed heroism, its skaldic portentousness, its blood revenge and sacred oaths and warrior deaths; and a reach-me-down dramatic structure that based all on unsuspected identities astonishingly revealed.

Such 'meaning' as the play has polarizes out about a North–South—and thus, by extension, a pagan–Christian—axis. By accepting as the initial situation the circumstance that a Viking warrior, wounded on a raid far from his Northern home, is saved from death by the tender care of a local girl, the play is able to contemplate—'explore' would

be too forceful a word—the notion of the reciprocal influences of
Nordic strength and Southern gentleness. The growth of his understanding of Christian humility as he sees it practised by her, and the
growth of her passion for the Northern lands and peoples as she hears
them described by him—these things herald the kind of reconciliation
of opposites that the final curtain speech proclaims. And finally, after
all the vicissitudes of the plot, the union of the gentle Southern maiden
with her warrior husband is blessed by the ageing Viking in terms that
very obviously underline the symbolic meaning: in speaking of 'this
pact combining Nordic strength with Southern mercy', he enjoins
the girl to 'plant Southern flowers there in the pine trees' haunt, and
spread the light of truth throughout the North'. It was the first dramatic
treatment of a polarity that appears again and again in Ibsen's later
work in different guises; one has only to think of Rosmer and Rebecca,
of Hedda and Tesman, of Solness and Hilde to see this dialectic re-
enacted with varying degrees of complexity and in subtly differing
variations.

Despite the flattering device of putting the praise of Nordic life
into the mouth of a Southern girl, many of the public and some of the
press were far from satisfied with the general image of Viking man
conveyed by the work. In Oehlenschläger they had become accustomed not only to a more fulsome kind of praise for the Viking
tradition but also to a more rigorous denunciation of the effeteness
and flaccidity of Southern ways. When Ibsen came to re-write this
play for performance in January 1854—and his revision was quite far-
reaching—among the adjustments he made was to give the North-
South opposition rather more forceful expression. The setting, which
for the 1850 version was Normandy, is displaced further south to
Sicily. The 'South' becomes more languidly and lushly Mediterranean.
The sense of a decayed civilization is emphasized by the new opening
speech, a monologue by the girl Blanka, who sees in the dead marble
monuments around her merely the remnants of a vanished world, the
epitome of the decrepit or 'sunken' South; by contrast, the life of the
North is bright and vigorous and alert. In the South, she complains,
all is but a crumbling ruin, drowsy, slothful, heavy and dull, whilst
in the North life is a plunging avalanche, the coming of spring and the
death of winter. Her dreams, in the revised version, became much
more vividly idealized, and she tells of her vision of a youthful hero, a
copper helmet on his blond hair, with blue eyes and a deep and manly
chest, and gripping in his mighty hand a sword. Ibsen's determination

to fashion something to the popular taste, to make the play acceptable at all costs to the Norwegian public, strikes one now as rather pathetic, perhaps even somewhat distasteful. In mitigation, one might perhaps remember that in 1854, after the resounding failure the previous year of *St. John's Night* to win favour with the public, he was desperately anxious to achieve a popular success. He was disappointed.

It takes no great effort of imagination to recognize that 2 January 1853 was a crucial day in Ibsen's early career. This was the date on which his first *commissioned* drama was to be performed. This was the first chance, since he had been invited fifteen months earlier to 'assist the theatre as dramatic author', that his employers would have of assessing the creative talents of the man they had appointed. It was the first opportunity for the Bergen public to gauge the quality of their young playwright. The management loyally laid out a little extra on new costumes and props. The public bought tickets in encouraging numbers for the first night. Ibsen chose to write a 'fairy tale comedy', *St. John's Night*, which in its own way was both 'national' and 'romantic'; and to that extent was thus in the current idiom. Alas, the play was a resounding failure. Ibsen's audience left him in no doubt that the writing of *such* plays was decidedly not how they viewed his poetic mission; and public opinion brought him very sharply to heel. The bitterness of his disappointment must have been profound.

Why, one wonders, did the Bergen audience turn so single-mindedly against the play? Probably not because of any dismay at the creaking complexities of the plot—a highly contrived story of denied inheritance, long-lost documents, a scheming widow, a comically senile old man, and two pairs of lovers who re-align themselves to affirm a kind of elective affinity of true love—a plot which was no better but no worse than those of a score of similar dramas current in the theatre of the day. Nor was it likely to be impatience with the obtrusive fairy-tale elements; after all, the fairy-folk—the goblin, the mountain king, the elves and the rest—were of impeccably Norwegian origin, and therefore acceptably 'national', and the by-play with the magic potion had been a not unfamiliar device in plays that had found a ready acceptance. (Some commentators, incidentally, have been encouraged by the midsummer-night setting of Ibsen's play and by the superficial resemblance between the goblin's pranks with the potion and Puck's antics to draw parallels with Shakespeare's *Midsummer Night's Dream*; but the cross-reference seems to offer little reward.)

Doubtless, what principally upset the Bergen audience was the fact that Ibsen had allowed his naturally irreverent cast of mind too free a rein in treating what was for those days a very sensitive range of topics. On the other side, Ibsen probably failed to realize just how dangerously two-edged irony is as a weapon, and that careful handling is essential. It is not improbable that a number of things that were meant as comically grotesque nevertheless succeeded in giving serious offence. It was far from obvious to Ibsen's contemporaries—something which is surely clear enough today—that the transposition of this highly conventional subject matter into a satirical key was the most individual and in a sense the most original thing about the entire play. Without it, the play might well be nothing more than a simple variant of a pattern which a number of well-known plays of the day had combined to create: plays like Heiberg's *Day of the Seven Sleepers*, for example, or Hostrup's *Master and Apprentice*. With it, and despite Ibsen's own later protestations to the contrary, the play is a recognizably Ibsenist thing.

It is worth stressing—although the point was very largely lost on his public—that Ibsen's intent was not to mock the nationalist ideal, only spurious nationalism; not the romantic spirit as such, only bogus romanticism. And in pursuit of this, his creation of the ludicrous Julian Poulsen was a considerable achievement. Casting himself as a Byronic figure, intent on impressing others as a wild and dark and demonic poet, Poulsen nevertheless betrays the most commonplace and unimaginative of minds. His account of his struggle to remain 'primitive' and 'national' is hilarious; he explains how he was devoted to that 'most national of all things national', the hulder, holding it to be the ideal of feminine beauty until by chance he discovers that hulders, despite their more apparent allurements, have tails, whereupon he suffers a great crisis of conscience. Is he to abandon his nationalist convictions because of this? He tries to revive his nationalist zeal, to recapture some of his earlier audacious primitiveness by taking to wearing a sheath knife, starting to spell phonetically and writing nouns with small initial letters (i.e. in bold defiance of the traditional Danish practice), but all in vain: 'Weltschmerz' seems the only refuge. So there, in his own self-dramatization, he stands like a typical Romantic 'Zerrissener', his nationalistic Self at war with his aesthetic Self, his primitive nature in conflict with his sophisticated mind, rustic ideals with urban, anxious on the one hand to show fitting allegiance to the hulder and other nationalistic fairy-folk, yet quick to explain them

away as merely 'symbolic concepts', and mis-identifying the Mountain
King as a member of the Festival Committee.

It is at this point, possibly, that Ibsen can be seen making a genuine
though in the event largely unsuccessful effort to give depth to the
otherwise largely two-dimensional quality of his play. If he had indeed
read Hettner's *Das moderne Drama* in the summer of 1852 when at work
on *St. John's Night*, he must have been struck by what was said there
about the nature and purpose of the 'Märchenlustspiel'. (Ibsen calls
his own play on its title page an 'Eventyrcomedie', a close equivalent.)
Briefly, Hettner's argument is that this particular genre best fulfils
itself by exploring, in its own distinctive and idiosyncratic way, the
relationship between illusion and reality, truth and fiction. There
must be an interpenetration of the real and the fairy-tale world,
whereby each sheds light on the other. Ibsen, instead of using the
device of the magic potion merely to increase the surface complexity
of things, makes of it an instrument for interrelating illusion and
reality. The potion, the goblin explains, will allow a glimpse of things
beyond any merely outward appearance; for those who drink it, the
mists that cloud the vision will be dispelled by the leaping flames of
dreams; and a true sense will be vouchsafed of those inner forces that
reign in the hidden chambers of the mind; he whose mind is empty,
however, will remain as blind as ever before, and sleep. When, in the
following Act, the visions on Midsummer Hill are seen poetically by
Birk and Anne, prosaically by Julian and Juliane, the dramatic discussion is at once, by implication, widened to embrace the limits of
rationality, the validity of the visionary, and the nature of reality.

For some years after its production in Bergen (it was played for
only two nights, the second occasion to an almost empty house) Ibsen
continued to include reference to it among his works when making
official applications for fellowships and grants and the like. But in
later life, with his reputation assured, his repudiation of it was complete; he not only refused to contemplate having it included in a
collected edition of his works, but he also denied that he was in any
real sense the author of it. It had been constructed, he said, upon a
rough, botched-up sketch which he had received from a fellow
student called Bernhoft; all he had done was re-draft this and put his
name to it; but he could not possibly acknowledge it as his own.

Certainly it would be going too far to suggest that *St. John's Night*
is in any way an impressive play in itself; but it does display certain
qualities of freshness and naturalness that immediately mark it off

from the other plays of these years, which by contrast give the impression of having been commissioned by a public looking for cultural reassurance and a measure of oblique flattery of themselves. It may well be that the fiasco of its reception determined him not to try to be so 'clever' another time; that his policy must be to assess popular demand and to write for it; to play safe, and to experiment only within cautious limits; not to yield too readily again to his delight in satire; and to hesitate before again adopting a contemporary setting.

Nationalistic fervour struck a rather more strident and more overtly polemic note in Ibsen's next play. *Lady Inger*, written probably in the summer and early autumn of 1854 and played in Bergen on 2 January 1855, is a historical drama in prose, a play not merely assertively Norwegian in theme but also pointedly anti-Danish in its implications. By its preoccupations it echoed the tradition of patriotic literature associated with Wergeland and his supporters of the earlier generation of the 1830s, the keynote of which in its turn had been struck by Nicolai Wergeland, the poet's father, with his book of 1816 entitled *A True Account of Denmark's Political Crimes against the Kingdom of Norway from 955 to 1814*. In this he had claimed 'that Norway, having suffered the insult of Denmark through the course of generations, had gained nothing and lost all . . . lost its kings, its freedom, its courts, its fleet, its flag, its language, its territories, its resources and its name in the political and literary world.' Like reformist movements everywhere, the new spirit that followed the adoption of the Eidsvoll constitution of 17 May 1814 was never happier than when being reminded of the bad old days.

Lady Inger did just that. The action of the play is set in 1528 when Norway's fortunes were at their nadir, and when her subjugation to Denmark was at its most humiliating. Henrik Jaeger in his biography of Ibsen of 1888 put it succinctly: 'The Danish nobles sat firm in the land; they took command of the best regions, took possession of the richest estates by marriage or by other less honourable methods, and did virtually as they pleased. Conditions were almost completely lawless: violent feuding, robbing, annexing of land, plundering, even small-scale wars made up the order of the day. Things never looked so black in Norway as they did then; and if one holds to the old image of "the four hundred year night" as a description of Norway's age of subservience, the beginning of the sixteenth century must be characterized as the midnight hour.'

Stimulated as it may well have been by the publication in the spring of 1854 of Paludan-Müller's two-volume history of the conflicts of these years, *Lady Inger* is nevertheless more invention than history. Whether Ibsen took his cue here from Hermann Hettner's *Das moderne Drama* (which he is thought to have read on his study tour to Dresden in 1852) is unsure; what is certain, however, is that in discussing the nature of historical drama, Hettner makes his point very firmly: 'What then, in poetry, does history mean for us *qua* history? From the moment it enters the realm of poetry does it not forfeit all independent rights?' Ibsen's play is very much in the spirit of this declaration.

Again it was Jaeger who was one of the first to catalogue the many divergences in the play from the established facts of history; and both Georg Brandes and William Archer, in their introductions to the German and English translations of the play respectively, made much of these: Lady Inger, though an able and wealthy woman in her day, was never in any real sense a focus of anti-Danish activity in Norway; she quite happily married her daughters into the Danish nobility, motivated probably by simple social ambition; the notion that Nils Stensson, the 'Dale-junker', was Lady Inger's own son is purest invention, and in actual fact Lady Inger betrothed one of her daughters to him; Nils Lykke was in real life married to Eline, one of Lady Inger's daughters, and after her death he took her sister Lucia as his mistress; this in the eyes of the day was incest, however, and he was arrested and executed in 1535. There was thus no real attempt in this drama to re-create the events of history, tempestuous enough though they were; rather, as Archer puts it, 'the Fru Inger of Ibsen's play is, in her character and circumstances, as much a creation of the poet's as though no historic personage of that name had ever existed'.

The plain events of history deserved, and indeed invited, the kind of treatment that was stark and simple. Instead, Ibsen succumbed to the allurements of the play of intrigue. The result was a play of daunting complexity. Improbability follows implausibility in wilful, relentless progression. The characters are herded towards their contrived fate by misunderstandings of almost unbelievable artificiality. Identities are mistaken; documents fall into wrong hands; the wildest suppositions are formed on the flimsiest of evidence and then used as the basis of the extremest of actions; relationships—of blood, of marriage, of liaison—are asserted, denied, anticipated, renounced; oaths are imposed, silences enforced, events concealed, confidences betrayed, all within a shifting pattern of dramatic irony bewildering beyond belief. Even the sympathetic Brandes was unable to conceal his dismay: 'Right at the beginning of the play, Olaf Skaktavl knows for example that he is to meet a man at Østråt, but does not know who that man is. When Nils Lykke, who hopes to find Count Sture there, hears of the arrival of a stranger, he presumes Skaktavl to be Sture; whilst Skaktavl for his part, who is to meet Nils Stensson, naturally takes Nils Lykke for Stensson. Although therefore the Danish knight does not know whom he is dealing with in the person of Skaktavl, he nevertheless very skilfully gives the impression that he himself is the man the other person is to meet. Then Nils Stensson arrives. He too is to meet a stranger at Østråt who has not been described to him in detail but to whom he is to hand over papers and documents. By cunning, Nils Lykke succeeds in getting documents intended for Olaf Skaktavl handed over to him, thereby gaining access to secrets, knowledge of which gives him advantage over the others. This advantage is enhanced when Lady Inger involuntarily reveals to him the crucial secret of her life. Nils Lykke learns that Nils Stensson is the son of Sten Sture and Lady Inger; he reveals to the young man the identity of his real parents of which he was previously unaware. It might then have seemed possible to lead the plot to its conclusion without any complications other than those arising from the situation and the characters—but the obscurity which has scarcely begun to clear is once again increased. Namely by the fact that Nils Stensson, as the result of an oath into which Nils Lykke has inveigled him, finds his lips so firmly sealed that he cannot reveal himself even to his own mother as her son, with the result that Lady Inger—who beyond all probability has never seen her own darling child and believes instead that Stensson is her son's rival for the throne—kills this son of hers from ambitious mother-love.' (The passage is strongly reminiscent of the famous occasion in the *Hamburgische Dramaturgie* where Lessing pours scorn on Corneille's *Rodogune* for much the same reasons as here: for absurdly complicating a dramatic situation that was immeasurably more powerful without the complications.)

If only, one feels, Ibsen had heeded the warning uttered elsewhere in Hettner—that a basic law of all tragedy is that Chance has no place in it—much might have been saved. As it is, however, the play is not wholly devoid of genuine dramatic power, despite its obvious deficiencies. The inner conflict within Inger herself, for example, is authentic and moving. Bold and yet fearful, confident and yet strangely uncertain, she is recognizable as a typical Ibsenist creation, even though as yet the draughtsmanship is crude. The final Act contains in Inger's own words the central tragic theme: 'I am hated there on high, because I bore you into the world . . . I was born with wealth and brains and a famous name that I should be God's standard-bearer on earth. But I went my own way . . . and that is why I have had to suffer so much and so long.' It is a recognition that she has failed in her duty, her mission, because of human weakness—because she 'went her own way'.

When Ibsen himself looked back fifteen years later at what he called the 'inner history' of the play, he passes over the literary patriotism in silence; what remains in his memory is the emotional background to the play. The play, he said, 'is based on a quickly formed and violently broken love affair, to which are linked also a number of minor poems, like "Wild Flowers and Pot Plants", "A Bird Song", etc.' The reference is doubtless to Rikke Holst, whose company Ibsen enjoyed in these months until her father rather firmly set his face against the association; though it must be admitted that the immediate relevance of this affair to *Lady Inger* is not very obvious, apart from the fact that the love scenes between Nils Lykke and Eline have a spontaneity about them that might well be supposed to have derived from Ibsen's own experience.

No other play of Ibsen received such exhaustive and formally authenticated commentary from its author as *The Feast at Solhoug*. Not that this occurred immediately: at the time of its first performance, in 1856, Ibsen was glad to let the audiences of Bergen, Christiania, and Trondheim show by their applause the extent of their appreciation; in Bergen, indeed, the citizens actually serenaded Ibsen after the performance. It was the first ever of Ibsen's plays to be performed outside Norway: Stockholm saw it in the autumn of 1857; and the occasion of its performance in Copenhagen four years later made of it the first Ibsen play to be produced in Denmark. The succession of hostile press notices was something that Ibsen was for the moment prepared to suffer in silence; whilst for the theatrical success, long delayed as it had been, Ibsen was deeply grateful and much sustained.

Yet in 1870 he was quite prepared to disown it. In his letter to Peter Hansen of 28 October 1870, he dismissed it in an afterthought as 'a study I no longer acknowledge', though even at this point in time he was anxious to add that 'also this play had a personal origin'. By 1883, however—perhaps because of the attention Vasenius accorded the play in his dissertation of 1879 and his book of 1882, based in part on personal discussion with Ibsen—he was anxious to bring out a second revised edition of the play, for which he suggested a preface 'like that for *Catiline*' written by himself.

This preface (see pp. 369–74) is in many respects a precise and detailed document. In it Ibsen records his application to the study of Norwegian medieval history that had accompanied the writing of *Lady Inger*; how this had led him first to the study of the kings' sagas—which he found too cold and too distant for immediate dramatic use—and subsequently to the Icelandic family sagas, notably in N. M. Petersen's translation, with their emphasis on personal conflict and confrontation, 'man and man, woman and woman, person and person'; how this subsequently led to the first vague shaping of *The Vikings at Helgeland*, whereupon various factors (including his discovery of Landstad's collection of *Norwegian Folk Songs*) had once again led him back to medieval romance. This encouraged him to incorporate these early tentative plans for a Viking drama into a different kind of lyrical historical play, to transform first Hjørdis and Dagny into the figures of Margit and Signe, and then Sigurd into Gudmund, and to ameliorate the starkness of the original tragic mood.

The motives that led Ibsen, exceptionally, into giving such a *compte rendu* of the genesis and growth of the play seem on the surface obvious enough. He had been greatly irritated by the dismissive way in which the critics and the press had received his play, in contrast to the approval accorded it by the theatre-going public. Published criticism, with few exceptions, had marked it down as a merely derivative piece within the general tradition of the Danish romantic drama; some critics indeed went further, and labelled it a simple imitation of the manner of Heiberg and Hertz; whilst Georg Brandes, in company with several others in both Norway and Denmark, declared in 1868 that the play was 'nothing more or less than a colourless imitation of [Hertz's] *Svend Dyring's House*'. Ibsen's preface of 1883, and especially his bitter comments in the opening pages on those qualifications that apparently served to make a critic, are evidence enough of the depth of the hurt this criticism occasioned him.

To this extent, the preface is explicit enough. But in some important respects, the document is neither greatly persuasive nor wholly candid. Anxious though Ibsen was to defend himself against the imputation of 'literary influence', in effect the preface merely substituted one kind of literary influence for another: not Heiberg but Petersen's translations, not Hertz but Landstad's folk-song collection. And where he might have more vigorously defended himself against charges of being derivative and secondhand by spelling out the personal statement his play might claim to make, he is unexpectedly evasive. Writing of the switch in plan from a saga-type tragedy to a lyric drama, he is disappointingly uncommunicative about concrete details: 'At that time I had not drafted any complete and consistent plan. Yet it was clear to me that some play of that kind was the first I should now have to write. But then many things intervened. Most of these were indeed of a personal nature and were, I presume, decisive in a most forceful and immediate way; but then neither do I believe that it was entirely without significance that just at that time I was also engaged on an intensive study of Landstad's collection of *Norwegian Folk Songs*. . . .' This emphatic though enigmatic insistence that personal experience of some crucial kind had intervened at a key moment in the composition of the play has bothered commentators ever since. The usual refuge has been to link it to Ibsen's brief affair with Rikke Holst; not only is the chronology of events awkward here, however (he had broken with Rikke Holst in 1853, and *The Feast at Solhoug* was probably written in the summer of 1855), but the relevance of that affair to the play is far from obvious.

Many years later, when Ibsen was an old man, Brandes wrote another preface to this play for the German collected works edition; his phrases give the impression—whether deliberately or not, it is hard to say—that not only was it right to emphasize the fact that associated with the play there was some distinctly personal experience, but also that he (Brandes) could possibly guess what it was, though friendship with the author and natural scruples were perhaps preventing him from revealing what it was. Discussing the remarks Ibsen had made in his preface of 1883, Brandes commented: 'The personal element, of which moreover we learn nothing, was therefore the main thing. One could already guess this from the content of the play, especially since variations on this theme are frequently found in Ibsen's youthful works, and most importantly in *The Vikings at Helgeland* which appeared two years later. Where this personal nucleus lies must be left unsaid by a critic who has received no confidential communication from the author. . . . Here one finds the contrast between on the one hand the violently passionate married woman, distraught, seductive, and prepared to use criminal methods, and the wholly naïve and devotedly loving woman on the other. The chief male character, finally, is a poet. . . . *The Feast at Solhoug* shows in fictive form how fate frees the young knight and minstrel from the net in which he has enmeshed himself. . . .'

The facts of Ibsen's life as we have them do indeed suggest an association here. The only awkward thing is the chronology. For instead of life inspiring art, art seems to realize itself in life. It is recorded that among the audience on the first night of *The Feast at Solhoug* on 2 January 1856 were the Rev. Johan Thoresen and his (third) wife Magdalene. As they were making their way home, Magdalene apparently persuaded her husband to invite the young dramatist to their home. Five days later he came; there he met and fell in love with one of the daughters of the house, nineteen-year-old Suzannah; within weeks he was formally engaged, and the marriage took place two years later.

Our attention today is, however, drawn mainly to Suzannah's step-mother, Magdalene. She was at the time thirty-six years old, some nine years older than Ibsen, of striking appearance with dark eyes and a fine Mediterranean complexion. From her earliest days—and she was of humble origins—she had determined to be a writer. After a turbulent youth and a tempestuous love affair with a brilliant but poor young Icelandic poet, she eventually gave her life some stability by accepting an offer of marriage from a widower, the Rev. Johan Thoresen. She made no secret of the fact that she was marrying not for passion but for companionship and security; and her new husband was happy to accept this arrangement. There is no very good reason to suppose that the party she gave after *The Feast at Solhoug* was the first time she had met Ibsen. She had both written and translated for the theatre, and three at least of her plays—*The Princess's Plea* and *A Witness* in the season 1852–3 and *Herr Money* in 1853–4—had been played at the Bergen Theatre. She has left behind a brief pen-portrait of Ibsen in his early years in Bergen, in which she stresses his reserve, his awkwardness in company, and adds that 'even towards the woman who approached him with ready admiration he appeared to lack the ability to yield to her charms'. Equally, one cannot be wholly sure that Ibsen and Suzannah had not met before. Certainly she had already seen some of his work performed in the theatre, for she apparently spoke to him of her admiration for *Lady Inger*; and there is significance, possibly, in the fact that after what is claimed to be their second meeting, only three weeks or so after the first, Ibsen sent her a proposal of marriage in the form of a poem.

There are grounds for wondering what precisely it was that led Magdalene, in the January of 1856, to decide that the time had now come to invite the young Ibsen to her home. Ibsen's own daughter-in-law, writing nearly a century later, must also herself have wondered; for she wrote: 'It must have both amazed and annoyed popular Magdalene Thoresen when young Ibsen gave all his attention to her stepdaughter instead of to herself.'[1] It is wholly consistent that when Ibsen left Bergen, Magdalene transferred her attention to the young Bjørnson who replaced him; and that in later years she took an equally close interest in the still younger Georg Brandes. When, after leaving Norway and after some years of silence, Ibsen took up again with Magdalene by correspondence, his letter (of 3 December 1865) is full of the kind of portentously veiled and ambiguous phrases he was inclined to use when writing to women who had figured significantly in his life:

Dear Mother-in-law!

I decided some time ago that I wanted to write to you; for now I can. Previously I was really never wholly myself *vis à vis* you. What I had to say from my real inner self always found a false expression; and as I myself was only too conscious of this, I closed up. . . . Your finest work *Signe's Story* [*sic*] we have down here; when we meet again, I can talk to you about it; previously it was as though something came between. That was surely what you meant when you said, as we parted, that things would be different and get better. I already understood you well enough then; but these things have to happen before they can be fully and completely understood. Yes, you may believe me when I say that I now understand you as you deserve to be, and as you always have deserved to be; but I had to get away from the swinishness up there in order to become in some measure cleansed. . . . Suzannah has written you two letters. . . . If there is anything about these letters that prevents you from answering them, at least answer this one! . . . With this I must conclude for this time. I am sure I can count on your replying with a few words. As you will understand, Suzannah will not be allowed to see this letter. . . .

Magdalene survived her husband by some forty-five years, and continued to exist as a presence in the life of the Ibsens. She is generally regarded as having contributed many details to the figure of Ellida Wangel in *The Lady from the Sea*. One could make a claim for her having been one of the most influential women in Ibsen's entire

[1] Bergliot Ibsen, *The Three Ibsens* (London, 1951), p. 17.

career. One final footnote is possibly not out of character. When, in the spring of 1895, Suzannah wrote from Italy accusing her husband of contemplating divorce, Ibsen was moved to fury: 'It made me extremely sad to read your last letter of 1 May. And I hope that after considering things further you now regret having sent it to me. It's that stepmother of yours, that damned old sinner, whose been at it again, trying to make mischief by setting us off against each other.'

At the very centre of the play itself, in among all its folksy importations, its ludicrously contrived misunderstandings and misinterpretations, its cups of cold poison variously raised and set down again, its hasty operetta-like resolution by way of violent death, swift repentance, magnanimous withdrawal, timely restitution, and the promise of marriage bells—in among all this is the genuinely moving history of Margit. (In parenthesis, one may remark that although the scene involving the poisoned goblet 'perhaps now reads like a parody', as one perceptive modern critic has written,[1] 'yet it is instructive': instructive in that it illustrates—though without the disciplined control of the corresponding scene in *Hamlet*—a method whereby action as a separate and self-sufficient thing can manufacture (by means of such objects as the goblet) a whole succession of exciting situations. Our impatience with the scene as it now reads in *The Feast at Solhoug* is rather because Ibsen's 'dramatic speech . . . is deliberately contrived to increase the confusion', since the author wanted no more of the language 'than that it should keep the confusion of the action going'.) Hers is the history of the proud, impassioned woman who has 'sold' herself in marriage to the wealthy, insensitive, and weak-willed Bengt, and who, finding herself in competition within her own household with a younger unmarried woman for the love of a young poet, bitterly regrets 'the wealth' of happiness she has lost.[2] There seems to be in all this—in the character of Margit as also in the situation itself—something observed, something direct and immediate, something that impresses

[1] Raymond Williams, *Drama in Performance* (London, 1954), pp. 80 ff.

[2] There is just possibly a tempting, even beguiling, encipherment here, of which it would doubtless be a mistake to make too much. One begins by relating Suzannah and Magdalene Thore*sen* to *Si*gne and Margit Gautes*ön*; this might further be linked to Suzannah and (her sister) Marie Thoresen, who have more than once been likened to Hjørdis and Dagny (in *The Vikings at Helgeland*) and who according to Ibsen's preface of 1883 were transmuted into Margit and Signe in *The Feast at Solhoug*; to which might be added that Ibsen himself, in his letter to Peter Hansen of 28 October 1870, acknowledged that for Hjørdis he had 'used the same model as for Svanhild in *Love's Comedy*'.

one as not to be explained by reference to merely literary sources. For the accusation of plagiarism from Hertz is nothing short of ludicrous. 'Literary influence' there still is in the play, admittedly; for Ibsen here is still deep in the toils of the tradition of the play of intrigue: the kind of play that Ibsen, month in and month out, was being required to produce almost to the point of nausea. But in some of its aspects—the torment of Margit particularly, and the slightly grotesque ineffectualities of Bengt, for example, though not the reaction of the two young lovers who are merely pasteboard figures—there is conveyed a sense of genuine feeling.

In 1856, and for the second time during his years in Bergen, Ibsen took out from among his papers one of his earlier manuscripts in order to help him meet his annual deadline: the requirement that he should complete a new play every year for performance on the anniversary of the theatre's foundation day. In 1853, when *The Burial Mound* was the play in question, he had been able to start with a complete play to re-work, and one moreover that had already seen the boards. This time he had at his disposal only a fragment—an act and a half— of a play originally planned in four acts, entitled 'The Grouse in Justedal' and written in 1850. The new play that he made of it, *Olaf Liljekrans*, was performed in Bergen on 2 and 4 January 1857. In most of its essentials it became a very different play from the earlier fragment, and none of the original dialogue was retained. Nevertheless, enough of the earlier piece remained residually in the completed work to give it in a number of respects an air of being strangely out of place in the strict chronological order of Ibsen's dramas.

This—the residual romanticism that lingered on from the play's original design—is the first of three constituent elements that can be separated out from the play without great difficulty. The second is related to the enthusiasm for folk poetry as a possible source of dramatic material that Ibsen conceived in these years, and in particular his interest in that collection of *Norwegian Folk Songs* published by M. B. Landstad in the early fifties. The third is linked with the instruction Ibsen had accepted—unconsciously perhaps, unwillingly even—from those Parisian dramatists and their imitators to whose plays he devoted so much of his time and energy as producer in the theatre.

'The Grouse in Justedal' was an early product of Ibsen's surrender to the spell of national romanticism. Drafted probably some time in the second half of 1850, it was explicitly defined on the title page of the manuscript as a 'national play'. Taking for its starting point the myth of the unspoilt child of nature, a descendant of survivors from the Black Death living a primitive and idyllic life deep within the mountains and far from the corrupting society of men, it at once proclaims its link with that folk tale on the same theme in the collection of *Norwegian Tales* published by Andreas Faye in 1844: even the place names of Justedal and (with slight emendation) Birkehaug are taken over from the tale into the drama. It embodied a myth that carried an immediate appeal for Norwegian society of this mid-century, incorporating as it did the notion that Norway's mountains constituted some great safe-deposit of cultural values, that their isolation and remoteness provided a simple but effective protection against the contagion of social evil, and that simple goodness endured though (as presumably the unfinished fragment would have gone on to show) it was sorely vulnerable if abused or insensitively treated. The trials and possible triumphs of such a fey creature are presumably what the drama would have been concerned to show in a plot clearly designed to trace the clash between romantic love and dutiful marriage—a theme which, in infinitely subtler fashion than here, was to become a constant preoccupation of Ibsen's dramas in later years.

Noteworthy too at this early stage is the introduction of the Minstrel. Here he is given the conventional form of the skaldic or bardic figure: prophetic, in league with the mysterious forces of nature, attuned to the world of the supernatural, dedicated to poverty and the simple life but of a powerful natural dignity, to offend which is to invite dire retribution. It represented for Ibsen a persona he would have been glad himself to adopt. Not only are variants of it to be found in the works of these years—in the figure of Hemming in the two versions of *The Burial Mound*, for example, or in the poem 'Møllergutten' ('The Miller Boy'), written probably in 1850—but also in the later Jatgeir (in *The Vikings at Helgeland*), Falk (in *Love's Comedy*), Maximos (in *Emperor and Galilean*), and even Rubek (in *When We Dead Awaken*), though the connections admittedly become more tenuous as the years pass.

Superimposed on these early elements from 1850 is first the influence of Landstad's collection in particular and of the medieval ballad in general. In Landstad, Ibsen found the ballad of Olaf Liljukrans. The theme of the young man struck down by the elves whilst riding in the forest the evening before his wedding is one that recurs with a range of variations in the folk poetry of many lands—one finds the Scandinavian version transposed into German in the poem 'Erlkönigs

Tochter' in Herder's *Stimmen der Völker*, for example. Apart from this isolated element of plot and the adoption of the name Olaf Liljekrans direct from the Landstad volume, the final drama has little directly in common with the corresponding ballad. Of the more important but more diffuse effects that Ibsen's ideas about the ballad form had on this play, the theories he outlined in his essay on 'The Heroic Ballad and its Significance for Literature' (see pp. 672–84) offer the best commentary.

Basically then what Ibsen did when he took out this early fragment in 1856 was to fuse the Alfhild theme of 'The Grouse in Justedal'—the myth of Innocence Survived—with the new theme of Olaf the Spell-bound ('pixilated' is a word that also suggests itself) taken from Landstad. Ibsen also seems to have been concerned to diminish the rawness of the supernatural element by relegating it to the safer confines of merely superstitious belief. Finally, however, he took pains to interweave all these mythical and folk elements into a framework of intrigue and complication and contrived misunderstanding which in its pattern would not have been out of place in the most representative Parisian play of the age.

Again there is the basic tension, of a highly conventional type, between an arranged marriage and the unpredictability of romantic love. The arrangement is for Olaf to marry Ingeborg, whereby the man provides a solution to his family's economic problems, the girl raises her family's social status, and the enduring feud between the two families is settled. But shortly before the wedding day, Olaf's heart is captured by Alfhild, the fey innocent girl of the mountains; Ingeborg, meanwhile, is being wooed by her father's lowly-born servant Hemming. The man's domineering mother Kirsten, and the girl's bluff father Arne complete the mirror-image nature of the design. Thereupon there follows a plot in which misunderstanding, double talk, wilful ambiguity, theatrical trick and surprise twist succeed each other in earnest succession: first to tie a formidably complicated knot and then to shake it free again with artificial and deceptive ease. The conversation between Lady Kirsten and Alfhild in Act II, for example, with its asides to the audience and its painfully contrived misunder-standings, is an excruciating example of dramatic intrigue of a deservedly discredited kind.

If one nevertheless moves on from its (very deficient) intrinsic worth to its importance as a document of Ibsen's development as a dramatist, it can be seen as a significant item in the tireless exploration

which Ibsen conducted into the conflict between the claims of illusion
and reality. The 'happy ending'—almost like a musical comedy in the
bathos of its resolution—is nevertheless totally out of harmony with
the nature of the shock which is felt when naïve idealism meets deceit
and self-seeking and the harsher edges of reality. One of the earliest
critical commentaries on this play—that of Henrik Jaeger in 1887—
defined 'the idea' of it as 'the struggle between reality and romanticism'. The piquant thing is that, even at this early and unsophisticated
stage, the play considers this from two opposing points of view. The
destruction of innocence is seen as a double-edged thing: in one light
pathetic, and in the other satirical. Georg Brandes saw a clear link here
with *Love's Comedy*: both the earlier and the later play, in their inquiry
into love and marriage, betray a scepticism about romantic values
however much they may seem to be in their toils. On the one hand
there is Alfhild, the embodiment of simple, untutored romantic
innocence, who comes into sad conflict with the painful realities of the
real world: the 'Dichtung' of her father's account of death is shattered
after its encounter with the 'Wahrheit' of a real funeral, of a mother's
actual grief at the loss of her child, of the stark significance of the
coffin; her daydreams of the distant world, of the nature of society,
and of community living are roughly dispelled when she leaves her
mountain fastness; and the hurt she feels at the deceptions of love drive
her in the end to murderous deeds. Olaf's warning to her is urgent:

'Tis often so
That life itself turns out like this!
Don't come too close—it's so easily done—
You may find you have burnt your fingers.
In truth it may shine like the stars of heaven,
But only when seen from a distance.

This is balanced by the irony in Ingeborg's and Hemming's reaction
to the demands of the simple life. Theirs is the Alfhild situation in
reverse. They flee from the complexities of community living to the
supposed delights of a simple cottage life, but their awakening is both
rapid and comic: Hemming declares he will hunt and fish, but remembers with dismay that he has brought neither bow nor fishing rod
with him; Ingeborg, who is to pick berries and see to the house,
realizes that she now has no servants at hand to do her bidding. She
has no clothes but the outrageously impractical wedding dress she
stands up in; and Hemming refuses to go back for others, fearing he
will be hanged for a thief. And at once reality has imposed itself:

INGEBORG. . . . . What about when the long winter comes? No people up here, and never the sound of singing or dancing. . . . Hemming! Should we stay here, or . . . ?

HEMMING. Where else could we go?

INGEBORG [*impatiently*]. But nobody can live here.

HEMMING. Of course they can.

INGEBORG. You can see for yourself they are all dead! Hemming! I think it would be best if I went back to my father.

HEMMING. Then what will become of me?

INGEBORG. You shall ride to the wars!

HEMMING. To the wars! And be killed!

INGEBORG. Certainly not! You shall perform some famous deed, and then you'll be knighted, and then my father will not stand against you.

HEMMING. Yes, but what if they do kill me?

INGEBORG. Well, we can always think about that. . . .

It is only at such times—like also the delicious moment when Lady Kirsten finds comfort in the notion that Alfhild, too, probably can expect to inherit extensive lands, and will therefore make an acceptable daughter-in-law—that the play really comes to life in among the rather dreary progression of pasteboard figures through the creaking plot. When one of the contemporary newspaper critics complained that he found it impossible to sort out the sense of this confused play after only one performance, and accused the author of lacking knowledge both of the world and of human nature, Ibsen was very cross and wrote an angry letter to the newspaper in his own defence. But even today one sees what the critic meant, and one has sympathy.

As one more product of the struggle for ascendancy between the romantic tradition and Ibsen's individual talent, *Olaf Liljekrans* helps to define the path of artistic development he was following. Though diffuse, slack, contrived in its structure, clumsy in its motivation, shallow in its psychology, the play nevertheless has something of significance to say to the present-day reader as a further variation on the theme of the authenticity of individual existence, and the necessity to search for it; though at the time of its composition Ibsen was apparently not prepared to give serious consideration to the relevance of this to his own search for dramatic form.

Among the pressures—social, political, professional, and others—acting from without to impose a shape upon a creative talent in its most formative years, two are thus conspicuous: the obligation to serve the Norwegian Myth; and the requirement to conform to the skaldic image. Like some monstrous piece of corsetry, they constricted and contorted Ibsen's talent to a sadly unnatural shape; and it took sheer physical release—an escape by voluntary exile from Norway in 1864—before this talent was allowed to find its natural configuration. Only great resilience of mind and spirit could have survived; and inevitably one speculates whence it was that this resilience drew its strength.

The notion that emerged from a discussion of *St. John's Night* is helpful again here: that of Ibsen's natural irreverence. Perhaps not one of the more obvious, more immediately striking qualities of his work and personality, it is nevertheless always recognizable, not only in his early years but also in later life beneath the layered accretions of decorum, as an enduring element in his make-up. His childhood friends repeatedly testify to his delight in tricks and practical jokes; he has himself confessed that his antics as an apprentice shocked the bourgeois society of Grimstad; alongside the highly conventional love poems of his youth there are many lampoons of great exuberance; against the solemn pieties of his occasional poems and prologues one must set the irreverent satire of his journalism; and countering the high-flown sentiments of *The Burial Mound* there is always the dry mockery of *Norma*. Almost always, in literary debate and polemic, he is at his most effective when flicking at his target with scorn rather than when taking an earnestly argued line of rectitude.

Nowhere is this duality between Ibsen's natural irreverence and the conformist pressures of the Zeitgeist so graphically illustrated—in the strictly literal sense of these words, indeed—as in his paintings and drawings of these years. From his earliest boyhood days in Skien and all through the years he spent in Grimstad, Christiania, and Bergen, Ibsen was greatly devoted to drawing and painting. From the very beginning—to judge from the testimony of his boyhood friend Boye Ording—his work seems to have fallen into two quite distinct categories: on the one hand there were romantic landscapes in water-colour; and on the other there were cartoons, caricatures, and satirical sketches. Few works have survived from these earliest years; but characteristically one is a tight, stiff, and formalized landscape water-colour painted in 1842 (the year before he left home), in which conspicuous in a primitively composed picture of green and blue vegetation with red and white farm buildings is a flag-pole carrying the Norwegian flag; whilst two of the other extant works are caricatures painted in oils on wood, said to be of his two brothers: one as a fox and the other as an ape.[1] In Grimstad he continued to paint earnestly: mainly portraits and landscapes in oils, views of deeply cleft fjords and waterfalls and log houses and snow-covered pines in sunset glow. But alongside these more contrived pieces he also—as the reports of at least two of his contemporaries in the town bear witness—indulged his more private passion for cartoon and caricature. Christofer Due, one of his closest friends, writes admiringly of the quick and ready pencil Ibsen had when it came to caricaturing and satirizing those with whom he came in contact. He tells of the wicked pleasure it gave them in the long evenings in the apothecary's house to write comic verse which Ibsen would then illustrate: 'Ibsen had an astonishing facility for writing free-flowing verse, and he had a great talent for drawing. His pencil could make the point swiftly, deftly, and tellingly when some-thing had to be conveyed by an illustration.'[2] This same gift found later outlet in the satirical drawings he contributed to the periodical *Manden/Andhrimner*—works which though primitive in their technical quality (they are printed from crude woodcuts) nevertheless have an animation and a simple directness that is largely lacking from his more ambitious landscapes. When he finally came to Bergen, he appears to have concentrated mostly on the more conventional kind of work, producing landscapes of a generally naturalistic though sentimentalized style, in which the influence of his teacher Johan Ludvig Losting—a painter whose enthusiasm and versatility outran his talents—is very marked.

In these pursuits as elsewhere he was clearly under strong compul-sion to do, to say, to write, to draw, and to paint what was expected of him. But beneath it all was the dedicated joker. Throughout his entire career, even as the top-hatted, frock-coated, much decorated dignitary of his later years, he was in the habit of referring to his plays as 'galskaber'—monkey tricks, practical jokes, pieces of tomfoolery.

Finally, it would be a mistake to imagine that Ibsen's eventual

[1] See Otto Lous Mohr, *Henrik Ibsen som maler* (Oslo, 1953), pp. 17 ff.
[2] Ibid., p. 19.

flight to Italy in 1864 betokened a mere closing of the chapter. It was not a simple escape from this conflict between literary convention and individual talent, with a new start. There was an enduring consequence: and it assumed the proportions of a revelation. It did not take long—as many of his letters from Italy testify—for him to reach an awareness of the full significance of what it was he had undergone; and how, generalized, it was relevant to vast areas of life. The experience of those years—it would not be an exaggeration to call it 'traumatic'—then invaded his later dramas in a multiplicity of guises. In essence, what emerged was the conviction that any submission to conventional 'duty', any surrender to traditional or institutional or social pressure was an affront to the integrity of the individual and therefore something to be passionately resisted in the interests of genuine self-realization, which alone justifies our existence. It is a notion with which few of his maturer dramas are not in some way preoccupied, sometimes even obsessed. Duties and responsibilities call for detached scrutiny and subjective evaluation. Only 'the call' or 'the mission'—which might be thought of as a Self-orientated 'duty'—can properly claim our attention. Duty to the Self, responsibly defined and responsibly pursued, must always come first. To Theodor Caspari on 27 June 1884 he wrote: '. . . I believe that none of us can do anything other or anything better than realize ourselves in spirit and in truth.' In a hundred different ways his mature dramas offer a commentary on this view: to subordinate one's life to the effort to meet the obligations of family or state or church (they say) is to turn one's back on authentic living, is to be absorbed into pattern and routine and stereotype, is to fall victim to drab conformity. Only by throwing off these constraints and escaping into a condition of life that allowed the unforced realization of one's potential, that allowed one to follow a natural bent and develop innate talents, obeying inner imperatives unhampered by the dictates of organized society and guided only by an individual sense of responsibility and propriety—this alone (the later dramas insist) must be the motive force of genuine living. This is the common factor that informs many of the key phrases of these works—notions like 'the joy of life', 'the man who stands alone', 'nobility of mind', 'freedom with responsibility', 'the robust conscience', 'the miraculous'. Individual fulfilment following some independent recognition or act of courage is the aim; and 'duty' ('pligt' in Norwegian) is—as Hilde Wangel declares—a nasty word both in sound and in implication.

Not until Ibsen had quit the North, however, had put a continent between himself and that overpowering sense of Nordic duty, and had set aside the skaldic persona he had so eagerly assumed in obedience to the call of the age; not until he had known at first hand the liberating experience of Mediterranean skies, of brilliant light and classical art and all the life of the South—it was not until he had done all these things that he became fully aware of the nature of the bondage under which he had suffered. The essence of his release and the extent of his emancipation then became clear to him. Many years later, in 1898, he described this revelation: 'I travelled South, through Germany and Austria, and crossed the Alps on 9 May [1864]. The clouds hung like great dark curtains over the mountains; we drove in under them and through the tunnel and suddenly found ourselves at Mira Mora, where the beauty of the South—gleaming strangely like white marble— suddenly stood revealed to me. It left its mark on all my later work, even though not everything there was beautiful.' It was, he said, like 'a feeling of being released from darkness into the light, escaping through a tunnel from mists into sunshine'.

CATILINE
[*Catilina*]

DRAMA IN THREE ACTS

BY

BRYNJOLF BJARME

(1850)

CHARACTERS

LUCIUS CATILINE, a Roman nobleman

AURELIA, his wife

FURIA, a vestal

CURIUS, a young man related to Catiline

MANLIUS, an old warrior

LENTULUS
COEPARIUS
GABINIUS } young Roman noblemen
STATILIUS
CETHEGUS

AMBIORIX } envoys of the Allobroges
OLLOVICO

A VESTAL

AN OLD MAN

Servants in the Temple of Vesta; waiters, gladiators, warriors, and the suite of the Allobroges

A PHANTOM

The first and second Acts take place in and near Rome, the third in Etruria

ACT ONE

*A road near Rome. The towers and walls of the city loom up in
the background. It is evening.*
    CATILINE, *deep in thought, is leaning against a tree, left.*

CATILINE [*after a pause*]. I must! I must! Deep down within my soul
  a voice commands, and I will do its bidding; . . .
  I feel I have the courage and the strength
  to lead a better, nobler life than this . . .
  one endless round of dissipated pleasures! . . .
  No, they can never still my inner urge!
  . . . Mad ravings! . . . All I crave is to forget.
  It is too late! I have no aim in life! . . .

  Ah, what became of all my youthful dreams?
  Like light and airy phantoms they have vanished, . . .
  to leave behind but bitter disillusion,
  and fate has robbed me of each daring hope!

                [*With vehemence.*]

  Despise, despise yourself then, Catiline!
  You feel the force for good within your soul, . . .
  but what, pray, is the goal of your endeavours?
  Mere sensual satisfaction, nothing more!

                [*More calmly.*]

  Yet still at times, as at this moment now,
  A secret dream will smoulder in my breast!
  Ah, as I gaze upon that city, proud
  and lofty Rome . . . and the depravity
  and rottenness in which it long lies steeped
  stand out in sharp relief before my soul . . .
  at once an inner voice cries out aloud:
  'Wake, Catiline, awake and be a man!' . . .

                [*He breaks off.*]

Yet these are all illusions, dreams of night-time,
and figments born of solitude, no more;
the slightest murmur from the world that's real
and down they flee to silent depths within! . . .

——————

[AMBIORIX *and* OLLOVICO, *with their party, enter from the right without noticing* CATILINE.]

AMBIORIX. Behold our journey's end: the walls of Rome's proud city;
and towering in the sky the lofty Capitol.

OLLOVICO. So that is Rome? Now Italy's almighty ruler,
soon Germany's, and Gaul's perhaps as well!

AMBIORIX. Alas, indeed, . . . that may one day be so,
and Roman rule is stern and hard to bear;
it tramples those it conquers in the dust; . . .
thus we have come as envoys of our people
to seek redress for injuries at home,
and peace and quiet for Allobrogian lands.

OLLOVICO. It will be granted.

AMBIORIX.   Let us hope it will.
We cannot say for certain that it won't.

OLLOVICO. You have misgivings?

AMBIORIX.   Rightly so perhaps;
for Rome was always jealous of her might; . . .
and then remember, Ollovico, this proud empire
is not, as we are, ruled by tribal chiefs;
way back at home we choose the wisest man, the best,
the shrewdest in the council, the boldest in the fight;
him we elect, the foremost of our clan,
as leader and as ruler of our people; . . .
but here . . .

CATILINE [*steps forward swiftly*]. . . . here sordid selfishness prevails; . . .
here artfulness and bribery take you to the top!

OLLOVICO. Ye gods above! He has been spying on us!

AMBIORIX. Is that how Roman noblemen behave?
It's what the women do where we come from!

CATILINE. No need to fear . . . I'm not a spy by trade . . .
    I merely chanced to hear your conversation; . . .
    it's from the Allobroges you have come?
    You think there's justice to be found in Rome?
    How blind! Turn back! Injustice here and tyranny
    are far worse now than they have ever been.
    Republic certainly it is in name,
    and yet its citizens are held in bondage,
    each one a debtor, slavishly dependent
    upon a Senate men must buy and bribe.
    That liberality which once was Rome's,
    that lofty Roman spirit, rule no more.
    Security and life, I tell you, are a gift
    the Senate grants, and must be matched with gold!
    The order of the day is might, not right;
    the good man is eclipsed by naked power.

AMBIORIX. Then who are you who sweep away the ground
    upon which we had built up all our hopes?

CATILINE. A man who always warms to freedom's cause,
    an enemy of arbitrary power . . .
    a friend of the defenceless and oppressed,
    with pluck and strength to bring the mighty down!

AMBIORIX. The noble Roman people? Tell me, Roman, . . .
    you doubtless would deceive those from abroad: . . .
    is Rome no longer what it used to be . . .
    the tyrant's dread, protector of the weak?

CATILINE [*gravely*]. Look westwards, Allobroges, and see how
    the haughty Capitol there on the hill
    is blazing in the reddish glow of evening,
    caught by the last light of the western sun.
    Rome's evening sky is also red with flame
    as thraldom's night enshrouds her liberty; . . .
    yet in her heavens soon a sun shall shine
    and darkness swiftly flee before its rays.

[*They depart.*]

————————————

A colonnade in Rome.

[LENTULUS, STATILIUS, COEPARIUS, *and* CETHEGUS *enter, in lively conversation.*]

COEPARIUS. Yes, you are right. Things go from bad to worse . . .
  I can't imagine what the end will be.

CETHEGUS. Oh come! . . . I never think about such problems . . .
  I just enjoy each moment as it comes;
  I pick the fruits of gladness for myself
  and for the rest I let the world go hang.

LENTULUS. How nice for those who can. I lack the gift
  of viewing with serene indifference
  a future day when nothing more is left
  and obligations can't be met in full.

STATILIUS. And never any prospect of improvement;
  but still there's no denying that this way of life . . .

CETHEGUS. Oh, stop it! . . .

LENTULUS.   They distrained this very day
  upon the last of my inheritance!

CETHEGUS. Have done with care and come with me. We will
  forget it in a Bacchanalian revel.

COEPARIUS. Yes, that we will! . . . Come on, my merry men!

LENTULUS. No, wait a bit. Our old friend Manlius
  is on his way, I see. He'll want to join us.

MANLIUS [*storms in*]. To hell with all of them, the dirty curs!
  They haven't any sense of justice left!

LENTULUS. Why, what has happened? Why are you so furious?

STATILIUS. Have creditors been plaguing you as well?

MANLIUS. No, nothing of the sort. As you all know,
  I once served honourably under Sulla;
  a piece of farming land was my reward,
  where since the war I've lived in peace and quiet;
  it brought in just enough to make ends meet.

It's now been taken from me . . . as they put it:
state property is all to be called in
for purposes of equal allocation;
it's daylight robbery, that's what it is;
they're only thinking of their own advantage.

COEPARIUS. That's how they trifle with our lawful rights.
The men in power are lording it like tyrants!

CETHEGUS [*cheerfully*]. I say, that *is* bad luck. But I've been hit
by even worse misfortune, as you'll see, . . .
why, think of it: my charming mistress, Tullia,
has gone away and left me, shameless creature,
just when I'd squandered everything on her,
and now I haven't got a penny left!

STATILIUS. Your love of luxury explains it all.

CETHEGUS. Explain it how you will. I'll not give up
the things I want. I mean to satisfy
my wishes quite as long as I am able!

MANLIUS. And I who bravely fought to win the power,
the glory, of which they boast so proudly now! . . .
I shall . . . if only they were with us still,
that brave old band of comrades from the field!
No, most of them, alas, are dead and gone,
and those who live are scattered round the world . . .
what are you younger men compared with them?
You bow to might and grovel in the dust;
you lack the pluck to break the chains that bind you;
you'd rather have this life of servitude!

LENTULUS. By all the gods! . . . strong words admittedly,
but there is truth enough in what he says.

CETHEGUS. Of course, of course, we must concede him that.
But how to set about it . . . that's the point.

LENTULUS. Yes, it's the truth! For ages we've put up
with this oppression. But now the time has come
for casting off the fetters which injustice
and morbid lust for power have forged around us!

STATILIUS. Ah, Lentulus, I understand. But wait . . .
    for that we shall require a forceful leader . . .
    with pluck and vision. Where are we to find him?

LENTULUS. I know a man who has the strength to lead us . . .

MANLIUS. Do you mean Catiline?

LENTULUS.   The very man!

CETHEGUS. Yes, Catiline, he is the only one!

MANLIUS. I know him well; I was his father's friend;
    we fought in many battles side by side.
    His son, though still a lad, went soldiering with him . . .
    a wild unruly fellow even then . . .
    but he's endowed with quite unusual gifts:
    nobility of soul, unflinching courage.

LENTULUS. I think that we shall find him keen and willing.
    I caught him terribly depressed this evening;
    he's brooding over secret plans of his,
    a daring scheme he's had in mind some time.

STATILIUS. He's long been trying for the consulship . . .

LENTULUS. He'll not succeed . . . his enemies have been
    attacking him most bitterly . . .
    it happened he was present at the meeting;
    he walked out wild with fury, planning vengeance.

STATILIUS. He's sure then to agree to our proposal!

LENTULUS. I hope he does. We'll go and look him up.
    Just come with me; . . . the time is opportune.

[*They go out.*]

The temple of Vesta.

[*The sacred fire is burning in a niche at the back.* CATILINE *and* CURIUS *sneak in behind the pillars at the front.*]

CURIUS. What, Catiline, it's here you're bringing me,
    to Vesta's temple?

CATILINE [*laughing*]. . . . Well, yes, as you see!

CURIUS. Ye gods, how rash! . . . today when Cicero,
  your enemy, has been denouncing you . . .
  and yet you can . . .

CATILINE.   Oh, let's forget about it! . . .

CURIUS. You are in danger and would forget it
  by rushing blindly into further peril!

CATILINE [*cheerfully*]. I like variety; I've never had
  a vestal virgin for my mistress yet.
  That's why I've come here now to try my luck!

CURIUS. Ye gods above! But surely you are joking?

CATILINE. A joke? Of course, as my love always is,
  but what I told you now was meant in earnest. . . .
  At the last festival along the streets of Rome
  I saw the priestesses as they filed past
  in slow procession, when I chanced to gaze
  on one of them, and with a fleeting glance
  her eyes met mine . . . they pierced my very soul . . .
  and the expression then in those dark eyes
  I never saw before in any woman.

CURIUS. I can believe it . . . tell me though: what followed?

CATILINE. I found my way into the temple here . . .
  and several times I've seen and talked to her.
  Ah, what a gulf there is dividing her
  from my Aurelia. . . .

CURIUS.   And you love them both
  at once. No, that I cannot understand . . .

CATILINE. It's curious . . . more than I can grasp myself,
  and yet it is exactly as you say . . .
  but what a world of difference in my love . . .
  Aurelia is so kind; her tender words
  will often put me in a gentle mood,
  while Furia . . . listen, quiet, there's someone coming . . .

FURIA [*enters*]. These hateful halls that witness all the pain
  and agony to which I am condemned!

Each cherished hope, each glorious ambition
extinguished in my heart . . . pervaded now
with chilling fever, now with glowing fire,
a passion burning hotter than that flame.
Ah, what a fate . . . what can have been the crime
for which I was imprisoned in this temple,
and was deprived of every joy of youth,
of harmless pleasures in life's lovely springtime? . . .
Yet never shall these eyes be moist with tears . . .
for only hate and vengeance stir this heart!

CATILINE [*steps forward*]. Do you not nurse another passion, Furia?
Not even tend a gentler flame for me?

FURIA. Ye gods! Oh reckless man . . . you here again!
Do you not fear . . . ?

CATILINE.   Fear is unknown to me,
and facing danger always was my joy.

FURIA. Oh wonderful! I think the same as you,
and so I hate this temple all the more,
because I live secure in peace and calm,
and danger never lurks behind the walls . . .
this empty round of inactivity,
life faintly flickering like a dying lamp.
Ah, what an outlet here for all the wealth
of proud and lofty plans within my breast!
How it is crushed between these narrow walls,
where all life ossifies and hope is quenched,
where drowsily the weary day drags on,
where thoughts can never find a concrete goal!

CATILINE. Ah, Furia, how uncanny are your words,
like sounds which seem to come from my own breast;
as though with characters of flame you would
depict my every warm and throbbing wish . . .
my heart is likewise in the grip of anguish,
and hatred tempers it, like yours, to steel . . .
I too was robbed of every hope I cherished;
my life is just like yours . . . without a goal. . . .
But I hide my agony in silence

and none suspects the fire that glows within . . .
these worthless men look down on me and scorn me . . .
they do not know how fast this heart is beating
for right and freedom, for each noble cause
which ever stirred in any human breast!

FURIA. Oh wonderful! No other soul but yours
was made for me . . . a voice which does not lie
proclaims it from the bottom of my heart. . . .
So come, oh come with me; we will obey . . .

CATILINE. What do these raptures mean, my lovely one?

FURIA. Yes, let us flee away now from this place
and find a better country of our own . . .
here soaring pride of spirit is repressed . . .
here baseness stifles every spark of brilliance
before it bursts forth into leaping flame. . . .
Oh, come and let us flee. . . . The motherland
of freedom's children is the globe itself!

CATILINE. You draw me with the magic of your words . . .

FURIA. So let us then this very moment flee . . .
across the mountain tops, beyond the seas;
far from Rome our flight shall first be stayed . . .
your friends are sure to follow you in strength;
we will set up our home in distant lands . . .
there we shall rule, and will no more conceal
that no heart yet did beat like yours and mine! . . .

CATILINE. Oh beautiful! But why, pray, should we flee?
. . . here too the flame of freedom can be fed . . .
here also there is ample scope for deeds,
as great as any even your soul asks . . .

FURIA. What, here, you say? In Rome, this wretched place
of tyranny and men with minds in bondage? . . .
Ah, Lucius, are you also one of those
who must shamefacedly recall Rome's past?
What was she once? What has she now become?
A band of heroes then, and now a crowd
of wretched slaves . . .

CATILINE.   You too are mocking me?
  Then you shall know: to keep alive Rome's freedom,
  to see her lofty splendour once again,
  I would, like Curtius, gladly hurl myself
  in the abyss below. . . .

FURIA.   Oh say no more!
  A strange fire lights your eye . . . you spoke the truth . . .
  but go . . . the priestesses will soon be here,
  according to their custom at this hour.

CATILINE. I'll go . . . but soon you'll see me here again . . .
  some magic power binds me to your side . . .
  I never saw a woman proud as you . . .

FURIA [*with a wild smile*]. Then one thing you must promise me, and
      swear
  to keep your promise . . . will you do so, Lucius?

CATILINE. I will do anything my Furia asks;
  in my heart you alone hold sovereign power . . .

FURIA. Then listen: though I live here in this temple,
  there is one man among you all in Rome; . . .
  to him I'm sworn in mortal enmity,
  and hate beyond the gloomy grave itself.

CATILINE. And so . . .

FURIA.   So swear this man shall also be
  your mortal enemy. Well, Lucius, will you?

CATILINE. I here do swear by all the gods on high,
  by my mother's memory, my father's name,
  I solemnly do swear . . . what is it, Furia?
  . . . there is a strange fire burning in your eyes,
  your cheeks are white as marble, pale as death!

FURIA. I do not know myself . . . like fire my veins
  are glowing . . . but, go on . . . swear yet again . . .

CATILINE. Ye gods on high, pour down upon my head
  the fulness of your vengeance; thunderbolts
  of wrath shall blast me, if I break my oath;
  I shall pursue him like a very demon!

FURIA. Enough, I trust you; ah, that eased my heart . . .
and now my vengeance truly rests with you!

CATILINE. I shall perform the task, but tell me, Furia,
who is he, and what crime did he commit?

FURIA. Far from the walls of Rome, close by the Tiber,
my birthplace lies; it was my peaceful home
until my ordination as a vestal; . . .
I lived there with a sister I loved dearly;
. . . some scoundrel visited our peaceful haven . . .
he saw the pure and lovely lily there . . .

CATILINE [*surprised*]. By all the gods above! . . .

FURIA.   and he seduced her. . . .
She sought her grave beneath the Tiber's waters!

CATILINE [*uneasy*]. You know the man?

FURIA.   I never saw him there . . .
I did not know a thing until too late!
But now I know his name . . .

CATILINE.   What was it then?

FURIA. I'm sure you know him: it was Catiline!

CATILINE [*shrinks back*]. Oh ghastly. . . ! Furia . . . what was that you
said?

FURIA. Is something wrong? Keep calm! How pale you are. . . .
Why, Lucius, can he be a friend of yours?

CATILINE. My friend! No, Furia, no! . . . Not any more. . . .
I've cursed, and sworn for evermore to hate . . .
myself . . .

FURIA.   Yourself! You . . . you are Catiline?

CATILINE. I am . . .

FURIA.   So you it was seduced my Tullia?
Then Nemesis indeed has heard my prayer . . .
yourself you've called down vengeance on your head;
alas for you, seducer! . . .

CATILINE.   Ah, your eyes,
   how hideously they stare! . . . ah, in this moonlight
   you might well be the dead girl's shade.

               [*He departs hastily.*]

FURIA [*after a pause, in a frenzy*].
   Ah, now I understand . . . at last the veil
   has fallen from my eyes and I see all.
   Hatred it was which rooted in my breast
   when first I saw him in that city street . . .
   a strange sensation and a wild, a blood-red flame!
   Yes, he shall feel what hatred such as mine,
   a flame for ever burning, unconfined
   and never ending, shall bring down on him!

A VESTAL [*enters*]. Time's nearly up now, Furia, you may go . . .
   that's why I've come . . . but by the sacred goddess! . . .
   what's this? . . . Alas for you, the flame is out!

FURIA [*wildly*]. Is out, you say? . . . It burns as fierce as ever . . .
   it never will go out . . .

THE VESTAL.   Ye gods, what *is* this?

FURIA. The fire of hate is not put out with ease . . .
   the flame of love flares up, and in a trice
   it dies away again, but hatred . . .

THE VESTAL.   Celestial goddess!
   Oh help! Bring help! Why, this is madness, help! . . .

       [*A number of temple servants rush in.*]

SOME. What's wrong? . . .

OTHERS.   The flame of Vesta has gone out! . . .

FURIA. Here in my heart the flame is burning still!

THE VESTAL. Away with her, away with the offender!

          [*They take her away.*]

CURIUS [*steps forward*]. They are taking her away to die.
   No, no, by all the gods, that must not be!
   Shall she, this proud, this noble creature suffer

the shameful death of common criminals?
Oh, I have never felt like this before!
How deep her image has engraved itself
within my heart; ah, what is wrong with me?
I wonder, is this love? Yes, love it is. . . .
Then I will save her . . . oh, but Catiline?
She will pursue him with eternal hate; . . .
are there already not enough who hate him?
Shall I increase the number of his foes?
Why, he has long since been a father to me . . .
my duty now demands that I protect him; . . .
but love itself? Ah, what does that demand?
And would proud Catiline, would he be one
to tremble at a woman's wrath? Not he!
It must be carried out with no delay!
Yes, Furia, I . . . I shall deliver you
from death, although it might cost me my life!

[*He departs hastily.*]

A room in Catiline's house.

CATILINE [*enters in great agitation*].
'Then Nemesis indeed has heard my prayer;
yourself you've called down vengeance on your head.' . . .
Such were the words on those ecstatic lips . . .
remarkable . . . perhaps it was an omen,
a sign of what the future holds in store. . . .
So I have bound myself on solemn oath
for ever to avenge my own transgression!
Ah, Furia, still I see your fiery gaze,
like savage eyes of some avenging goddess;
your words still echo hollow in my soul,
my oath I shall remember evermore . . .

[*He breaks off. During the following* AURELIA *approaches him
unnoticed.*]

Yet it is utterly absurd to dwell
upon such nonsense . . . it is nothing more . . .
I have a better line of thought to follow . . .

my soul has bigger things to focus on; . . .
my projects press their claims imperiously,
on them I now must concentrate my mind;
my inner self is like a storm at sea . . .

AURELIA [*seizes his hand*]. And may Aurelia not be told the reason;
may she not know what stirs within your breast,
what savage conflict now is raging there . . .
may she not comfort you with kindliness
and banish all the darkness from your soul?

CATILINE [*gently*]. How sweet and kind you are, Aurelia dear!
But why should I embitter life for you;
why should you share with me my every sorrow? . . .
I have inflicted on you pain enough;
for is it not enough that on my head
a hostile and oppressive fate has heaped
the curse inherent in that combination
of noble spiritual energies,
of ardent fervour for a life of deeds,
with sordid bonds which cramp the striving soul. . . .
Must you drain too, in long and cheerless draughts,
my bitter cup of sorrow to the dregs?

AURELIA. A woman's role is to console and comfort,
although she cannot dream like you of greatness; . . .
when man is fighting for his proudest dream,
and reaps but disillusion and distress,
her words sound kind and tender in his ear . . .
and she will lull him into peaceful slumber;
then he discovers that the quiet life
itself has joys which frantic turmoil lacks.

CATILINE. Yes, you are right; . . . I feel it in my bones,
and yet I cannot tear myself away . . .
a ceaseless ferment works within my breast . . .
life's turmoil has alone the power to still it.

AURELIA. Is your Aurelia not enough for you?
Although she cannot bring your soul to rest . . .
at least unlock your heart to words of kindness,
to words of love and comfort from your wife.

Though she can't satisfy this frantic urge,
and cannot follow you in flights of thought:
yet you shall know that I can share each sorrow . . .
with courage and the strength to ease your load!

CATILINE. Then I will tell you why, Aurelia dear,
my spirits are so very low just now; . . .
you know that for some time I have been trying,
without success, to get the consulship. . . .
You know the story . . . how to win more votes
I've squandered . . .

AURELIA.   Do not talk of it, my dear.
It grieves me so . . .

CATILINE.   Do you reproach me too? . . .
was any other course still open to me? . . .
The whole lot gone with not a thing to show! . . .
Disgrace and ridicule are all I've gained. . . .
Now Marcus Cicero, my enemy,
has bitterly reviled me in the Senate . . .
he spoke about my life, and drew a picture
so foul that even I was forced to shudder; . . .
contempt is written large on every face,
the name of Catiline is said with loathing
and will be handed to posterity
to be a grim and ghastly symbol
of baseness coupled to licentiousness,
of mocking scorn for what is high and noble.
No deed will ever save his reputation
and testify against these shameful lies,
for people will believe what rumour says. . . .

AURELIA. But I do not believe it, Catiline!
Let all the world express its condemnation,
just let it load disgrace upon your head;
I know you hide within your lofty soul
a seed that one day can bear noble fruit . . .
but here it has no chance to sprout and grow,
and soon it will be choked by harmful weeds. . . .
Let us depart then from the home of sorrow.
What ties have you? Why should we stay here longer?

CATILINE. What do you mean? Am I to go away?
  Shall I abandon all my proud ideals? . . .
  A drowning man . . . although without all hope . . .
  will still cling tightly to the shattered timbers; . . .
  and when the wreck is sucked down to its grave,
  with every hope of rescue long since faded,
  with his last ounce of strength he still holds on
  and sinks with the last timber to the bottom . . .

AURELIA. But if some friendly coast should smile on him,
  with groves of green along the ocean waves,
  then hope is reawakened in his breast; . . .
  he strives to reach the light and airy woods . . .
  there all is perfect . . . all is peace and calm,
  there friendly waves come rippling to the shore,
  and there he lays his weary limbs to rest
  while cool winds from the west caress his brow,
  dispelling every gloomy cloud of care,
  to leave him with a sense of peace and calm.
  He lingers in this haven and, refreshed,
  forgets the gloomy days which now are past; . . .
  the distant echo from the noisy world
  is all that penetrates his quiet abode . . .
  and this does not disturb his inner peace,
  but calms his soul and gladdens it the more,
  reminding him of times that have gone by,
  his shattered plans and his tumultuous joys; . . .
  he finds this life of quiet now twice as fair,
  and would not change for any Roman's honour!

CATILINE. Your words are beautiful, and I could go
  away with you at once from this life's turmoil . . .
  but tell me, where are we to find our refuge,
  where shall we find a peaceful place to live? . . .

AURELIA [*happy*]. You will come, Catiline? How wonderful!
  My heart cannot contain itself for joy. . . .
  What are we waiting for? . . . Why, we can go
  this very night . . .

CATILINE.   And where are we to go? . . .
  Where shall we find a spot for me to rest
  my head in peace? . . .

AURELIA.   How can you speak like that?
  Do you forget the little country place
  where I was born, and where we later, gay
  and happy in our calm of utter bliss,
  have spent so many a carefree summer day?
  Where else, I wonder, was the grass so green?
  Where else such coolness in the forest's shade?
  The little house peeps forth between the trees
  and beckons with its cosy air of peace.
  That's where we'll flee, and dedicate our lives
  to peaceful country ways, to quiet pleasures.
  There you shall have a loving wife to cheer you,
  whose tender kisses shall dispel your sorrows . . .

                         [*Smiling.*]

  and when with blossoms gathered from the fields
  you seek your sovereign lady in her bower,
  I shall at once proclaim you Prince of Flowers,
  and wind the laurel wreath around your brow ! . . .
  But tell me, what is wrong? You clutch my hand
  convulsively . . . a strange glint lights your eyes . . .

CATILINE. Alas, your hopes are all in vain, Aurelia;
  it's more than I can do to take you there; . . .
  I cannot . . .

AURELIA.   Goodness, how you frighten me !
  You surely must be joking, Catiline?

CATILINE. Me joking? Am I capable of that? . . .
  when all your words, sharp arrows of revenge,
  transfix this poor tormented breast of mine,
  which fate has never yet allowed to rest . . .

AURELIA. Ye gods! Why, tell me what you mean . . .

CATILINE.   Here, look !
  Here is your house, your future happiness.

      [*He pulls out a purse of gold and flings it on to the table.*]

AURELIA. Oh, you have sold . . .

CATILINE. Indeed, this very day. . . .
What for? . . . For purposes of bribery . . .

AURELIA. Enough! Enough! . . . Let's not think any more
about it . . . it will only cause us pain!

CATILINE. Your gentleness is much more shattering
than any words of bitter accusation.

[*An* OLD SOLDIER *enters and approaches* CATILINE.]

THE SOLDIER. Forgive me, sir, for walking in like this,
so late at night and unannounced. Forgive . . .

CATILINE. Yes, out with it! What have you come here for?

THE SOLDIER. My errand is a humble prayer, which you,
I'm sure, will hear. I am just a pauper, one
whose strength has been devoted to Rome's glory; . . .
now I am spent . . . I can no longer serve . . .
my arms are rusting on the walls at home; . . .
my hopes were wholly centred on my son,
who kept me with the labour of his hands.
Alas, he is in prison now for debt,
and I am desperate. Oh help me, sir!

[*He kneels.*]

Please spare a coin! I have tramped from door
to door, but all were bolted long ago . . .
I can't go on . . .

CATILINE. Just what you would expect!
You see, Aurelia, that's the way they treat
our brave old company of veterans . . .
we have no gratitude left here in Rome! . . .
There was a time when I in righteous anger
had gladly sought revenge with fire and sword,
but there, I cannot do it now . . . my heart
is gentle as a child's . . . I can't take vengeance . . .
relieving sorrow is a good deed too . . .
take this, my man. Now you can pay your debt . . .

[*He hands him the gold.*]

THE SOLDIER. Oh gods above! Can I believe your words?

CATILINE. Yes, hurry, man, and free him from his chains!

[*The* SOLDIER *departs hastily.*]

A better use for it than bribery,
Aurelia, and corruption, don't you think?
It may be pleasant bringing tyrants down . . .
but simple kindness has its own reward!

AURELIA. Oh, still you are magnanimous and noble!
Once more I recognize my Catiline!

A subterranean vault.

[*A lamp burns faintly. A large iron door at the back.* FURIA, *dressed in a black gown, is standing in the middle of the vault and seems to be listening to something.*]

FURIA. A hollow rumble! Thunder up above!
The distant sound comes echoing down to me . . .
but all is still here in the underworld!
Ah, am I doomed to drowsiness for ever?
Am I not even here to thread my way
along untrodden paths . . . my joy of old?
[*After a pause.*] How strange a life it was, and strange the fate
which like a comet swiftly came and vanished!
He met me. Some compelling magic power . . .
some inner sympathy brought us together; . . .
I the avenging goddess, he my victim . . .
but punishment soon followed the avenger!
[*A pause.*] How all is silent up above . . . am I
still moving further from the sphere of light?
Ah, good, if that is so . . . and if my spell
inside this cavern is in fact a flight
on wings of lightning down to lands of darkness,
if I am now approaching the dread Styx!
There leaden waves are rolling on the shore,
there Charon rows his boat and makes no sound . . .
and soon I shall be there . . . there I will sit
in silence by the ferry . . . ask each spirit,

E1

each fleeting shade which from the realm of life
steps lightly onward to the land of death,
inquire of him how Catiline is faring
among the living in the world above,
inquire how Catiline has kept his oath!
And I will shine my blue sulphureous torch
deep into every phantom's lifeless eye; . . .
in all the thousands I shall pick out Catiline . . .
and when he comes, then I shall follow him . . .
and we shall make the crossing both together,
we both shall enter Proserpine's abode; . . .
for even as a shade I'll dog his steps . . .
where Catiline is, Furia too shall be.

[*A pause.*]

The air in here is growing close and stuffy,
and breathing harder than it was before; . . .
then I am drawing near the gloomy swamps
where silently the streams of Hades flow . . .

[*She listens. A faint noise can be heard.*]

. . . A muffled sound . . . as though of thudding oars . . .
the ferryman of death already come
to fetch me . . . no, 'tis here I wish to wait! . . .

[*The iron door at the back opens softly and* CURIUS *appears, beckoning gently.*]

I greet you, Charon. Are you here so soon
to take me as a guest to halls of death?
It's here I wish to wait . . .

CURIUS.   Hush! Follow me . . .

ACT TWO

A room in Catiline's house.

[CATILINE *is pacing up and down.* LENTULUS *and* CETHEGUS.]

CATILINE. No, I'm telling you . . . you miss the point,
just do not understand me. . . . What, shall I
become a traitor? Start a civil war?
The blood of fellow citizens shall stain
my hands? . . . No, I'll not do it! No! May Rome
condemn me if . . .

LENTULUS.   You will not, Catiline!

CATILINE. I will not . . .

CETHEGUS.   Tell me, have you no old scores
to settle . . . nothing personal to gain?

CATILINE. Let those who want seek vengeance; I'll not do so . . .
yet there is vengeance too in silent scorn . . .
that is the only kind I'll take . . .

CETHEGUS.   Ha! ha!
I see the moment is inopportune,
but I am sure that when tomorrow comes
you'll view things in a different light . . .

CATILINE.   How so?

CETHEGUS. There are peculiar rumours going round; . . .
just now a vestal has been led to death . . .

CATILINE [*surprised*]. A vestal has? Ah, What was that you said?

LENTULUS. Indeed, a vestal! . . . and as rumour says . . .

CATILINE. What does it say?

CETHEGUS.   . . . That you yourself are not
entirely ignorant of this affair . . .

CATILINE. So that is what they say! . . .

LENTULUS.   Yes, that's the rumour!
   Of course, for those of us who are your friends
   this is a matter of indifference . . .
   the general public judges sternly though!

CATILINE [*sunk in thought*]. And she is dead! . . .

CETHEGUS.   Most certainly she is . . .
   one hour's immurement in the convicts' tomb
   is ample time . . .

LENTULUS.   Well, let's forget about it!
   We didn't mention her because of that . . .
   but listen, Catiline! Just think a moment:
   you tried to get the consulship . . . you pinned
   your hopes exclusively on the success
   of your attempt . . . and now that too has failed . . .

CATILINE [*as before*]. 'Yourself you've called down vengeance on your
   head.'

CETHEGUS. Now stop this brooding! It will do no good. . . .
   Act like a man; things still can be put right;
   a quick decision . . . you have friends enough,
   All ready to obey a sign from you . . .
   your answer, Catiline . . . well, will you?

CATILINE.   No, I will not!
   And why do you all wish for this conspiracy?
   Is noble love of liberty the reason?
   Would you in order to restore Rome's greatness
   lay all in ruins? . . .

LENTULUS.   I can't exactly say,
   but private hopes of greatness, you'll agree,
   are adequate incentive, Catiline!

CETHEGUS. And means sufficient to enjoy life's pleasures
   are not entirely to be ruled out either . . .
   that's all I aim for . . . I am not ambitious!

CATILINE. Ah, I knew it. You are prompted solely
   by base and personal considerations. . . .
   Oh no, my friends, I have a better goal . . .

I tried, it's true, to win the consulship
by dint of bribery; . . . but my intentions
were better than the methods used would lead
you to suppose. The goal of my endeavours
was freedom and the welfare of us all.
I was misjudged, appearances belied me.
My fate decreed it thus. It must be so!

CETHEGUS. You will not, Catiline? You will not save
your friends from utter ruin and disgrace? . . .
A lot of us, please note, will soon be forced
to beg our way, because of riotous living . . .

CATILINE. Well stop in time then . . . that is my decision!

LENTULUS. What, Catiline, do you intend to change
your mode of life? Oh no, you must be joking!

CATILINE. I am in earnest, by the gods on high!

CETHEGUS. Hm, so we'll not get anywhere with him!
Come, let us hurry up and tell our friends
the outcome of our meeting. They will be
carousing down at Bibulus's place . . .

CATILINE. With Bibulus? Ah, many a riotous night
we've spent together down at his place, friends!
But that's all over now and done with . . .
I'm leaving here before the night is out . . .

ENTULUS. What's that? Leave here . . .

CETHEGUS.   Before the night is out?

CATILINE. This night, together with Aurelia
I shall be taking leave of Rome for good; . . .
we'll make our new home in the dales of Gaul . . .
a little plot of land will do to feed us.

CETHEGUS. Ah, Catiline, you mean to leave us then . . . !

CATILINE. I do, I must. The shame here weighs me down. . . .
Oh, I can stand up to my poverty,
but when I see the scorn and deep contempt
on every Roman's face, no that is too much! . . .

. . . Out there I'll lead a settler's quiet life,
I will forget the man I used to be,
I'll wipe out every thought about my plans,
and see my past as in a hazy dream!

LENTULUS. Farewell it is then, and the best of luck!

CETHEGUS. And mind you don't forget us, Catiline.
We'll always think of you. . . . Now we must tell
our friends of the decision you have made.

CATILINE. And say goodbye for me with warm regards!

[LENTULUS *and* CETHEGUS *depart.* AURELIA *enters, but stops apprehensively when she sees* LENTULUS *and* CETHEGUS. *When they have left she goes up to* CATILINE.]

AURELIA [*reproaching him gently*].
Those wild friends of yours again,
Catiline . . .

CATILINE. And that time was the last.
I merely said goodbye . . . and now my ties
with Rome have all been well and truly severed,
in all eternity . . .

AURELIA.   I have been packing
our few belongings. Nothing very much . . .
enough for simple needs though, Catiline!

CATILINE [*lost in thought*]. Yes, quite enough, now all is lost for me!

AURELIA. Oh, think no more about what can't be helped . . .
forget . . .

CATILINE. I would be happy if I could,
if I could pluck the memory from my soul,
finally forget my dreams, my plans!
Oh no, I'm not yet capable of that,
but I will try my hardest . . .

AURELIA.   I will help you,
and you will find a cure for all your pain.
But we must leave here now as soon as may be . . .
your soul is haunted here by memories . . .
we leave this very night then, you agree? . . .

CATILINE. Of course, this very night, Aurelia!

AURELIA. I have collected up the little bit
of money left . . . sufficient for the journey!

CATILINE. Good! I will trade my sword in for a spade . . .
what further use have I got for a sword? . . .

AURELIA. You dig the ground and I shall till the soil;
soon you will have a lovely show of flowers,
a hedge of roses, sweet forget-me-nots,
as symbols that the time has now arrived
when you can welcome as a childhood friend
each memory returning from the past!

CATILINE. Oh no, oh no, Aurelia, such a time
belongs still to the dim and distant future.
[*After a pause.*] But now go in and rest awhile, Aurelia,
at midnight we will set off on our way,
the hour when Rome is sunk in deepest slumber
and not a soul suspects where we are fleeing. . . .
The radiance of the morning sky shall find us
far far from here, and in the heart of nature
we'll rest upon our bed of soft green grass. . . .

AURELIA. A new life is about to dawn for us,
more joyous than the life we're soon to leave.
But I'll be going now. A quiet hour's rest
will give me strength. Good night, my dearest one!

[*She kisses him and goes.*]

CATILINE. She's gone at last! . . . Ah, what a great relief!
And now I can discard this burdensome
pretence, this semblance of tranquillity,
which is the very least of all my feelings. . . .
She is my better spirit . . . it would grieve her
to see my sorrow and I must conceal it . . .
but I will dedicate this silent hour
to meditation on my wanton life; . . .
that lamp though is distracting to my dreams . . .
I must have darkness, dark as in my soul!

[*He extinguishes the lamp. The moon shines in between the columns at the back.*]

Ah, it is still too light, but never mind!
The pallid moonlight harmonizes well
with this dim twilight gloom which now enshrouds,
which ever has enshrouded all my steps. . . .
So this day, Catiline, will be your last . . .
when morning comes you will no longer be
the selfsame Catiline as hitherto.
Away in distant Gaul my life will flow
unnoticed in the darkness of the forests. . . .
Ah, this is my awakening from those dreams
of greatness, of a proud life rich in deeds,
which I once cherished . . . deep within my soul
they had their only being, known to no man!
It isn't the oppressive peace and calm
far from this world's bustle which alarms me . . .
no . . . just to shine forth for one single second
and blaze with meteoric brilliance,
just by some splendid exploit to inscribe
my name on rolls of everlasting glory . . .
ah, that very moment I could quit
this life; . . . for then I would have lived indeed; . . .
I could away and flee to foreign shores,
and I could plunge the dagger in my heart . . .
yet this is nothing but a living death!
So, Catiline, you are to perish thus!
A sign, ye gods above me, that it is
my fate to vanish from this life forgotten,
without a trace! . . .

FURIA [*behind the pillars at the back*]. It is not, Catiline!

CATILINE [*shrinks back*]. That ghastly sound! What kind of voice was
   that?
   A spirit speaking from the world of shades?

FURIA [*comes forward into the moonlight*].
   I am your genius! . . .

CATILINE [*horror-struck*].   Ah, Furia!

FURIA. You have sunk low indeed to be afraid
   of me! . . .

CATILINE. Ah, you are risen from
the grave's dark depths in order to pursue me . . .

FURIA. Pursue, you said? I am your genius!
Wherever you go, there I too must be . . .

[*She comes nearer.*]

CATILINE. Oh gracious gods of mercy, she is real,
she is no ghost . . .

FURIA. No matter whether ghost
or not. I shall be staying by your side . . .

CATILINE. With everlasting hate! . . .

FURIA. Hate vanishes
with death . . . like love and every other feeling
that thrives in mortal breasts . . . one thing alone,
one thing alone remains unchanged for ever . . .

CATILINE. And that? Speak out! . . .

FURIA. The fate of Catiline!

CATILINE. My fate is known but to the gods on high,
to no one else . . .

FURIA. And me, it's known to me!
I am your genius, uncanny bonds
link us together . . .

CATILINE. Bonds of hatred . . .

FURIA. No!
Did any spirit rise up from the grave
with hate at heart? I tell you, Catiline,
the rivers of the underworld have quenched
the fire of hatred blazing in my breast; . . .
why, Catiline, no longer am I now
the selfsame Furia, wild and full of vengeance,
whom you once knew . . .

CATILINE. You do not hate me then?

FURIA. Not any more. For down there in that cavern,
as I stood on the path which leads across

from life to death, and, evermore cut off
from realms of light, prepared to make my stay
within the underworld, a curious mood
came over me . . . I don't know what it was . . .
I underwent the strangest transformation,
my hate, revenge, my soul itself . . . all vanished;
each memory, each earthly longing vanished . . .
just one name . . . 'Catiline' . . . remains engraved
in fiery letters on my heart for ever . . .

CATILINE. Uncanny! Ah, whoever you may be,
a mortal, or a spirit from below,
there is in truth a curious fascination
in those dark glances, in the words you speak! . . .

FURIA. Your soul is proud like mine, and yet you would,
despondent and afraid, give up all hope
of future greatness. . . . Like a coward you
would quit the stage where all your lofty plans
were due to grow and reach maturity. . . .

CATILINE. I must! I must! My fate is driving me!

FURIA. Your fate? Have you then not the strength and courage
to fight against this thing you call your fate?

CATILINE. Oh, I have fought enough! Was not my life
a constant fight? . . . And what was my reward?
Contempt and scorn . . .

FURIA.   Ah, you have fallen low.
You set yourself a bold and lofty goal . . .
you strive to reach it, yet you are dismayed
by every hindrance . . .

CATILINE.   Fear is not the reason . . .
my goal was daring and my plans were lofty; . . .
the whole thing was a fleeting dream of youth!

FURIA. No, Catiline, oh no. You would deceive yourself.
Each single thought was centred on this goal . . .
your soul is noble, fit to govern Rome,
and you have friends. Ah, why then hesitate?

CATILINE [*meditating*]. Am I . . .? What do you mean? . . . With Roman
    blood . . .

FURIA. You weakling! You have not a woman's courage!
    Have you forgotten that proud Roman daughter
    who seized the throne across her father's corpse?
    I feel I'm cast in Tullia's mould . . . but you?
    Despise, despise yourself, oh Catiline!

CATILINE. Shall I despise myself because my breast
    no longer is the seat of wild ambition?

FURIA. You now stand at the parting of the ways . . .
    on one path quiet solitude awaits you . . .
    a life which is part death, part lethargy . . .
    but on the other side you can descry
    a monarch's throne; . . . so choose then, Catiline!

CATILINE. Ah, your words have such seductive charm!

FURIA. Come, Catiline, just one audacious step
    and proud Rome's destiny lies in your hands!
    Look, greatness, sovereign power await you here,
    and yet you waver, do not dare to act!
    you leave us for your distant forests, where
    each hope you ever nursed will be snuffed out; . . .
    ah, Catiline, is there not any trace
    of pride remaining somewhere in your heart? . . .
    And is this noble soul, for honour born,
    to vanish in some backwood quite unknown? . . .
    Oh, go then . . . knowing you have lost for good
    what you could win with forceful action here!

CATILINE. Go on! Go on!

FURIA.   Your name will be remembered
    with dread and horror by posterity. . . .
    Your life was nothing but a reckless gamble . . .
    yet it would shine with brilliant clarity
    across the ages, if with strength and vigour
    you forced a passage through the madding crowd;
    and through your radiant spirit clouds of thraldom
    had given way to new-born skies of freedom . . .
    if you had . . .

CATILINE.   Oh, no more. For you have touched
   that string which sounded in my deepest soul . . .
   those words of yours were like a ringing echo
   of what my heart has whispered for so long!

FURIA. This is the Catiline I used to know.

CATILINE. I shall not go! . . . You have recalled to life
   my youthful nerve, my manhood's proud ambitions;
   ah, I shall be a light to abject Rome,
   and blaze forth with a comet's awesome splendour!
   You haughty wretches, you shall now discover
   I am not broken yet, though for a time
   my strength was sapped in battle . . .

FURIA.   Catiline!
   Now hear! Whatever fate may will, and spirits
   of darkness may decree, we must obey . . .
   and so . . . my hate is gone, fate willed it thus . . .
   it had to be . . . your hand on our alliance
   in perpetuity . . . why hesitate?
   you are unwilling? . . .

CATILINE.   Oh, those frightening eyes,
   like lightning flashing in the dark of night; . . .
   that ghastly smile . . . just how I've always thought
   of Nemesis . . .

FURIA.   What? . . . She is to be found
   deep down in your own breast; . . . do you forget your oath?

CATILINE. No, I remember, yet you seem to me
   a spirit of revenge . . .

FURIA.   Indeed, I am
   an image from your soul . . .

CATILINE [*brooding*].   What did you say?
   Ah, dim forebodings, weird and clouded visions,
   rise up before my inner eye. And yet
   I cannot make them out. It is too dark within!

FURIA. It must be so . . . our realm is of the dark;
   and there we rule. Now come, your hand upon
   our dark and everlasting bond. . . .

CATILINE [*wildly*].   Fair Nemesis!
My genius and image of my soul!
Here is my hand on our eternal bond.

[*He seizes her hand violently; she looks at him with a wild smile.*]

FURIA. Now we shall never part! . . .

CATILINE.   Ah, when you touched
my hand a fire shot blazing through my veins.
No longer flowing blood, but savage flames!
I feel already that my heart is bursting;
I find it dark; but soon a blazing light
shall spread above the city of the Romans!

[*He draws his sword from its scabbard.*]

My sword! My sword! Ah, see the way it gleams!
Yet soon it shall be stained with streams of blood!
My brow aglow, my heart is pounding madly,
and strangest visions flit across my soul.
It is revenge, revenge and proud wild dreams
of greatness, power, and everlasting fame; . . .
now 'Blood and Flames' shall be my battle cry. . . .
Away! Away! I've found myself at last!

[*He dashes out, with* FURIA *following.*]

A tavern.

[STATILIUS, GABINIUS, *and* COEPARIUS *enter, together with several other young noblemen.*]

STATILIUS. Well, here we can amuse ourselves, my friends;
it's safe in here. We can't be overheard!

GABINIUS. Yes, we'll enjoy each moment as it comes;
for who can say how long we'll have the chance?

COEPARIUS. No, let us wait and hear what news Cethegus
and Lentulus are going to bring us first.

GABINIUS. Oh, they can bring whatever news they like,
and meanwhile we will while away the time . . .
Come on, my friends, let's have a jolly song!

[*As the servants hand round the cup the following song is sung.*]

Bacchus we hail thee,
brimful we gaily
fill up the goblet,
drink to thy praise.
Red wine is flowing,
mellow and glowing,
drink of the wine-god,
all men's delight.

Liber is jovial,
smiling approval;
gladness now beckons,
clear is the grape.
Bliss let us capture
wines bring us rapture,
ever with gladness
filling our hearts.

Bubbling Falernian,
sparkling and clearest,
we love thee dearest,
first among wines.
Source of elation,
joy thy creation,
thou to our spirits
bringest good cheer.

Bacchus we hail thee,
brimful we gaily
fill up the goblet,
drink to thy praise.
Red wine is flowing,
mellow and glowing,
drink of the wine-god,
all men's delight.

———————————

[LENTULUS *and* CETHEGUS *enter.*]

LENTULUS. No time for songs and merriment!

STATILIUS.   What now?
  Are you not bringing Catiline along?

GABINIUS. Well, surely he agreed? . . .

COEPARIUS.   What was his answer?
  Come, out with it! . . .

CETHEGUS.   His answer was
  the opposite of what we thought . . .

GABINIUS.   Well, well!

LENTULUS. He simply turned our offer down, and won't
  have any more to do with our proposals!

STATILIUS. Ah, is that true? . . .

COEPARIUS.   And why is he unwilling?

LENTULUS. He doesn't want to, as I said; he's walking
  out on all his friends; . . . he plans to leave us. . . .

STATILIUS. Did you say leave? . . .

CETHEGUS.   Yes, he is setting off
  this very night; we cannot blame him though; . . .
  he had good reasons . . .

LENTULUS.   Cowardice, that's why;
  breaks faith and leaves us in our hour of need!

GABINIUS. Ha, so much for his friendship!

COEPARIUS.   No, oh no!
  Why Catiline has never yet played false!

LENTULUS. But still, he's leaving . . .

STATILIUS.   And our hopes leave with him!
  Who would, I ask you, make as good a leader?

COEPARIUS. No, that's true. We must give up our plans . . .

LENTULUS. Not yet, my friends! . . . First listen to what I
  have got to say. . . . We have made up our minds
  that we will use armed force to gain those things
  denied us by a harsh relentless fate;

we are kept under now . . . we wish to govern;
we suffer want . . . our aim is affluence!

SEVERAL. Yes, power and affluence are what we want . . .

LENTULUS. Well now, we chose a man to be our leader
whom each of us was proud to call his friend;
he has betrayed our trust, is making off;
so come, my friends, and let us prove to him
that we can help ourselves . . . the only thing
we want is someone steadfast and courageous,
prepared to lead . . .

SEVERAL.   And where can he be found?

LENTULUS. My friends, if he came forward would you then
consent to have him as your leader? . . . Well?

SEVERAL. Yes, that we would . . .

OTHERS.   Yes, yes, indeed we would! . .

STATILIUS. Then what's his name? . . .

LENTULUS.   What if it were myself?

GABINIUS. Yourself! . . .

COEPARIUS and OTHERS [*doubtfully*]. You, Lentulus? You want to lead
us?

LENTULUS. I do! . . .

CETHEGUS.   You think you can? Why it requires
the strength and daring of a Catiline. . . .

LENTULUS. I have no lack of daring . . . nor of strength;
let's set to work . . . you are not backing out
just when the crucial moment has arrived,
I trust? . . . when all the indications point
to our success? . . .

STATILIUS.   No, we will follow you!

SEVERAL. We'll follow you! . . .

GABINIUS.   Indeed, if Catiline
abandons us you are the only man
now capable of leading . . .

LENTULUS.   Listen then
to what I plan. The first thing we must do . . .

CATILINE [*ushers in*]. Well, here I am, friends! . . .

ALL.   Catiline! . . .

LENTULUS [*aside*].   Be damned,
I say! . . .

CATILINE.   Come on, what do you ask of me?
No, as you were. . . . I now am offering
myself as leader; will you follow me?

ALL [*except for* LENTULUS]. Yes, Catiline, yes, we will follow you!

STATILIUS. They have deceived us . . .

GABINIUS.   and told shameful lies about
you!
Would you have left us really, Catiline?

CATILINE. I would, but that's past history now. Henceforth
I mean to live entirely for my plans. . . .

LENTULUS. But what exactly are these plans of yours?

CATILINE. My aim is high, a higher aim than you,
than anyone perhaps suspects. . . . Now listen!
We shall win over to our side each Roman,
each freedom-lover, who would give his all
for Rome's good name and ancient liberty.
Why friends, the Roman spirit still exists,
the last remaining spark is not quite dead!
Indeed, it shall be fanned to brilliant flames,
so high, so bright, as never yet before;
the gloom of servitude, as black as night,
has all too long been hanging over Rome!
This empire, proud and mighty though it seems,
is tottering now and is about to fall.
A forceful hand must therefore seize the helm . . .
but first, my friends, we must pluck out the weeds;
our ancient Rome must be recalled to life,
annihilated all the abject baseness

F1

which prospers here and soon will suffocate
all vestiges of freedom in men's minds.
For it is freedom, freedom, I would sow,
as pure as any which in bygone days
has blossomed here . . . I will bring back again
the time when every Roman gladly bought
the honour of his country with his life,
and to preserve her splendour . . . gave his all! . . .

LENTULUS. You let your fancy run away with you.
That wasn't what we meant . . .

GABINIUS.   What is the good
of rehabilitating ancient times
with their absurd naïvety . . .

SOME.   No, no!
We ask for power, the wherewithal to live
a gay and carefree life . . .

OTHERS.   Hear, hear! That's what we want!

COEPARIUS. What use to us is Roman glory, friends!
No, we are out for pleasure. . . .

CATILINE.   Worthless breed!
Are you descended from those noble forebears?
Why, your way of protecting Roman splendour
is heaping infamy upon her name.

LENTULUS. You dare to jeer, when you have long since been
the symbol of monstrosity. . . .

CATILINE.   Yes, true,
I was the dread of decent folk, and yet
I've never equalled you in turpitude. . . .

LENTULUS. Mind what you say! We'll take no jibes from you! . . .

SEVERAL. No, no, we will not . . .

CATILINE [*calmly*].   Miserable cowards!
Do you still dare to have a will! You are . . .

LENTULUS. Down, down with him! . . .

OTHERS.   Yes, down with Catiline!

[*They draw their daggers and rush at* CATILINE, *who calmly pulls back his toga from his breast and looks at them with a cold contemptuous smile; at this they lower their daggers.*]

CATILINE. Thrust! Stab! You dare not? Cowards bred and born!
   I would respect you for it if you plunged
   your daggers in my breast, in Catiline; . . .
   you haven't got a spark of courage left! . . .

SEVERAL. No, no, he is our friend! . . .

OTHERS.   We have deserved his scorn!

CATILINE. You have indeed! . . . Yet now the hour has come,
   the chance for you to wipe away your shame. . . .
   Come, let us all forget what's past and finished! . . .
   a new existence beckons close at hand.
   [*Bitterly.*] . . . Oh no! how can I pin my hopes on you?
   What courage is there here, what Roman spirit? . . .
   [*Passionately.*] I once had lovely dreams, and glorious plans
   were teeming in my breast . . . but that is past!
   If I, like Icarus, had wings to soar
   on high, across the deep aetherial blue,
   and if the gods above endued my hand
   for one brief moment with a giant's strength,
   then I would seize the lightning in its flight
   and hurl it at the city down below;
   and when the vivid tongues of flame leapt high
   and Rome collapsed amid the crumbling ruins,
   then from the grave I'd summon back to life
   the long-departed spirits of old Rome. . . .
   Alas, these are but dreaming visions! Ah,
   those bygone days will never more return,
   nor will the spirits of proud ages past.
   [*Wildly.*] All right, if ancient Rome is not to be
   restored to life, then modern Rome shall fall!
   Where stately rows of marble columns stand,
   ah, soon there shall be but a heap of ash!
   The temples shall come tumbling down in ruins,
   and soon the Capitol shall be no more. . . .

So swear, friends, swear. If you will follow me,
then I will be your staunch and steadfast leader.
Well, will you? . . .

LENTULUS.   Yes, yes, we will follow you!

[STATILIUS, GABINIUS, COEPARIUS, *and the others whisper together.*
CATILINE *watches them with a contemptuous smile.*]

LENTULUS [*in an undertone*]. Indeed, we'll follow him, for ruins are the place
where we are likeliest to reach our goal. . . .

ALL. Yes, Catiline, yes, we will follow you. . . .

CATILINE. So swear to me by every god on high
you will obey all my commands! . . .

ALL.   We will!
We solemnly do swear we will obey you!

CATILINE. In that case let us start without delay.
You will find weapons over at my house. . . .
We'll gather there for further consultation! . . .

                    [*They rush out.*]

LENTULUS. Quite so, but listen to me, Catiline:
you know that there has just arrived today
a delegation from the Allobroges . . .

CATILINE. Yes, yes, go on . . . indeed . . . why you are right!

LENTULUS. We'll win them over to our project, and
with them the whole of Gaul as well; that would
increase our strength not inconsiderably . . .

CATILINE [*pondering*]. Barbarians? You suggest that they . . . ?

LENTULUS.   It is . . .
essential. . . .

CATILINE [*bitterly*]. Ah yes, Rome has fallen low.
Within her walls there's neither strength nor pluck
enough to bring a tottering ruin down.

                    [*They depart hastily.*]

———————

[*A garden to the rear of* CATILINE's *house, which is visible in the background. Left, a side-building.* CURIUS, CETHEGUS, *and others enter cautiously from the right, conversing in whispers.*]

CURIUS. But is it really true what you are saying?

CETHEGUS. It is . . . and no more than a moment since
  it all was settled . . .

CURIUS.   He's prepared to lead you?

CETHEGUS. He is to lead us . . . he will soon be here.

[*They enter the house, except for* CURIUS.]

CURIUS. A weird night this . . . my thoughts are whirling round
  in circles, just as though all were a dream; . . .
  and yet throughout this strangely changing scene
  I find her image almost everywhere.

CATILINE [*enters*]. So here you are then, Curius! I have missed you;...
  the outcome of our visit to the temple
  was unexpected. . . .

CURIUS [*confused*].   Ah, yes, you are right!

CATILINE. I will not think about it any more . . .
  a curious thing to happen, most mysterious!
  The furies rise up from the underworld,
  so we are told, in order to pursue
  us mortals; . . . ah, supposing it were true!

CURIUS. You mean you've seen . . . ?

CATILINE.   Yes, not an hour ago!
  But let's forget about it . . . listen, Curius,
  we're planning something pretty big just now . . .

CURIUS. I know the facts. Cethegus has been telling . . .

CATILINE. Just so! The gods alone know what the end
  will be . . . perhaps it is my destiny
  to be destroyed in mid-career, before
  I have achieved my goal; ah well, so be it! . . .
  But, my dear Curius, you've been dear to me

since you were just a lad . . . I'll not have you
caught up in danger's maelstrom. Promise me
to stay behind in Rome till all is over . . .

CURIUS [*touched*]. My father! Catiline! Oh, how considerate!

CATILINE. That is a promise! Now we'll say goodbye.
Wait here for me. I will be back quite soon.

[*He goes indoors.*]

CURIUS. He loves me still the same . . . has no suspicions . . .

[LENTULUS *and several of* CATILINE's *friends enter.*]

LENTULUS. Say, Curius, was that Catiline who went
into the house? . . .

CURIUS.   Yes, he is waiting for you!

[*They go in.*]

CURIUS [*pacing up and down in great agitation*].
I can't control myself for sheer impatience . . .
this restless vehemence which drives me on. . . .
Ah, Furia, such a strange mysterious woman,
who stirs my passions deeper every moment; . . .
she took herself away at lightning speed
when I had brought her from that cave of death . . .
and then those wild and terrifying words,
in her eyes that dim mysterious glow; . . .
ah, what if it were madness . . . no, oh no!
it cannot be . . .

FURIA [*approaches*].   No, no, my pale young man!

CURIUS [*shrinks back*]. Furia . . . you here?

FURIA.   Catiline dwells here,
so here it is that Furia too must be! . . .

CURIUS. Oh, Furia, come with me and I will bring
you into safety; . . . what if someone saw you?

FURIA. Bring me, young man? You have forgotten then
that I belong no more among the living? . . .

CURIUS. Ah, once again those terrifying words . . .
  come to your senses; listen to me, Furia! . . .

[*He tries to seize her hand.*]

FURIA [*wildly*]. Audacious youth, are you then not afraid
  of me, the child of darkness, risen up
  to life for no more than one fleeting moment! . . .

CURIUS. Afraid? Indeed I am, but just such fear,
  this wondrous thrill of terror, is my joy! . . .

FURIA. No more, young man; your words are all in vain,
  my home is in the grave; there I belong . . .
  from death's dark valley I am risen forth . . .
  there I will flee again when daylight dawns,
  for there among the pallid shades I live,
  in Pluto's halls is Furia to be found; . . .
  for, Curius, I am risen even now
  up from the underworld of darkness . . .

CURIUS.   Ah,
  then take me there. I am prepared to follow,
  although your path may lead through death's dark vale!

FURIA. Not I, young man! What shadows of the grave
  conceal is past the reach of mortal eye!
  My time is short and I must use it well;
  I am conceded only night's brief span . . .
  my work is of the dark, there I belong. . . .
  Tell me, is Catiline not there . . . indoors?

CURIUS. It's him you want? You still pursue him then?

FURIA. Why should I rise up from the underworld
  unless it was to follow Catiline? . . .

CURIUS [*vehemently*]. Why, terrifying woman, this is madness . . .
  yet you are lovely even as you rage!
  Oh Furia, think no more of Catiline;
  now come . . . you'll have me at your beck and call,
  before you on his bended knees your slave [*He kneels.*]
  shall beg one single glance. Oh hear me, Furia!
  I love you; but the very flame consumes me . . .
  the sufferings of Hercules were less
  when poison seared his breast . . .

FURIA.   How dare you! Stop!
  Yet tell me first what they are doing there
  at Catiline's. . . .

CURIUS [*rises*].   And there you go again.
  You think of nothing else but him. Ah, I could . . .

FURIA. Look, Curius, is he willing to accept
  the invitation?

CURIUS.   So you know?

FURIA.   I do!

CURIUS. Well then, I'll tell you! Catiline's assumed
  the leadership. . . . However, that's enough
  of him . . .

FURIA.   No, Curius, answer me one question . . .
  it is the last: will you be going with him?

CURIUS. I must . . .

FURIA [*with a wild smile*]. With him . . . with Catiline?

CURIUS.   That name
  rekindles all the fire within my breast!
  How I detest him! I could murder him!

FURIA. You said just now you were prepared to do
  whatever I might ask? . . .

CURIUS.   Indeed I am!
  But please, I beg: forget your Catiline; . . .

FURIA. What, forget, you say! . . . No, first he must descend
  into his grave . . .

CURIUS.   Ah, Furia, I am then . . . ?

FURIA. No, not in person . . . just betray the plot . . .

CURIUS. How dreadful! He my foster-father and . . .

FURIA. Your rival! Spineless creature! Do you dare
  to talk of love and yet you lack the nerve
  to strike him down? How I despise you! . . .

                    [*She is about to leave.*]

CURIUS [*holds her back*].   No!
  Don't leave me! I'll do anything you ask.
  Ah Furia, you are terrifying, yet
  I cannot break apart this magic net
  enmeshing me . . .

FURIA.   You are agreed then?

CURIUS. I must! I must! For have I now a will?
  Your gaze is like the snake's which fascinates
  the bird that circles round in horror, nearer
  and ever nearer to the dreaded jaws. . . .

FURIA. Well, go and do it then . . .

CURIUS.   And once that I
  have sacrificed my duty to my love?

FURIA. Then I shall not be tied to Catiline; . . .
  my task will be accomplished. Ask no more. . . .

CURIUS. I shall . . . ah Furia, how my heart is raging!

FURIA. You still hold back, you coward . . .

CURIUS.   No, I will,
  ye spirits of the dark! For he alone
  divides us. He shall die . . . each spark is quenched
  of all that once blazed brightly in my heart!
  Ah fearful woman, every gentle feeling
  which stirs inside me turns at once to stone
  when you are near; my love itself is more akin
  to hate than to affection . . . now I know
  myself no longer . . . blindly I am leaping
  into the deep abyss to follow you . . .
  Yes, he shall die. I will this moment go
  and give the plot away. Wait here for me! [*He hurries out.*]

FURIA [*after a pause*]. My task will soon be over, Catiline!
  You're making rapid strides towards your goal!

  [AMBIORIX *and* OLLOVICO *leave* CATILINE'S *house without noticing*
  FURIA.]

AMBIORIX. So that is settled then, and in all truth
  a daring move . . .

OLLOVICO. It is a risk,
but our reward awaits us . . . well worth winning
and facing even greater dangers for
than that about to threaten us . . .

AMBIORIX. Indeed! . . .

OLLOVICO. The liberation from Rome's tyranny,
our ancient freedom, is well worth a fight . . .

AMBIORIX. We'll hasten back as soon as we are able,
and surreptitiously the whole of Gaul
shall arm itself for battle with the tyrants,
and join the ranks of Catiline's supporters.
It won't be easy, Rome is powerful still; . . .
but done it has to be. Come, Ollovico!

FURIA [*admonishing*]. Alas, alas for you! . . .

AMBIORIX [*terrified*]. Ye gods above!

OLLOVICO [*likewise terrified*]. That sound is coming from no earthly voice!

FURIA. Alas, alas for you! . . .

OLLOVICO. See, there she stands,
a pale prophetic goddess in the moonlight!

FURIA. Alas for you; go not with Catiline!

AMBIORIX. Come, Ollovico, come, a spirit's voice is speaking; . . .
away, away now, we must do its bidding! [*They hurry away.*]

CATILINE [*comes out of the door at the back*].
Ah, what a desperate hope it is in truth
to think of crushing Rome with such a mob
of good-for-nothings, motivated solely
by want and by rapacity; and what
have I to gain? . . .

FURIA [*behind the trees*]. Revenge, my Catiline!

CATILINE. Ye gods! Why, what was that? A voice which came
from deep inside my soul? Revenge! Indeed,
so be it then! Revenge for every hope
they took from me, revenge for every plan
of mine a hostile destiny destroyed!

[*The conspirators come out of the door at the back. They are armed.*]

LENTULUS. The Roman capital still lies in darkness,
  the time has come . . .

SEVERAL.   Yes, now, away! away!

AURELIA [*comes out of the side-building without noticing the conspirators*].
  You, Catiline, my dearest, here! . . .

CATILINE.   Aurelia!

AURELIA. Have you been waiting . . .?

      [*She stops as she becomes aware of the conspirators.*]

                    Oh, great gods of mercy!

CATILINE [*wildly*]. Go, woman, go! . . .

AURELIA.   Oh, what does all this mean?
  You are going. . . .

CATILINE [*as before*].   Yes, by night's black spirits!
  A merry trip; . . . see how my sword is flashing!
  And streams of blood are soon to dye it red!

AURELIA. Ye gods! Oh, then my hope was but a dream,
  and terrible is my awakening . . .

CATILINE.   Quiet!
  Come, woman, if you will; no longer shall this breast
  be moved by tears of yours. How brightly, see,
  Rome's pinnacles are lit by Luna's beams. . . .
  Before she rises in the east again
  the flames shall leap up into heaven's blue
  and bring Rome down in one grey heap of ruins; . . .
  and when on bright nights in the distant future
  upon the crumbling ruins still she shines
  a single pillar standing in the rubble
  shall show the wanderer where Rome once did lie! . . . [*They go out.*]

ACT THREE

CATILINE's *camp in wooded country. His tent is visible on the right, with an ancient oak-tree to one side. It is night. The moon breaks through the clouds intermittently. A campfire is burning outside the tent and there are several more among the trees in the background.* STATILIUS *is dozing by the fire;* MANLIUS *is pacing up and down in front of the tent.*

MANLIUS. How very like them! Such a thoughtless crowd!
   They slumber there so peacefully and soundly
   you'd think that they were lying safe and snug
   in mother's arms, and not in some wild forest; . . .
   as though expecting to wake up and play
   and not to fight a battle which may prove
   to be their last. . . .

STATILIUS [*awakes and rises*]. You still on guard, old soldier?
   Not feeling weary? I'll relieve you now!

MANLIUS. No, just you have your sleep. A young man needs
   refreshing sleep; . . . his wild exuberance
   takes energy; . . . it is a different tale
   when once your hair grows grey, your blood runs slow,
   and you can feel the burden of your age . . .

STATILIUS. Yes, you are right. And one day I shall also,
   an old and hardened warrior . . .

MANLIUS.   Are you then
   so sure that this has been decreed by fate . . .
   that ripe old age has been accorded you?

STATILIUS. Dear me, why not? I say, what puts such thoughts
   into your head? . . .

MANLIUS.   I take it that you mean
   we have no need to fear; why, you young fool!

STATILIUS. We've had strong reinforcements, haven't we? . . .

MANLIUS. Of slaves and gladiators, yes indeed!

STATILIUS. Yes, may be so, but their combined effect
    amounts to something; and the whole of Gaul
    is sending help. . . .

MANLIUS.   Which still has not arrived.

STATILIUS. Are you in any doubt? . . .

MANLIUS.   I know these people.
    Well, never mind, for time will soon reveal
    what fate the gods have specified for us.
    But go along, Statilius, and make sure
    the sentries are alert and at their posts. . . .
    We must secure ourselves against a night attack; . . .
    there's no harm done in taking all precautions.

[STATILIUS *goes out.*]

And now the clouds are gathering apace . . .
the night is dark and threatens to be stormy,
a clammy fog, so heavy and oppressive,
is weighing on an aged warrior's chest.
I am no longer light of heart, as when
I used to hurl myself into the fray;
it is not just old age . . . it's like a weight
upon my mind; but curiously enough
the others too seem strangely ill at ease.

[*A pause.*]

Indeed, the gods shall know revenge was not
the reason why I followed Catiline.
My anger flared up for a fleeting moment,
when first I felt that I'd been wronged, insulted; . . .
the old blood's still not absolutely cold,
it still at times flows warmly through my veins.
But the offence is now forgotten and forgiven; . . .
I only came because of Catiline . . .
I shall watch over him with greatest care. . . .
He stands here all alone among the crowds
of worthless scoundrels and of scatterbrains; . . .
they cannot understand him, whereas he
is far too proud to wish to make them out.

[*He puts a few branches on the fire and remains standing in silence.*
CATILINE *comes out of the tent.*]

CATILINE. Already midnight . . . everything so still . . .
and mine the only eyes which sleep eludes.
The wind blows cold tonight, it will refresh my spirits
and give me strength . . . ah, I can do with some!

[*He notices* MANLIUS.]

Ah Manlius, is it you who faithfully
keeps watch on this cold night? . . .

MANLIUS.   And fitting too!
I guarded you when you were just a lad; . . .
why, do you not recall? . . .

CATILINE.   Those days are past . . .
my peace went with them; everywhere I go
I am pursued by strangely changing figures;
my bosom, Manlius, harbours everything
except for peace . . . that is no longer there.

MANLIUS. Dispel such thoughts and rest now, Catiline,
remember that tomorrow may demand
each ounce of strength and calm that you can muster . . .

CATILINE. I cannot, Manlius; . . . if I shut my eyes
to snatch a moment's sleep and to forget,
I live in a fantastic world of dreams; . . .
as I lay dozing on my bed just now
the visions once again appeared before me,
more strange than ever, more mysterious
and puzzling. Ah, if I could only grasp
what they all mean, but no. . . .

MANLIUS.   Confide your fear in me.
Perhaps I can advise you, Catiline.

CATILINE [*after a pause*].
Was I waking, was I sleeping, that I cannot say,
thoughts and projects by the thousand darted through my soul.
Of a sudden all goes dimmer in the deepening gloom,
night descends upon my bosom, with her wings unfurled.

Save for flashing thoughts which pierced it, dark and terrible,
there I see a vaulted chamber, black as any grave; . . .
high the ceiling like the heavens, thick with thunder clouds,
and the strangest swarm of visions, as some phantom chase,
whirled around in wild confusion, like a hurricane
when it sweeps in fury over foam-topped ocean waves.
But amid the crazy turmoil now and then emerge
figures from a better home, garlanded with flowers. . . .
Round about them all the darkness turns to radiant light. . . .
In the middle of the chamber stands a curious pair;
both are women, one is tall and dark as night is she,
and the other fair as evening when the daylight fades.
Ah, so curiously familiar both did seem to me,
one of them was smiling gently, with a look of peace;
from the other's haughty glances savage lightning flashed.
Terrible, and yet with pleasure I observed this sight.
One is standing proudly and the other meanwhile leans
on the table where these women played at some mysterious game . . .
all the time the crowding visions floated up and down.
Then at last their game is over and she sinks into the ground,
she who gazes with such radiant gentle eyes of love,
and the fair resplendent figures vanished with her too.
Now the din is growing wild and wilder all the time,
and the darker woman's glances burned like fiery flame.
Then before me all things faded, her alone I saw,
but what else I dreamed of later in my fevered sleep
now lies hidden deep inside me, veiled from memory;
could I but recall what followed; it has gone, alas.

MANLIUS. Catiline, upon my word this dream
  is very strange . . .

CATILINE [*meditating*].   If I could just remember,
  but no, it's useless . . .

MANLIUS.   Well, forget about it.
  Don't think of it; for what are dreams in fact? . . .
  imaginings and empty fantasies,
  quite meaningless and lacking all foundation.

CATILINE. Yes, you are right! I will dismiss these thoughts,
  it is unmanly brooding on such things,

yet sometimes in the still hours of the night
the most peculiar moods come over me.
It's nearly over. You can go then, Manlius.
Have some rest now, if you wish; I'll take a stroll
a moment, with my thoughts for company.

[MANLIUS *goes out and for a time* CATILINE *paces up and down in
silence. A* PHANTOM *enters slowly from the back without being noticed
by* CATILINE.]

CATILINE [*becomes aware of the* PHANTOM].
Ye gods, but what is this old . . .

PHANTOM.   Greetings, Catiline!

CATILINE. What do you want? Who are you? Speak, my man.

PHANTOM. Quiet, it is *my* place here to ask the questions
and yours to answer them. Do you not know
this voice again from ages long since past?

CATILINE. I seem to; tell me though, whom do you seek
in such a spot at midnight's silent hour?

PHANTOM. It's you I seek. And, mark you, this one hour
is granted me; I must make use of it.

CATILINE. By all the gods, who are you? Tell me!

PHANTOM.   Silence!
I come here now to call you to account.
Why do you never let me rest in peace?
Why have you driven me to rise again
from my deep grave at midnight hour, that I
may guard the honour I so dearly bought?

CATILINE. Ah, I feel dark forebodings rising up within.

PHANTOM. What is there left now of my sovereign power?
Just nothing. That went with me to the grave.
Ah, what it cost; the price I paid was high.
My peace in life; my rest within the grave
were bartered for it; yes, that was enough!
And now in your audacity you would
deprive me of the little I have left!

Are there not paths enough to deeds of fame?
Why do you have to follow in my tracks?
My power I relinquished here on earth;
my name I thought should be for ever blazoned,
not like the friendly twinkle of some star,
no, like a flash across the sky at night.
I had no wish, as hundreds had before me,
to be remembered for the gentle virtues,
for magnanimity . . . I had no wish
to be admired . . . such was, will always be,
the lot of, oh, so many; no, I wished
posterity to see my bloody splendour.
In fear and trembling, tinged with admiration,
men would look up to me, whom none before
or since has ever dared to emulate.
Such was my dream; yet it was an illusion!
I knew you; why then did I not suspect
what lay concealed there deep inside your soul!
Beware though, Catiline, for I can see
beyond the veil of things to come what lies
in store for you . . . what fate has predetermined . . .

CATILINE [*eagerly*]. You know? Then tell me what it is!

PHANTOM. No, first beyond the grave's dark portal
the mist shall vanish which enshrouds
the horrible, the truly great,
that seas of time shall wash away.
But hear a spirit from the grave
now quoting from your book of fate:
'Though thou shalt fall by thine own hand
yet shall another strike thee down.'

[*The* PHANTOM *vanishes.*]

CATILINE [*looks round after a pause*].
Why, he has vanished! Was it then a dream?
No, here he stood with moonbeams shining down
upon his face; ah, I know who he was.
It was the man of blood, the old dictator,
who rose up from the grave to frighten me.
He was afraid that I should take away

GI

. . . no, not his honour . . . that horrific glare
which lights his memory. Does ambition then
survive the very shadows of the grave?

[*A pause.*]

I am assailed on all sides; . . . first Aurelia
speaks words of gentle admonition, then
my bosom echoes with what Furia said . . .
and now, arisen from the grave itself
the pallid shadows from a bygone age.
They threaten me and say I should turn back!
No, I'll not waver. I will boldly stride
towards my goal and soon I shall be there. . . .

CURIUS [*rushes in, greatly agitated*]. Catiline! . . .

CATILINE [*surprised*].   What, you here, my dear Curius!

CURIUS. I had to . . .

CATILINE.   Why did you not stay in Rome?

CURIUS. I couldn't. I just had to come and find you!

CATILINE. How rash of you! But come into my arms . . .
for my sake you are rushing into danger. . . .

[*He is about to embrace him.*]

CURIUS [*shrinks back*]. No, no, you must not touch me, Catiline!

CATILINE. Ye gods, what is this . . . ?

CURIUS.   Flee! You are surrounded
by enemies . . .

CATILINE.   Why, Curius, calm yourself!
You are delirious. Has the journey tired you?

CURIUS [*in despair*]. Oh no, but save yourself while there is time.
You are betrayed. . . . [*He kneels before him.*]

CATILINE [*shrinks back*].   Betrayed! What did
you say?

CURIUS. It was among your friends . . .

CATILINE.   No, Curius, no!
  No, all my friends are loyal just like you.

CURIUS. Then I am sorry for you, Catiline.

CATILINE. Come, pull yourself together. It is love,
  concern about my safety, causing you
  to notice dangers which do not exist.

CURIUS. These words of yours cut through me like a knife . . .
  but flee, by all the mighty gods in heaven, flee!

CATILINE. Compose yourself and answer calmly now;
  why should I flee? Am I in danger here?

CURIUS [*in despair*]. Yes, yes, you are betrayed; your plan revealed.

CATILINE. What, are you mad? No, that's impossible!

CURIUS. Yes, it is as I say; but flee at once,
  there's still a chance for you if you are quick.

CATILINE. Oh, could it be . . . but no, impossible!

CURIUS [*tearing out his dagger and handing it to* CATILINE].
  Here, take it, Catiline, and pierce my breast. . . .
  Now stab me! Stab me! It was I betrayed you!

CATILINE. Why, this is madness! . . .

CURIUS.   No, by all the gods
  I swear it: I have given you away . . .
  do not ask why. Oh, this is crushing me.

CATILINE [*bitterly*]. Am I to lose my faith in friendship too?

CURIUS. Oh, run me through and cease tormenting me
  with this forbearance . . .

CATILINE [*gently*].   No! Get up then, Curius!
  You erred . . . and I am now forgiving you.

CURIUS [*overwhelmed*]. Oh stop it, Catiline, you shatter me.
  But quick, away, it soon will be too late.
  The Roman army will attack you soon;
  they're on their way and soon they will be here.

CATILINE. And what about my friends in Rome?

CURIUS. Alas,
they are in prison, put to death perhaps!

CATILINE [*distressed*]. Oh fate, oh fate!

CURIUS [*in despair holds out the dagger to* CATILINE *again*].
Now plunge it in my breast!

CATILINE [*gently*]. No, you were just the tool; . . . what could you
do? . . .

CURIUS. Oh, let me pay for my offence with death . . .

CATILINE. I have forgiven you . . .

[*As he goes.*]

and now there is
but one thing left . . .

CURIUS [*rises*]. Yes, flight!

CATILINE. A hero's death! [*He goes out.*]

CURIUS. Quite useless. Certain death awaits him now!
This kindliness is fearful punishment . . .
I'll go and find him; *one* thing shall not be denied me . . .
to fall in battle by the hero's side! [*He hurries out.*]

[LENTULUS *and* TWO GLADIATORS *enter stealthily from behind the trees.*]

LENTULUS [*softly*]. Someone was speaking here . . .

FIRST GLADIATOR. It's quiet now.
Perhaps it was the sentry as he went
off duty.

LENTULUS. Yes, perhaps. We'll wait just here . . .
be at the ready . . . I suppose your swords
are sharp and gleaming . . .

SECOND GLADIATOR. Aye, mine gleams like lightning;
it really has some bite. At the last fights
I finished off two gladiators with it . . .

LENTULUS. Then go and stand behind that bush just there,
and when I give the signal rush out quick
and strike him down . . .

FIRST GLADIATOR. Aye, aye, it shall be done!

[*They remain standing where they were.* LENTULUS *goes downstage, spying out the land.*]

LENTULUS [*half to himself*]. It is a risky game, there's no denying . . .
but still, if it is done at all it must
be done tonight; . . . if Catiline should fall,
apart from me there's no one who can lead them. . . .
Tomorrow we will start our march on Rome
and men will rally to us all the way.

[*He goes in among the trees.*]

FIRST GLADIATOR. I say, who is this unknown man that we
have got to kill?

SECOND GLADIATOR. Shut up! That's no concern
of ours. If Lentulus has paid us for it
he must accept responsibility.

LENTULUS [*returns hastily*].
Get ready now. He'll be here any moment . . .

[*The* GLADIATORS *and* LENTULUS *stand behind the bushes.* CATILINE *enters immediately afterwards.*]

LENTULUS. Now! Strike him down! Come, run your swords right
through him!

[LENTULUS *and the* GLADIATORS *rush at* CATILINE.]

CATILINE [*draws his sword and defends himself*].
You scoundrels! You have the nerve to . . .

LENTULUS. Strike him down!

CATILINE [*recognizes him*]. You, Lentulus, would you kill Catiline?

SECOND GLADIATOR [*terrified*]. It's him!

FIRST GLADIATOR [*likewise*]. What, Catiline! We'll not
fight him!
Come, quick . . . let's go! [*They run away.*]

LENTULUS. Then you shall fall by
my hand.

[*They fight;* CATILINE *strikes the sword from* LENTULUS's *hand.*
LENTULUS *tries to run away, but* CATILINE *holds on to him.*]

CATILINE. Assassin! Traitor!

LENTULUS [*imploringly*]. Mercy, Catiline!

CATILINE. I get your plan. You meant to murder me . . .
and then take on the leadership yourself.

LENTULUS. That was so, Catiline!

CATILINE [*aside*]. He's no idea
what's happened.

[*Aloud. Hypocritically.*]

Well then, so it shall be.

LENTULUS. Explain . . . what do you mean?

CATILINE. I shall resign.
Lead them yourself; you're worth it.

LENTULUS [*astonished*]. You are willing?

CATILINE. I am. Take care though, Lentulus, take care!
Your job is dangerous; you see, our plan
has been betrayed. But I will call our friends
to introduce their new commander to them
and then stand down. [*He is about to go.*]

LENTULUS [*surprised, detains him*]. No, Catiline, one moment!

CATILINE. Our time is precious . . . for the Roman army
will soon be here . . .

LENTULUS [*anxiously*]. No, listen, Catiline!
You must be joking . . . it just can't be true.

CATILINE. Our plan, as I have told you, is betrayed!
Now show your strength and capability.

LENTULUS. Alas for us! . . .

CATILINE [*contemptuously*]. You're trembling, wretched
coward . . .
yet think of crushing me . . . of leading them? . . .

LENTULUS. Forgive me, Catiline!

CATILINE.   Quick, off with you
and save your skin, if you can get away. . . .

LENTULUS. Ah, you allow me . . .

CATILINE.   Do you really think
I meant in earnest to resign this post
in hour of danger? . . . Little do you know me.

LENTULUS [*hypocritically*]. Oh Catiline! . . .

CATILINE [*haughtily*].   You have no time to waste.
Just flee to safety. . . . I know how to die.

LENTULUS [*aside, as he departs*].
I thank you for this piece of information.
I'll make good use of it to save my skin.
I know the district well . . . I shall escort
the Roman army here by secret paths. . . .
The serpent which you trample in the dust
so haughtily has not yet lost its sting. [*He departs.*]

CATILINE [*after a pause*]. This is the trust which I relied upon.
Thus they betray me one by one, ye gods!
Disloyalty and cowardice are all
you find in base and worthless souls like these.
I am a fool, I must say, with my plans;
I would destroy that nest of vipers there . . .
why, Rome was long since nothing but a ruin!

[*The sound of arms is heard approaching.*]

Ah, there they come . . . so there is still some pluck
among them; . . . hear the lively clash of swords . . .
it brings back all my energy again;
I felt just now so listless and depressed; . . .
but that is over; courage is revived
by danger . . . I will go and face it boldly.

[MANLIUS, STATILIUS, GABINIUS, *and many other conspirators enter.*]

MANLIUS. I've brought your friends here with me, Catiline,
all ready and prepared to follow you.

STATILIUS. Yes, Catiline, we'll go along with you
   in life or death, wherever you command.

CATILINE. My gallant comrades, I am grateful to you.
   But I must tell you we have now no choice
   of life or death, but simply one of death
   in glorious combat by the sword of foes,
   or under torture after grim pursuit,
   when we are trapped like wild beasts in the forest.
   Then do you choose by means of abject flight
   to gain brief respite for a worthless life,
   or like your proud and noble ancestors
   to go down fighting boldly, sword in hand?

STATILIUS. That's what we choose . . .

OTHERS.   Yes, yes, with sword in hand!

CATILINE. Then let us go. Our death shall be our seal
   of immortality . . . and distant times shall think
   of us with admiration.

FURIA [*who has approached him unobserved*]. Or with horror!

SOME [*stepping back in astonishment*]. Ah, a woman!

CATILINE [*surprised*].   Furia, you are
      here?
   Tell me, what do you want?

FURIA.   I must escort
   you to your goal!

CATILINE.   Where is my goal then? Speak!

FURIA. Men seek to reach their goal in different ways . . .
   you seek your own by means of violent conflict,
   and conflict sows the seeds of death, destruction . . .

CATILINE. Yet also honour and eternal fame.
   Go, woman, Fine and noble is this hour!
   My breast is closed to all your raucous cries! . . .

   [AURELIA *comes out of the tent and is astonished to see the assembled
   group.*]

AURELIA. Why, Catiline, my dearest!

CATILINE.   Oh, Aurelia!

AURELIA. What is all this . . . ?

CATILINE [*distressed*].   To have forgotten you!
  What will fate do to you?

FURIA [*contemptuously*].   Why, Catiline,
  already wavering in your lofty purpose? . . .
  Is this your courage?

CATILINE [*vehemently*].   No, by all the gods!

AURELIA. Oh, tell me, Catiline, what's going to happen? . . .

FURIA. What time is this for whimpering and wailing?

MANLIUS. No, let us go. Don't linger, Catiline!

CATILINE [*struggling with himself*].
  Oh, what a turmoil in my heart, and yet . . .
  there's nothing we can do about it; . . . right,
  come, follow me, away!

AURELIA [*throws herself into his arms*].   Oh, Catiline!
  You must not go, or I am going too.

CATILINE. No, no, Aurelia . . .

FURIA [*contemptuously*].   Yes, let it be so . . .
  that's all a feeble wretch like you is worth . . .
  to fall in battle by a woman's side!

CATILINE [*violently thrusts* AURELIA *away*].
  Me . . . feeble! No, ye shades of darkness, no!
  [*Wildly.*] I'll pluck out every feeling from my breast,
  where only lust for bloody battle burns.

FURIA. Ah, that's the spirit, noble Catiline!

CATILINE. May certain death await me, soon to strike . . .
  that is my wish . . .

AURELIA.   Oh listen, Catiline!
  Please do not cast me out; by all my love
  I do implore you . . .

CATILINE [*wildly*].   Silence! In this heart
  there is no longer any love . . .

AURELIA.   Oh gods of mercy!

  [*She leans wearily against the tree by the tent.*]

CATILINE. But now away . . .

MANLIUS.   That was the sound of arms!

SEVERAL. They're coming nearer . . .

CATILINE.   We will face them boldly!
  Loud speaks the voice of honour in our breasts;
  we will obey . . . to perish by the sword!
  Away! With Roman valour and by Roman sword
  the last of Roman sons shall shed their blood! [*They rush out.*]

FURIA. He is gone and I have won. My purpose is achieved;
  soon he'll lie on field of battle; death will claim him, stiff and cold.

AURELIA [*lost in thought, without noticing* FURIA].
  In his heart now filled with anger love no more can find a place.
  Was I dreaming? No, I heard the fury pouring from his lips.

FURIA. Swords are clashing; Catiline already hovers at the brink; . . .
  soon he shall, a fleeting shadow, hurry to the land of death.

AURELIA [*becomes aware of* FURIA].
  Who are you, oh voice of terror sounding over there . . .
  like the frenzied hooting of some owl upon its bough!
  Are you risen from the lightless lands of shades below
  to escort my Catiline off to your gloomy home?

FURIA. Home is every journey's end, and he has followed paths
  leading deep through life's morass . . .

AURELIA.   But never did he stay!
  Great and noble was his heart, at one time he was good,
  till the root of evil grew deep down within his breast.

FURIA. Flowers too at one time stood in colourful array,
  but they lost their lustre and were claimed at last by death.

AURELIA. Dreaded woman! Well indeed this voice's sound I know;
  from the lips of Catiline so often did it speak.

My life's finest fruit you've taken, spirit from the dark; . . .
locked my Catiline's dear heart against my tenderness.
I have seen you mid the figures flitting through my dreams . . .
you it was who came between us, menacing and grim . . .
side by side with Catiline so happily I dreamed
of a life adorned with love, a haven of true peace!
And a flower-bed I planted in his splendid heart . . .
with my love, the garden's showpiece, in a sheltered spot.
But the flower has been uprooted by your hostile hand.
Where of late it stood and flourished in the dust it lies!

FURIA. Feeble fool! You seek to guide the steps of Catiline . . .
do you not know his heart has never yet belonged to you?
Woman, yours are not the flowers to thrive in such a soil,
only in the warm spring sunshine does the lily grow,
henbane though unfolds its chalice under clouded skies,
and his soul has long since been a cloudy autumn day.
Soon the final gleam of light will vanish from his breast
and he'll lie, the prize of darkness, in the arms of death.

AURELIA [*with ardour*].
No, by all the gods in heaven that shall not be so!
Even yet my tears shall find a way to reach his heart.
If he lies already bleeding mid the battle's roar . . .
I will throw my arms about him, round his breast so cold,
breathe upon his pallid lips the fulness of my love,
soothe the storm within his soul and gentle peace bestow.
Spirit come from darkness, from your grasp I'll wrest your prize,
chain him to the realm of light with fetters forged of love;
should his heart now beat no longer and his eyes be dimmed
we shall leave this life together, claspt in tight embrace.
Grant me then, ye gods above us, for my sufferings here,
by the side of Catiline the quiet of the grave! [*She goes.*]

FURIA [*stares out through the trees in the background*].
Then go, deluded one . . . I have no fear;
the victory is securely in my hands . . .
hark, sounds of battle, soon the hour is come.
I hear the hollow screams, he still fights on.
The moon goes in, how blissful is this hour. . . .
Soon he will lie there with a glassy stare.

I would behold him thus before I go
to seek him out among the pallid shades.

[*She listens.*]

Ah, now the sounds are dying right away . . .
the fight will soon be still . . . his soul may be
already racing home on weightless wings. . . .
Oh, how delightful in this forest gloom,
and in the dark of night, to hear breasts heave
their final sigh as they contend with death.

[*In a frenzy of joy.*]

Such sweet and lovely music to my ear . . .
hark how the owl chimes in . . . he bids them all
a cheerful welcome to his gloomy realm.

[*After a pause.*]

The stillness of the grave lies all around; . . .
the victors are departing from the field.
The silent dead now rest out there alone . . .
there they will slumber many days and more
while all the time the sun will bleach their bones
and greedy ravens hover overhead.

[*A pause.*]

What is that floating there above the meadow,
like some dense patch of early morning mist
that glides across the marshes damp and grey.
It's drawing near, and I can see more clearly . . .
it is a warrior, staggering, exhausted.
Ah, from the fallen heroes comes a shade.

[*She draws back slightly.* CATILINE *enters with drooping head and a
haggard expression.*]

CATILINE [*without noticing* FURIA].
   'Though thou shalt fall by thine own hand
   yet shall another strike thee down.'
   Those were his final words before he vanished.
   What did he mean? . . . I cannot read the riddle!

FURIA. So, welcome from the battle, Catiline!

CATILINE. Ah, who are you? . . .

FURIA.   You do not know me now?

CATILINE. Why, Furia, it is you! You bid me welcome.

FURIA. I am your genius, the goddess who rewards you!
Here now, accept the wreath of victory.

[*She picks some flowers, with which she weaves a wreath during the
following lines.*]

CATILINE. What do you mean? . . .

FURIA.   I'm going to wreathe your temples.
But tell me, why have you come here alone?
Why do your friends not keep you company?

CATILINE. They slumber, Furia . . .

FURIA.   They slumber did you say?

CATILINE. Yes, yes; they slumber; go beyond that forest
and there they lie so silent in the moonlight . . .
there you will find them stretched out in their rows;
they fell asleep, lulled by the song of swords.
But tell me, Furia, can you understand:
I used to think that slumber would be peaceful,
when once the stream of life blood ceased to flow . . .

FURIA. Well, is it not so?

CATILINE.   No, as you shall hear!
I led my company in savage fighting,
I sought my death among the slashing swords,
and round about me all my comrades fell,
to sleep in death; 'twas only I who failed; . . .
and when they all lay prostrate on the ground,
and when the enemy had gone away . . .
I stood there still half-dazed, where just before
the din of battle roared. . . . All was so quiet . . .
the moon shone down between the broken clouds
and faintly lit the pallor of the fallen; . . .
with glassy stare they lay there all around me,

grotesque the smile upon their twisted lips;
it seemed to me as though they lay there dreaming,
and grinned at me in ominous contempt . . .
as though they were demanding back their blood.

FURIA. No, Catiline, no, that was not the case . . .
they merely beckoned you to follow them.

CATILINE. I would be happy if I could; . . .

FURIA.   Now think
no more about it. Come, I will adorn
you with the victor's crown, your victory prize!

[*She holds out the wreath to him.*]

CATILINE. Ugh, what is this . . . a poppy wreath. . . .

FURIA [*in wild merriment*].   Why, yes!
But aren't they pretty flowers? . . . See, the moon
makes them all glisten just like fresh-spilt blood. . . .

CATILINE. Throw them away. It's ghastly how they shine.

FURIA [*with laughter*]. Well if you like your colours dull and pale
then you shall have the garland of green weeds
which Tullia wore upon her dripping locks
that day her corpse was floating on the Tiber!

CATILINE. Alas, what memories! . . .

FURIA.   Should I perhaps
fetch you instead some grass from Roman fields
tinged brown with stains of your compatriots' blood,
which you, dear Catiline, have caused to flow?

CATILINE. No, stop . . .

FURIA.   Or shall I bring you from the woods
a brown wreath of the leaves which shrivelled up
that time they witnessed all the imprecations
which sounded on the ravished woman's lips. . . .

CATILINE. Are you some demon then . . . ?

FURIA.   No, one who would

remind you in all kindness of your past. . . .

CATILINE. But why must this be now . . .?

FURIA. A weary traveller
once at his goal looks back the way he came.

CATILINE. Have I then reached my goal? . . .

FURIA. If you so will . . .

CATILINE. So will? I do! Oh, you have conjured forth
a host of ghastly visions in my soul . . .

[*Vehemently.*]

What do you want of me, you pallid shades?
Leave me in peace, what claims have you on me?

FURIA. Compose yourself, your heart is in a turmoil . . .
come, let me thread this wreath now through your hair,
it has a healing virtue, strong and sure,
it will induce repose . . . bestow oblivion.

CATILINE [*lost in thought*].
You said oblivion! Ah, the very word.
So press the wreath then tight upon my brow.

FURIA [*puts the wreath on his head*].
Now you are crowned, and thus you shall appear
before the prince of darkness, Catiline!

CATILINE. Yes, yes, I will . . . I hanker after peace . . .
my soul has grown so weary in life's struggles; . . .
and now would slumber; . . . all is black within,
as is this night, and yet I still perceive
a twinkling star through the pervading gloom. . . .

[*He puts his hand on his breast.*]

FURIA [*aside*]. Ah, it is she . . .

CATILINE. It's standing in my way.
I cannot follow you until its light
is well and truly out. . . . There was a time
when it shone clear and radiant as that star
in heaven there behind the cloud's dark lining.
And now it gleams but faintly through the mist. . . .

FURIA. Then put it right out. . . .

CATILINE.   Ah, what do you mean?

FURIA. You have your dagger still . . . an inch or two
    will do, and then that heart will beat no more,
    which came and stood in enmity between us.

CATILINE. I understand . . . Aurelia . . . no, oh no!
    I had forgotten her, I don't know why,
    it seems to me as though all would be well
    and peaceful in my soul could I but lean
    my head against her bosom and forget . . .
    forget it all . . .

FURIA.   No, it is foolishness
    still harping on such things . . . yet as you will.
    Now I am going. See if you can find
    with her that long-lost sense of peace and calm. . . .

            [*With increasing vehemence.*]

    You foolish man! Do you imagine then
    the pale-faced dead will let you rest in peace? . . .
    Oh no! They'll gather round in frenzied mobs; . . .
    will stare at you with hideous, hollow eyes,
    demanding bloody vengeance. . . .

CATILINE.   Ah, how true!

            [*He looks round.*]

[*Wildly.*] There is to be no peace for me on earth . . .
    with you then to the shadow land of death.
    Yes, she shall die! She is the only bond
    still chaining me to life. . . .

BOTH.   Yes, she must die.

    [*A flash of lightning lights up the stage and the thunder rolls.*]

FURIA. The powers above have heard the oath you swore.
    Look, Catiline, your victim's on her way. . . .

AURELIA [*comes from the back and looks round anxiously*].
    Where is he to be found? I cannot see him . . .
    ye gods on high, please give me strength!

[*She notices him.*]

Oh heavens!

[*She rushes towards him.*]

Oh Catiline!

CATILINE [*wildly*].   Ah, what do you want, woman?

AURELIA. You're still alive!

[*She is about to throw herself into his arms.*]

CATILINE [*pushes her away*]. Be gone. I hate you! Go!

AURELIA. Oh gods of mercy!

CATILINE.   Would you once again
clap me in chains . . .? Ah, you will not succeed; . . .
don't gaze at me like that. I tell you, woman,
those tender looks are more than I can bear;
they cut like daggers through me to the heart. . . .
I can no longer bear it . . . you shall die.

[*He draws his dagger and seizes her violently by the arm.*]

AURELIA. Watch over me, oh lofty gods in heaven!

CATILINE [*with mounting vehemence*].
You shall, you must . . . you are my only tie
in life . . . and soon that bond shall burst apart.

[*A loud clap of thunder is heard.*]

[*In a frenzy.*] Hear, woman, how the hollow thunder rumbles! . . .
You hear, you hear? It is the gods who speak
their last word of farewell to Catiline! . . .

[*He rushes at her and she flees from the stage; he pursues her.*]

FURIA [*watches them go with wild glee*].
My victory is now assured . . . he lifts the dagger . . .
in vain she stretches up her hands to heaven;
he strikes the blow . . . she falls in her own blood. . . .

CATILINE [*enters slowly*].
Now it is done; . . . soon I shall be no more . . .
the peace of death descends upon my soul.

H1

Yet something is amiss . . . I know not what . . .
it seemed to me that when she sighed her last
my heartstrings snapped. I feel so ill at ease,
as though the whole wide world had all at once
become one great enormous wilderness
and in it none but you and I remain.

FURIA. That is so, Catiline!

CATILINE [*brooding*].   Now I discern
more clearly what I long had dimly sensed. . . .
Is life then not an unabating struggle
between the hostile forces in the soul? . . .
And in this struggle lies the soul's true life; . . .
but in my breast the struggles now are silent. . . .
[*Vehemently.*] All right! I am no longer Catiline . . .
here, take my dagger; quench the dying flame!

FURIA [*seizes the dagger*]. So die then by my hand and I shall follow
beyond the very shadows of the grave.

[*She thrusts the dagger into his breast. He sinks down at the foot of the tree.*]

CATILINE [*after a pause, faintly*].
Now, oh enigmatic shade, the words you spoke to me are clear!
'I shall fall both by my own and by another's hand.'
When I crushed her tender heart there vanished from my soul
all inherent good and beauty; hideous and grim,
only night was left . . . which soon shall be eternal dark.
Dash your waves now, murky Styx, against the shore and swell
high above your banks. Soon you shall carry Catiline
off to gloomy Tartarus, towards his future home.
Of the two paths leading downwards, only one is mine,
to the left . . .

[AURELIA *staggers in. She is pale and her bosom bloody.*]

AURELIA.   No, to the right, towards Elysium!

CATILINE [*terrified*]. How her shade so wan and pallid makes my blood
run cold; . . .
are you risen from the dead, or are you still alive?

AURELIA [*kneels at his side*].
　I can tell your soul is seething like a raging sea . . .
　let me gently press my heart against your breast and die.
　Only sleep, which heralds death, had settled in my soul,
　yet I followed you with eyes grown dim, I saw it all . . .
　and my love for you did give me strength at point of death.
　Breast to breast, dear Catiline, down to our grave we sink.

CATILINE [*distressed*].
　Oh how gladly! Yet you cherish such a hope in vain; . . .
　in my heart wild cries of vengeance raise their dreaded sound.
　No, Aurelia! You shall soar to realms of everlasting light . . .
　Nemesis is taking me down to the dark.

[*Day dawns in the background.*]

AURELIA [*in a kindly voice, pointing to the east*].
　No, for ever love dispels the terrors and the gloom of death.
　See, the thunder clouds depart, the star is gleaming faint and pale.

[*Weakly.*]

Light has conquered . . . see Aurora smiling soft and warm;
come then, Catiline, for death already grips me tight.

[*She sinks down.* CATILINE *grasps her hands.*]

CATILINE [*with a last burst of strength*].
　Ah, how sweet! Now I remember my fantastic dream,
　how that hall's thick darkness was dispersed by streams of light
　from the brilliant rays of sunshine, from the new-born day.
　Oh, my eyes are growing dim, my strength is running out;
　but my soul is full of light as never yet before . . .
　and my life, my past erratic course, is clear to me. . . .
　Yes, my life was midnight, lurid in the lightning flash,
　but my death is morning twilight, tinged with rosy hues!
　From my soul the gloom you've banished; calm lies in my breast,
　now with you I come to dwell in realms of light and peace!

[*He quickly tears the dagger from his breast and speaks as his voice fails.*]

Reconciled the gods in heaven smile down from on high . . .
All the powers of darkness you have vanquished with your love.

[*During the foregoing* FURIA *has gradually withdrawn into the background and disappears as the final lines are spoken.* CATILINE's *head sinks down on to* AURELIA's *breast. They die.*]

AUTHOR'S NOTE

The factual background of this present drama is too familiar for it not to be immediately obvious how far it differs from historical truth; and also that history has only been utilized to a limited extent, so that it must be considered primarily as a vehicle for the underlying idea of the play.

The author hopes to be excused for having made use of the names of historical persons who, both in character and other details, do not appear here as one knows them from history—all the more so as their names are scarcely eminent enough for their appearance in unhistorical contexts to create a confusing impression.

[1850]

CATILINE

PREFACE

TO

THE SECOND EDITION

(1875)

Catiline, the drama with which I embarked on my literary career, was written in the winter of 1848-9, that is, in my twenty-first year.

I was in Grimstad at the time, dependent on my own efforts for the necessities of life and to pay for the tuition which would enable me to reach university entrance standard. Those were turbulent times. The February Revolution, the uprisings in Hungary and elsewhere, the war over Schleswig—the powerful influence of all this furthered my development, however immature I may have remained for long to come. I wrote resounding poems to the Magyars encouraging them, in the cause of freedom and humanity, to hold out in their just struggle with the 'tyrants'; I wrote a long series of sonnets to King Oscar primarily containing, as far as I remember, a plea to set aside all petty considerations and without delay to march at the head of his troops to the aid of our brothers on the very frontiers of Schleswig. As I now doubt, although at the time I did not, whether my high-flying appeals would essentially have profited the cause of the Magyars or the Scandinavians I consider it fortunate that they were confined to the semi-privacy of the manuscript stage. Yet I could not refrain from expressing myself, on more elevated occasions, along the same passionate lines as in my poetry—from which, however, I derived only dubious benefit, both from those who were and those who were not my friends: the former acclaimed my talent for being unintentionally funny, while others found it utterly remarkable that a young man in my subordinate position should actively discuss matters which not even they themselves ventured to have views about. For the sake of truth I must add that my behaviour on a number of occasions did not justify any great hopes that society had in me someone in whom the solid middle-class virtues might confidently be expected to flourish, just as I also, through my epigrams and caricatures, quarrelled with many who had deserved better of me and whose friendship I in fact prized. The long and short of it was that, while big things were happening in the tumultuous world outside, I found myself at logger-heads with the small community in which I lived, cramped as I was by private circumstances and by conditions in general.

Such was the position when, studying for my examination, I went through Sallust's *Catiline* and Cicero's speeches attacking Catiline. These works I simply lapped up and some months later my play was finished. As will be seen from my book, I did not at the time share the views of the two ancient Roman authors on Catiline's character and conduct and I am still inclined to believe that there must have been much that was great or significant about a man whom Cicero, the indefatigable spokesman of the majority, did not find it expedient to tackle until circumstances had so changed that he could attack him with impunity. One should also remember that there have been few people in history whose posthumous reputation has been more com-pletely at the mercy of their adversaries than Catiline's was.

My play was written at night. I virtually had to steal the time for my studies from my employer, a kind and good-natured man, although entirely absorbed by his business, and from this stolen time I stole in turn odd moments for writing. Thus there was practically nothing but night available. This I think is the unconscious reason why nearly all the action of the play takes place at night.

In such a milieu the incomprehensible fact that I was occupied in writing plays had of course to be kept dark; but it is difficult for a twenty-year-old author not to have someone to share his secrets, so I confided to two friends of my own age what I was doing on the quiet.

The three of us expected great things of *Catiline* when it was finished. First of all a fair copy was to be made so that it could be sub-mitted under a pseudonym to the theatre in Christiania, and it was also to be published. One of my two trusting and loyal friends under-took to produce a neat and legible copy of my rough, uncorrected draft, a task he performed so conscientiously that he didn't even forget a single one of the innumerable dashes I put in whenever, in the heat of composition, the right expression momentarily eluded me. The second of my friends, whom I shall mention here by name as he is no longer among the living, Ole C. Schulerud, a student at the time and later to become a lawyer, went off with the copy to Christiania. I still remem-ber a letter of his telling me that *Catiline* had been submitted to the theatre; that it would shortly be performed—there could of course be no doubt about it, since the theatre was run by very discerning men; and there could be equally little doubt that every publisher in the city would gladly pay a sizeable royalty for the first edition; it was simply a matter, he said, of finding out who would make the highest bid.

However, after a long and tense period of waiting, some snags emerged. My friend had the play returned from the theatre with an extremely polite but equally firm rejection. He then went the round of the publishers with the manuscript; but to a man they took the same line as the theatre. The highest bidder wanted so and so much for printing the play, and there were to be no royalties.

But none of this remotely destroyed my friend's belief in victory. On the contrary, he wrote to me that it was all for the best; I was to publish my play myself; he would advance the necessary funds; we were to share the profits, for which he was to look after the business side of things—except for proof-reading, which he considered super-fluous because they had such a clean and legible copy to print from. In a later letter he said that in view of such promising future prospects he was thinking of giving up his studies so as to be able to devote himself entirely to the publication of my works; I could easily write two or three plays a year, he imagined, and according to his calculations the profits would probably enable us before long to take that trip through Europe and the Orient we had often discussed and agreed on.

For the time being, however, my travels were limited to Christiania. I arrived there in the early spring of 1850, *Catiline* having appeared in the bookshops shortly before. The play aroused interest and created a stir in student circles, but the critics dwelt on the faulty versification, as well as finding the work immature. A more appreciative verdict came from only one quarter, but this was from a man whose appreciation I have always cherished and valued and to whom I now once more express my gratitude. Not many copies of the limited edition were sold, to be sure. My friend had some of them in his keeping, and I remember that one evening when the difficulties of our domestic economy seemed insurmountable we fortunately disposed of this pile of printed matter to a dealer as so much waste paper. For the next few days we did not lack any of the necessities of life.

Back home in Norway last summer, and particularly since my return here, I saw the changing scenes of my literary career come more clearly and sharply into focus than ever before. Among other things I had another look at *Catiline*. I had almost forgotten the details of the work, but on re-reading it I found that it did contain a great deal I could still acknowledge, especially if one bears in mind that it was my first work. Much of what my later writings have been about—the clash of ability and aspirations, of will and possibility, at once the tragedy and the comedy of mankind and of the individual—is already adumbrated here. I therefore decided to prepare a new edition, a jubilee edition, as it were—a decision my publisher readily approved as usual.

But obviously I could not just reprint the original edition as it stood, because, as indicated above, this is no more than a copy of my uncorrected and not yet finalized manuscript version, or of the very first rough draft. Reading it through I remembered clearly what had originally been in my mind and I saw too that virtually nowhere did the form satisfactorily express what I had wanted to say.

I therefore decided to revise this work of my youth in such a way as I believe I could have done even then, if I had had the time at my disposal and circumstances had been more propitious. On the other hand I have left ideas, thoughts, and development of plot untouched. It is still the original book, except that it now appears in its finished form.

In the light of what I have said I hope it will be acceptable to my friends in Scandinavia and elsewhere; I hope that they will accept it as a greeting from me at the conclusion of what has been for me a period full of changes and rich in contrasts. Much that I dreamt of twenty-five years ago has become a reality, even if not in such a way or as soon as I then hoped. But now I think it was all for the best; I would not have been without any of the experiences of the intervening years, and when I look back on the sum of my experience, I do so with a feeling of gratitude for everything and to everyone.

HENRIK IBSEN

Dresden, 1 February, 1875

CATILINE

SECOND VERSION 1875

Extract from revised Act III
(cf. above pp. 96 ff, and Appendix I, 3, p. 581)

[AURELIA *appears at the opening of the tent.*]

AURELIA. Why, Catiline, my dearest . . . !

[*She stops, frightened at the sight of the assembled crowd.*]

CATILINE [*distressed*].　　　　　　Oh, Aurelia!

AURELIA. What is all this? This uproar in the camp . . .
　What's happening here?

CATILINE.　　　　　To have forgotten you!
　What will fate do to you . . .?

FURIA [*whispers contemptuously, unnoticed by* AURELIA]. Why, Catiline,
　already wavering in your lofty purpose?
　Is *this* your dauntless courage?

CATILINE [*flaring up*].　　　　No, ye gods!

AURELIA [*comes closer*]. Oh speak, my dearest, set my mind at rest....

FURIA [*behind him, in an undertone*].
　Flee with your wife . . . while all your friends are dying!

MANLIUS. Don't linger now; quick, lead us out to battle. . . .

CATILINE. Oh, what a choice! And yet . . . there is no choice; . . .
　I have to finish . . . dare not stop halfway.

[*He calls out.*]

Come, follow me to battle!

AURELIA [*throws herself into his arms*]. Catiline . . .
　you must not go away . . else take me with you!

CATILINE. No, you must stay, Aurelia!

FURIA [*as before*].   Take her with you!
  You'll die full worthy of your name and life,
  when you are cut down . . . in a woman's arms.

CATILINE [*thrusts* AURELIA *aside*].
  Away, you would deprive me of my fame! . . .
  I'll be with men when death shall strike. My life
  must be atoned for and my name be cleared . . .

FURIA. Ah, that's the spirit, noble Catiline!

CATILINE. I'll pluck out from my soul all things which bind
  me to my past and to its empty dream!
  It is as though what lies behind me now
  had never been. . . .

AURELIA.   Oh, do not cast me out!
  By all the love I cherish, Catiline,
  let us not part . . . I do implore you!

CATILINE.   Silence!
  My heart is dead, my eyes are blind to love.
  From this life's trumpery I turn my gaze
  upon that faint and mighty star in skies
  of posthumous renown!

AURELIA.   Ye gods of mercy!

    [*She leans wearily against the tree by the tent.*]

CATILINE [*to the men*]. And now away!

MANLIUS.   That was the clash of arms!

SEVERAL VOICES. They're coming nearer!

CATILINE.   Good! We'll face them
  boldly.
  Long was our night of shame; soon day shall dawn. . . .
  We'll plunge in battle's bright red morning clouds!
  So come! By Roman sword, with Roman valour
  the last of Roman sons shall shed their blood!

    [*They hurry out through the forest; noises and battle cries are heard
    from the camp.*]

FURIA. He is gone. I have achieved the purpose in my life.
Rising sunshine on the plain will find him cold and stiff.

AURELIA [*to herself*].
In his heart now filled with anger can then love not find a place?
Was I dreaming? No, I heard the fury pouring from his lips.

FURIA. Swords are clashing; Catiline already hovers at the brink;
soon he shall, a silent shadow, hasten to the dead men's land.

AURELIA [*starts*].
Who are you, oh voice of evil omen that I hear,
like the eerie warning of some owl upon its bough!
Are you risen from the clammy land of shades below
to escort my Catiline off to your murky home?

FURIA. Home is every journey's end, and he has followed paths
leading through life's foul morass . . .

AURELIA.   But never did he stay!
Free and noble was his heart, his soul was strong and good,
till around him poison tendrils wound their serpent coils.

FURIA. So too does the plane-tree spread its foliage fresh and green,
till its trunk is smothered in some twining plant's embrace.

AURELIA. Now you have betrayed your source, because this voice's
     sound
from the lips of Catiline so often echoed forth.
Deadly serpent, you have poisoned my life's fruit for me,
serpent who have locked his heart against my tenderness.
From my waking dreams at night-time I know you so well,
see you standing there between us, ominous and grim.
At my dearest husband's side I longed so happily
for a quiet secluded life, a haven of repose;
and a bed of flowers I planted in his weary heart,
with our love, the garden's showpiece, in a sheltered spot.
Ah, that plant has been uprooted by your spiteful hand;
where it lately stood and flourished in the dust it lies!

FURIA. Feeble fool; you seek to guide the steps of Catiline?
Do you not perceive his heart was never wholly yours?
Do you think that flowers of yours can thrive in such a soil?
Only in the sunny springtime does the violet bloom,

henbane though spreads most profusely under clouded skies;
and his soul has long since been a cloudy autumn day.
All is lost to you! The spark will die soon in his breast,
and he'll lie, the prey of vengeance, in the arms of death!

AURELIA [*with mounting ardour*].
No, by all the gods of daylight, that shall not be so!
Even yet my tears shall force a way towards his heart.
If I find him pale and bleeding when the battle's done,
I will throw my arms about him, round his breast so cold,
breathe upon his silent lips the fulness of my love,
soothe the pain within his soul, to bring him peace and calm.
Messenger of vengeance, from your grasp I'll wrest your prey,
bind him to the home of light with fetters forged of love;
if his heart's no longer beating and his eyes are dimmed,
we shall leave this life together, claspt in tight embrace.
Grant me then, ye powers of mercy, for my sufferings here,
by my husband's side the endless quiet of the grave. [*She goes.*]

FURIA [*gazing after her*].
Seek him, deluded one; . . . I have no fear;
I hold the victory safely in my hands.
The sound of battle grows, its roar now mingled
with shrieks of death and clash of broken shields.
Perhaps he's dying? Maybe still alive?
Oh, blissful is this hour! The sinking moon
conceals itself behind thick thunder-clouds.
For one brief moment night will fall again
before day comes; . . . and with the coming day
all will be over. In the dark he dies,
as in the dark he lived. Oh blissful hour!

[*She listens.*]

The wind is rushing past like autumn squalls,
and far off in the distance fades away;
the cumbrous armies slowly clear the plain.
Relentlessly they trample down the dead,
roll on and on like angry ocean waves. . . .
Out there I hear the wails and sighs and groans . . .
the final cradle-song . . . with which they lull
themselves to rest, and all their pale-faced brothers.

The owl is chiming in. He bids them welcome
into the kingdom of the gloomy shadows.

[*After a pause.*]

How still it is. So now then he is mine . . .
he's mine alone, and mine for evermore.
We both can go together now to Lethe . . .
and cross the stream where no day ever dawns.
Yet first I will go out and find his corpse
and I will feast my eyes upon that fine
and hated face, before it is disfigured
by rising sunshine and by waiting ravens.

[*She is about to go, but suddenly steps back, startled.*]

What's that? What's gliding there across the meadow?
Is it some image formed by marshy vapours
solidifying in the morning chill?
It's drawing near . . . the shade of Catiline!
His ghost . . . ! Now I can see his lifeless eye,
his shattered shield, his sword without a blade;
I see the dead man clearly, one thing though . . .
how strange . . . I do not see—the fatal wound.

[CATILINE *comes through the forest, pale and weary, with drooping
head and a haggard expression.*]

CATILINE [*to himself*].
'Though thou shalt fall by thine own hand . . .
yet shall another strike thee down.'
That was his prophecy. Now I am fallen . . .
though no one struck me. Who can solve the riddle?

FURIA. I greet you after battle, Catiline!

CATILINE. Ah, who are you?

FURIA.   I am a shadow's shadow.

CATILINE. Why, Furia, it is you! Do you greet me?

FURIA. Yes, welcome to our common home! Now we
—two ghosts—can go to Charon's boat together.
Yet first . . . accept the wreath of victory.

[She picks some flowers and weaves them into a wreath during what follows.]

CATILINE. What's that?

FURIA.   I'm going to adorn your brow.
   But why have you come here all by yourself?
   The leader's shade should be escorted by
   ten thousand of the slain. Where are your friends?

CATILINE. They slumber, Furia!

FURIA.   Are they slumbering still?

CATILINE. They slumber still . . . and they will slumber long.
   They slumber, all of them. Steal through the forest;
   look out across the plain . . . hush; don't disturb them!
   There you will find them in their endless rows.
   They fell asleep, lulled by the song of swords,
   they fell asleep . . . and did not wake like me
   when far away that song died in the hills.
   A ghost you called me. Yes, I am a ghost
   of what I used to be. But do not think
   that those men slumber now in perfect peace,
   in dreamless sleep. Do not think that!

FURIA.   Then tell me!
   What are your comrades dreaming?

CATILINE.   You shall hear. . . .
   I led the fight, despairing in my heart,
   and sought my death among the slashing swords.
   Both right and left they fell, each man of them;
   Statilius fell . . . Gabinius, Manlius too.
   My Curius died while he was shielding me;
   all perished by the gleaming Roman swords . . .
   those same swords which rejected only me.
   Yes, Roman steel rejected Catiline.
   Half-dazed I stood there with my broken blade,
   alive to nothing as the waves of battle
   swept over me. I first came to my senses
   when all grew still around, and I looked up
   and saw the battle raging . . . far behind me!

How long did I stand there? I know just this . . .
I stood alone among my fallen friends.
But there was life yet in those glassy eyes;
the corners of their mouths curled in a smile;
and smile and eyes they focused straight on me,
who stood alone erect among the corpses . . .
on me who fought his best for them and Rome . . .
on me, left standing there despised, rejected
by Roman swords. . . . Then Catiline did die.

FURIA. You are quite wrong about your dead friends' dreams;
you are quite wrong about what caused your death.
Their smiles and glances were inviting you
to sleep alongside them. . . .

CATILINE.   Yes, if I could!

FURIA. An erstwhile hero's shade must not lose heart;
your hour of rest is near. Come, bend your head; . . .
I will adorn you with the victor's crown.

                    [*She offers it to him.*]

CATILINE. Ugh . . . what is this? A poppy wreath . . . !

FURIA [*in wild glee*].   Why, yes;. . .
aren't poppies pretty things? And they will glisten
around your brow just like a fringe of blood.

CATILINE. No, throw the wreath away! I hate this red.

FURIA [*with a loud laugh*].
Do you prefer your colours dull and pale?
Good! I will fetch the garland of green rushes
which Silvia wore upon her dripping locks
that day the Tiber brought her corpse afloat.

CATILINE. Alas, what visions . . . !

FURIA.   Would you rather then
that I should bring you thistles from the forum,
tinged brown with stains of your compatriots' blood,
which you, dear Catiline, have caused to flow?

CATILINE. No, stop!

FURIA.   Or would you like a wreath of leaves
  picked from the holm-oak near my mother's house,
  which shrivelled up that time a ravished girl
  with piercing screams leapt wildly in the river?

CATILINE. Pour out at once all measures of revenge
  upon my head . . . !

FURIA.   I am your very eye . . .
  your very memory, your very doom.

CATILINE. But why must this be now . . . ?

FURIA.   A weary traveller
  once at his goal looks back the way he came.

CATILINE. Oh, have I reached my goal? Is this the goal?
  I am alive no more . . . nor yet interred.
  Where is the goal?

FURIA.   Close by . . . if you so will.

CATILINE. I haven't any will now. My will died
  when nothing came of all I once had willed.

> [*With a sweeping gesture.*]

Be gone, away now all you sallow shades!
What do you, men and women, ask of me?
I cannot grant to you . . . ! Oh, this great throng . . . !

FURIA. Your shade is even yet attached to earth.
  Break all these thousand threads enmeshing you!
  Come, let me press the wreath upon your hair; . . .
  it has amnesic virtue, power to heal;
  it kills the memory, will induce repose.

CATILINE [*in a flat voice*].
  It kills the memory? Dare I trust your words?
  Press tight your poison wreath then on my brow.

FURIA [*puts the wreath on his head*].
  Now you are crowned, and thus you shall appear
  before the prince of darkness, Catiline!

CATILINE. Let us be gone! I yearn to be below; . . .
I long now for the homeland of all shades.
Together let us go! . . . What ties me here?
What shackles me? Behind me I can sense
a misty star upon the vault of dawn; . . .
it holds me back here in the land of life;
it draws me as the moon will draw the sea.

FURIA. Away! Away!

CATILINE.   It twinkles and it beckons.
I cannot follow you until this light
is well and truly out, or veiled by clouds. . . .
Now I can see it; that is not a star,
it is a heart, a warm and throbbing heart;
it binds me here; it fascinates and draws me,
as does the evening star a small child's eye.

FURIA. Then stop this beating heart!

CATILINE.   What do you mean?

FURIA. You have your dagger in your belt. One thrust . . .
the star will fade away, this heart which stands
in enmity between us will be crushed.

CATILINE. Am I to quench . . .? The blade is sharp and gleaming. . . .

[*With a cry.*]

Where are you now, Aurelia? Where, Aurelia?
If you were near. . . ! No, no . . . I must not see you!
And yet it seems to me all would be well,
that peace would come if I could lay my head
upon your breast and then repent . . . repent!

FURIA. And what would you repent?

CATILINE.   All I have done!
That I was born, and that I ever lived.

FURIA. Too late now to repent! From where you stand
there's no road leading back. . . . Go, fool, and try!
Now I am going home. Just lay your head
upon her breast, and see if you find there
the peace your weary soul is looking for.

I1

[*With mounting frenzy.*]

The thousand dead will soon rise up again;
dishonoured women too will join their ranks;
and every one of them will ask of you
the life, the blood, the honour that you stole.
In terror you will flee into the night . . .
will flee past every shore around the globe,
like some Actaeon by his hounds pursued . . .
a shade pursued by all the thousand shades!

CATILINE. I see it, Furia! I'm an outcast here.
I have no home now in the world of light!
I'll go with you down to the land of shades; . . .
the bond that binds me I will cut asunder.

FURIA. Why fumble for your dagger?

CATILINE.   She shall die!

[*The lightning strikes and the thunder rolls.*]

FURIA. The mighty powers rejoice at your resolve! . . .
Look, Catiline . . . your wife is on her way.

[AURELIA *comes through the forest, searching anxiously.*]

AURELIA. Where is he to be found? Where can he be?
He's not among the dead . . .

[*She catches sight of him.*]

                          Great heavens above; . . .
Oh Catiline!

[*She rushes towards him.*]

CATILINE [*bewildered*].   Don't ever speak that name!

AURELIA. Alive!

[*She is about to throw herself in his arms.*]

CATILINE [*repulsing her*].   Begone! I am no living man.

AURELIA. Oh, listen to me, dearest. . . !

CATILINE.   No, I will not!
I hate you! I see through your cunning trick;
you'd chain me to the hell of life in death.
Don't gaze at me like that! Your eyes are torture; . . .
they are like daggers piercing through my soul!
Of course, the dagger! Shut your eyes and die. . . !

        [He draws the dagger and seizes her arm.]

AURELIA. Watch over him and me, oh gods of mercy!

CATILINE. Come, shut your eyes; shut them, I say; . . . I can
see starlight in them and the morning sky. . . .
Now I shall quench that morning star in heaven!

        [The thunder rolls again.]

Your heart-blood! Now the gods of life call out
their last farewell to you and Catiline!

    *[He raises the dagger to her bosom; she flees into the tent; he pursues
her.]*

FURIA *[listening]*.
She is entreating him with arms outstretched.
She's pleading for her life. He will not hear.
He strikes the blow! . . . She lies in her own blood.

    *[*CATILINE *comes slowly out of the tent with the dagger in his hand.]*

CATILINE. Now I am free. Soon I shall be as nothing.
My soul is sinking into dense oblivion.
My sight is blurred, my hearing is confused,
as if through rushing waters. Do you know
what I have slaughtered with this little dagger?
Not her alone . . . but all the hearts on earth . . .
all living things, and all that blooms and blossoms; . . .
I have put out the stars, the moon's bright disc,
the fiery sun. You see . . . it does not rise,
will never rise again; the sun is dead.
The whole great globe itself is now transformed
into one vast and chilly sepulchre
whose vault is leaden grey; . . . beneath this vault
stand you and I, cast out by light and darkness,
by death and life . . . two never resting shadows.

FURIA. We stand before our goal now, Catiline!

CATILINE. No, one step more . . . before my goal is reached.
Release me from my burden! Don't you see,
the corpse of Catiline weighs down on me?
A stake to pierce the corpse of Catiline!

[*He shows her the dagger.*]

Oh Furia, set me free! Come, take this stake; . . .
with this I speared the starry eye of morning; . . .
Here, take it . . . take it, drive it through the corpse,
which then will lose its power . . . and I am free.

FURIA [*seizes the dagger*].
So be it, spirit whom in hate I loved!
Shake off your dust, and come where men forget!

[*She plunges the dagger deep in his breast; he collapses at the foot of the tree.*]

CATILINE [*regains consciousness after a time, strokes his hand across his fore-head, and speaks faintly*].
Now, oh enigmatic shade, your prophecy is clear!
I shall fall both by my own and by another's hand.
Nemesis has done her deed. Enshroud me, gloom of death!
Raise your waves now, murky Styx, and let the crests swell high!
Take me over; speed the boat unhindered on its course
to the silent prince's realm, the home of all the shades.
A divided path leads downwards. Mutely I shall go
to the left . . .

AURELIA [*staggers from the tent. She is pale and her bosom is bloody.*]
No, to the right, towards Elysium!

CATILINE [*startled*]. How this vivid apparition makes my blood run cold!
She herself it is! Aurelia . . . speak . . . are you alive?

AURELIA [*kneels by him*].
Yes, I live that I may calm the sea of your afflictions; . . .
live that I may lay my bosom on your breast and die.

CATILINE. Oh, you are alive!

AURELIA. I fell into a swoon, no more;
yet I followed you with eyes grown dim; I heard it all . . .
and my love for you restored to me my wifely strength; . . .
breast to breast, dear Catiline, down to our grave we go!

CATILINE. Oh, how gladly! Yet you cherish your blithe hope in vain.
We must part now. Vengeance calls me with its hollow cries.
You may hasten swift and carefree on to peace and light;
over Lethe I must go, descend into the dark.

[*Day dawns in the background.*]

AURELIA [*points to the growing light*].
No; for ever love dispels the terrors and the gloom of death.
See the thunder clouds departing; faintly beckons morning's star.

[*With arms uplifted.*]

Light has conquered. See, in warmth and splendour dawns the day!
Come then, Catiline, for death already grips me tight.

[*She sinks down over him.*]

CATILINE [*clutches her tightly and speaks with a last burst of strength*].
Oh what bliss! Now I remember my forgotten dream,
how that chamber's darkness was dispersed by streaming rays,
how the song of little children hailed the new-born day.
Ah, my eyes are growing dim, my strength is running out,
but my mind is full of light as never yet before,
and my past erratic wanderings lie there clear to see.
Yes, my life has been a storm beneath night's lightning flash,
but my death is morning twilight, tinged with rosy hues.

[*He leans over her.*]

From my soul the gloom you've banished; calm lies in my breast.
Now with you I come to dwell in realms of light and peace!

[*He quickly tears the dagger from his breast and speaks as his voice fails.*]

Reconciled, the powers of dawn smile gently from on high;
You have vanquished with your love the spirit of the night!

[*During the last scene* FURIA *has gradually withdrawn into the background, where she disappears among the trees.* CATILINE'*s head sinks down on to* AURELIA'*s breast. They die.*]

THE BURIAL MOUND
[Kæmpehøjen]

DRAMATIC POEM IN ONE ACT
BY
BRYNJOLF BJARME
[1850]

First performed in Christiania on 26 September 1850

CHARACTERS

BERNHARD, an old recluse

BLANKA, his foster-daughter

GANDALF, a Viking chief from Norway

ASGAUT, an old warrior

HEMMING, Gandalf's scald

JOSTEIN, standard-bearer

HROLLOUG along with several Vikings

The action takes place on the coast of Normandy, called at that time Valland, before the introduction of Christianity into Scandinavia

Forest district near the sea, which can be glimpsed in the background between the trees. In the middle of the stage a warrior's mound, with a monumental stone; in front of the mound a little moss-grown altar, upon which is a cross bedecked with flowers. The roof of a cottage can be seen through the foliage; beneath a tree in the foreground sits BERNHARD *writing on a roll of parchment; at his side stands* BLANKA *in a reflective attitude. It is evening.*

BERNHARD [*writing*].
  'Then it is said—when Ragnarok has stilled
  The wild forces, and purified this life,
  Odin, Baldur and the gentle Freia
  Will once again rule over men in peace.'

       [*He puts the parchment on one side, and rises.*]

  But, Blanka! Dreaming yet again, I see!
  You are wearied by these saga tales
  Of Northern peoples you have never known,
  And find delight instead in your own world.
  So be it then! I do just the same.
  I love these ancient memories of the past,
  Of the times when I went ranging far and wide
  On Northern seas, among Thule's barren fells.
  Faithfully in my mind I stored each song
  From the poet's lips—the exploits of our kin
  From the glorious days of the dark and ancient past—
  And cannot now dismiss them from my mind.
  And now that I have settled down in peace
  On Valland's strand, to me they are doubly dear.
  For if I now recite them, it is to me—
  As if I lived my whole life through again.

BLANKA [*eagerly*]. I wearied? No, no, it is not so.
  The North was the very substance of my dreams.
  Longing, my ardent soul had set its course
  Thither on an urgent stream of thought.
  Each tale you told, dear father, speaks so true,
  And the spirit rises up and knows no peace
  Until in fleeting dream it greets the North.

BERNHARD. Your heart is quickly moved, my little Blanka!
  Often when you hear these ancient tales
  From out the distant North, your cheeks will glow—
  And Valland's flowers are very nigh forgotten.

BLANKA [*vehemently*]. How can I help it? What is this Southern life
  Against the heroic world of the Northern folk
  Amidst their mountains; as different as the bulrush
  from the sturdy pine that defies the tempest's rage!

            [*More amiably, as she seizes his hand.*]

  But tell me why it puts you out of humour
  To be reminded of your own life in the North?
  It almost seems as though you wished to banish
  From living memory all your youth on earth!

BERNHARD [*evasively*].
  Please ask no more, my daughter! It is enough
  You know I found you as a little girl,
  Abandoned, helpless, shortly after a band
  Of Viking raiders had attacked the coast.
  Your father met his death beneath their swords.
  His castle stands in ruins on the cliffs.
  But vengeance followed hard upon their deeds—
  Their cruel chieftain fell in mortal combat.
  But ask no more about the North, nor yet
  About my life there—I grow sad at heart.

BLANKA [*quickly*]. And can you still not bear to see again
  The glistening icefield set among the meadows
  Of the North, from which an echo of the past
  Still trembles through the harp strings of the heart?

BERNHARD. Do not call these hopes to life again.
  Let these yearnings slumber deep in the soul,
  Since my heart must banish thoughts like these
  If I'm to rest content on Valland's strand.
  Speak no more about it—Now I'll take
  My usual evening saunter through the forest.

BLANKA. I'll come with you and pick some forest flowers
  Where spreading oak-tree leans towards the sea.
  Then by the dead man's grave I shall offer

My daily prayer that his soul may rest in peace.
Soon the cross will bear a fresh, green wreath
To greet in tranquil trust the twilight hour.

[*They go out into the forest.* GANDALF *enters from the opposite side,
followed by his* VIKINGS.]

GANDALF. Here we stand, ready and armed for the fray,
With sword in hand on Valland's verdant coast.
Here a son has led his Viking band
Where a father's blood was spilt by a hostile sword!
Straw-thatched cottage roofs come into view—
Which scarlet flames will very soon consume.
Yonder the sound of song and evening bells—
But the women's joyous cries shall turn to lament,
And the song of the men in the tranquil hour of evening
Shall turn to a croak of death from their speechless mouths!
I shall collect my father's scattered ashes,
And round the urn shall place a new-made wreath
Of the oak-tree's leaves; and in his native soil
His ashes then shall find eternal rest.

[*He draws his sword.*]

The goal is reached.
Revenge has found
Its way over foaming seas.
The sword is ready
To spatter with blood
The Viking chieftain's grave!
Hear my promise,
Thor and All-Fader,
Pronounced with binding force;
Whomsoever we find,
Be it woman or man,
Shall bleeding sink to the ground!
This day, by its end,
Will witness bloodshed,
Or else I destroy myself.
And should I not keep
This oath that I swear
Then send me, oh gods! to Hell!

HEMMING [*who up till now has timidly held back, rushes forward, his harp in his hand, and shouts vehemently*].
Swear not revenge by the gods of heaven, Gandalf!

GANDALF [*darkly*].
You here, Hemming? Why don't you stay with the ship?

HEMMING. I cannot. Always I must accompany you,
Wherever you go, like a tireless shadowing spirit!

GANDALF. This is no place for the scald. . . .

HEMMING.   Yet see, Gandalf!
Is it not peaceful here, by this open shore,
Between these beeches and those oak trees tall?
See yonder how the swelling sea is bathed
In the golden light of Odin's fatherly eye,
And the tree-clad cliff observes with tranquil gaze
The sportive waves that ripple at its feet,
And yet no glacier spreads its protective shield
Across the mountain's peak or its sloping sides!

ASGAUT [*approaches, whilst* HEMMING *retires to the rear*].
Odin soon will descend to Saga's halls
And darkness then will spread across the land.
Here it is cool, with greensward under foot.
Here could be a place to pitch our camp.

GANDALF. Indeed—but look! Yonder stands a cottage
Among the forest trees . . .

JOSTEIN.   A splendid find!

HROLLOUG. And those who dwell there?

GANDALF.   We shall send to Hell!

THE WARRIORS. Yes, yes, to Hell!

ASGAUT.   And that without delay—
Audun shall be revenged with blood and fire.
But first spy out the forest. Go now, men—
But cautiously, that none might notice us.

[*The* VIKINGS *go.* HEMMING *remains standing in the background.*]

GANDALF. Well, this is the place, from what you've always said.
Beside the cliff-top castle by the rocky point,
There, you said, he fell. Its walls were long
ago reduced to ruins—a consolation!

[*He notices the burial mound.*]

But stay! What do I see? Am I deceived?
No, no! By Odin and by Asathor!
A memorial stone is set above the mound.
This is a Viking grave in the style of old!

ASGAUT. Indeed it is! Suppose . . . ! No, no, impossible!

GANDALF. You do not mean . . . my father's grave?

ASGAUT.   No, no!
The forest birds have long devoured his corpse.
The winds of night dispersed his mortal dust!

GANDALF. I swore by mighty Thor my solemn oath—
His killer is to perish by my sword,
Given he is still alive. . . .

ASGAUT.   Someone approaches.

GANDALF. A woman fair as Freia!

ASGAUT.   Make her the first
Of the sacrificial victims of our revenge.

GANDALF. Must I murder a woman! Yet my oath
Requires me to. . . .

ASGAUT.   Thus you swore, Gandalf!
If it please you, wait here by this oak,
I shall summon the Vikings back again.

[*He goes.* BLANKA *returns with her lap full of flowers; she kneels before the altar in silent prayer, after which she rises, hangs a fresh wreath on the cross and strews flowers over the burial mound.*]

BLANKA. Here I've made my Viking raid
In the lovely land of the world of flowers.
Each little flower had to yield,
Conquered by the language of force.

How rich my plunder by compare
With gold that's dearly bought for blood.
O Viking, asleep within this mound,
Why did you plough the swelling sea,
Why did you harry that foreign strand
And burn and pillage those peaceful homes?
Why did you only seek joy in power?
Why did you not remain at home?
Had you remained there, you might still be
A man enjoying serene old age.
And the colourful tints of joyous peace
Would light the winter of your years!
—I still remember well that night:
The castle there was lit by flames,
And through the trees and undergrowth
A clash of swords and cries of death.
And still I often seem to glimpse
The ebb and flow of battling men.
And when in the sea the sun sinks low,
And when the breezes rustle the leaves,
It often seems as if I see
A Viking bold with his belted sword—

[*Becomes aware of* GANDALF.]

Great God above!—

GANDALF [*approaches*].   Fear not, my child!

BLANKA. A vision from the realm of dreams?
An apparition ready poised
To vanish? No, I see it plain.
You are a man from the Viking North. . . .

GANDALF. Do not be afraid, my child!
But tell us why you decorate
That burial mound with sprigs of green?

HEMMING [*interrupting, as he comes forward*].
Come, Gandalf! Come! Can't you see this woman
Is no earthly maid. . . .

GANDALF [*vehemently*].   Stand back, Hemming!

[HEMMING *goes.*]

BLANKA. Who is that man?

GANDALF.   Oh, just a poor scald.
  He is at times a little feeble-minded.
  Only when he takes his harp, and strikes
  The swelling chords, and sings a funeral lay
  Is he aroused from that unruffled dream
  In which he wanders silently through life.

BLANKA [*eagerly*]. So the hearts of Norway's sons are also filled
  With fervent longing and with secret dreams!
  More and more this land appears to me
  Resplendent in a glorious magic light,
  The more my inner eye refines its vision!
  But tell me, Viking! Why not rest awhile
  In the cool and shady refuge of this glade,
  With the oak trees' leafy canopy above.
  I shall watch for you, and you may slumber.
  And should you thirst, I can bring for you
  A cool refreshing drink from yonder spring
  That gushes crystal-clear from out the grass.
  Oh, tell me, will you not?

GANDALF [*vehemently*].   Be silent, woman!
  I clearly see your guile! You want to lull
  My mind with wheedling words and lying talk!
  But angered Vikings seeking stern revenge
  Are not to be lulled to sleep by women's words!

BLANKA [*smiling*]. You do but jest! You merely try to scare me!
  You won't succeed—I know the sons of Norway!

GANDALF. You know them?

BLANKA.   I've known of them for years.
  My father's told me countless splendid things,
  And many glorious tales of the people there.

GANDALF. You are not afraid of this fierce and war-like man?

BLANKA. Why should I be? Clearly, you are strong,
  And I am just a weak, defenceless woman.
  Would any valiant man debase himself
  By using force against this weak. . . ?
K1

GANDALF.   Enough!
  It's well you choose your words, fair woman!
  But since you do not fear me—answer this:
  Who slumbers there beneath the burial mound?

BLANKA. Only my father knows—though I believe
  He was a Viking who came from the distant North.

GANDALF. Who met his death in combat! But tell me this:
  Who raised this mound above him in the forest,
  In this foreign land, and planted tiny flowers,
  And decked the warrior's grave with greenest grass?

BLANKA. I was the one. And still today I plant
  Further tender shoots at the approach of spring.
  You see how well they thrive—how every leaf
  Turns in loving trust towards its neighbour,
  And hand in hand they seem to form a circle,
  A ring of flowers about the burial mound,
  As if they would protect the quiet grave
  And make of it a haven of spring flowers!

GANDALF. How very strange! I do not understand!
  He was your foe; he came intent on plunder!
  He left your country bathed in streams of blood.
  He took away your people to live as slaves
  In a distant land. And yet, dear girl,
  You decorate this Viking's grave with flowers!

BLANKA. This our faith instructs us. A precept there
  Commands: Forgive your foe, and hold the hand
  Of reconciliation out towards him.

GANDALF [*pondering*]. Reconciliation? I know not the word.
  Yet wait! I do believe I have it!
  But it applies a different way with us!

BLANKA. How is it then? Tell me, and I shall listen.

GANDALF.   When in his bosom
                           Rancour is blazing,
                           Ready the Viking
                           Makes for the fight.
                           Sets on the helmet

Steel-bright for combat,
Then to the duel
Bravely he strides.
—Swords are set clashing
Wounds are left reddening,
Slashed to the bone the
Enemy's breast.
Sooner or later
Follows the other
On to Valhalla,
Home of the brave;
Holds to his bosom
Kinsmen and comrades,
Greets as a brother
His enemy there!

BLANKA. Yes, that's fine! But I have heard it said
That your Valhalla is a place of strife,
That savage combat is your joy in death,
And after death in Odin's company too.

GANDALF. What would this life be if not for strife?
A sunless day, a man deprived of honour,
A frozen well in winter's icy grip,
A listless doze in Hela's dismal halls!

BLANKA. Ah yes! The inner strife, the spirit's battle,
And light's resounding victory over dark.
Such a strife gives life its purpose, heathen!
But it's clear you cannot grasp its meaning!

GANDALF [*reflectively*]. No, you are right! I do not grasp your words—
And yet my soul is lit by fleeting insights,
And visions which I never saw before.

BLANKA. There is a myth embodied in your faith,
About which father often used to tell:
And that is the lovely tale of Baldur's death.
He walked secure, safe in love's protection;
Your gods kept watch at every step he took.
But evil Loki worked his baleful tricks
And Baldur quickly found himself in Hell.
But after night there comes the shining day

And Baldur was united with the gods.
The power of evil was, like the leaf, swept off,
And the giant's guile defeated by the gods.

[*With fiery vehemence.*]

Yet here you come, a man of violent hates,
To start a reign of terror in these dales!
Can you conceive no better form of strife
Than that dispute the sword's red tongue contests?
Where could one find a field of combat fairer
Than that where love and faith contest the prize?
Where the victor's cry is but a humble prayer?
And God the one to whom we swear our faith?
Can Viking really find no better goal,
As through the stormy seas of life he sails,
Than that where human blood discolours the sword
And the homestead burns within the quiet wood?
Is your heart as cold and hard as armoured steel?
Is your soul not large enough to grasp
The heavenly riches and the endless worth
Of the glorious golden treasure of the spirit?
So why not take to your wintry mountain land
This priceless treasure with you from the South,
And teach that tender care and brotherly love
Count more than force of arms and sword's constraint!

GANDALF [*vehemently*]. Be silent, woman! You speak with the tongues
of trolls,
And fill my soul with pestilence and poison!
Till now my pride resided in my sword.
Valhalla's sweet rewards were what I craved.
But now my troubled spirit is divided,
My aim confused—here the fame of war,
First chanted by the sword, then etched in blood,
And carried across the sea to distant places;
And yet, on the other hand, a gentle light,
A distant gleam from Freia's holy grove,
In which is heard a curious sound of harps,
And wondrous songs from fairest elfin lips!—

[*Sadly.*]

But if I thus betray Asathor, Odin,
And all the powerful ancient Nordic gods,
Consign me then to slumber in that earth
Where the quiet beech-tree droops across the mound!

[*The* VIKINGS *enter with* BERNHARD; HEMMING *follows them.*]

ASGAUT. See what a splendid catch we bring you, Gandalf!

BLANKA. Oh God! My father in their cruel hands!

GANDALF. Fear not, maiden!

BERNHARD [*greatly moved, pointing to* GANDALF].
                              Is this man your leader?

JOSTEIN. Indeed he is. [*To* GANDALF.] He can tell you something
About your father's death! He knows what happened!

BERNHARD [*moved*]. Are you a son of the Viking chief who landed
Nearby on the coast a good many years ago
And fell by yonder castle, now in ruins?

GANDALF. I am, old man!

ASGAUT.   The reason he is here
Is to take a blood-revenge.

GANDALF.   Quiet! Let him speak!

BERNHARD. Our life is held in the Lord the Father's hand.
I do not fear these murdering swords of yours.
But spare at least the life of this young child
Whose foster-father I have been so long.
She also lost her father in that battle.
He was the one-time owner of the castle
Your savage Viking hordes attacked and plundered!

BLANKA [*to* GANDALF]. Oh! You a son of the man who killed my
    father!
And yet . . . may God forgive him!

BERNHARD.   There you see,
You heathens, a magnanimous mind's revenge!
A quiet prayer to the Lord for a fallen foe!
And what is yours? Further bloody deeds!—

HEMMING. By Baldur, Gandalf! This old man is right!

ASGAUT. You sound just like a woman! Silence, man!
You'll never be a fighter. . . .

HEMMING.   That's a calling
All too far removed from that of scald.

GANDALF. A son of the man who killed her father! No!
It isn't true! Oh, woman, that's not so!
The man who struck him down is over there!
But take me to the spot my father died.

BERNHARD [*points to the burial mound*].
He slumbers in this mound!

THE WARRIORS.   It's Audun's mound!

GANDALF. My father's burial place!

ASGAUT.   And the memorial stone?

BERNHARD. I set the stone upon his grave; and she,
My daughter, decks it every day with flowers.

GANDALF. How strange and puzzling are the ways of the Norns!

ASGAUT. And now away to seek the man who killed him,
Exact your blood-revenge!

THE WARRIORS.   A blood-revenge!

GANDALF. No, no! I will not seek revenge just yet!

ASGAUT. What ails you, man?

GANDALF.   My mind is sore confused!
I know not why—but all my soul's in ferment!

[*He places his hand on his breast.*]

BERNHARD. You will not take revenge?

GANDALF.   I cannot do it.
This maiden here has spoken gladsome words
That still reverberate within my soul.
These tender glances! Yes, this gentle voice!
It's thus I picture Folkvang's beauteous goddess!

BERNHARD. You will not seek revenge! You feel compassion!
No longer is there aught to bind my tongue!
See! This is the hand by which your father fell!

GANDALF [*starts back*]. Ah, Loki!

THE WARRIORS.   Down with him! To Hell with him!

BLANKA [*throws herself into her father's arms*].
Oh, father, what are you saying! That's not true!
Oh, listen, warriors. Listen, listen, Gandalf!
I found him in the forest, bleeding, weak,
That dreadful morning following the battle.
I brought him . . .

ASGAUT.   Silence, woman! That's enough!
On, on, you men!

THE WARRIORS [*with drawn swords*]. Away to Hela's shades!

GANDALF [*stepping in front of* BERNHARD].
Stay! Spare him! Do not touch this man!

ASGAUT. He must be out of his mind! Collect your wits!
That is the man who killed your father, Gandalf!

GANDALF. I tell you once again: Don't touch this man!

BLANKA. Take back, oh father dear, those dreadful words!
You did not kill the Viking . . .

BERNHARD.   Calm your fears,
My daughter! Many things will soon be clear to you!

ASGAUT [*to* GANDALF]. Do you forget that as you strode ashore
You swore by Asathor a solemn oath
To revenge your father's death. And these your words:
'He or I shall fall as a sacrifice.'

GANDALF [*with emotion*].
Alas, my heart is crushed within my breast
As though the Midgard serpent cast his coils
With giant strength around it, and destroyed
The last remaining power of my will.
Ah, maiden! You have sown these seeds of doubt,
And raised a tempest in my inmost soul.

My blood is glowing hot, like Hela's fire,
And nothing can assuage this inner pain.

BLANKA [*moved*]. Oh, Gandalf! Now I come to see at last
How fond of you my heart has grown to be!

GANDALF. Ah, maiden! Are your words indeed the truth?

BLANKA. Believe me, Gandalf!

GANDALF.   Blanka, say no more!
Ill-fated is the oath which I have sworn.
I cannot take revenge—so I must die!

ASGAUT. What do you mean?

GANDALF.   He or I—so ran
My words—must pay the sacrifice in blood!
He shall not die, for he has fostered her—
This woman who has wakened in my soul
A whole new world of strange and wondrous thoughts!
My oath must hold—so go, prepare my ship.
I shall on Muspel's wings ascend on high
To join my father's spirit in Valhalla!

THE WARRIORS. Ah, Gandalf!

GANDALF.   Yes, in ancient Nordic style
I'll seek my death. The evening wind is blowing
From off the shore. Then go, bedeck my ship
With victory signs. And then I'll go aboard,
The way so many Vikings have before!

BLANKA. Oh, do you mean. . . ?

GANDALF.   For me there is no choice.
I cannot now betray my father's gods!
To me this present hour is like the gleam
Of Odin's splendour through the autumn mists.
My life has been a world of war and strife—
The life that beckons now is like a day
In spring, with golden fruit and lovely flowers.
Is this the glory I shall now forsake!

[*Seizes her hand.*]

It must be so. Farewell then, dearest Blanka!
We shall not meet again . . .

BLANKA.   We shall . . . in heaven!

GANDALF. No, never Blanka! Your immortal soul
Will soar on high beyond the myriad stars,
While mine will sweep away to Odin's burg.
And there I'll give myself to warlike combat,
Forgetting for a while perhaps my grief,
Though never will it still my ardent longing!—
From you forever parted! Hapless thought!
At darkest hour of night my shade will roam
From shore to shore in restless agitation,
Until the sun shows red on heaven's edge.
And when my spirit ship, beflecked with foam,
Transports the Viking's spirit across the sea,
On yonder clouds as light as air you'll sit
By moonlight in the company of Christ!
Ah, cruel fate! For wherein was my crime?
But now, farewell! This is our final meeting.
The raging Northern seas shall hold my body
Far, far from you—far from your flowery grave!

BLANKA. Oh, turn away from these dark gods of yours!
Yet, Gandalf, no!—Your eye proclaims your purpose.
Your heart has formed a resolute decision.
But when below the blue-black waves you slumber,
Then I'll be free to follow my desire—
To speed towards the North across the sea
And spread the word of Christ among your folk!

BERNHARD [*who during the previous speeches has been visibly struggling with
    himself, starts forward and seizes* BLANKA's *hand*].
Oh, Blanka, hold! I can no more subdue
The violent storm that rages in my breast

[*Sinks to his knees.*]

Forgive me, child! Forgive me if you can!
You are deceived in everything I've done . . .

BLANKA [*raises him up*].
Oh, God in heaven! Father, you're confused!

GANDALF. Ah, what is this!

BERNHARD.   Forgive, forgive me, Blanka!
  My son, my Gandalf! See! I am your father!

GANDALF. Oh, gentle Baldur!

BLANKA.   God! What are you saying!

ASGAUT. You're lying, man!

BERNHARD [*exposing his arm and holding it out to* ASGAUT].
                    You recognize this scar?
  A scar which you yourself, once long ago,
  Did slash across my arm with rusty steel?

ASGAUT [*seizes his hand in astonishment*].   Thor's hammer! Audun,
  it is you!

BLANKA. Oh merciful heaven!

GANDALF.   Father! Oh, my father!

                    [*They sink in his arms.*]

THE WARRIORS [*beating on their shields*].
  Hail, Audun! Hail to Norway's warrior of old!

BLANKA. See how all things resolve in glorious concord!

AUDUN. Not yet! Oh, Blanka, can you ever grant me
  Forgiveness?

BLANKA [*throws her arms about him*].
                    Father, that you should ask me that!
  Have you not always been so good to me,
  And guided all my steps with loving care,
  And often borne me safely in your arms?

AUDUN. Compared with what I owe to you, it's little.

GANDALF. But, Father, tell me how it came to be
  That you remained behind on Valland's shores?

AUDUN. I'll tell you. Down I sank beside the castle—
  The battle was by that time nearly over—
  Unconscious, bleeding, by the cliff I lay,
  Concealed from sight by overhanging branches.
  My people mourned the killing of their chief.

They sailed away—and I alone remained.
And when the sun next morning rose resplendent,
I heard a rustling in the nearby branches.
It was my Blanka, then a little girl
Of scarcely five years old. She stood there, fearful;
But when she saw me bleeding and exhausted,
She brought me water from the nearby stream,
Cupped in her tiny hands, and tended me.
She was the only one who was not murdered.
The entire coast was ravaged and deserted.
With tender words she soothed away my pain.
I lived on here quite happy in the forest—
I felt no urgent longing to go home,
For you, my Gandalf, had from earliest youth
Been ranging far and wide on Viking raids.
I heard the words of Christ from this child's lips,
And then my inner soul grew light and pure!

GANDALF. But why this burial mound? Oh, tell me, father!
How can I make sense of what you've said?

AUDUN. I buried there my armour and my sword!

[*After a pause.*]

To me it seemed as if the savage spirit
That once inspired the blood-drenched Viking life
Had altogether vanished from my soul.
To me it seemed as if a quiet repose
Already more and more possessed my mind,
When at the altar foot, with childlike faith,
My Blanka prayed for the peace of the Viking's soul.

ASGAUT [*seizes* BLANKA's *hand*].
Forgive my harsh behaviour, fairest maiden!

GANDALF. Oh, Blanka mine, come let me now embrace you!
From you I've learnt a better goal in life.

BLANKA [*affectionately*]. And what of your gods?

GANDALF.   These I can't betray!
However could you trust my love for you
If I were faithless to my people's gods?

BLANKA. Ah well . . . in time, dear Gandalf, one may hope!
And yet one thing I know you'll promise me:
You'll never more embark on Viking raids!

GANDALF. I swear a solemn oath I will not go!
My Kingdom I'll defend with proper courage,
But never, never plunder peaceful lands.
My friends, what say you? Are you not prepared
To follow me?

HROLLOUG.   All hail, our gallant leader!
We all will follow loyally as before!

GANDALF. So now away, towards the distant North!

BLANKA. The heart-felt goal of all my fondest dreams!
Oh, fairest land of snow and Northern lights,
I'll soon greet you as my proper home!

[*To* AUDUN.]

And you, beloved father . . .

AUDUN [*with suppressed emotion*]. No, dear Blanka!
I cannot make the journey with you, Gandalf!

GANDALF *and* BLANKA. Oh, Father!

AUDUN.   No, this is my resolute
Decision—never can I leave this coast.
The burial mound conveys its quiet welcome;
This aged Viking soon will slumber there.
I'll miss you sorely when we part, believe me.
Oh, often at the midnight hour I'll go
And seat myself beneath the memorial stone
And stare across the wide expanse of sea
And when those faintly distant Northern lights
Like a spirit's smile illuminate the sky,
In gratitude I'll clasp my hands together
And greet this bright aurora as a sign,
A message that a Day of Light has dawned
In all its splendour in my fatherland!
But, Gandalf, you my son have solemn duties
Towards your people; here you must not linger.

Whilst you, my daughter, have a pious mission—
To guide his steps through life with sweet devotion.
Fear not, my child, for where it's clear that love
Has made its home, so also faith will there
Be blended soon in blessed harmony!

HEMMING [*steps forward with his harp in his hand*].
I likewise cannot make this journey, Gandalf!
This moment is engraved upon my soul.
The darkness of my bosom will be banished
By Christendom's pellucid, gentle flame.

>   [*He sings to the harp.*]
>   Rock hugely towering
>   High in the heavens,
>   Time will devour
>   With ravenous fangs.
>
>   Sword which at one time
>   Clashed on the battlefield,
>   Wild as the tempest,
>   Crumbles to rust.
>
>   Hero who forges
>   Through the wild oceans
>   Slumbers at last in
>   His burial mound.
>
>   Though mighty forces
>   Rule in Valhalla,
>   Ragnarok's tempest
>   Them shall disperse.
>
>   After the darkness
>   Of bloodshed and conflict,
>   Of savage aggression,
>   Dawns a new day.

At the foot of the cross I lay my harp to rest,
My final song a lament for Asa's faith!

>   [*Places his harp before the altar.*]

GANDALF. And you, my father, will not come with us?

BLANKA. And your children may not close your eyes?

AUDUN. It cannot be. See, Hemming shall remain.
He'll care for me . . .

HEMMING.   . . . With filial piety.
And maybe on some distant future day
My harp will sound again in blessed prayer.

GANDALF [*dejected, but composed*].
So be it then . . .

BLANKA.   Oh, God! Are we to leave him!

AUDUN. That is decided. Kneel before me, children,
In order that my hands may bless your union!

[*They kneel, one on each side of him, holding each other's hands.*
AUDUN *places his hands on their heads in blessing.*]

Eternal blessing be upon this pact
Combining Nordic strength with Southern mercy.
Be good and pious, Gandalf! Guard the treasure
Which you have taken from these Valland forests!
And you, my daughter, guard the sacred mission
Which God has made of woman's lot on earth.
Plant Southern flowers there in the pine trees' haunt
And spread the light of truth throughout the North!

[*He embraces them silently as they rise.*]

THE WARRIORS [*as they beat their shields*].
All hail, our chieftain! Hail to his young bride!

[AUDUN *sits by the burial mound, and* HEMMING *at his feet.*]

HROLLOUG. Already sail is set! The ship is ready!

BLANKA [*with spirit, seizing the banner from* JOSTEIN's *hand and stepping
forward*].
And now away! Towards the North we course
Across the ocean blue, through wave and foam.
Upon the glacier's peak the day soon dawns,
Naught but a memory soon these Viking raids!

Already the Viking sits upon his mound.
The time is past when he would swiftly sail,
And harry from coast to coast with savage sword.
The thunder-god's great hammer sinks to dust;
The Nordic lands become a warrior's grave!
Do not forget the promise of All-Fader:
And when the grave is flanked with moss and flowers
The Viking's spirit shall fight at Idavold—
The North shall also rise from out the tomb
To purer strife on silver seas of thought!

THE BURIAL MOUND
[*Kæmpehøjen*]

DRAMATIC POEM IN ONE ACT
BY
HENRIK IBSEN
(1854)

Performed in Bergen on 2 January 1854, and subsequently printed in *Bergenske Blade*, nos. 9–13, 1854.

CHARACTERS

RODERIK, an old recluse

BLANKA, his foster-daughter

GANDALF, a sea-king from Norway

ASGAUT, an old Viking

HROLLOUG

JOSTEJN

SEVERAL VIKINGS

HEMMING, a young scald in GANDALF's service

The action takes place on a little island near Sicily, shortly before
the introduction of Christianity into Norway

An open space surrounded by trees near the shore. To the left in the background the ruins of an ancient temple. In the middle of the stage a large burial mound, upon which there is a monument, decked with garlands.

[RODERIK *sits writing, right. Left,* BLANKA *in a reclining position.*]

BLANKA. Evening sunset's dying flames
swelling like a sea ablaze.
Temple-still along the shore,
still as in a wooded glade.
Summer evening's gentle calm
descends upon us like a dove,
hovers like a swan above
forest flower and ocean wave.

In the orange thicket slumber
gods and goddesses of yore;
marble monuments remind one
of a world that is no more.
Honour, courage, integrity,
all turned to stone, so dead, so rich.
What more fitting image is there
of the whole decrepit South? [*Rises.*]

But my father used to tell me
of a land beyond the waves
where one finds a vital life,
not a carved or painted copy!
Here the god-like lives no more;
stone alone its features bears.
There it breathes a vigorous air,
like a warrior strong and bold!

And when the sultry calm of evening
settles heavily on my breast,
the image of the North emerges

in my mind's eye, bright with snow!
Here it's all a crumbling ruin,
drowsy, slothful, heavy, dull.
There a plunging avalanche,
a life of spring, a winter death!

Had I but the swan's plumage . . .

RODERIK [*after a pause, writing*].
'Then, it is said, when Ragnarok has stilled
The wild forces, and purified this life,
Odin, Baldur and the gentle Freia
Will again rule the race of men in peace!'

[*After having observed her for a moment.*]

But, Blanka! You are dreaming there again.
Lost in thought, you gaze out into space—
What do you seek?

BLANKA [*approaches*].   Forgive me, father dear!
My thoughts were flying with the snow-white swan
that wings its way across the distant sea.

RODERIK. And if I had not stopped you in your flight,
stopped my young and lovely little swan!
Who knows how far you might indeed have flown—
perhaps to Thule?

BLANKA.   And indeed why not?
For does the swan not fly there every spring,
yet every autumn he returns again?

[*Sits down at his feet.*]

Yet I'm no swan. Rather should you call me
a captive falcon, sitting tame and true,
a golden ring upon its leg.

RODERIK.   What is the ring?

BLANKA. That is my love for you, my dearest father,
with which you have secured your youthful falcon!
It cannot fly—not even if it wished to.

[*Gets up.*]

Yet you must see—that when the swans go skimming
across the waves like clouds before the wind,
then I remember all that you have told me
of that heroic life in distant Thule.
Then, in my mind, the bird becomes a longship
with dragon's head and wings of burnished gold.
And there in the prow I glimpse the youthful hero,
a copper helmet over his yellow hair,
with eyes of blue, a deep and manly chest,
his sword gripped firmly in his mighty hand.
And as my hero speeds upon his way,
my dreams disport themselves about his boat
in gay abandon, like a school of dolphins
that play about in fancy's cooling waves!

RODERIK. You live within a dream world, my good child!
Sometimes I fear your thoughts too often dwell
upon the people in the distant North.

BLANKA. And whose the fault then, Father, if it's so?

RODERIK. You mean that I myself. . .?

BLANKA.   Indeed, what else?
You live your own life wholly in the memory
of the youth you spent among those doughty Norsemen.
Do not deny that once you start to speak
of Viking raids, of battles, single combat,
your cheek begins to flush, your eye to glow.
To me you seem to find your youth again.

RODERIK. Perhaps. But I have also reason for it.
Did I myself not live among these heroes?
And all the things that memory whispers to me
are also pages from my personal saga.
But you, however, fostered in the South,
who never saw the winter-silvered mountains,
who never heard the lur-horn's echoing sound—
why should my stories have appeal for you?

BLANKA. But tell me! Does one always have to see
and hear such things through outer senses only?
Has not the soul its eyes and ears too,

with which it can both see and hear clearly?
My corporeal eye can plainly see
the richly glowing colour of the rose.
The spirit's eye can see within the bloom
the lovely fairy with her butterfly wings
behind the crimson petals roguishly hiding,
and singing of that secret power from heaven
that gave the blossom all its colour and perfume.

RODERIK. That's true, my child!

BLANKA.   I almost could believe
because I have not seen these things myself
they take on greater beauty in my thoughts.
And that, at least, is how it is with you!
The ancient sagas, all the heroic lays—
these you recall and talk about with pleasure,
recording them in runes upon your parchments.
But when I ask about your own career
in Northern lands, your eyes grow often dark,
your lips grow silent, and it seems at times
as if your bosom houses gloomy thoughts.

RODERIK [*rises*]. Ah, speak no more about it my good child!
Where will you find the man whose youthful memories
do not contain a measure of bitter remorse?
You know the Norsemen are a savage race.

BLANKA. But are the warriors of the South less fierce?
Do you forget that night, ten years ago—
that time those strangers landed on the coast
and plundered. . .?

RODERIK [*with visible disquiet*]. Enough of that! Come, away!
The sun begins to set already. Come!

BLANKA [*as they go*]. Give me your hand! [*Stops.*] No, wait!

RODERIK.   What is it?

BLANKA. Never before today have I forgotten. . . .

RODERIK. Forgotten what?

BLANKA [*pointing to the mound*]. The wreath upon the stone!

RODERIK. It is . . .

BLANKA. The withered one from yesterday.
I have forgotten to make the change today.
Yet let me take you to your cottage first;
then I shall venture out in search of flowers.
The violet's scent is best when evening's dew
has bathed it in a mist of glittering pearls;
the budding rose is never quite as fair
as when in childlike slumber it is plucked!

[*They go out, right, rear.*]

SCENE TWO

[GANDALF *and the* VIKINGS *enter, right.*]

ASGAUT. We'll soon have reached the place.

GANDALF. Where? Let me see!

ASGAUT. No, wait a while till we're behind the wood.
Upon the rocky slope beside the sea, as we left,
there stood, as we withdrew, a ruined wall.
It probably remains there still, I fancy.

JOSTEJN. But tell us, King, what purpose we pursue
to range about this island here like fools?

HROLLOUG. Yes, tell us what we . . .

GANDALF. Silence, all! Be silent!
And blindly follow where your King commands!

[*To* ASGAUT.]

It seems to me, however, you did sweep
the board a bit too clean, when last you came.
You might, I think, have tried to leave a little
for me and my revenge!

HROLLOUG. You are our King.
To you we pledged our loyalty at the Thing.
But when we followed you upon this raid,
our purpose was to win our fame and glory.

JOSTEJN. And gold and treasure, Hrolloug, gold and treasure.

SEVERAL. Yes, that is the law, Gandalf. Pay heed to that!

GANDALF. I think I know the law as well as you.
　　But is it not, from times long past, a custom
　　and covenant with us that when a kinsman
　　is slain by enemy hand, and then his corpse
　　is left unburied, a prey to any raven,
　　this calls for bloody vengeance?

SEVERAL.　　　　　　　　　　　Yes, that is so.

GANDALF. Then stand prepared to use your swords and shields—
　　You have a king to avenge, and I a father!

　　　　　　　[*Commotion among the* VIKINGS.]

JOSTEJN. A king?

HROLLOUG.　　　A father?

GANDALF.　　　　　　　　　Wait, and I shall tell you
　　what occurred. You know my father was
　　a mighty Viking. Twelve years ago it was
　　when last he sallied forth one spring to raid
　　with Asgaut there and all his trusted men.
　　Two years he ranged about from strand to strand,
　　and sailed to Bratland, Valland, even Blaaland.
　　At length he turned to harry Sicily,
　　and there he heard reports about a chieftain
　　who lived upon this island in a castle
　　with sturdy walls built high upon a rock.
　　And in this place were costly treasures hidden.
　　At dead of night he landed on the shore,
　　attacked the stronghold there with fire and sword.
　　An angry bear, he led the charge himself,
　　and in his berserk fury did not see
　　how round about him all his men fell dead.
　　And when the light of dawn first filled the east,
　　the entire fortress lay in smouldering ruins,
　　and only Asgaut and some few survived—
　　my father and a hundred others with him
　　had ridden to Valhalla through the flames.

ASGAUT. I hoisted high the sail upon our ship
and set a course for home in the distant North.
Once there, I sought for Gandalf—but in vain.
The youthful eagle, it was said, had flown
across the sea to Iceland or the Faroes.
I voyaged after him, but found no trace—
though all men knew his name wherever I went,
for though his longship sped like a fleeting cloud,
his fame was borne on even swifter wings.
And then this summer I tracked him down at last
in Italy. I then reported to him
what things had happened, and how his father died.
And Gandalf swore by all Valhalla's gods
to wreak with fire and sword a bloody vengeance.

JOSTEJN. This is established law, and should be honoured!
Yet—if I had myself been King Gandalf,
I should have stayed behind in Italy,
for there one knows that gold is to be won.

HROLLOUG.   And honour.

GANDALF. Is this your loyalty to your fallen king?

JOSTEJN. Come, now! Let's watch our words! I only meant
perhaps the dead could wait.

ASGAUT [*with suppressed fury*]. Contemptible pack!

JOSTEJN. But seeing that we *are* here now . . .

HROLLOUG.   Yes,
we'll find a fitting way to mark his memory.

SOME. Yes, yes!

OTHERS.   With fire and blood!

ASGAUT.   This suits me well!

GANDALF. And now away to spy around the island.
This very night blood-vengeance must be mine;
if not, I suffer death myself.

ASGAUT.   He swore it.

GANDALF. I swore it thus by all Valhalla's gods!
  And once again I swear it . . .

HEMMING [*with a harp over his shoulder; during the foregoing, he has come
  forward among the* VIKINGS, *and he cries out imploringly*].
                    Swear not, Gandalf!

GANDALF. What ails you?

HEMMING.   Do not swear here in this wood!
  For here our gods can never hear your words.
  Aboard our ships, upon our Northern hills
  they hear you well enough. But never here!

ASGAUT. The pestilential South has smitten you!

HEMMING. I heard the pious priests in Italy
  recounting gentle stories of the Christ;
  and what they said remains within my mind
  by night and day, and will not be forgotten.

GANDALF. I brought you here because from boyhood days
  you showed the signs of rich poetic talent.
  You were to see my bold and valiant deeds,
  and when King Gandalf, an aged grey-haired man,
  would sit among his men at festive board,
  the King's young scald could while away the hours
  of winter-time by singing heroic lays,
  and finally compose my funeral song.
  The monument the poet's tongue creates
  outlives the memorial stone upon the mound.
  Now go! And cast away your harp, and don
  the monkish cloak, if such is what you wish!
  Ha! What a splendid singer is the king's!

      [*The* VIKINGS *go into the wood, left;* HEMMING *follows them.*]

ASGAUT. Oh, what a stagnant time is this we live in!
  Our faith and customs from the olden days
  are everywhere unhappily in decline.
  How lucky for me my back is bent with age;
  my eyes shall never see the North's decay.
  But you, King Gandalf, you are young and strong;

wherever you may roam in distant lands,
remember that it is your royal call
to guard the people's gods and keep their powers!

[*He follows after the others.*]

GANDALF [*after a pause*]. He does not have much confidence in me.
It's good he went! It feels like some great burden
about my shoulders whenever he is near.
This grim old man with rugged, graven face—
he looks like Asathor as, hewn in stone,
he stands with Mjölnir and the belt of strength
within the grove upon my father's lands.
My father's lands! Who knows how things now look
at home and in those old familiar places!
The woods and hills are doubtless much the same
—but the people's heart? Does *it* beat as before?
A blight has fallen on this present age,
that's sapping all the goodness of the North,
just like a poison feeding on its blooms.
I shall go home! And save what still there is
to save, before it all falls down in ruins.

[*Pauses, during which time he looks about him.*]

How pleasant here within this Southern grove!
My pine woods cannot boast so strong a scent.

[*He notices the mound.*]

What's this? A warrior's grave? No doubt it holds
One of our kind from earlier, livelier days.
A burial mound in the South! That seems but just!
For the South it was that struck our mortal blow.
How pleasant this place is! It brings to mind
one winter's night when as a little boy
I sat by the hearth upon my father's knee,
the while he told me stories of our gods,
of Odin, Baldur and the mighty Thor.
And when I spoke to him of Freia's grove,
he then described a grove as it is here.
But when I asked to hear more of Freia,
and how in fact she looked, the old man smiled

and answered, as he set me on the floor:
'Some woman will, I fancy, tell you that.'

[*Listening.*]

Sh! Footsteps in the forest! Quiet, Gandalf—
they bring the first occasion for revenge!

[*He steps aside, so that he is half concealed among the bushes to the right.*]

SCENE THREE

[GANDALF; BLANKA, *with oak leaves in her hair and a basket of
flowers, enters left.*]

BLANKA [*sits left, and busies herself weaving a wreath of flowers.*]
The rippling rivers course through verdant valleys;
the sea-fresh breakers splash upon the shore.
Yet neither rippling river nor murmuring breaker
can rival the appeal of yonder flowers,
that huddle by the edge of the warrior's grave,
transporting me away by night and day.
How good it is to yearn thus, and to dream.
And now the wreath is done. The hero's grave,
so hard and cold, is ready for adornment.
Yes, it is beautiful!

[*Indicating the mound.*]

A life departed,
So strong and brave, now moulders in the ground.
And all that speaks of this man's great renown—
the ice-cold stone that stands upon his mound.
But then comes art, and with beneficent hand
it plucks the fragrant flowers from nature's breast,
and covers the hard insentient monument
with snow-white lilies, sweet forget-me-nots.

[*She climbs up on the mound, hangs the wreath over the gravestone,
and says after a pause:*]

So once again my flock of dreams goes flying
like migrant birds above the ocean's waves.
I'm drawn towards the country of my yearnings;
and to that secret power I gladly yield,

which has its royal seat deep in the soul.
I am in Norway. I'm a warrior's bride,
and like an eagle on a peak I watch.
Across the shining sea the ship appears.
Oh, fly like a gull towards your native strand!
I am a child of the South, I cannot wait.
I snatch the wreath of oak leaves from my head.
Accept, my hero, this—the second token
to mark my welcome—my yearning was the first.

[*She throws the wreath.* GANDALF *steps forward and seizes it.*]

What's this? Who stands . . .?

[*She rubs her eyes and stares in astonishment at him.*]

                                    No, it is no dream.
Who are you, stranger? What is it you seek
here on the strand?

GANDALF.   First come down from the mound,
then we can talk together.

BLANKA [*steps down*].   Here I am!

[*Aside, as she looks at him.*]

Chain-mail across his breast, the copper helmet—
Exactly as my father once described.

[*Aloud.*]

Take off your helmet!

GANDALF.   Why?

BLANKA.   Do as I ask!

[*Aside.*]

Two clear blue eyes, and hair like a field of corn—
exactly as I saw him in my dream.

GANDALF. Who are you, woman?

BLANKA.   I? A simple child!

GANDALF. Yet certainly the fairest on the island.

BLANKA [*laughing*]. The fairest? Yes, I think that's not unlikely,
   For here there's no one else.

GANDALF.   No one at all?

BLANKA. Unless you think my father . . . But he's old,
   and has a silvery beard as long as this.
   I rather think perhaps *I* win the prize.

GANDALF. You are a merry soul.

BLANKA.   Alas, not always!

GANDALF. But tell me now how all this hangs together.
   You're living all alone here with your father;
   and yet I've heard it said beyond dispute
   the island here was richly populated?

BLANKA. Indeed it was, about three years ago.
   But then—it makes a melancholy tale—
   yet you shall hear it, if it is your wish.

GANDALF. Indeed, it is!

BLANKA.   You see, three years ago . . .

[*She sits down.*]

Come, sit you down!

GANDALF [*takes a step back*]. No, you sit. I shall stand.

BLANKA. Three years ago, coming from God knows where,
   a band of warlike raiders reached the isle,
   and everywhere they went they robbed and plundered,
   and murdered every living thing there was.
   The one or two who could, escaped by flight,
   and sought a refuge in my father's castle,
   which stood upon the cliffs beside the sea.

GANDALF. You say your father's?

BLANKA.   Certainly, my father's.
   The evening of their assault was overcast.
   They stormed the castle gate, they forced the walls
   and broke into the court-yard, killing wildly.
   Afraid, I ran away into the darkness

and found a place of hiding in the forest.
I saw our home go raging up in flames;
I heard the clash of arms, the dying's cries.
At last it all grew silent—all were dead.
The savage band retreated to the shore
and sailed away.—The next day there I sat
upon the cliff beside the smoking ruins.
I was the only one whom they had spared.

GANDALF. And yet you told me that your father lives.

BLANKA. My foster-father. Wait, and I shall tell you!
I sat there on the cliffs, in grief and sadness,
and listened to the terrifying silence.
Then from a rocky cleft there came a sigh,
a feeble sound that issued near my feet.
In fear I listened; then at last climbed down
to find a stranger, pale and badly bleeding.
I went to him, though I was sore afraid,
and bound his wounds, and nursed him.

GANDALF.   What of him?

BLANKA. As time went by, he once more gained his strength,
and told me how a trading ship had brought
him to the island on the self-same day
the castle was attacked; he'd come to us
and bravely done his best to fight the raiders,
until he'd fallen, faint with loss of blood,
into the rocky cleft in which I found him;
since when we two have made our home together.
For us he built a cottage in the woods,
and now I love him more than any other.
But now it's time you met him. Come!

GANDALF.   No, wait!
I fancy we must surely meet in time.

BLANKA. It shall be as you wish. But rest assured—
he would be glad to see you under his roof.
I need not say that hospitality
is not peculiar to the North.

M1

GANDALF.   The North?
  You know then. . .?

BLANKA.   Where you come from? Yes, indeed!
  My father has so often talked of you
  that I knew from the very start. . . .

GANDALF.   And yet
  you weren't afraid?

BLANKA.   Afraid? Why so?

GANDALF. Well, did he never tell you. . .? Has he not. . .?

BLANKA. Explained what fierce men you are? Oh, yes!
  But why should that cause any fear to me?
  I know you seek your fame in distant lands
  in virile combat against a doughty foe.
  But I have neither coat of mail nor sword.
  Why should I then be. . . ?

GANDALF.   You are right, of course!
  But tell me more of those who stormed the castle.

BLANKA. What of them?

GANDALF.   Well, I only meant . . . did not
  your father tell you whence they came?

BLANKA.   No, never.
  They were as strange to him as they to us.
  But if you wish, I'll go and ask it of him.

GANDALF [*quickly*]. No, let it be.

BLANKA.   Ah, now I understand!
  You want to know where you can find the men
  on whom to wreak blood vengeance, as you call it.

GANDALF. Blood vengeance! Yes! I thank you for those words.
  I almost had forgotten . . .

BLANKA.   Yet you know
  it is a hideous custom.

GANDALF [*walks to the rear of the stage*]. Fare you well!

BLANKA. You go?

GANDALF.   We'll meet again.

[*Stops.*]
                                    But one thing more.
Who lies at rest beneath the burial mound?

BLANKA. I do not know.

GANDALF.   You do not know, and yet
 you place fresh flowers upon this warrior's grave!

BLANKA. One morning early, father brought me here
 and showed this burial mound, all newly made.
 I'd never seen it on the strand before.
 He bade me say my morning prayers beside it,
 remembering in my supplications those
 who cruelly harried us with fire and sword.

GANDALF. And you?

BLANKA.   Each morning from that day to this
 I've said a quiet prayer for their salvation,
 and every evening made a wreath of flowers
 to place about their grave-stone.

GANDALF   Strange! How strange!
 How can you offer prayers to help a foe?

BLANKA. My faith commands.

GANDALF [*vehemently*].   That is a coward's faith!
 The kind of faith that saps a warrior's strength,
 and killed stone-dead the great heroic life
 that once the South had known!

BLANKA.   And yet suppose
 my coward's faith, as you are pleased to call it,
 to be transplanted to your virgin soil—
 I know full well it would produce a wealth
 of flowers so abundant as to cover
 the naked mountain side.

GANDALF.   Oh, leave the mountain
 to stand there naked till it falls to dust.

BLANKA. Oh, take me with you there!

GANDALF.   What do you mean?
  I shall be sailing home . . .

BLANKA.   Yes, let me come.
  I've often done that journey in my thoughts—
  up to the land in which you have your home,
  mid ice and snow and sombre forest pines.
  The house would ring with gaiety and mirth,
  if I had any hand, you must believe.
  For I like laughter. Do you have a scald?

GANDALF. I had one once; but in these Southern climes
  the balmy air has slackened all his harpstrings.
  They play no more. . . .

BLANKA.   Then I can be
  your scald.

GANDALF.   And you . . . you wish to come and join us,
  and leave your home and father?

BLANKA [*laughing*].   Ha! ha! ha!
  You think I am in earnest?

GANDALF.   You mean
  you only jest?

BLANKA.   A foolish dream, alas,
  I often dreamed before we met each other—
  and which I know I'll often dream again,
  when you . . .

                [*Breaks off suddenly.*]

            Why are you staring at me?

GANDALF.   Am I?

BLANKA. You are! What are you thinking of?

GANDALF.   Of nothing!

BLANKA. Of nothing?

GANDALF.   Well, I scarce know what to think.
  And yet I do—and now I'm going to tell you.
  I think of how, up in the distant North,

you wish to plant your flowers—and thinking thus,
I recall to mind the faith that is my own.
There is an aspect of it which, till now,
I've never understood. But now you've taught me.

BLANKA. And what is that?

GANDALF.   Valfader, it is said,
receives but half the warriors slain in battle.
The other half belongs by rights to Freia.
All this I've never fully understood.
But now I comprehend. I am myself
a beaten warrior, and my better half
passed into Freia's possession.

BLANKA [*startled*].   What do you mean?

GANDALF. In brief, I think it means . . .

BLANKA [*quickly*].   No, do not say!
I can no longer linger here tonight—
my father waits and I must go. Farewell!

GANDALF. You're going?

BLANKA [*takes the wreath of oak leaves which he has let fall and places it on
his helmet*].
                    There, something for you to keep.
What I once gave you in my dreams before,
Awake I now present again.

GANDALF.   Farewell!

[*He goes out quickly, right.*]

                    SCENE FOUR

BLANKA [*alone*].
He is gone! A breathless stillness
Falls upon the barren coast.
Breathless stillness, grave-like stillness
Also falls upon my breast.

Did he only come to vanish
Like the sunlight in the mist?
Will he like a gull go winging

Far into the realm of night?

What is left behind to cherish?
Only a flower for my dreams,
Solitude in which to hover
Like a petrel round his boat.

SCENE FIVE

[BLANKA; GANDALF *enters right.*]

GANDALF [*aside*]. It is too late!

BLANKA.   Oh, there he is again!
What do you want?

GANDALF.   Go quick! Go quick! Away!

BLANKA. What do you mean?

GANDALF.   Away! For danger threatens!

BLANKA. What danger?

GANDALF.   Death!

BLANKA.   I do not understand!

GANDALF. I wished to keep it from you. So I left
to call my men to return aboard the ship,
and sail away. You never would have known.
But the sound of trumpets shows it is too late.
They're coming here.

BLANKA.   Who are? Who?

GANDALF.   Listen!
The strangers who did earlier raid the isle
were Vikings like myself.

BLANKA.   From Norway?

GANDALF.   Yes.
My father fell, and he was King among them.
And he must be avenged.

BLANKA.   Avenged?

GANDALF.   Such is
  our rule and custom.

BLANKA.   Now I understand!

GANDALF. They're coming. Stand behind me!

BLANKA.   Killer, be gone!

SCENE SIX

[*As above;* ASGAUT, HEMMING *and the* VIKINGS *enter, leading*
RODERIK *between them.*]

ASGAUT [*to* GANDALF]. A meagre catch, but always something, Gandalf.

BLANKA. My father!

                [*She throws herself into his arms.*]

RODERIK.   Blanka! Oh, my child!

JOSTEJN.   A woman!
  Someone to keep him company.

ASGAUT.   Yes, to Hell!

BLANKA. Oh father! why is it you never told me. . . ?

RODERIK. Hush! hush! my child!

              [*Points to* GANDALF.]

                    Tell me, is this your chieftain?

ASGAUT. That he is.

              [*To* GANDALF.]

          And this man can inform you
  how your father died; for he was there,
  he says, but managed to escape alive.

GANDALF. Be silent. I've no wish to hear.

ASGAUT.   All right!
  Now we can set to work!

BLANKA.   Oh God! What now!

GANDALF [*in a low voice*]. I cannot, Asgaut!

ASGAUT [*similarly*].   Is our chief a coward?
Has woman's evil tongue bewitched his mind?

GANDALF. Well, be that as it may! I said . . .

ASGAUT.   Be warned—
for this affects your honour among men.
You gave Valhalla's gods your solemn oath;
to break it is to earn the contempt of all.
Do not forget how insecure our faith,
and how it falters. One blow could bring it low.
And if the blow were dealt by our own King,
it would inflict a mortal wound.

GANDALF.   Alas!
That was a most unhappy oath I swore.

ASGAUT [*to the* VIKINGS]. Prepare, you warriors!

BLANKA.   Will you murder him,
an old defenceless man?

ASGAUT.   Down with them both!

BLANKA. Oh, God!

HROLLOUG.   No, stay! The woman is too fair!
We'll take her in the ship.

JOSTEJN [*laughing*].   As battle-maid.

GANDALF. Stand back!

RODERIK.   Oh, spare, please spare at least my child!
And I will bring the man who slayed your king,
if only you will spare her.

GANDALF [*quickly*].   Bring him here,
and she goes free. Agreed?

THE VIKINGS.   Yes, yes! Agreed!

BLANKA [*to* RODERIK]. How so?

ASGAUT.   Then fetch him!

RODERIK.   Here he stands!

SEVERAL. Ha! this old man!

GANDALF.   Woe! woe!

BLANKA.   Ah no, you shall not. . . .

RODERIK. Behold the hand that struck the Viking dead.
And now he rests within that burial mound!

GANDALF. My father's grave!

RODERIK.   A warrior strong and brave!
I buried him according to his custom.

GANDALF. Since he received this burial . . .

ASGAUT.   Nonetheless
the fallen King cries out for blood—now strike!

BLANKA. He hoodwinks you.

[*To* GANDALF.]

Oh, don't you understand
that all he wants to do is save his daughter?
But you've no feeling for a loving heart
that sacrifices . . .

GANDALF   I . . . not understand?
I do not understand?

[*To the* VIKINGS.]

He shall not die!

ASGAUT. How so?

BLANKA.   Oh father! He is good like you!

ASGAUT. You'll break your oath?

GANDALF.   By no means! I shall keep it!

JOSTEJN. What will you do?

HROLLOUG.   Speak!

GANDALF.   Did I not swear
   that I'd revenge the King or die myself?
   Well, *he* is free—and I shall seek Valhalla.

BLANKA [*to* RODERIK]. What does he mean?

ASGAUT.   This is your firm intent?

GANDALF. Go and prepare for me a ship of mine,
   and hoist the sail, and light the ritual pyre.
   I'll go aboard her in our time-honoured way!
   The evening wind is blowing off the shore—
   I'll sail on crimson wings into Valhalla!

                  [JOSTEJN *goes out, right.*]

ASGAUT. I fear this woman has enchanted you!

BLANKA. No, you must live!

GANDALF.   I live? I must keep faith—
   and I shall not betray my fathers' gods.

BLANKA. Your oath is bloody. Baldur surely hates it.

GANDALF. Ah! Baldur lives no longer here among us!

BLANKA. For you he lives. You have a gentle soul.

GANDALF. And that has been my downfall! As King it was
   my task to keep our way of life intact—
   alas, my powers fail me! Asgaut, come!
   For you shall take the royal sceptre from me.
   You are a Viking of the proper metal.
   The poisonous South has sore afflicted me.
   But if I cannot serve my people living,
   I yet can die for them.

ASGAUT.   Well said, King Gandalf!

BLANKA. And thus the die is cast! You die a hero,
   in faithful loyalty to gods you love.
   But now that we must part for ever, know
   that as you die yourself to keep your oath,
   so you deliver me to death as well!

GANDALF. Deliver you to death!

BLANKA.   My life was like
a flower, transplanted to a foreign soil,
that slumbered, captive in its folded bud.
But then from distant home there came a sunbeam—
ah! that was you, my Gandalf! One brief moment,
and then the sunlight paled—the flower died!

GANDALF. Ah, do I rightly understand? You would . . . ?
Ten times more wretched then becomes my oath!

BLANKA. We'll meet again!

GANDALF.   Ah, never, nevermore!
Your heaven awaits you, and the holy Christ.
But I shall reach Valhalla, take my seat
in silence at the table, near the door.
The pleasures of the hall are not for me.

JOSTEJN [*returns with a banner in his hand*].
The ship is ready now, as you requested.

ASGAUT. How glorious is your end! Full many a man
will surely envy you.

GANDALF [*to* BLANKA].   Farewell!

BLANKA.   Farewell!
Farewell for this life and eternity!

RODERIK [*struggling with himself*].
Oh, stop!

[*Prostrates himself before* BLANKA.]

Sweet mercy! Please, oh please forgive me!

BLANKA. Oh God!

GANDALF.   What does he mean?

RODERIK.   I will confess!
You are deceived in everything I've done!

BLANKA. Oh! Terror has confused his mind!

RODERIK.   No, no!

[*To* GANDALF, *after he has risen.*]

You are released for ever from your oath.
Your father's shade demands no blood revenge!

GANDALF. How so? Explain!

BLANKA.   Oh, speak!

RODERIK.   Here stands King Rörek!

SEVERAL. The fallen King?

BLANKA.   Great heavens!

GANDALF [*doubtfully*].   You—my father?

RODERIK. Do you remember still the scar, Asgaut,
  you gave to me on our first Viking raid—
  the time we fought about the booty?

                    [*He bares his arm and shows it to* ASGAUT.]

ASGAUT.   Yes,
  by Thor, it is King Rörek!

GANDALF [*throws himself in his arms*].   Father! father!
  Now for the second time you give me life.
  Oh, heartfelt thanks!

RODERIK [*downcast, to* BLANKA]. And now—what can you give
  to this old Viking?

BLANKA.   Love, just as before!
  I am your daughter! Have not these three years
  of love expunged all blood-stains from your shield?

ASGAUT. Explain however how you're still alive!

GANDALF. She saved his life.

RODERIK.   Yes, like a friendly elf
  she healed my wounds and took good care of me.
  And all the while she spoke to me so sweetly
  of the faith these gentle Southern people held,
  that even my tough breast was softened by it.
  And day by day I kept my secret from her.
  I did not dare . . .

GANDALF.   But what of the burial mound?

RODERIK. I buried there my armour and my sword.
To me it was as if the wild old Viking
were buried past recall. Each day my child
sent up a prayer for him beside the mound.

ASGAUT. Farewell!

GANDALF.   Where are you going?

ASGAUT.   I'm sailing North!
I clearly see that now my time is past—
the same with Viking life. So I shall go
to Iceland. This infection has not spread there yet.

[*To* BLANKA.]

Young woman, take my place beside the King!
For Thor can do no more—and Mjölnir's powerless.
From now on Baldur rules through you. Farewell!

[*He goes.*]

GANDALF. Yes, henceforth Baldur rules through you, my Blanka!
At last I grasp the sense of Viking life.
It wasn't desire for fame or lust for riches
that drove me from my home and native land.
Not so! What guided me was secret longing,
a quiet desire for Baldur. Now you see
my yearning satisfied. Now we go home.
And I shall live in peace among my people.

[*To the* VIKINGS.]

And you will follow me?

ALL.   We'll follow you!

GANDALF. And you, my Blanka?

BLANKA.   I? I too was born
a Northern child. For deep among your fells
the fairest blossoms of my heart took root.
To you it was I hastened in my dreams.
From you it was that I have won my love!

RODERIK. So now away!

GANDALF.   But you?

BLANKA.   You'll come with us!

RODERIK. No, I stay here.

> [*Points to the burial mound.*]

> My burial mound awaits me.

BLANKA. And I am to leave you here alone?

HEMMING.   No! no!
Be not afraid! For I shall close his eyes
and sing his funeral saga from the mound.
My final song.

> [*He seizes* GANDALF's *hand, deeply moved.*]

> Farewell, farewell, my king!
Now you have found a better scald than I.

RODERIK [*with firmness*].
Thus it must be. You are the King, my Gandalf,
and you have weighty duties to your people.

> [*He places their hands together.*]

You are the children of the coming dawn—
go you where a royal throne awaits you.
I am the last of an epoch in decline,
the grave my royal throne—please grant me that!

> [GANDALF *and* BLANKA *embrace him silently.* RODERIK *ascends the mound.* HEMMING *with his harp sits down at his feet.*]

GANDALF [*with resolution*]. And now to Norway!

HROLLOUG.   Home!

ALL.   To Norway!
Home!

BLANKA [*with spirit, as she seizes the banner from* JOSTEJN's *hand*].
And now away! Towards the North we course
across the ocean blue, through gale and foam.
Above the glacier peak the day soon dawns.
Naught but a memory soon these Viking raids!

Already the Viking sits upon his mound.
The time is past when he would swiftly sail
and harry from coast to coast with fire and sword.
The thunder-god's great hammer sinks to dust.
The Nordic lands become a warrior's grave.
Do not forget the promise All-Fader gave:
And when the grave is flanked with moss and flowers
the Viking's spirit shall fight at Idavold—
The North shall also rise from out the tomb
to purer deeds of spirit on seas of thought.

NORMA
OR
A POLITICIAN'S LOVE

[Norma
eller
En Politikers Kjærlighed]

TRAGIC OPERA IN THREE ACTS

(1851)

PROLOGUE

The other day I found myself in the gallery of the Storting; the nature of the matter under discussion was like most of these things, so I no longer remember what it was about. Schydtz happened to be speaking; and as there was nothing for me to attach my attention to, I gave free play to my imagination and yielded myself up to that agreeable state of suspended animation, partly in the domain of reality, partly unreality, to which we readily submit ourselves in leisure moments when either the soul feels weary or the surrounding world produces the appropriately soporific impressions. I then thought as follows: Within these 106 heads—some with and others without wigs—is to be found the quintessence of all the excellence, of all the cultural talent which Old Norway has to show from the North Cape to Lindesnes, from Svinesund to Stavanger (where of course Natvig was elected). Here is to be found genius, eloquence, patriotism, liberality compressed into a compact mass. And of all these excellent qualities even the rarest manifestations have their representatives; thus, for example, a certain nuance of genius is represented by *Skjerkholdt*, a certain ditto of eloquence by *Parneman*, etc. etc. Lyric talent naturally finds expression through Natvig, who thus in a certain way forms an intermediate link between poetry and politics.

I pursued my contemplations in this direction for some hours, until Schydtz finished and my undisturbed flights of fancy were thus interrupted.

In the evening I saw *Norma*, and suddenly I realized: 'The Storting is a dramatically talented company!' I will not attempt to account either to myself or to the reader for the chain of argument that led me to that conclusion, for who does not know the power of music, who does not know that it is granted to music to cut through the Gordian knots and the threads of thought with an Alexandrian sword, to shoot us forward with the speed of lightning on the spiral path of logic and bring us to a point which we had least expected? But the closer I examined the matter, the clearer and more illuminating it became for me. Holmboe is the respected father in the play; Motzfeldt, Lange and Harris the old, peevish uncle who has lost all feeling for the poetry of life but who, however, is good to have in reserve, however hostilely his prosaic worldly commonsense operates against the fantastic plans, the castles in the air of the young lovers. The Opposition in general is the coquette, which every young fellow wants to pay court to, but of whom finally he usually has doubts about taking to wife (especially when her rival tends to bring a more substantial dowry). Stabell is of course the hero of the intrigue; he is one of those genuinely dramatic characters Heiberg talks about, 'whom one must rather guess about than observe, and who eventually at the end of the play stands where—judging from the beginning—one would have least expected'.

It was these considerations which moved me to arrange the opera 'Norma, or a Politician's Love', the printed text of which follows, and which I hereby invite Parliament to perform on some festive occasion or other. They will have to see to the music themselves; and as they have virtuosi in all possible instruments from trumpet to drums and trombone, one hopes that this will not present any difficulties. True, I know that 'until further notice' Parliament has its hands full; but it is perhaps not impossible that His Majesty, fearing dangerous consequences from these excessive exertions, especially in the dog-days, might one fine day grant it a holiday 'until further notice', in which case it would be good if it had a useful and pleasant pastime with which to divert itself.

CHARACTERS

NORMA	performed by	The Opposition
ADALGISA, her good friend	,, ,,	The Government
SEVERUS, the lover of both ladies	,, ,,	A 'Liberal' (or, failing that, Herr Stabell)
ARIOVIST, Norma's father, an old Druid	,, ,,	Herr Ueland

(N.B. The druids were heathen dogs, who like owls and bats preferred to perform their activities in dark forests, where enlightenment—from sun and moon—found difficulty in penetrating.)

THE TWO CONSUMPTIVE SONS OF NORMA AND SEVERUS	,, ,,	The Address of 1848
	,, ,,	Ditto of 1851
CHORUS OF DRUIDS	,, ,,	Sensible members of the Opposition, together with Skjerkholdt
DITTO OF FEMALE DRUIDS	,, ,,	The silent members of Parliament

ACT ONE

A dense forest, with the semi-darkness appropriate to it; in the background 'the rocks of Norway'; blue anemones and 'liberty cockades' bloom in the shelter of the pines. In the middle of the stage, a sacred idol, in which 'Freedom's Work' is mounted, glazed and framed.

SCENE ONE

[ARIOVIST, MALE *and* FEMALE DRUIDS *appear, led by trumpeters.*]

ARIOVIST. Here we stand on freedom's freest land,
　In the good old, ancient North!
[*Aside.*] For Norway is indeed a confoundedly ancient land.

CHORUS OF MALE AND FEMALE DRUIDS.
　Yes, yes, yes, yes!
　Yes, yes, yes, yes!

ALL. In the good old, ancient North!

ARIOVIST. As strong as the trunk of the lofty oak
　Stands 'Freedom's Work' in its glass and frame!—
　Mounted in stone so fast and firm
　—'Tis pity it somewhat lacks esteem!

CHORUS OF DRUIDS.
　'Tis pity it somewhat lacks esteem!
　'Tis pity, 'tis pity, 'tis pity, 'tis pity!!!

ARIOVIST.
　But we must watch, and we must pray,
　And we must protect our sacred shrine;
　For barbarian hordes would tear it down
　And carry it off to another place,
　Where the sun shines down the live-long day
　(And the moon at night, at certain times).
　Our duty then is clear to all.
　Our treasured freedom we must defend!
　Something must be done—so much is clear!

THE DRUIDS.
Something must be done—the thing is: what?

ARIOVIST.
Look now, children! Now is a time
When we must act as all deem right!
I'd place it myself in a thief-proof chest,
Secure in a vault under lock and key,
That it may be found, when the world is dust,
As fresh and as new as of yesterday.
For the mountains of Norway (as well you know)
Will stand though the rest of the world do fall.
But, come, let us now adjourn a while
To rest, and to summon our strength for the fight.

[*Aside.*]

It has always been my practice, from my very earliest days,
To keep myself in any case a horse's length behind the times.[1]

[*They go.*]

SCENE TWO

[SEVERUS *enters, in declamatory emotion à la 'Morgenblad'.*]

SEVERUS. Oh, forest shade, thou in thy bosom
Conceal our sanctified 'Freedom's Work'!—

[*Looks about him.*]

Damn it, they have all gone; and I could have saved myself all that
nonsense.
Hush! Best to observe some caution—
This was always my golden rule.
Ah, woe! If Norma should find me here,
Who knows what ideas might fill her head!
She's a woman of considerable irritation,

[1] One will notice that the lines spoken in aside are constructed differently from those intended to be heard by each and everybody; this is in no sense carelessness, but deliberately observed; for as all well-informed people know, our political actors even for everyday use employ a special metre when they speak in aside. [*Ibsen's note.*]

And although to such things she's not unused,
She's pretty strict on duty and morals.
That's why I must, as I've just said,
Politico modo, show some care,
Bring suitable offerings to her altar,
Burn incense in her leafy columns.
But who comes there in the darkling wood?
It's Adalgisa. My heart beats faster;
My errant thoughts I scarce can master;
I am a prey to secret desire!

SCENE THREE

[SEVERUS, ADALGISA.]

ADALGISA [*recitative*]. In as far as you, S.T. O Severus!
  Did summon my presence in this grove,
  I herewith respectfully take this chance
  Of humbly announcing my arrival!

SEVERUS. Oh, sweetest voice! Ah, words enchanting!—
  Hear now the secrets of my heart!

  [*Makes to kneel, then thinks better of it.*]

Yet, no! *Unter uns gesagt*, don't you really know what's in my heart?

ADALGISA. As a modest and virtuous maid
  I strictly hold to form and decorum.
  The heart is not the proper forum
  For me. . . .

SEVERUS. Ah, woe is me! Then I must die!
  Do you not meet justice with mercy,
  I must present a pretty picture.
  I know indeed my sins are many,
  (For the 'leafy columns' are pretty lengthy).
  But he who stands on conversion's way,
  Is one I know you will never repulse!

ADALGISA. But how can I place any faith in your words,
  When I find you declaring your love for *two*?

SEVERUS. Ah, Norma, you mean! This you must not believe!

ADALGISA. Yet she was the flame of your younger days.

SEVERUS. She was, I confess—though I do it with shame.
  Now all that is past; it was naught but a fancy,
  Naught but a fleeting, poetic dream,
  A bursting bubble upon life's stream.
  My aberration please let me describe—
  Straight from my beard my words must come:
  Once I belonged to the Radicals
  (Who go under the name of the Liberals)
  Who speak with scorn of gilded halls,
  Who rally themselves with 'rock' and 'valley',
  Who steadfast in Germanic fashion
  Boast of the North, from its trance aroused,
  Who vie in song with the swallows of spring
  On Freedom's Day—in short, to the madmen!
  But now I'm too weary to ride any more
  This aged hobby-horse; things more substantial
  Are what I yearn for—you understand?

ADALGISA [*overwhelmed*].
  Come to my breast, O lamb redeemed!

  [*Touching embrace; the curtain falls for the sake of the proprieties.*]

ACT TWO

A private chamber, where people can talk together in complete comfort.

SCENE ONE

[NORMA *enters with her two* CHILDREN.]

NORMA. Poor little trembling, stumbling creatures,
  On their feeble legs they can barely stand.
  What a wretched thing it is to be
  The mother of this shameful brood,
  Who, from the moment of their birth
  Made for the grave with seven-league boots.
  The blame for it all on Severus lies;
  Had he not been in such a haste
  I'd surely then have been the mother
  Of a couple of strong and sturdy lads.

SCENE TWO

[*As above;* ADALGISA.]

ADALGISA [*aside*].
  It's her! just watch me now torment
  The simple fool. How will she not lament
  And throw her arms about in frenzy
  When I proclaim myself her rival?

[*Aloud.*]

Ah, is it you, my dearest friend!
  How nice that I should find you here,
  And with your children—still alive!

NORMA. Indeed they live! But such life is grim!

ADALGISA. Yes, my dear, it's a frightful shame!
  Yet it couldn't well be otherwise.
  Severus is playing a cunning game.

He is—shall we say—unfaithful to you.
And only where one finds trust and love
Do children grow up straight and strong.

NORMA. Unfaithful, you say? Oh, spare me such tales!
They're sheer invention—nothing but lies.
He knows full well where his duty calls—
He's acknowledged it often enough in the press.

[*A thought strikes her.*]

But one thing *has* roused my suspicion.
He's slinking around within the wood.
Who knows what is passing through his mind—

SCENE THREE

[*As before;* SEVERUS *enters without noticing* NORMA.]

SEVERUS [*embraces* ADALGISA].
Darling! That I should find you here!

NORMA. Traitor! Traitor!

SEVERUS [*disconcerted*]. In Heaven's name, Madam! Why are you here!

NORMA. Traitor! Traitor!

SEVERUS. Hush, I beg you! I beg you, be silent!

NORMA. Trai . . .

SEVERUS [*heatedly*]. Oh, keep your mouth shut, won't you. How can any man of culture be expected to stand and listen to stupid women yelling about things they don't understand?

[*Whispers to a stage-hand in the wings.*]

Oh, let the curtain down, this is a scandalous scene.

[*The curtain says:* 'You're right there', *whereupon it drops quickly.*]

ACT THREE

The same forest as in Act One.

SCENE ONE

[It is already quite late in the day; but most of the Druids, who as is well known always hold themselves a little behind the times, are still lying fast asleep under the trees; some of them are nevertheless awakened when alarm drums and wild shouts are heard backstage, as in 'The Hulder's Home'.]

A WAKENED DRUID.

What is that noise, what are those shouts?

ANOTHER.

Surely the signal for bloody war.
Just listen to that embittered roar.
You know that Norma is about to set
About Severus—I myself did hear her swear.

FIRST.

Ah well, the damage will not be great.
He isn't really one of us.
I doubt if I'd shed many a tear
Though lifeless he lay upon his bier!

SCENE TWO

[As before. NORMA *enters in a berserk fury, as if somebody had proposed amending the constitution.]*

NORMA. Awake, ye Druids! Oh, come, oh come!
Listen, one and all—to my decree.

> *[The Druids start up in great terror.]*

A DROWSY DRUID *[furiously]*.

Well, I'll join the Government! What a sight this is!

ANOTHER *[terrified]*.

Has our leader dissolved the wise men's council?

A THIRD [*plaintively*].
My three dalers a day! Farewell, farewell, to the good old days.

NORMA. Gather your wits again, I pray you!
I refer to Severus, the shameless traitor!

SCENE THREE

[SEVERUS *is led forth, entangled in his own snare.*]

NORMA. He's here! Let's now dispense quick justice.
Confess your sins. . . .

SEVERUS [*aside*]. Ah, what a relief!
The length of the list is so substantial
It'll gain me time—might even save me.

[*Aloud.*]

My first confession is that the masses
Were once the golden calf I worshipped.
Yet this was but my cunning game.

NORMA. Then you must die. . . .

[*Raises the dagger in Opposition-like rage, but naturally does not strike.*
ADALGISA *enters at that moment in the form of an angel and transforms
him into a demi-god, or—as people express it today—into a Cabinet
Minister.*]

THE DRUIDS [*disconcerted.*]
Your respectful servant, at your service!

[*Bow deep.*]

SEVERUS [*striking an imposing attitude*].
As once was said by wise Lycurgus:
'A splendid unity prevails
Among the state's distinctive powers.'
So I hope I may depart in peace!

NORMA [*ingratiatingly*].
Indeed, in Heaven's name, how could
Your Excellency think anything else . . .

[SEVERUS *leaves.*

The curtain falls.]

ARIOVIST [*remains standing pensively, and says in an aside*]:
That was the devil of a story; who knows but perhaps I too. . . .
Ah, well, time will tell. . . !

[*End.*]

ST. JOHN'S NIGHT
[*Sancthansnatten*]

FAIRY-TALE COMEDY IN THREE ACTS

[First performed 2 January 1853]

PROLOGUE[1]

for the performance of *St. John's Night*
2 January 1853

Wherever we go on life's way, one word accompanies us which binds many blue forget-me-nots in our garland of old memories—acting as a quiet comforter in our longing, in our deprivation, whispering in familiar voices—and that word is the name of home.

Did you not see how, in the late autumn, the swallow left for the Southern summer? Yet with the next spring it will return again to the North. The nest where its mother sang it can never forget; thither it is driven by some secret urge—there it has its home.

If on foreign strand you voyage—your yearnings fly across the sea to the dear old country, buried in the distance behind the waves. To the place where your cradle stood, you wander in waking dreams, and would gladly exchange the blood of the grape for a draught of the mountain stream.

If you sit some winter's evening lonely in your quiet chamber, dipping into the well of memory, staring into the flames of the stove—does not thought in its flight make for the old nursery, where once as a child you sat nicely and meekly by the glow of the hearth?

And the tales of your childhood, and the old melodies which remain silent under the cape of forgetfulness in the noise and bustle of life—see, they rise again once more, reminding you of vanished days, whilst your thoughts turn to that quiet family home.

The power of home, which in our bosom loyally accompanies us to the grave, is also felt strong and warm like some sun in the garden of art. If a flower is to thrive there, it must embrace homely soil, or else it will lose its colour—the flower's best adornment.

And where is home not rich? Like a hedge red with roses, like a gentle, delightful poem life surges towards us. Are not the quiet lives of the people, high on the hillside and deep in the valley, images which are well worth being painted by an artist's hand?

Southern plains may well be resplendent with orange and plane

---

[1] *Editor's note:* The original is in eleven 8-line stanzas, four stresses to the line, and generally rhyming a, b, a, b, c, d, c, d.

trees, but on the North's proud mountains there grow the erect fir-trees. Do their branches not offer shelter, and is this not shady and fragrant? Why should art build its pavilion only in Southern lands?

The clear sound of the sæter girl's lur is heard on the green hillsides; the plaintive melodies of the hulder are heard on the mountain scree. The girl's breast is light as spring, the hulder's bosom is full of yearning —this torment and this joy is precisely the characteristic of the people's mind.

And when our breast is too confined, and when it can no longer contain its fulness, we must seek release in song; joy and melancholy find a voice. Then we seek the home of art, for it is there that the people can demand that its life be interpreted and clarified and expressed.

But not every bird was given the scaldic tongue of the lark, and yet it tries from its cover to sing as well as it can. So receive generously what is offered you today. Remember that an artistic career can only be opened up foot by foot!

CHARACTERS

MRS. BERG

JØRGEN KVIST, a student } children of Mrs. Berg's
JULIANE, his sister } first marriage

ANNE, her step-daughter

BERG, former estate-owner, her late husband's father

JOHANNES BIRK }
JULIAN POULSEN } students

A Goblin

Elves and fairies, etc.

The action takes place on Mrs. Berg's estate in Telemark

ACT ONE

MRS. BERG's *garden. In the background, a fence with a gate separating it from the road. On the right, a big house in the finest modern style; further back, left, an old-style log house.* ANNE *is standing in the background, busy fastening a birch twig over the door of the old house.* MRS. BERG *and* JULIANE *enter immediately.*

ANNE [*singing as she continues with her job*].
> 'Oh, say, little bird on the fir tree branch
> As you sing your plaintive lament . . .'

MRS. BERG [*comes out on to the steps*]. Anne, Anne!

ANNE [*turns for a moment and then continues with what she is doing, still singing*].
> 'Why do you not sing in the lady's bower
> Where all is so joyful and gay!'

MRS. BERG. Why don't you answer me? What is it you are doing?

ANNE [*points silently to the birch twig over the door and then continues with what she is doing*].
> 'The sparrow grey is my sister's child,
> My uncle the swift white hare . . .'

MRS. BERG. Oh dear, she gets worse and worse.

ANNE [*continuing*].
> 'In the festive hall no man can know
> The songs I sing on the hill.'

MRS. BERG. Anne! Seriously now, you must stop all this nonsense! Have you completely forgotten that the visitors will be here at any moment—or perhaps you don't intend to change?

ANNE [*turns round*]. No! [*Continues with her work.*]

MRS. BERG. Really! Do you mean to say you are going to appear in what you have on?

ANNE [*as before*]. No!

MRS. BERG. Then what are you going to do?

ANNE. Nothing!

MRS. BERG [*goes down the steps*]. Anne, I advise you immediately to . . .

[ANNE *continues with her work, humming*.]

JULIANE [*enters from the left with some flowers*]. Oh, mother, don't speak to her so harshly. . . . You know it does no good.

MRS. BERG. But what am I to do? If this goes on . . . she'll end up completely crazy.

JULIANE. You know why she's like that. If only you are kind to her, then . . .

MRS. BERG [*kindly, to* ANNE]. Now Anne, just to please your mother, do go in now and put on another pinafore. You can't be seen in that one.

ANNE [*immediately puts down the birch twigs*]. All right, I will, straight away. [*Goes into the house.*]

MRS. BERG. Poor child! I really am most awfully sorry for her.

JULIANE. It's the old man with his stupid talk that's to blame for it. Every blessed evening he sits in there telling her stories until now she thinks she sees elves and fairies and goblins in broad daylight. . . . If only he knew how to make it somehow poetic, it would be all right.

MRS. BERG. And as for that broken down old shack there [*points towards the log house*] that he won't give up at any price. . . . Heaven knows what possessed my late husband to promise him that for the rest of his days. If it hadn't been for that, I'd have had it pulled down long ago.

JULIANE. Oh, but that would have been a shame, mother! That old house reminds one so vividly of those parsonages in Swedish novels. It's probably haunted by goblins from the old days . . . and there'll be some beautiful young girl with an idyllic name like Thekla or Linda or something like that. . . . Oh, it's so tiresome having a name like Juliane . . . it's so ordinary . . . so . . .

MRS. BERG. Now, now! Let's have no more of these fancies. You are beautiful, and what's more important you are rich. . . . Go along in now and see if everything is in order.

JULIANE. And get myself dressed up.

MRS. BERG. I don't have to ask you to do that.

JULIANE. No, don't you worry. . . . [*She goes.*]

MRS. BERG [*to herself*]. Rich? Everybody thinks so at least, but . . . it's not all settled, not yet at any rate. . . . Once the engagement is announced, they will soon be married and then he will be my son-in-law and all my worries will be over. . . . Or will they? What if the papers were still in existence. . . . And that's not impossible. . . . If only I knew for certain. . . . There is only one place to look . . . that jackdaw's nest over there. . . . But nobody sets foot in there but the old man and Anne. But he's in his dotage . . . it can't be long now . . . then I shall be able to tidy up that old rubbish dump. I shan't rest until I know for certain. [*Goes into the house.*]

[ANNE *crosses the stage to the left during* MRS. BERG'*s speech.*]

SCENE 2

BERG [*opens the door of the log house and calls*]. Isn't there anybody out there? Anne, Anne! . . . They don't answer. . . . I've been sitting here ringing till I'm tired, but they don't take any notice. Anne! Do you hear?

SCENE 3

[BERG; ANNE *enters from the left holding a bowl in her apron.*]

ANNE. I'm here, grandfather! I'm here!

BERG. So you've come at last.

ANNE. Have you been waiting for me? I was in the garden. Come and sit over here in the sun, it will do you good. [*Leads him to a seat, left, front.*]

BERG. I got weary in there. Pasop was away as well. Where is he?

ANNE [*aside*]. Heavens, Pasop died a year ago; he's forgotten that too. [*Changing the subject.*] Can you guess what I've got here, grandfather? [*She sits at his feet.*]

BERG. No, I can't.

ANNE. Open your mouth. [*Pops a strawberry in his mouth.*]

BERG. Strawberries! You are good to me, child.

ANNE. Of course I am. . . . But what was it you wanted?

BERG. Let me see now . . . what was it? Oh, now I remember. I want to know what's going on over there. . . . They are turning the house upside down. . . . All that noise and shouting. . . .

ANNE. And you don't know what it's all about?

BERG. No, I haven't been told anything, have you?

ANNE. Yes, indeed! They're expecting visitors. Jørgen is coming home.

BERG. Jørgen? Ah, yes, that's the student.

ANNE. And he's bringing someone with him.

BERG. Really! And who is that?

ANNE. He is engaged to Juliane. . . . But nobody knows about it yet.

BERG. Is that so! But I want to know . . . I want . . . Oh, my poor old head is going round and round. I'm just an old dodderer who . . .

ANNE. Yes, grandfather, I know what you're going to say. . . . But you are forgetting the strawberries. Come along, let me feed you as I used to feed the little doves, in the old days.

BERG. Yes, that was before your stepmother had them destroyed.

ANNE. Yes, but she had to, you know. . . . They went and pecked up all the corn in the fields, the thieving little things. [*Drying her eyes.*] But can you wonder that those in there . . . that mother and Juliane treat you differently from the way I do. They are more like strangers here . . . but we two were born and bred together.

BERG. We two. . . . Yes, perhaps you're right. . . .

ANNE. Yes, it's true, isn't it? Ever since I was tiny you have talked to me about all the things that have happened here . . . about my dear old grandmother and my real mother and all the other things we loved. All the things you have told me . . . you know, I feel as if I have lived through them myself. And it's the same with the old songs and stories. Often I feel as if I had been there myself, as if I had been inside the mountain and seen and heard all the wonderful things you told me about. So when the others over there don't understand me, and speak harshly to me, then . . . [*Throws her arms round his neck.*] Grandfather, grandfather, I have nobody in the world but you.

BERG. Don't say that, child! As long as this old house stands, this place will never be completely damned. Your dear mother sang you to sleep here, until she herself fell asleep. Your father lived here contentedly and happily, until we got this new wife around the place . . . and then everything was too small and too ordinary, and the new house had to be built with all those splendid rooms and that enormous drawing room. . . . And then your father died, and soon there was nobody left in the old log house, but you and me.

ANNE. And the old goblin in the loft.

BERG. He'll stick to the old place longest of all. . . . And when the young bride moves in over there. . . .

ANNE. Juliane, you mean?

BERG. Yes, the young lady. . . .

ANNE. Oh, but Juliane isn't going to live here, grandfather!

BERG. Oh, so they're going to live in fine style in town?

ANNE. Not at all. The newly-weds are getting the farm at Birkedal as a wedding present and . . .

BERG. What . . . what did you say?

ANNE. I said . . .

BERG. What did you call it? What did you say the farm was called?

ANNE. Birkedal. You know, the place father won in that lawsuit against Arne, who owned it.

BERG. Birkedal, Birkedal! Yes, yes . . . now I begin to remember. . . . But how did you know it was going to be a present?

ANNE. I heard her over there. . . . Mother, I mean . . . talking about it yesterday. . . . But nobody must know about it beforehand, and . . .

BERG. This must not happen. . . . Anne . . . this must not happen!

ANNE. Grandfather! What's bothering you?

BERG. Nothing, child, nothing. . . . I'm just beginning to remember something that has long been forgotten. . . .

MRS. BERG [*calls from inside the house*]. Anne, Anne!

ANNE. What is it, grandfather?

BERG. Nothing, nothing, child! Go in, I think they are calling for you.

MRS. BERG [*in the house*]. Anne! Do hurry up!

ANNE. All right. . . . I'm coming!

BERG. Go along now. But as soon as it gets dark, look in and see me. . . .

ANNE. I will. But meanwhile, don't get excited!

BERG. Don't worry about me, Anne. My poor old brain, my poor old brain . . . it's become so feeble and forgetful.

[ANNE *takes him into the log house and then goes towards the big house where she meets* MRS. BERG *and* JULIANE *on the steps.*]

SCENE 4

[ANNE; MRS. BERG; *and* JULIANE.]

MRS. BERG [*to* ANNE]. Heavens, where have you been! Hurry up now and get the table laid, they are already coming down the hill!

[ANNE *arranges the table in the foreground, while she hums a folk tune.*]

JULIANE [*tidying her hair*]. Mother! Does that look all right now?

MRS. BERG. Yes, relax now.

JULIANE. Oh Mother, how my heart is beating. . . . I'm all strung up.

MRS. BERG. And you are doubtless too tightly laced up as well, my child.

JULIANE. Oh, it has nothing to do with that! A girl always feels nervous when she's waiting for her young man, especially at the start. . . . And Birk and I haven't had a chance to see much of each other. I left Christiania immediately after we got engaged, and he hasn't been here since. . . . And then I am in such an awkward position. . . . Nobody here knows about the engagement until it is announced tomorrow. . . . But just fancy if Birk forgets himself and rushes up and embraces me right here on the road. . . . Then the secret's out . . . and . . .

MRS. BERG. You don't have to worry your head about that. After all, you have asked him to keep it quiet. Besides, Birk isn't the demonstrative type; he's not one of the passionate sort.

JULIANE. Oh no, God knows he isn't. You can tell that from his letters. In that respect, he might just as well be my husband already. Mother . . . I must say I would rather the engagement weren't announced quite so quickly. . . .

MRS. BERG. But, Juliane, what sort of talk is this!

JULIANE. You can't put yourself in my place, Mother. When one has other memories that linger on. . . .

MRS. BERG. Memories? You mean all that nonsense when you were at the Academy. I would advise you not to say anything to Birk about that. And as for the engagement, that is all settled. There is nothing more to be said about it.

JULIANE. Ah, well. I see I must suffer in silence. That is woman's lot in life. Heavens, here they are! Look, Mother! Is my dress all right?

SCENE 5

[*As above.* BIRK *and* JØRGEN *enter from the rear with rucksacks on their backs.*]

JULIANE. Johannes!

BIRK. Juliane, my dear Juliane! [ANNE *makes to go into the house, but at the sound of* BIRK'S *voice she stops and gazes at him intently.* BIRK *and* JULIANE *shake hands.*] This handshake will have to do for an embrace. . . . You did ask me not to betray anything.

JULIANE. Yes, I did.

[BIRK *greets* MRS. BERG.]

JØRGEN. And as there is a friend coming who isn't in on the secret . . .

JULIANE *and* MRS. BERG. A friend?

JØRGEN. Yes, someone I have brought with me. An excellent fellow. . . . You probably know him from the papers, Juliane. He is the critic, Julian Poulsen. . . . He is very well known in Christiania. He is the one who founded the Society for the Restitution of Old Norse.

MRS. BERG. Really! Is it a sort of temperance society?

BIRK. Well . . . no. I don't think you could call it temperate, exactly. . . .

JØRGEN. No, you see . . . it is a society for. . . . Well, you see, it's rather difficult to explain before the society has got its programme drawn up.

BIRK. Yes, I dare say that's where the difficulty is.

JØRGEN. Nonsense! It's a piece of cake for Poulsen. . . . He said so himself. 'You see, Jørgen,' he said to me once . . . because he and I are on Christian-name terms. . . . We many a time go about arm in arm, smoking our cigars. . . . Don't we, Birk?

BIRK. Yes, indeed.

ANNE [*who has meanwhile approached* BIRK, *holds out her hand*]. May I welcome you as well.

BIRK [*surprised*]. I beg your pardon. . . .

MRS. BERG. But, Anne!

BIRK. I'm afraid I didn't notice. . . . You must be one of the family?

MRS. BERG. My step-daughter. [*Whispers.*] Poor child, she isn't quite all there. [*To* ANNE.] Run along and get on with your work.

[ANNE *goes over to the table.*]

BIRK [*whispers*]. Ah, that's how it is! Yes, that's right, now I remember, Juliane said something about her.

JØRGEN. But what has happened to the poet?

JULIANE. Poet! What, is he a poet, too?

JØRGEN. Yes, indeed he is. . . . A real poet, wild and sombre. . . . His forte is nationalism.

JULIANE. Really?

JØRGEN. True, he hasn't actually published anything yet. But everybody is agreed that when he does, it really will be something.

JULIANE. But how interesting. . . .

MRS. BERG. He will be very welcome. But won't you take off your rucksacks. Supper is ready.

JØRGEN. Excellent. Actually we are very hungry and thirsty.

[*They all go in*; BIRK *and* JULIANE *last, hand in hand.*]

SCENE 6

POULSEN [*enters from the rear and stands by the gate watching* BIRK *and* JULIANE]. What's this? On such intimate terms already. . . . Hand in hand. . . . So help me, they were hand in hand. [*Comes forward.*] That's what I call an intro . . . getting worked in quick! To the best of my knowledge, he's never set foot in the house before. . . . Nice people they must be here. . . . Simple probably, and spontaneous. . . . But no matter . . . simplicity . . . the . . . the primitive has something to be said for it. After all it is a national trait . . . and. . . . But if I appear here now, all sombre and neurotic, and upset this quiet domestic scene—which I am almost certain *will* happen—[ANNE *enters with a tea urn which she puts on the table.*] Perhaps I had better slip away while there is still time. . . . But what is this I see: a girl and a meal ready. . . . If I slip away, I'll just cause an upset somewhere else. For I know I cannot escape my fate. . . . That is settled, then. . . . I stay. Sh! She's singing. . . . Ah, the pure true music of the forest, I do declare. [*Listens.*]

ANNE [*singing without noticing him*].
<blockquote>
'Hundreds of birds on the green hill side,
But none of them is my kind;
And so I must sit in the heather grey
And grieve the live long day.'
</blockquote>

POULSEN. None of them . . . none of them your kind, you say? That's just as it is with me. Oh, in heaven's name, dear lady! Sing another verse, just one. . . .

ANNE [*looks at him with a half smile*]. H'm, no! I don't want to sing any more.

POULSEN. I am just such another grey bird, understood by nobody. I am all alone, too.

ANNE [*turns away and continues with her work*]. Go in . . . go in. . . . The others are in there.

POULSEN [*aside*]. Yet another person whom my presence has cast gloom on. . . . Should I go in, or . . . I think I shall. [*Straightens his clothes.*] If

I were vain, I would find my position most interesting. . . . To have oneself introduced by one's friends before one arrives. Then when they are all keyed up with anticipation and one makes one's entrance, then they start nudging each other and whispering among themselves: Is that him . . . is that him? Intelligent face! Clever look . . . bit melancholy . . . but interesting . . . damnably interesting . . . you can see immediately he . . . but here they come!

SCENE 7

[*As above.* MRS. BERG, JULIANE, BIRK *and* JØRGEN.]

JØRGEN. Ah, there he is! Welcome at last, Julian!

POULSEN. I beg your pardon, Madam! I am compelled to introduce myself. I presumably haven't the honour. . . .

MRS. BERG. Not at all! We know all about you already and . . .

JULIANE [*whispers*]. Let me . . . let me! [*To* POULSEN]. And the sort of things that make us doubly grateful to you for coming along.

POULSEN. Oh, I beg you. . . !

MRS. BERG. Please have a seat.

POULSEN. Thank you, thank you.

[*They sit round the table.* MRS. BERG *pours tea and* ANNE *hands it round. It begins to grow dusk.*]

POULSEN. Here at last I attain my heart's desire. . . . Surrounded by proud wild nature. . . .

BIRK. I beg your pardon, but this is a garden. . . .

POULSEN. Much the same. A bit of imagination and it's all one. . . . Here surrounded by proud wild nature . . . if ever I am to recapture my primitive self, it must be here.

JULIANE [*to* JØRGEN]. Gracious me, what interesting ideas he has!

BIRK [*aside*]. What, she too!

JØRGEN. Ah, but they haven't the right ring. No, you should hear him when he propounds them in the old dialect tongue!

JULIANE. But can anybody understand it?

JØRGEN. Good gracious, no! That's precisely what one is to learn.

POULSEN. I have long been looking forward to this trip with pleasure.
... That is to say, as much as I am capable of feeling pleasure at anything. I have never spent midsummer night in the country before,
and it is precisely at this time that the national ... the ... the primitive life manifests itself free of all restraint. ... You have—have you
not, my friend—promised to take me up to Midsummer Hill?

JØRGEN. Yes, you can rest assured about that. We must all go up
together, and enjoy ourselves till morning. Nobody goes to bed on
midsummer night. ...

POULSEN. Not go to bed?

JØRGEN. You'll have to accept that, it's an old national custom.

POULSEN. Is that so! That's really what I meant. Oh, how good it will
be to bathe one's soul in the fresh night air. ...

JULIANE [*aside, to* BIRK]. Heavens, how sweet he is!

BIRK [*ironically*]. Yes, isn't he!

MRS. BERG. So you are a nature lover, then. My late husband was
too. ...

POULSEN. Really? So Mr. Berg was of a poetic disposition?

MRS. BERG. Mr. Berg? No, quite the contrary, he was a solicitor. It was
my first husband I meant, Jørgen's and Juliane's father.

POULSEN. Really ... that I can well believe. [*To* JULIANE.] A poetic disposition is usually hereditary. However, when you believe me to be
a nature lover, this is not strictly true, if by 'loving' you mean that
blind abandonment to things ... that ... I was in love once, but
that is past. ...

BIRK [*whispers*]. That was the one with ...

POULSEN. I beg you, Birk, do not touch my feelings on the raw. Now
what was it I wanted to talk about?

BIRK. About yourself, of course. You said ...

POULSEN. That's right, now I remember. ... What I wanted to say
was. ... What I find fascinating are those mysterious beings with
which superstition populates nature.

Pi

[*The* GOBLIN *pokes his head through a shutter in the loft of the log house.*]

JULIANE. Yes, aren't they? That's just what I say.

POULSEN. For my part, I regard goblins and fairies and the like as symbolic concepts which in the past wise men used to express ideas for which they did not have the correct abstract terminology. And nature is so interesting in consequence . . . so philosophically significant.

BIRK. Piffle!

POULSEN. Ah, I know it is an audacious thought, but it is a peculiarity of mine to think audaciously. . . . I can't help myself.

JULIANE. Heaven knows it is poetic, anyway!

BIRK [*aside*]. Ugh . . . what a . . . ninny!

POULSEN [*to* JULIANE]. Yes, isn't it? You agree with me? What is the point of fairy tales and legends if we who are endowed with poetic insight don't invest them with significance and with philosophical value, we who . . .

GOBLIN. Ho, ho, ho, ho! [*He disappears.*]

POULSEN *and* JULIANE [*terrified*]. Ugh, what was that?

JØRGEN. Ha, ha, ha, ha! Take care, Poulsen!

BIRK. Who knows, perhaps it was a real goblin. The old log house looks as if it is capable of anything.

ANNE [*who has listened to the conversation intently, breaks out vehemently*]. Stop talking like that! Shut up, all of you! I won't have it. . . .

POULSEN. Heavens above . . . I . . .

MRS. BERG. Anne, Anne. . . . What's got into you!

ANNE. Nobody is to make fun of the old house. . . . I won't have it. [*Points to* POULSEN]. I don't understand everything he said . . . but there can't be any good in it. . . . I feel it. . . .

BIRK. But Anne, my dear. . . . [*Gets up.*]

ANNE [*laying her hand on her brow, whispers*]. Nobody here can possibly understand how I feel. . . . They don't understand that these things they laugh at mean more to me than all the treasures on earth.

[*Goes into the house.*]

BIRK [*watches her*]. What's the matter with the child?

POULSEN [*aside*]. Again my unconventional ideas have caused another upset. [*To* MRS. BERG.] I should be most distressed if . . .

MRS. BERG. Oh, no! On the contrary, I must beg your pardon. I shall give her a good scolding, believe me.

BIRK. No, really, you mustn't, Mrs. Berg.

JULIANE. She isn't always quite . . . you know what I mean.

JØRGEN. It's grandfather's stories have made her a bit queer in the head. . . . But, to change the subject, I thought somebody said something about punch. . . . Well, anyway, I propose we have something to fortify us before we go to the festivities on Midsummer Hill.

POULSEN. Hear, hear! [*They all get up.*]

MRS. BERG. Then you must come and lend a hand, Jørgen. You are an expert at making punch, aren't you?

JØRGEN. I should just think I am.

[MRS. BERG *and* JØRGEN *go into the house.*]

JULIANE. Meanwhile I'll go and fetch my hat. Goodbye for now, Mr. Poulsen. [*To* BIRK, *in passing.*] He hasn't the faintest idea we are engaged. [*Goes in.*]

BIRK. Naturally not.

POULSEN. Heavens, how adorable she is! There is something . . . something Nordic about her that appeals to me so strangely. . . .

BIRK [*to himself*]. 'They don't understand here that these things they laugh at mean more to me than all the treasures on earth.' Yes, yes . . . I think I begin to understand her.

POULSEN [*slaps him on the shoulder*]. Birk! You are my friend!

BIRK. Well, what do you want?

POULSEN. I say, you are my friend!

BIRK. Yes, I know. . . .

POULSEN. I'm so happy tonight! Birk, did you notice that look she gave me. . . ?

BIRK. No, I did not take the slightest notice of the lady's looks.

POULSEN. Oh yes, you did! When she . . .

BIRK. I have no wish to hear.

POULSEN. Very well, as you please. . . . All the same, I don't think it is very friendly of you to answer me in that tone of voice when you can see I am cheerful for once. You know how little it takes to make me gloomy and bitter. . . .

BIRK. You know something? I'm sick of this interminable talk about your gloom and suffering and all that rot. . . . It's sheer affectation. . . .

POULSEN. Dear God, so I'm affected! That's something I didn't know before!

BIRK. That's something your friends omitted to tell you.

SCENE 8

[As before. JØRGEN with two punch glasses.]

JØRGEN. Here's the advance party, boys! It doesn't do to stand around with parched lips. . . .

POULSEN. You're an excellent fellow, Jørgen.

JØRGEN. Did you ever doubt it? [*Goes in.*]

POULSEN [*to himself*]. He can sulk if he likes, I'm going to have a drink. Punch is a bath of rejuvenation in which man may drown all his dispiritedness. . . . Dispiritedness. . . . Low in spirits! That's a good expression . . . he shall hear that one, so help me, whether he wants to or not. [*Takes a glass.*] I must try to make it up with him. I say, Birk, shall we drink to each other?

BIRK. Oh, rubbish! We've already done that once.

POULSEN. All the same, I thought . . .

BIRK. Some other time. . . . [*Goes into the garden, left.*]

POULSEN. Well, just look at that. Off he goes . . . but what the devil's got into him? Oh, what a numskull I am . . . what a witless creature, I should say . . . I've supplanted him with the girl and he's annoyed about it . . . that's it. Now I remember . . . he really looked as if he was getting somewhere before I came, but then that passed. . . . He went into the garden . . . good! I must forestall him and invite her to take my arm for the walk. [*Goes into the house, meets* ANNE *on the steps and makes her a deep bow.*]

SCENE 9

[ANNE *enters with a punch bowl and glass which she puts on the table. The* GOBLIN *appears later.*]

ANNE. Something strange is happening to me this evening, but what it is I don't know. I have never felt like this before. [*The* GOBLIN *appears at the loft shutter.*] It is like when I have been trying to remember an old song for a long time and then suddenly I think I have got it. . . . But, Grandfather! Oh dear, I promised to look in on him as soon as I could. . . . I very nearly forgot. [*Goes into the log house.*]

SCENE 10

THE GOBLIN [*climbs down and comes forward; he is dressed in grey, with a red cap on his head; he brushes the dust off his clothes and pulls up his shirt collar*].

Midsummer night is a great celebration;
A festival time for Goblins as well.
Each and all in the light green hall
Enjoys himself as best he can.
Twigs of birch in the peasant's room
Fills the night with its quiet perfume.
The meanest hillock is bedecked
With little plants and flowers wild.
. . . . The goblin is busy the whole year through.
He haunts the loft and he haunts the cellar;
And he stays in the stable the live-long day,
To guard, as he must, the old homestead.
But midsummer night is his time for fun;
And then he dons his festive clothes
And visits his friends and his nearest kin
Who live in the hill where the bonfire burns.
There the mortals disport themselves,
They sing and dance in briar and copse,
But little they know that the fairy folk
Do sit in the hill and watch it all.

[He takes out a pocket watch.]

But now I must be on my way. . . .

[Makes to go, but notices the punch bowl.]

What's this?

[Dips his finger in the punch, tastes and spits.]

Ugh no! . . . that's not for me!
This is the stuff that mortals drink,
It clears their vision for many a thing
As loudly they speak of friendship's call,
And all the world seems rich and fine;
They laugh, and all forget their sorrow—
At least, that is . . . until tomorrow!

[Pauses, and says happily.]

But, wait! I think I have something!
Tonight I could play a little joke;
The Goblin has an inventive mind
Whenever it comes to playing a trick.

[Goes into the garden and returns with a little flower in his hand.]

There's a plant that grows on every path
That has some remarkable powers.
But few are they who seek it out,
And most will pass it heedlessly by.
Forth it sprang from Suttung's mead
Which Odin spilled at Valhalla's gate,
And whosoever tastes its sap
Will lose his eye for outward show.

[Squeezes the sap from the flower into the bowl.]

The mists that once did veil their eyes
Will clear in the leaping flames of dreams;
Then they will sense the inner power
In the secret places of the mind.
But he who has nothing to ponder on
Will wander as blind as before and . . . sleep.

[Bows and disappears into the ground.]

SCENE II

[MRS. BERG, JØRGEN, POULSEN *and* JULIANE *come out of the big house, and* ANNE *comes from the log house.*]

POULSEN. And now out into the glorious summer night, into proud, wild nature, into the. . . . [*To* JULIANE.] Isn't that right? You have promised to take my arm.

JULIANE. Yes indeed, you shall be my cavalier.

JØRGEN. But first a glass of punch. [*He takes the glass* BIRK *has left untouched and fills the other glasses from the bowl.*]

POULSEN. Yes, let's. . . . [*To* ANNE.] May I take the opportunity of drinking reconciliation with our charming protectress of goblins and trolls. I should be unspeakably sorry if my bizarre ideas had distressed you.

MRS. BERG. Oh, how could you think . . .

ANNE. I haven't given it another thought.

JØRGEN. Come on, hold out your glasses!

POULSEN. And drink to all the spirits of midsummer night.

[*Everybody drinks except* MRS. BERG.]

JØRGEN. Hurrah!

POULSEN. Hurrah!

[*Voices from the background, among them the* GOBLIN *who sticks his head out and waves his cap, shouting* 'Hurrah!']

MRS. BERG *and* JULIANE. Oh, good heavens.

POULSEN. What was that?

JØRGEN. Oh, it's probably the village people at their party on the hill.

POULSEN [*sniffs his glass*]. Lord, what remarkable punch!

JULIANE. M'm, I agree!

JØRGEN. It's made from the old recipe. But now . . . forward march.

POULSEN [*very lively*]. I don't know why it is but I feel so bright and breezy. . . . May I? [*Offers her his arm.*] Ah, here comes Birk. [*Calls out to the left.*] You've missed your chance, my friend. It's like a party game . . . every man for himself. . . .

JULIANE. Ha, ha, ha! See you later!

[MRS. BERG, JØRGEN, JULIANE *and* POULSEN *go out, back.*]

SCENE 12

[ANNE; BIRK *enters left.*]

BIRK. 'Every man for himself' . . . I could almost be tempted to say 'Help yourself!' [*Goes and fills a glass.*]

ANNE. Aren't you going with the others?

BIRK [*surprised*]. Oh, you're here! . . . No, I'm not . . . are you? Perhaps you're like me . . . odd man out?

ANNE. More or less.

BIRK. But what a strange child you are. What made you so angry with poor old Poulsen because. . . .

ANNE. Please don't say any more about it, I know I shouldn't have. . . . Anyway, it wasn't Poulsen who made me so furious. . . .

BIRK. Wasn't it? Who was it then?

ANNE. You.

BIRK. Me?

ANNE. Yes, you. It didn't bother me that Poulsen and the others joked about the things I care about and believe in. . . . But that you could laugh at them . . . that . . . I don't know why, but I couldn't bear it.

BIRK. But, my dear little Anne!

ANNE. Well, all right. I should have held my tongue, but I get like that occasionally, so I warn you . . . don't do it again. I won't have it.

BIRK. There's no need to be so vehement about it. I realize I was a bit hasty. I have no childhood memories of my own to cherish, but I realize I must respect other people's.

ANNE. Have you no childhood memories?

BIRK. Practically none. My life has been divided into two sections. What happened to me before I left my childhood home I have practically entirely forgotten. I was only nine or ten then and soon after that I had a serious illness. . . . Meningitis, or whatever it was . . . and from the day I got up again, life in a way began anew. But let's not talk about that any more. Once again I beg your pardon.

ANNE. I have already forgiven you. [*Fills a glass.*] And now I drink to *our* reconciliation.

BIRK. And to old memories.

ANNE. To all old memories. [*They drink.*]

BIRK [*after a pause*]. Ah, that tasted good! [*Growing more and more cheerful.*] I feel like a new man. Here, we have something else to drink to.

ANNE. What's that?

BIRK. We are going to be related and . . .

ANNE. Related? Yes, that's right, we are. . . . But isn't it odd, I never think about that.

BIRK. Don't you? Yet it's all signed and sealed . . . at least it will be tomorrow. However, the time . . . the sorrow . . . the joy, I should say. . . . Come on, we must drink to each other!

ANNE. Yes, let's!

BIRK. Thanks. [*They drink.*] To you! [*Takes her hand.*]

ANNE. To you! But I must leave you now. We could have another chat tomorrow.

BIRK. Oh, but must you go already?

ANNE. Yes, I must. Grandfather is waiting for me.

BIRK. Just when I'd got my good spirits back. Do you know I would just love to sit here at your feet on this beautiful night and listen to your stories.

ANNE. Another time. It's impossible tonight.

BIRK. No, dear little sister-in-law, it's not. I am just in the mood tonight. You may not believe me, but I wouldn't mind if you took me by the hand and led me through the quiet, dew-drenched valleys and fields and forests and experienced with me all the fabulous events of mid-summer night.

ANNE. Would you like to do that?

BIRK. There's nothing I would rather do.

ANNE. It could be done, but only if . . .

BIRK. Really? Could it?

ANNE. Only if you go up to the hill in the right frame of mind.

BIRK. Well! You are quite sure about it. . . . Perhaps you yourself have. . . .

ANNE. That's what the legend says.

BIRK. Well then, it must be so.

ANNE. But it must be after twelve o'clock.

BIRK. Of course, it would be impolite to bother the little people with visitors before midnight. . . . But you will come with me?

ANNE [*steps nearer and looks at him intently*]. Are you really serious?

BIRK [*a little surprised, but still jokingly*]. But heavens, how could you think otherwise!

ANNE. And you are not afraid?

BIRK. Not when I am with you.

ANNE. Good. . . . Then I'll come!

BIRK. What . . . how do you mean?

ANNE. I'll come. Goodbye for now.

[*She goes into the log house.*]

BIRK. Now what? What does that mean? 'I'll come', she said, and she sounded as if she really meant it in real earnest. Perhaps she is a bit crazy, as Juliane says. No, no, surely not. But she did behave a little oddly. . . . If I were conceited, I might be tempted to think that she . . . . But perhaps I too have been a bit indiscreet. . . . After all, I am engaged. Engaged! That word has a positively distasteful ring about it tonight. The short time I have been here has revealed more to me of Juliane's character than all her letters. What is she, after all? She's a flirt, conceited, flighty. . . . We were to pretend not to be engaged until it was announced. Yes . . . she plays that role well enough, I'll grant her that . . . but what about me? [*Vehemently.*] Yes, what on earth has got into me! Perhaps the punch has gone to my head? It must be. Ah, well, if the worst is going to happen, I may as well make a job of it. [*He drinks off a couple of glasses of punch.*] Ah, well, I'll just sit here. [*Sits on a bench, right, front.*] And if she doesn't come as she promised . . . the little one . . . and help me enjoy the night in wakeful dreams . . . then I can at least have a dreamful sleep. That's another way of killing time . . . and then comes tomorrow and the engagement celebrations and congratulations. Yippee. . . . Hurrah! What fun! . . . O my God! [*Rests his head on a tree and falls asleep. Men and girls, led by a fiddler, cross the stage, back, singing.*]

CHORUS.

> The fiddle sounds on field and hill
> As we make for Midsummer Hill.
> We need to hurry because we know
> That midsummer soon is over.
> We throng together towards the hill,
> But homeward we shall go in twos.
> > Never too narrow
> > Never too long
> Will we then find the road.

SCENE 13

[MRS. BERG *and* JØRGEN *enter, back.*]

JØRGEN. It's a nice idea in theory to enjoy the night up on the hill, but in practice I would much rather spend it in bed.

MRS. BERG. I fancy the others think so, too. Let us go indoors and wait for them. [*They go in.*]

SCENE 14

[*After a moment,* JULIANE *enters hurriedly from the back, followed by* POULSEN.]

JULIANE. No, no, I'm telling you straight, I daren't in all conscience go one step further with you when you talk so wildly.

POULSEN. Wildly? It is my nature to be wild, I cannot help it.

JULIANE. Then explain yourself. I haven't understood a word up to now.

POULSEN. You haven't? Really? But I have tried to clothe my ideas in as popular a form as possible.

JULIANE. But in heaven's name! Can't you just say what you mean!

POULSEN. All right then, short and to the point. . . . At least I'll try. But first answer me one question. What sort of an impression have I made on you?

JULIANE. But Mr. Poulsen! Who says you have made any impression on me?

POULSEN. Well, what I mean is, how do I appear to you? You remain silent. . . . Good. . . . I know how to interpret your silence. I shall tell you what you think of me. You regard me as a wild and reckless creature, as a . . .

JULIANE. No, how could you think such a thing! . . . You are most certainly a very well-behaved young man.

POULSEN. Oh, never. You don't mean that. You see me as wild . . . eccentric, though I say it myself. . . . No, no, there's no denying it, I am convinced of it. . . . That's the impression I make on everybody. You're afraid of me, aren't you?

JULIANE. If you go on like that, I really must confess . . .

POULSEN. There you are. . . . You see, I was right. You shrink from me . . . it's quite natural. You do not understand the workings of my mind and therefore you judge by outward appearances. There goes a spirit. . . .

JULIANE [*startled*]. Oh . . . where?

POULSEN [*similarly*]. Oh, what was that?

JULIANE. You make me quite nervous.

POULSEN. Allow me to continue. . . . There goes a spirit on the downward path, you say to yourself. . . . A spirit who has broken with society, who has set himself against convention . . . because that is what I have done . . . who fights for an idea that no one understands and that therefore must go under. Isn't that true . . . isn't that what you think?

JULIANE. No, I assure you. . . .

POULSEN. But that's not the way it is. You shall know everything, for . . . I must confess to you . . . in you I believe I have found a soul in whom I can place my secret.

JULIANE. A secret! Yes, out with it.

POULSEN. Well, you see, I'm not what I seem to be.

JULIANE. Good gracious! Who are you then?

POULSEN. I am not the wild, neurotic creature the world takes me for. . . . I love . . .

JULIANE. But, Mr. Poulsen! [*Aside.*] Lord, how my heart thumps!

POULSEN. An ideal!

JULIANE. Flatterer!

POULSEN. Or rather, I did love her.

JULIANE. Oh!

POULSEN. Yes, because now she is dead.

JULIANE. Dead!

POULSEN. Dead to me . . . now you know.

JULIANE. But who are you talking about?

POULSEN. I'll try to explain myself a little more clearly. Well, you see. . . . There was once a time when I was still a child. . . .

JULIANE. Yes, that's understandable, but . . .

POULSEN. And a highly intelligent child, from what I'm told. I grew up under the purest nationalistic influences. . . . My father was a country shopkeeper, you see. . . . And so you can easily comprehend how my breast became a sounding-board for all the popular sentiments I had received in my childhood. But then life's conflicts began. I went to Christiania, became a student and began, like the others, to go in for aesthetics and criticism and all that unpatriotic nonsense. God knows what would have happened to me if I hadn't had my eyes opened in time. Poulsen, I said to myself, if you continue thus, then you deliver your national Self a mortal wound. You must make an end of it! The which I did and bade farewell to city, aesthetics and art and went on a hiking trip to Drammen. I thus rediscovered my original Self and fell in love. . . .

JULIANE. In Drammen?

POULSEN. No, on the way, of course. In those delightful, fresh pine forests. I chose the most national creature that ever existed. Can you guess what that is?

JULIANE. Most national? Yes, a dairy maid.

POULSEN. No, no. . . . I tell you . . . it was no dairy maid. It was the *hulder*, the wood nymph.

JULIANE. What! The *hulder*?

POULSEN. As I said, the *hulder* . . . that adorable, evanescent creature who sits under the linden tree in the dark forest and sings her delightful songs in a minor key. . . .

JULIANE. Sometimes in C major, too.

POULSEN. Quite true, sometimes . . . but not so often. Well, as I said, I loved her and I was happy in my love. I read our poets and constantly discovered in them fresh sustenance for my passionate nationalism. And then, one day, I got hold of a collection of folk-tales. . . . Oh, the monster who wrote that book! He has robbed me of all my peace of mind.

JULIANE. But, in heaven's name, how?

POULSEN. I read it and do you know what I discovered?

JULIANE. Not really. . . .

POULSEN. Ah well, it has to come. . . . It will reopen the wound, but nonetheless, it has to come. I discovered that the *hulder* had . . . had . . . a tail!

JULIANE. Oh, no! What are you saying!

POULSEN. Yes, just think . . . and such a long one, and what's more one that can't be concealed. I can't tell you how I suffered. Aestheticism and nationalism fought a life and death struggle in my breast. . . .

But I may as well tell you at once that on this occasion . . . culture triumphed over nature. I had to renounce my love. . . . Believe me, it cost me dear, but it had to be. . . .

JULIANE [*after a pause*]. I understand your distress. I realize only too well what it means to have an unfortunate attachment . . . but tell me more.

POULSEN. What more is there to tell? My world, my original Self . . . my primitive Self, I mean . . . was lost. . . . But I could never escape the reproachful voice that reminded me I had renounced my love from paltry prejudice. I did my best to revive my nationalist zeal; I started wearing a sheath knife and began to spell phonetically. . . . The world was deceived by it . . . but I knew it was no use. Do you know what is stirring in me now? It's rather like what the Germans call 'Weltschmerz'. [*He drinks off a glass of punch.*]

JULIANE. And what are your plans for the future, then?

POULSEN. Until today, I haven't had any, but hope now begins to spring anew. . . . I have met a kindred spirit. You shall reconcile me to life. . . . Come, Juliane . . . I beg your pardon, Miss Juliane! With you I shall immerse myself in . . .

JULIANE. Heaven save us! What are you thinking of!

POULSEN. With you I will immerse myself in immediacies . . . that is to say, the higher . . . the artistic immediacies. Let us waste no more time. . . . Look, they are setting the bonfire on the hill aflame, and the people are dancing round it. . . . All the shades of national life are displayed. . . . We will accompany each other thither. . . . Are you coming?

JULIANE. Strange man! What sort of language is this you speak. No one has ever talked to me like this before.

POULSEN. It is the language of enthusiasm I speak. Will you not heed the call?

JULIANE. Yes, yes, I will. I must! [*Aside.*] Heavens, I do believe he has bewitched me.

POULSEN. Well then, let us join in the national life.

JULIANE. Free and beauteous nature beckons.

POULSEN. In search of immediacies. [*They go.*] May I offer you my arm?

[*They depart, back.*]

SCENE 15

[BIRK *still asleep;* JØRGEN *comes down the steps and looks round.*]

JØRGEN. What's happened to them! Poulsen and Juliane left us on the way, and Birk has gone too. Surely they can't have taken the joke seriously at supper time about staying up there all night. It's just like Poulsen's crazy ideas. And if he and Juliane are wandering about up there now, I wonder how Birk will take it. I must go and look. Ah, I see something white there. It must be them. [*As he goes.*] Wait a minute, I say, wait! No, they don't hear me. [*Goes out, back.*]

SCENE 16

[BIRK *sleeps.* ANNE *comes slowly out of the log house and approaches him.*]

ANNE [*almost in a whisper, laying her hand on his shoulder*]. Wake up, wake up! It's time.

BIRK [*gets up and gazes at her in astonishment*]. Anne! Are you here?

ANNE. Yes. Come along, we must go, it's nearly midnight.

BIRK [*rubs his eyes and looks round*]. Am I dreaming or. . . ?

ANNE. Look, the moon is high in the sky. . . . Follow me . . . I know the way. [*Goes slowly to the rear.*]

BIRK. But what does all this mean? Is it really her . . . or am I going crazy? . . . I think I must be. See there, she's waiting. She's beckoning. Ah, I feel dizzy . . . everything is going round. I must go with her . . . I must. [ANNE *goes, followed by* BIRK.]

SCENE 17

[THE GOBLIN *suddenly appears between the trees. The lighting changes and soft music can be heard.*]

> Along the dewy path they stride
> While the *hulder* sits on the fir-clad hill;
> She sings and strums her dulcet song,
> And the scalds lie listening to her there.

The sprite sits combing his beard green
By rowan and cherry on river bank,
And elves do dance in the alder glade—
They cannot sleep—it's too cold for them.
Ah well! You walk in the land of dreams
But whether your brow be clouded or clear,
I've trapped you all within my snare.
This goblin will have fun tonight!

[*He disappears.*]

ACT TWO

A forest path. In the background, a rounded hilltop on which the remains of a bonfire periodically flares up. Left front, a large rock. It is night and the moon is shining.

SCENE I

[*As the curtain rises, there is violin music and singing which fades into the distance.* THE GOBLIN *enters backstage and listens.*]

GOBLIN.   Dance and song and play are ended,
        Now the night belongs to us.
        Each sprite and elf shall be my guest—
        Come forth! Our Midsummer feast begins.

        [*He disappears behind the trees.*]

INVISIBLE ELVES. Gently, gently! Night is coming,
        Come, you ranks of elfin folk!
        Hear our call, you forest flowers,
        Open wide your scented leaves!
        Elves awaken from your slumber,
        Gather here within the glade,
        Flower's cup is now too sultry,
        Summer night is now so cool.

        Sit you quiet by the willow,
        Work away with nimble hands,
        Plait from lilies of the valley
        Ribbons white and dainty shoes.
        Dress yourselves in festive garments
        Deftly woven from the rose,
        Add the scent of midnight violet
        Sweetly bathed in evening dew.

        See the brilliant jewels glitter,
        Many thousand precious stones
        Gently bend the blue-green lily
        Down towards the mossy ground.

See how bright the centre sparkles,
Shining from each jewelled drop;
Deep within it is the image
Of the stars that shine by night.

Take these drops that now do twinkle
From the petals and the leaves,
Intertwine them in your tresses,
Make of them a string of pearls.
Light as air we then shall hover
Over the dewy meadow green,
Whilst the swelling sound re-echoes
From the river spirit's harp!

SCENE 2

[POULSEN *and* JULIANE *enter, left.*]

POULSEN. This can't possibly be right. We must have come the wrong
way.

JULIANE. No, I assure you. The path goes up there. You can trust me.

POULSEN. I do, implicitly. I follow you blindly, wherever you will. . . .
But to return to what we were saying. . . . You see . . .

[*They go out, right, talking.*]

SCENE 3

[*After a moment,* JØRGEN *rushes in from the left, stops and looks round.*]

JØRGEN. They've gone again! This is the very devil's art! . . . If I saw
aright, she still had Poulsen hanging round her. You can't afford to
be even the slightest bit indiscreet, my dear sister . . . giving your
arm to one person in the evening like this, when you're going to give
your hand to another in the morning. Oh, but Poulsen only has
platonic affairs, as he himself says . . . besides one is allowed a bit of
licence on Midsummer night . . . to relax the formalities somewhat
. . . but all the same . . . all the same . . . I think I had better try and
catch them up. [*Goes out, right.*]

SCENE 4

[POULSEN *and* JULIANE *enter from the left.* THE GOBLIN *shows himself in the background, rubbing his hands and laughing gleefully.*]

POULSEN [*gesticulating eagerly*]. Well, you see . . . this hypothesis leads nowhere and so I have abandoned it. It is wholly contrary to my nature to go round in circles and . . . [*Looks round.*] But what is this? We have gone completely round the hill and come back to where we were before.

JULIANE. Yes, it looks like it.

POULSEN. Ah well, never mind. The populace also seems to have pretty well disappeared up there. . . . I can't see a soul.

JULIANE. Yes, we had really best be thinking about going home. I am terribly tired.

POULSEN. Do you want to go already. . . ? I have so much to tell you. Look at the moon, so beautiful behind the pine trees! And the tall pines so dark against the moon. O, nature's bosom is so delightful to rest in.

JULIANE. Yes, if only it weren't so dirty.

POULSEN. Yes, but one has to rise above that. Come and sit on this soft mossy stone. . . . Wait a moment, I will spread my handkerchief over it, otherwise you will get yourself dirty . . . and then I will lie down here in the grass before you. . . . Ugh, it is rather wet. . . . Well, at least I'll stand here on the grass before you.

[JULIANE *sits down.*]

JULIANE [*after a moment*]. Now you are all serious again, Mr. Poulsen.

POULSEN. I'm rarely cheerful for more than half an hour at a time, especially when I don't have anything to drink. It is characteristic of me.

JULIANE. But what is the matter?

POULSEN. I will tell you. You see, to put it bluntly . . . I'm still not absolutely clear about myself. . . . I vacillate.

JULIANE. But you only just said you had found a firm basis in . . .

POULSEN. Exactly! In theory I really have . . . but it's one of the peculiarities of my theories that they don't always work out in practice.

JULIANE. Really?

POULSEN. Yes, it's because the world is out of joint. That's an axiom I always cling to. But enough of this. You shall know what it is that disquiets me. It is, as you might say, my national Self warring with my aesthetic Self. And this conflict I must have resolved or else . . . enough said. . . .

JULIANE. Heavens!

POULSEN. You see, my national Self reasons like this: 'You are a man of the people, you wear a sheath knife at your belt and write all your nouns with a small initial letter, how can you possibly admit to renouncing a creature which our national poets cling so fast to.'

JULIANE. Yes, that seems quite sensible reasoning.

POULSEN. But that is precisely the dilemma, because then my aesthetic Self says: 'No, it is a lie! For it conflicts with all your notions of aesthetics to feel this way about a creature endowed with the afore-mentioned abnormal appendage, so incompatible with any theories of beauty.' What am I to do? Which of my two Selves is right? Upon my soul, I don't know myself. So here I am confronted with one of the enigmas of life, which man must either conquer or be defeated by. But what was that? I thought I heard voices. . . .

JULIANE. Yes, it seems like. . . .

[*They talk in whispers.*]

SCENE 5

[*As before.* BIRK *and* ANNE *enter, back left, and walk downstage.* THE GOBLIN *appears later.*]

BIRK. Where are we? I feel as if this place were familiar and dear to me, yet I have never been here before. Anne, where are we going?

ANNE. To Midsummer Hill. Look, there it is up there. The fire has gone out. Everything is quiet. Come, keep beside me . . . there are lots of ways up, but they aren't easy to find. Lots of people search and search and never find them. . . . Stay close to me.

BIRK. Strange! My mind seems to be reeling. . . .

ANNE. Hear how quiet it is here! Listen! Can you hear how quiet it is?

BIRK. Anne!

ANNE. Was that a bird twittering among the alders? Do sing, little bird, do sing! You may join us. . . .

BIRK. Have I really gone mad too? . . . Because she, she . . . I don't know what to believe any more.

ANNE. Look, I found some cowslips . . . enormous yellow cowslips. I used to play with them when I was a child. There. . . ! [*She hands him some flowers.*] Three for you and three for me. Keep them . . . keep them safe. [*Fastens the other flowers on her breast.*] Don't you know the tale about the boy who could open up the hillside with a shining cowslip and who entered the hall that stood on four golden pillars. . . .

BIRK. Look, look!

[*Soft background music. The hill opens and reveals a large brilliantly lit hall. The mountain king sits on a high throne in the background. Elves and mountain fairies dance round him.*]

ANNE. There it is. Shining like gold in the moonlight!

BIRK. Ha! What does all this mean?

POULSEN (*to* JULIANE). Just look at that! It must be the bonfire they're lighting again. [*He rubs his spectacles.*] It's got a good hold. . . . Surely they must have got hold of a whole tar barrel.

JULIANE. Look, look, how they leap about. Ugh, don't let us go up there, I'm sure they are drunk.

POULSEN. You're right. It's safest to observe them from a distance.

BIRK. But, Anne, do please explain . . . I feel as if I had seen all this before . . . as if . . .

ANNE. Sh, sh! I feel the same.

POULSEN [*to* JULIANE]. But this is charming. This scene is straight out of the folk tradition. You do have your lorgnette with you?

JULIANE. Yes.

POULSEN. I could only wish there were an artist here.

JULIANE. Or a photographer.

POULSEN. Yes, you are right. That would be better. I would never have believed that our folk dances could be so genuinely national, so. . . . Just look at those steps, those movements.

[*In the hall, a young girl is led forward. The mountain king descends from his throne and approaches her.*]

BIRK. Anne, do you know who that is?

ANNE. Yes, it's little Karin. Don't you remember the song:

'Little Karin entered the mountain so fine;
So sweetly smells the rose in spring;
Little Karin was to be the mountain king's bride. . . .'

BIRK. Now I remember. Look, he is asking her:

'And where were you born and where were you bred?
And where in this world was your bridal dress cut?'

POULSEN. But who do you suppose the old man can be?

JULIANE. I have no idea.

POULSEN. Oh, he's probably a member of the festival committee, since he is receiving the guests. But how extraordinary that they are so civilized up here. I'd never have thought it, I do declare.

BIRK. See, now she's answering.

ANNE. Yes, I remember this well:

'On the green green sward stood my father's farm;
So sweetly smells the rose in spring.
I wore golden rings and flowers in my hair.
In the valley I was born, in the valley I was bred,
In the green green valley my bridal dress was cut.'

BIRK. He's speaking to her again. . . . Look. . . !

POULSEN. He seems to be having an animated conversation with her. He is clearly a man of culture.

BIRK. Now he's offering her a golden crown and silver-buckled shoes if she will be kind to him.

ANNE. But little Karin won't. . . . You'll see, she won't.

BIRK. So he offers her all the wealth which the mountain holds.

ANNE. But still she won't. Not for all the treasures on earth. . . . She declines them. . . .

BIRK. Look, now the mountain king is taking the golden horn!

POULSEN. Heavens, I do believe the fellow carries a flask in his pocket.

ANNE.   'And the mountain king fills the horn with red gold.
How beautifully fades the rose in spring.'

BIRK. She puts it to her mouth. . . . She drinks. . . .

ANNE.   'And then little Karin drains the wondrous drink. . . .'
Listen, listen!
'In the mountain was I born, in the mountain was I bred,
Within the mountain here my bridal dress was cut!'

[*The girl throws herself into the arms of the mountain king. Both disappear.*]

JULIANE. Poor girl . . . she has fallen!

POULSEN. I do believe she's fainted.

[*In the mountain, a warrior and a young girl meet.*]

JULIANE. There are soldiers among them. I can see one with a sword.

POULSEN. This is how things should be, all classes happily mixing together. Only then does the picture take on that . . . that rounded form, that . . . Oh, it is astonishing how attracted I am by it. And while we sit here, receptively contemplating the poetic aspect of life, Birk and the others are probably lying sound asleep somewhere, dreaming some trivial dream or other. . . .

JULIANE. Ah yes, a poetic disposition is a good thing, that's perfectly true.

ANNE. Here come Erik and Swanwhite. Do you remember the song?

BIRK. Oh, I remember it well.

'Young Erik was going to the wars:
"Oh, hear me Swanwhite my lass,

"To wield my sword in the world I must go,
And return when I've proved myself worthy of you.
You will wait for me here at home!"

ANNE. Sh! She's answering, Do you hear?

'"Fifteen years I will wait for you
And fifteen days besides!"

BIRK. '"And if by then I don't return
Tell me Swanwhite, my fairy maid,
How much longer will you wait?"

ANNE [*listening and with subdued voice*].

'"Then I will wait fifteen years more,
And a little while longer still. . . .
And if you don't come, my hair will grow white;
In my coffin they will lay me down
And I'll wait on the floor of the grave!"'

[BIRK *and* ANNE *speak in whispers.*]

JULIANE. I feel so horribly melancholy seeing all these happy people dancing about like this. It reminds me so vividly of the first grown-up ball I went to when I was at Madame Olsen's Academy.

POULSEN [*animatedly*]. Madame Olsen's Academy! Did you go there?

JULIANE. Yes, I did. But I have such painful memories of this ball I mentioned. . . . It was at the Harmony Hall. . . .

POULSEN. Harmony Hall! . . . Heavens, it's the same with me. . . . Tell me more.

JULIANE. Yes, I will repay your confidences. I will tell you about the memory that torments me. At the ball there was a pale young man with dreamy eyes.

POULSEN [*with mounting excitement*]. With dreamy eyes?

JULIANE. He didn't speak to me, but he kept staring at me with these strangely expressive eyes.

POULSEN. Go on, go on!

JULIANE. In the end, he plucked up courage and asked me for the last dance, but . . .

POULSEN. He asked you to dance, then what?

JULIANE. The first time round, he trod on my foot. I had white shoes on, and I let out a yell . . . I wouldn't dance any more.

POULSEN. And he? Tell me, what did he do?

JULIANE [*anguished*]. He threw me a despairing glance, left the dance floor . . . and I . . . I have never seen him again.

POULSEN. A despairing glance! And he . . . he had a bright yellow waistcoat . . . and . . .

JULIANE. Yes, yes. But what is wrong with you?

POULSEN. Juliane! The pale youth with the despairing glance and the bright yellow waistcoat, that was . . . me!

JULIANE [*jumps up*]. What do you say? You? Heavens, is this true?

POULSEN. Yes, yes! [*With animation.*]

> I once was a youth with hair so fair,
> And fair it is still, as you can see!

JULIANE. With shoes and black cotton socks on your feet!

POULSEN.   I beg your pardon, my socks were silk!
> I remember as though it were yesterday.
> I had no great command of speech,
> So I said not a word, but my eye was bright,
> And warm and expressive my glance, as you said.
> But then at the final, painful scene,
> In utter confusion I left the room.

JULIANE. And you didn't commit suicide?

POULSEN. Not likely, I didn't. . . . Well, that's to say, I was near to it, but something happened to prevent me. As I was saying:

> But then at the final, painful scene,
> In confusion I must have left the room
> And afterwards found myself stumbling alone
> By the light of the moon in the dark of night.
> From that time on I went my wild way,
> And sought for peace in a hopeless love.
> But Julian has found his Juliane now. . . .

[*He seizes the handkerchief* JULIANE *has been sitting on, spreads it out and kneels on it.*] Thus the secret is out!

GOBLIN [*appears suddenly in a bush, which opens up*]. Ho, ho, ho! [*The bush closes up again.*]

JULIANE [*shrieks*]. Oh, merciful heaven, what was that?

POULSEN [*jumps up*]. Run, run! But don't be afraid. . . . I shall defend you. . . . [*They rush out separately.*]

JULIANE [*offstage*]. Poulsen, Poulsen!

POULSEN [*also offstage*]. Juliane, where are you? Miss Juliane!

BIRK. But what is all this! To me it seemed as if delightful images of a long forgotten past went gliding past me in the uproar there. And these sounds! They have long been trembling in my inmost soul, but when I tried to reach out and grasp them and arrange them in a melody, they always evaded me . . . fled further and further away. . . . But now I have them and I'll never forget them again. And you, Anne. . . . I seem to have known you so long, too, even if perhaps it was only in a dream. Ah, listen! Do you hear?

ANNE. Quiet!

[*Chorus of* INVISIBLE ELVES.]

ANNE. Johannes, Johannes, my childhood friend!

[*She throws herself into his arms.*]

BIRK [*jubilant*]. Anne! Now I recognize you again!

[*They each go to their own side.*]

GOBLIN [*in the background*].

> The sun is rising behind the hill. . . .
> The games of Midsummer Night are done!
> This goblin will be a delighted man
> If you have had such fun as he!

[*The music dies away, little by little.*]

ACT THREE

The garden outside MRS. BERG's *house. It is early morning.*

SCENE I

[POULSEN *sits sleeping on the steps of the big house.* BERG *and* ANNE *walk up and down in the foreground.*]

ANNE. So you didn't sleep well either last night, Grandfather?

BERG. No child! Scarcely a wink. I couldn't help thinking about that business your father told me to see to. It was just before he died. . . . But now I've got it all confused again.

ANNE. Well then, you must stop thinking about it. I'm sure you've got it wrong, Grandfather, and . . .

BERG. No, no, I haven't. And when you told me yesterday that . . . what was it was going to happen today?

ANNE. Juliane's engagement.

BERG. Engagement. Yes, yes, that's right. And the deeds of that estate. . . . I felt certain for the moment there that I must still have the papers today. But where am I to find them? That I don't know.

ANNE. So you and I, Grandfather, would do best not to think any more about it. Now let's talk about something else. Do you know, I had the strangest dream last night. I dreamt that I was up on Midsummer Hill . . . where we used to go so often when I was small, and where you used to sit and tell me stories.

BERG. Well, it isn't so strange that you should dream about Midsummer Hill. You were forever going up there. Do you remember the time you fell asleep up there. . . ?

ANNE. No! Did I?

BERG. Don't you remember? Oh, no, you weren't very big then, but I have a better memory for those days. Yes, you see . . . you had wandered off with something . . . what was it now. . . ? A signet, or something of the sort. . . . It belonged to your father and you had thrown it away up there. Your father scolded you and you cried . . . so you went up there to look for it. Everybody was in a panic because nobody knew what had become of you. . . . But eventually, in the morning, we found you.

ANNE. Well, I think I ought to remember that. . . . But really, Grandfather, I'm sure I walked in my sleep last night. . . . You know I used to often as a child. And the dreams I had used to be most strange. . . . Besides, do you see this? [*Produces an old key.*] I dreamt I picked some big yellow flowers up there and fastened them here on my dress, but when I woke up, instead of the flowers, I found this. [*Shows him the key.*]

BERG. But . . . but . . . goodness me, it's . . .

ANNE. What is it? What do you mean?

BERG. That's what you threw away up there. . . . I recognize it again. . . . It's the key to the old chest. Anne, Anne, now I've got it. . . . That's where they are, they couldn't be anywhere else. . . . Come with me.

ANNE. But, Grandfather, what on earth. . . ?

BERG. Child, this is the work of Providence. I would never have had any peace if. . . . Come with me . . . just come with me.

[*They go into the log house.*]

SCENE 2

[POULSEN *still sleeps.* BIRK *enters slowly from the back.*]

BIRK. I still can't explain tonight's strange events to myself. It has all been a dream—I can scarcely be in any doubt about that. . . . But this dream has clarified all my confused childhood memories; and moreover . . . I have found her . . . she who was once so dear to me and is doubly so now . . . and yet I have to give her up.

SCENE 3

[*As before.* JØRGEN *comes out on to the steps.*]

JØRGEN. Ah, here they are . . . both of them. Poulsen! . . . He's still snoring. [*He comes down the steps.*] And you? . . . Have you had a good night's sleep?

BIRK. I suppose so. I don't rightly know. But what is the matter with Poulsen?

JØRGEN. How do you mean?

BIRK. I was sitting half asleep on the bench there until an hour ago, since when he has lain on the steps and drivelled the most ridiculous nonsense about a ball and Midsummer Hill and that he was in love . . . and goodness knows what else.

JØRGEN [*aside*]. Damn! Suppose he's let something out? [*Aloud.*] Oh, it's probably his old unhappy attachment, you know. . . .

BIRK. Definitely not. . . . He's got over that. I'm sure there's something more in it. I heard him say several times that he had found her here, and . . .

JØRGEN. Oh, I think I can tell you what it is. [*Aside.*] I must think of something. [*Aloud.*] It is Anne who . . .

BIRK. Anne! Surely not. . . . It can't be!

JØRGEN [*aside*]. He is definitely suspicious. [*Aloud.*] Yes, I assure you . . . I am almost certain that . . . But where were you last night?

BIRK. Up on Midsummer Hill, I think . . . but I wouldn't like to say for certain.

JØRGEN. Ha, ha, ha, ha! I dare say you looked a little too deep into the punch bowl last night.

BIRK [*half to himself*]. That's it . . . I have looked too deep. . . .

JØRGEN. Yes, I could well imagine that.

BIRK. Not into the punch bowl though . . . into myself. I have seen to the depths of my being. And it is as well that I have . . . it was high time, otherwise I should have been like the girl who drank from the golden horn and forgot home and valley and forest and self.

JØRGEN. Out of the golden horn? Damn me, what sort of a story is that?

BIRK. Oh, it doesn't matter. The thing is that I can now penetrate the mists that have veiled my childhood. . . . It is not as I have believed until now . . . that time or absence or something of the sort had lulled me into forgetfulness. . . . It was the empty, heartless, yet dazzling life of the town. It was he [*pointing to* POULSEN] and his cronies who dragged me into the gilded, sham life they themselves lived. Oh God, if I had only known two years ago what I know now. [*He goes into the garden, left.*]

JØRGEN. Upon my soul, he must have noticed Poulsen making sheep's eyes, or else he's got a screw loose as well. I must take him to task about this and find out the truth. [*Shaking* POULSEN.] Poulsen, Poulsen! Wake up, man!

POULSEN [*in his sleep*]. Run, run. Oh, there he is!

JØRGEN. It looks as if he's going crazy too. [*Shakes him again.*] Can't you hear me? Wake up! It's late.

POULSEN [*waking*]. Ah, it's you.

JØRGEN. Yes, it's me. How are you feeling?

POULSEN. Oh, I had a fantastic night. Have you had breakfast?

JØRGEN. No, not yet.

POULSEN [*continuing*]. A fantastic night . . . full of adventure and strange romances.

JØRGEN. Yes, you and Juliane carrying on in the moonlight.

POULSEN. Yes, while Birk and you and all the other prosaic people were curled up between the sheets, we sat out there in the bosom of nature and observed the life of the people. It's perfectly true that he who is incapable of viewing life with a poetic eye is only half alive. Oh, it was magnificent. The time went like lightning.

JØRGEN. Yes, especially coming home, from what Juliane says.

POULSEN. Oh, I know what you mean. A country bumpkin came along drunk and bawled the most disgusting nonsense at us and we didn't know what it was all about.

JØRGEN. And so you ran away. Ha, ha, ha!

POULSEN. Ran? I never ran. I returned home . . . at somewhat faster tempo, it is true. . . . But where is your sister?

JØRGEN. My sister?

POULSEN. Yes, yes. We were interrupted yesterday at a most interesting point in our conversation and I must continue, I really must. [*Makes to go in.*]

JØRGEN. But look here, Poulsen, there's something I must tell you.

POULSEN. You know what? I have something I want to confide in you, too. Jørgen, embrace me. . . . I am going to be your brother-in-law.

JØRGEN. The devil you are!

POULSEN. Yes, really I am. All that remains is for me to propose and for her to say 'yes'.

JØRGEN. But who do you mean, man? . . . Juliane?

POULSEN. Yes, who else? Please let me go in. I really must talk to her.

JØRGEN. Well, since you are quite mad then I had better apprise you of something which should really be a secret. . . .

POULSEN. Well?

JØRGEN [*whispers*]. Well, you see, there is a snag. . . . Let me tell you the tale. . . .

POULSEN [*shrinks back*]. What are you saying, man? A tail . . . that's the second one!

JØRGEN. Not that kind of tail. . . . The snag is, in short, she's engaged.

POULSEN. Eng . . . engaged.

JØRGEN. Engaged to Birk. Now you know.

POULSEN. But Jørgen, my best and dearest friend! I can only hope you are lying.

JØRGEN. Be a man and pull yourself together. It's as I say.

POULSEN. Oh, I feel faint. Well then, he must release her . . . he must. . . .

JØRGEN. Hush! . . . Are you crazy!

[ANNE *comes out of the log house and goes into the garden, left.*]

POULSEN. I can't give her up! Where's Birk? I must find him!

JØRGEN. But think, man. . . . You'll create a scandal and . . . Is this the way to go on?

POULSEN. It's all right for you to talk. You have no conception of what it means to lose your first love twice over. Tell me where he is.

JØRGEN. Oh well then, he's somewhere down the road there. [*Points backstage. Aside.*] He won't meet him there, I hope.

POULSEN. Good, then I must go. Jørgen, you will see me next time as your brother-in-law . . . or never again.

JØRGEN. No, I'll come with you, my friend! I can't leave you alone in all your trouble. Wait . . . wait. . . .

[POULSEN *hurries out, back, followed by* JØRGEN.]

SCENE 4

[BIRK *and* ANNE *enter, left.*]

BIRK. Yes, there are some things that become more and more incomprehensible the longer you think about them. . . . It makes no difference whether it was a dream or the work of the mysterious powers that rule the hill and forest, still I have found my little playmate again.

ANNE. And I mine. Come and sit down, Johannes! You must tell me what has happened to you since we were children together. [*They sit on the bench, right.* ANNE *gazes at* BIRK *intently.*] I can't understand now why I didn't recognize you immediately . . . you, who used to come here so often. . . .

BIRK. It's not so strange. I remembered well enough that my father used to take me to a strange house occasionally where there was a little girl who used to play with me and an old man who told us stories. . . . But it was all quite different here then. The big house wasn't built, and the garden here was a field, and your father was a widower. . . . I never came again after he remarried.

ANNE [*sits making a flower posy meanwhile*]. But how have things gone for you since then?

BIRK. That's quickly told. You see . . .

ANNE. Wait a moment. Who do you suppose these flowers are for?

BIRK. I don't know.

ANNE. Guess.

BIRK. Me perhaps.

R1

ANNE. Yes, and do you know why?

BIRK. No.

ANNE. Well, because if you had some flowers, I know who you would give them to.

BIRK. Really?

ANNE. To me. Wouldn't you?

BIRK. Yes, yes of course. If I didn't give them to Juliane.

ANNE [*laughing*]. Oh yes, Juliane, that's right. Isn't it odd, I never can remember that you and she are engaged. Come here, let me put them in your button-hole. [*Fastens the flowers on his jacket.*] What was it you were going to tell me now?

BIRK. You see, when my father died, I was barely seven years old, and it soon became apparent that he had left me practically nothing. So my aunt in Christiania took me, though God knows she scarcely had enough for herself. She got me to use the name Birk because it sounded less provincial. . . . I must confess she did tend to be a bit vain . . . but that's by the way. Well, things would have looked pretty grim for me if I hadn't had help from another quarter. . . .

ANNE. How do you mean?

BIRK. Someone else supported me . . . until your father died.

ANNE. My father?

BIRK. Yes, it was your father. It was only after he died that I learned who I had to thank for my upbringing. And this puzzled me even more for I knew that in my father's last years the relationship between him and Berg had been very strained as a result of the lawsuit between them that my father lost.

ANNE. But I didn't know a word of all this. And she . . . my step-mother has never told me anything about . . .

BIRK. I don't know if she knows the connection though I would assume she does. Because when she spent the winter in Christiania two years ago and I met her, she treated me with all the kindness and consideration that sensitive people always show to those who are indebted to them and can't repay. And since she never referred to it, I never felt it was proper for me to mention it either, so . . . [*Stops.*]

ANNE. Well?

BIRK. Eventually I became like a member of the family and then Juliane and I got engaged [*vehemently, and half to himself*] without my really knowing how it happened!

ANNE. And you can talk about it with such a serious face. Puh, you should be ashamed of yourself. You should be happy about it . . . because you see, when we become relatives we can enjoy all our old memories together and visit all the places where we used to play as children.

BIRK. But, Anne, how are we to do that? We won't be together.

ANNE. No, not yet, I know that. But when you and Juliane are married then. . . . Let me tell you how we'll arrange things. . . . I shall of course come and visit you. . . .

BIRK. Visit us?

ANNE. Yes, visit you, otherwise it can't be done. You know I'd rather we were together for all time, but we daren't even think of that. . . . Grandfather has to be looked after, and besides. . . . No, it wouldn't work. But I will come for long, long visits, I promise you. . . .

BIRK. But, I say, Anne. . . !

ANNE. No! Now it's you who must listen. I will tell you how we will arrange it. . . . Since neither of us is Juliane's type . . . she calls it being poetic. . . .

BIRK. So that's Juliane's type?

ANNE. Yes, she says so herself. . . . But since neither of us is like that, we will live in our own way. . . . We will take ourselves off on our own, like now, and ask each other 'Do you recall the time?' and 'Do you remember that?' and . . . But what is the matter? Why have you become so serious?

BIRK. Anne, what a child you are! And I must tell you . . . that all this you suggest is impossible.

ANNE. Impossible? What do you mean by that?

BIRK. Well, since an explanation is necessary. . . . Anne, you are a child.

ANNE [*laughing*]. But what gives you that idea? I'm over . . .

BIRK. In thought and mind you are. You have grown up here . . . I might almost say in solitude, because your grandfather wasn't able to contribute anything to your development. On the contrary, he has kept you back in a world of ideas which are bound to make you a stranger to the outside world. And your step-mother . . . well, she seems to have been taken up with her own affairs, and she . . .

ANNE [*gets up*]. Ah, that's how it is. Now I understand you. You are ashamed of me.

BIRK. But what on earth gives you that idea?

ANNE. I'm well aware what everybody here says. . . . 'Anne is silly . . . she's mad.' Perhaps they were right, until yesterday. . . . But not any more! They thought it was grandfather's stories, but I know better. It was something here . . . [*She lays her hand on her breast.*] . . . here inside of me that I brooded over and pondered on. But all that is over now. Johannes, I promise you I'll be different, if you want me to.

BIRK. You misunderstand me, Anne! You misunderstand me! I see you as you really are. But let me continue . . . I must. Anne, you love me!

ANNE. Yes, but of course I do. . . . Can you doubt it?

BIRK. No, and just because I don't doubt it. . . . You don't realize that the situation has changed between us since we were children. I . . . I am engaged, and someone else must occupy first place in my heart. . . . And you, Anne, let me tell you this . . .

ANNE. But I know all this!

BIRK. But what you don't know is that you love me . . . no longer as a brother.

ANNE [*smiling*]. No longer as . . . [*growing suddenly serious, then adding slowly*] . . . no longer as a brother.

BIRK. You must see that, for your own sake, I . . .

ANNE [*whispering while she looks around*]. No longer as . . . Johannes, tell me, how do you love Juliane?

BIRK. What do you mean?

ANNE [*apprehensively*]. When you see her, is it like in the old song?
'Wherever you step with dainty feet,
The tiny flowers, it seems, take root.
Wherever you tread on field or floor,
Both lilies and roses sweetly grow.'
[*She grasps his hand*]. Tell me, Johannes, is it like that?

BIRK [*with averted face*]. Yes, yes, it is.

ANNE [*growing more apprehensive*]. And when she speaks to you . . .
when she looks at you, does your heart beat faster and faster?

BIRK. Yes, it does.

ANNE [*releases his hand*]. Perhaps you are right then. [*After a pause.*] I
feel like the man who was sleep-walking on a mountain top, and
when someone called his name, he fell into the abyss. Johannes, you
shouldn't . . . [*Gazes at him for a second then walks upstage, pauses and
breaks into tears.*]

BIRK. Anne, dear Anne, compose yourself! Calm yourself!

ANNE [*brushes away her tears and grows more vehement*]. Calm? I am calm.
Why shouldn't I be? And moreover . . . you mustn't think what I
said just now was anything more than a joke. I didn't mean anything
by it . . . do you hear? You're not to believe it . . . you're not to
remember it. Give me those. [*She takes the flowers from him, breaking
into tears.*] I made a mistake, it wasn't you who . . . it was Grandfather . . . [*Goes quickly into the log house.*]

BIRK [*after a moment*]. Anne, it was hard for me, but I had to. . . . But
then supposing I were to recant, suppose I . . . It was after all her
mother who was responsible for it all, it was she who made the first
moves and I . . . Ha, ha, ha! Weak, spineless fool that I am. But
shouldn't I now have the right to break it off? . . . And suppose I did?
What would people think of me? It's common knowledge that
Mrs. Berg's financial position hasn't improved lately. . . . Quite the
reverse. . . . And besides . . . the debt of gratitude I owe the family.
No, no, I can't. Things must take their course!

SCENE 5

[BIRK; MRS. BERG *and* JULIANE *come out of the big house.*]

MRS. BERG. Ah, here he is at last. I have scarcely exchanged a word with
you yet. . . . And as our guests are already due for dinner, then . . .

BIRK. For dinner already? Yes, indeed. . . . Let us have it as soon as possible.

JULIANE [*aside*]. My goodness, how impatient he has become.

MRS. BERG [*smiling*]. You would seem to be in a hurry. . . . Juliane isn't nearly so anxious. . . .

BIRK. Isn't she?

JULIANE. Mother, how can you say such things?

MRS. BERG. It's just my little joke. But let us have a little talk about our plans for the future, Birk. . . . Young people live only for the moment and for love. They never give a thought to tomorrow.

[MRS. BERG *and* BIRK *walk up and down, left.*]

JULIANE [*to herself*]. But where can Poulsen be? I must find an opportunity to explain everything to him. I must in any case prepare him. Because if he finds out suddenly, there will be a disaster, of that I'm sure. And Birk, he has become so ardent too. If I were to break it off, or even ask for a postponement . . . it would be the death of him. Oh dear, how horrid is this conflict between duty and inclination.

SCENE 6

[*As before.* JØRGEN *rushes in from the back.*]

JØRGEN [*whispering to* JULIANE]. Hasn't Poulsen been here?

JULIANE. Here? No! What is going on?

JØRGEN. He's like a man possessed. You've got him completely by the ears, and he intends to declare himself to you on the spot.

JULIANE. Now?

JØRGEN. What was I to do? I told him straight that you were engaged already and . . .

JULIANE. Then what?

JØRGEN. Well, then he went quite mad. He wanted to get hold of Birk and rushed off down the road to find him, with me in pursuit, but he had a start on me and I lost sight of him.

JULIANE. Oh, heavens . . . didn't I know there would be a disaster. If he gets hold of Birk, then . . .

JØRGEN. Yes, that must be prevented at any price.

JULIANE. But it was also very rash of you to come straight out with it like . . .

JØRGEN. But what was I to do?

SCENE 7

[*As before.* BERG *and* ANNE *come out of the log house.*]

MRS. BERG [*aside*]. My God, what does this mean? What does he want?

JULIANE. Grandfather, out here!

BIRK. I recognize him again . . . every line on his face!

BERG. Yes, it's true that it's the first time for years I've ventured out here when there was anybody about. But today I had to. No, stay, Anne! Stay! What's the matter with you—that you won't stay with your grandfather? [*Approaching the others.*] There is to be an engagement here, I hear.

MRS. BERG. Yes, that was what I thought.

BERG. And you intend to make the young people a present of the Birkedal estate.

BIRK. What? The estate . . . to me. [*Aside.*] Oh, it's this charity that makes me so unhappy.

MRS. BERG [*to* BERG]. So you know all about it? It is doubtless Anne who . . .

BERG [*raising his voice*]. It is Anne who keeps an old man informed about what goes on in his son's house. I suppose you think it doesn't concern him. . . .

MRS. BERG. Yes, it's true, I thought . . .

BERG. Yet, in a way it clearly does. . . . See here, Ma. . . . [*He produces some old papers.*]

JULIANE [*to* JØRGEN]. Ugh, how common he is! He calls Mother 'Ma'.

MRS. BERG. But what is it?

BERG. Look! These are papers which my son—your late husband—entrusted to me to hand over. . . .

MRS. BERG. Good, good, give them to me.

BERG. No, not to you. They belong to the son of the former owner of the estate. . . .

MRS. BERG. What? They belong . . .

BERG. And if he is still alive and we can track him down . . .

BIRK. But that is me!

BERG. You? Are you. . . ?

BIRK. Yes, certainly I am. Grandfather, if I may still call you that . . . don't you recognize me? Don't you remember how often I used to come here with my father in the old days. . . .

BERG. With Arne. . . . Yes, yes, now I remember. . . . Yes, that was when my son was alive. But then it all changed here; then the strangers came. . . .

MRS. BERG [*pointing to* BIRK]. We are not strangers to him anyway. . . . You must realize that. . . .

BERG. I understand very well. So it's Arne's son you are going to marry your daughter to, then?

MRS. BERG. Yes, I have never made any attempt to conceal it. But now that the papers are more or less superfluous, then. . . . [*Makes to take them.*]

BIRK. Oh, no. I must see what they contain.

MRS. BERG [*aside*]. My God, supposing they are all there.

BERG. But, Anne, you didn't say a word about it being him.

ANNE. I only found out yesterday. . . .

[*They whisper together.*]

BIRK [*aside*]. No! Is this possible?

JULIANE [*to* MRS. BERG]. Mother, what are those papers?

MRS. BERG [*tense with apprehension*]. Oh, how should I know? Old family documents, I imagine. It is unpardonable of him to produce things like this today.

BIRK. So there has been good reason for all this charity . . . this deference. [*Bitterly, to* MRS. BERG.] You, of course, can't guess what these papers contain?

MRS. BERG. Me? How should I?

BIRK [*as before*]. No, of course not. How could you guess that if these papers had been produced at the time of the lawsuit with my father, then Birkedal would have been mine today and I wouldn't have had to accept it from you as a present.

MRS. BERG. But I don't understand. . . .

BIRK. Don't you really? All right, I believe you, and I shall endeavour to explain. How these papers came into your hands I don't know; but I do know that Berg was your attorney and from what I hear your suitor as well. Now, under such circumstances it is difficult to refuse to do a small service if it were asked. It is quite natural that Berg should be entrusted with these papers. He had to know all sides of the case, of course. . . .

MRS. BERG. And you believe then . . .

BIRK. I only say that it could be explained thus. Nothing more, Mrs. Berg, nothing more! On Berg's conduct, I will make no comment. He won the case for you and shortly afterwards you consented to marry him. . . .

MRS. BERG. But, Birk!

BIRK. You must allow me to have my say. It is, I would point out, the first time we have spoken openly to each other . . . for I too have something I have concealed from you . . . that your late husband in some measure made up for the wrong he did me. It is him I have to thank for my upbringing, my education.

MRS. BERG. Did he. . . ?

BIRK. He has supported me, but until today I was unaware of the real motives. Of the motives for your kindness, Mrs. Berg, I am still not quite clear. Whether it was an uneasy conscience, or the fear that these papers might not be completely destroyed, as Berg no doubt assured you—I don't know, I say, which of them it was that prompted you. But now our account must be settled.

MRS. BERG. My God, Birk you wouldn't. . . ?

BIRK. Make use of the papers? No, you may rest assured. I am very glad, I must say, that Berg cannot have entertained any fears in that direction, otherwise he wouldn't have dared to ease his conscience by delivering them into my hands.

MRS. BERG. Then what is your intention?

BIRK. Firstly, to reassure you in this respect. [*He tears up the papers and hands them to her.*] And secondly . . .

MRS. BERG. Yes?

BIRK. Secondly, I will sever all ties between us.

MRS. BERG. You want. . . ? You mean. . . . Juliane. . . ?

BIRK. Correct! I will not marry her.

MRS. BERG. You don't care about her reputation? What about the gossip?

BIRK. I don't see that. . . . The engagement is still secret. I have only now really got to know Juliane and I have come to the conclusion that we wouldn't be happy together. Besides [*with emphasis*] I scarcely need remind you of the part you have played in our engagement and . . .

MRS. BERG [*quickly*]. Enough, enough . . . if that's the way it is to be. But I expect you to keep silent . . . silent about everything.

BIRK. You can rely on me. It's strictly between us. [*Aside.*] Ah, at last I am free!

JULIANE. But, Mother, what is going on?

MRS. BERG. Quiet, child! Compose yourself. . . . It's possible that there won't be any engagement today.

JULIANE. No engagement? Heavens above, what does that mean?

JØRGEN [*quietly, to* JULIANE]. Poulsen must have given himself away, that's obvious. [*To* MRS. BERG.] But what have the papers to do with it?

MRS. BERG. Oh, the papers have nothing to do with it. . . . It is family business . . . old documents.

SCENE 8

[*As before.* POULSEN *enters from the rear.*]

POULSEN. At last I've found him!

BIRK [*aside*]. What is the matter with him? Could it really be Anne. . . ?

POULSEN. I say, Birk. . . . A word or two in private. I've seen through you. . . . I know who you are in love with. . . . Your secret . . .

BIRK. How do you know? [*Aside.*] Jørgen was right, then. . . .

POULSEN. Never mind! But I love her, too. . . . I am hopelessly in love . . . and you must release her.

BIRK. Release! What do you mean?

POULSEN. What I say. I have the prior claim.

BIRK. You have?

POULSEN. Yes, by God, I have. I have trodden on her foot, you haven't. I have been unhappy about it for years, and you haven't!

BIRK. But I don't understand a word. Who are you talking about?

POULSEN. About Juliane, of course. Who else?

BIRK. And it is she who . . . ?

POULSEN. Yes, yes.

MRS. BERG [*to* JØRGEN]. Now the secret is coming out.

JØRGEN. It's already out.

BIRK [*to* JØRGEN]. But you said it was Anne!

JØRGEN [*confused*]. Yes, yes . . . I said . . . because I thought . . . I had no idea that . . .

POULSEN [*to* BIRK]. I'm telling you, you must . . . or there will be a disaster!

BIRK [*raising his voice*]. Poulsen, you are mistaken. . . . I am not engaged to Miss Juliane. . . .

JULIANE [*to* MRS. BERG]. Lord! So it's all over between us then!

MRS. BERG. Be quiet.

POULSEN. Not . . . not engaged. What do you mean?

BIRK. What I say.

POULSEN [*to* JØRGEN]. But, upon my word, you said . . .

JØRGEN. Well, I didn't know for certain. . . . Or rather . . . it was . . .
ha, ha . . . it was really all just a joke . . . to put the wind up you a bit.

POULSEN. Well, thanks very much. [*Goes over to* JULIANE.] Juliane . . .
then I am your only love, just as I was your first.

JULIANE [*holds out her hands to him*]. My friend.

MRS. BERG. But Mr. Poulsen, what am I to make of this?

JØRGEN [*making faces to* POULSEN]. You have forgotten your proposal.

POULSEN. Not at all. I have already made it . . . last night on Midsummer
Hill.

JULIANE [*confused*]. Well, no . . . that is to say . . . not properly. . . .
[*To* BIRK.] You mustn't think . . .

JØRGEN [*aside*]. The damned bletherer!

BIRK [*softly, to* JØRGEN]. Aha, so this is the way it all fits together. Poulsen
and Juliane had already come to an arrangement yesterday. Now I
see why it had to be Anne who . . .

JØRGEN. Sh, sh, I beg you.

BIRK. All right, relax!

POULSEN. Then where is this mysterious beloved you are so secretive
about?

BIRK. Beloved? What do you mean?

POULSEN. Well, you are engaged, you admitted it. . . . Then where is
she now? Come on, out with it!

BIRK. Very well. . . . Here she is, here! [*Points to* ANNE.]

ALL. Anne!

ANNE. Heavens, what does this mean?

JULIANE [*aside*]. What self-sacrifice.

BERG. Anne? Is it she. . . ?

BIRK. Yes, it is. The engagement has been secret, in the proper meaning of the word. But Mrs. Berg and Juliane and Jørgen and I, we also know how to keep a secret, don't we?

MRS. BERG. I hope so.

BERG. But Anne, why have you never told me?

ANNE [*in a whisper*]. Gracious me, Grandfather, I knew nothing about it myself.

BIRK [*also in a whisper*]. Yes! You see, Anne, I skipped the proposal, like Poulsen. What have you to say to it?

ANNE. Johannes! You know . . . [*quickly*] what you know.

POULSEN. But what an agreeable situation it is—to be engaged. It is as if all the puzzling contradictions of existence were resolved in one . . . one . . . how can I put it . . . one essence. . . . Then we know for the first time why we are alive.

JØRGEN. But all your theories about love, these will have to be abandoned now.

POULSEN. My theories? Never in this world. . . . But I won't apply them of course. When in love, one takes a theoretical view of love. Betrothal and marriage, on the other hand . . . these are practical matters, and theories—as one knows—can't always be made to work in practice.

MRS. BERG. Well, as things turn out, we have two engagements to announce today instead of one.

JØRGEN [*laughing*]. And we have Poulsen's inflammable heart to thank.

BIRK [*glancing at* ANNE]. No, we have old memories to thank.

ANNE [*throws herself into his arms*]. Johannes!

BIRK. Anne!

POULSEN [*wistfully to* JULIANE]. Old memories.

JULIANE. Julian!

POULSEN. Juliane!

[*They embrace and kiss.*]

LADY INGER
[Fru Inger til Østeraad]

HISTORICAL DRAMA IN FIVE ACTS
[1855]

CHARACTERS

INGER OTTISDAUGHTER, widow of Lord Steward Henrik Gyldenløve

ELINE, her daughter

NILS LYKKE, a Danish knight

OLAF SKAKTAVL, an outlawed Norwegian nobleman

NILS STENSSON

JENS BJELKE, a Danish commander

BJØRN
FINN   } Lady Inger's retainers
EINAR

Swedish soldiers, retainers, etc.

The action takes place at Østeraad Hall, on the Trondheim Fjord, in the year
1528

ACT ONE

A room at Østeraad. Through an open door at the back can be seen the Great Hall, only half of which is lit by the moon as it shines in from time to time through a large arched window in the opposite wall. Right, an outside door. Left, a door to the inner rooms. Downstage right, a window. Left, a fire, which lights up the room. It is a stormy evening.

SCENE ONE

[BJØRN *and* FINN *are sitting by the fire. The latter is busy polishing a helmet. Several pieces of armour, a shield, a sword, etc., lie near them.*]

FINN [*after a pause*]. Who was Knut Alfson?

BJØRN. Norway's last knight.

FINN. And the Danes killed him in Oslo fjord?

BJØRN [*grumpily*]. If you don't know, go and ask any boy of five. He'll tell you.

FINN. So Knut Alfson was our last knight, was he? And now he's dead and gone! [*Holding up the helmet.*] Then you might as well resign yourself to hanging all bright and polished in the Great Hall, because you are nothing but an empty nutshell now; yes, the kernel was eaten up by the worms many winters ago. . . . I say, Bjørn, couldn't we also speak of Norway as a hollow shell, like this helmet—bright on the outside and worm-eaten inside?

BJØRN. Shut up and get on with your job! [*After a pause.*] Is the helmet done?

FINN. Bright as silver in the moonlight!

BJØRN. Then put it down. Look here, scrape the rust off this sword.

FINN [*looking at it*]. But is it worth it?

BJØRN. What do you mean?

FINN [*maliciously*]. The edge has gone!

BJØRN. That's no business of yours. Give it me; here, take this shield. [*Hands it to him.*]

FINN [*as before*]. The strap's missing!

BJØRN [*aside*]. Why, I'd like to get a strap to you ... [FINN *hums to himself.*] Now what?

FINN. An empty helmet, a sword without an edge, a shield without a strap, and that's the whole blessed lot. You can't blame Lady Inger for hanging weapons like these all nice and polished on the the wall instead of letting them rust in Danish blood.

BJØRN. Nonsense; why, the country's at peace.

FINN. Peace? Yes, when the farmer has shot his last arrow and the wolf has stolen his last lamb from the fold there's peace between them; it's a strange friendship, though. Well, well, let it pass. It is quite logical, as I said, for the armour to hang gleaming on the wall. You know the old saying: Only a knight is a real man. And now we've no more knights left in the country, we haven't any real men either, and where there are no men the women have to be in charge, and that's why. ...

BJØRN. That's why—that's why I charge you to stop this revolting drivel! [*He rises.*] It's getting late. There now, you can hang up the helmet and armour in the hall again.

FINN [*in a low voice*]. No, it's better left till morning.

BJØRN. What, you're not afraid of the dark, are you?

FINN. Not by day. And it wouldn't be my fault if I were at night, believe me. Yes, you may well look at me, but things get said down in the servants' room, let me tell you. [*Whispering.*] There are some that say a tall figure in black walks there every single night.

BJØRN. Old wives' tales!

FINN. Yes, but they all swear it's true.

BJØRN. That I can quite believe.

FINN. The strangest thing is that Lady Inger shares our view.

BJØRN [*starting*]. Lady Inger! Well, what is her view?

FINN. Her view is, er—I can't exactly say; but she's certainly pretty restless. Can't you see how she's getting paler and thinner every day? [*With a searching glance.*] They say she never sleeps . . . and that it's because of the ghost. . . .

> [*During the last few words* ELINE *comes out of the left door. She stops and listens, unobserved.*]

BJØRN. And you believe such nonsense!

FINN. Well, yes and no. There are some others with a different explanation, but that's sheer malice, you see. I say, Bjørn, do you know that song that's going round the country?

BJØRN. Song?

FINN. Yes, everybody's singing it. It's barefaced slander, of course, but it's quite a catchy little thing. Just listen:

> [*Sings in a low voice.*]

> 'Dame Inger lives over at Østeraad Hall, —
> She's clad in costly fur,
> She's clad in velvet and ermine and all,
> She twines precious beads of red gold in her hair, —
> But there's no peace of mind for her.

> Dame Inger is sold to the Danish King—
> Her folk she lets suffer a foreigner's rule—
> And in return . . .'

> [BJØRN *grabs him furiously by the chest.* ELINE *withdraws, unnoticed.*]

BJØRN. And if you utter one more disrespectful word about Lady Inger I'll see you suffer in hell, and there'll be no return.

FINN [*tearing himself free*]. Now then, was it me who wrote the song? [*A horn is heard from the right.*]

BJØRN. Hark, what's that?

FINN. A horn. So we're having guests tonight.

BJØRN [*goes to the window*]. They are opening the gate. I can hear the sound of hoofs in the courtyard. It must be a knight.

FINN. A knight? That's hardly likely.

BJØRN. Why not?

FINN. Our last knight is dead and gone. You said so yourself.

[*Goes out, right.*]

SCENE TWO

[BJØRN. ELINE *enters immediately, left.*]

BJØRN. The damned scoundrel! He sees too much. I've done my best to shelter Lady Inger. I've tried to keep things from her children and the servants. What's the use? People are already talking, and it won't be long before they are all shouting out that Lady Inger has betrayed her people in their hour of need.

ELINE [*with suppressed emotion*]. Are you alone, Bjørn?

BJØRN. Is it you, Miss Eline?

ELINE. I say, tell me one of your stories. I know you can . . .

BJØRN. A story? But it's so late.

ELINE [*bitterly*]. Yes, it *is* late, if you count from the time it grew dark at Østeraad.

BJØRN. What is the matter with you? Has something gone wrong? You are so restless.

ELINE. Perhaps!

BJØRN. Something has happened. I've hardly recognized you these last six months.

ELINE. Remember that for six months now my sister Lucia has been sleeping six feet below the ground.

BJØRN. That's not the reason, Miss Eline, not the only reason you go round pale and quiet and thoughtful, or else all wild and excited like tonight.

ELINE. You don't think so? And why not? Wasn't she as mild and gentle and lovely as a summer's night? I tell you, Bjørn, she was as dear to me as life itself! Have you forgotten when we were children how we often used to sit on your knee on a winter's evening—you would sing to us and tell us stories . . . .

BJØRN. Yes, in those days you were so gay and happy.

ELINE. Yes, Bjørn, in those days! It was a wonderful life of tales and dreams. I don't know whether the beach used to be as desolate as it is now, but if it was I didn't notice. I went out there and made up lovely stories. My heroes would come and go and I lived among them and went with them on their travels. [*She sinks down on a chair.*] Now I'm so weak and weary—my stories cannot sustain me any more— they don't exist any more—they are only—stories. [*Vehemently, as she rises.*] Bjørn, do you know what has made me ill? A truth, an ugly truth which preys on me night and day!

BJØRN. What do you mean?

ELINE. Do you remember how you sometimes gave us good advice and practical maxims? My sister Lucia followed them, but I alas . . . !

BJØRN [*kindly*]. There now!

ELINE. I know—I was proud, haughty; when we used to play I always wanted to be queen, because I was the biggest, the prettiest, the cleverest. I know!

BJØRN. That's true!

ELINE. Once you took me by the hand and looked at me gravely and said: You must not be proud of your beauty and cleverness, but be as proud as the mountain eagle every time you think to yourself that you are Inger Gyldenløve's daughter!

BJØRN. You had reason to be proud of it.

ELINE. Yes, Bjørn, you told me so often enough! Oh, you told me so many stories in those days. [*Pressing his hand.*] Thank you for all of them! Tell me another; it might make me light-hearted again, as I used to be.

BJØRN. Why, you're not a child any longer.

ELINE. Of course not! But let me pretend. Now, begin!

[BJØRN *sits down by the fireside.* ELINE *flings herself down by the side of the chair.*]

BJØRN. Once upon a time there was a handsome knight . . .

ELINE [*who has been listening restlessly in the direction of the hall, clutches his arm and exclaims in a vehement whisper*]: Ssh, don't shout so loud; I'm not deaf! A story shouldn't be bellowed out like a nasty piece of common gossip; no, it should be whispered, quietly— [*with her eyes on the door to the hall*] as quietly as a ghost at midnight.

BJØRN [*whispering*]. Once upon a time there was a handsome knight about whom there was a strange story—

[ELINE *half rises and listens, tense and anxious, in the direction of the hall.*]

BJØRN. Miss Eline, what is wrong with you?

ELINE [*sits down again*]. Me? Nothing! Keep on!

BJØRN. Well, as I was saying, once he had looked straight into a woman's eyes she never forgot it, and her thoughts went with him wherever he went, and she pined away with grief.

ELINE. I've heard that one. Anyhow it's a true story you are telling me, not a proper one, because the knight you are talking of is Nils Lykke, who to this day is the first of the Danish King's men.

BJØRN. May be!

ELINE. Ah well, never mind; go on!

BJØRN. And one day it happened . . .

ELINE [*rising suddenly*]. Hush! Be quiet!

BJØRN. What now? What's come over you?

ELINE [*listening*]. Can you hear?

BJØRN. What?

ELINE. It's there. Yes, by Christ, it's there!

BJØRN [*rises*]. What is there? Where?

ELINE. *She* is—in the Great Hall. [*She goes quickly towards the back.* BJØRN *likewise.*]

BJØRN. How can you think . . . ? Miss Eline . . . go to your room!

ELINE. Hush, keep still! Don't move! Don't let her see you! Wait, the moon's coming out. Can you see that figure in black?

BJØRN. By all the saints . . . !

ELINE. You see, there she is turning Knut Alfson's portrait to the wall. Ha! ha! I bet it's looking her too straight in the eye!

BJØRN. Listen, Miss Eline!

ELINE [*moving downstage*]. Now I know what I know!

BJØRN [*aside*]. So it is true then?

ELINE. Who was it, Bjørn? Who was it?

BJØRN [*depressed*]. You know as well as I do.

ELINE. Well then?

BJØRN. It was Inger Gyldenløve, your mother!

ELINE [*half to herself*]. Night after night I've heard her steps in there. I have heard her whispering and moaning like some restless spirit. And what does the song say—ah, now I know; I know that . . .

BJØRN. Quiet!

[LADY INGER *enters hastily from the hall without noticing the others. She goes to the window, listens, and stares out for a while, as if looking for someone along the road, and then goes back into the hall.*]

ELINE [*aside, when* LADY INGER *has gone*]. She is as white as a shrouded corpse. A brow so clouded must mean autumn storms within.

[*Noises and voices can be heard outside the right-hand door.*]

BJØRN. And now what's that?

ELINE. Go and see what it's all about!

SCENE THREE

[*As before.* EINAR *and several* RETAINERS *enter, right, followed immediately by* LADY INGER *from the back.*]

EINAR [*at the door*]. In here, in here! And don't be shy now!

BJØRN. What do you want?

EINAR. Lady Inger!

BJØRN. Lady Inger? So late at night?

EINAR. Yes, it's late; but still time enough, I think.

SEVERAL. Yes, that's right. She's got to listen to us!

[*The crowd gets noisy.* LADY INGER *appears at the door. A sudden silence.*]

LADY INGER. What do you want of me?

EINAR. We were looking for you, your ladyship, to . . .

LADY INGER. Yes, speak up!

EINAR. Well, we are here in a good cause; in short, we have come to beg leave . . .

LADY INGER. Leave? For what?

EINAR. You see, there is a rumour in Østeraad tonight that the Swedes in Dalecarlia have taken up arms and are marching against King Gustav.

LADY INGER. The Swedes?

EINAR. Yes, so it is rumoured; and they say it's a fact.

LADY INGER. Even so, what's it to do with you if the Swedes take up arms?

SEVERAL. We want to join them!

OTHERS. We want to help them!

LADY INGER [*aside*]. So the time has come, then!

EINAR. Countryfolk from all the border regions are crossing over into Sweden and making for the Dales. Even outlaws who've been wandering round for years up in the mountains are venturing down into the valleys again, looking for people to sharpen their rusty swords.

LADY INGER [*after a pause*]. Tell me, have you thought it over carefully? Have you worked out the cost if King Gustav's men should win?

BJØRN [*in a half whisper to* LADY INGER]. Work out what it would cost the Danes if King Gustav's men should lose.

LADY INGER [*proudly*]. That's not for me to work out. [*To the others.*] You know King Gustav can count on support from Denmark; King Frederick is his friend and will protect him. I am sure of that.

EINAR. But if the people were now to rise up all over the country, if we all of us rose up together—to the last man. . . . Yes, Inger Gyldenløve, we have only been waiting for our chance. Now it's come. That's why things are starting up—and so out with the Danes.

ALL. Yes, out with the Danes.

LADY INGER [*aside*]. Ah, there's good stuff in them yet!

BJØRN [*aside*]. She's wavering. [*To* ELINE.] What's the betting Miss Eline that you have misjudged Inger Gyldenløve?

ELINE [*softly*]. If only I had! I'll tear my eyes out if they have been deceiving me.

EINAR. Don't you see, your ladyship, the first thing is King Gustav; once he's out of the way the Danes won't last long here and then we shall be free—we shall have no king any longer and we'll be able to elect one from our own people, just as the Swedes did before us.

LADY INGER [*with emotion*]. A king from the people? You mean from the Sture family?

EINAR. The Danes have made a clean sweep of our landed aristocracy; the best of the knights are homeless outlaws on the mountain tracks, if they are still alive; but still there might be a chance of finding a descendant of one of the old families, who . . .

LADY INGER [*hastily*]. Enough! [*Aside.*] Ah, my fondest hope! [*Aloud.*] I have warned you now; I've told you what a risk you are running; but if your minds are made up it would be foolish of me to forbid what you can manage on your own in any case.

EINAR. Then we have your consent to . . .

LADY INGER [*evasively*]. You have a strong will of your own; consult it. Another thing: there might well be quite a few serviceable weapons in the Great Hall. . . . Ah well, you are in control of Østeraad tonight. You may do as you wish. Good night!

[*General excitement among the crowd. They bring in candles and fetch weapons of all kinds from the hall.*]

BJØRN [*seizes* LADY INGER's *hand as she prepares to leave*]. Thank you, Inger Gyldenløve! I've known you since you were a child and I've never doubted you.

LADY INGER [*whispering*]. Quiet, Bjørn! It's a dangerous game I've embarked on tonight. The others have merely their lives at stake, but I have—infinitely more, believe me!

BJØRN. How? I don't understand you. Is it your power, your reputation . . . ?

LADY INGER [*scornfully*]. My power! Good heavens!

EINAR [*enters with a sword*]. How's this for a wolf's fang to tear through the Danes to the marrow of their bones!

A MANSERVANT [*to another* MANSERVANT]. What's that you've brought?

SECOND MANSERVANT. Herlof Hyttefad's breastplate!

EINAR. It's too good for you; here's a lance which belonged to Sten Sture. Hang the breastplate on it and you'll have the proudest banner a man could ask for.

SCENE FOUR

[*As before.* FINN *enters with a letter, left.*]

FINN [*to* LADY INGER]. I have been looking for you all over the house.

LADY INGER. What do you want?

FINN [*hands her the letter*]. A messenger from Trondheim has brought you a letter.

LADY INGER. Let me see! [*Half aloud, as she opens the letter.*] From Trondheim! What can it be? [*She glances through the letter.*] My God! From him! And in Norway . . . [*She reads on in great agitation while the others keep bringing weapons from the hall. Aside.*] So he's coming here, coming tonight. Now it will have to be a battle of wits, not swords.

EINAR. Right then. Now we are armed, so off we go!

LADY INGER [*hastily and firmly*]. No one is to leave the house tonight!

EINAR. But, my lady, the wind is favourable—we'll race along the fjord and—

LADY INGER. It is to be as I say!

EINAR. Not till tomorrow then. . . ?

LADY INGER. Not tomorrow either. Let no one leave Østeraad yet awhile.

[*Commotion among the crowd.*]

EINAR. We're going all the same, Lady Inger!

THE MEN. Yes, we're going!

LADY INGER [*reaching for Knut Alfson's sword, which has been left on the table*]. Who dare? [*Deathly silence. A pause.*] I have been doing your thinking for you. That's something you are not very good at. Put your weapons away! You'll learn my pleasure later. Go now! [*They take the weapons into the hall and go out, right.*]

ELINE [*aside to* BJØRN]. Do you still think I have misjudged Inger Gyldenløve?

LADY INGER [*motions* BJØRN *to her*]. Have a guest room ready!

BJØRN. Certainly, Lady Inger!

LADY INGER. And the gate open to anyone who knocks.

BJØRN. But . . .

LADY INGER [*peremptorily*]. The gate open!

BJØRN. The gate open! [*He goes out, right.*]

SCENE FIVE

[LADY INGER. ELINE.]

LADY INGER [*as* ELINE *starts to go*]. Stay here! . . . Eline, my child, I'd like a word with you.

ELINE. I am listening!

LADY INGER. Eline, you think ill of your mother!

ELINE. I think what your actions force me to think.

LADY INGER. And you answer me in the hardness of your heart.

ELINE. My hardheartedness is your own doing. From my childhood I had grown to respect you as a great, high-minded woman. I used to imagine those women in the old tales looked like you—those women who emerged in times of danger and roused the people to action. I felt that the Lord God himself had set a seal upon your brow and marked you out as the leader of the many thousands around you. In the banqueting hall knights and pages sang your praises, and country-folk throughout the land called you the mainstay of Norway's hopes! And all thought the old times would return through you! All thought that through you day would dawn again in Norway; . . . night is with us still, and the morning will scarcely come through you, Inger Gyldenløve!

LADY INGER. I know very well what puts such spiteful words into your mouth. You have been listening to the unthinking masses, which, like a flock of sheep, blindly follow a cunning leader wherever he goes.

ELINE. Truth is in the mouths of the people; that's what you always used to say when they sang and spoke your praises.

LADY INGER. Well, may be. But even if Inger Gyldenløve had failed her people, don't you think her burden would be heavy enough without your adding to the load?

ELINE. What I add to your load weighs as heavily on me as you. I have lived my finest days believing in your greatness; for I cannot live without pride, and I would rightly have been proud if you were still the same as ever!

LADY INGER. And what proof have you that I am not, Eline? Why are you so sure that you are not doing your mother an injustice?

ELINE [*with sudden feeling*]. Oh, if only I were!

LADY INGER. Quiet! A daughter has no right to call her mother to account. In one word I could tell you—but it would not be good for you to hear. You must wait and see what time will bring—it may be that . . .

ELINE [*prepares to go*]. Sleep well, mother!

LADY INGER [*hesitantly*]. No, wait! There's something else which. . . . Come closer, you must listen! [*She sits down at the table.*]

ELINE. I am listening!

LADY INGER. You may not say much but I am well aware that you often long to get away from here. It's too dead and lonely for you at Østeraad.

ELINE. Can you wonder, mother?

LADY INGER. It's up to you whether things are different from now on.

ELINE. How?

LADY INGER. Listen! I am expecting a guest tonight!

ELINE [*taken aback*]. A guest?

LADY INGER. A guest whose identity must not be revealed. No one may know where he comes from, nor where he is going.

ELINE [*throws herself at her mother's feet and grasps her hands*]. Mother, oh, mother! Can you forgive me the wrong I have done you?

LADY INGER [*astonished*]. What do you mean? I don't understand, Eline.

ELINE. So they were all mistaken; you are still true at heart.

LADY INGER. But stand up and tell me . . .

ELINE. Oh, do you think I don't know who your guest is?

LADY INGER [*surprised*]. You know, and yet . . .

ELINE. Do you imagine the gates of Østeraad are shut so firmly that no sounds of distress can reach me from our friends outside? Do you imagine I don't know that many a son of the old nobility is an outlaw roaming round without roof or shelter while the Danish lords are masters of his ancestral home?

LADY INGER. And then? . . . Go on!

ELINE. I'm well aware that many a knight of noble birth is being hunted in the forest like a hungry wolf; he has no hearth to rest by, not a bite of bread!

LADY INGER [*coldly*]. That's enough. I understand.

ELINE [*continues, ignoring her*]. And that is why you open the gates of Østeraad by night; that is why your guest's identity must not be revealed and no one can know where he comes from nor where he is going. You are flouting the strict ban on harbouring and helping fugitives.

LADY INGER. That's enough, I say. [*After a struggle.*] You are mistaken, Eline. It is no outlaw I am expecting.

ELINE [*rises*]. Then I have badly misunderstood you, Inger Gyldenløve!

LADY INGER. Listen, my child, but listen calmly, that is if you can control that temperament of yours.

ELINE. I will control it, until you have finished.

LADY INGER. Then hear what I have to tell you. . . . I have done everything in my power to keep you in ignorance of all our country's misery and woe. What would be the good of filling your young heart with sorrow and anger. No tears, no woman's sobs can save our suffering people—we need courage and the strength of men.

ELINE. And who told you that I lack courage and the strength of a man should they be needed?

LADY INGER. Quiet, child, I might take you at your word!

ELINE. What do you mean, mother?

LADY INGER. I might ask for both; I might—but let me finish first. You should know then that the time is approaching which the Danes have worked for years to bring about; the time for them to deal the final blow to our freedom. Therefore we must . . .

ELINE [*eagerly*]. Have at them, mother!

LADY INGER. No, we must play for time. The Privy Council is meeting now in Copenhagen to consider how best to tackle the matter. The majority are of the opinion that the disputes cannot be settled unless there is a union of Norway and Denmark, for if we retain our privileges as a free people it is likely that the feud will break out openly when the next king comes to be elected. That is what the Danish rulers seek to prevent.

ELINE. And we should tolerate that! We should look on quietly . . .

LADY INGER. No, we shouldn't tolerate it; but taking up arms and fighting openly would be of little help, as long as we are not all united. No, if we are to achieve anything it must be done secretly and on the quiet. We must, as I have said, play for time. In the south of Norway the nobility are pro-Danish, but up here in the north there is still some doubt, so King Frederick has sent up one of his knights to see for himself how we feel about things.

ELINE [*tense*]. Yes, and so . . .

LADY INGER. He is the man coming to Østeraad tonight!

ELINE. Here? Tonight?

LADY INGER. A trading vessel brought him to Trondheim yesterday. He has just sent word that he is to visit me; we may expect him within the hour.

ELINE. Mother, haven't you considered the danger to your reputation in agreeing to meet the Danish envoy like this? Aren't the people suspicious enough of you as it is? How can you hope that they will let you lead them and rule them one day, once it gets about . . .

LADY INGER. Don't worry! I've thought it all over carefully, but there is no danger. His errand in Norway is a secret; that's why he came incognito to Trondheim and is also visiting Østeraad as an unknown stranger.

ELINE. And you don't know his name?

LADY INGER. I do, and a fine-sounding name it is. You couldn't find a nobler name in Denmark.

ELINE. But what have you in mind then? I still don't follow.

LADY INGER. You will soon understand. Since we can't crush the serpent we must bind it.

ELINE. Then mind the rope doesn't snap.

LADY INGER. It's up to you how tightly it is tied.

ELINE. Me?

LADY INGER. I have seen for some time that you feel caged in at Østeraad. The young falcon is fretting behind the iron bars.

ELINE. My wings are clipped. If you were to set me free it would be of little use.

LADY INGER. Your wings are clipped only as long as you will.

ELINE. Will? My will rests with you; be what you were and I will also . . .

LADY INGER. Enough of that! I have more to tell you! You wouldn't object strongly to leaving Østeraad.

ELINE. Perhaps not, mother!

T1

LADY INGER. You once told me that the best time in your life was spent in a world of tales and stories; such a life may well be yours again!

ELINE. What do you mean?

LADY INGER. Eline, if some mighty lord were to come and take you off to his castle, where you found pages and ladies-in-waiting, robes of silk and lofty halls!

ELINE. Some lord, you said?

LADY INGER. A lord!

ELINE [*moving slightly further away*]. And the Danish envoy is coming tonight?

LADY INGER. Tonight!

ELINE. Then I shudder to think what you mean.

LADY INGER. There is no need for alarm, unless you deliberately mistake my meaning. I have certainly no intention of forcing you. You shall be your own mistress in this matter and choose for yourself.

ELINE [*taking a step nearer and looking her straight in the eye*]. Inger Gyldenløve, have you heard of the mother who drove over the mountains one night with her little children in the sledge? The pack of wolves was after her; it was a matter of life and death—and one by one she threw out her little ones to play for time and save herself.

LADY INGER [*heatedly*]. Fairy tales! A mother would tear her heart from her breast rather than let her child go from her arms.

ELINE [*bitterly*]. If I weren't my mother's daughter I would say you were right; but you are that mother and you have thrown your daughters to the wolves, one by one. Five years ago your eldest daughter Merete left Østeraad. Now she lives in Bergen as Vincents Lunge's wife. But do you think she is happy as the wife of the Danish knight? Vincents Lunge is powerful, virtually a king: she has pages and ladies-in-waiting, robes of silk and lofty halls, but there is no sunshine in her day and no rest at night, for she has never loved him. He came here and wooed her because she was the richest heiress in Norway and he needed at the time to get a firm footing in the country. I know, I know all about it!... Merete submitted to your will; she went with the foreign lord—but what did it cost her? More tears than a mother should wish to answer for at the day of judgement.

LADY INGER. I know my reckoning and I am not alarmed.

ELINE. That is not the end of your reckoning. Where is Lucia, your second child?

LADY INGER [*pointing to heaven*]. Ask God who took her.

ELINE. I am asking you; for it is you who must answer for her leaving this life so young. As happy as a bird in spring she left Østeraad to visit Merete in Bergen. A year later she was back in her mother's home; her cheeks were white and death had eaten into her breast! Yes, mother, you are surprised! You thought the secret was buried with her, but she told me all. A chivalrous knight had won her heart; he wished to wed her; you knew her honour was at stake, but you were adamant—and your child had to die. I know everything, you see!

LADY INGER [*aside*]. Everything! [*Aloud.*] Then she told you his name as well?

ELINE. No, I didn't ask.

LADY INGER [*aside*]. Ah, so you don't know everything! [*Aloud.*] What you have told me, Eline, I have known for a long time, but there is something you haven't thought of: the young knight was a Dane.

ELINE. I knew that too.

LADY INGER. And his love was false; he had ensnared her with his subtle ways and smooth talk.

ELINE. I know, but she loved him all the same, and if you had had a mother's heart your child's honour would have come first!

LADY INGER. Not before her happiness. Do you think that with Merete's fate staring me in the face I would sacrifice my second child to a man who was not fond of her?

ELINE. Your smooth tongue may fool the world, but not me. Don't imagine, Inger Gyldenløve, that I am completely ignorant of what is going on in Norway. I see perfectly well what you are doing. I know that in your heart you do not like the Danes. Perhaps you hate them; but you fear them too. When you gave Merete to Vincents

Lunge the Danes were everywhere on top; three years later when you forbade Lucia to wed the man to whom she had joined her life—although he had seduced her—then things were very different. The Norwegians were beginning to come to life again, and it was not wise to be on friendly terms with the foreign tyrants. And what have you done to avenge the girl who had to die so young? Nothing! Well, I will act in your stead; I will avenge all the disgrace which has befallen our people and our family!

LADY INGER. What do you mean to do?

ELINE. I shall go my way, as you go yours. I don't know myself what I mean to do, but I feel I have the strength and dare do anything for our just cause.

LADY INGER. Then you have a hard fight ahead of you. I once vowed to do the same, and my hair has grown grey under the burden of my vow.

ELINE. I will go now; your guest will soon be here and I would be in the way. Perhaps there is still time for you. . . . Well, God guide you and give you strength in what you do! Don't forget that the eyes of the people are upon you! Think of Merete, weeping night and day over her wasted life! Think of Lucia, sleeping in her black coffin! [*She is about to go, but comes back again.*] And one thing more. Don't forget, Inger Gyldenløve, when you play tonight that the stake is your last child! [*She enters the room on the left.*]

SCENE SIX

[LADY INGER *alone.*]

LADY INGER [*after a pause*]. My last child? She little knows the truth of what she says; but there's not just my child at stake. God help me! Tonight we are playing for the future of Norway! Ssh, isn't that someone riding through the gateway? [*Listening.*] No, not yet; it was only the wind. Brr, it's blowing with a graveyard chill out there tonight! And I seem to hear the sigh of a storm as it sweeps through the Great Hall [*pressing her hands to her heart*] and through my breast! [*Pauses.*] How strange, how strange! Fate made me a woman, but burdened me with a man's work. The welfare of my people is in my hands; I am rich and strong; it is within my power to make them all rise as one man to win back what treachery and force have taken

from us. They are waiting for the signal from *me*, and now is the
time, now or never! Dare I delay, then? Is it right to sacrifice many
for the sake of one? Would it not be better if I could—no, I can't, I
won't. [*She starts in terror.*] . . . Ah, there they are again, those pale
phantoms which come when I am alone; . . . my departed ancestors,
my fallen kinsfolk! . . . Ugh, how they stare at me! How stern and
silent! I know them. [*Screaming.*] Sten Sture! Knut Alfson! Olaf
Skaktavl! Back! Stand back! What do you want of me?

SCENE SEVEN

[LADY INGER. OLAF SKAKTAVL, *who has entered slowly from the Great
Hall.*]

SKAKTAVL. Greetings to you, Inger Gyldenløve!

LADY INGER [*turns with a scream*]. Ah, the Lord protect me!

[*She falls back in the chair.* OLAF SKAKTAVL *stares at her, motionless and
leaning on his sword.*]

ACT TWO

The same set as in Act One.

SCENE ONE

[LADY INGER, *sitting at the table on the right.* OLAF SKAKTAVL.]

SKAKTAVL. For the last time, Inger Gyldenløve! You are firmly resolved then?

LADY INGER. I can do nothing else; and my advice to you is: do what I do! If it is the will of heaven that our people shall perish, perish they will, whether we help or not.

SKAKTAVL. And do you think I shall be content to believe that? Am I just to sit still and watch, now the time has come? Have you forgotten the old scores I have to pay? . . . They have plundered and stolen the home of my fathers; my son, my only child, the last of my line, they have slaughtered like a dog; and myself they outlawed and drove into the forests and mountains twenty years ago. People have long since presumed me dead, but it is my belief that I cannot go to my grave before I have taken my revenge.

LADY INGER. Then you have a long life ahead of you. What do you intend to do?

SKAKTAVL [*flaring up*]. Do? How should I know? I've never been one for thinking and planning; that's where you must help. You have brains; I have only my two arms and my sword.

LADY INGER. Your sword is rusty, Olaf Skaktavl! All the swords in Norway are rusty!

SKAKTAVL. That's because the younger generation only fights with its tongue. . . . You have changed, Inger Gyldenløve! There was a time when a man's heart beat in your breast.

LADY INGER. Don't remind me of what *was*.

SKAKTAVL. But that is why I have come; you *shall* listen to me, even if . . .

LADY INGER. Very well, but make it short, because—I'll have to tell you —this is no safe place for you.

SKAKTAVL. Not safe for an outlaw at Lady Inger's house. I've known that a long time; but you forget that an outlaw has nothing to forfeit but a life whose loss would be a gain!

LADY INGER. Then say what you have to say. I shall not prevent you.

SKAKTAVL. I first saw you some thirty winters ago; it was at Akershus in the house of Knut Alfson and his wife. You were scarcely more than a child at the time, but you were as bold as the mountain eagle, wild and tempestuous as the storm which is raging round Østeraad tonight. Many a gallant knight lay at your feet; you were dear to me too; dear as no woman before or since. Yet you had only one thought in those days: your people and your country!

LADY INGER. I had only seen fifteen summers then. Remember that we have both been frozen by the snow of thirty winters since those days.

SKAKTAVL. You came from the noblest families in Norway; power and riches were to be yours; and you had an ear for the grievances of our people. The old and experienced among us thought it was written in heaven that you were the one who would break our bonds and restore our freedom; and you yourself thought the same at that time.

LADY INGER. That was a sinful thought, Olaf Skaktavl. It was pride and not the Lord's calling which spoke through me.

SKAKTAVL. You *could* have been the chosen one if you had wanted. Do you remember that night when the Danish fleet lay off Akershus? The commanders offered peace terms and, trusting in his safe-conduct, Knut Alfson went on board. Three hours later we were bearing him through the gate . . .

LADY INGER [*distressed*]. His corpse!

SKAKTAVL. The finest heart in Norway burst when the Danish bandits struck him down. I can still see that long procession of mourners filing into the Knights' Chamber, two by two. There he lay on the bier, white as a spring cloud, with the axe wound above his brow. And in the stillness of the night the bravest men in Norway gathered round the corpse. Lady Margaret stood by her lifeless husband's head, and every one of us swore to risk his life and all he had in the

fight for freedom and revenge. Then there was a movement behind
the pillar in the corner and into the circle of men stepped a girl,
scarcely more than a child, but with fire in her eyes and steel in her
voice. She solemnly swore—shall I repeat your words?

LADY INGER. I swore to stay by you in life and death; to fight like you
for freedom and revenge.

SKAKTAVL [*bitterly*]. You remember your oath, yet you have forgotten
it!

LADY INGER. And how did the others keep their promise? I am not
speaking of you, Olaf Skaktavl, but of your friends, the whole
nobility of Norway. Not one of them has the courage to be a man,
yet they reproach me for being a woman!

SKAKTAVL. I know what you mean: why did they submit instead of
defying their tyrants to the last? True, there is poor stuff in our
nobility nowadays, but if they had held together who knows what
would have happened; and you could have held them together.
They would all have bowed to you.

LADY INGER. I could give you an answer, but you would scarcely understand. So let us talk no more about what cannot now be changed.
Tell me instead what really brings you to Østeraad. Do you need
shelter? Good, I will hide you. Do you need care and attention? You
shall have it!

SKAKTAVL. For twenty years I have been homeless; my hair has grown
grey up in the mountains; I have lived with the wolves and the bears.
You see, Lady Inger, *I* can manage without you, but the people need
you.

LADY INGER [*shrugging her shoulders*]. The old refrain!

SKAKTAVL. Yes, it grates on your ears, I know; but you must hear it just
the same. In short, I have come from Sweden. There's trouble
brewing there; the Dales are about to revolt!

LADY INGER. I know!

SKAKTAVL. Peter Kanzler[1] is on our side, but secretly, you understand.

LADY INGER [*with a start*]. Indeed!

[1] i.e. Peter the Chancellor.

SKAKTAVL. It is he who has sent me to you.

LADY INGER [*tense*]. Peter Kanzler, you say?

SKAKTAVL. Himself—but perhaps you no longer remember him?

LADY INGER [*aside*]. Only too well. [*Aloud.*] But tell me, do tell me what message have you brought me.

SKAKTAVL. When rumours of the revolt reached the Jämtland mountains where I was at the time, I went over at once into Sweden. I had an idea that Peter Kanzler would have a finger in the pie. I looked him up and offered him my sword and my services. He knew me from earlier days, as you are aware. He knew I was to be trusted, and so he sent me here.

LADY INGER [*with impatience*]. Yes, yes, he sent you here to . . .

SKAKTAVL [*confidingly*]. Lady Inger, there's a stranger coming to Østeraad tonight!

LADY INGER [*surprised*]. What? You know that. . . ?

SKAKTAVL. Indeed I do. I know all about it; after all, it was to meet him that Peter Kanzler sent me.

LADY INGER. To meet him? It can't be, Olaf Skaktavl! Impossible!

SKAKTAVL. It is as I say. If he has not arrived it won't be long before . . .

LADY INGER. No, it won't, but . . .

SKAKTAVL. So you were expecting him?

LADY INGER. I was; he sent word. That is why they let you straight in when you knocked.

SKAKTAVL. Hush! There's someone riding down the road. [*He goes to the window.*] They are opening the gate!

LADY INGER [*looks out*]. It's a knight and his man. They are dismounting in the courtyard.

SKAKTAVL. There he is then. And his name?

LADY INGER. You don't know his name?

SKAKTAVL. Why should I know? Peter Kanzler simply told me to come and I came.

LADY INGER. Then I'll show you to your room. You'll be needing some refreshment. You can talk to the visitor presently.

SKAKTAVL. Just as you wish. [*They go out, left.*]

SCENE TWO

[FINN *shows in* NILS LYKKE *and* JENS BJELKE *from the right.*]

NILS LYKKE [*to* FINN]. Then we can depend on you entirely?

FINN. The commandant at Trondheim has always testified to my reliability.

NILS LYKKE. Good, good; he said as much to me. First of all then . . . has there already been a visitor at Østeraad tonight?

FINN. Someone came an hour ago.

NILS LYKKE [*aside to* BJELKE]. He's here. [*Aloud to* FINN.] Would you recognize him? Did you see him?

FINN. No. No one did except for the lodge porter, as far as I know. He was shown straight in to Lady Inger, and she . . .

NILS LYKKE. Well, and she? He's not gone again already, has he?

FINN. No, but she'll be hiding him in one of her rooms, because . . .

NILS LYKKE. Good!

BJELKE [*whispering*]. Then the first thing is to put a guard on the gate and we've got him.

NILS LYKKE [*smiling*]. You think so? [*To* FINN.] I say, is there any way out of this place apart from the gate? I mean, can anyone get out of Østeraad unobserved when the gate is shut?

FINN. Well, I don't know. It's true they talk of secret passages down in the vaults, but no one apart from Lady Inger will know about them.

BJELKE. The devil!

NILS LYKKE. Right then, you may go.

FINN. Very good. If you should want me for anything you just need to open the second door on the left in the Great Hall and I'll be there at once.

NILS LYKKE. Good. [*He points to the door.* FINN *goes out, right.*]

SCENE THREE

[NILS LYKKE. JENS BJELKE.]

BJELKE. I say, Nils old man, you know this is going to be a pretty miserable campaign for both of us.

NILS LYKKE [*smiling*]. Hm! Not for me, I hope.

BJELKE. Really? In the first place there's not much glory chasing a mere overgrown boy like this Nils Sture. Look at the way he's been behaving. First he goes stirring up bad blood among the country-folk, promises them help and I don't know what, and when it comes to the event he dashes away and hides behind a petticoat. What's more, I'm frankly sorry I followed your advice instead of acting on my own initiative.

NILS LYKKE [*aside*]. It's rather late to be sorry, old man!

BJELKE. I don't mind telling you I've never enjoyed poking round for badgers. I had been expecting something quite different. I ride all the way with my men from Jämtland; in Trondheim I get a warrant from the Danish commandant to look for the trouble-maker any-where I like; I know from a reliable source that he is in league with Lady Inger—so what was more likely than to find the gates guarded? Then we could have hit out, stormed the house . . .

NILS LYKKE. Instead of which they are polite enough to open the gates for us. You see: if I know Lady Inger she'll entertain us royally.

BJELKE. And then it was your idea to leave my horsemen a mile or so from the house. If we had come in greater numbers . . .

NILS LYKKE. She would still have made us most welcome. But remember that the affair would then have created a stir; the peasants would have taken it as an act of violence against Lady Inger; she would again have risen in the popular estimation, and that, you see, would not have been a good thing.

BJELKE. That may be so. But what am I to do now? Count Sture is in Østeraad, true enough, but what use is that? Lady Inger will have as many hide-outs as a fox, and more than one exit. We could go nosing round here for ever. To hell with the whole business!

NILS LYKKE. Well, since you don't like the turn things have taken you had better leave the field to me.

BJELKE. To you? What are you going to do?

NILS LYKKE. In this case shrewdness and cunning will perhaps accomplish what force cannot. To tell the truth, I've had something of the sort in mind since we met in Trondheim yesterday. That's why I got you to . . .

BJELKE. The devil you did! I really should have known that you would be up to your usual tricks!

NILS LYKKE. Yes, but you know this is just where we need a few tricks, if both sides are to fight with equal weapons. You have shown more than once what you can do. Now I feel like proving myself, and here is the chance. My lord, the King of Denmark, has entrusted me with more than one awkward assignment in which I have acquitted myself quite well, but . . .

BJELKE. I'll say you have. God and men alike know that you are the craftiest devil in the three kingdoms.

NILS LYKKE. Many thanks! But, you see, so far I've only had men to pit myself against, and that is not saying much; whereas now it's a question of outwitting a woman!

BJELKE. Ha! ha! ha! That's a skill in which you proved yourself a master long ago, old man! Do you think I don't know the song:

> 'Every fair maiden sighs with a tear:
> God grant that Nils Lykke should hold me dear.'

NILS LYKKE. Yes, that refers to women of twenty or thereabouts, but Lady Inger is getting on for fifty, and, what's more, is as cunning as they make them. If I succeed in beating her I shall have the confidence to take on anything. So you'll leave Lady Inger to me then? Remember, when you visited the Court in Denmark I gave up more than one young lady to you.

BJELKE. You shouldn't remind me of that piece of generosity, you know. It only caused me annoyance, and apart from that you had them all where you wanted them. But never mind, seeing that I've set off on the wrong foot I shall be glad to let you take over. But it's a promise: if young Count Sture is here you will hand him over, dead or alive.

NILS LYKKE. You shall have him alive and kicking. I don't intend to kill him. But now you must get back to your men. Keep guard on the road. If I should notice anything suspicious you'll be informed without delay.

BJELKE. Very good; but how do I get out?

NILS LYKKE. The fellow in there will help you out. But quietly does it. . . .

BJELKE. Of course. Well, good luck!

NILS LYKKE. My luck has never let me down in my battles with women. Now hurry! [BJELKE *goes out, right.*]

SCENE FOUR

[NILS LYKKE, *alone.*]

NILS LYKKE [*after a pause*]. So at last I am in Østeraad, that old ancestral home a child told me so much about two years ago. Lucia—yes, two years ago she was still a child, and now, now she is dead. [*He shrugs his shoulders.*] Flowers wither quickly up here in the north! A young girl gets hurt—snap, and it's over once and for all. I wonder whether it's through anger and shame at losing her so-called honour, or whether it is through sorrow and grief at finding herself deceived by the man she has given herself to. Well, in either case she is a fool, and one fool more or less in the world. . . . [*Smiling, after a pause.*] Hm, my life's young spring has been rich enough; early each year I have seen a rose-bud bloom; each autumn I have seen a lily wither! [*He looks round at the room.*] I know this place as though I had been born here. That is the Great Hall in there, and down below is—the burial vault; Lucia will be there too. . . . If I believed in such things I might have imagined that she turned in her coffin when I set foot inside the gates of Østeraad; that when I came across the courtyard she lifted the lid—and when I mentioned her name just now it was as though something summoned her up from the vaults. Perhaps she is this moment groping her way up the stairs. She is hampered by the grave clothes, but still she gropes forward. Perhaps she is standing now in the Great Hall, watching me through the chink in the door. Come closer, child! I am not one to be frightened! Come closer! I think I was in love with you once! Talk to me a little!—Lady Inger is keeping me waiting. You helped me to while away so many a tedious hour, I remember well. The best part of love is the memory, and I . . . have many memories. [*He puts his hand on his forehead and paces up and down several times.*] There now! . . . Right, there is the big window with the silk curtains. That's where Inger Gyldenløve usually stands gazing out over the road, as if waiting for someone who never comes. Lucia told me so. . . . In there [*pointing to the left door*] is sister Eline's room . . . sister Eline? Yes, that's her name. She's a remarkable one is sister Eline: so shrewd and so brave! A pity she's seen so damned little of the world. She can't have left the precincts of Østeraad. And they say she's beautiful by the way—plump like an overripe apple probably! Well, well, you shall keep sister Eline unscathed when I go. Wild flowers are not to my taste. The stalk is too soft. It's as though they thanked you for the honour of being picked. [*He looks at a bunch of flowers he is wearing on his chest.*] Yet only today I picked these poor things when I set foot for the first time on Østeraad estate. They were the last survivors of autumn—Østeraad's fair spring flower perished one stormy night two summers ago! [*He pauses.*] How will Lady Inger receive me? Will she burn down the house over all our heads tonight? Will she open a trap-door to swallow me up? Or perhaps she will be content to stab me with a knife in the back of my neck at dinner? She would certainly win my respect if she thought of some such thing. [*Listening.*] Well, we'll soon see. . . .

SCENE FIVE

[NILS LYKKE. LADY INGER *enters from the Great Hall.*]

LADY INGER. I bid you welcome, Sir Nils!

NILS LYKKE. Ah, the Lady of Østeraad!

LADY INGER. And I thank you for letting me know of your visit.

NILS LYKKE. No more than my duty. I had reason to suppose that my visit would surprise you.

LADY INGER. Indeed, Sir Nils, in that you are not mistaken. Nils Lykke was certainly the last person I expected to see as my guest at Østeraad.

NILS LYKKE. And even less had you expected him to come as a friend?

LADY INGER. As a friend? You add mockery to all the pain and shame you have heaped upon Inger Gyldenløve's house? You bring my child to her grave and still dare . . .

NILS LYKKE. If I may say so, Lady Inger, we shall scarcely reach agreement on that point because you have not taken into account what *I* lost on the same occasion. My intentions were honourable, I was tired of my disorderly life—I have lived life to the full, I can tell you. I was thirty at the time. I needed a wife who was young, beautiful, and gentle. Add to this the good fortune of becoming Lady Inger Gyldenløve's son-in-law . . .

LADY INGER. Take care, Sir Nils. I have concealed what happened from the eyes of the world, but don't imagine that what is out of sight is out of mind. There might well be an opportunity . . .

NILS LYKKE. Are you threatening me, Lady Inger? I have offered you my hand in reconciliation; you refuse to take it. So from now on it is to be war between us?

LADY INGER [*haughtily*]. I was unaware that there was ever anything else.

NILS LYKKE. On your part perhaps. Myself I have never been your enemy, although as a subject of the King of Denmark I had good reason.

LADY INGER [*bitterly*]. I know what you mean; I have not been tractable enough. Winning me over to your party has not gone as smoothly as was expected? But it seems to me you have nothing to complain of. My daughter Merete's husband is your countryman. I can go no further; my position is difficult, Nils Lykke!

NILS LYKKE. I fully understand: your people have a long-standing claim on you, a claim which, it is said, you have only partly satisfied.

LADY INGER. If I may say so, Sir Nils, I am accountable for my conduct to none other than God and myself. If you please then, tell me what brings you here.

NILS LYKKE. At once, Lady Inger! The purpose of my mission to this country cannot, I take it, be unknown to you.

LADY INGER. I know the task which is generally ascribed to you. It is of importance for our King to know where he stands with the Norwegian nobility.

NILS LYKKE. Yes, indeed.

LADY INGER. That is why you are visiting Østeraad then?

NILS LYKKE. Partly. But I have certainly not come to ask for any verbal assurance.

LADY INGER. Well then?

NILS LYKKE. Listen, Lady Inger! You have just said yourself that your position is difficult. You stand between two parties, neither of which dare rely on you entirely. Self-interest must necessarily tie you to us; on the other hand you are bound to the disaffected elements by nationality and—who knows?—perhaps by some secret bond as well.

LADY INGER [*aside*]. Secret bond! . . . My God, can he know . . . ?

NILS LYKKE [*aside*]. She is uneasy. There must be something in it! [*Aloud.*] You will see for yourself that your position is not tenable in the long run. Now suppose it were in my power to free you from a situation which . . .

LADY INGER. In your power, you say?

NILS LYKKE. First of all, Lady Inger, I beg you to attach no importance to any rash words which escaped me just now. Don't imagine that I have forgotten for one moment the debt I have incurred. Suppose that it had long been my intention to make amends for my crime as far as possible. Suppose that was why I procured this mission for myself.

LADY INGER. Explain yourself more precisely, Sir Nils! I don't understand.

NILS LYKKE. I am perhaps not mistaken in assuming that you know as well as I about the disturbances threatening in Sweden. You know, or at any rate you suspect, that these disturbances have a wider aim than is generally ascribed to them, and you will understand therefore that our King cannot look idly on while events take their course. Is that not so?

LADY INGER. Go on!

NILS LYKKE [*searchingly, after a pause*]. There is a possible contingency which might endanger Gustav Vasa's throne.

LADY INGER [*aside*]. What is he getting at?

NILS LYKKE. Namely, the contingency that there might be a man in Sweden who by reason of birth had a claim to be elected king.

LADY INGER [*evasively*]. The Swedish nobility has been as savagely crippled as ours, Sir Nils! Where would you look for . . . ?

NILS LYKKE [*smiling*]. Look? The man has already been found!

LADY INGER [*aside*]. Ah, can he know . . . ? No, he can't possibly!

NILS LYKKE. And he is too close to you, Madam, for you not to have thought of him. [*Watching her fixedly*.] The late Count Sture left a son . . .

LADY INGER [*aghast*]. Holy Saviour, so you know then . . .

NILS LYKKE [*taken aback*]. Be calm, Madam, and let me finish. This young man has so far been living quietly with his mother, Sten Sture's widow.

LADY INGER [*aside*]. He means the other one. Dear me—I almost revealed . . .

NILS LYKKE. But now he has come out into the open and has emerged in Dalecarlia as the peasants' leader. Their numbers are growing daily and, as you may know, they are finding friends among the common folk on the Norwegian side of the mountains.

LADY INGER [*who in the meantime has regained her composure*]. You seem certain, Sir Nils, that I am acquainted with the events of which you speak. What reason have I given you to suppose any such thing? I know nothing and do not wish to know. My intention is to live quietly on my own estate. I am not lending my support to the trouble-makers, but neither should you count on me if it is your intention to suppress them.

NILS LYKKE [*in a low voice*]. Would you still stand idly by if it were my intention to support them?

LADY INGER [*tense*]. How am I to understand you?

NILS LYKKE. So you haven't grasped what I have been driving at all this time? Well then, I will be quite frank about things. The fact is that the King and his Cabinet see clearly that in the long run we can have no firm footing in Norway while the people feel wronged and oppressed. We fully understand that an honourable ally is better than a reluctant subject, and therefore we wish for nothing better than to loosen bonds which in effect bind us as much as you. You

U1

will also understand, I am sure, that the attitude of the Norwegians to us makes such a step too dangerous until we have reliable support behind us.

LADY INGER. Well?

NILS LYKKE. The obvious place to look for such support is Sweden, but not, mark you, as long as Gustav Vasa is at the helm, because his account with Denmark is not yet settled and probably never will be. On the other hand, a new monarch who had the people on his side and who owed his crown to Danish aid. . . . Well, do you begin to understand me? Then we could safely say to our Norwegian brothers, 'Take back your ancient inherited rights, choose yourselves the ruler you want, and be our friends in need, as we will be yours!' And please observe, Lady Inger, that our magnanimity is not in fact as great as it seems, because you will see that, far from being weakened, we shall be strengthened by it. And now I have spoken candidly to you, you too must abandon all mistrust. Therefore . . . [*firmly*] the knight from Sweden who arrived here an hour before me . . .

LADY INGER. Then you know already?

NILS LYKKE. Everything! He's the one I am looking for!

LADY INGER [*aside*]. Strange! So it is as Olaf Skaktavl said. [*Aloud.*] Wait here, Sir Nils! I will go and fetch him. [*She goes out through the Great Hall.*]

SCENE SIX

[NILS LYKKE, *alone.*]

NILS LYKKE. That's the way, Nils Lykke, that's the way! . . . The battle is won! I must say, it took less than I thought. She's gone to bring Count Sture to me, just like that! Yes, my words must have gone home as though they came from her own heart, because when I first mentioned Sten Sture's son she was clearly overcome with fear and on the point of collapse. Now that Lady Inger has been gullible enough to walk into the trap, Nils Sture shouldn't cause any trouble. They say he's still only a boy. It won't be hard to throw the dust into his eyes. He'll set off with my promise of help—unfortunately he'll get picked up on the road and the whole enterprise is killed. And once things have prospered thus far it won't hurt to do a little

extra on my own account. One might drop a hint that the young
Count Sture has been here, that a Danish envoy has had a secret
meeting with Lady Inger, as a result of which young Count Nils
has been picked up by his pursuers just outside the gates of Østeraad.
However high Inger Gyldenløve's reputation with the people, it
would have difficulty in surviving a blow like that!... But, damn it,
what if I have miscalculated? What if Lady Inger has smelt a rat?...
Perhaps he has just this moment slipped through our fingers. Ah, no,
no need to worry. Here they come!

SCENE SEVEN

[NILS LYKKE. LADY INGER *and* OLAF SKAKTAVL *enter from the Great
Hall.*]

LADY INGER [*to* NILS LYKKE]. Here is the gentleman you are waiting for.

NILS LYKKE [*aside*]. Hell! What does this mean?

LADY INGER. I have told this gentleman your name and everything you
said.

NILS LYKKE. Really? Well now—[*Aside.*] Does she take me for a fool or
is there some misunderstanding? I mustn't let them notice anything.

LADY INGER. And I won't hide from you that he has no great faith in
your support.

NILS LYKKE. He hasn't?

LADY INGER. You can scarcely wonder—since you know who he is.

NILS LYKKE. Who he is? Yes, indeed.... [*Aside.*] The devil I do.

SKAKTAVL [*to* NILS LYKKE]. But since it was Peter Kanzler who summoned us both to this meeting ...

NILS LYKKE [*aside*]. Peter Kanzler? What can he mean?

SKAKTAVL. In short—I prefer not to worry my head about it.

NILS LYKKE. No, quite right. We certainly mustn't do that.

SKAKTAVL. I prefer to come straight to the point. So tell me your
errand here.

NILS LYKKE. Certainly. I was just about to.

SKAKTAVL. Peter Kanzler mentioned something about papers which . . .

NILS LYKKE. The papers? Oh, yes!

SKAKTAVL. Have you got them on you then?

NILS LYKKE. Of course! [*Aside, pretending to look for them.*] What the devil shall I think up? It might be best to confess there's been a misunderstanding. No, I may be able to discover something. [*Aloud.*] Ah, I see Lady Inger is having dinner served. We could discuss our business at table.

SKAKTAVL. Very well, as you will.

[*The servants have meanwhile laid the table and lit the lamps in the Great Hall.*]

NILS LYKKE [*aside*]. That'll give me time to find out the lie of the land. [*Aloud.*] And meanwhile we might learn what part Lady Inger intends to play in our scheme.

LADY INGER. I? None!

NILS LYKKE *and* SKAKTAVL. None?

LADY INGER. Can you wonder, gentlemen, that I dare not stake all by joining in your game? Particularly as neither of my allies dare trust me fully.

NILS LYKKE. That reproach does not apply to me. I trust you blindly. I beg you to be assured of that.

SKAKTAVL. Who would dare rely on you if not your countrymen?

LADY INGER. Indeed, such confidence gladdens me! [*She goes to a cupboard at the back and fills two goblets with wine.*]

NILS LYKKE [*aside*]. Damn, is she going to back out? If she falls in with the rebels she's in our power.

LADY INGER [*hands each of them a goblet*]. And since that is so I offer you this cup of welcome to Østeraad. Drink, gentlemen, drink up! [*She looks at them in turn when they have drunk and says gravely:*] But now I must tell you that one goblet contained a welcome for my ally, the other death for my enemy!

NILS LYKKE [*throws down his goblet*]. Ah, I've been poisoned!

SKAKTAVL [*at the same time, clutching his sword*]. Death and damnation! Have you murdered me?

LADY INGER [*to* SKAKTAVL, *laughing and pointing to* NILS LYKKE]. That is Denmark's trust in Inger Gyldenløve! [*To* NILS LYKKE, *pointing to* SKAKTAVL.] And likewise my countrymen's faith in me! [*To both of them.*] Yet you expect me to place myself in your power? Gently, my lords, gently! Inger Gyldenløve still has all her wits about her!

SCENE EIGHT

[*As before.* ELINE *enters from the left.*]

ELINE. I heard a noise and the sound of swords—what is happening?

LADY INGER [*to* NILS LYKKE]. My daughter Eline!

NILS LYKKE [*aside*]. Eline? That wasn't how I imagined her!

[ELINE *notices* NILS LYKKE *and stops in surprise, looking at him.*]

LADY INGER [*to* ELINE]. My child, this knight is . . .

ELINE [*still staring at him*]. No need—I see who it is; it is Nils Lykke.

NILS LYKKE [*softly, to* LADY INGER]. What? Does she know me? Can Lucia . . . ? Can she know . . . ?

LADY INGER. Quiet! She knows nothing!

ELINE [*aside*]. I knew it; Nils Lykke just had to look like that!

NILS LYKKE [*to* ELINE]. Well, you have guessed correctly, and since I am, as it were, known to you, you will not deny me the bunch of flowers you are wearing on your bosom; as long as it is fresh and fragrant I shall have in it a picture of yourself.

ELINE [*proudly, but still staring at him*]. I am sorry, Sir Nils. It was picked from my own garden and no flower grows there for you!

NILS LYKKE [*offering her his own bunch of flowers*]. Ah, then I'm sure you won't disdain this humble present—the first flowers I found when I set foot in Østeraad. Mark my words, my dear young lady, were I to offer you a gift fully worthy of you, it would need to be a princely crown!

ELINE [*who has unthinkingly taken the flowers*]. And even if you held out to me the royal crown of Denmark . . . rather than share it with you I would crush it in my hands and hurl the pieces at your feet! [*She throws the flowers at his feet and goes into the Great Hall.*]

SKAKTAVL [*to himself*]. Bold as Inger Gyldenløve at Knut Alfson's bier!

LADY INGER [*softly, after looking at* ELINE *and* NILS LYKKE *in turn*]. The wolf can be tamed! We have to forge the chain.

NILS LYKKE [*picking up the flowers and gazing in rapture after* ELINE]. My God, how proud and beautiful she is!

ACT THREE

The Great Hall. A high arched window in the background. A smaller one in the foreground, left. Several doors on each side. The ceiling is supported by massive wooden pillars, which, like the walls, are hung with all kinds of weapons. Portraits of knights and ladies hang all round the hall. A large lamp hanging from the ceiling is lit. Front right, an old-fashioned carved seat of honour. In the centre of the hall a table with the remains of dinner.

SCENE ONE

ELINE [*enters slowly and dreamily from the left. Her movements show how she is reliving in her thoughts the scene in the previous Act. Finally she makes a violent gesture as if throwing down the bunch of flowers, and then says in a low voice*]: And then he gathered up the fragments of the Danish crown—the flowers, that is—and . . . [*After a pause.*] . . . 'My God, how proud and beautiful she is!' Had he whispered those words in the most secluded spot, a thousand miles from Østeraad, I would still have heard them! How I hate him! How I have always hated him, this Nils Lykke! I have heard his name since I was a child of ten. 'There is no man like him,' they said, 'he thinks of woman simply as a toy, and discards her when she has ceased to amuse him.' And it was to him my mother wanted to offer me, to him she thought to say: 'Make my daughter your wife, and I will give you property and gold in return.' . . . How I hate him! They say that Nils Lykke is different from other men; it is not true; there is nothing unusual about him; they are many, many like him! When Bjørn used to tell me stories, all the heroes looked like Nils Lykke. When I sat here all alone in the Great Hall and dreamed out my stories, and my knights came and went, they were all like Nils Lykke! How strange and how good it feels to hate! I never fully realized that until I stood face to face with him tonight. No, not even for a thousand years of life would I give the moments I have lived since I saw him! . . . 'My God, how . . .' [*She goes slowly to the back, opens the window, and looks out.*]

[ELINE. NILS LYKKE *enters from the right, still wearing the flowers on his chest.*]

NILS LYKKE [*to himself*]. 'Sleep well at Østeraad, Sir Nils', Lady Inger said as she rose from table and left me to myself. Sleep well—yes, it is easily said, but outside—sky and sea in tumult, in the burial vault below a young creature on her bier, the future of two kingdoms in my hand, and on my chest a withered bunch of flowers which a woman hurled at my feet. Indeed, I fear sleep will take its time. [*He notices* ELINE, *who leaves the window and starts to go out, left.*] There she is. She has a thoughtful look in those proud eyes. Ah, if I dared . . . [*Aloud.*] Miss Eline!

ELINE [*stopping at the door*]. What do you want? Why are you pursuing me?

NILS LYKKE. You are wrong. I am not pursuing you. It is I who am pursued.

ELINE. You are?

NILS LYKKE. By a multitude of thoughts. So sleep is like you—it eludes me!

ELINE. If you go to the window you will find compensation—a stormy sea. . . .

NILS LYKKE [*smiling*]. A stormy sea? I can find that in you as well.

ELINE. In me?

NILS LYKKE. Our first meeting has convinced me of it.

ELINE. And do you complain?

NILS LYKKE. No, not at all, but I would like to see you in a more gentle mood.

ELINE [*proudly*]. Do you think you will?

NILS LYKKE. I am sure of it, because I have welcome news for you.

ELINE. Which is?

NILS LYKKE. Farewell!

ELINE [*coming nearer*]. Farewell! You are leaving Østeraad?

NILS LYKKE. Tonight!

ELINE [*seems to hesitate for a moment, then says coldly*]: Then fare you well, Sir Nils! [*She bows and is about to go.*]

NILS LYKKE. Eline Gyldenløve! I have no right to detain you, but it would be impolite to refuse to hear what I have to tell you.

ELINE. I am listening, Sir Nils!

NILS LYKKE. I know you hate me!

ELINE. Your perspicacity is unimpaired, I observe!

NILS LYKKE. But I also know that I have fully merited your hatred. The words with which I referred to you in my letter to Lady Inger were ill-chosen and offensive.

ELINE. Quite possibly. I have not read them.

NILS LYKKE. But at least the gist is not unknown to you. I know your mother has not kept you in ignorance of the matter. You know that I praised the good fortune of the man who was chosen to be Lady Inger's son-in-law. You know the hope I cherished . . .

ELINE. If that is what you wish to speak of, Sir Nils . . .

NILS LYKKE. I wish to speak of it solely to excuse my conduct, for no other reason, I swear. If my reputation, as I have reason to suppose, reached you before I came in person to Østeraad, you must know enough about my life not to wonder that in such matters I proceed somewhat boldly. I have known many women, Eline Gyldenløve, but none has given me cause to complain of hardness of heart. Under the circumstances a man grows somewhat smug, you know; he gets out of the way of being diplomatic. . . .

ELINE. I don't know what Danish women are like, but you had no reason to think we are made of the same stuff.

NILS LYKKE [*smiling*]. If you will pardon me, Miss Eline, I did have reason.

ELINE. Have you been in Norway before, then?

NILS LYKKE [*a little embarrassed*]. In Norway? No, indeed not, but nevertheless . . .

ELINE. Well, no matter. You are wrong, by the way, if you think it was your letter which stirred up bitterness and hatred towards you in my heart. My reasons go back further.

NILS LYKKE [*anxiously*]. Go back further? What do you mean?

ELINE. It is as you said—your reputation preceded you to Østeraad, as it did over the whole country, and when your name was mentioned it was always in conjunction with some woman you had charmed and then abandoned. I despised those weak-minded creatures who let themselves be taken in by your smooth talk. But I am proud, Nils Lykke, and it offended me to the bottom of my soul to know that my sex was so bitterly scorned by a man whose praises echoed on all lips. That was when my hatred towards you was conceived; you were constantly in my thoughts and I felt a burning desire to meet you face to face, so that you should know there are women on whom your subtle talk is wasted . . . should you be thinking of trying it.

NILS LYKKE. You judge me unfairly, if you judge from hearsay. There may be some truth in all you have heard, but you do not know the underlying causes. I began my round of pleasure as a young gentleman of seventeen; I have lived another fifteen years since then. I have picked many a flower for myself, but beautiful women have given me even more of their own accord. You are the first to throw them scornfully at my feet. Don't think I am complaining. On the contrary, I respect you for it as I have never yet respected any woman. What I do deplore is that fate did not lead me to you sooner. [*With growing ardour.*] Eline Gyldenløve, your mother has told me about you—while life pursued its hectic course far away from here you went your own quiet way in the solitude of Østeraad, living in your world of make-believe and dreams. Therefore you will understand what I have to tell you. Well, I too lived the same sort of life as a boy. My most pleasant memories are of those days. I thought that when I went out into the great wide world I would meet a fine and noble woman whose love would give me strength and point the way to some splendid goal. [*With a change of tone.*] I was deceived, Eline Gyldenløve. The aspirations of youth are a shameless fraud, as false as the Nils Lykke rumour paints. Even before I had grown to manhood I had learnt thoroughly to despise your frivolous sex and to consider them all as creatures who merely deserved to be ensnared and abandoned, which, in all honesty, I have done. [*More vehemently.*] Was it my own fault then? Why were the others not like you? I know that the fate of your country weighs heavily on your mind. You know my part in these affairs; . . . they say that Nils Lykke is as faithless as the seas. That may well be, but if he is, it is woman who has taught him. Had I found sooner what I sought, had I met sooner a woman proud, noble, and high-minded like you, my course would have been different indeed. Then I would have followed my youthful urge to fight with better weapons. Maybe at this moment I would have been standing at your side as the spokesman of a noble people. For a woman is the greatest power in this world, and only through her can a man fully realize his potentialities.

ELINE [*to herself*]. Can it be as he says? No, there is falsehood in his eye and a lie on his lips. And yet no song sounded sweeter to me than his words.

NILS LYKKE [*giving her a searching glance*]. How often you will have sat here alone at Østeraad with all your different thoughts and have felt a tightness in your breast; and roof and walls seemed to shrink and crush your soul, and you have longed to be outside, have wished to fly far away, and knew not where. How often you will have walked alone by the fjord, mistress of a whole world in your dreams, a world as fair and rich as only thoughts can make it—but it was not enough for you. . . . Far out a fine sailing ship has glided past, with knights and ladies, with songs and melodies on strings; the vague rumour of great events has reached your ears—and you have felt a longing in your breast, an irrepressible yearning to know what lies beyond the sea and the distant mountains. But you have not understood your need; at times you believed it was the fate of your native land which filled you with all these restless thoughts. You deceived yourself: a girl of seventeen has other things to brood on. Eline Gyldenløve, have you never imagined mysterious forces in nature? Has it never struck you that there is a strong and inexplicable power which binds men's destinies together? When you dreamed of the colourful life out in the wide world, when you dreamed of tournaments and festive gaiety, did you never see in your dreams a knight standing amid the life and merriment with a smile on his lips and bitterness in his heart—a knight who once had dreamed a dream as lovely as yours, of a fine and noble woman, whom he sought in vain midst those around him?

ELINE. Who are you who have this power to clothe my most secret thoughts in words; who can teach me what I have borne in my inmost heart, yet did not know until I heard you speak? How do you know. . . ?

NILS LYKKE. What I have told you I read in your eyes.

ELINE. No man has spoken to me like you. I have only dimly understood and yet—all, all seems changed since. . . . Now at last I see why they said Nils Lykke is different from the rest.

NILS LYKKE. If there is one thing in this world which can drive a man insane it is brooding on what might have been if only *this* had happened or *that* had happened. If our paths had met while my tree of life was fresh and green perhaps at this moment you would have been. . . . But forgive me, my dear young lady, our little talk has made me forget how things stand between us. It was as though a secret voice had told me from the outset that with you I could talk frankly, without flattery and pretence.

ELINE. You can!

NILS LYKKE. There, and this frankness may already have partly reconciled us. Yes, I am even bold enough to hope that there may yet be a time when you will think of that knight who came to Østeraad without hatred and bitterness in your soul. No, do not misunderstand me, I do not mean at once, but at some later time. And to make it easier for you—as I have begun to talk openly and candidly —let me say . . .

ELINE. Sir Nils!

NILS LYKKE [*smiling*]. Ah, I see that my letter still frightens you; but you can set your mind completely at rest. I would give anything not to have written it, because—I know you will not be unduly distressed, so I may as well be frank—I am not in love with you and never shall be. You may rest assured then, as I said; I shall never try —but what is wrong with you?

ELINE. With me? Nothing! Nothing at all! . . . Tell me just one thing. What do you want those flowers for?

NILS LYKKE. These? Aren't they the gauntlet which outraged womankind through you has thrown down at Nils Lykke's feet? When I sit

once more among the lovely ladies at the Danish Court, when the
strings fall silent and the hall is hushed, I will take out my flowers
and tell a tale of the young woman who sits alone in a gloomy
timbered hall in the far-off north. [*He breaks off and bows respectfully.*]
But I fear I detain the noble daughter of the house too long. We
shall not meet again: before daybreak I shall be gone. So I bid you
farewell.

ELINE. Farewell, Sir Nils!

NILS LYKKE. Now you are deep in thought again, Eline Gyldenløve! Is
the fate of your country still preying on your mind?

ELINE [*shaking her head and staring absently in front of her*]. My country? I
am not thinking of my country!

NILS LYKKE. Then you are worrying about the strife and misery of
the times.

ELINE. The times? I had forgotten them. . . . Didn't you say you were
going to Denmark?

NILS LYKKE. Yes, to Denmark!

ELINE. Can I see from here where Denmark lies?

NILS LYKKE [*pointing to the left window*]. Yes, from this window. Denmark lies over there to the south.

ELINE. And is it far from here—more than a hundred miles?

NILS LYKKE. Much more. The sea lies between Denmark and you.

ELINE [*half to herself*]. The sea? Thought has wings like gulls; no sea can
stay its flight. [*She goes out, left.*]

SCENE THREE

[NILS LYKKE, *alone.*]

NILS LYKKE. If I were prepared to sacrifice a couple of days, or even one,
she would be in my power like all the rest. There is rare stuff in that
young woman though, I must say. She is proud. Ought I really to go
ahead and . . . ? No, sooner humiliate her. A woman's sweetest
victory lies in being vanquished and that I begrudge her. [*After a
pause.*] I do believe she has set my blood on fire. She has struck

deeper roots in my soul than I would now have thought possible. No matter, I will pluck her up by the roots. It is high time I thought of extricating myself from the mess I've landed myself in. [*He sits in a chair, right.*] I can hardly get the situation in proper perspective. Let me see—both Skaktavl and Lady Inger seem blind to the mistrust they may incur when it is rumoured that I am in league with them. Or can Lady Inger in fact have grasped my intentions? Can she have realized that my promises were simply calculated to draw Nils Sture out of his hiding-place? [*Jumping up.*] Damn! What shall I do in that case? Is it in fact I who have been fooled? Most probably Count Sture is not at Østeraad at all. Perhaps the rumour of his flight was just a blind and he is sitting at this moment safe and sound among his friends—while I . . . [*He paces up and down in great agitation.*] And to think I was so sure of myself. If I had Count Sture here he would be in custody within the hour, the whole plot would be crushed and I, in consequence, released from my promise; whereas now. . . . Sooner or later Lady Inger will see through my plans. Naturally she won't hush things up and then I'll be the laughing-stock of the whole country. Instead of leading Lady Inger into the trap I've been of the greatest service to her cause, her popularity will rise, and—ah, I could almost sell my soul to any devil willing to help me get my claws into Count Sture. What the . . . ! [*The window at the back is thrust open.* NILS STENSSON *appears outside.*]

SCENE FOUR

[NILS LYKKE. NILS STENSSON.]

STENSSON [*jumping down on to the floor*]. Well, here I am at last!

NILS LYKKE [*aside*]. What does this mean?

STENSSON. God be with you, sir!

NILS LYKKE. Thank you, sir! You have chosen a strange way to come in, incidentally.

STENSSON. Well, what the devil could I do? The gate was locked; the people in this place must have hibernated or something.

NILS LYKKE. Thank God! One sleeps best on a clear conscience, you know.

STENSSON. That must be so. For all my hammering and banging . . .

NILS LYKKE. You still didn't get in?

STENSSON. Dead right! So I said to myself: as you must get into Østeraad, though it means going through fire and water, you may just as well jump in through the window.

NILS LYKKE [*aside*]. Ah, the devil—I've just thought of something—supposing it's . . . [*Aloud.*] So it's vitally important for you to reach Østeraad tonight?

STENSSON. Important? I'd say it is. I don't like to keep people waiting, I can tell you.

NILS LYKKE [*aside*]. I bet my life it's Nils Sture. [*Aloud.*] So Lady Inger is expecting you?

STENSSON. Lady Inger? Well, I can't exactly say about that, but there might be someone else here. . . . [*Aside.*] I shouldn't wonder if he's the one.

NILS LYKKE [*aside*]. Quite right. This is our man!

STENSSON. I say, do you belong here?

NILS LYKKE. Me? Yes, inasmuch as I have been Lady Inger's guest this evening.

STENSSON [*aside*]. Aha, it all fits. But Peter Kanzler told me to be smart, so I'll let him begin.

NILS LYKKE [*aside*]. This is a matter of feeling one's way. If he knows only some of the facts, like Skaktavl, I might be able to pump something out of him. [*Aloud.*] I trust you will soon be able to meet the lady of the house—so far as I know she has not gone to bed yet. But while you are waiting you can take a seat and rest awhile. Look, here is a bottle of wine left over, and you'll probably find something to eat. Well, help yourself. You'll be needing to fortify yourself.

STENSSON. You are right, sir! That wouldn't be a bad idea. [*He sits down at table and eats and drinks during what follows.*] You live like lords here. When you've been sleeping out in the wet like me, and living on bread and water for four or five days . . .

NILS LYKKE [*looks at him with a smile*]. Yes, that must be hard when one is used to sitting at high-table in a count's castle.

STENSSON [*aside*]. Count's castle? What does he mean by that?

NILS LYKKE. But now you can have a good rest at Østeraad for as long as you like.

STENSSON [*cheerfully*]. I say, can I really? Then I don't have to be off again so soon?

NILS LYKKE. Well, I don't know. That's for you to say.

STENSSON [*aside*]. Oh, the devil, that wasn't very smart of me. [*Aloud.*] Er, actually that's not quite decided. For my part I wouldn't mind staying here a bit, but . . .

NILS LYKKE. But you are not entirely your own master. There are other obligations, other things to consider. . . .

STENSSON. Yes, that's just the trouble. If it were left to me I would at least relax here at Østeraad for the winter. When you've spent most of your time roughing it as a soldier, like me. . . . [*Pours out some wine and drinks.*] Your health, sir!

NILS LYKKE [*aside*]. Roughing it! The braggart! I know full well he was at home being coddled by his mother.

STENSSON. Apart from that I have been dying to meet Lady Inger for a long time—she has such a great reputation. She's a splendid woman, don't you think? The only thing I can't approve of is that she's so damned reluctant to get going.

NILS LYKKE. Get going?

STENSSON. Yes, you understand; I mean she is so reluctant to take a hand in driving the foreigners out of the country.

NILS LYKKE. Yes, true enough. But now you must do what you can and it will be all right.

STENSSON. Me? Why, God help me; a lot of use it would be if I . . .

NILS LYKKE. But it's strange that you should visit her if you have no great hopes.

STENSSON [*aside*]. What an odd conversation. [*Aloud.*] I say, do you know Lady Inger?

NILS LYKKE. Naturally, since I am her guest . . .

STENSSON. Yes, but that doesn't mean you know her. I'm her guest too and have never so much as seen her shadow.

NILS LYKKE. But you were able to speak of...

STENSSON. Common gossip—that's fair enough. Besides, I so often heard from Peter Kanzler.... [*He stops suddenly and begins eating with gusto.*]

NILS LYKKE. You were going to say something.

STENSSON [*eating*]. I was? Oh no, it doesn't matter. [NILS LYKKE *laughs.*] What are you laughing at, sir?

NILS LYKKE. At nothing, sir!

STENSSON [*drinks*]. It's a superb wine you keep in this place.

NILS LYKKE. Listen, isn't it time to throw off the mask?

STENSSON. The mask? Well, you must do as you think fit. [*Aside.*] Now for it.

NILS LYKKE. Then stop pretending. You are known, Count Sture!

STENSSON [*aside*]. Ha! ha! ha! Now he thinks I'm a count. [*Aloud, as he rises from the table.*] You are mistaken, sir. I am not Count Sture.

NILS LYKKE. Really? Who are you then?

STENSSON. Nils Stensson's the name!

NILS LYKKE [*smiling*]. But you are not Sten Sture's son? The name fits at any rate.

STENSSON. Quite true, but God knows what right I have to it. I never knew my father; my mother was a poor country woman who was robbed and killed in one of the old feuds. Peter Kanzler happened to be on the spot. He took charge of me, brought me up, and taught me to be a soldier. As you know he has been hunted by King Gustav for many years and I've been following him faithfully around.

NILS LYKKE [*aside*]. He's craftier than I expected. [*Aloud.*] Well then, you are not Nils Sture, but you *have* come from Sweden. Peter Kanzler has sent you here to find a stranger, who...

STENSSON [*smiling*]. Who has already been found.

NILS LYKKE [*somewhat uncertainly*]. And whom you don't know?

WI

STENSSON. As little as you know me, because I swear by God himself I am not Count Sture.

NILS LYKKE. Seriously, sir?

STENSSON. As sure as I am alive! Why should I deny it if it were true?

NILS LYKKE. But where is Count Sture then?

STENSSON [*whispering*]. Ah, that's the secret.

NILS LYKKE [*whispering*]. Which you know the answer to, don't you?

STENSSON [*nodding*]. And which I am to tell you.

NILS LYKKE. Me? Well, where he is then? [STENSSON *points upwards.*] Up there! Lady Inger has got him hidden in the loft?

STENSSON. No, indeed not. You misunderstand me. [*He looks round cautiously.*] Nils Sture is in heaven!

NILS LYKKE. Dead? Where?

STENSSON. At his mother's castle, three weeks ago.

NILS LYKKE. Ah, you are deceiving me. He crossed the frontier into Norway five or six days ago.

STENSSON. Oh, that was me.

NILS LYKKE. But shortly before that the Count had appeared in Dalecarlia. The people, who were already restless, revolted outright and elected him king.

STENSSON. Ha! ha! ha! That was me too!

NILS LYKKE. You?

STENSSON. I'll tell you how it all happened. One day Peter Kanzler summoned me and told me that big things were brewing. He ordered me to go as quickly as I could to Østeraad, where I was to meet a stranger. . . .

NILS LYKKE. Correct, that's me!

STENSSON. From him I was to receive further instructions, and also I was to tell him that the Count had died suddenly, but that no one knew except his mother, the Countess, along with Peter Kanzler and a few old retainers at the Stures' castle.

NILS LYKKE. I understand. The Count held things together. If the news of his death got about, the peasants' party would disintegrate and the whole thing would come to nothing.

STENSSON. Maybe. I don't understand that sort of thing.

NILS LYKKE. But why did you think of passing yourself off as the Count?

STENSSON. Why did I think of it? Hm, how should I know? I've thought up some stupid things in my time. And it wasn't my idea, by the way, because everywhere I went in Dalecarlia the people crowded round and hailed me as Count Sture. However much I denied it it didn't help. Count Sture had been there two years before, they said, and the merest child knew who I was. Well, here goes, I thought, you'll never be a count again in this life. You might as well see what it's like for once.

NILS LYKKE. Yes, and what else did you do?

STENSSON. Me? I wined and dined and lived in style. It was just a pity that I had to leave so soon. But when I set off . . . ha! ha! ha! . . . I I promised them I would soon be back with three or four thousand men, God knows how many, and then things would really get started.

NILS LYKKE. And it never occurred to you that you were acting rashly?

STENSSON. Yes, it did, afterwards; but then, of course, it was too late.

NILS LYKKE. I am sorry for you, my young friend, but you'll soon feel the effects of your folly. You are a wanted man. The King's men are after you.

STENSSON [*laughing*]. After me? Ha! ha! ha! Why, that's a good one! And when they come and think they've got hold of Count Sture. . . . Ha! ha! ha!

NILS LYKKE [*gravely*]. That's the end of you.

STENSSON. Of me? Why, I'm not Count Sture.

NILS LYKKE. But you have called the people to arms, you have made seditious promises, and fomented civil strife.

STENSSON. Oh, but it was only a joke.

NILS LYKKE. King Gustav will view the matter differently.

STENSSON. Yes, indeed, there's something in what you say. I'd never have thought of it if you hadn't. . . . Ah well, there's time to think of that later. You will take care of me. Besides, the Swedes are not on my heels yet.

NILS LYKKE. But what else have you to tell me?

STENSSON. Me? Nothing! Once I've given you the packet.

NILS LYKKE [*without thinking*]. The packet?

STENSSON. Certainly, you know . . .

NILS LYKKE [*recovering*]. Ah yes, that's right. The papers from Peter Kanzler.

STENSSON. Of course! Here they are. [*He hands him a packet which he has taken from a breast pocket*].

NILS LYKKE [*aside*]. Letters and papers for Olaf Skaktavl. [*Aloud.*] They are open. So you know what is in them?

STENSSON. No, I'm not fond of reading. I have my reasons.

NILS LYKKE. And what are they?

STENSSON. Oh, in the first place, I've never learnt.

NILS LYKKE. Well, that's a good enough reason. [*He looks through the papers.*] Aha, more than enough information to find out what's brewing. This little packet done up with a silk thread. . . . [*He examines the address.*] Also to Olaf Skaktavl. Should I . . . ? I already know what I need to know, sure enough, but all the same . . . since I've spent the whole evening pretending to be the owner of all this I suppose I may. . . . [*He opens the packet and continues speaking as he glances through the contents.*] From Peter Kanzler. I might have guessed. He is hard pressed, he says, because . . . yes, quite right, here it is: young Count Sture has been gathered to his fathers just when the revolt was due to break out. 'But all may yet be remedied.' What now! [*He reads on to himself in astonishment.*] 'I must tell you then, Olaf Skaktavl, that the bearer of this letter is a son of . . .' Good heavens, am I seeing things? Yes, my God, that's what it says! [*With a glance at* NILS STENSSON.] It says he's . . . ah, if that were so. [*He reads on.*] 'I have brought him up since he was a year old, but to this day I have constantly declined to give him back, thinking I would have in him an effective hostage guaranteeing Lady Inger's loyalty to us and to our friends; but he has been of little use in that. . . . You will wonder perhaps that I did not tell you this secret when you were with me here in Sweden, but if that is so I frankly confess that I was afraid you would hold him for the same reason as I. However, now you have met Lady Inger and presumably have confirmed her reluctance to concern herself with our affairs, you will see that it would be wisest to give her back what is hers as soon as may be. Then it might well happen that gratitude—that is now our only hope.' Aha, what a letter! It's worth its weight in gold!

STENSSON [*aside*]. I can see I've brought him important news all right. Yes, Peter Kanzler has many irons in the fire, they say.

NILS LYKKE [*aside*]. What is it to be? I've a thousand schemes running round blindfold in my head, all tumbling over each other. [*Pondering.*] If I—no, where would that lead? But if—if I—ah, yes, that would be an idea! If it comes off I shall be out of my quandary and I'll be sure of Lady Inger. Indeed, I'll risk it. [*Aloud.*] A word, my young friend!

STENSSON [*approaching*]. Well, you look as though the game is going well.

NILS LYKKE. Yes, I'll say it is. Nothing but court cards in my hand, queens and jacks and . . .

STENSSON. But what about me who brought you all this good news? Is there nothing more for me to do?

NILS LYKKE. You? Yes, I'll say there is. You are part of the game. You are the king, and king of trumps, what's more.

STENSSON. I am? Oh yes, now I understand. You are thinking of the elevation you promised me.

NILS LYKKE. Elevation?

STENSSON. You know, if King Gustav's crowd laid hands on me you prophesied that . . . [*He goes through the motions of hanging.*]

NILS LYKKE. True enough, but don't let that worry you any more. It's now up to you whether within a month you will be wearing a hempen noose or a gold chain round your neck.

STENSSON. A gold chain? And it's up to me? [NILS LYKKE *nods*.] Then I'm damned if there are two ways about it. Just tell me what I have to do.

NILS LYKKE. I will, but first, you must take a solemn oath that no living soul in the whole wide world shall know what I am going to confide to you.

STENSSON. Is that all? You can have ten oaths, if you like.

NILS LYKKE [*severely*]. Be serious, sir! I am not joking!

STENSSON [*somewhat abashed*]. All right then, I'll be serious!

NILS LYKKE. In Dalecarlia you called yourself a count's son, didn't you?

STENSSON. Oh, you're not going to lecture me about that again? . . . I've made an honourable confession.

NILS LYKKE. You don't understand. What you said on that occasion was the truth!

STENSSON. The truth? What are you getting at now? But tell me . . .

NILS LYKKE. Your oath first, the most sacred and binding oath you know.

STENSSON. Good, you shall have it. There's a picture of the Virgin Mary on the wall . . .

NILS LYKKE [*shrugs his shoulders*]. The Virgin Mary has been on the decline of late. Haven't you heard what the monk of Wittenberg is claiming?

STENSSON. Fie, why do you take notice of him? Peter Kanzler says he's a heretic.

NILS LYKKE. Well, we won't argue about that. [*Aside.*] Indeed, one oath is as good as another to me, but I must be sure of him. These are bad times we are living in. The beloved saints are no longer reliable. [*With a glance at* NILS STENSSON, *as he looks round the room.*] But damn it, he's scarcely twenty! People of that age usually think there is something sacred in this world. Let me see, isn't there a. . . . [*He notices a picture hanging on one of the pillars.*] Aha, there we are. I couldn't do better. [*Aloud.*] Then swear to keep silent until I myself loose your tongue, silent as truly as you hope for eternal salvation for yourself and for the man whose picture hangs there.

STENSSON [*approaching the picture*]. I swear! So help me God. [*He shrinks back in surprise.*] Christ in heaven!

NILS LYKKE. What now?

STENSSON. This picture! Why it's me!

NILS LYKKE. It is old Sten Sture, as he was in his youthful days.

STENSSON. Sten Sture! . . . And the likeness and . . . Didn't you say I was speaking the truth when I called myself a count's son?

NILS LYKKE. I did!

STENSSON. Ah, I've got it, I've got it! I am . . .

NILS LYKKE. You are his son, the last of Sten Sture's line.

STENSSON [*with silent astonishment*]. Me—Sten Sture's son!

NILS LYKKE. On your mother's side too you are of high birth. Peter Kanzler lied when he told you a poor country woman had entrusted you to him.

STENSSON. Strange! How strange! Then I can believe . . . ?

NILS LYKKE. You can believe anything I tell you, but bear in mind that all this will be the ruin of you if you forget what you have sworn by your father's salvation.

STENSSON. Forget? Oh no, you may be sure I won't. But tell me, who are you that I've given my word to?

NILS LYKKE. Nils Lykke is my name!

STENSSON [*astonished*]. Nils Lykke? The Danish statesman?

NILS LYKKE. Precisely.

STENSSON. And you were to . . . ? That's strange! How do you come . . . ?

NILS LYKKE [*interrupting*]. . . . to receive messages from Peter Kanzler? That surprises you, I shouldn't wonder.

STENSSON. Yes, I don't deny it. He's always mentioned you as our bitterest enemy.

NILS LYKKE. And therefore you mistrust me?

STENSSON. No, not exactly, but—well, I'm damned if I'm going to bother my head about it!

NILS LYKKE. You are right. Do things your own way and you're as sure of the rope as you are of the Count's title and the gold chain if you rely on me.

STENSSON. Which I will, implicitly. Here's my hand upon it. You do the thinking for me as long as necessary. When it's a matter of fighting I can take care of myself.

NILS LYKKE. Good. If you come into this room with me you shall learn the whole situation and what you have to do. [*He goes out, right.*]

STENSSON [*with a glance at the picture*]. Me, Sten Sture's son! Strange! If only I'm not dreaming. [*He follows* NILS LYKKE.]

ACT FOUR

The Great Hall. The dining table has been taken out. Smaller tables are standing one on each side in the foreground.

SCENE ONE

[LADY INGER *with some papers in her hand.* OLAF SKAKTAVL *and* BJØRN *enter from the left. The latter is carrying a branched candlestick which he places on the table.*]

LADY INGER [*to* BJØRN]. And you are sure my daughter was talking to Sir Nils here in the hall?

BJØRN. Quite sure. I met her coming out into the corridor.

LADY INGER. And she looked upset, you said?

BJØRN. She looked quite pale and distracted. I asked her if she was unwell, but instead of answering she said: Go and tell my mother that Sir Nils is leaving before daybreak. If she has any letters or messages for him ask her not to delay him. I'm inclined to think he's been at Østeraad too long already.

LADY INGER. And where is Sir Nils?

BJØRN. In his room, I think, across the corridor.

LADY INGER. Good. I have here the things I want to give him. Go and tell him that I am waiting for him here in the hall.

[BJØRN *goes out, right.*]

SCENE TWO
[LADY INGER. OLAF SKAKTAVL.]

SKAKTAVL. You know what, Lady Inger? I may be as blind as a bat in such matters, but it does seem to me that . . .

LADY INGER. Well?

SKAKTAVL. That Nils Lykke has taken a fancy to your daughter.

LADY INGER. Then you are not so blind after all, for unless I am very much mistaken you are right. Don't you remember at dinner how eagerly he listened to every little thing I said about Eline?

SKAKTAVL. He forgot to eat and drink.

LADY INGER. And our secret business as well.

SKAKTAVL. Yes, and what's more, the papers from Peter Kanzler he was supposed to be bringing.

LADY INGER. And from all this you conclude . . .

SKAKTAVL. From all this I conclude chiefly, as you know Nils Lykke and his reputation, particularly where women are concerned . . .

LADY INGER. . . . . that I would be glad to see him the other side of the gate?

SKAKTAVL. Yes, and today rather than tomorrow.

LADY INGER [*smiling*]. No, precisely the opposite, Olaf Skaktavl!

SKAKTAVL. What do you mean?

LADY INGER. If things are as we both think, he mustn't leave Østeraad just yet on any account.

SKAKTAVL. Going your wicked ways again, Lady Inger? Are you thinking up yet another scheme which will increase your power but will harm and stifle the cause you are called on to defend?

LADY INGER. Once again your shortsightedness makes you unfair to me. If you'll let me speak I will explain all. Perhaps you believe I mean to choose Nils Lykke as my son-in-law? If such were my intention why should I have refused to take part in the plots now being concocted in Sweden and which Nils Lykke and the entire Danish faction seem willing to support?

SKAKTAVL. But if that's not your intention, what are you thinking of doing then?

LADY INGER. I'll explain briefly. In the letter telling me he was coming to Østeraad Nils Lykke hinted at something of what you have just mentioned. Whether it was really in earnest I can't rightly say, but there is at any rate reason to suppose so; and to be honest with you, I'll admit frankly that I really did consider the proposal.

SKAKTAVL. There, you see?

LADY INGER. Wait a moment! Allying Nils Lykke to my family would be the first step towards a reconciliation of the conflicting parties in this country.

SKAKTAVL. I should have thought your daughter Merete's marriage to Vincents Lunge might have shown you what such alliances lead to. They give the Danes a firmer foothold in the country and help them to rob us of the last remnants of our freedom.

LADY INGER. Quite true, I didn't overlook that either. But at the same time I had all kinds of other thoughts running through my mind. I was thinking of something which I can't confide to you and which does not affect our common concern, only me personally. I spoke to Eline of the suggestion Nils Lykke had hinted at, though without saying who it came from. But she just answered with bitterness and scorn. And I respect her for it. Because to choose a Dane as my son-in-law for the second time is an expedient I will adopt only in the last resort, and we have not yet come to that, thank heaven.

SKAKTAVL. But if that's how things are why do you intend to detain him at Østeraad?

LADY INGER. Because I hate him. Nils Lykke has done me more grievous harm that anyone and I shall not rest until I have taken my revenge on him. You don't understand? Just suppose Nils Lykke took a liking to my daughter, and it all points to such a possibility, suppose that I could prevail on him to stay here awhile, and that he got to know Eline better—she is beautiful and she is clever: it might well be that he would come to me one day with true love in his heart and ask for her hand—to be able then to chase him away like a dog, to heap scorn and contempt on him—oh, I would give my last drop of blood to see the day.

SKAKTAVL. Cross your heart, Inger Gyldenløve—*is* that what you mean to do to him?

LADY INGER. That and nothing else, as sure as there is a God! You must believe that my intentions towards my countrymen are honourable. But I still haven't a free hand. I have a secret; and anyone who knows it can do me mortal harm. But it can't and mustn't go on like this. And once I am safe from that quarter you'll see whether I have forgotten what I swore at Knut Alfson's bier.

SKAKTAVL [*shakes her hand*]. Thank you for those words. I would be most reluctant to think ill of you, but as to your plan for Nils Lykke, it seems to me you are playing a risky game. What if you had miscalculated—what if your daughter—they say, you know, that no woman can resist this insinuating devil. . . .

LADY INGER. Do you think my daughter . . . ? No, you needn't be alarmed; I know her better than that. Ever since she heard his name as a child she has hated him. I think their first meeting must have reassured you fully on that account.

SKAKTAVL. Yes, but a woman's mind is shaky ground to build on; and you may well live to see the truth of my words.

LADY INGER. All right, I'll be on the alert, and if he should succeed even so in getting her on the hook I have only to whisper a couple of words in her ear and . . .

SKAKTAVL. And?

LADY INGER. She will curse him as though he were a veritable messenger of hell. Quiet, Olaf Skaktavl! Do be careful now. Here he comes.

SCENE THREE

[*As before.* NILS LYKKE *enters from the right.*]

NILS LYKKE [*aside*]. There she stands like a lofty mountain pine. But just you wait. A storm is brewing which will break you. [*Aloud.*] You sent for me, Madam?

LADY INGER. I have learned through my daughter that you are thinking of leaving us tonight.

NILS LYKKE. Yes, alas, my business at Østeraad is finished.

SKAKTAVL. Not until I have my papers.

NILS LYKKE. Quite true. I had almost forgotten the most important part of my errand. But that, of course, is the fault of our gracious hostess. She entertained her guests at table so skilfully and pleasantly. . . .

LADY INGER [*interrupting*]. That you no longer remembered what had brought you here. I am glad, because that was precisely my intention. I saw that if my guest, Nils Lykke, felt contented at Østeraad he would be sure . . .

NILS LYKKE. To do what, Madam?

LADY INGER. To forget his errand in the first place, and whatever else had gone before.

NILS LYKKE [*to* SKAKTAVL]. The papers from Peter Kanzler. You will find here complete lists of our supporters in Sweden.

SKAKTAVL. Good! [*He sits down at the table on the left, where he glances through the packet.*]

NILS LYKKE [*aside*]. I'll keep the letter to myself. [*Aloud.*] And now, as far as I know, there is no more for me to do here.

LADY INGER. Inasmuch as it was simply business which brought us together you may be right. But I am reluctant to believe that.

NILS LYKKE. You mean?

LADY INGER. I mean that it is not solely as a Danish statesman or as the ally of Peter Kanzler that Nils Lykke has visited me. Should I be wrong in imagining that even in the Royal Palace you have been told things which made you anxious to get to know the Lady of Østeraad rather better.

NILS LYKKE. Indeed . . . Lady Inger's fame is too far-flung for me not to have desired long since to see her face to face.

LADY INGER. You must see those you would know not face to face but soul to soul. Lady Inger has a shrewd head, and the Lord God has been far too bountiful to you yourself for you not to esteem the like in others. But you deceive yourself, Sir Nils! You deceive yourself if you think that an hour's small talk at dinner is enough to plumb my depths. Yes, you smile. You see I am honest or proud enough to say myself what would come better from others. Well, that proves at least that we are beginning to draw closer to each other. That is always a step towards a better understanding. Moreover, on these remote shores a guest like you is such a rare occurrence that it cannot seem unreasonable to seek to keep him as long as possible. Extend your stay here for some days then. I dare not persuade Olaf Skaktavl —he has duties calling him to Sweden—but as for you I am sure you will have organized things with such sagacity that your presence is scarcely required. Believe me, you will not find it tedious here; at least both my daughter and I will do all we can to make your stay in my house a pleasant one.

NILS LYKKE. I do not doubt that you and your daughter are well disposed towards me. Of that our first meeting has fully convinced me. When I tell you, nevertheless, that it is impossible to extend my stay at Østeraad, I am sure you will realize that my presence elsewhere is vitally necessary.

LADY INGER. So it is like that! You know, Sir Nils—if I were malicious I might think you had come to Østeraad to cross swords with me, and having lost, you found it distasteful to linger on the field among the witnesses of your defeat.

NILS LYKKE [*smiling*]. There might be good reason for you to suppose so, but in fact I still do not look upon the battle as lost.

LADY INGER. Be that as it may, if you stay with us for some days you could at any rate regain your losses. You see, it would not be distasteful for me to be defeated, since I myself am persuading my formidable adversary not to quit the field. . . . Frankly then, and without mincing matters, the point is this: your alliance with the disaffected elements in Sweden still strikes me as somewhat—somewhat fantastic. The idea which prompted you to take this step is indeed most sensible, most astute, but it stands in stark contrast to your countrymen's actions in previous years. You must not wonder therefore that my faith in your promises needs to strike firmer roots if it is to become a sturdy plant.

NILS LYKKE. In that case my stay at Østeraad would hardly get us anywhere, since I intend to make no further attempt at shaking your resolve.

LADY INGER. Then I pity you from the bottom of my heart. Yes, Sir Nils, you may trust an old woman's words, and I prophesy that you will derive little pleasure from your visit to Østeraad.

NILS LYKKE [*smiling*]. Is that your prophecy, Lady Inger?

LADY INGER. Certainly it is! What shall I say, Sir Nils? The world is such a cynical place. Within six months you will be the talk of the town. You will have malicious tongues singing their satirical songs. Men in the street will stop and stare, and say: 'Look, look, there goes Nils Lykke, the knight who went to Østeraad to trap Inger Gyldenløve and got caught in his own snare.' . . . Come, come, Sir Nils, do not be so impatient! That is not my view, but such will be the verdict of this cynical world. Yes, it's a bad thing, but true it is:

ridicule will be your reward—ridicule because your enemies out-witted you. Cunning as a fox he stole into Østeraad, they will say—and sneaked away like a dog with its tail between its legs. And another thing: don't you think that Peter Kanzler and his friends will seek to be rid of your support once it gets around that Inger Gylden-løve refuses to fight under your banner?

NILS LYKKE. You speak wisely, Madam. Hence in order not to expose myself to ridicule and not to put an end to the good understanding with our friends in Sweden, I am forced . . .

LADY INGER [*quickly*]. To extend your stay at Østeraad?

SKAKTAVL [*aside*]. Now he's going to walk into the trap.

NILS LYKKE. No, Madam! I am forced to reach agreement with you here and now.

LADY INGER. But if you should not succeed?

NILS LYKKE. I shall!

LADY INGER. You seem sure of yourself.

NILS LYKKE. What is the betting that the victory will be mine?

LADY INGER [*proudly*]. Østeraad Hall against your knee-buckles!

NILS LYKKE. Østeraad Hall is yours no longer!

LADY INGER. Nils Lykke!

SKAKTAVL [*who has meanwhile risen from the table*]. What now?

NILS LYKKE. I will not accept the wager, for in a moment you will be glad to give me Østeraad and more besides to be freed from the trap in which you yourself are caught, not I.

LADY INGER. Your pleasantry is growing somewhat amusing, Sir Nils!

NILS LYKKE. It will be even more amusing, for me, at least. You boast of having seen through me, you heap on me bitterness, scorn, and ridicule; . . . ah, you should take care not to arouse my lust for vengeance, for with two words I can have you kneeling at my feet.

LADY INGER [*laughs scornfully*]. Ha! ha! . . . [*She stops suddenly, as if seized with misgivings.*] And these two words, Nils Lykke? These two words . . .

NILS LYKKE. The secret of Sten Sture's son and yours!

LADY INGER [*with a shriek*]. Oh, my God! [*Kneeling.*] Mercy! Mercy!

SKAKTAVL [*flabbergasted*]. Lady Inger's son! . . . What did you say?

NILS LYKKE [*raises her up*]. Compose yourself and let us talk calmly.

LADY INGER [*whispering, somewhat bewildered*]. Did you hear, Olaf Skaktavl, did you hear? Or was it just a bad dream, some trick of hearing?

NILS LYKKE. You heard correctly!

LADY INGER. But where have you got him then? . . . Where? What are you going to do to him? . . . You mustn't kill him. Give him back to me! Give me my child! . . . Nils Lykke, listen to me! Take all I have, take my wealth, my gold, but give me my child, just give me back my son!

SKAKTAVL. Ah, I begin to understand . . .

LADY INGER. And this fear, this choking dread which I have borne these twenty years! . . . God! Oh God, is it right of Thee? Was it for this Thou gavest him to me, that I should endure all this pain and anguish! Ah, I know, I know—I am hated in heaven because I have betrayed the calling which was laid upon me from above. . . . You look at me in amazement, Olaf Skaktavl! Those were hideous words I spoke? Yes, that I well believe. But when this fear sinks its iron claws in my breast I no longer have the power to curb my thoughts. . . . Nils Lykke, tell me one thing: where have you got him? Where is he?

NILS LYKKE. With his foster-father!

LADY INGER. Still with his foster-father? . . . With the man who has persistently refused me—but this cannot go on. Olaf Skaktavl, you must help me.

SKAKTAVL. I must?

NILS LYKKE. That will not be necessary, if only you . . .

LADY INGER. Listen, Olaf Skaktavl! Listen both of you—for now I think I have the strength to . . . Well then, you reminded me this evening of that night when Knut Alfson was slain at Oslo. You reminded me of the promise I made as I stood by his bier among the bravest men in Norway. I was little more than fifteen, but I felt the Lord's strength within me, and on that day there was born in me and in all of us the firm belief that heaven had set its mark on me and chosen me to lead the struggle for our sacred cause. Whether it was pride or a revelation from above which inspired me I know not, but woe betide anyone who has been given a great mission in life to which he is not equal. It is said that a woman shall leave her father and mother and shall follow her husband; but she who is chosen to be the instrument of heaven may hold nothing dear; not spouse nor child, not kinsfolk nor home; and there, I say, lies the curse of being chosen to do a deed of glory. . . . For ten years I kept my promise faithfully. I stood by my countrymen in their trials and tribulations. When I was twenty-five everywhere my childhood friends were wives and mothers; I alone was in the fight, in danger. Mine was not the normal lot of woman—such were the words for ever echoing in my ears, words which I myself was far too ready to believe. It was then I first set eyes on Sten Sture, at that time in the full flower of manhood.

NILS LYKKE. Quite true, and according to what I have been told he had come on a secret mission to Norway. . . . No one but you would know that he was well disposed towards your party.

LADY INGER. He lived near me for a whole winter, incognito and disguised as a knight's squire. It was then I learned there are other longings, other dreams in a woman's soul than those I had so far cherished. The following winter he came back, and when he left again he took with him a little child, whose existence no one knew of . . . not that I was afraid of popular prejudice, but our cause would have suffered harm had it got around that Sten Sture enjoyed my confidence. The child was given to Peter Kanzler to rear until the better times we were vainly waiting for. Sten Sture was married two years later in Sweden, and when he died he left a widow . . .

SKAKTAVL. . . . and with her a lawful heir to his name and rights!

LADY INGER. In vain I appealed to Peter Kanzler to give me back my child, the only creature I could lavish my affection on, but he persistently refused. Join us once and for all, he said, and I will return your son, but not before. How dared I? The disaffected faction was

XI

weak. If our enemies were victorious and my child fell into their hands—oh, I know: to make sure of the mother they would have inflicted on the child the fate King Christian would have suffered had he not fled to safety. But the Danes were also active. They spared neither threats nor promises to win my support.

SKAKTAVL. That was understandable; you still had a fine-sounding name in Norway. The eyes of the people were still on you as the one who was called to break their chains.

LADY INGER. Then came Herlof Hyttefad's revolt. Spring had returned to the land; there was hope in the hearts of men. 'The hour of freedom has come. Strike, strike now,' they shouted, but I—I stood and doubted, far from the strife in my lonely home. True, at times it seemed to me as though God himself had called me to arms on behalf of our people, but I hesitated, for again that deadly fear came over me. 'Who will win?' . . . that was the question which for ever echoed in my ears and paralysed my will. . . . It was a short spring that had come to Norway. Herlof Hyttefad was killed and hundreds with him. No one could call me to account because I had remained aloof from events, yet there was no lack of veiled threats from the Danish Court. Once more my fear was awakened. . . . What if they knew the secret? Gyldenløve, the Lord Steward, asked my hand in marriage. A month later he was my husband. Then came a cry of condemnation throughout the land. 'She has betrayed us, she has left her people in the lurch!' Inger Gyldenløve had no home in the hearts of her countrymen. Events marched on; the policy of oppression grew daily more intense; but *my* activity was over. There were times when I loathed myself; for what had I to do? Only to fear, to suffer scorn, and bring daughters into the world. My daughters! May God forgive me if I have no motherly feelings for them; but my conjugal duties were sheer slavery to me . . . how could I enjoy their fruits? Oh, it was different with my son. He was the child of love, all I had to remind me of the time when I was really and truly a woman. And him they had taken from me. He was growing up among strangers who might be sowing the seeds of corruption in his soul. Olaf Skaktavl, if I had been naked and forsaken in a raging mountain storm with my child clutched in my arms, even though he were so wretched and puny that no wolf would have devoured him while other food was to be had—believe me, I would not have sorrowed and wept from his birth to this very hour.

SKAKTAVL. Here is my hand. I have judged you too harshly, Lady Inger, but now let our differences be forgotten. Henceforth you may command me as before; I shall obey. Yes, by all the saints, I know what it means to sorrow for one's child.

LADY INGER. The enemy's sword has taken yours, but what is death to the unending terror of twenty long years?

NILS LYKKE. Well, now it is within your power to end this terror. If you reconcile the two parties neither will need to abduct your child as a pledge of your loyalty.

LADY INGER [*aside*]. This is the vengeance of heaven! [*Aloud.*] Tell me, what do you demand?

NILS LYKKE. That you call your countrymen to arms in support of the disaffected elements in Sweden.

LADY INGER. Go on!

NILS LYKKE. That you help the young Count Sture to assert his ancestral claims to the throne of Sweden.

LADY INGER. Him? You ask me to. . . ?

SKAKTAVL [*softly*]. It is the wish of the Swedes and it would serve our purpose too.

NILS LYKKE. How can you hesitate, Madam? You tremble for your son's safety. . . . What better can you wish than to see his half-brother on the throne?

LADY INGER [*meditating*]. True, true!

NILS LYKKE [*looks at her sharply*]. Unless there are other plans brewing.

LADY INGER. What do you mean?

NILS LYKKE. That Inger Gyldenløve might be thinking of becoming—a king's mother!

LADY INGER. No, no! Give me back my child and you can give the northern crown to anyone you please. But are you certain that Count Sture is willing. . . ?

NILS LYKKE. He himself can assure you of that.

LADY INGER. Himself? When?

NILS LYKKE. This moment!

SKAKTAVL. How?

LADY INGER. What did you say?

NILS LYKKE. In a word, Count Sture is at Østeraad!

SKAKTAVL. Here?

NILS LYKKE [*to* LADY INGER]. You have been told perhaps that two of us rode through the gate. The Count was my attendant.

LADY INGER [*aside*]. I am in his power; there is no longer any choice. [*Aloud.*] Very well, you shall have my assurance of support.

NILS LYKKE. In writing?

LADY INGER. As you wish. [*She goes to the table on the left.*]

NILS LYKKE [*aside*]. So I win at last!

LADY INGER [*after a moment's thought turns suddenly to* OLAF SKAKTAVL *and says in a low voice*]: Skaktavl, I am certain that Nils Lykke is a traitor!

SKAKTAVL [*softly*]. What? You think . . . ?

LADY INGER. He is planning treachery. [*She sits down at the table to write.*]

SKAKTAVL. And yet you are going to write this document which may be your downfall?

LADY INGER. Quiet! Leave things to me! [*They whisper together.*]

NILS LYKKE [*aside*]. Ah, talk things over together as much as you like. The danger is past now: in a moment I shall have her written word which will, if necessary, brand her as a rebel. I must slip word to Jens Bjelke before the night is out. Now I can assure him with a clear conscience that the young Count is not here. And tomorrow, when it's safe, I'll bring our man in there to Trondheim; my ship will take him on to Denmark, and then we can make Lady Inger any conditions we want. If this little effort doesn't make me famous it means people have no sense of greatness left.

LADY INGER [*to* SKAKTAVL]. Well, you understand?

SKAKTAVL. Absolutely! It shall be as you command! [*He goes out, back right.*]

[*As before.* NILS STENSSON *enters through the door at the front, right, unnoticed by* LADY INGER, *who goes on writing.*]

STENSSON [*in a low voice*]. Sir Nils! Sir Nils!

NILS LYKKE. What rashness is this? What are you doing here? Didn't I say you were to wait in there till I called you?

STENSSON. How could I? Now you have told me Inger Gyldenløve is my mother I long more than ever to see her face to face. Oh, there she is! How proud! How noble! Yes, I knew she would look like that. I can't explain it, but since I learned this secret I've grown older and wiser, as it were. I'll not be wild and scatter-brained again; I will be a man, a hero. I say, does she know I'm here? I suppose you'll have prepared her?

NILS LYKKE. Indeed I have, but . . .

STENSSON. Well?

NILS LYKKE. She does not recognize you as her son.

STENSSON. She does not recognize me? Why, she's my mother. [*He takes out a ring which hangs round his neck.*] Oh, if that's all, show her this ring which I have worn since my earliest childhood; she must know about it.

NILS LYKKE. You don't understand. Lady Inger has no doubt that you are her child, but . . . well, look around you; look at all this wealth; . . . look at all these mighty ancestors whose portraits are hanging on the walls; then look at Lady Inger herself, this proud woman, used to authority like a queen. Do you think she will fancy parading the poor ignorant lad for all men to see, saying: Behold my son!

STENSSON. Yes, doubtless you are right. I am poor and ignorant; I have nothing to give in return for what I ask; oh, never have I felt my poverty so bitterly as at this moment. But tell me, what do you think I should do to win her over? Tell me, surely you will know!

NILS LYKKE. You must win the kingdom, but primarily you must take good care not to offend her ears by breathing one word about kinship and the like. She will look on you as Count Sture till you make yourself worthy of being called her son.

STENSSON. Oh, but tell me then . . .

NILS LYKKE. Quiet, be quiet!

LADY INGER [*rises and hands him the paper*]. Here is my word, Sir Nils!

NILS LYKKE. I thank you.

LADY INGER [*noticing* NILS STENSSON]. Ah, this is . . .

NILS LYKKE. Count Sture!

LADY INGER [*aside*]. Every feature. Yes, by heaven, it is Sten Sture's son! [*Aloud.*] Welcome to my house, Count Sture! It rests in your hands how far we shall bless this meeting a year from now.

STENSSON. In my hands? Oh, tell me what I have to do. I have the strength and the will, believe me.

NILS LYKKE [*listening*]. Shouts and the clash of arms? Someone is coming. What does it mean?

LADY INGER [*triumphantly*]. It is the spirits awaking!

SCENE FIVE

[*As before.* SKAKTAVL, BJØRN, FINN, RETAINERS *and* SERVANTS *enter from the back, right.*]

RETAINERS. Long live Inger Gyldenløve!

LADY INGER [*to* SKAKTAVL]. You have told them what is afoot?

SKAKTAVL. I've told them all they need to know.

LADY INGER. And now, loyal friends and servants, arm yourselves as best you can. What I forbade you earlier tonight you are now at full liberty to do. And here, here I present to you Count Sture, King of Sweden and of Norway too, if God be willing.

ALL. Hail, hail Count Sture!

NILS LYKKE [*aside*]. The fire is smouldering under the ashes more fiercely than I thought. I pretended to conjure up the demon of revolt . . . heaven help me if he gets out of hand.

[*General commotion. The* RETAINERS *choose weapons, put on armour, etc.*]

LADY INGER [*to* NILS STENSSON]. Here, to be going on with, you have from me thirty horsemen who will form your bodyguard. Believe me, before you reach the frontier thousands will have rallied to your banner. Go now, and God be with you!

STENSSON. Thank you, Lady Inger. Thank you, and rest assured that you will not be ashamed of—of Count Sture! If you see me again I shall have won the kingdom!

NILS LYKKE [*aside*]. Yes, *if* she sees him again!

SKAKTAVL. The horses are waiting. Everything is ready!

NILS LYKKE [*uneasy*]. What? You mean now, tonight . . . ?

LADY INGER. This moment!

NILS LYKKE. No, that is impossible!

LADY INGER. It shall be as I say.

NILS LYKKE [*softly, to* NILS STENSSON]. Don't obey her!

STENSSON [*whispering*]. What else can I do? I will, I must!

NILS LYKKE [*as before*]. But it means your ruin.

STENSSON. No matter! She has the right to command.

NILS LYKKE [*peremptorily*]. And I?

STENSSON. I will keep my word to you. The secret shall not cross my lips until you yourself release me. But she is my mother!

NILS LYKKE [*aside*]. And there's Jens Bjelke lying in wait! Damnation, he'll snatch the prey out of my hands! [*To* LADY INGER.] Wait until tomorrow!

LADY INGER. Count Sture, are you going to obey me or not?

STENSSON. To horse! [*He goes towards the back.*]

NILS LYKKE [*aside*]. Poor fellow! He doesn't know what he is doing. [*To* LADY INGER.] Well, since it must be so, farewell. [*He is about to go.*]

LADY INGER [*detains him*]. No, stay! Not so, Sir Nils, not so!

NILS LYKKE. What do you mean?

LADY INGER [*in a low voice*]. Nils Lykke, you are a traitor! Quiet! Quiet! Let no one see that there is trouble in the generals' camp. You have gained Peter Kanzler's confidence by some devilish trick which I am unable to fathom; you have forced me to take up arms, not to support our cause but to further your own designs, whatever they may be. I cannot withdraw now, but do not think therefore that you have won; I shall know how to render you harmless.

NILS LYKKE [*puts his hand involuntarily on his sword*]. Lady Inger!

LADY INGER. Be calm. Your life is not in danger; but you will not pass through the gates of Østeraad before the victory is ours!

NILS LYKKE. Death and damnation!

LADY INGER. Resistance is quite useless; you will not get away! So your wisest course is to keep quiet.

NILS LYKKE [*aside*]. Ah, I am outwitted; she has been too clever for me.

LADY INGER [*softly, to* SKAKTAVL]. You will go with Count Sture and his men to the frontier; then you will make straight for Peter Kanzler and fetch my child. He has no reason now for detaining him. [*As* SKAKTAVL *is about to leave.*] Wait . . . how will you recognize him? . . . The man wearing Sten Sture's ring is the one.

SKAKTAVL. By all the saints, you shall have him!

LADY INGER. Thank you, thank you, my faithful friend!

NILS LYKKE [*whispering to* FINN, *whom he has beckoned to unobserved*]. Right, off you go, for all you're worth! The Swedes are lying in ambush about a mile away; let Jens Bjelke know what I have told you about Count Sture's death; the young man *there* must not be touched—his life is worth thousands to me!

FINN. It shall be done!

LADY INGER [*who has meanwhile been keeping an eye on* NILS LYKKE]. And now go, all of you, and God be with you! [*Pointing to* NILS LYKKE.] This noble gentleman cannot bring himself to leave his friends at Østeraad so hastily; he is going to wait until the news of victory comes.

NILS LYKKE [*aside*]. The devil!

STENSSON [*seizes his hand*]. You won't have long to wait, believe me!

NILS LYKKE. Good, good! [*Aside.*] All may yet be well, if only my message reaches Jens Bjelke in good time.

LADY INGER [*pointing to* FINN]. And *that* man is to be placed under close guard in the dungeon.

FINN. Me?

THE RETAINERS. Finn!

NILS LYKKE [*aside*]. There goes my last hope!

LADY INGER [*peremptorily*]. To the dungeon!

[*Two* RETAINERS *lead* FINN *out, left. Everyone else, except* NILS LYKKE, *goes out at the back, right, shouting:*] Away! To horse! To horse! Long live Inger Gyldenløve!

LADY INGER [*to* NILS LYKKE, *as she goes out after the others*]. Who wins?

SCENE SIX

[NILS LYKKE, *alone.*]

NILS LYKKE [*after a pause*]. Who? Yes, alas for her! The victory will cost her dear. I wash my hands of it; she herself is murdering him, not I. But, all the same, my prey is slipping out of my grasp and the revolt is under way. Oh, this is a reckless crazy game I've embarked upon. . . . [*Listening.*] Hark, there they go riding through the gates already, and I am left behind as a prisoner—no chance of getting out! Within half an hour the Swedes will be on him. He has thirty well-armed men with him. It'll be a fight to the death! But what if they take him alive after all? . . . If only I were free I could catch the Swedes up and make them hand him over before they reach the frontier. Damn it, is there no way out? [*He paces rapidly up and down, then stops suddenly and listens.*] What is that? Singing and music! It's coming from Eline's room; so she's still up. [*As though he has a sudden idea.*] Eline! Ah, if it were possible? A drowning man clutches at a straw! And why shouldn't it be feasible? Am I not the same Nils Lykke? As it says in the song:

> 'Every fair maiden sighs with a tear:
> God grant that Nils Lykke should hold me dear.'

And she . . . ? Yes, indeed, Eline shall save me!

ACT FIVE

The Great Hall. It is still night. The hall is only faintly lit by a branched candlestick standing on the table, front right.

SCENE ONE

[LADY INGER *is sitting at the table deep in thought.*]

LADY INGER [*after a pause*]. Who is shrewdest on this earth? One who stands to gain a kingdom by using his wits? One whose grave will bear a monument of shame should his inmost self be revealed and his intimate thoughts displayed in the full light of day? [*Shaking her head.*] Neither. The one who stands to gain a kingdom—if he were shrewdest—would fight to lose his gain, not to win it. The one faced with a monument of shame—if he were shrewdest—would say to himself that when he lies six feet below the ground no man's hands can erect a monument which could crush him. Who is then the shrewdest? [*She rises.*] The shrewdest is a mother fighting to save her child! *That* is what sharpens the wits! No one is so shrewd and no one so astute as Inger Gyldenløve, so they say in the three kingdoms of Scandinavia. [*Whispering.*] I have fought this fight; for twenty years I have struggled to save my child—that is the key to the riddle! [*After a pause, during which she runs her hand over her forehead, as though to collect her thoughts.*] I don't know why it is, but at times I feel as though my thoughts were deserting me, that I had to reach out, as it were, and hold them tight. Is it that the fight is over now and I no longer need my wits? No, it comes more likely from this gnawing fear that presses on my brain. Can my reason. . . ? Oh, it will pass, there is nothing to be afraid of, it will pass! [*After a pause.*] How peaceful it all is in the house tonight; everyone asleep, and now I too am going to rest. How many a sleepless night I have spent here alone with my worries! My ancestors have looked down at me, sombre and menacing, and I have turned their faces to the wall to avoid their angry scowls. Tonight they all look so friendly; there is a spirit of reconciliation in their souls and [*putting her hand on her heart*] so there is in mine! For now I am at my goal; I shall have my child again! [*She takes up the light and is about to go, but stops.*] My goal? My goal? Is that really my ultimate goal—to have him back? *That*, and that alone? [*She puts the light down on the table again.*] Nils Lykke dropped a casual remark—a remark which fell into my soul like a seed into fertile ground. . . . It has already begun to sprout. No, that is not so. It had long lain dormant there, but like a thought unborn, which first came to life when he called it by name. [*Whispering.*] A king's mother; . . . a king's mother, he said! And why not? Have my fathers before me not ruled as kings, though they did not bear the title? Has my son not the same claim as the other to the rights of the Stures? In the sight of God he has, if there is truly justice in heaven. And I have extravagantly relinquished these rights as a ransom for his freedom! . . . Could they still be retrieved? While I feared for his life the thought lay unspoken in my soul, shy as the forest deer which fears the light; now it plucks up courage again and sneaks from its hiding-place. . . . No, I will not entertain the thought: I have aroused the wrath of heaven by going my own way; . . . now I will renounce power and fame. That is the sacrifice which shall reconcile me with God! And would he, my child, be worthy of what I have suffered for him, if my love alone did not suffice him? [*She picks up the light again.*] Away with all reckless thoughts. I have fought for twenty years: my day of battle is at an end and now I will seek peace and rest! [*She goes towards the back, but stops, and says in a meditative voice:*] A king's mother! [*She goes out slowly, back left.*]

SCENE TWO

[NILS LYKKE *and* ELINE *come in through the left door at the front.* NILS LYKKE *has a small lantern in his hand.*]

NILS LYKKE [*after spying out the land*]. All quiet. I must be gone!

ELINE. Oh, let me look into your eyes once more before you leave me.

NILS LYKKE [*embraces her*]. Eline!

ELINE [*after a pause*]. Will you never come back to Østeraad?

NILS LYKKE. How can you be in doubt? Are you not henceforth my betrothed? But will you also be true to me? Will you not forget me before we meet again?

ELINE. You ask *will* I be true? Have I a will now? Could I be untrue to you even if I would? You came by night, you knocked upon my door, and I let you in. You spoke to me, you looked deep into my eyes with all that mysterious power which, like a magic net, ensnares a woman's soul. I gave you all a woman can give to the man she loves. Thus I am yours, and I must be true to you—true in all eternity!

NILS LYKKE. Upon my honour as a knight, before the year is out you shall be the lady of Nils Lykke's castle.

ELINE. Quiet, Nils Lykke, quiet! Make no promises!

NILS LYKKE. What is wrong? Why do you shake your head so sadly?

ELINE. Because I know that you have whispered these fair words which captivated my heart to hundreds before me. No, understand me aright! I do not reproach you, as I did until I knew you. Now I know you are in every way a man, a man to whom fate has entrusted mighty talents and a great task in life. How then can love be other than a game to you, and woman a mere toy?

NILS LYKKE. Eline, listen to me!

ELINE. Right from my childhood I heard your name in songs and stories. I hated that name because I thought woman's pride was dishonoured by your conduct. And yet, how strange; when I pictured in my dreams the story of my own future you were always my hero, although I did not know. Now all is clear to me; it was not hate I felt; it was a thought without a name, a mysterious longing for you, whom destiny had chosen to come my way and reveal the whole glory of life to me!

NILS LYKKE [*aside, putting down the lantern on the left table*]. I don't know what has happened but I feel as though she had grafted a fresh and sturdy branch on to my life's withered tree. If this is how love feels, oh, then I have never known it until tonight. Why was none of the others like her? But is it too late now? Poor me! Lucia, Lucia! [*He sinks into the chair.*]

ELINE. What is it?

NILS LYKKE. Oh, it's nothing, Eline! I am going to be honest with you. Until this moment my words were false. What I whispered to you tonight I have told to hundreds; but, believe me . . .

ELINE. Quiet! No more of that! My love is as nothing in return for what you give me. Oh no; I love you because every look of yours is a royal command which bids me do so. [*She throws herself down at his feet.*] Oh, let me once more stamp that command deep into my soul, though well I know it is already imprinted there in time and eternity! ... Dear God, how blind I have been to my true self. Only tonight I said to my mother, 'I cannot live without my pride'. But what is my pride? Is it to know my people are free or my family famous in many lands? Oh no! My love is my pride! A little dog is proud to sit at his master's feet and eat crumbs out of his hand—and so I too am proud to sit at your feet, while your words and glances feed me with the bread of life. ... I say to you then what I said to my mother just now, 'I cannot live without my love', for there lies my pride from this hour forth!

NILS LYKKE. No, not at my feet—your place is by my side, however high fate shall think to raise me. Yes, Eline! You have led me on to better paths, and should it once be my lot in life to do some illustrious deed the honour shall be yours as much as mine.

ELINE. Oh, you talk as though I were still the same Eline who last evening hurled the flowers at your feet. I have read in my books of the colourful life in far-off lands. To the sound of the horn the knight rides forth into the green of the grove with his falcon on his wrist; so too do you ride forth through life; your name resounds before you everywhere you go. All I want of this glory is to rest like the falcon on your arm. Like him I too was blind to light and life until you loosed the hood from my eyes and sent me soaring high above the forest trees; yet, believe me, however boldly I may spread my wings I shall always come back to my cage.

NILS LYKKE [*rises*]. Then I too bid defiance to the past! Come now; ... take this ring and be mine before God and men, mine, even though the dead be troubled in their dreams!

ELINE [*standing up*]. You make me feel uneasy. What is it that ...

NILS LYKKE. It is nothing! Come, let me put the ring on your finger. There; ... now you are pledged to me!

ELINE. Nils Lykke's bride! All that has happened tonight seems like a dream. Oh, but it is a lovely dream. I am so light of heart; there is no more bitterness and hate in my soul; I will make up for all the wrong I have done. I have been unkind to my mother. Tomorrow I shall go down to her; she must forgive me where I have erred.

NILS LYKKE. And give her consent to our union.

ELINE. She will! . . . Oh, I am sure she will. . . . She is kind, everyone is kind; now I harbour no resentment to a single soul—except for one!

NILS LYKKE. Except for one?

ELINE. Alas, it is a sad story. I had a sister . . .

NILS LYKKE. Lucia?

ELINE. You knew her?

NILS LYKKE. No, I have merely heard the name.

ELINE. She too gave her heart to a knight. He deceived her; . . . now she is in heaven!

NILS LYKKE. And you?

ELINE. I hate him!

NILS LYKKE. If there is mercy in your heart, forgive him his sin. Believe me, he bears his punishment in his own breast.

ELINE. I cannot, even though I would, for I have sworn—hush, can you hear?

NILS LYKKE. What?

ELINE. A distant rumble, like the tramp of horses' hoofs.

NILS LYKKE. Ah, it's them! Alas, I had forgotten. . . . I must be gone! I must be gone!

ELINE. But why? Tell me why . . .

NILS LYKKE. Tomorrow; I swear to be back by then. Quick now, where is the secret passage you mentioned?

ELINE. Through the burial vaults. Look, here's the trap-door!

NILS LYKKE. The vaults? [*Aside.*] No matter, he must be saved!

ELINE [*listening at the window*]. The riders are drawing nearer . . . [*She hands him the lantern.*]

NIL LYKKE. Here I go! [*He begins to descend.*]

ELINE. Go straight ahead to the coffin with the death's head and the black cross; it is Lucia's . . .

NILS LYKKE [*comes up rapidly and shuts the trap-door*]. Lucia's! Ugh!

ELINE. What is it?

NILS LYKKE. The smell of death makes my head reel.

ELINE. They are knocking on the gate!

NILS LYKKE. Ah, it is too late!

SCENE THREE

[*As before.* BJØRN *comes in from the right, carrying a light.*]

ELINE. What is it? What has happened?

BJØRN. An ambush! Count Sture . . .

ELINE. What of him?

NILS LYKKE. Has he been killed?

BJØRN [*to* ELINE]. Where is your mother?

SCENE FOUR

[*As before.* LADY INGER *enters from the left with a branched candlestick. Two* RETAINERS *enter from the right.*]

RETAINERS. Lady Inger! Lady Inger!

LADY INGER [*entering*]. I know everything. Begone with you! Keep the gate open for our friends but closed to the rest.

[*She puts the candlestick on the left table.* BJØRN *and the two* RETAINERS *go out, right.*]

LADY INGER [*to* NILS LYKKE]. So *that* was the trap!

NILS LYKKE. Inger Gyldenløve, believe me . . .

LADY INGER. An ambush to pounce on him as soon as you had that written word which could ruin me.

NILS LYKKE [*taking out the paper and tearing it up*]. Here is your word. I shall keep nothing which can be used in evidence against you.

LADY INGER. What are you doing?

NILS LYKKE. From now on I shall protect you! If I have sinned against you, by heaven I will make good my crime! But I must be gone, even if I have to fight a way through with my sword. Eline, tell her everything! And you, Lady Inger, let bygones be bygones! Be generous! Believe me, you will not regret it. [*He hurries out, back right.*]

SCENE FIVE

[LADY INGER. ELINE.]

LADY INGER. Just as it should be! I understand! [*To* ELINE.] Nils Lykke—well?

ELINE. He knocked on my door and put this ring on my finger!

LADY INGER. And he loves you with all his heart?

ELINE. That's what he said, and I believe him.

LADY INGER. Good work, Eline! Ha! ha! And now, sir, this is where I come in!

ELINE. Mother—you are so strange! Oh yes, I know: it is my unkindness which has made you angry with me.

LADY INGER. Not at all! Not at all! You are an obedient daughter. You let him in; you listened to his fair words. I know what it cost you, because I know your hatred . . .

ELINE. But, mother—

LADY INGER. Quiet! Our plans have converged. You will be able to kindle love in Nils Lykke's soul; it has already begun; I could tell from his words and from the way he looked. Hold him fast now, draw the net tighter about him, and then. . . . Ah, if we could tear apart the perjured heart within his breast.

ELINE. Alas! . . . What did you say?

LADY INGER. Do you need more courage to go along with me further? Very well, I need only whisper two words into your ear; in them is the girdle of strength which shall sustain you. I must tell you then. . . . [*Listening.*] The fighter is coming closer! Steady! Now comes the moment. [*She turns to* ELINE *again.*] I must tell you: Nils Lykke was the man who brought your sister to her grave!

ELINE [*with a shriek*]. Lucia?

LADY INGER. It was he as truly as there is a god in heaven!

ELINE. Then heaven help me!

LADY INGER [*horrified*]. Eline!

ELINE. I am his betrothed in the sight of God.

LADY INGER. Unhappy child! What have you done?

ELINE [*in a flat voice*]. Forfeited my peace of mind! . . . Goodnight, mother! [*She goes out, left.*]

LADY INGER. Ha! ha! ha! Inger Gyldenløve's family is going downhill! *There* goes the last of my daughters! Why could I not have kept the secret to myself? If she had known nothing she would have been happy—after a fashion. But that is my fate. It is written above that I shall break off one green branch after the other until only the leafless trunk remains. Well and good! I shall have my son again. I will not think of the others, of my daughters. What would be the use of brooding and remorse? There is no hurry. Not until the great day of wrath shall man give an account of himself, and that will not be yet awhile!

NILS STENSSON [*outside*]. Hey there, shut the gate!

LADY INGER. Count Sture's voice!

SCENE SIX

[LADY INGER. NILS STENSSON *enters from the right, followed immediately by* OLAF SKAKTAVL.]

STENSSON [*with a laugh of despair*]. Well met, Inger Gyldenløve!

LADY INGER. What are your losses?

STENSSON. My crown and my life!

LADY INGER. My men—what have you done with them?

STENSSON. You'll find the carcasses along the road. Who has taken the rest I cannot say!

SKAKTAVL [*outside*]. Count Sture, where are you?

STENSSON. Here! Here!

[SKAKTAVL *enters with his right hand bandaged with a cloth.*]

LADY INGER. Skaktavl! You've come back?

SKAKTAVL. It was impossible to get through!

LADY INGER. Are you hurt?

SKAKTAVL. Oh, I'm a finger short, that's all!

STENSSON. Where are the Swedes?

SKAKTAVL. On our heels. They are breaking open the gate!

STENSSON. Oh God, no! I can't, I won't die!

SKAKTAVL. A hiding-place! Isn't there some odd corner where we can hide him?

LADY INGER. But if they search the house . . .

STENSSON. Yes, they'll find me! . . . And to be hauled off to prison or to be strung up. . . . Oh no, Inger Gyldenløve, I'm sure you'll never stand for it!

SKAKTAVL. There, they've forced the lock!

LADY INGER. They are storming into the courtyard!

STENSSON. To lose my life now; now when it was just beginning; now, just when I had learnt I had something to live for. . . . No, don't think me a coward . . . if I could only have repaid you what I owe.

LADY INGER. I can hear them in the servants' hall already. [*Firmly.*] He must be saved—at all costs.

STENSSON [*seizes her hand*]. Oh, I knew it; . . . you are noble and good!

SKAKTAVL. But how are we to do it?

STENSSON. Ah, I've got it, I've got it! The secret . . .

LADY INGER. The secret?

STENSSON. Yes, yours and mine!

LADY INGER. Heavens above! You know it?

STENSSON. From beginning to end, and now when this is a matter of life and death . . . where is Nils Lykke?

LADY INGER. Fled!

STENSSON. Fled! Then God help me, for he alone can loose my tongue! But life is worth more than a promise; . . . when the Swedish captain comes . . .

LADY INGER. What then? What will you do?

STENSSON. Buy my life and my freedom! Reveal all!

LADY INGER. Oh no, no! Have mercy!

STENSSON. It is the only hope. When I have confessed what I know . . .

LADY INGER [*looks at him with suppressed emotion*]. You will be safe?

STENSSON. Yes! Nils Lykke will plead my cause. It's my last chance, you see!

LADY INGER [*composes herself and says meaningly*]: The last chance? You are right, that is something any man may take. [*She points to the left.*] Look, you can hide in there meanwhile.

STENSSON. Believe me, you will never regret it.

LADY INGER [*half to herself*]. God grant that you speak the truth!

[STENSSON *goes out hastily, back left.* SKAKTAVL *starts to follow;* LADY INGER *detains him.*]

SCENE SEVEN

[LADY INGER. OLAF SKAKTAVL.]

LADY INGER. Did you understand what he said?

SKAKTAVL. He's going to betray your secret, the scoundrel! He means to sell your son's freedom to save himself.

LADY INGER. When life is at stake, he said, we must seize our last chance. Very well, let it be as he said.

SKAKTAVL. What do you mean?

LADY INGER. One life against another! One of them must perish!

SKAKTAVL. You would . . . ?

LADY INGER. If that man in there is not silenced before the sands run out, my son is lost to me. If he is killed my child will inherit his rights . . . then you will see that Inger Gyldenløve still has good stuff in her. Believe me, you shall not thirst long after the revenge you have waited for these twenty years. . . . Listen, listen, they are coming! It rests with you alone whether tomorrow I am childless or . . .

SKAKTAVL. So be it! My sword still has an edge. I still have one good hand left. [*He gives her his hand.*] Inger Gyldenløve, your name shall not die out through any fault of mine! [*He goes into the room to* NILS STENSSON.]

LADY INGER. But dare I really? [*A noise is heard from the room. She hurries towards the door.*] No, no, it must not be! [*A heavy thud is heard within. She covers her ears with her hands and rushes downstage with a wild look. After a pause she removes her hands, listens, and says:*] Now it is over! All is quiet in there. . . . Thou didst see it, God! I thought better of it, but Olaf Skaktavl was too quick on the draw!

[OLAF SKAKTAVL *comes in.*]

LADY INGER [*without looking at him*]. Is it done?

SKAKTAVL. You are safe from him. He'll not see sun nor moon again.

LADY INGER [*as before*]. He is silenced then?

SKAKTAVL. Six inches of steel in his breast—I killed him with my left hand!

LADY INGER. Yes, the right hand was too good for work like that!

SKAKTAVL. That is your business—it was your idea. And now to Sweden! Peace be with you meanwhile! The next time we meet at Østeraad there will be two of us. [*He goes out, right.*]

SCENE EIGHT

[LADY INGER. BJØRN *enters immediately from the right with several Swedish soldiers.*]

LADY INGER. Blood on my hands. So it had to come to that! Now I'm beginning to pay dear for him!

A SOLDIER [*as he enters with the others*]. Begging your pardon, if you are the lady of the house . . .

LADY INGER. Is it Count Sture you are looking for?

SOLDIER. That's right!

LADY INGER. In that case you are on the right track. The Count has sought protection with me.

SOLDIER. Protection? With respect, your ladyship, you have no power to protect him, because . . .

LADY INGER. The Count has doubtless realized the truth of what you say and therefore he—well, see for yourselves—therefore he has taken his own life.

SOLDIER. Taken his own life!

LADY INGER. As I said, see for yourself. You will find the body in there, and since he already stands before another judge it is my will that he should be taken from here with such decorum as befits his rank. Bjørn, my coffin has been standing ready for many years in the secret room. [*To the* SOLDIERS.] You are to take Count Sture's body in it to Sweden!

SOLDIER. It shall be as you command! [*To one of the others.*] Take this news to Sir Jens. He is still keeping guard on the road. The rest of you come in here with me! [*One soldier goes out to the right,* BJØRN *and the others to the left.*]

SCENE NINE

[LADY INGER. *Later,* BJØRN.]

LADY INGER. If Count Sture had not been in such a hurry to bid this world adieu he would have been hanging on the gallows within a month, or sitting in a dungeon for the rest of his days. Would he have been better off with such a lot? Or he would have bought his freedom by delivering my child into the hands of my enemies. Is it I then who have killed him? Does not even the wolf defend her young? So who will pass judgement on me for digging my claws into one who would have robbed me of my own flesh and blood? It had to be. Any mother would have done what I did. . . . But there is no more time for idle thoughts. I have work to do. [*She sits down at the left table.*] I will write round to my friends in Norway. They shall all support our cause. [*She begins to write, but stops, and says:*] Whom will they elect as king in the place of the one who's killed? . . .

A king's mother—fine words. I have only one thing against them: they sound so horribly like those others; . . . king's mother and . . . king's murderer! A king's *murderer* is one who takes a king's life. A king's *mother* is one who gives a king life! [*She rises.*] Very well, I will give back what I have taken. My son shall be king! [*She sits down, sets to work, puts what she is doing to one side again, and leans back in the chair.*] It's always a little uncanny when there is a corpse in the house. That is why I feel so strange. [*As though speaking to someone.*] No? What else can the reason be? [*Pondering.*] Is there any difference between slaying a man in open fight and killing him like this? Knut Alfson had cleft many a brow with his sword, yet his own was as unruffled as a child's. Why then do I go on seeing this—[*she makes a stabbing motion*] this thrust to the heart and then the red blood pouring out? [*She rings, and continues talking as she rummages among the papers.*] I'll have no more of such ghastly sights. I will keep busy day and night and within a month my son will come to me.

BJØRN [*enters*]. You rang, my lady?

LADY INGER [*writing*]. Fetch more candles; in future I want lots of candles in the room. [BJØRN *goes out again, left. After a pause* LADY INGER *rises impetuously.*] No, I cannot put pen to paper tonight. I have a splitting headache! [*Listening.*] What is that? Oh, they are screwing the lid on the coffin in there. . . . When I was a child they told me the story of Aage, the knight who came with a coffin on his back; . . . what if the man in there took it into his head one night to come with his coffin on his back to thank me for the loan? [*Smiling.*] Hm! Inger Gyldenløve has no business with childhood fancies! [*Vehemently.*] Such tales are a bad thing anyhow, they give you disturbing dreams. When my son is king they shall be banned! [*She paces up and down several times and then opens the window.*] How long is it usually before a corpse begins to smell. All the rooms shall be aired; until that is done it will be unhealthy living here!

[BJØRN *comes in with two branched candlesticks, which he puts on the table.*]

LADY INGER [*sets to work at the papers again*]. That's right. Mind you remember what I said: lots of candles on the table! What are they doing in there now?

BJØRN. They are still screwing the lid on the coffin.

LADY INGER [*as she seals a letter*]. Are they screwing it good and tight?

BJØRN. As tight as it needs to be.

LADY INGER. Yes, you never know how tight it needs to be. See they make a good job of it. [*She goes close up to him, with the letter in her hand.*] You are an old man, Bjørn, but one thing I would like to impress upon you: be on your guard against all men—both those who have yet to die and those who are dead. Now go in there—go and see that they screw the lid down tight.

BJØRN [*shaking his head*]. I can't make her out! [*He goes out again, left.*]

LADY INGER [*begins to seal a letter, but throws it down, paces to and fro several times, and then says vehemently*]: If I were a coward I would never have done this, not in all eternity! If I were a coward I would have screamed to myself: Stop, while you still have some hope of salvation for your soul! [*Her gaze falls on Sten Sture's portrait; she turns it hurriedly to the wall.*] Ugh, what a face! Was it because I wronged your son? But the other, isn't he your son too? And he is mine as well, mark you!... There is something strange about tonight, or else all these knights and ladies have hit on the comic idea of rolling their eyes and staring at me everywhere I go. [*She stamps her foot.*] But I will not have it; I will have peace in my house! [*She begins to turn all the pictures to the wall.*] Yes, even if it were the Virgin Mary herself. She's in it too. Dost thou think this is the time? Why didst thou never hear my prayers when I prayed to have my child again?... Why? Because the monk of Wittenberg is right: there is no intermediary between God and man! What is this saint I have wasted my words on? A yard of linen, perhaps from the same piece which my father's servant patched his breeches with. [*More and more confused.*] It is well I know about these matters! There is no one who saw what happened in there. There is no one to testify against me! [*Whispering.*] My child! My lovely son! Come to me! Here I am! Hush, I have something to tell you: I am hated up there because I brought you into this world; ... I was born with wealth, a keen brain, and a famous name, so that I might be God's standard-bearer on earth. But I went my own way; ... that is why I have had to suffer so much for so long!

BJØRN [*enters*]. My lady, I have to report—God help me—what is this?

LADY INGER [*who has mounted the seat of honour by the right-hand wall*]. Silence! I am the king's mother! My son has been elected king of all Scandinavia! It was a hard struggle to get so far—it was with God I had to fight!

SCENE TEN

[*As before.* NILS LYKKE *rushes in from the right.*]

NILS LYKKE. He is safe! I have Jens Bjelke's promise; I rode like mad to find him. . . . Lady Inger, I must tell you . . .

LADY INGER. Silence, I say; look at the swarms of people! They have come to see the coronation procession; they all acclaim the King's mother; indeed, she fought for her son until her hands were red! Where are my daughters? I do not see them!

NILS LYKKE. My God! What has happened here?

LADY INGER. My daughters, my beautiful daughters! I haven't any now! I had one left and I lost her when she was to mount her bridal bed! [*Whispering.*] Lucia lay there dead. There was no room for two.

NILS LYKKE. Ah, so it has come to this! God's judgement on my deeds.

LADY INGER. Can you see him? Can you see him? It is the King. It is Inger Gyldenløve's son—I know him by the crown and by Sten Sture's ring which he wears round his neck. [*A funeral hymn is heard from the left room.*] Hear the joyful sounds. He is coming. Soon I will have him in my arms! Ha! ha! Who is the victor, God or I? [*The* SOLDIERS *come in with the coffin.*] The corpse! Ugh, it is a horrid dream! [*She sinks back on to the seat of honour.*]

SCENE ELEVEN

[*As before.* The SOLDIERS *with the coffin.* JENS BJELKE *and* SOLDIERS, *from the right.*]

BJELKE [*surprised*]. Dead!

A SOLDIER. He took his own . . .

BJELKE [*with a glance at* NILS LYKKE]. His own . . . ?

NILS LYKKE. Hush!

LADY INGER [*whispering to herself*]. Yes, that's right. Now I remember it all.

BJELKE [*to the* SOLDIERS]. Put the body down. That is not Count Sture!

A SOLDIER. Begging your pardon, sir, but this ring he was wearing round his neck . . .

NILS LYKKE [*whispering*]. Be quiet!

LADY INGER. The ring! The ring! [*She rushes up and snatches it violently from the soldier's hand.*] Sten Sture's ring! [*With a scream.*] Oh God, oh God, my son! [*She throws herself over the coffin.*]

THE SOLDIER. Her son?

BJELKE [*at the same time*]. Inger Gyldenløve's son?

NILS LYKKE. That is so.

BJELKE. But why didn't you tell me. . . ?

BJØRN [*who tries to lift her up*]. Help! Help! My lady, is there anything. . . ?

LADY INGER [*in a faint voice, half raising herself*]. Anything. . . ? Six feet of earth. A grave beside my child!

[*In a state of collapse she sinks down again over the coffin.* NILS LYKKE *hastens out, right. General commotion.*]

LADY INGER OF ØSTRÅT
(Fru Inger til Østråt)

PLAY IN FIVE ACTS
1874

When Ibsen, in the summer of 1873, was thinking of revising *Lady Inger* he asked Ludvig Daae for comments on the historical accuracy of the play. Daae replied that the play was entirely inaccurate. Short of abandoning the project there was little Ibsen could do but drop the word 'historical' from the title page. Consequently the content of the revised *Lady Inger*, published at the end of 1874, is in its essentials identical with that of the first version. The revision, and there are many changes on every page, concentrates on dramatic technique and language. Selective details of the new version are given in Appendix VI, pp. 694–5. Something of its quality may be seen in the following extract from Act II, which corresponds to Act II, Scenes 2–7 inclusive, of the original play (see pp. 290–301).

[*After a brief pause* FINN *enters cautiously through the door on the right, looks round the room, peeps into the Great Hall, goes back to the door again, and motions to someone outside. Immediately* NILS LYKKE, *a Danish privy councillor, and* SIR JENS BJELKE, *the Swedish Commander, enter the room.*]

NILS LYKKE [*in a low voice*]. No one there?

FINN [*likewise*]. No, my lord!

NILS LYKKE. And we can depend on you entirely?

FINN. The commandant at Trondheim has always testified to my reliability.

NILS LYKKE. Good, good; he said as much to me. First of all then . . . has there already been a visitor at Østråt tonight?

FINN. Yes, a man came an hour ago.

NILS LYKKE [*to* JENS BJELKE, *in a low voice*]. He's here. [*He turns to* FINN *again.*] Would you recognize him? Did you see him?

FINN. No. No one did except for the lodge porter, as far as I know. He was shown straight in to Lady Inger, and she . . .

NILS LYKKE. Well? And she? He's not gone again already, has he?

FINN. No, but she'll be hiding him in one of her rooms, because . . .

NILS LYKKE. Good!

JENS BJELKE [whispers]. Then the first thing is to put a guard on the gate and we've got him.

NILS LYKKE [with a smile]. Hm! [To FINN.] I say . . . is there any way out of this place apart from the gate? Don't just stand there looking stupid! I mean can anyone get out of Østråt unobserved when the gate is shut?

FINN. Well, I don't know. It's true they talk of secret passages down in the vaults; but no one will know about them, apart from Lady Inger; . . . and, yes, perhaps Miss Eline.

JENS BJELKE. The devil!

NILS LYKKE. Right then, you may go.

FINN. Very good. If you should want me for anything you only need open the second door on the right in the Great Hall, and I'll be there at once.

NILS LYKKE. Good. [He points to the entrance-door. FINN goes out.]

JENS BJELKE. I say, my dear friend . . . you know this is going to be a rather shabby campaign for both of us.

NILS LYKKE [smiling]. Oh . . . not for me, I hope.

JENS BJELKE. Really? In the first place there's not much glory chasing a mere overgrown lad like this Nils Sture. What am I to make of him, the way he's been carrying on? Is he mad or sane? First to go stirring up bad blood among the countryfolk, promising them help and heaven on earth; . . . and then, when it comes to the point, running away to hide behind a petticoat.

What's more, I'm frankly sorry I followed your advice instead of acting on my own initiative.

NILS LYKKE [to himself]. It's rather late to be sorry, my good fellow!

JENS BJELKE. I don't mind telling you I've never been one for staying put and poking round for badgers. I had been expecting something entirely different. I rode all the way with my men from Jämtland, and got a warrant from the commandant in Trondheim to look for the rebel anywhere I liked. Every trail leads to Østråt . . .

NILS LYKKE. He *is* here! He *is* here, I tell you!

JENS BJELKE. Yes, but in that case what would have been more likely than to find the gate locked and securely guarded? If only we had; then I could have found a use for my soldiers. . . .

NILS LYKKE. Instead of which they are polite enough to open the gate for us. You see: if Lady Inger Gyldenløve lives up to her reputation she will not let her guests go short of food and drink.

JENS BJELKE. Yes, to side-track me! . . . And how could you hit on the idea of having me leave my horsemen a good mile or so away from the house? If we had come in full force . . .

NILS LYKKE. She would have made us just as welcome nevertheless. But remember that our visit would then have created a stir. The peasants hereabouts would have taken it as an act of violence against Lady Inger, she would again have risen in the popular estimation, and *that*, you see, would not have been a good thing.

JENS BJELKE. That may be so. But what am I to do now? Count Sture is in Østråt, you say. Yes, but what use is that to me? Lady Inger Gyldenløve will have as many hiding-places as a fox, and more than one exit. With only two of us we could go nosing around here for ever. To hell with the whole affair!

NILS LYKKE. Well, my dear fellow . . . if you don't like the turn your mission has taken you had better leave the field to me.

JENS BJELKE. To you? What are you going to do then?

NILS LYKKE. In this case shrewdness and cunning may well accomplish what we cannot achieve with force of arms. . . . To tell the truth, Sir Jens . . . I've had something of the sort in mind since we met in Trondheim yesterday.

JENS BJELKE. Was that why you persuaded me to leave my men behind?

NILS LYKKE. Our respective purposes at Østråt could best be served without them; and so . . .

JENS BJELKE. Go to the devil . . . I almost said! And me too! I might have known that you were always up to your tricks.

NILS LYKKE. Yes, but you know this is where a few tricks will come in handy if both sides are to fight with equal weapons. And I'm bound to tell you that it is of the utmost importance to me to discharge my mission well and in all secrecy. You see, when I left I was scarcely in favour with my lord the King. He thought he had good reason, though I believe I have served him as usefully as anyone in more than one awkward assignment.

JENS BJELKE. You can certainly plead your credentials in that respect. God and men alike know that you are the craftiest devil in all three kingdoms.

NILS LYKKE. Many thanks! Though that's not saying much. But what I'm faced with now I certainly count as the supreme test: this is a question of outwitting a woman . . .

JENS BJELKE. Ha! ha! ha! That's a skill in which you proved your mastery long ago, my dear man! Do you think we don't know the song in Sweden?:

'Every fair maiden sighs with a tear . . .
God grant that Nils Lykke should hold me dear.'

NILS LYKKE. Alas, that song refers to women of twenty or thereabouts. But Lady Inger is getting on for fifty and, what's more, is as cunning as they make them. It will be hard going to get the better of her. But it *must* be done . . . at any price! If I succeed in winning certain advantages over her which the King has long desired I can reckon on the mission to France next spring. I suppose you know I spent three whole years at the University of Paris? My heart is set on going down there again, especially if I could appear in the elevated role of royal ambassador. . . . So you'll leave Lady Inger to me then? Don't forget, when you last visited the Court at Copenhagen I gave up more than one young lady to you.

JENS BJELKE. That was not so generous either, you know. You had them all where you wanted them. But never mind, seeing that I've started off on the wrong foot I'd rather you took over. But it's a promise: if young Count Sture is in Østråt you will hand him over, dead or alive!

NILS LYKKE. You shall have him alive and kicking. I certainly don't intend to kill him. But now you must ride back to your men. Keep guard on the road. If I should notice anything suspicious, you'll be informed without delay.

JENS BJELKE. Very good; but how do I get out . . . ?

NILS LYKKE. The fellow who was here will see you right. But quietly does it . . .

JENS BJELKE. Of course. Well . . . good luck!

NILS LYKKE. My luck has never let me down in my contests with women. Now hurry!

[JENS BJELKE *goes out, right.*]

NILS LYKKE [*stands still for a moment, walks about in the room a little, and looks round; then he says in a low voice*]: So at last I am in Østråt, that old ancestral home a child told me so much about two years ago. Lucia. Yes, two years ago she was still a child, and now . . . now she is dead. [*He hums, with a half smile:*] 'Flowers are plucked and flowers wither . . .' [*He looks round again.*] Østråt. It's as though I had seen it all before; as though it were my home. . . . That is the Great Hall in there. And down below is the burial vault. Lucia will be there too.

[*More softly, half seriously, half with forced levity.*]

If I were a timid man I might have imagined that she turned in her coffin when I set foot inside the gate of Østråt; that when I walked across the courtyard she lifted the lid. And that when I mentioned her name just now it was as though a voice summoned her up from the vaults. . . . Perhaps she is this moment groping her way up the stairs. She is hampered by the grave clothes, but still she gropes forward.

Now she has reached the Great Hall! She is standing looking at me behind the doorpost. [*He jerks his head back over his shoulder, nods, and says aloud:*]

Come closer, Lucia! Talk to me a little! Your mother is keeping me waiting. It is tedious waiting; . . . and you helped me to while away so many a tedious hour. . . .

[*He runs his hand over his brow and paces up and down several times.*]

There now!... Right; there is the deep window with the curtains. That's where Inger Gyldenløve usually stands gazing out over the road as if waiting for someone who never comes. ... In there ... [*he looks towards the door on the left*] somewhere in there is sister Eline's room. Eline? Yes, Eline is the name.

Can I really believe she is as remarkable ... as shrewd and as brave as Lucia said? She's beautiful, too, they say. But as a wife ...? I shouldn't have written quite so bluntly. ...

[*Lost in thought, he is about to sit down at the table, but stands up again.*]

How will Lady Inger receive me? ... She won't set fire to the house over our heads. She'll not try shooting me through a trap-door. A knife from behind is not the sort of thing either. ...

[*He listens towards the hall.*]

Aha!

LADY INGER GYLDENLØVE [*enters from the hall and says coldly*]: I bid you welcome, Lord Nils!

NILS LYKKE [*bows deeply*]. Ah ... the Lady of Østråt!

LADY INGER. ... and I thank you for letting me know of your visit.

NILS LYKKE. No more than my duty. I had reason to suppose that my visit would surprise you. ...

LADY INGER. Indeed, Lord Nils, in that you are not mistaken. Nils Lykke was certainly the last person I expected to see as my guest in Østråt.

NILS LYKKE. And even less you had expected him to come as a friend, I imagine.

LADY INGER. As a friend? You add mockery to all the pain and shame you have heaped upon my house? You bring a child of mine to her grave and still dare ...

NILS LYKKE. If I may say so, Lady Inger Gyldenløve ... we shall scarcely reach agreement on that matter, because you have not taken into account what *I* lost on that unhappy occasion. My intentions were honourable. I was tired of my disorderly life; ... I was already over thirty at the time; I longed to find a good and gentle wife. Add to this the happy prospect of becoming *your* son-in-law ...

LADY INGER. Beware, Lord Nils! I have done all I can to hush things up about my child. But don't imagine that out of sight is out of mind. There might soon be an opportunity . . .

NILS LYKKE. Are you threatening me, Lady Inger? I have offered you the hand of peace; you refuse to take it. So from now on it is to be open conflict between us?

LADY INGER. I was unaware that there was ever anything else.

NILS LYKKE. On *your* part perhaps. I have never been your enemy . . . although as a subject of the King of Denmark I had good reason.

LADY INGER. I know what you mean. I have not been tractable enough. Winning me over to your camp has not gone as smoothly as you wished. . . . But it seems to me you have nothing to complain of. My daughter Merete's husband is your countryman. I can go no further. My position is difficult, Nils Lykke!

NILS LYKKE. I fully understand. Both the nobles and the common people here in Norway think they have a long-standing claim on you . . . a claim which, it is said, you have only partly satisfied.

LADY INGER. If I may say so, Lord Nils . . . I am accountable for my conduct to none other than God and myself. If you please then, tell me what brings you here.

NILS LYKKE. At once, Lady Inger! The purpose of my mission to this country cannot, I take it, be unknown to you . . . ?

LADY INGER. I know the task which is generally ascribed to you. It is of importance for our King to know where he stands with the Norwegian nobility.

NILS LYKKE. Yes, indeed!

LADY INGER. That is why you are visiting Østråt then?

NILS LYKKE. Partly. But I have certainly not come to ask for any verbal assurance . . .

LADY INGER. Well then?

NILS LYKKE. Listen, Lady Inger! You have just said yourself that your position is difficult. You stand midway between two opposing camps, neither of which dare rely on you entirely. Self-interest must

Z1

necessarily tie you to us. On the other hand you are bound to the disaffected elements by nationality, and—who knows?—perhaps by some secret bond as well.

LADY INGER [*to herself*]. Secret bond? My God, can he . . . ?

NILS LYKKE [*pretends not to notice her emotion and adds in a natural voice*]: You will see for yourself that your position is not tenable in the long run. Now suppose it were in my power to free you from a situation which . . .

LADY INGER. In your power, you say?

NILS LYKKE. First of all, Lady Inger, I beg you to attach no importance to any thoughtless words I may have used when talking of the matter that divides us. Don't imagine that I have forgotten for a second the guilt I have incurred. Suppose that it had long been my intention to make amends for my crime as far as possible. Suppose that was why I procured this mission for myself.

LADY INGER. Explain yourself more precisely, Lord Nils; . . . I don't understand that.

NILS LYKKE. I am perhaps not mistaken in assuming that you know as well as I of the disturbances threatening in Sweden. You know, or at any rate you suspect, that these disturbances have a wider aim than is generally ascribed to them, and you will understand therefore that our King cannot look idly on while events take their course. Is that not so?

LADY INGER. Go on!

NILS LYKKE [*searchingly, after a short pause*]. There is one possible contingency which might endanger Gustav Vasa's throne . . .

LADY INGER [*to herself*]. What is he getting at?

NILS LYKKE. . . . namely the contingency that there might be a man in Sweden, who by reason of birth had a claim to be elected King.

LADY INGER [*evasively*]. The Swedish nobility has been as savagely crippled as ours, Lord Nils! Where would you look for . . . ?

NILS LYKKE [*smiling*]. Look? The man has already been found. . . .

LADY INGER [*with a start*]. Ah! He has been found?

NILS LYKKE. . . . and he is too close to you, Madam, for you not to have thought of him. [*Looking at her fixedly.*]
The late Count Sture left a son . . .

LADY INGER [*with a cry*]. Holy Saviour, how do you know . . . ?

NILS LYKKE [*taken aback*]. Be calm, Madam, and let me finish. This young man has so far been living quietly with his mother, Sten Sture's widow.

LADY INGER [*breathes more freely*]. With. . . ? Ah yes; . . . of course!

NILS LYKKE. But now he has come out into the open and has emerged in Dalecarlia as the peasant's leader. Their numbers are growing daily and, as you may know, they are finding friends among the common folk on the Norwegian side of the mountains.

LADY INGER [*who in the meantime has regained her composure*]. You seem certain, Lord Nils, that I am acquainted with the events of which you speak. What reason have I given you to suppose any such thing? I know nothing and do not wish to know. My intention is to live quietly on my own estate. I am not lending my support to the troublemakers; but neither should you count on me if it is your intention to suppress them.

NILS LYKKE [*in a low voice*]. Would you still stand idly by if it were my intention to support them?

LADY INGER. How am I to understand you?

NILS LYKKE. So you haven't grasped what I have been driving at all this time? . . . Well then, I will be quite frank about things. The fact is that the King and his Cabinet see clearly that in the long run we can have no firm footing in Norway if the nobles and the people continue, as now, to feel wronged and oppressed. We fully understand that willing allies are better than reluctant subjects; and therefore we have no more heart-felt wish than to loosen bonds that restrict *us* as much as *you*. But you will also recognize, I am sure, that the attitude of the Norwegians to us makes such a step too dangerous . . . until we have reliable support behind us.

LADY INGER. And this support . . . ?

NILS LYKKE. The obvious place to look for such support is Sweden. But not, mark you, as long as Gustav Vasa is at the helm; because *his* account with Denmark is not yet settled, and probably never will be. On the other hand a new king of Sweden who had the people on his side and who owed his crown to Danish aid. . . . Well, do you begin to understand me? *Then* we could safely say to you Norwegians: 'Take back your ancient inherited rights, choose yourselves the ruler you want, and be our friends in need, as we will be yours!' . . . And please observe, Lady Inger, that our magnanimity is not in fact as great as it may seem; because you will see that, far from being weakened, we shall be strengthened by it.

And now I have spoken candidly to you, you too must abandon all mistrust. . . . Therefore . . . [*firmly*] the knight from Sweden, who arrived here an hour before me . . .

LADY INGER. Then you know already?

NILS LYKKE. Everything! He's the one I'm looking for.

LADY INGER [*to herself*]. Strange. So it is as Olaf Skaktavl said. [*To* NILS LYKKE.] Please wait here, Lord Nils. I will go and fetch him. [*She goes out through the Great Hall.*]

NILS LYKKE [*looks after her awhile, exultant and astonished*]. She's fetching him! Yes . . . she's really fetching him! The battle is half won. I didn't think it would be so easy. . . . She's deeply involved with the rebels. Started with terror when I mentioned Sten Sture's son. . . .

And so? Hm! Now that Lady Inger has been gullible enough to rush into the trap Nils Sture won't cause much trouble. A mere boy, excitable and thoughtless . . . he will set off with my promise of help . . . unfortunately Jens Bjelke will pick him up on the road . . . and the whole project is killed.

And then? Then a little extra on my own behalf. It will get spread around that the young Count Sture has been in Østråt; . . . that a Danish envoy has had a meeting with Lady Inger . . . as a result of which young Count Nils has been picked up by King Gustav's soldiers a mile from the house. . . . However high Lady Inger's reputation with the people, it would have difficulty in surviving such a blow. [*He starts, suddenly uneasy.*]

Damn it . . . ! What if Lady Inger has smelt a rat! This very moment he may be slipping through our fingers. . . . [*Reassured as he listens towards the Great Hall.*] Ah, no need to worry. Here they come!

[LADY INGER GYLDENLØVE *enters from the hall, accompanied by* SIR OLAF SKAKTAVL.]

LADY INGER [*to* NILS LYKKE]. Here is the gentleman you are waiting for.

NILS LYKKE [*to himself*]. Hell! . . . What does this mean?

LADY INGER. I have told this gentleman your name and everything you said . . .

NILS LYKKE [*uncertainly*]. Really? You have? Well, now . . .

LADY INGER. . . . and I won't hide from you that he has no great faith in your support.

NILS LYKKE. He hasn't?

LADY INGER. Can you wonder? You know the sort of man he is and the harsh fate he's . . .

NILS LYKKE. This man's . . . ? Why . . . yes, indeed . . .

OLAF SKAKTAVL [*to* NILS LYKKE]. But since it was Peter Kanzler himself who summoned us to meet here . . .

NILS LYKKE. Peter Kanzler. . . ? [*He recovers quickly.*] Yes, that's right . . . I am on a mission from Peter Kanzler. . . .

OLAF SKAKTAVL. And he must know best whom he can rely on. So I prefer not to worry my head about how . . .

NILS LYKKE. No, quite right, my dear sir; we certainly mustn't do that.

OLAF SKAKTAVL. Preferably straight to the point . . .

NILS LYKKE. To the point; no beating about the bush; . . . that's always my way.

OLAF SKAKTAVL. Then will you tell me your errand here?

NILS LYKKE. I think you can pretty well guess my errand . . .

OLAF SKAKTAVL. Peter Kanzler mentioned something about papers which . . .

NILS LYKKE. Papers? Oh yes, the papers!

OLAF SKAKTAVL. I take it you have them on you?

NILS LYKKE. Of course; well taken care of; almost too well for me immediately to . . . [*He pretends to search inside his doublet and says to himself:*] Who the devil is he? What shall I think up? I may be able to discover something important. [*He notices that the servants are laying the table and lighting the lamps in the Great Hall, and says to* OLAF

SKAKTAVL:] Ah, I see Lady Inger is having dinner served. Perhaps it would be better to discuss our business at table.

OLAF SKAKTAVL. Very well; as you wish.

NILS LYKKE [*to himself*]. Time is everything! [*To* LADY INGER, *in a most friendly manner.*] And meanwhile we might learn what part Lady Inger Gyldenløve intends to play in our scheme.

LADY INGER. I? . . . None.

NILS LYKKE *and* OLAF SKAKTAVL. None?

LADY INGER. Can you wonder, gentlemen, that I dare not stake all by joining in your game? Particularly as neither of my allies dare trust me fully.

NILS LYKKE. That reproach does not apply to me. I trust you blindly; I beg you to be assured of that.

OLAF SKAKTAVL. Who would dare to rely on you, if not your countrymen?

LADY INGER. Indeed . . . such confidence gladdens me.

[*She goes to a cupboard at the back and fills two goblets with wine.*]

NILS LYKKE [*to himself*]. Damn! Is she going to get out of the trap?

LADY INGER [*hands each of them a goblet*]. And since that is so I offer you this cup of welcome to Østråt. Drink, gentlemen! Drink up!

[*She looks at them in turn when they have drunk, and says gravely:*]

But now I must tell you . . . one goblet contained a welcome for my ally, the other . . . death for my enemy!

NILS LYKKE [*throws down the goblet*]. Ah, I've been poisoned!

OLAF SKAKTAVL [*at the same time, clutching his sword*]. Death and damnation! Have you murdered me?

LADY INGER [*to* OLAF SKAKTAVL, *laughing and pointing to* NILS LYKKE]. That is the Dane's trust in Inger Gyldenløve . . . [*To* NILS LYKKE, *pointing to* OLAF SKAKTAVL.] . . . and likewise my countrymen's faith in me!

[*To both of them.*]

Yet you expect me to place myself in your power? Gently, my lords . . . gently! The Lady of Østråt still has all her wits about her.

THE FEAST AT SOLHOUG
[Gildet paa Solhoug]

PLAY IN THREE ACTS
(1856)

PREFACE TO THE SECOND EDITION (1883)

[When Ibsen came to revise the play for a second edition in 1883, he made no major changes in it; such minor modifications as he did make are summarized in Appendix VII, p. 699. For this second edition, however, he wrote a preface of considerable interest.]

I wrote *The Feast at Solhaug* [*sic*] in Bergen in the summer of 1855, that is, about 28 years ago. The play was first performed, in the same town, on 2 January 1856, a gala performance on the anniversary of the *Norwegian Theatre*.

At the time I held the post of Instructeur at the Bergen Theatre and consequently took the rehearsals of the play myself. It was done supremely well and with rare feeling. Given with pleasure and enthusiasm, it was received in the same way. The 'Bergen poetic temperament', which is said to have decided the latest elections up in those parts, rose to a high pitch in the packed theatre that evening. The performance ended with numerous calls for the author and actors. Later the same evening I was serenaded by the orchestra, accompanied by a large part of the audience. I have an idea I was so carried away that I made some sort of speech to the assembled crowd; at all events I know I felt very happy.

A couple of months later *The Feast at Solhaug* was performed in Christiania. There too it was very well received by the public, and the day after the first performance Bjørnson wrote a warm, kind, and typically youthful article about it in *Morgenbladet*. This was not in fact a notice or critical review; it was more of a free poetic improvisation on the play and its performance, full of phantasy and feeling. But then came criticism proper, written by the proper critics.

How did one become a proper literary critic, particularly a dramatic critic, in the Christiania of those days—I mean the years between 1850 and 1860 or thereabouts?

As a rule it went like this: after a trial run in *Samfundsbladet*, and after having listened frequently to the discussions held at Treschow's café or 'at Ingebret's' after the play, the would-be critic went to Johan Dahl's bookshop and ordered from Copenhagen a copy of J. L. Heiberg's *Prose Works*, which contained, so he had heard, an essay *On the*

Vaudeville. He then read the essay, pondered on it, and perhaps even partly understood it. Furthermore, he learned from these works about a controversy which Heiberg had once been engaged in with Professor Oehlenschläger and with Hauch, the Sorø poet. He would also learn, incidentally, that J. I. Baggesen (the author of *The Letters from the Dead*) had at an even earlier date started a similar campaign against the great author who wrote *Axel and Valborg* and *Hakon Jarl.*

Much other information of use to a critic could be culled from these works. One learned, for example, that a proper critic, in the interests of good taste, felt in duty bound to be scandalized by hiatus. If they discovered a verse containing such a monstrosity one could be sure that the young critical Jeronimuses of Christiania would exclaim with their forerunner in Holberg: Bless my soul, the world won't last till Easter!

And then there was one peculiar feature about contemporary criticism in the Norwegian capital whose origin baffled me for a long time. Whenever a new author published a book or had some small thing performed, our critics were in the habit of flying into an uncontrollable rage, of behaving as though they personally, and the papers they wrote for, had been grievously insulted by the publication of the book or the performance of the play. As I said, I pondered on this peculiarity for a long time. At last I got things straight. Reading the Danish periodical *Månedskrift for Literatur* I noticed that old Molbech, the state-councillor, had in his day been seized with fury whenever a young author published a book or had a play performed in Copenhagen.

Such, more or less, was the constitution of the court which now summoned *The Feast at Solhaug* before the bar of criticism in the daily press of Christiania. It was mainly composed of young men who, for their criticism, lived on loans from various quarters. Their critical thoughts had long been thought and expressed by others; their views had long since been formulated elsewhere. Their whole aesthetic theory was borrowed; their whole critical method was borrowed; the polemical tactics they employed were borrowed in each and every detail, big or small. Yes, even their attitude of mind was borrowed. Borrowed; the whole lot borrowed. The only original thing about them was that their borrowings were without fail inappropriate and misapplied.

No one will be surprised that this body, whose members, as critics, subsisted on borrowings, thought it must assume something similar of me as as an author. So one or two, perhaps more, of the newspapers up there discovered sure enough that I had borrowed this and that from Henrik Hertz's play, *Svend Dyring's House.*

This assertion is unjustifiable and without foundation. It was clearly prompted by the fact that the metre of the old ballads is used in both plays. But the tone of my language is quite different from that of Hertz; the diction in my play has quite a different ring from his. There is a light summer breeze wafting over my rhythm; there is a feeling of autumn hanging over his.

Nor do the two plays, with respect to characters, plot, and contents in general, show any other or any greater similarity than what necessarily follows from the fact that the subject matter of both was taken from the old ballads with their narrow range of ideas.

With equal, or perhaps even greater, justification one could assert that Hertz in *Svend Dyring's House* had borrowed here and there, and more than a little at that, from Heinrich von Kleist's *Käthchen von Heilbronn*, which was written at the beginning of this century. Käthchen's relationship to Count Wetter vom Strahl is essentially the same as Ragnhild's to the knight, Stig Hvide. Like Ragnhild, Käthchen is driven by a mysterious and inexplicable power to follow the man she loves wherever he goes, to steal secretly after him, like an automaton to lie and sleep near him, to return to him from inner compulsion however often she is chased away. There are, moreover, further examples of supernatural intervention, both in Kleist's and Hertz's play.

But can anyone doubt that it would be possible, given a little good will or malice, to ferret out some play among still older dramatic literature from which it might be claimed that Kleist had borrowed a thing or two for his *Käthchen von Heilbronn?* *I* at any rate do not doubt it. But such indications of sources would be pointless. What makes a work of art its creator's spiritual property is the fact that he has impressed upon it the stamp of his own personality. My view is therefore, despite the similarities pointed out, that *Svend Dyring's House* is as unquestionably and exclusively an original work by Henrik Hertz as *Käthchen von Heilbronn* is an original work by Heinrich von Kleist.

In my case I make the same claim for *The Feast at Solhoug*. I hope too that in future each of the three namesakes may be allowed to retain in full what is his by right.

George Brandes, writing on the relationship of *The Feast at Solhoug* to *Svend Dyring's House*, said that the former was not specifically in any way based on the latter but that it was affected by the influence of the older author on the younger. He says, incidentally, such kind things about my work that I have every reason to be grateful to him for this idea, as for so much else.

Nevertheless I must insist that the facts are not as Brandes sees them either. Henrik Hertz has never particularly appealed to me as a dramatist. I cannot therefore bring myself to believe that he should ever, unknown to me, have been able to exert any influence on my own dramatic production.

In this connection, and on this point in particular, I could confine myself to referring the reader to Dr Valfrid Vasenius, lecturer in aesthetics at the University of Helsingfors. In his Ph.D. thesis: *Henrik Ibsen's Dramatic Poetry in its First Period* (1879), and also in *Henrik Ibsen. Portrait of a Poet* (Stockholm, Jos. Seligmann & Co., 1882, 343 pp.), he has given an account of his views on the play under discussion—the latter work being supplemented with what I very briefly told him when we were together in Munich three years ago. I could, as I have said, refer the reader to these. But in order to keep the record straight I will myself outline in the following pages the genesis of *The Feast at Solhaug*.

I said at the beginning of this Preface that the play was written in the summer of 1855. The previous year I had written *Lady Inger*. The work on this drama had of necessity led me to immerse myself in the literature and history of the Middle Ages in Norway, particularly in the later parts of it. I tried, as far as it was possible, to live myself into the ways and customs of that period, into the emotional life of its people, into their patterns of thought and modes of expression.

It is however not a particularly rewarding period to dwell long in; nor does it offer material particularly well suited to dramatic treatment.

Thus it was that I soon turned to the saga times proper. But the Kings' Sagas and the generally stricter historical accounts from that distant time did not attract me; at that time I could not, with the literary plans I then had, make any dramatic use of the conflicts between kings and chieftains, between parties and factions. That did not come till later.

On the other hand I found in rich measure in the Icelandic Family Sagas what I needed in the way of personal embodiment of certain ideas, thoughts, and moods which were occupying me at the time, or of which I was at least more or less vaguely conscious. These Old Norse literary contributions to the history of our saga time I had not known previously; I had hardly even heard them mentioned. Then N. M. Petersen's splendid translation—splendid at least as far as the tone of the language is concerned—came by chance into my hands. In these family chronicles with their changing fortunes and the encounters between man and man, between woman and woman, and between individuals generally, I was conscious of a rich and vital tradition. And from thus living together with all these distinctive, fully-formed, and individualized men and women, the first rough vague outline of *The Vikings at Helgeland* began to grow in my mind. How many of the details took shape in my mind, I cannot say any longer. But I well remember that the two figures I first got my eye on were the two women who later became Hjördis and Dagny. In the play there was to be a great feast, with a fateful clash and much provocative talk. Moreover I wanted to include those aspects of character, feeling, and conditions generally that seemed to me to be most typical of saga life. In a word: what had been treated in epic fashion in the Volsungasaga, I wanted to present directly in dramatic form.

I probably did not draft any complete and consistent plan at that time. But it was clear to me that such a play would have to be the next thing to write.

But then all sorts of things intervened, mostly of a personal nature, and presumably therefore more influential and more decisive than the rest; but I also believe that it was not altogether without significance that just at this time I began a close study of Landstad's collection of Norwegian folksongs, which had been published a few years before. The frame of mind I found myself in at that time was more in tune with the literary romanticism of the Middle Ages than with the events of the sagas, more with verse than with prose, more with the musicality of the ballads than with what is characteristic of the sagas.

Thus it happened that the rather formless plans for a tragedy of *The Vikings at Helgeland* changed for the moment to the lyric drama *The Feast at Solhaug*.

The two women characters, the foster-sisters Hjördis and Dagny in the originally projected tragedy, became the sisters Margit and Signe in the completed lyric drama. That the two last-named derive from the two saga women becomes obvious, once one's attention is drawn to it. The family resemblance is unmistakable. The hero vaguely planned for the tragedy—the far-travelled Viking chieftain Sigurd, who was well known at foreign courts—was transformed into Gudmund Alfsøn, a knight and minstrel, who had also travelled far in foreign lands and lived in royal households. His position between the two women was altered to conform to the different circumstances and conditions of the time; but the relation of the two sisters to him remained in essentials the same as in the originally planned and ultimately completed tragedy. The fateful feast which I had felt it to be of the utmost importance to portray, according to my first plan, became in the drama the stage on which the characters appeared throughout; it became the background against which the action stood in relief, and informed the whole picture with the general atmosphere I had intended. The ending of the play was toned down and softened, true enough, to harmonize with its nature as drama and not tragedy; but orthodox aestheticians could perhaps argue none the less how far this ending retains a touch of sheer tragedy in witness of the origin of the drama.

I shall not go into this matter any further just now. I only wished to assert and show that the present play is the inevitable result of my life at a given time, just as much as all my other dramatic work. It grew from within and not from any external inspiration or influence.

This is the only correct version of the genesis of *The Feast at Solhaug*.

HENRIK IBSEN

Rome, April 1883

BENGT GAUTESON, Master of Solhoug

MARGIT, his wife

SIGNE, her sister

GUDMUND ALFSON, their cousin

KNUT GJÆSLING, the King's sheriff

ERIC OF HÆGGE, his friend

FIRST RETAINER

SECOND RETAINER

THE KING'S MESSENGER

AN OLD MAN

A GIRL

Lady and gentleman guests

Gudmund's men

Knut Gjæsling's men

Serving-men and maids at Solhoug

The action takes place at the beginning of the fourteenth century

ACT ONE

A stately room with doors at the back and on both sides. Right, a table with a number of fashionable feminine ornaments. Left, a larger table with silver tankards, goblets, etc. The door at the back leads out to a gallery, beyond which can be seen glimpses of a wild fjord landscape.

SCENE ONE

[BENGT, MARGIT, KNUT, *and* ERIC *are sitting round the left table.* KNUT'*s men at the back. As the curtain rises, bells from a nearby church are heard ringing to mass.*]

ERIC [*rising from the table*]. And now, in short, what answer have you to my proposal of marriage on behalf of Knut Gjæsling?

BENGT [*with an anxious look at his wife*]. Er, I . . . I think . . . [*As she remains silent.*] Well, Margit, let's hear your opinion first.

MARGIT [*rises*]. Sir Knut, what Eric of Hægge has told us about you I have known for a long time. I am fully aware that you come from an illustrious family; you have a great deal of property and money, and our sovereign lord is most favourably disposed to you.

BENGT [*to* KNUT]. Most favourably . . . I confirm that.

MARGIT. And my sister, it is true, could not choose a better husband.

BENGT. None better; that is exactly what I think.

MARGIT. That is, if you can get her to like you.

BENGT [*anxiously and half aside to* MARGIT]. But . . . but, my dear wife!

KNUT [*jumping up from the table*]. So that's it, Lady Margit! You think your sister . . . ?

BENGT [*seeks to calm him*]. No, wait, Knut Gjæsling! Wait a moment. You must get us right.

MARGIT. There is nothing in my words to give offence; my sister, remember, only knows you by reputation, and your reputation grates on the ears of gentlefolk.

A11

Your ancestral home is an unsafe place
with its swarms of riotous guests; . . .
you carouse together all day and all night,
God help the poor maiden who weds you!
God help the poor maiden you tempt with your gold,
with chattels, and vast green forests . . .
soon you will see how she pines away,
a-yearning to sleep in her coffin!

ERIC. Yes, it's true Knut Gjæsling is a little wild and unruly; but that will change all right once Signe becomes his wife.

KNUT. And please note, Lady Margit: I was over at Hægge drinking with Eric here—it will be about a week ago—and the ale was strong; and as the evening wore on I made a vow that your beautiful sister Signe should be my wife before the year was up. Never shall you say of Knut Gjæsling that he broke a vow; so you see that you must choose me as your sister's husband, whether you like it or not.

MARGIT. Before that can happen, I'll not hide the fact,
you must say goodbye to your drunken companions;
you'll stop charging round with your horses and coaches,
shouting and bawling all over the place;
you will have to allay the widespread horror
when Knut Gjæsling comes to a wedding feast.
Remember your manners when off to a banquet;
your axe leave at home in its place by the door;
you know how it's loose in your hand, whenever
you are flushed and fuddled with mead and ale.
Modest young ladies shall be left unmolested;
let each man retain what is his;
you must not send anyone insolent warnings
that he would do wisely to pack his shroud
should ever his path cross yours!
And if that's how you shape by the end of the year,
you might make my sister your bride indeed.

KNUT [*with suppressed fury*]. You have a subtle way of putting things, Lady Margit. You really should have been a priest, not your husband's wife.

BENGT. Oh, as far as that goes I could also . . .

KNUT [*continues, ignoring him*]. But let me tell you; if any fighting man had spoken to me like that, he . . .

BENGT. Here, I say, Sir Knut, you must understand us!

KNUT [*as before*]. Well, in short, he would have learnt that the axe is loose in my hand, as you said just now.

BENGT [*aside*]. There we are! [*Softly to* MARGIT.] No good will come of this, Margit.

MARGIT [*to* KNUT]. You asked for a straight answer and I've given you one.

KNUT. All right, all right; I'll not take your words too much to heart, Lady Margit. You are cleverer and have more sense than the rest of us put together. Here is my hand; you may well have good reason for all your hard words.

MARGIT. I'm glad to hear you say so; you're already well on the road to reform. And by the way: we are having a feast here at Solhoug today.

KNUT. A feast?

BENGT. Yes, Sir Knut. It's our wedding anniversary you know. Three years ago today I became Lady Margit's husband.

MARGIT [*interrupts him somewhat impatiently*]. As I said, we are having a feast today. Ride back here after church, when you've done all your business, and join the party. Then you can meet my sister.

KNUT. Thank you, Lady Margit, that's fine. But I wasn't on my way to church when I rode down here this morning. It's a relative of yours, Gudmund Alfson, I've come to see.

MARGIT [*surprised*]. My cousin, Gudmund! Where are you going to find him?

KNUT. As you know, his home is beyond the headland on the other side of the fjord.

MARGIT. But he himself is miles away.

ERIC. I wouldn't say that; he might be nearer than you think.

KNUT [*softly*]. Be quiet!

MARGIT. Nearer? What do you mean?

KNUT. Haven't you heard that he is back in Norway? He came with the Chancellor, Audun of Hægrenæs, who was sent to France to fetch our new Queen.

MARGIT. That is true; but there is the royal wedding at Bergen just now and Gudmund Alfson is taking part in the festivities.

BENGT. Yes, and we could have been among the guests too if my wife had wanted it.

ERIC [*softly, to* KNUT]. Then Lady Margit doesn't know?

KNUT [*softly*]. So it seems; but don't give the game away. [*Aloud.*] Well, Lady Margit, I'll have to go all the same and chance it; I'll be back this evening.

MARGIT. And then you must show whether you can manage to control that wild spirit of yours.

BENGT. Yes, take note!

MARGIT. Hands off your axe, do you hear, Knut Gjæsling!

BENGT. Off your axe and your knife, and any other weapon you bring.

MARGIT. Or else you can never hope to be one of my family.

BENGT. No, our minds are firmly made up.

T [*to* MARGIT]. No need to worry!

BENGT. And when our minds are made up we stand firm.

KNUT. I'm glad to hear it, Lord Bengt. I'm made the same way; and I have already drunk to our future kinship. You'll see whether I too don't keep firmly to my word. Till this evening then, and God be with you! [*He goes out at the back with his men;* BENGT *accompanies them to the door. The bells have stopped ringing in the meantime.*]

SCENE TWO

[MARGIT. BENGT.]

BENGT. I had a feeling he was threatening us as he left.

MARGIT [*absently*]. Yes, it seemed like it.

BENGT. Knut Gjæsling is not a man to come up against; and come to think of it we did say rather a lot of unkind things to him. Well, don't let's worry about that; today we must be merry, Margit, and I do declare we both have good reason to be.

MARGIT [*with concealed bitterness*]. Yes, of course!

BENGT. It's true I was not in my first youth when I asked you to marry me. But I do know I was the richest man within miles. You were a beautiful girl of noble birth; but your dowry would not have attracted many suitors.

MARGIT [*to herself*]. Yet I was so well off in those days.

BENGT. What did you say, Margit?

MARGIT. Oh, nothing, nothing! I am going to put on my pearls and my rings. It is after all a joyful occasion for me this evening.

BENGT. Good, that's what I like to hear; let me see you dress in your best so our guests can say it's a happy woman who got Bengt Gauteson for a husband. But now I must go and see about the catering. There's a great deal to attend to today. [*He goes out, left.*]

SCENE THREE

[MARGIT, *alone.*]

MARGIT [*sinks down into a chair, right, and says after a pause*]:
Thank goodness he's gone. When I see him in here
it feels just as though my blood had stopped flowing;
it feels like a cold, constricting band
pressing so tightly round my heart!

[*Vehemently, bursting into tears.*]

He is my husband, I am his wife! . . .
What is the span of our life on this earth?
God help me! It could be quite two score and ten . . .
and I am, alas, in my . . . twenty-third year!

[*Calmer, after a moment's silence.*]

It is hard to sit sighing behind gold walls,
it is hard to be shut in a cage so long!

[*She mechanically picks up her jewels, which are lying on the table in front of her, and begins to put them on.*]

He asked me to wear my pearls and rings,
to put on my very best jewels.
If this were my funeral here today
I would find it a gayer occasion! . . .
But I must stop brooding about it all;
I know of a song to drive sorrow away.

[*She sings.*]

The Mountain King rode the country through,
—My days are all sadness and yearning—
To seek the fair maiden he wished to woo.
—Oh, when is my loved one returning?—

The Mountain King did to Lord Haaken's ride,
—My days are all sadness and yearning—
Little Kirsten stood combing her hair outside.
—Oh, when is my loved one returning?—

The Mountain King wedded the maiden fair,
—My days are all sadness and yearning—
A girdle of silver he gave her to wear.
—Oh, when is my loved one returning?—

The Mountain King wedded the lily wand,
—My days are all sadness and yearning—
With fifteen gold rings upon each tiny hand.
—Oh, when is my loved one returning?—

And three summers passed, and there passed some five,
—My days are all sadness and yearning—
In the mountain dear Kirsten was scarce alive.
—Oh, when is my loved one returning?—

And five summers passed, and there passed some nine,
—My days are all sadness and yearning—
Little Kirsten ne'er saw the sun on the pine.
—Oh, when is my loved one returning?—

The valley has blossoms and birds in song,
—My days are all sadness and yearning—
The mountain has gold and its night is long.
—Oh, when is my loved one returning?—

How oft of an evening would Gudmund sing
that song in my father's hall;
there's something about it . . . I cannot tell what . . .
there is something which I could never forget.
There is something it has which took me by storm,
which I never could grasp and keep pondering on still.

[*In horror, as she notices her rings and the other jewels.*]

Rings of red gold! The belt round my waist!
And with gold the Mountain King wedded his wife!

[*She sinks down in the chair and covers her face with her hands.*]

I am, alas, the Mountain King's bride!
And no one is coming to set me free!

SCENE FOUR

[MARGIT. SIGNE *comes hurrying in from the back.*]

SIGNE. Margit! Margit! He's coming!

MARGIT [*jumps up, trying to keep calm*]. Coming? Who's coming?

SIGNE. Gudmund, our cousin!

MARGIT. Gudmund Alfson here . . . how can you think . . . ?

SIGNE. Oh, I am sure of it.

MARGIT. Why, Gudmund Alfson is at the royal wedding. You know
that as well as I do.

SIGNE. Perhaps; but I am sure it was he all the same.

MARGIT. Did you see him then?

SIGNE. Oh, indeed not; but let me tell you about it!

MARGIT. Yes, do.

SIGNE. When early this morning I heard the bells ring
I felt I must ride in to worship;
from sallows and birches above and around
the wild birds were chirping and singing.
All heaven and earth were throbbing with joy;
'twas almost too late now for service . . .
for as I rode on down the path in the shade
each rosebud invited and beckoned.
I crept into church, not making a sound; . . .
there stood the priest by the altar;
he changed and read while, devout in their hearts,
the flock was imbibing God's message.
Then a voice rang out from the blue of the fjord,
I fancied I saw how the statuettes turned,
straining to listen to every sound.

MARGIT. And then what, Signe? Go on! Go on!

SIGNE. As though a profound and inscrutable call
bade me go forth from the holy church
over hill and dale, across field and rock.
Past the silver birches I strode as I heard,
I was walking as though in a dream . . .
behind me stood empty the house of the Lord;
for priest and the faithful were coming with me
while the ravishing strains poured forth.
A hush lay over that path from the church,
I sensed that the birds were pausing to hear,
the lark descended, the cuckoo was still,
and echoes gave answer from hill and fell.

MARGIT. Yes . . .

SIGNE.   Men and women all crossed themselves.

[*She lays her hands on her breast.*]

But strange were the thoughts which rose up inside me. . . .
That glorious song . . . I knew it so well.
Gudmund has sung it many a time;
Gudmund has sung it many an eve;
and all of his songs I so clearly recall.

MARGIT. And you think it could be . . . ?

SIGNE.   I'm quite sure it is!
You'll see for yourself soon, I promise.
Doesn't every wee songster come home in the end
and leave foreign lands far behind him?
I do feel so happy but cannot say why; . . .
I've just had a thought . . . do you know what I'll do?
His harp has been hanging for ages
in there on the wall; I will take it down
and I'll give it a polish, tune its gold strings
and put it out ready for playing.

MARGIT [*lost in thought*]. Do what you want to . . .

SIGNE [*looks at her reproachfully*].   Don't say it like that;

[*In a friendly manner, embracing her.*]

When Gudmund comes you'll feel light of heart,
as you did when Signe was tiny.

MARGIT [*half to herself*].
A great deal has altered since then!

SIGNE. Margit, you *shall* be happy and gay!
Why, lasses and lads there to serve you,
and the walls lined with rows of the costliest clothes;
dear heart, there's no end to your riches!
Each day you can ride through the shady grove
and go out hunting the wild deer;
each night you can sleep in your lady's bower
on cushions worked in blue silk.

MARGIT [*ignoring her*].
To think that he's coming to Solhoug . . . our guest!

SIGNE. What did you say?

MARGIT [*controls herself*]. Nothing! . . . Go, put on your best!
  These blessings of mine which you praise to the skies
  might be waiting for you.

SIGNE.   What is it you mean?

MARGIT [*looks at her affectionately and strokes* SIGNE's *hair to one side*].
  I mean . . . ah well, you'll see for yourself . . .
  I mean, if some suitor should ride here tonight . . . ?

SIGNE. A suitor? Who for?

MARGIT.   For you!

SIGNE [*laughing*].   For me?
  In that case, I fear, he'll have come the wrong way.

MARGIT. What would you reply if he graciously asked
  for your hand?

SIGNE.   I am too gay at heart, I'd reply,
  to be thinking of suitors and things of that kind!

MARGIT. But if he were rich and a man of power?

SIGNE. Why, even a king with a palace full
  of costly raiment and bright red gold
  would really be no great temptation!
  I feel I am well enough off in myself,
  with the song of the river, the summer and sun,
  with you and the birds on the branches!
  This, my dear sister, is where I will live;
  as for giving a suitor my word and my hand . . .
  I just have not the time; I'm too happy and gay.

                    [*She runs out singing, left.*]

SCENE FIVE

[MARGIT. BENGT *enters almost immediately from the back.*]

MARGIT [*after a pause*]. Gudmund Alfson coming here, here to Solhoug?
  No, no, it can't be true. Signe heard him singing, she says; . . .
  when I heard the pines rustling deep in the forest, when I heard
  the roar of the waterfall and the twittering of the birds in the

treetops I never tired of fancying that Gudmund's songs were mingled with them . . . yet he himself was miles away. Signe must be mistaken; Gudmund is not coming.

BENGT [*enters hurriedly from the back*]. Margit, here's someone we don't often see!

MARGIT. Who is it?

BENGT. Your cousin, Gudmund! [*He calls out to the right.*] Get the best guest-room ready, and quick about it!

MARGIT. Is he here already then?

BENGT [*looks out through the door at the back*]. No, not quite; but it won't be long now! [*He calls out to the right.*] The carved oak bed with the dragon heads! [*To* MARGIT.] His squire brings greetings from him; he himself is following.

MARGIT. His squire? Is he bringing a squire?

BENGT. Yes, I'll be bound! He has a squire and six armed men accompanying him. Ah well, he is a very different man from the one who left the district seven years ago. But I must go out and receive him. [*He calls out.*] Put the best gilded saddle on! And all my men are to march down to the beach. And don't forget the bridle with the serpent heads! [*Fastening his sword.*] Such a fine gentleman . . . Heavens above! . . . We must receive him with honour, with great honour! [*He goes out at the back.*]

SCENE SIX

[MARGIT. *Three serving girls enter almost immediately.*]

MARGIT. He went from these parts just a penniless lad;
now he comes back with his squire and armed men.
What for? Does he want perhaps to see
if I am embittered with gnawing grief?
Does he desire to probe and find out
what I'm able to bear till my heart has to burst?
Can he imagine . . . ? Just come and try,
the joy you derive will be slight indeed!

[*She makes a sign; the girls come in.*]

I want you to listen to what I say:
go off and fetch my blue silk gown
then come straightaway with me to my room
and there you will robe me in velvet and fur;
two of you shall dress me in ermine and gold,
the third shall thread strings of pearls through my hair.
And bring along all my jewels as well.

[*The girls go out with the caskets etc., left.* MARGIT *continues after a momentary silence.*]

So be it! Margit is the Mountain King's bride.
Good! The royal robes are for me to wear. [*She goes out, left.*]

SCENE SEVEN

[BENGT *shows* GUDMUND ALFSON *in from the back.*]

BENGT. And once more, welcome to my wife's cousin at Solhoug Hall!

GUDMUND. I thank you; . . . and how is she? Flourishing in every way, I imagine?

BENGT. Yes, you may be sure she is. She has all she wants. No fewer than five girls at her beck and call; a mount ready saddled whenever she feels so inclined; yes, in short, she has all that a lady of quality can desire to make her lot a happy one.

GUDMUND. And Margit, is she happy then?

BENGT. God knows, anyone would think she must be; but oddly enough . . .

GUDMUND. What do you mean?

BENGT. Well, believe it or not, I have the impression that Margit was much more cheerful when she hadn't a penny than as the Lady of Solhoug.

GUDMUND [*to himself*]. I knew it; it was bound to be so.

BENGT. What did you say, cousin?

GUDMUND. I said I am highly astonished at what you tell me about your wife.

BENGT. And don't you think I feel the same? As sure as I am a knight I cannot see what more she can want. . . . She has my company all day long and no one could call me strict; I've also taken on all the running of the house and estate; and yet . . . ah well, you were always a jolly fellow; I expect you'll have brought a ray of sunshine. Hush; here is Lady Margit! Don't let her see that I . . .

SCENE EIGHT

[*As before.* MARGIT, *splendidly attired, from the left.*]

GUDMUND [*hastens to meet her*]. Margit, my dear Margit!

MARGIT [*greeting him with a blank look*]. You must forgive me, my lord, but . . . [*As though just recognizing him.*] Indeed, Gudmund Alfson, unless I am mistaken! [*She holds out her hand.*]

GUDMUND [*without taking it*]. So you didn't recognize me at once?

BENGT [*laughing*]. Come, Margit, what were you thinking of? [*Still laughing.*] Why, I told you just now that Gudmund . . .

MARGIT [*crossing to the table, right*]. Twelve years is a long time, Gudmund. Long enough for the sturdiest plant to have died ten times over. . . .

GUDMUND. It's seven years since we last met.

MARGIT. It must surely be longer.

GUDMUND [*looking fixedly at her*]. I'm tempted to think so, but it is as I say.

MARGIT. Most strange! But I was only a child then and it seems an eternity since I was a child. [*She throws herself down into a chair.*] Well, cousin, be seated! Rest and relax; this evening you shall dance and regale us with your songs. [*With a forced smile.*] I expect you know we are all feeling happy here today . . . we are having a feast.

GUDMUND. So I was told as soon as I got here. [*Aside.*] Had I known earlier I would scarcely have come.

BENGT. Yes, three years ago today I became . . .

MARGIT [*interrupting*]. My cousin has heard all about that. [*To* GUDMUND.] Won't you take your cloak off?

GUDMUND. Thank you, Lady Margit; but I find it cold here . . . colder than I expected.

BENGT. Well, upon my sword, I feel hot enough for the two of us, but then I've so many things to attend to. [*To* MARGIT.] Keep our guest entertained in the meantime; . . . you can talk over old times together [*About to go.*]

MARGIT [*dubiously*]. Are you going? Wouldn't you rather . . . ?

BENGT [*comes back; to* GUDMUND, *laughing*]. You see, Lord Bengt of Solhoug has a way with women. My wife can't do without me for a single moment. [*To* MARGIT, *chucking her under the chin.*] Rest assured, I'll soon be back. [*He goes out at the back.*]

MARGIT [*aside*]. Oh, it drives me mad having to endure all this!

SCENE NINE

[MARGIT. GUDMUND.]

GUDMUND [*after a pause*]. How is your sister Signe these days?

MARGIT. Very well, thank you!

[*A pause.*]

GUDMUND.   They said she was here
with you!

MARGIT.   She has been here ever since I . . .

[*Abruptly, correcting herself.*]

She came with me to Solhoug three years ago.

[*A brief pause.*]

I dare say she'll join us in here before long.

GUDMUND. She used to be such a likeable girl,
nothing sly or deceitful about her.
Whenever I think of those big blue eyes
I am always reminded of angels.
But so much may happen in seven years.
Tell me . . . while I have been gone on my travels,
has she changed too in so striking a fashion?

MARGIT [*with constrained banter*].
　She too? Can it be at Court that you learn
　such diplomatic language?
　You make me remember how time erodes . . .

GUDMUND. Margit, you know very well what I mean.
　You both were once so kind towards me;
　you wept when the day came for me to leave you.
　We vowed to stick close like brother and sister,
　for better for worse, in joy and in sorrow.
　Like a sun you outshone all the other young girls,
　and the fame of your beauty had spread far and wide.
　You still are as lovely as ever you were,
　but the Lady of Solhoug, I see, has forgotten
　her penniless cousin. So hard in your manner,
　you who were once the most friendly of souls.

MARGIT [*with an outburst of feeling*].
　Yes, once . . . !

GUDMUND [*watches her with kindly interest and, after a pause, says in a
　subdued voice*]. Your husband said pass the time
　reviving old memories dear to us both.

MARGIT [*vehemently*]. Oh no, not that!

　　　　　　　　　　　[*Calmer.*]
　　　　　　　　　　　　　　I find it so hard
　to remember. I've never wanted to learn.
　Tell me instead of the years since you left us;
　they were not uneventful, of that I am sure.
　There must be so much you can talk of;
　the richness and warmth of the world outside
　make for lightness of heart and of mind.

GUDMUND. The Royal Palace never saw me so gay
　as I was when a lad in my humble home.

MARGIT [*without looking at him*].
　And I . . . each day living at Solhoug here . . .
　thanked the Lord for making my lot so pleasant.

GUDMUND. A good thing for you that you can give thanks . . .

MARGIT [*vehemently*].
   Why, am I not honoured, am I not free?
   Can I not give orders in what way I please?
   Am I not the mistress, to rule as I fancy?
   I always come first here; my place is not shared,
   and that, as you know, suits me in every way.
   You'll have thought you would find me all weary and sad,
   but you see I am gay and light of heart.
   So clearly you need not have gone to the trouble
   of coming to Solhoug; much good it will do you!

GUDMUND. What do you mean, Lady Margit?

MARGIT.   I'm fully aware
   what it is brings you here to my lonely home.

GUDMUND. You know why I've come? And you do not approve?

[*He picks up his hat.*]

   Farewell then, my lady, and God be with you!

MARGIT [*who has risen in the meantime*].
   It would have redounded far more to your credit
   had you stayed where you were, at the Royal Palace.

GUDMUND. Royal Palace! Can you mock at my plight!

MARGIT. At your plight! You've set your sights high then, my cousin;
   I'm curious to know where you're thinking of stopping!
   You are able to dress in robes of red velvet,
   are close to the King, have lands and gold . . .

GUDMUND. *You* must know best if fortune's my friend;
   you said only now you were fully aware
   what brought me to Solhoug.

MARGIT.   I have no doubt at all!

GUDMUND. Then you also know of my recent experience; . . .
   you know that I am an outlaw now!

MARGIT [*utterly astonished*].
   Outlaw! You, Gudmund!

GUDMUND.   I am! It is true!
  But I solemnly swear by our Lord Jesus Christ,
  had I known how you thought and felt about things
  I'd not have set foot in Solhoug Hall!
  I thought you would still be gentle and kind,
  as you were at the time when I left;
  but I'll not be a beggar; the forest is vast,
  and I can rely on my hand and my bow; . . .
  for board and lodging I'd rather the moors
  and the den of the mountain bear.

                    [*He is about to go.*]

MARGIT. Outlawed! No, stay! I give you my word,
  I knew not a thing about it!

GUDMUND. It is as I tell you. My life is at stake,
  and life is what we all cling to!
  Three nights I've slept like a dog in the open,
  resting my weary limbs up in the hills,
  and laying my head on the rocky slopes.
  I just could not bear to go knocking on doors,
  begging for shelter and somewhere to sleep;
  so sure did I feel, and hope was fresh!
  I thought: once you get to Solhoug now
  then all your trials are over for good,
  you have friends you can safely depend on there. . . .
  But hope is as tender as flowers by the wayside!
  Your husband met me in pomp and style
  and welcomed me here with open doors,
  but I find everything bleak and bare,
  gloomy your hall, and my friends are gone.
  Ah well, I'll take to the hills again.

                    [*He is about to go.*]

MARGIT. Oh, hear me!

GUDMUND.   I'm not made with the soul of a slave!
  Life now seems to me a gift not worth having,
  its value I put at virtually nothing.
  You have cast to one side all I ever held dear,
  you force me to bury my fondest of hopes!
  Farewell, Lady Margit!

Bɪɪ

MARGIT.   No, Gudmund, listen!
  By God almighty . . .

GUDMUND.   Stick to your pleasures;
  just live for your pleasures and honours;
  for Gudmund will scarcely darken your door,
  and never will cause any trouble.

MARGIT. That is enough now! Your bitter words
  will bring you much harm and sorrow!
  Had I known that you were a hunted man,
  outlawed all over the country . . .
  it would have been, believe me, the day of my life
  when your steps brought you here to Solhoug Hall,
  and I would have had my merriest feast
  when the outlaw invited himself as a guest.

GUDMUND. You say. . . ! What *am* I to think and believe?

MARGIT [*holding out her hand to him*].
  That kinsfolk at Solhoug are kind folk too.

GUDMUND. But what you just said . . . ?

MARGIT.   Forget about that.
  Listen to me and you'll understand. . . .
  My life is as dark as the blackest night,
  no stars in my sky and no sunshine . . .
  there *is* no cure for the anguish I feel;
  alas I have bartered my youth away!
  My carefree nature I traded for gold,
  I shackled myself with gaudy chains;
  you can take my word for it, money itself
  is poor compensation for sorrowing souls!
  When we were children how happy I was!
  We had little enough, our home was poor,
  but hope in abundance I had in my breast.

GUDMUND [*who has been looking at her fixedly*].
  You were even then an exquisite beauty.

MARGIT. May be, but the lavish praises I heard
  were soon to ruin and wreck my life.
  You had to travel to foreign lands,

but each of your songs was deeply engraved
in the recesses of heart and mind,
and a tissue of dreams veiled my brow.
Your songs had ranged over every joy
the human breast can encompass and hold.
Your songs had sung of the cheerful life
which knights and their ladies lead. And then . . .
there came suitors from east and suitors from west,
until . . . I became my husband's wife! . . .
Believe me, it was not very long after that
before I was shedding bitter tears.
Just thinking of you, my cousin, my friend,
was all the joy I had left.
How empty it seemed at Solhoug Hall,
how bare its vast apartments!
We had knights come to see us, and lords with their ladies,
I was honoured in many a minstrel's song;
but there was not one who could understand,
not one who fathomed my sorrow!
I froze as though locked in the mountain fastness,
yet my head was throbbing, my blood was on fire!
As for my husband, I never loved him,
it was only his gold that attracted me;
whenever he spoke, when he sat by my side,
my mind was distracted with anguish!
And that's how I've lived for three whole years;
a life of incessant, unending woe.
We heard you were coming. You are aware
how fierce is the pride which burns in my heart . . .
I hid my sorrow, concealed my distress;
for you were the last who should know the truth.

GUDMUND. And that is the reason you turned away?

MARGIT [*without looking at him*].
     I thought you had come to poke fun at my grief.

GUDMUND. Margit, how could you believe . . . ?

MARGIT.   In short,
     I had reason enough for thinking so.
     But that, thank heaven, is over and past.

I'm not on my own any more,
I feel so free and so light of heart,
like a child they've let out to play!

[*With sudden terror.*]

But where are my thoughts? How could I forget;
by all the merciful saints above!
Outlawed, you said . . . ?

GUDMUND.   Not now I'm home;
for now the King's men will leave me in peace.

MARGIT. But not long ago your credit stood high;
tell me how you . . .

GUDMUND.   The story's soon told.
You know that I went on a visit to France
when the Chancellor, Audun of Hægrenæs,
sailed there from Bergen in pomp and style
to bring back the princess, the King's bride-to-be,
together with pages and maidens and wealth.
A fine handsome man Lord Audun was,
the princess a woman of charm unsurpassed.
Her eyes were so warm and appealing; . . .
they talked to each other, they whispered in private.
Of what? That was hard to discover. . . .
One night I was leaning against the rail . . .
I was sitting there in silence;
with the seagulls my thoughts were speeding ahead
towards the coast of Norway.
I heard a voice whisper behind my back,
I turned round to look . . . and there they were!
They didn't see me, I was safe where I sat,
but I could recognize them.
She gazed at him with sorrowful eyes
and whispered: 'If only our course were set
for southern lands of enchantment,
and alone on the ship just the two of us,
my heart, I believe, would surely find peace,
and the fever would leave my brow.' . . .
And softly he whispered, her answer was bold;

she answered in words so ardent and fierce;
I saw how her eyes were flashing like stars;
she said: ...

[*He breaks off.*]

I was utterly shocked and appalled!

MARGIT. Go on!

GUDMUND.   I stood up; they both of them fled; ...
and there I was alone on the deck ...

[*He takes out a small phial.*]

but where they'd been sitting I picked up this.

MARGIT. And that?

GUDMUND [*in a low voice*]. Contains a mysterious fluid;
one drop of this in your enemy's glass
and his strength will gradually ebb away;
no cure known to man can help him then!

MARGIT. But tell me ...?

GUDMUND [*whispering*].   The phial was meant for the King!

MARGIT. By all the saints ...!

GUDMUND [*replacing the phial*]. I've kept it carefully ever since. ...
Three days later the voyage was over,
and I secretly fled with all my men.
I knew well enough that, once at Court,
Audun would scheme and my downfall was sure ...
and that is what happened.

MARGIT.   Now all your troubles
are over, and all is back where it was.

GUDMUND. All? No, Margit, you used to be free.

MARGIT. You mean ...?

GUDMUND.   Mean? Nothing! Oh, let me collect
my thoughts; it makes me so happy and glad
to be at long last with you two once more.
But tell me ... Signe ...?

MARGIT [*points with a smile to the left door*]. She'll soon be here;
  she has to dress up for her cousin, you know,
  and that's not a thing you can rush, I dare say.

GUDMUND. I must see if she still can recognize me. [*He goes out left.*]

SCENE TEN

[MARGIT, *alone.*]

MARGIT. How handsome and manly he is! [*With a sigh.*] There is not
  much resemblance between him and . . . [*She tidies up the tables etc.*]
  You used to be free, he said. Yes, used to be! [*A pause.*] That was a
  strange story about the princess who . . . she loved another, and
  then; . . . yes, these foreign women—so I've heard said—are not meek
  like us; they are not afraid of putting their thoughts into action.
  [*She picks up a goblet standing on the table.*] When he went away, Gudmund and I drank from this goblet to our happy reunion. It's virtually
  the only heirloom I brought to Solhoug. [*She puts it into the cupboard.*]
  A real summer day . . . how mild it is! It is so light in here. For
  three years we've not had such glorious sunshine.

SCENE ELEVEN

[MARGIT. SIGNE *and* GUDMUND *enter from the left.*]

SIGNE [*laughing as she comes through the door and runs up to* MARGIT].
  Ha! ha! ha! He won't believe that it's me!

MARGIT [*smiling, to* GUDMUND].
  You see, while you have been gone on your travels,
  she *too* has changed in as striking a fashion.

GUDMUND. She certainly has! But that she should. . . . No,
  that had simply never entered my mind.

[*He grasps* SIGNE'*s hands and looks into her eyes.*]

  And yet as I look into these blue eyes
  I can still see the innocent child;
  what possible reason then is there to doubt!
  I laugh when I think of the many times
  I've imagined you, Signe, as you were,
  the wisp of a child I bore in my arms . . .
  and now you're the *hulder* who teases and charms us.

SIGNE [*mischievously, as she steps back and shakes a finger at him*].
Take care! Once you make a *hulder* cross,
she'll soon have you caught in her nets . . . so beware!

GUDMUND [*aside*]. I rather believe she already has.

SIGNE. One moment, though; you still have to see
the way I have tended and cared for your harp.

[*As she goes out, left.*]

And now you shall teach me your songs, every one!

GUDMUND [*aside, as he watches her go*].
As the loveliest rose she has now blossomed forth,
who was yet a mere bud at the coming of dawn!

SIGNE [*returning with the harp*]. Here you are!

GUDMUND.   My harp! As sparkling as ever!

[*He strikes a few chords.*]

There's music still in the dear old strings;
You shall not go back on the wall again.

MARGIT [*looking out at the back*].
Our guests are arriving!

SIGNE [*as* GUDMUND *plays the opening chords of the following song*].
                        Hush! Quiet! Oh listen!

GUDMUND [*sings*].
        So sadly I wandered alone in the hills,
        from bushes and boughs there came twitters and trills;
        they twittered so slyly, those small birds above:
        Now hear while we sing to thee all about love!

        It grows like the oak through the years slow and long,
        it feeds on our musing and sorrow and song,
        Yet quickly it sends forth the first tender shoot,
        in no time at all in our heart it strikes root.

[*During the final bars he walks to the back.*]

SIGNE [*watches him dreamily, places her hand on her heart, and repeats to herself*]:

> Yet quickly it sends forth the first tender shoot,
> in no time at all in our heart it strikes root!

MARGIT [*absently*]. Were you speaking to me? . . . I didn't quite catch . . .

SIGNE. I? No, I wasn't; I only meant . . . [*Again going off into a reverie.*]

MARGIT [*half to herself*].

> It grows like the oak through the years slow and long,
> it feeds on our musing and sorrow and song.

SIGNE [*waking up*]. You were saying . . . ?

MARGIT [*running her hand over her forehead*]. Oh, it was nothing. Come, we must go and meet our guests.

SCENE TWELVE

[*As before.* BENGT *enters with the* GUESTS *from the back.*]

CHORUS OF GUESTS.

> We fiddle and sing as we enter the hall;
> we've come to feast and play.
> God bless our kind hostess, so say we all,
> we wish her both happy and gay.
> The skies above Solhoug's fair mansion, we pray,
> > as bright as today
> > ever may be!

ACT TWO

A birch grove adjoining the house, part of which is seen on the left.
Paths lead up the hillside at the back. Back right, a waterfall, the
lower part of which is hidden by boulders. It is a light summer night.
The windows in the house are lit up.

SCENE ONE

[CHORUS OF GUESTS *in the house. Later,* KNUT *and* ERIC.]

CHORUS [*offstage*].

> Let music begin; while fiddlers play
> we will all dance till night turns to day,
> for many a merry long hour!
> The maiden's cheeks are flushed and aflame;
> then up steps a youth so bold and game,
> and holds tight the slender flower!

[KNUT *and* ERIC *come out of the house. The sound of music and merriment continues in the background during what follows.*]

ERIC. As long as you don't regret it, Knut!

KNUT. That's my business.

ERIC. Indeed, but it's risky. You are the King's sheriff; you are ordered on the highest authority to catch Gudmund Alfson wherever you can lay hands on him; and now that you have him in your grasp you offer him your friendship and let him go about freely, just as he pleases.

KNUT. I know what I am doing. I looked for him in his own home and he wasn't to be found there. And if I tried to seize him here do you think Lady Margit would feel like letting me marry Signe?

ERIC [*slowly*]. No, it would hardly be with her blessing, but . . .

KNUT. And I am reluctant to proceed against her will. Then again, Gudmund is an old friend of mine and he can be useful to me. [*Firmly.*] So it shall be as I said; no one here must know tonight that Gudmund Alfson is an outlaw; tomorrow he can fend for himself.

ERIC. Yes, but the King's peace!

KNUT. Oh, the King's peace! You know as well as I do that the King's
   writ scarcely runs out here in the country; if it were enforced many
   a stout fellow among us would have to pay the price for killing and
   bride-snatching. . . . Come on! [*They go out, right.*]

SCENE TWO

[GUDMUND *and* SIGNE *come down a path among the trees at the back.*]

SIGNE. Oh do go on! Let me hear you speak;
   Your voice is sheer music upon my ears.

GUDMUND. Signe, my fair one, my exquisite flower!

SIGNE [*secretly delighted and astonished*].
   I . . . I am dear to him!

GUDMUND.   Dearest of all!

SIGNE. I am the one who can bind your will,
   I am the one who can bind your heart!
   Oh, dare I believe you?

GUDMUND.   You dare, indeed.
   Signe, I'll tell you. As the years flew past,
   summer and winter, I was true in my thoughts
   to both of you, to my loveliest flowers.
   But I couldn't quite fathom my feelings aright.
   You, Signe, were like a wee elf when I left,
   like the tiny wee elves that live in the woods,
   who are busy at play while we dream in our beds.
   But now when I entered Solhoug here
   I became quite clear in my mind,
   quite clear that Margit's a lady proud
   and you are the sweetest of charming young girls.

SIGNE [*who has only been half listening to his words*].
   One winter night—it was long ago—
   we sat, I recall, by the glowing hearth . . .
   you sang to me of the little maid
   the sprite had lured to his watery lair.
   There she forgot both father and mother,
   there she forgot both sister and brother;

she quite forgot both heaven and earth,
forgot the good Lord and each Christian word.
But close by the bank a young lad stood,
and he was so weary and sad at heart;
he plucked at his harpstrings, full of woe,
and far the sounds spread, both loud and long.
The dear little maid from the depths of the pool
heard them and woke from her heavy sleep;
the sprite could do naught but let her go free,
and up through the lilies she rose to the top;
then once more she knew both heaven and earth,
and grasped the full meaning of God and his word!

GUDMUND. Signe, my loveliest flower!

SIGNE.   Like her,
I too have been dreaming and fast asleep;
those mysterious words you have spoken tonight
of the power of love were a joyful awakening.
The heavens have never seemed so blue,
never so fair the wide wide world;
I feel I can tell what the birds are saying
as I stroll on the hillside with you.

GUDMUND. Yes, such is the power of love; . . . it can stir
longings and thoughts and delight in our breast!
But let us go in to your sister now.

SIGNE [*shyly*]. Are you going to tell her . . .?

GUDMUND.   She ought to know all.

SIGNE [*as before*].
Then go by yourself . . . for I am quite sure
I would blush if I went in too.

GUDMUND. All right, I'll go.

SIGNE.   And I will wait here;

[*She looks out to the right.*]

Or better . . . down by the river there.
I can hear Knut Gjæsling with the lasses and lads.

GUDMUND. You'll be waiting there?

SIGNE.   While you talk to her. [*She goes
out, right.* GUDMUND *enters the house.*]

SCENE THREE

[MARGIT *enters from behind the house.*]

MARGIT. The fun and the frolics they're having inside;
    young men and the ladies all dancing away.
    I felt so hot I could scarcely breathe.
    Gudmund was not there among them.

[*She takes a deep breath.*]

It's pleasant out here, so peaceful and quiet,
with the cool night air to refresh me.

[*A pause.*]

That horrible thought; . . . I don't understand . . .
it follows me round wherever I go!
The phial . . . contains a mysterious fluid . . .
one drop of this in my . . . enemy's glass
and his strength will gradually ebb away.
No cure known to man can help him then!

[*A pause.*]

If I knew that Gudmund . . . were he fond of me . . .
then little I'd care . . .

SCENE FOUR

[MARGIT. GUDMUND *comes out of the house.*]

GUDMUND.   Why, Margit, you here?
    And alone? I've looked for you everywhere.

MARGIT. It's stifling indoors and so cool outside.
    Look at the way all those white mists there
    glide so softly across the fen.
    It's not really dark or light out here,
    about halfway between. [*Aside.*] Just as in my breast!
    [*Aloud.*] Don't you find when you're out on a night like this
    that there's something about it you don't understand? . . .

But you sense how life stirs so mysteriously
in bushes and leaves, in flowers and reeds!

[*Switching abruptly.*]

Do you know what I wish?

GUDMUND.   Well?

MARGIT.   I wish that I were
the elf-maid that lives on the hill-slope up there;
how artfully I would weave my spells!
Why . . . !

GUDMUND.   Tell me, Margit, is something the matter?

MARGIT [*continuing*]. How I would sing my soulful song!
Singing and sighing all night and all day!

[*With mounting vehemence.*]

How I would lure the bold young man
past green forest slopes to my mountain den;
there I could forget the woes of the world,
there with my darling I could burn in love's fire!

GUDMUND. Margit! Margit!

MARGIT [*without listening to him*]. At midnight hour
sleep would be sweet on our hillside lea;
and if death should strike with the rising sun,
how pleasant a way to die, don't you think?

GUDMUND. You're not well.

MARGIT [*laughing violently*]. Ha! ha! ha! Oh, let me laugh!
Let me laugh! It does do me good!

GUDMUND.   I can see
you still have the same uncontrollable spirit
as ever . . . !

MARGIT [*suddenly becoming serious*]. You must not wonder at that. . . .
It's only at midnight when folk are asleep;
in daytime I'm always as shy as a deer.
And what of it, I ask you, when all's said and done?
Just remember those women in foreign parts . . .

why, she *was* a wild one . . . that lovely princess;
compared with her I'm as meek as a lamb.
She was not one to stop at wistful sighs;
no, she meant business, and that . . .

GUDMUND.   I am glad
you've reminded me of it; I won't keep the thing
any longer; I've little need for it now.

[*He takes out the phial.*]

MARGIT. The phial! You mean. . . ?

GUDMUND.   I kept it because
I thought I might use it to set myself free
if the King's men should ever bring me to bay.
But after this evening its value is gone;
now I will fight with my arm and my sword,
summon family and friends to strive to the last
in defence of my life and my freedom.
Here goes! [*He is about to throw it away.*]

MARGIT [*holds him back*]. No, wait! Let me have it!

GUDMUND.   What for?

MARGIT. To send to the sprite in the water.
So often his playing has given me joy
and many a song of strange beauty he's sung me!
Give it me!

[*She takes the phial out of his hand.*]

There!

[*She pretends to throw it into the waterfall.*]

GUDMUND [*goes to the back and looks down into the depths*].
Did you throw it down?

MARGIT [*hiding the phial and descending in the foreground*].
Of course, why you saw me. . .!

[*Aside.*] So help me God!
Now it's a case of sink or swim!
[*Aloud.*] Gudmund!

GUDMUND [*approaching*]. What is it?

MARGIT.   Teach me one thing:
  You must tell me the sense of the ancient lay
  that is sung of the church down below.
  There was once a young swain and a lady fair
  who held one another so dear.
  The day they were bearing her to her grave
  he by his own sword died.
  They buried her close to the south church wall,
  and him they interred to the north. . . .
  No willow or cherry had flourished before
  in that consecrated ground.
  But springtime came and on those two graves
  the fairest of lilies grew;
  up they rose, past the roof of the church,
  and together they bloomed the whole year long.
  Can you tell me the meaning?

GUDMUND [*with a searching glance at her*]. I don't rightly know!

MARGIT. You can take it of course in several ways;
  but I think the best sort of sense is this:
  No church can divide those who hold each other dear!

GUDMUND [*aside*]. By the saints! If she. . . . The time has come
  for her to be told the whole truth!
  [*Aloud.*] Margit, have you my welfare at heart?

MARGIT [*in great excitement*].
  Your welfare?

GUDMUND.   Yes, I mean . . .

MARGIT.   Speak out!

GUDMUND.   It's this:
  You could make my life so happy and rich . . .

MARGIT. Gudmund!

GUDMUND.   Listen; I've something to tell.

  [*Voices are heard, offstage right; he breaks off suddenly.*]

SCENE FIVE

[*As before.* SIGNE, KNUT, ERIC, *and several guests enter from the right.*]

KNUT [*still upstage*]. Wait a moment, Gudmund Alfson. I must have a word with you. [*He stops, engaged in conversation with* ERIC, *who, during the following, goes out with the other guests, left.*]

MARGIT [*aside*]. Make him so happy and rich . . . what else can he mean but . . . [*Aloud.*] Signe, my dear dear sister! [*They move upstage as they converse.*]

GUDMUND [*aside, with a glance at* MARGIT]. Yes, that would be wisest. Signe and I must leave here. Knut Gjæsling has shown he's my friend; he must help.

KNUT [*softly, to* ERIC, *who is going behind the house*]. Gudmund is her cousin; he must plead my cause. [*Aloud, as he approaches* GUDMUND.] I say, Gudmund!

GUDMUND [*smiling*]. Well, have you come to tell me that you daren't let me go free any longer?

KNUT. Dare? Don't worry about that; Knut Gjæsling dare do anything he wants. No, it's about something else. . . . As you know, I have the reputation in these parts for being a wild unruly fellow.

GUDMUND. Yes, and if rumour doesn't lie . . .

KNUT. Oh no, a lot of it may well be true. But now I want to tell you . . . [*They go upstage, conversing.*]

SIGNE [*to* MARGIT, *as they move downstage*]. I don't understand you. You speak as though some unexpected happiness had come your way. What is it all about?

MARGIT. You are still a child, Signe; you don't know what it means to go in constant terror of . . . [*She breaks off suddenly.*] Just imagine it, Signe, to have to wither and die without having lived! [SIGNE *shakes her head and looks at her in amazement.*] No, you don't understand; . . . never mind. [*They go upstage in conversation.* GUDMUND *and* KNUT *come forward again.*]

GUDMUND. Well, if that's how it is, if this wild life doesn't appeal to you any more I'll give you the best advice a friend has to offer: marry some nice young girl!

KNUT. There now. And if I were to tell you that only today I had exactly the same thought.

GUDMUND. Good luck to you then, Knut Gjæsling. And now it is my turn to tell you . . .

KNUT. You? Are you thinking along the same lines?

GUDMUND. Indeed I am . . . but the King's displeasure . . . I'm an outlaw, you know.

KNUT. Pah, I wouldn't bother too much about that. There's no one here, apart from Lady Margit, who knows about it; and as long as I am your friend you have someone to rely on. . . . Well now, I . . .

[*He continues in a whisper as they return upstage.*]

SIGNE [*to* MARGIT, *as they both move downstage*]. But tell me then . . . !

MARGIT. I cannot tell you any more.

SIGNE. Then I will be more frank with you. But answer me one question first: has no one said anything to you about me?

MARGIT. About you? No, what would it be?

SIGNE [*shyly*]. You asked me this morning, if a suitor came riding here tonight . . .

MARGIT [*aside*]. That's true; Knut Gjæsling . . . has he already . . . [*Aloud.*] Well?

SIGNE. He's come! I didn't know at the time whom you meant; but now . . .

MARGIT. And what answer did you give him?

SIGNE. Oh, I don't know. [*She throws herself round* MARGIT'*s neck.*] But the world has seemed so rich and beautiful since he told me he loved me.

MARGIT. But, Signe, I don't understand how you could so soon. . . ! You scarcely knew him before today.

SIGNE. Oh, I still know so little about love; but I do know that the words in the song are true:

> Yet quickly it sends forth the first tender shoot,
> in no time at all in our heart it strikes root.

CII

MARGIT. So be it; and now I needn't keep anything from you.

KNUT [*to* GUDMUND, *as both move downstage*]. That's what I like! Here is my hand.

MARGIT [*aside*]. Ssh, what's this?

GUDMUND. And here is mine! [*He gives him his hand.*]

KNUT. But now we must tell each other who is . . .

GUDMUND. Good! Among all the pretty women here at Solhoug I have found the one who . . .

KNUT. So have I. And I'll take mine away tonight, if need be.

MARGIT [*who has approached unobserved*]. Ye saints!

GUDMUND [*to* KNUT]. That is also my intention.

SIGNE [*who has also been listening*]. Gudmund!

GUDMUND *and* KNUT [*both whispering at once and pointing to* SIGNE]. There she is!

GUDMUND [*taken aback*]. Yes, mine!

KNUT [*likewise*]. No, mine!

MARGIT [*aside, half out of her mind*]. Signe!

GUDMUND [*as before*]. What do you mean?

KNUT. Why she's the one I am going . . .

GUDMUND. Her? Signe is mine in the sight of God.

MARGIT [*with a shriek*]. It was her! Oh no!

GUDMUND [*aside, as he notices her*]. Margit! She's heard everything!

KNUT. Aha, is that how things are! Come, Lady Margit, you needn't look so surprised. I see it all.

MARGIT [*to* SIGNE]. But you just said. . . ? [*Suddenly grasping the situation.*] It was Gudmund you meant!

SIGNE [*amazed*]. Yes, didn't you know? . . . But what is wrong with you?

MARGIT [*in an almost toneless voice*]. Oh, nothing! Nothing!

KNUT [*to* MARGIT]. And this morning when I gave you my word to keep the peace at Solhoug tonight . . . you knew all the time that Gudmund was coming! Ha! ha! Don't you imagine you can make a fool of Knut Gjæsling! I've fallen in love with Signe. This morning it was still my rash vow which drove me to ask for her hand . . . but now . . . !

SIGNE [*to* MARGIT]. Him? He was the suitor you were thinking of!

MARGIT. Quiet! Quiet!

KNUT [*to* MARGIT]. Lady Margit . . . you are the elder sister. You must give me an answer.

MARGIT [*struggling with herself*]. Signe has already made her choice; I have nothing to say.

KNUT. Good, then I've no further business at Solhoug! But the day ends at midnight, remember . . . then I dare say you'll be seeing more of me, and fortune must decide whether Gudmund or I shall take Signe away.

GUDMUND. Yes, just you try . . . if you want a crack on the skull!

SIGNE [*alarmed*]. Gudmund! By all the saints!

KNUT. Steady on, steady on, Gudmund Alfson! You'll be in my power before sunrise . . . and she, your sweetheart . . . [*He calls out towards the left.*] Come along, Eric! We'll away to our own people! [*Menacingly, as he goes out.*] Woe betide the lot of you when I get back! [*He and* ERIC *go out, back right.*]

SCENE SIX

[MARGIT. SIGNE. GUDMUND.]

SIGNE [*to* GUDMUND]. Oh tell me, what does it all mean?

GUDMUND [*whispering*]. We must both leave Solhoug, now, tonight.

SIGNE. Heaven help me! You intend. . . !

GUDMUND. Hush! Not a word to a soul; not even your sister.

MARGIT [*aside*]. Signe! She's the one! And he's scarcely given her a thought before tonight! . . . If I had been free I know whom he would have chosen all right. . . . Yes, free!

SCENE SEVEN

[*As before.* BENGT *and* GUESTS *come from the house.*]

CHORUS OF GUESTS.

Out here in the open we'll feast and play,
while sleepy song birds doze.
And dance midst the flowers, happy and gay,
where the birch wood grows.

Out here in the open you'll hear us jest,
we'll banish all our woes.
When fiddles are tuned not a soul is depressed,
where the birch wood grows.

BENGT. That's the spirit! Just what I like to see. I feel merry, my wife
does too, so you must all be merry together!

ONE OF THE GUESTS. And now let's play making up verses.

MANY [*shouting*]. Yes, yes!

ANOTHER. No, better not; it will only upset the party. [*Lowering his
voice.*] Bear in mind that Knut Gjæsling is here tonight.

SEVERAL [*whispering together*]. Yes, that's true . . . you remember the
last time that. . . . Better be on our guard.

AN OLD MAN. You now, Lady Margit! Your family has always had a
good fund of stories, I know, and you yourself could tell many a
fine tale even as a child.

MARGIT. I've forgotten them all, alas. But ask my cousin, Gudmund
Alfson . . . he knows quite an amusing tale.

GUDMUND. Margit!

MARGIT. Why, what a miserable face! Be cheerful, Gudmund! Be
cheerful! Yes, I can well believe you don't find it so easy. [*Laughing
to the guests.*] He's seen the elf-maid tonight. She tried to entice him,
but Gudmund is a steadfast fellow. [*She turns to* GUDMUND *again.*]
Ah well, the story isn't finished. When you take your sweetheart
up over the moors and through the forests, never turn round, never
look back . . . the elf-maid will be sitting and laughing behind every

bush, and in the end . . . [*In a low voice as she goes up close to him.*] you will get no further than she means you to. [*She crosses to the right.*]

SIGNE [*aside*]. Oh God! Oh God!

BENGT [*contentedly mixing with the guests*]. Ha! ha! ha! Lady Margit knows how to make things up; when she puts her mind to it, she is much better at it than I am.

GUDMUND [*aside*]. She's threatening me. She'll not find peace of mind until I've dashed her last hope. [*Aloud to the guests.*] There is a song I know, if you would like . . .

SEVERAL GUESTS. Yes please, Gudmund!

[*They settle down, sitting on boulders, lying in the grass, or leaning against the trees.* GUDMUND *stands in the middle;* MARGIT *right;* SIGNE *left.*]

GUDMUND [*sings*].

> I rode into the forest,
> I sailed across the sea,
> and yet it was way back at home
> I won my bride-to-be.
>
> Then said the elfin fairy,
> she was so bad and grim:
> No, never shall that maiden pure
> walk up the aisle with him.
>
> Hear me now, elfin fairy,
> your trouble you can spare;
> you cannot separate two hearts
> that for each other care!

AN OLD MAN. That's a pretty song. Look where the young lads' eyes are roving. [*He points to the girls.*] Ah well, each will have his own, I dare say.

BENGT [*making eyes at* MARGIT]. Yes, I have my own, sure enough. Ha! ha! ha!

MARGIT [*aside*]. Oh, to have to suffer all this scorn and ridicule! No, I won't. There's only one thing for it now.

BENGT. What is wrong? You look so pale.

MARGIT. It will soon pass. [*To the guests, as she comes forward.*] I believe I said I had forgotten all my tales, but there's one I think I can remember.

BENGT. That's right, Margit! Let us have it!

MARGIT. I'm rather afraid you won't much like it, but that can't be helped.

GUDMUND [*aside*]. Ye saints, surely she's not going to . . . !

MARGIT. There once was a maiden choice and fair,
   who dwelt in her father's hall,
   embroidering linen, embroidering silk,
   though scant was the joy she found.
   She sat all alone with her horror and grief,
   and hall and bower felt bare;
   the maiden she was proud at heart,
   she fain would be a fine lady of rank. . . .
   And then rode the Mountain King down from the north,
   came to the hall with his suite and his gold.
   At night on the third day he went home again,
   taking her with him . . . his bride!
   Full many a summer in the mountain she lived,
   from horns of gold she could drink her mead;
   but fair grow the flowers in the valley below,
   she gathered them only in dreams. . . .
   There was a young man so good and bold,
   whose fingers had mastered the golden strings;
   to the core of the mountain his music pierced,
   where our maid had lived for so long.
   So strange was her mood when she heard those notes . . .
   wide open the mountain-gates sprang!
   The valley lay steeped in the peace of God,
   the earth in its glory her eyes could see.
   It now seemed to her that, as never before,
   she had wakened to life at the strains of that harp,
   that now for the first time she knew how to count
   the blessings this life has in plenty!
   For each one and all of you shall know

that captives enchained in the mountain-side
the sound of the harp can soon set free!
He saw her imprisoned, heard how she screamed,
but there as he stood he flung down his harp,
hoisted forthwith his sail of silk,
and speeding across the salt sea-wave
he took his betrothed to foreign shores. . . .

[*With mounting vehemence.*]

So sweetly you played on those golden strings . . .
that my bosom heaves and my heart grows bold!
Let me out! Let me out to where valleys are green!
Here in my mountain halls I shall die! . . .
He only derides me! He clasps his bride,
and off he speeds on the salt sea-wave!

[*In despair.*]

All is over with me; the mountain is locked!
The sun shines no longer, the stars have gone out.

[*She sinks back, senseless.*]

SIGNE [*weeping, as she grasps her in her arms*]. Margit! My sister!

GUDMUND [*at the same time*]. Help! Help! She is dying!

[*General commotion among the guests.*]

ACT THREE

The same room as in Act One. It is still night, but it is beginning to grow light in the room.

SCENE ONE

[BENGT *is standing outside the door at the back, holding a tankard of ale. A* SERVANT GIRL *is tidying up the room.*]

BENGT [*talking to someone offstage*]. Goodbye then and come back to Solhoug again soon! You could have stayed the night, you know, like the rest. Ah well. . . . No, wait, I'll see you down to the gate; I must drink to you once more. [*He goes out.*]

[*After a pause the following chorus can be heard softly in the background.*]

CHORUS.
Farewell and God bless you all, we say,
from whom we now are parting!
We must over the hills and far away; . . .
tune up; it's time we were starting!
With dance and with song
we will shorten the road so hard and long.
Heigh ho, merrily we go!

[*The song fades away in the distance.*]

SCENE TWO

[*The* SERVANT GIRL. MARGIT *enters from the left.*]

SERVANT. Good gracious, my lady, are you up?

MARGIT. I'm perfectly well; you can go and get some sleep. . . . Wait a minute; tell me . . . have all the guests gone?

SERVANT. No, not all. Some are staying overnight; they're already asleep.

MARGIT. And Gudmund Alfson?

SERVANT. He'll be asleep too. He went to his room there just over the corridor a few moments ago. [*She points to the right.*]

MARGIT. Very well; you may go. [*The* SERVANT *goes out, left.*]

SCENE THREE

[MARGIT, *alone.*]

MARGIT [*sits down by an open window, right*].
 Tomorrow then Gudmund is going away,
 he's going out into the wide wide world,
 while I'm to be left with my husband . . . and then . . .
 my fate will be that of the flowers under foot,
 the languishing plant, and the broken-off stem;
 I shall live but to suffer and wilt. . . .
 I once heard a tale of a child born blind,
 who lived in a world of playtime and fun;
 a web of enchantment the mother wove
 enfolded its eyes in an aura of light.
 And the child looked out with wonder and joy
 over hill and dale, over sea and shore.
 Then all of a sudden the magic failed;
 the child lived once more in the dark of night; . . .
 that was the end of fun and games.
 With grief and longing its cheeks turned pale,
 the little thing pined and wasted away,
 and it whimpered and wailed without stopping! . . .
 My eyes too were blind, alas,
 and saw neither summer nor radiant light. . . .
 [*She jumps up.*] And now imprisoned inside this cage!
 Why no, my youth is too precious by far!
 Three years I have sacrificed to him
 and I've come to the end of my tether!
 Were I to stand any more of this,
 meek as a dove I would have to be.
 I'm weary to death of the petty rows;
 the world all around me is throbbing with life . . .
 I will follow Gudmund with shield and bow,
 share in his joys and soothe him in grief,
 guard him by day, watch over his sleep;

and folk in amazement will stand and will stare
when they see the bold knight and Margit his wife. . . .
His wife! Forgive me! Forgive me, oh Lord!
I know not what I am saying!
Grant me thy peace which comforts and heals!
[*A pause.*] Signe, my sister . . . it would mean that I sent
her down to an early grave.
And yet, who knows, she is still so young,
her feelings towards him may well not go deep.

[*She takes out the small phial.*]

This phial contains . . . and with it I could . . .
my husband would sleep then for evermore.
[*Horrified.*] Not that! It shall go to the river's bed!

[*She stops as she is about to throw it out of the window.*]

And yet I could at this moment now. . . .

[*In a whisper, with a thrill of horror.*]

To think how the power inherent in sin
tempts us and charms us and leads us on!
I feel that it puts a premium on joy
when it's paid for with blood, with my soul's perdition!

SCENE FOUR

[MARGIT. BENGT, *from the back. He is noticeably tipsy.*]

BENGT. Oh my, that was a feast they'll talk of for miles around. [*He notices* MARGIT.] What, you here? You are better . . . that's fine.

MARGIT [*who has meanwhile hidden the phial*]. Have you locked up?

BENGT [*sits down, left*]. I've dealt with everything; I saw the last of the guests to the gate. But what became of Knut Gjæsling tonight? . . . Fill up the goblet, Margit, I'm thirsty.

MARGIT [*fills the goblet, which stands on the table in front of him, and says, as she crosses to the right with the flagon of mead*]: You were asking about Knut Gjæsling.

BENGT. Indeed I was. That braggart! I haven't forgotten how he threatened me yesterday morning.

MARGIT. He used worse language when he left tonight.

BENGT. Did he now? That's good. I'm going to kill him. [MARGIT *smiles contemptuously.*] I'm going to kill him, I say; I'm not frightened of standing up to ten fellows like him. My grandfather's axe is hanging up on the wall in there. Its shaft is inlaid with silver, and when I turn up with that . . . [*He thumps the table and takes a drink.*] Tomorrow I shall arm myself, take all my men, and go and kill Knut Gjæsling. [*He takes another drink.*]

MARGIT [*aside*]. To have to live here with him! Oh God! Oh God!

[*She is about to go.*]

BENGT. Come here, Margit! Fill up my goblet again. [*She approaches. He tries to pull her on to his knee.*] Ha! ha! ha! Margit, you're pretty! I'm fond of you.

MARGIT. Let me go! [*She tears herself free and crosses to the right with the goblet.*]

BENGT. You are in an awkward mood tonight. Ha! ha! ha! I don't suppose you mean any harm.

MARGIT [*softly, as she fills the goblet*]. If only this were the last goblet I were filling for you. [*She is about to go out, left.*]

BENGT. You know, Margit, one thing you can thank heaven for is that I married you before Gudmund Alfson came back. [MARGIT *stops.*] Yes, he doesn't own one tenth of what I do . . . and I am certain he would have proposed to you if you hadn't been the Lady of Solhoug.

MARGIT [*with a glance at the goblet*]. Do you think so?

BENGT. Yes, I would swear to it. Bengt Gauteson has a keen pair of eyes in his head. But he can have Signe now of course.

MARGIT. And you think he will. . . ?

BENGT. Have her? . . . Yes, since he can't get you. But if you had been free. . . . Ha! ha! ha! Gudmund is like the rest . . . he envies me for being your husband. That's what I like about you, Margit. Fill up the goblet . . . right to the brim! [MARGIT *goes to the right and does as he says.*] Knut Gjæsling was after Signe of course, but I'm going to kill him! Gudmund shall have her; he is a good fellow. Just imagine, Margit, how nice it will be to have them as neighbours; we will go visiting each other in the summer, and in the winter we will sit indoors the whole day long, each with his wife on his knee, drinking and chatting about this and that. . . . Ha! ha! ha! I expect Gudmund will look a bit glum to begin with when I put my arms round you; but I'm sure he'll soon get over it.

[MARGIT's *inner conflict has clearly become more intense as* BENGT *speaks; she finally takes out the phial.*]

BENGT [*without noticing*]. Well, fill up the goblet!

MARGIT [*aside*]. This is more than a woman can bear. [*She empties the contents into the goblet, throws the phial out of the window, and says:*] Your goblet is full!

BENGT. Good!

[MARGIT *goes to the left, but stops as she struggles with herself; she then returns to the goblet, as though regretting what she has done.*]

BENGT [*laughing as he settles back in his chair*]. Well, well, are you expecting me? Off you go; I'll be along soon.

MARGIT [*her mind suddenly made up*]. Your goblet is full. There it is! [*She hurries out, left.*]

SCENE FIVE

[BENGT. *A* RETAINER *enters almost immediately from the back.*]

BENGT. I like her; I'm not sorry I married her, even though she had inherited no more than that goblet and the brooches she wore at her wedding. [*He goes to the right and grasps the goblet.*]

RETAINER [*enters in terror*]. My lord, my lord, you must go out as quick as you can. Knut Gjæsling is riding up to the house with a band of armed men.

BENGT [*puts the goblet down*]. Knut Gjæsling? Who said so?

RETAINER. Some of your guests saw him down on the road and they've come back to warn you.

BENGT. Good, then I shall . . . ! Fetch my grandfather's axe!

[*They go out at the back.*]

SCENE SIX

[GUDMUND *and* SIGNE *enter from the right*.]

SIGNE. Then it must be so?

GUDMUND.   There's no other way;
  we are compelled.

SIGNE.   Oh, to flee
  like this from the place where I was born!

[*She dries her eyes*.]

  No, I will not complain;
  for your sake it is I am going away.
  Gudmund, if you weren't a wanted man
  I'd stay with my sister.

GUDMUND.   And then next day
  Knut Gjæsling would come with sword and bow,
  he'd whisk you up on the back of his horse,
  and Signe would be his wife!

SIGNE. Oh, let us flee! But where shall we go?

GUDMUND. Down by the fjord I have a friend;
  he'll find us a ship. Over salt-sea waves
  southward we'll sail to the Danish coast;
  there, believe me, it is pleasant to dwell,
  there you will find it delightful to live,
  there the most exquisite blossoms grow
  where the beech trees spread their shade!

SIGNE. My poor dear sister, farewell and goodbye!
  You have sheltered me with such motherly care,
  have guided my steps, and devoutly prayed
  that heaven should prosper me!
  Come, Gudmund, let us take this goblet
  and drink her health; let us wish she may soon
  be herself once again and lucid in mind;
  and that God may remove her affliction.

[*She takes up the goblet*.]

GUDMUND. We will; we will drain it and think of her.
[*With a start.*] No, stop! I should know whose goblet this is.

[*He takes it from her.*]

SIGNE. It is Margit's goblet.

GUDMUND.   By heaven, why yes!
I well remember how the day when I left,
the wine in this goblet was glowing;
she drank to me and our happy reunion,
but for her the result was grief and woe.
No, Signe, never must you drink wine
from this goblet here.

[*He pours the wine out of the window.*]

We must away!

[*Noises in the background.*]

SIGNE. Hush, quiet, I hear voices and the sound of feet.

GUDMUND [*listening*]. Knut Gjæsling's voice!

SIGNE.   Oh save us, Lord!

GUDMUND. Don't worry! I shall defend my bride!

SCENE SEVEN

[*As before.* MARGIT *enters from the left.*]

MARGIT [*aside*]. What does it mean? Is my husband . . . ?

GUDMUND *and* SIGNE. Margit!

MARGIT. Gudmund and Signe . . . you here!

SIGNE. Margit, sister dear!

MARGIT [*horrified as she notices the goblet which* GUDMUND *is still holding*].
The goblet! Who drank from it?

GUDMUND [*bewildered*]. Drank . . . ? Signe and I, we wanted . . .

MARGIT [*in despair*]. Mercy! Mercy! Help! They will die!

SIGNE. Margit! Oh God! What ails you?

MARGIT. Help! Help. Won't anyone help?

SCENE EIGHT

[*As before. A* RETAINER *and, later, a* SECOND RETAINER *enter from the back.*]

FIRST RETAINER. Lady Margit, your husband!

MARGIT. My husband . . . did he drink too . . . ?

GUDMUND [*aside*]. Ah, now I understand . . . !

FIRST RETAINER. Knut Gjæsling has killed him!

SIGNE. Killed!

GUDMUND [*draws his sword*]. Not yet, I hope. [*Softly, to* MARGIT.] Keep calm; no one has drunk from that goblet!

MARGIT. Praise be to God for saving us all! . . . [MARGIT *sinks down in a chair, left.*]

SECOND RETAINER [*enters and stops* GUDMUND *as he is about to rush out*]. You are too late! Lord Bengt is dead!

GUDMUND. So it's true!

SECOND RETAINER. The guests and your men have overpowered the assailants. Knut Gjæsling and his men are all tied up . . . here they come.

SCENE NINE

[*As before.* GUESTS *and* RETAINERS *enter, escorting* KNUT GJÆSLING, ERIC OF HÆGGE, *and several of* KNUT'S *men, all bound.*]

KNUT [*pale and subdued*]. I've killed a man, Gudmund! What have you to say?

GUDMUND. Knut, oh Knut, what have you done?

KNUT. It was an accident, I'll swear. . . . He ran into me in the gallery outside. It was dark and I struck him with my axe without meaning to.

ERIC. That's the truth!

KNUT. Lady Margit, ask any sum you like. I'm ready to pay the penalty.

MARGIT. I ask for nothing; . . . God must be our judge. . . . No, one thing I ask: give up your evil designs on my sister.

KNUT. Never again shall I try to redeem that wretched vow. Believe me, I'm going to reform; if only my old mother . . . that's what upsets me most. Gudmund, if ever you are restored to a position of favour, put in a good word for me with the King.

GUDMUND. Me? I must be out of the country before dawn. . . .

[*Astonishment among the guests. In a whisper* ERIC *explains the situation.*]

MARGIT [*looking first at* GUDMUND, *then at* SIGNE]. And Signe is going with you? [SIGNE *approaches her imploringly.*] God be with you both!

SIGNE. My dear sister!

GUDMUND. Thank you, Margit! But let us be brief. [*Listening.*] Hush! I can hear the sound of hoofs in the courtyard.

SIGNE [*alarmed*]. Visitors!

SCENE TEN

[*As before. A* RETAINER *from the back.*]

RETAINER. The King's men are outside. They are looking for Gudmund Alfson!

SIGNE. Oh God!

MARGIT. The King's men!

GUDMUND. So all is over! . . . Oh Signe, to lose you now would be the hardest thing of all.

KNUT. No, Gudmund! You must sell your life dearly; we are all ready to fight for you.

ERIC [*looks out*]. It's no use; we are outnumbered.

SIGNE. They're coming in. Oh God! Oh God!

SCENE ELEVEN

[*As before. The* KING'S MESSENGER *with his escort enters from the back.*]

MESSENGER. I seek you, Gudmund Alfson, in the name of the King!

GUDMUND. Very well. But I am innocent. I swear it by all that is holy and dear.

MESSENGER. We know!

ALL [*except for the new arrivals*]. What?

MESSENGER. I am instructed to invite you to the Royal Palace as the guest of the King. He offers you his friendship and rich fiefs as well.

GUDMUND. Signe!

SIGNE. Gudmund!

GUDMUND. But tell me, why . . . ?

MESSENGER. Your enemy the Chancellor, Audun Hugleikson, has fallen.

ALL. Fallen!

MESSENGER. Three days ago he was beheaded in Bergen. [*He lowers his voice.*] He had offended against the Queen of Norway.

[*At the moment the sun rises and sheds its light in the room.* MARGIT, *who has been sitting there lost to the world, stands up and steps forward between* GUDMUND *and* SIGNE.]

MARGIT. Thus punishment follows hard on crime!
Guardian angels, gentle and kind,
looked down on me in their mercy tonight,
and saved me before it was too late.
I know now that life means more by far
than earthly pleasures and worldly power.
I have felt the remorse, the frantic fear,
which come upon those who hazard their soul . . .
and now to St Sunnifa's convent I go.

[GUDMUND *and* SIGNE *try to speak.*]

There now, Gudmund, take home your bride;
your contract is hallowed and safe in God's care!

GUDMUND. Signe, my wife! . . . See, the dawn has come.
This is the dawn of our fresh young love!

D11

SIGNE. My fairest memories, my sweetest of dreams
to you and the strains of your harp I owe.
My noble minstrel, in sorrow and joy,
pluck at your harpstrings with all your skill.
There are chords, believe me, deep down in my breast,
which shall answer to you in grief and in bliss!

CHORUS.

Over earth there watches light's clear eye,
guarding the paths of the righteous with love,
sending rays of comfort from above; . . .
praises to the Lord Our God on high.

'THE GROUSE IN JUSTEDAL'
[*Rypen i Justedal*]

NATIONAL PLAY IN FOUR ACTS

BY

BRYNJOLF BJARME
[1850]

CHARACTERS

BENGT OF BJERKEHOUG, a rich yeoman

BJØRN, his son

MERETA, his foster-daughter and ward

EINAR, a young yeoman

ALFHILD, a young girl

MOGENS, a priest

KNUD, an old minstrel

PAAL, an old hunter

INGEBORG and other servants at Bjerkehoug

ACT ONE

*Wild mountainous region; left, an old sæter cottage; in the background, high
mountains rise one above the other.* BJØRN *and* PAAL *come down the hillside
with bows and other hunting equipment on their backs; it is evening.*

PAAL. We must press on if we still want to get
to Bjerkehoug while it's still daylight, Bjørn!
It'll soon be dark.

BJØRN. There's no great hurry; come
and sit upon this slope, and rest awhile.

PAAL. Oh, are you tired?

BJØRN. That's not the reason, Paal!
But it's so cool and beautiful up here.
See there the mountain glowing red as gold.
One might suppose it was the elfin folk
displaying all their rich and secret hoard.

PAAL. Again your thoughts go straying off once more
to elfin folk and hulders, and God knows
the names they're called. . . .

BJØRN. Do you then not believe
such things exist?

PAAL. That these things still exist
I think I surely know as well as you.
But that's precisely why you shouldn't talk
about such matters as the sun goes down.

BJØRN. You mean you think it's not impossible
they might appear?

PAAL. Indeed, why shouldn't they?
I've seen before such things.

BJØRN. You have?

PAAL. Indeed,
and that not very long ago . . .

BJØRN. Where?

PAAL. The sæter north of here, where once I stayed
one Saturday last summer.

BJØRN.   Doubtless you
were up there courting?

PAAL.   That is largely true.
I should explain that Gunborg—she I nearly
became engaged to, then it all fell through—
was staying at the sæter.

BJØRN.   That old woman
we met up there this morning?

PAAL.   Well, in truth
she isn't all that old, and anyway
she makes a quite delicious porridge cream.

BJØRN. That may well be. But tell me what you saw.

[*He takes his pack of food out, as* PAAL *continues.*]

PAAL. I'm going to tell you . . . if you'll wait a little.
The time was evening, more or less as now,
and I was plodding on, quite lost in thought,
when all at once a grouse went flying up
from underneath my feet into the thicket.

BJØRN. And then?

PAAL.   I quickly drew and aimed my bow.
Alas, the bird was gone.

BJØRN.   The which I well believe.

PAAL. But listen now . . .

                    [*In a low voice.*]

                    . . . for when I looked again
a hulder stood upon the slope, just where
the grouse had disappeared not long before.

BJØRN. Oh, that was surely only Gunborg.

PAAL.   Oh!
Do you imagine that I can't distinguish
a hulder from a Christian girl—now, come!
I know exactly who it was. And the grouse?
I'm quite prepared to swear it was a troll-bird.

BJØRN. But tell me how she looked? Did she look lovely?

PAAL. The girl was nicely shaped, I will say that. . . .
But more than that I didn't stay to see. . . .

BJØRN. You ran away?

PAAL.   They do say that is best
in such a case; for people say the hulder
will wait to seize her chance; and if she can,
she tempts all likely lads to go with her.

BJØRN. She much prefers them young!

PAAL.   All right, I know!
I'm not so very ancient even now,
and thirty years ago I was but still
the merest youngster . . .

BJØRN.   Well, you might say that.

PAAL. Well, thirty's no great age, I'd have you know.
But all the same, to run away was best.
Remember how it was with Eivind Bolt . . . ?

BJØRN. The hulder lured him deep inside the mountain.

PAAL. And let him stay there many many years,
and when at last he came to light again,
they didn't recognize him any more.

BJØRN. I cannot see that that's a disadvantage.

PAAL. You mean you might feel drawn to go along
if ever the hulder tempted you?

BJØRN.   Why not!

PAAL. I thought you might—I've noticed for some time
that all your thoughts of late inclined to turn
to fairy tales and stories; so you tend
to roam about this place from morn till night.
I met you yesterday—so tell me now,
where had you been?

BJØRN.   You mean you cannot guess?

PAAL. Upon the heights, as always?

BJØRN.   Even further—
as far as Justedal!

PAAL.   May God protect you!

In Justedal—the place where mortal man
has never set his foot for countless years!
It lies there all deserted since the plague.

BJØRN. All this I know. . . .

PAAL.   And people also say
the land is full of ghosts, and that the dead
that lie unburied there still haunt the place.

BJØRN. That could well be!

PAAL.   But you've not seen a thing?

BJØRN. I have not *seen* . . . but heard . . .

PAAL.   What have you heard?

BJØRN. Oh . . . whispering in the trees, the songs of birds,
and things you always hear upon the heights . . .

PAAL. And nothing else?

BJØRN.   Oh please don't let us talk
of things like this so late at night now, Paal!

PAAL. They say the hulder owns the entire valley.

BJØRN. The hulder?

PAAL.   Also that she grazes there
her flock of beasts.

BJØRN.   Oh, that might well be true.
I saw no one. . . .

PAAL.   Yet nonetheless I've heard
the sæter girls around this district say
that often on a summer's evening they
have heard the hulder blowing on her lur.

BJØRN [*leaps up*]. What's that they say they hear?

PAAL.   What ails you now?

BJØRN. It's nothing much. You did however say
they heard the hulder's call from up the hill?

PAAL. I listened to them only yesterday
as they were talking in the sæter there.
You see this old abandoned cottage here?
The reason is that no girl ever dares
to stay here overnight. . . .

BJØRN.   How very strange!
But let us take a little drink for now.
There's no great haste; we may as well sleep here
as any other place.

[*He drinks and hands* PAAL *the horn.*]

PAAL.   Just as you please!

[*He drinks.*]

You don't seem very sociable these days,
and much prefer to stay up in the forest.
Well, each man to his taste. If you prefer
to stay here overnight, I'll try to find
some bench to sleep on in this cottage here.

[*He gets up.*]

BJØRN. Yes, you go on. I'll sit a moment here
and polish up my bow a little.

PAAL.   Good!
But don't be long—it's getting late already.

[*He goes into the cottage.*]

BJØRN [*after a pause*].
No matter how I struggle to resist,
I cannot rid my mind of all these thoughts!
Across the hill I heard it loud and clear,
the tempting call she sounded on her lur.
And ever since the time that first I heard it,
I feel as though some strange and unseen force
were driving me up there—each day it seemed
I had to go there, even against my will.
—What noise was that? [*Listens.*] Oh, nothing but a cuckoo
beginning his song up there on the firtree branch.
I've heard it said that such can mean good luck.
I only hope it's true. . . . Hush! what was that?
Do I hear footsteps? . . . There is someone coming!

HARALD [*comes down from the hill-side with his fiddle in his hand*].
Good evening!

BJØRN.   Good evening to you! Where are you going
so late at night. . . ?

HARALD.   I'm making for the village!

BJØRN. You live, I take it, on the other side
of the mountain?

HARALD.   Yes, you might indeed say that,
though no more there than any other spot.
My home is where I chance to find a place.

BJØRN. I'm not sure what you mean.

HARALD.   I travel round
and never stay too long in any spot.
I am a minstrel, as you doubtless see,
and sing in any house I find a hearing.

BJØRN. And you have no real home?

HARALD.   Each single tree
on yonder fir-clad slope gives splendid shelter.

BJØRN. Indeed you're right. So long as one is young,
that serves one well. . . . But . . .

HARALD.   Do not speak of age!
For one might live a hundred winters through,
and still remain as young as ever, lad!

BJØRN. You speak so strangely!

HARALD.   Yes, I doubtless do.
But that's because you do not understand.
And now I must be on my way again.
—This path will take me on to Bjerkehoug?

BJØRN. To Bjerkehoug? You're making there tonight?

HARALD. Such was my plan. It's many many years
since last I called there. What I want to know
is whether—as there always was before—
a place by the hearth awaits the weary wanderer!

BJØRN. You may depend on that. . . .

HARALD.   I think so too!

BJØRN. So now farewell. . . . I hope you will not find
the road too long. . . .

HARALD [*preparing to leave*].
                    Too long? Why should it be?
The forest only needs the proper mood

and company you'll find in plenty there.
How can you think it ever could be lonely,
when hill and mountain are so full of life?
Not so, you think? Yet it is as I say,
and if you neither see nor hear what's there,
the only reason is you don't possess
the proper sight and hearing! Now, goodnight!

[*He goes.*]

BJØRN [*watches him go*].
How very strange the things he said just then.
But what he meant—I don't quite understand.

[*The sound of a lur is heard from the background.*]

Ah, listen! there's that sound again up there.

[*Listens.*]

I recognize the notes. . . . It must be her.

[*He listens silently and expectantly. The sounds of the lur are heard once more and* ALFHILD *appears in the background on the high ground.*]

ALFHILD [*sings without noticing* BJØRN].
        'So hushed is all in wood and hill,
        The brook alone makes murmur;
        The thrush tonight so sadly sings
        His song from the birch's branches.

        Behind the leaves of green, his mate
        Sits waiting there at home,
        And listens glad and joyfully
        To that beloved voice.'

[*She takes a few steps forward and notices* BJØRN; *surprised, she remains standing there for a moment, then disappears among the trees.*]

BJØRN. So fair she stood on yonder birch-clad slope—
as, lur in hand, she sang her lilting song.
Yes, she was lovely—pretty too her voice!
And very different from the valley girls.
There was some truth in what the old man said—
that hill and field are full of life. I mean
to talk with him again this very night.

[*Shouts into the cottage.*]

Get up and let us be upon our way!

PAAL [*comes out*].
What is afoot? Perhaps you've seen some game!

BJØRN. I have indeed. But let us now go home.

PAAL. You're sure your eyes have not again deceived you,
as they have often done of late, it seems.

BJØRN. I did not fire a shot.

PAAL.   So much the better.

BJØRN. It was a mountain bird . . .

PAAL.   A grouse perhaps?

BJØRN. Exactly like the one which once you saw;
it disappeared at once behind the hill!

PAAL. So there you see. . . . Admit now I was right. . . .
It's just as well I have some steel in hand,
for thus the elfin people cannot harm us!

BJØRN. Ah yes, of course not. . . . Hurry, let us go!

[*They go out, left.*]

[*An old-style hall built of logs at Bjerkehoug; up-stage, the high seat; on one wall the hearth, on the other a door.*
MERETA *and* INGEBORG *enter, the latter carrying a horn of mead.*]

MERETA. The horn goes on the table, Ingeborg!
Our guest will doubtless need some entertainment
or otherwise the time may seem to drag.

INGEBORG. Oh, you don't need to worry on that score.
Young Einar would, if I am not mistaken,
quite gladly spend his life at Bjerkehoug. . . .

MERETA. I don't know what you mean?

INGEBORG.   Oh, yes you do!
You've known for long enough just what I mean.

[*She leaves, as* EINAR *enters.*]

EINAR. Again you ran away from me out there
and left me all alone. . . .

MERETA.   I simply went
to see if I could find refreshment for you.
You've talked to me about so many things,
your throat must now be dry and painful, Einar.

EINAR. If you keep leaving, there is never time
for you to hear what I must say to you!

MERETA. That's probably the wisest thing to do!

EINAR. You laugh at me, and won't believe my words.
My honour you cast doubt upon. . . .

MERETA.   Don't speak
of honour—honour isn't found in cities,
and you have lived there ever since your childhood.

EINAR. And do you think I ever could forget
the lovely country flower in the valley?

MERETA.   Ah,
I see you've learnt to make a pretty speech;
that art we have no sense for . . .

EINAR.   I never thought
I'd see the day at Bjerkehoug when you
refused to listen to words sincerely meant.

MERETA [*gaily*].
Well, do not let us argue more about it,
but come and let us once again be friends.

EINAR [*tries to take her hand*].
Mereta!

MERETA.   Please don't be upset, young Einar!
You must not think that we've forgotten you!
You ought to see the little apple tree
you planted here some seven years ago.

EINAR. You still remember that?

MERETA.   Oh, every day
I look at it . . . we call it Einar's tree!

[*She goes.*]

EINAR. I do not know quite what to make of her;
at times she holds me off with scorn and censure,
at other times she draws me on, as if
she seemed to like me really rather well.

[MOGENS *enters.*]

MOGENS. God's peace, my son! are you here all alone? I have a message for Sir Bengt. I don't suppose you know where I might find him?

EINAR. I'm sure he won't be long.

MOGENS. In that case I'll wait. [*He sits down.*] Well, now you have returned to be our neighbour again . . . taken over your father's estate again yourself.

EINAR. Yes, reverend father! I am tired of court life. I thought I would take things easy for a while. . . .

MOGENS. You do right—*beati sunt agricolæ*. But what have you got in that horn . . . Ah! mead. . . . I think a little drop might well do me some good. . . . [*He drinks.*] Ah yes, Bengt of Bjerkehoug has many good things in his cellar, but they rarely come to light these days. . . . Life is not as gay here now as it was in the days of good old Thormod, Einar!

EINAR. I feel the same! Bengt seems generally rather sad and gloomy.

MOGENS. Yes, that is so. Pray God it doesn't become any worse. . . . It is the sins and vanities of his youth that weigh upon him in his old age. . . . He is now a child of the world, one who prefers *rumores ante salutem*, as it is called.

EINAR. Does it not date from the time his brother Alf disappeared?

MOGENS. Yes, it does. . . .

EINAR. But what happened?

MOGENS. I dare say I can tell you—there is nobody about, I suppose—for you are a good lad and your father was always open-handed with all kinds of gifts and presents for the monastery . . . [*Drinks.*] . . . You see, Alf was the eldest son; he was a quiet pious soul, whilst Bengt was wild and quick-tempered, just like Bjørn. Alf was to have the estate after the father's death, and Bengt could not come to terms with that idea, for he was now a child of the world. And he always tried to turn his father against Alf.

EINAR. And especially when Alf got married.

MOGENS. Exactly. The father was against the marriage, but this time Alf wanted his way. And when he went in to see his father after the wedding, he called down a curse upon him and swore he would never see him again. It cannot be denied that it was Bengt's fault. God forgive him . . .

EINAR. But what became of Alf?

MOGENS. Nobody knows. The couple disappeared after their marriage. The people of the village say the elfin folk took them; but he probably went off to a place he had up in the mountains. But then along came the Black Death and carried away everybody up there, and nobody has dared set foot up there since.

EINAR. That I've heard.

MOGENS. But since then, things have not been good at Bjerkehoug. The old man died soon after, and Bengt gave no sign. But the memory of Alf gnaws at him, as I can understand. He is now a powerful man . . . and Bjørn will be even more powerful, if it ever comes to anything between him and Mereta.

EINAR. Mereta? Is Bjørn thinking . . . ?

MOGENS. Well, I don't know. But his father is thinking about it. . . .

EINAR [*half aside*]. Now I understand why he turned me away.

MOGENS. What do you say? Sh! Here he comes!

[*He rises.*]

EINAR. Then I'm going. . . .

[*He goes out, left, as* BENGT *enters from the back.*]

BENGT. Well, Herr Mogens, so you are here. You've brought the papers with you?

MOGENS. They are all here.

BENGT. And there's no other heir apart from Mereta?

MOGENS. None. That is fortunate for her, for her late father's possessions were not great.

BENGT. No, you are right!

MOGENS. Now I cannot think that anything stands in the way of the wedding. . . .

BENGT [*flaring up*]. What is this, priest! Are you thinking that's why I've kept it secret. Do you think the aunt's bequest . . .

MOGENS. Far from it. But folk in the village . . .

BENGT. I don't worry about that. 'Straight ahead', that is my motto. Bjørn shall marry her. I have kept it secret because I wanted it so. Now it will be announced because I want it so.

MOGENS. But neither Bjørn nor Mereta know anything about it.

E11

BENGT. What need is there? Is Bjørn not my son? Have I not been her guardian? Would he do as Alf did . . . ? [*In a suddenly changed voice.*] God be with him. I have paid for masses to be said for his soul. I have given altar candles and other gifts to the monastery. . . .

MOGENS. That you have done like a good Christian.

BENGT. All the same . . . But let us not speak any more about it.

[*He walks across to the hearth.*]

Now what are you so merry about. . . ?

⟨MERETA *crossed out*⟩ EINAR. We are telling stories and fairy tales.

MERETA. Oh, Father, come and sit, and you shall . . .

BENGT.   No,
I fear I cannot bear this ancient custom.
One sleeps so restlessly, and has bad dreams. . . .

MERETA. But Grandpapa would often tell us stories,
and he enjoyed his sleep. . . .

BENGT.   He did, did he?

MERETA. Oh, you remember, Einar! When we were
still children, here we'd sit on winter evenings,
and I would sit upon the old man's knee. . . .

EINAR. And then he'd talk to us of Singer Knud.

MERETA. Ah yes, of Singer Knud—that was delightful. . . .

MOGENS. Who is this Singer Knud?

MERETA.   He is a minstrel
Who wanders round the valleys with his songs!

EINAR. Yet here he never came . . . ?

MERETA.   I do not know,
I never saw him. . . .

BENGT.   I hardly think he did.
The whole thing's nothing but a fairy tale. . . .

MERETA. It's not! He's still alive. . . . You just ask Paal. . . .

BENGT. Ah, Paal. . . . He also claims he's seen the hulder. . . .

MERETA. But you yourself have talked of Singer Knud.

BENGT. That was the time . . .

MERETA.   I'm sure you can remember,
   when I and Bjørn and Einar sat beside you,
   and as you told the tale, you grew so merry.
   Oh, Father, tell us. . . .

BENGT [*pats her cheek*].   Well, perhaps I will.

[*They sit down.*]

A minstrel went wandering far and wide
Through forest and distant valleys,
And at every house he was asked to perform
In silence they heard his story.
He plucked from the strings a delightful sound
Recalling the hulder's call,
And the birds in the trees all sang for joy
And they merrily danced in a ring.

In the clamour and noise of a wedding feast
A hush would fall over the guests,
For One stood among them erect and tall
Preparing to sing his song.
—But often he'd sit by the hearth and sing,
Relieving the bitterest pain.
Nor mountain nor fjord could bar his way;
He wandered so far and so free.

KNUD [*enters slowly*].
   God's peace unto you all, to women and to men!
   God's peace unto you all foregathered in this room!

BENGT. God's peace to one who comes so late at night,
   You must ⟨have travelled far; come, sit you down! *crossed out*⟩ have far to
   travel!

KNUD.   My name is Knud and I have my roof
                    beneath the bush like the fleeting hare.
                    My hall is the shady pine-tree wood;
                    I feel that my homestead is there.
                    I happily sing and play my tunes,
                    and the birds all know my voice.
                    But often some secret power impels
                    me to leave my forest retreat;
                    at times I rest on the lonely shore
                    at times I dream in the valley.

I halt my steps at the yeoman's house
and play a lilting tune.
I sing my songs and say farewell,
and nowhere I stay very long.

EINAR. You go your way in bitter cold and frost?

MERETA. The poor old man must sorely be in need.

KNUD. I need no silver, nor do I need gold;
I never sing at any time for money.

BENGT. Then sit you down and rest beside the hearth.

KNUD. My thanks to you.

MERETA.   And let me fetch you now
a stoup to drink that will restore your strength.

[She takes him the horn of mead.]

KNUD. I thank you, child.

[He drinks.]

EINAR.   And then perhaps, old man,
you'll sing for us some merry melody!

KNUD. If such is wanted, I am always ready.

BENGT. But none of those old fairy tales that tell of
elfin folk and such.

KNUD *[rises]*.   You don't believe
these ancient tales?

BENGT.   Such things are just for women
and children. . . .

EINAR.   Surely not! Do tell and sing!

BENGT *[proudly]*.
Well, if you mean to sing, then choose a song
about my gallant ancestors, of which
there are full many. . . .

KNUD.   I also know a song
about some other kinsmen—you might like
to hear that too—the one of Alf and Ingierd!

BENGT *[taken aback]*.
Damned villain! Silence! Are you here to mock me!

MERETA. Oh, Father, be not angry. . . .

EINAR.   What is wrong?

KNUD. I mean it well. . . .

MOGENS.   Keep silent, now, old man!

KNUD. I feel that it would profit you to hear it!

BENGT. Had you not drunk the horn of mead with us
and rested by my hearth, I would have had
you hunted from my house like any dog!

KNUD. No longer then is this a place for me;
but heed me well now, Bengt of Bjerkehoug!
if you will let me sing, it will bring luck
to you and all your family as well.

MOGENS. I think he must have lost his mind.

BENGT [*to* KNUD].
I have no wish to listen to your songs.
If there is anything you have to tell,
then tell it to me briefly.

KNUD.   That I cannot;
my power resides within my strings; by song
alone and story do I work—that's all. . . .

[BJØRN *and* PAAL *enter.*]

MERETA. Here's Bjørn come back!

BJØRN.   Why, surely, here we have
the minstrel man!

KNUD.   We meet again, it seems.
So this estate is where you have your home. . . .
It is not good to be here.

BENGT.   Do you know
this man?

BJØRN.   Why yes, I met him in the mountains.

BENGT [*suspiciously*].
You did not send him here by any chance?

BJØRN. He said himself he meant to call on you.

MERETA. Do not be angry. . . .

BENGT.   Silence, girl. I'm speaking. . . .

KNUD. I go, for here it is not good to be.
  Woe, woe the house where songs may not be heard;
  no luck finds there its home. —I say goodnight!
  It's not the last that you will hear of me!

                    [*He goes.*]

PAAL [*in terror*].
  In heaven's name! You haven't turned him out of
  the house, my master?

BENGT.   Why not, may I ask?
  I had no wish to hear.

PAAL.   Now by St Olaf!
  This is a doughty piece of work you've done. . . .

BENGT. What do you mean?

MERETA.   Who was he?

PAAL.   Saw you not
  the golden string upon his fiddle?

EINAR.   Yes!
  I think I did!

PAAL.   Well . . . that was Singer Knud!

     [*Commotion among the people of the house.*]

BJØRN. He! Singer Knud!

BENGT.   What is this that you're saying!

PAAL. It's as I say!

MERETA.   Can you be sure of that?

PAAL. Indeed, my father often used to talk
  of him—and how he brings good luck along
  wherever people listen to his stories.
  But if one's hard, and turns the man away,
  bad fortune then will come upon the house!

BENGT. Well, that we've had a good share of already.
  But now it's late, and time we all should go
  and rest.

      [MERETA *and the servant girls leave.*]

And you shall come with me, Herr Mogens!
Some things I wish to talk to you about.

[*He and the priest leave.*]

PAAL. And I will also take me to my bed. . . .
But Singer Knud! . . . God knows what happens now!

[*He goes;* BJØRN *sits down in an attitude of thought.*]

EINAR [*stands in front of him*].
Well, Bjørn! What think you now?

BJØRN.   I do not know!

EINAR. Has some misfortune been your lot today?

BJØRN. Whether fortune or misfortune, I can't tell. . . .

[*He gets up.*]

But there is something. . . . Listen, and I'll tell
you all about it. High up in the hills,
not far from Justedal, I chanced to meet
a young and lovely woman. . . .

EINAR [*laughing*].   Is that all?
Surely that is no misfortune, Bjørn!

BJØRN. Ah, hear me out. It was that barren spot
where sæter girls will never dare to go.

EINAR. Then clearly she had gone and lost her way. . . .

BJØRN. Ah no! Nor did she look like the other girls. . . .
She stood among the trees and sang a song,
and then at once she vanished.

EINAR [*murmuring*].   It couldn't
have been the hulder . . . ?

BJØRN.   Several times I heard
how she did blow some notes upon her lur.
But now that I have seen her . . . Listen, Einar,
I must go there again. . . .

EINAR.   I counsel you
to show a little caution. Do beware,
or else these sæter girls will turn your head. . . .

BJØRN. I tell you . . .

EINAR.   Very well, this hulder girl!
But listen, Bjørn! And now I speak in earnest—
your father has some different plans for you.
He'd rather like in time to see a match
between Mereta and you. . . .

BJØRN.   That cannot be!
Of this he's never spoken. She and I
regard ourselves as only brother and sister.

EINAR. But listen, Bjørn!

BJØRN.   No, no, it is no use.
It cannot be. My thoughts are all on her
I saw today. . . .

EINAR.   But this is madness, Bjørn!
It almost makes me think that witches' art
or trolldom's magic powers have you in thrall!

BJØRN. Well, be that as it may. . . . I can no more
resist this thing, though I have battled hard.
It is no use. Since I first heard the lur,
my thoughts are turned to her each waking moment.
I've often prayed to God and to St. Olaf
to strengthen me. Alas, that brings no help.
I must be off up there once more to find her!

ACT TWO

A wild but beautiful region in Justedal; trees and mountains in the background and at the sides; left, a little rocky cave hidden by branches and leaves.

BJØRN [*enters*].
  It's evening soon—and I have roamed around
  the whole long day among the hills and woods,
  to follow reindeer tracks across the scree,
  beneath the firtree's canopy above.
  This is the valley—a fair and lovely valley,
  but quite shut off by towering rocky cliffs.
  A hunter who has penetrated deep
  within the mountains hopes that he will find—
  some rare occasion on the other side—
  a pleasant valley filled with flowers and trees.
  It was up there, upon the peak, I stood
  when I first heard the lur's appealing tones.
  What must I think? For people say that when
  a bachelor first hears the hulder's call,
  he has to stop and listen then in silence,
  and afterwards he never can forget.

                    [*The sound of a lur is heard.*]

  But what is that? In truth, it is her lur. . . .
  and there I see her coming through the forest!

ALFHILD [*enters*].
  No more today is Alfhild glad at heart.
  He wasn't there, and will not come again. . . .

                    [*She becomes conscious of him.*]

  Why, there he is . . .

                    [*She hurries across to him.*]

                    . . . and you must never leave
Alfhild so soon again. . . .

BJØRN [*surprised*].   Fairest maiden!
  Who are you?

ALFHILD. Do you ask who Alfhild is?
For that you know. . . . But here you must remain;
you must not go so quickly as last night!

BJØRN [*wonderingly*].
Last night! What do you mean! I didn't spend
last night up here.

ALFHILD. Alas, you left so quickly. . . .

BJØRN. What do you mean?

ALFHILD. Just listen, and I'll tell you.
But come and sit beside me on the grass.

[*They sit down under a tree in the foreground.*]

It was so very strange. But you have heard
about the elves?

BJØRN. No, no . . .

ALFHILD. You do not know
those tiny creatures, those good elves, who play
among the flowers of the forest when
the Mighty Eye is closed behind the hill.

BJØRN. Indeed I know of them. But tell me more!

ALFHILD. When it is dark and Alfhild shuts her eyes,
they come and play their merry games nearby;
they also bring her flowers—then she's glad—
for all the woodland flowers belong to them.
But then last night the elves did not appear. . . .

BJØRN. Why not?

ALFHILD. Ah, Alfhild doesn't know that, either.
She thinks they were afraid of you, as she
herself did fear that time she saw you first.
Thereafter Alfhild only thought of you;
and then you came again; we walked together
within the forest—Alfhild was so glad!
But then today you'd gone away again!

BJØRN. You did but dream!

ALFHILD. What do you mean by that?
But now you must not go again tonight. . . .

BJØRN. I must not go?

ALFHILD.   No, no! You must not go!
You surely know yon little mountain flower
that grows so blue beside the spruce's root . . . ?

BJØRN. Oh yes, I know it.

ALFHILD.   As evening falls,
the Mighty Light comes up behind the hill
and shines upon its leaves; and all the lights,
the tiny ones up there, they shine as well—
and then the little flower is glad, so glad!
Alas, when Night is gone, they all depart—
and then it folds its little leaves and weeps.

                [*Passionately seizing his hand.*]

Oh, you must stay! For Alfhild is just like
that blue, that little mountain flower up there.

BJØRN. Yes, yes, I'll stay. But you must tell me then
how you first got up here; is no one there
to share your life up here?

ALFHILD.   What do you mean?

BJØRN. Well, don't you have a father or a mother?

ALFHILD. Oh yes! But they no longer live with Alfhild!
They are asleep; they won't come back again.
The time when Alfhild was a little girl,
she lived beside her father and her mother.
But that's so long, so very long ago.

BJØRN [*aside*].
I fear they surely must be dead, poor child!

ALFHILD. Oh, mother was so good . . . and Father too.
He looked like you. . . .

BJØRN.   And since that time you've lived
Alone up here. . . ?

ALFHILD.   No, Alfhild's not alone.
See, here are flowers, and here are little birds,
and Alfhild knows each one of them full well.
And Alfhild also has her little lambs
and all her goats . . . just now they're on the hills.
And there's the elves who live here in the forest,
and when she's glad, they play their games with her.

BJØRN. And no one else lives here . . . ?

ALFHILD.   Oh yes, sometimes,
For Alfhild's aged father also comes.

BJØRN. Your aged father! But you said just now
he wasn't any longer . . .

ALFHILD.   There's the other.
Oh, don't you know about the old, old man
who tells so many very lovely tales.
Then Alfhild sits and listens to them all,
and asks about those things she doesn't follow.
But now that you have come along, she would
prefer to hear the tales you have to tell.

BJØRN. And yet he never takes you with him. Why?
Why does he leave you staying on up here?

ALFHILD. Oh, that's a question Alfhild's never asked him.

[*A thought strikes her and she says suddenly:*]

But tell me—since the thought has only struck me—
Could Alfhild live some other place than here?

BJØRN. You could. Oh, Alfhild, if you'd come with me
down to my home. . . .

ALFHILD [*glad*].   You have a home as well?
A dale like this with flowers and with forests?

BJØRN. Indeed I have. So will you come with me . . . ?

ALFHILD. Yes, gladly, gladly Alfhild comes with you!

[KNUD *comes slowly out from the forest.*]

KNUD. Good evening, Alfhild!

ALFHILD [*hurries across to him*]. Father! Why are you here
so late?

KNUD.   I had to talk to you tonight!

[*He notices* BJØRN.]

Ah, so it's you. And how did you get here?

BJØRN [*astonished*].
I was out hunting . . .

ALFHILD.   Father! he has promised
that he will never leave Alfhild again!

KNUD. You've promised that?

BJØRN.   Yes, I have, old man!

ALFHILD. He says he also has a home, a dale
like this one—there he means to take Alfhild!
And Alfhild will so gladly go with him,
for she could not stay here when he is gone!

KNUD. You mean to take her to your father's house?

BJØRN. That is my plan.

ALFHILD.   And you must go there, Father,
and sing for him the things that you have sung
before for Alfhild. . . .

KNUD.   That I shall do, child!
For I must guard you still. . . .

BJØRN.   But say!
Why did you leave her living in the valley,
abandoned and alone?

KNUD.   I do not rule
her fate; moreover only in my strings
and songs is found what's in my power to do!

BJØRN. Who are you then, mysterious old man?

KNUD. I fear I cannot tell you that, my son,
but over you and her I shall keep watch!

ALFHILD. And won't you come and join us then, dear Father?

KNUD. I cannot do that, Alfhild! I must go
from place to place; for many are the hearts
that need the touch of comfort, many's the breast
in turmoil, pregnant with its own tormenting burden.
And things that stir within the people's bosom,
I must interpret through my vibrant strings.

[*He goes.*]

BJØRN. So you will join me then?

ALFHILD.   Yes, yes, I will!
Oh, surely you will then be good to Alfhild,
for when she leaves this fair and pleasant valley
she has no refuge then apart from you.

BJØRN [*seizes her hand*].
Yes always, Alfhild, I'll be good to you.
Oh, I will love you, love you all my life.

ALFHILD. What's that? . . . You'll love me? What is that you mean?

BJØRN. That I'll be good to you, and always think
of you alone as long as I may live.

ALFHILD. Ah, Alfhild now is glad. For now she thinks
she understands you. Say again you mean
to love me constantly.

BJØRN.   Yes, constantly.

ALFHILD. For otherwise would Alfhild surely die.
You know, two doves once built a nest up there
within the topmost branches of the fir;
along one day there came a stranger dove
and with it soon one dove did fly away.
The other sat and waited, night and day,
but never did the first, alas, return.
That dove could only die. . . .

BJØRN.   No, Alfhild, no!
On me you always may rely. But what
are you now listening for . . . ?

[*Soft music is heard.*]

ALFHILD [*quietly*].   You hear that sound . . . ?
The gentle elves are singing all around us!

BJØRN. That's but the evening breeze. . . .

ALFHILD.   And do you hear
them whispering among the flowers? . . . Hark!

[*During the following,* ALFHILD *stands silently listening, revealing her feelings
in line with the content of the song.* BJØRN *watches her with anxiety and wonder.*]

CHORUS OF ELVES.
                    Whispering elves by night
                    Take their fond farewell.
                    Soon we must, by fond moonlight,
                    Halt our dance under dew-drenched leaves.
                              Then we will,
                              Quiet and still,
                    Bathe the evening flowers in tears.

Your way cannot be ours,
Kind thoughts we'll think of you.
Up to our realms secure
you'll once more rise again.
     Then we will,
     Quiet and still,
Greet again the valley's maid!

[*The music gradually dies away.*]

BJØRN [*in a low voice*].
You whisper, Alfhild! Come, what is the matter?
I feel so sad in spirit. . . . Let us go!

ALFHILD [*grasps his hand*].
Now Alfhild comes to join you. She has whispered
farewell to all the little elves and flowers.

[*They go.*]

———————

[*The green at Bjerkehoug; trees in the background; left can be seen one wall of the house.*]

PAAL [*comes to meet* MERETA]. No, no, there is no good fortune at Bjerkehoug. . . .
Dear God! is this gaiety for a Midsummer Night? I managed to raise their
spirits a little over there on the hill. . . .

MERETA. And then?

PAAL. And then Bengt Alfsen came along, and everything went as quiet as in
a church. . . .

MERETA. Yes, Paal, I have noticed everybody is afraid of him. . . .

PAAL. God knows what is wrong. Everybody avoids him, even Bjørn, his own
son.

MERETA. Great God, do you think that?

PAAL. I have noticed this for some time. . . .

MERETA. And this is why he is always off hunting in the mountains, and never
feels settled at home?

PAAL. Yes, that was the initial reason, but since then . . .

MERETA. Since then? What . . . ?

PAAL. Oh, nothing. . . . Don't ask me anything more, here comes Bengt Alfsen!

MERETA. Then I'll go.

[She goes.]

BENGT ALFSEN *[enters]*. Who were you talking to here . . . ?

PAAL. It was your foster-daughter.

BENGT. And why did she leave when she saw me coming?

PAAL. She said she had something to see to in the house.

BENGT. Indeed—that's always happening when I come. That's the way it is with them all. If the girls are sitting spinning by the hearth they always have things to see to in the kitchen or the cellar when I come in.

PAAL. Bengt Alfsen, it is your own fault.

BENGT. Be silent. I don't want to hear any more about it.

PAAL. Well, I can just as well keep silent. It was only for your own good I said it.

BENGT. Yes, yes. . . . Have you seen anything of Herr Mogens this evening?

PAAL. He was in the servants' hall sitting in the dark.

BENGT. See if you can find him. . . . Tell him I am expecting him.

PAAL. I will!

[He goes.]

BENGT *[after a pause]*.
I'm not as quick and healthy as before;
a heavy burden weighs upon my shoulders,
and people notice things are not so well
with me—they go when once they see me coming.
But where's that priest! Damnation, where's he gone!
It sometimes brings relief to talk to him.
—You exact a heavy price, my brother Alf!

[He looks about him.]

There's movement in among the trees . . . St. Olaf!

[He crosses himself and goes into the house. EINAR *and* MERETA *enter.]*

EINAR. Why is it that you will not dance with me?

MERETA. Because I do not wish—that is the reason.

EINAR. You do not treat me as you should, Mereta!

MERETA. Indeed! And what do you desire?

EINAR. Oh, well . . .
I dare say . . . nothing. But you know full well
I'm fond of you. . . .

MERETA. Is that why you are cross
if I so much as talk to someone else?

EINAR. Oh, talking! . . . Laughing, whispering. . . .

MERETA [*gaily*]. Ha, ha, ha!
The more you sulk, the more amused I then
become. . . .

EINAR. I know, I see you do, Mereta!
I was like that myself when I first came,
but these few days have wrought a change in me.
Mereta, listen. . . .

MERETA. Please don't start again
with all that stupid nonsense. . . .

EINAR [*offended*]. Very well,
I'll say no more to you. . . .

[*He starts to go.*]

MERETA. You going, Einar?

EINAR. Farewell, Mereta!

MERETA [*roguishly*]. Happy journey to you!

[*As he reaches the way out.*]

Yet wait a moment. Let me talk to you.

EINAR [*turns*]. What do you want?

MERETA. Come here. Listen, Einar!
You promise me you'll keep a silent tongue
and speak no more of love. . . .

EINAR [*darkly*]. Yes, yes, I promise.

MERETA. And when I sometimes laugh at you a little
you mustn't look so sour.

EINAR. Do as you please.

F11

MERETA. Then that's all right. I thank you. You may go.
But for your journey I would like to make
a little present. . . .

EINAR.   What is that?

MERETA.   It's this!

[*She gives him her hand.*]

So there you are—my hand and heart.

EINAR [*embraces her*].   Mereta!
You mean it truly?

MERETA.   Yes, I mean it, Einar!

[BENGT ⟨*and* MOGENS added⟩ *enter.*]

God! There is father!

BENGT.   What is happening here?

EINAR. Bengt Alfsen! Listen!

BENGT.   Silence! There's no need.
I saw enough to understand. Mereta!
It would become you better if you spent
your time among the maids, and not with Einar.

[MERETA *leaves.*]

[*To* EINAR.]
And you, my friend! I can inform you now
that if you try to court Mereta's favours,
it won't do any good; for I have made
a different decision. Come, Herr Mogens!

[*They leave.*]

EINAR. So what the priest has told me is all true!
So be it, then. I know Mereta loves me,
and doubtless she knows how to get her way.
Moreover I can hope for fortune's help. . . .

[PAAL, *several musicians, peasants and peasant girls appear; there is music.*]

⟨*Here the manuscript ends.*⟩

OLAF LILJEKRANS
[*Olaf Liljekrans*]

PLAY IN THREE ACTS

[First performed in Bergen, 2 January 1857]

CHARACTERS

LADY KIRSTEN LILJEKRANS

OLAF LILJEKRANS, her son

ARNE OF GULDVIK

INGEBORG, his daughter

HEMMING, his page

THORGEJR, an old minstrel

ALFHILD

Wedding guests

Kinsfolk of Arne of Guldvik

Maids and servants of Lady Kirsten

The action takes place in the Middle Ages, in a mountain village

ACT ONE

*A thickly wooded hillside, sloping up to higher mountainous areas;
in a deep cleft, a swiftly-flowing river runs from the rear and out to
the right; a few old logs and the remains of a broken-down bridge lie
across the river. Huge boulders lie scattered in the foreground; in the
distance, the peaks of snow-capped mountains can be seen. The red
glow of evening hangs over the landscape; later the moon comes out.*

SCENE I

[THORGEJR *stands on a rock beside the river, listening to various choruses
which are heard off-stage.*]

CHORUS OF LADY KIRSTEN'S RETINUE [*deep in the forest, left*].

    With hymns of praise, and ringing of bells,
    We wander abroad in the valleys.
    Oh, Christian man, pay heed to our song,
    And wake from your drowsy enchantment.

KINSFOLK OF ARNE OF GULDVIK [*far away to the right*].

    Now, off we go
    To the wedding hall,
    And the foal runs light on the hill!
      With thundering hooves
      In the grass-green woods,
    Where the merry young men do ride!

LADY KIRSTEN'S RETINUE [*a little closer than before*].

    We summon you forth from hill and fell
    Wherever you sit enthralled.
    Be awakened thereby, and free your soul
    From the treacherous elves of the grove!

[THORGEJR *disappears into the cleft where the river runs; after a brief
interlude, the songs are heard much nearer.*]

ARNE'S KINSFOLK.

    Our way we shorten with jest and song
    All on the bridal night!

LADY KIRSTEN'S RETINUE.
>   In tears we wander the whole day long,
>   Searching up hill and down dale!

ARNE'S KINSFOLK [*close nearby, but still off-stage*].
>   To wedding banquet, song and dance,
>   Men and maids do make their way!

LADY KIRSTEN'S RETINUE [*nearer than before*].
>   Olaf Liljekrans! Olaf Liljekrans!
>   Why sleep you so long and so heavy!

SCENE II

[ARNE OF GULDVIK *appears with his kinsfolk, men and women, minstrels etc. at the rear, right, on the other side of the river; they are all in festive clothes. Shortly after,* HEMMING *appears from the same side.*]

ONE OF THE RETINUE. Look, this is the way!

ANOTHER. No, here it is.

A THIRD. Surely not! It must be this one.

ARNE OF GULDVIK. Well now, are we stuck again! [*Shouts.*] Hemming! Where is Hemming?

HEMMING [*enters*]. Here!

ARNE. Haven't I told you to keep close to me so that you can help me?

HEMMING. It was the Lady Ingeborg . . . she wanted . . . and so . . .

ARNE [*angrily*]. Lady Ingeborg! Lady Ingeborg! Are you Lady Ingeborg's maid? You are my page. You are to serve me. Isn't that what you get your wages and your keep for? Come now, tell us the way! We are stuck!

HEMMING [*uncertainly*]. The way? Well, I don't know these parts very well, but . . .

ARNE. Might I not have known! That is always what I get from you! Well, then we'll have to stay out on the moors all night, as sure as my name is Arne of Guldvik.

HEMMING [*who in the meantime has caught sight of the remnants of the bridge*]. Ah, there is no need for that. We go over here!

ARNE. Why did you not say so at once?

[*All cross the river and come forward on the stage.*]

ARNE [*looks around*]. Yes, now I know where I am again. The river there is the boundary between my land and Lady Kirsten's. [*Points to the left.*] Her estate is down there. Another hour or two and we can be sitting snug in the bridal house. But if so we must hurry. [*Shouts.*] Ingeborg! . . . Hemming! Where has Ingeborg got to?

HEMMING. Back there, up on the hillside. [*Points to the right.*] She is playing with her bridesmaids. They are pulling green twigs off the cherry trees and chasing each other with them, shouting and laughing.

ARNE [*exasperated, but in a low voice*]. Hemming! This marriage is causing me so many worries it's making me ill. [*Looks out to the right.*] Look! Just look at them running about over there! She was the one who had the idea of going over the mountain instead of following the road. We would get there quicker, she said. And in spite of that . . . huh! It's enough to make me mad. Tomorrow she goes to the altar. Is this the proper decorum she should be observing! What will Lady Kirsten say when she finds my daughter so badly brought up? [*As* HEMMING *starts to speak.*] Because she is! She is badly brought up, I say.

HEMMING. Master! You should never be marrying your daughter into Lady Kirsten's family. Lady Kirsten and her kinsmen are high-born folk and . . .

ARNE. You are stupid, Hemming! 'High-born, high-born!' A lot of good that is! You don't grow fat on that. If Lady Kirsten is high-born, then I am rich. I have gold in my chests and silver in my coffers.

HEMMING. Yes, but your neighbours are laughing at the agreement you have come to with her.

ARNE. Ha, ha, let them. That's because they wish me ill!

HEMMING. They say that you have surrendered your legal rights to get the Lady Ingeborg married to Olaf Liljekrans. I suppose I shouldn't really mention it, but they have made up a lampoon about you, Master!

ARNE. You lie in your throat! Nobody dare make up lampoons about Arne of Guldvik. I have power. I can have them thrown out of house and home anytime I like. Lampoon! A lot you know about lampoons! . . . If they have made up any songs, then they are in honour of the bride and her father! [*Flares up.*] In any case, it's a miserable bit of work, quite miserable, I tell you. He's got no poetic talent, the man who put it together. And if ever I get hold of him...

HEMMING. Ah, master! Then you know it? Has somebody been bold enough to sing it to you?

ARNE. Sing, sing! Don't stand there holding me up with all this nonsense. [*To the others.*] Come away, kinsmen, we must not dally if we want to reach the bridal house before midnight. You should have heard what Hemming was telling me. He was saying there's a reliable rumour that Lady Kirsten has baked and brewed for five whole days in order to receive us with honour. Is that not so, Hemming?

HEMMING. Yes, master!

ARNE. He says she does not own any piece of silver so costly but what she does not put it out on the table, shining and polished. She has not prepared so splendid a banquet since the King visited her late husband twenty years ago. Isn't that so, Hemming?

HEMMING. Yes, master! [*Whispers.*] But, master, it is unwise to say such things! Lady Kirsten is proud of her birth. She thinks she is doing you an honour by this marriage. Little you know how she means to receive her guests.

ARNE [*in a low voice*]. Oh, what nonsense! [*To the others.*] He says that Lady Kirsten gives herself no rest. Night and day she is busy in the pantry and in the cellar. Is that not . . . ? [*Starts, as he looks out to the left.*] Hemming! What is this! Do you see who is coming there?

HEMMING [*with a cry*]. Lady Kirsten Liljekrans!

ALL [*astonished*]. Lady Kirsten!

SCENE III

[As before. LADY KIRSTEN *enters, left, with her House Carls.]*

LADY KIRSTEN *[to her retinue, without noticing the others].* Now, just a little further and I'm sure we'll find him. *[Startled, aside.]* Arne of Guldvik! Heaven preserve me!

ARNE *[going to meet her].* God's peace, Lady Kirsten Liljekrans!

LADY KIRSTEN *[composes herself and holds out her hand to him].* God's peace to you! *[Aside.]* Does he not know?

ARNE *[in continuing good humour].* And well met at the boundary! What a pleasure this is! You do me almost too much honour!

LADY KIRSTEN. What do you mean?

ARNE. I mean you do me too much honour by coming miles through the hill and moor to bid me welcome to your land.

LADY KIRSTEN. Ah, my good Sir Arne! *[Aside.]* He knows nothing as yet!

ARNE. And on a day like today when you have quite enough to attend to. Although it is at your house that our children's wedding is to be held, since my own estate lies too far from the church, you nevertheless come to meet me with all your servants.

LADY KIRSTEN *[embarrassed].* I beg you, say no more about it.

ARNE. Yes, I will say it out loud. The people of the district are saying that you pride yourself on your noble birth, that you despise me and mine, and that you only agreed to the arrangement in order to put an end to the long disputes which bore heavily upon you, now that you are a widow and growing old. And if it had not been for that, then you would never . . .

LADY KIRSTEN. How can you bring yourself to listen to what evil tongues can invent! Let us think no more of these disputes, which have now been in existence since the days of your ancestors. I say our families have suffered grievously enough under them, yours as well as mine. Look about you, Sir Arne! Is the land here not like some wild and remote district, when in our fathers' days it was rich and populated? A bridge lay over the river, and a road led from

Guldvik to my father's. But on both sides they sallied forth with fire and sword, and laid waste to everything they encountered, because they thought they were too near neighbours. Now weeds of all sorts cover the road, the bridge is broken, and only wolves and bears make their homes here.

ARNE. Yes, they led the road round the mountain there below. It is a good deal longer and they were better able to keep an eye on each other. But we have little need of that now, which is well and good for both of us.

LADY KIRSTEN. Certainly, certainly! But Ingeborg, the bride, where is she? I do not see her, nor the bridesmaids either. Should she not...?

ARNE. She is following us. She'll be here any moment. But . . . listen to me Lady Kirsten! One thing I want to tell you, and it's as well now as later, although I daresay you probably know it. Ingeborg sometimes has strange moods and fancies . . . I assure you, she does, however well brought up she may be.

LADY KIRSTEN [*tense*]. Well, what then? [*Aside.*] Is she too . . . ?

ARNE. These things you must control. I could never manage to, as her father. But you will surely find a way.

LADY KIRSTEN. Yes, rest assured. [*Aside.*] And Olaf nowhere to be seen!

HEMMING [*who has looked out to the right*]. Here comes the Lady Ingeborg! [*Aside.*] How fine she looks, striding there at the head of them all!

LADY KIRSTEN [*in a low voice to her servants*]. You will keep silent about our errand up here.

A SERVANT. You may depend on that.

HEMMING [*aside, sighing, as he continues to look out to the right*]. Happy Olaf, to possess her!

SCENE IV

[*As before;* INGEBORG *and* THE BRIDESMAIDS *come across the bridge.*]

INGEBORG [*still in the background*]. Why do you run away from me? What is the use of that? Nothing can happen till I get there. [*Notices* LADY KIRSTEN *and her retinue.*] Lady Kirsten! Are you here? What a pleasure that is. [*Quickly, in passing, to the retinue.*] Greetings to you all! [*To* LADY KIRSTEN, *as she looks around.*] But Olaf, where is he?

LADY KIRSTEN. Olaf! [*Aside.*] Woe is me! Now it will all come out!

ARNE. Yes, indeed, Olaf! Ha, ha, ha! I must be blind. Good thing that the bride sees better. For I did not notice that the bridegroom was missing. But now I understand how it happens that we meet here. . . . He is the cause . . .

LADY KIRSTEN. He . . . you mean . . . you know that . . . ?

ARNE. I mean that time weighed heavily on him down there in the banquet hall. Yes, I well remember from my own wedding day, when I too was young. He greatly wanted to meet his bride as soon as it could be arranged, and then he got you to come with him.

LADY KIRSTEN. Indeed he greatly wanted to meet his bride, but . . .

INGEBORG. But what?

LADY KIRSTEN. Olaf is not here with us.

HEMMING [*approaches*]. Not with you!

ARNE. And why not?

INGEBORG. Speak out, I beg you!

LADY KIRSTEN [*reluctantly, jestingly*]. In truth, it seems the bride is also anxious! Come, come along with me to the wedding hall. There I think we must surely find him.

HEMMING [*whispers to* ARNE]. Master! Remember I warned you.

ARNE [*suspiciously, to* LADY KIRSTEN]. First answer my question, then we shall come.

LADY KIRSTEN. Well then . . . he has gone out hunting. [*As she is about to go.*] Come, it is quickly getting dark.

INGEBORG. Hunting?

LADY KIRSTEN. Aye! Does that surprise you? You know the song:

> 'A knight delights in a forest ride,
> To test his horse and his hound!'

INGEBORG. Does he have so little regard for his young bride that he goes hunting animals on the eve of his wedding?

LADY KIRSTEN. Now you are jesting. Come along, come along!

ARNE [*who in the meantime has been watching* LADY KIRSTEN *and her retinue*]. No, wait, Lady Kirsten! Perhaps I don't compare with you in cleverness, but one thing I nevertheless see clearly. And that is that you are concealing your real errand up here.

LADY KIRSTEN [*disconcerted*]. I! What makes you think that?

ARNE. I can see from a number of things that there is something you are keeping to yourself. You are sorely disturbed and yet you pretend to be in a jocular mood. But it won't do. . . .

LADY KIRSTEN. Nor is it anything new for you to think ill of me and mine.

ARNE. Perhaps. But never did I do it without good reason. [*Bursts out.*] As sure as I live, you are concealing something from me.

LADY KIRSTEN [*aside*]. What will this lead to?

ARNE. I let myself be fooled by you, but now I see things clearly enough. You said that you came to meet me at the boundary. How did you know we were taking the road across the mountains. It was Ingeborg who decided she wanted that, just as we were leaving Guldvik, and nobody could have told you about that. [*When* LADY KIRSTEN *does not answer.*] You are silent. I imagined you would be.

HEMMING [*in a low voice*]. You see, master! Now will you believe what I said?

ARNE [*likewise*]. Be silent!

LADY KIRSTEN [*who has in the meantime composed herself*]. Very well, my good Sir Arne! I will be honest with you. The rest is in the hands of fate.

ARNE. Then tell me . . .

INGEBORG. What do you mean?

LADY KIRSTEN. The contract between us was sealed by word and by handclasp. Many honourable men I see here can witness to that. Olaf, my son, was to marry your daughter. The wedding feast was to be held tomorrow at my house . . .

ARNE [*impatiently*]. Yes, yes!

LADY KIRSTEN. Dishonour to him who breaks his word, but . . .

ARNE AND THE GUESTS. But then! Speak out!

LADY KIRSTEN. The wedding cannot take place tomorrow, as was arranged.

ARNE. Not take place?

LADY KIRSTEN. We must wait.

HEMMING. Ah, disgrace and shame!

INGEBORG. No wedding?

ARNE. A curse upon you for playing me false!

THE GUESTS [*threateningly, as several of them draw their knives and rush at* LADY KIRSTEN'*s people*]. Revenge! Revenge on the house of Liljekrans!

LADY KIRSTEN'S MEN [*raise their axes and prepare to defend themselves*]. Strike them! Down with the men of Guldvik!

LADY KIRSTEN [*throwing herself between the assailants*]. Stop, stop! I beg you! . . . Sir Arne! Hear me out before you judge my conduct.

ARNE [*who has tried to pacify his kinsfolk, goes up to* LADY KIRSTEN *and says in a low voice, as he tries to control his agitation, which is nevertheless apparent*]: Forgive me, Lady Kirsten! I was too quick to anger. If I had stopped to think, I would surely have realized that it was all a jest on your part. I beg you, do not contradict me! It must be so! No wedding tomorrow. . . . How could anything like that happen! If you need ale or mead, if you are short of silver, or of embroidered linen, come to me!

LADY KIRSTEN. You are not marrying your daughter into any poor man's house, Sir Arne! Come along to the wedding feast with all your kinsmen and friends, come indeed with three times as many, if you like. . . . In my house you will find both accommodation and fine food, as much as you can eat. Do not think for one moment that such unworthy reasons could deter me.

ARNE. Then you have changed your mind, perhaps?

LADY KIRSTEN. Not that either! If I have given my word, then I am also prepared to keep it, today or any day. For this was always the custom and rule in my family. But in this instance it is not my affair. We are short of one person . . .

INGEBORG. One person? Who? I should think surely that if the bride is ready . . .

LADY KIRSTEN. Two are needed to make a wedding, the bridegroom as well as the bride . . .

ARNE AND THE GUESTS. Olaf!

INGEBORG. My betrothed!

LADY KIRSTEN. Yes, he! My son. . . . He fled this night from his home and his bride!

THE GUESTS. Fled!

ARNE. Fled! He!

LADY KIRSTEN. As I hope for the grace of heaven, I have no part in this!

ARNE [*with suppressed exasperation*]. And the wedding was to be held tomorrow! My daughter has put on her golden attire; I have sent invitations all round the district; my friends and kinsmen are coming from near and far to be at the celebrations. [*Flares up.*] Ah, take care not to expose Arne of Guldvik to the scorn of his neighbours. Little shall it profit you . . . that I solemnly swear!

LADY KIRSTEN. You build on shifting ground if you think that . . .

ARNE. Do not go on, Lady Kirsten, do not go on! We too have an old account to settle. It is not the first time that you set cunning snares for me and mine. The line of Guldvik has long had to endure you and your kinsmen plotting deception and guile! We had the power; we also had the materials and the money. But you were too cunning for us. You knew how to mislead us with deceptive words and fine phrases . . . these are wares which I am little able to value as I should!

LADY KIRSTEN. Sir Arne! Listen to me!

ARNE [*continuing*]. Now I see very clearly that I have behaved like a man who built his house on an ice-floe. Came the thaw, and down he went. But little joy you will have of this. I will hold you to account, Lady Kirsten! You must answer for your son; it was you who urged his suit. It is up to you to keep the promise which has been given to me! I was a fool. . . . Aye, ten times a fool, to trust your smooth tongue. Those who wished me well warned me. My enemies mocked me. But I paid little attention to either. I put on my festive clothes, and gathered together my kinsmen and friends. We set out for the wedding house with song and laughter, and then... the bridegroom has fled!

INGEBORG. A man who values me so lightly will never bring me to church.

ARNE. Be silent!

HEMMING [*in a low voice, to* ARNE]. Lady Ingeborg is right. Better break the agreement.

ARNE. Be silent, I tell you.

LADY KIRSTEN [*to* ARNE]. You may well be feeling angry and resentful. But if you suppose me deceitful, you do me a very grave injustice. You think some cunning trick is being played on you; but tell me, why should my son or I be tempted to any such thing? Does he not love Ingeborg? Where could he find himself a better bride? Is she not beautiful and vital? Is her father not rich and powerful? Is her family not referred to in honourable terms wherever it is known?

ARNE. But then how could Olaf . . . ?

LADY KIRSTEN. The lot I have suffered is worse than you think. You will feel more sorrow than anger for me when you hear what it is. Since sunrise this morning I have been on the move, looking for him here.

ARNE. Up here?

LADY KIRSTEN. Yes, up here. You will have to be told . . . though it will terrify you . . . nevertheless . . . Olaf is troll-struck!

THE GUESTS. Troll-struck!

INGEBORG [*at the same time*]. God save me!

ARNE. What is that you say, Lady Kirsten?

LADY KIRSTEN. He is troll-struck! What else can it be. . . . Three weeks ago, when the betrothal feast was held at Guldvik, he did not come home until late the following day. He was pale, and moody and

GII

quiet besides, in a way that I had never seen him before. The days went by; he spoke little; most of the time he lay in bed with his head turned away. But as evening approached, it was as if he were seized by some strange unrest. He would saddle his horse and ride away, far into the hills. Nobody dared follow him, and nobody knew where he went. Believe me, evil spirits have bewitched his mind. The power they wield in here is great. Ever since the great plague attacked the villages, one has never been quite safe here in the mountains. Hardly a day goes by without the cow-girls hearing strange music, though there are no people where it comes from.

ARNE. Troll-struck! Is that conceivable?

LADY KIRSTEN. Would to God it weren't, but I am no longer in any doubt about it. It is three days now since he left home.

ARNE. And nobody you asked could tell you where he was?

LADY KIRSTEN. That isn't it, alas. A hunter saw him up here yesterday, but he was as shy as a wild deer. He had picked all sorts of herbs, which he scattered about wherever he went and all the time he whispered strange words. As soon as I heard this, I set out with my people, but we have found nothing.

INGEBORG. And you met nobody who could tell you . . . ?

LADY KIRSTEN. The whole area is deserted, as you know!

ARNE [*catching sight of* THORGEJR *who is climbing up from the river*]. Here is somebody I will ask.

HEMMING [*fearfully*]. Master! Master!

ARNE. What is it?

HEMMING. Let him go! Don't you see who it is?

THE GUESTS *and* LADY KIRSTEN'S MEN [*whispering among themselves*]. Thorgejr the minstrel! Crazy Thorgejr!

INGEBORG. He has learnt the song of the nixies.

HEMMING. Let him go! Let him go!

ARNE. Even if he were a nixie himself . . .

SCENE V

[*As before; in the meantime,* THORGEJR *has moved to the edge of the stage, left; at* ARNE'*s last words he turns suddenly as if he had been directly addressed.*]

THORGEJR [*moving a few steps nearer*]. What do you want with me?

ARNE [*starting*]. What's that!

HEMMING. You'll hear!

ARNE. Let me deal with this. [*To* THORGEJR.] We are looking for Olaf Liljekrans. Have you met him in these parts today?

THORGEJR. Olaf Liljekrans?

LADY KIRSTEN. Yes, you know him well.

THORGEJR. Is he not one of those evil men from the villages down there?

LADY KIRSTEN. Evil?

THORGEJR. They are all evil there! Olaf Liljekrans curses the little bird when it sings on his mother's roof.

LADY KIRSTEN. You lie, minstrel!

THORGEJR [*with a cunning smile*]. So much the better for him!

ARNE. How so?

THORGEJR. You ask about Olaf Liljekrans? Has he got lost here? You seek him and cannot find him?

LADY KIRSTEN. Yes, yes!

THORGEJR. So much the better for him! . . . If that was a lie I told, he is in no danger.

INGEBORG. Tell us what you know!

THORGEJR. That would keep me busy a long time! [*Malevolently.*] This is the land of elves and sprites. Be of good cheer! . . . If you do not find him, then he's at play with the elves. They like those who are fond of little birds, and you said, didn't you, that Olaf . . . ? Go home! Go back home! Olaf is in the mountain and is in no danger!

LADY KIRSTEN. Curse you for saying that!

THORGEJR [*with a wild expression, and half to himself*].
> Once I was a bachelor gay
> And slept on the green hillside;
> When hard upon the midnight hour
> There came nine elfin maids!
> —Like the moon as it shines in the misty night,
> Like a shimmering light in the sea,
> Was the pallid gleam to the troll-girls fair
> As they danced by the river's edge.
> They gave me the cup of forgetfulness,
> Which thrice to the dregs I drained,
> And now in the hall of the mountain lord
> I sit and dream my dreams!

[*Then, as though waking up, he says to the others.*]

Olaf Liljekrans can sing that song if it so be . . . believe me! . . . Farewell! [*Goes.*]

ARNE [*to* LADY KIRSTEN]. Pay no attention to what he says.

THORGEJR [*approaches again*]. Away I go now to sing and play. Olaf Liljekrans is sitting in the mountain, and it's there his wedding shall be. . . . Crazy Thorgejr has to be there, for he can make the seats and tables dance, as soon as he touches his fiddle strings. But all of you take heed! Go back home. It is not good for you here. Have you not heard the saying:

> In faith I know a fair green vale
> Where elves, it is said, hold sway.
> You must beware when the elves do play
> For they know how to capture your mind!
> You must take care when the elves do play;
> They draw you into their game,
> And all things there that you hear and see
> You will never forget again.

[*Suddenly breaking out in wild joy.*] Here we have the wedding guests . . . ha ha! The ladies have their best dresses on, the men their best jerkins . . . now I understand! Olaf Liljekrans is a bridegroom in the village as well; he has another betrothed there! Well, such things have been known before! I know there was once . . . many years ago . . . but I remember it well . . .

[*Continues again after a moment's pause, wilder and ever wilder.*]

> Sir Alvar and Ingrid plighted their troth;
> A sprightly young maiden was she.
> Their wedding feast lasted for three glad days,
> With eating and drinking and song.
> And the bride was a maid both nimble and fair,
> As among her guests she danced,
> When the nixie came, that evil sprite,
> And sat on the edge of the bed.
> Sat like a minstrel on the edge of the bed
> And played a bewitching tune!
> And tables and benches all danced in a ring
> As lightly as servants and maids!
>
> The nixie, he left by the open door—
> There is little to gain by denying—
> And e'en as he played on his fiddle string
> The bride had to follow behind him.

[*Wildly, triumphantly.*]

> All spell-bound stood the knights and their men,
> The bridegroom transfixed in a trance.
> The nixie prepared little Ingrid's bed—
> Her bridal bed deep in the river!

[*Suddenly becomes quiet, and says in a low voice.*] That song I shall never forget! . . . But go home! Evening is coming on, and once the sun is down the forest belongs to the others. Farewell! I shall take messages and greetings to Olaf where he sits . . . in the mountain!

[*He goes out left.*]

SCENE VI

[*As before; excepting* THORGEJR.]

ARNE [*to* LADY KIRSTEN]. He is lying! Do not believe him!

HEMMING. All the same there is truth in that about the bride who disappeared on the eve of her wedding.

ARNE. Aye, that was many years ago; things like that don't happen any longer! But we will all set to and look for him.

INGEBORG. It was never sung at my cradle that I should run about in fields and forest to find my bridegroom again!

ARNE. Be silent!

INGEBORG. If he is in the mountain, bewitched, then let her who did it take him. I don't intend to share my husband's heart and mind.

HEMMING [*in a low and intense voice*]. The Lord bless you for those words!

INGEBORG [*with a haughty, disdainful look*]. What?

ARNE. Will you be silent, I say! [*To the* GUESTS.] Quickly now, my friends! Scatter and search for him on every slope and every hill! Away! Indeed! Tomorrow we'll celebrate the wedding!

[THE GUESTS *and* LADY KIRSTEN'S RETINUE *go out, right and left, in different groups.*]

ARNE [*in a low voice to* LADY KIRSTEN]. He must be found! It will be to my eternal shame if the wedding . . .

LADY KIRSTEN. Come, then! Come with me!

INGEBORG [*in a low voice to* HEMMING, *who stands dejected*]. Why don't you go with the others? It would be better if you brought me back my betrothed than stood there blessing me for words that I didn't really mean.

ARNE [*departing*]. Come, come!

INGEBORG [*to* HEMMING, *who is on the point of going*]. Wait, Hemming! Fasten my shoes!

[LADY KIRSTEN *and* ARNE *go out left.*]

SCENE VII

[INGEBORG; HEMMING.]

INGEBORG [*putting out her foot*]. There! Fasten it well!

[HEMMING *kneels down and does as she bids.*]

INGEBORG [*whilst he is occupied with this*].

> Sir Hjalmar sailed to a distant shore,
> And there laid down his young life;
> Whilst sitting at home in a lofty room
> Was the fair Ingeborg his dear wife!

[*She puts her other foot forward.*]

There! Fasten me that one, too!

[*Continues humming.*]

> And when she received the mournful news
> So sorrowful and sad grew she,
> That the belt burst open at her waist,
> And the buckles burst on her shoe.

That's how it was with me when I heard the news that the sprites had lured away my betrothed. [*She looks to see what impression this makes on* HEMMING.] That was why my buckles came undone! [*Impatiently, as he betrays nothing.*] Do you hear, Hemming! I say that was why . . .

HEMMING [*still occupied as before*]. Yes, yes! I hear well enough!

INGEBORG. You hear, you hear! . . . Nobody could see that you did! Well, why are you bending your head? Has something upset you?

HEMMING. Do you wish me honestly to tell you . . . ?

INGEBORG. Indeed I do!

HEMMING. Then you ought to know . . .

INGEBORG [*hastily*]. Oh no, there's no need! [*She moves away a few steps;* HEMMING *gets up.*]

INGEBORG [*hums, concealing a mischievous look*].

> And when she received the mournful news
> So sorrowful and sad grew she,
> That both her eye-balls burst at the news,
> And the blood spurted out of her breast.

[*Carelessly.*] Well, actually that didn't happen to me. But it might well happen . . . [*Turns suddenly to face him, and says vehemently:*] And then he says 'Lord bless you for those words', just as if . . .

HEMMING. Oh, Lady Ingeborg! You were so kind to me at one time. But now that you have grown up to be a proper lady . . . and mainly, I think, since you got betrothed . . .

INGEBORG. What?

HEMMING. Oh, nothing! . . . [*Pause.*] Can you remember we were up here once before?

INGEBORG [*curtly*]. I don't recall it!

HEMMING. You had gone chasing your spotted goat and I went with you as I always used to. . . . Yes, that was a long time ago. But I remember it as though it were yesterday. Just down there is the marsh which . . .

INGEBORG [*approaching*]. Was that the time we heard the bear?

HEMMING. Yes, the very time!

INGEBORG [*more and more excitedly*]. I found the goat again!

HEMMING. No, I was the one who found it first.

INGEBORG. Yes, yes! That was it. Up there on the slope.

HEMMING. And then you took your garter!

INGEBORG. And tied it up.

HEMMING. Yes, for we wanted to pick strawberries.

INGEBORG. On the hill over there, yes! And you had made me a basket of birch bark.

HEMMING. But just then we heard . . .

INGEBORG. The bear, ha ha ha! We had to cross the marsh where it was wettest . . .

HEMMING. Then I took you in my arms.

INGEBORG. And jumped with me from one tuft to another. [*Laughing.*] How frightened we both were!

HEMMING. I was mostly afraid on your account.

INGEBORG. And I on yours . . . [*Stops suddenly, and as she continues to regard him, her face assumes a haughty and offended look.*] Why are you standing here telling me all this? Why don't you go? Is it fitting to speak like this to your master's daughter? Go, go! You are supposed to find my betrothed!

HEMMING. Oh, I forgot about your betrothed. I forgot that you are my master's daughter!

INGEBORG. I promise you an embroidered jacket for Christmas if you find him. . . . I shall be so glad!

HEMMING. I don't wish for any jacket. I serve you for neither gold nor silver, nor yet for food nor fine clothes. But now I go. I shall do whatever I can, if I know it pleases you.

INGEBORG [*who has climbed up on a rock and is picking some flowering cherry twigs*]. Hemming! How rich is my betrothed?

HEMMING. How rich he is I cannot say. But of his grandfather it is said in the song:

> 'He can clothe in golden vestments
> A hundred bridesmaids for his bride.'

Quite so wealthy Olaf Liljekrans probably is not. But he owns both house and land.

INGEBORG [*occupied as before*]. And you? What do you own?

HEMMING [*sighing*]. My poverty! That is all!

INGEBORG. That is not much, Hemming!

HEMMING. No, that is not much, Lady Ingeborg!

INGEBORG [*hums, turned away from him, without changing her position and occupied as before*].

> Little my heart to him is drawn
> Whose wealth includes both house and land!
> The poor young swain much more appeals;
> He holds my thoughts; he is my friend!

HEMMING [*with unbounded joy*]. Ingeborg! Oh, if what you say is true, then I must prize my poverty tenfold!

INGEBORG [*turns her head and says coldly*]. I don't understand you. What I was singing was only an old ballad! [*Gets down from the rock with the cherry twigs in her hand and goes over to him, watching him fixedly.*] But I also know another song, and I'll sing you that one:

> In the palace yard stands a noble steed.
> The lover whose courage befits a knight
> Will shoe the fallow, will shoe the grey,
> The fleetest he'll saddle without delay!
> He sweeps up his bride on the stallion's back,
> She follows him willingly, trusting to him.
> And so they go galloping far far away;
> With him she will happily live and die!

HEMMING [*as though out of his mind*]. Ingeborg! Ingeborg! From now on I shall fear nothing! Not that you are betrothed, nor that you are my master's daughter. . . . As sure as I live, I shall make off with you this very night!

INGEBORG [*vehemently, as she tries to subdue a smile*]. God grant me help! What has come over you? What are you thinking of? Make off with your master's daughter? You must be either sick or mad to think a thing like that! And yet, it shall be forgotten—this time. Go now! And thank heaven you got off so lightly. For you well deserve a lash . . . [*She raises the twigs, but lets them fall, and says in an altered tone:*] . . . and my red gold bracelet. . . . There! Take it! [*She throws him a bracelet she has taken off her arm and hurries out, left.*]

SCENE VIII

[HEMMING. OLAF LILJEKRANS *enters shortly afterwards from the rear. The moon is rising.*]

HEMMING. This bracelet of gold to me she has given.
So I still hold her favour, still have her love!
She wasn't in earnest; it was but a jest—
Pretending she took such bitter offence.
All I will venture! Everything risk!

[*Dejected.*]

And yet I am only a penniless swain!
And tomorrow will witness her wedding day!

[*Quickly.*]

But deep in the forest the bridegroom is fled!
Ah! Think, were he never to come back again!

[*Is about to hurry off, but stops with a cry.*]

Olaf! There he is!

[OLAF *emerges slowly from among the rocks in the background. He walks dreaming, his head bare, and his hands full of flowers which he pulls to pieces and strews on the path; his entire behaviour during the following scene indicates a confused mind.*]

OLAF [*without noticing* HEMMING].
　　　　Could I but interpret
Those mysterious words, the appalling enigma!

[*Is about to go out, left.*]

HEMMING. Lord Olaf! Lord Olaf! What path are you taking?
Please hear me, Lord Olaf!

OLAF [*half awakening*].　　　Hemming! Is that you?
Do not try to stop me!

HEMMING.　　　　What preys on your mind?
For three long days you have wandered up here!

[*Looks at him more closely.*]

What mysterious game is this that you play?
Your cheeks are white, your brow is pale!

OLAF. Be not amazed that my cheeks are white;
Three nights I have fought so sore a fight.
And be not amazed that my brow is pale;
Three nights I have played in the elfin game!

HEMMING. Protect us, God!

OLAF.　　　　I am sick, I am faint!
I cannot distinguish the earth from the sky!

HEMMING [*anxiously*].
Lord Olaf! Let us go to your mother's house!

OLAF. My mother's house! Where is that to be found?
It is here that I feel I have my home!

The forest is now my ancestral house.
The sound of the river, the rustling firs
Mean more to me now than my mother's voice!

[*With growing ecstasy.*]

Ah! is it not quiet! Ah! is it not fair!
See how my hall is prepared for a banquet!
See all the tiny glittering pearls!

[*Vehemently, as he grasps* HEMMING's *arm.*]

Hemming, stand still! Beware how you go!
You are standing on all the sparkling jewels!

HEMMING. It is only the moon that shines upon
All the dew-drenched leaves!

OLAF. I tell you in truth they are tiny jewels!

[*Listens.*]

Hark, Hemming! Can you tell what my minstrels are singing?
Can you hear their enchanting song?

HEMMING. You are wrong! It's the rushing river below.

OLAF. I tell you in truth it is music and song;
I know the plaintive sound of the strings.
Hemming, look there! Do you see those maidens
Gliding in white in a stately dance?

HEMMING. Dear Lord! It is only the mist that rises
Above the river . . . [*Aside.*] Oh, help me, God!

OLAF. They are wedding attendants! My bride will come soon!

HEMMING. Your bride! You know then . . . !

OLAF [*continuing*].   At the close of the day,
When the cloud turns pale, and the birds all slumber,
She'll come to me here so young and proud!

HEMMING [*crosses himself*].
All heavenly saints! So it's true what they say!

OLAF. Do you know when it was I first beheld her?
I rode from Guldvik late one evening,

After a banquet, I seem to recall.
My spirit was heavy; at heart I was sad!
There was something had grieved me—what it was I forget.
I went riding alone up the mountain side;
At the midnight hour I came to the stream.
I heard the sound of melodious strings,
Filling the hills and dales with song.
It seemed an enchanting and plaintive lament.
I folded my hands; I tried to pray.
But my tongue was lame, and my thoughts as well.
I was drawn by the sound; I was lured away.
Now there'd be weeping, now there'd be laughter,
Now it was joyful, and now it resembled
The cry of pain of a breaking heart,
The anguished moan of a dying man,
Welling within this incantation,
Streaming about me! I could scarce draw breath!
My mind and soul grew sore confused.
Forces at once both strong and gentle
Drew me towards the mountain side.
I had to go, whether I wished to or no.
And still it beckoned, and still it called.
I no longer remember how far I rode!

HEMMING [*aside*]. And the bride about whom the minstrel sang—she
    also had to go along . . .

OLAF. My foal stopped short. I woke with a start.
    I looked all about me with wondering gaze.
    A fair and beautiful place! But where
    I had come to was far from clear!
    I stood in a valley—peaceful shade
    Enveloped all things like the dew of the night!
    The moon played content on the edge of the tarn,
    And seemed to smile as it dipped its face
    In the cooling, rippling waves!
    My head was heavy; my spirit was sore;
    I yearned for sweet repose.
    I laid myself down by a linden tree
    In the gently whispering grove.

HEMMING. Lord Olaf! Lord Olaf! How dared you risk that?

OLAF [*continuing*]. It was then that I danced with the elfin maids.
The loveliest of them brought me flowers,
Some snowdrops blue, and lilies white.
She looked in my soul with adoring eyes;
She whispered some secret words in my ear,
Some words I shall never forget:
'Olaf Liljekrans! Where does happiness grow?
Do you know the moment you'll find peace?
Of all the flowers that do abound,
You must find the loveliest one of all,
And pluck it, petal by petal, apart
And scatter it all to the fickle wind.
Then—only then will you happiness find!'

HEMMING. You were sleeping and dreaming!

OLAF.   From that time on
My mother's home seemed cramped and narrow!
Through the scree, up the hill, to the pleasant grove
I made my way with my bow and my arrows!
And again I met the elfin maid!

HEMMING [*steps back astonished*].
What then—while awake did you find . . . ?

OLAF. My betrothal ring I took and shot it
Through the air and above her head.
And now she is bound for ever!

HEMMING. And this is the bride you are waiting for here?

OLAF. This is the bride, who will soon be near.

HEMMING [*aside*]. His soul is enthralled; his mind is sick.
All this Lady Kirsten must know!

[*Aloud.*]

Yet you come and go, and feel no fear
Up here?

OLAF.   It feels so safe and sound
Cradled up here in dreams!

[*He walks slowly in among the rocks, right foreground.*]

HEMMING. Tomorrow already is his wedding day.
Yet he has no thoughts for his bride-to-be.
Little he knows that she is near,
Still less that she holds another man dear!—
He wanders wild in the trackless forest,
And Ingeborg gave me the golden ring!
His mother must know what I have seen—
The saints alone know how this will end!

[*He goes out, left.*]

SCENE IX

[OLAF LILJEKRANS *enters again, right.*]

OLAF [*plucking apart some flowers which he has gathered*].
'Of all the flowers that do abound,
You must find the loveliest one of all,
And pluck it, petal by petal, apart
And scatter it all to the fickle wind.
Then—only then will you happiness find!'
These mysterious words will not let me rest.
The loveliest plant? Where might it be found?
How shall I know it? Does its beauty reside
In the charm of its fragrance, its immaculate leaves?
Suppose it resides in some secret ideal
That I never can find though I seek it forever?
Like the precious worth of many a sword
Beneath a deceptive layer of rust;
Or the way a harp can hang, neglected,
Pushed in a corner, all forgotten,
Though quite the most enchanting music
May be held within its dusty strings!

SCENE X

[OLAF LILJEKRANS. ALFHILD *from the back of the stage. She is fantastically dressed, and adorned with wreathed leaves and flowers; she looks anxiously about her until she discovers* OLAF *and hurries joyfully over to him.*]

ALFHILD. Oh, stay, stay! Do not leave me!

OLAF [*as though suddenly brought to life*]. Alfhild! My lovely young bride!

ALFHILD. Olaf! My handsome knight! I grew weary of waiting. I had to come and meet you!

OLAF. But tell me, why do you always fear to come here?

ALFHILD. I told you I was never outside this valley until you came to visit me. My father told me that evil forces ruled out here. Only in among the mountains could I live safe and secure! Oh, let what forces rule that will. You are here, and that is enough for me! Come, let me look into your eyes! Yes, I have you again!

OLAF. Have me! Ah yes, Alfhild! You enchanting, you delightful woman, indeed you do have me again! My soul is deep in thrall to you. Lead me wherever you will—within the mountain, deep under the hill, to the grassy meadow where music and song sweetly echo at eventide, on the river's bed, deep below the waterfall, where its harps make great lament—wherever *your* home is, there I am ready to make my life!

ALFHILD. Why do you speak like this? Surely you know better than that?—Spirits and elves live in the hills and mountains, and the nixie lives on the river's bed—all this my father told me. Do you believe me to be an elf, or . . . ?

OLAF. You are the fairest in all the world! Be what you will, so long as you are mine!

ALFHILD [*smiling*]. If I were an elfin maid, then indeed it would go ill with you!

OLAF. With me!

ALFHILD. Yes, with you! As you came riding along your lonely path, I should approach you and hand you the golden horn with its potion. In it I should so blend my charms that you forgot both heaven and earth, forgot where you were born and bred, forgot your name and where your kinsmen lived. One thing alone you would recall; one thing alone would remain in your heart and mind.

OLAF. Then indeed you are that elfin maid! For from the very first moment you have so blended your charms for me.

ALFHILD. I have?

OLAF. Along the green hillside I rode, deep below where the river runs. . . . It was night, and all around me was the strange sound of song and lament. . . .
   I lost my way, and I strayed far, far into the mountains, and discovered that lovely valley where no foot had trod, and on which no eye had feasted before mine. . . .
   A heavy slumber came over me, but the elfin maids were playing and drew me into their game. . . .
   But when I woke there was a sadness in my soul. Homeward I rode, but there no longer throve. It seemed I had left behind the richest and best things of life; or as if a splendid treasure awaited me there if only I went and sought it. . . .
   I had to return to the valley before I could find peace. . . .
   You came to meet me, lovely and ardent as you are now. I seized your hand, I looked into your eyes. . . . Heaven and earth and all the loveliness of creation were in your eyes! . . .
   Then I forgot friends and kinsmen . . . !
   I came the following night, put my arm round your waist, crushed you to my breast, the glory of heaven was in your embrace. . . .
   Then I forgot my Christian name and the home of my fathers! . . .
   And the third night I came. I had to come. I kissed your red lips and my eyes penetrated your soul. . . . More than the glory of creation was there! I forgot God and home, forgot heaven and earth, and more . . . I forgot myself! [*Throws himself down before her.*] Alfhild! Alfhild!

ALFHILD. If that was a potion of forgetfulness, then I am a victim of it myself. I am like that minstrel who taught himself the nixie's song in order to charm his sweetheart . . . then spun and spun his charms until they enmeshed his own soul and he never could win free.

[*Stops, and remains standing pensively.*]

OLAF [*getting up*]. What are you thinking?

ALFHILD. High on the mountain is a rock face so steep that not even the eagle can find a claw-hold there. There stands a solitary birch tree, stunted and poor in leaf. But it bends its branches down toward the valley lying far below, as though longing for its sisters in the

Hɪɪ

fresh and verdant grove, as though yearning to be transplanted to the sun-warmed life below. . . .

My own life was like that mountain birch. I yearned to be away, I yearned for you a long, long time, before I even knew of your existence. The valley grew too narrow for me. What I did not know was that there was another valley like mine beyond the mountains. The knights and the ladies who came to me every night brought no satisfaction—nor did they tell me anything of the life outside!

OLAF. Knights and ladies? You told me that you never met anyone.

ALFHILD. Nobody like you! But every evening my father sang me his songs. And when it was night and my eyes had closed, they came to call upon me, all those who lived in my father's songs. Among them were brilliant knights and fair ladies, falcons on their wrists, riding on proud steeds. They danced in the meadows, and gaiety and laughter followed them everywhere. The elves listened silently behind each flower, and the birds on the branches had fallen asleep. But with the coming of day, they vanished all. Lonely I walked, and decked myself with flowers and green leaves, for I knew that the next night they would come once again. That life, alas, was not enough. A great yearning filled my breast; it would never have been stilled, had you not come!

OLAF. You speak of your father. Never did I see him there!

ALFHILD. He comes now but seldom. He has not been there since the evening we first met!

OLAF. But tell me, where is he?

ALFHILD. You told me you rode one summer night along the green hillside where the river runs. And there you heard strange songs you but half understood, but which so haunt you that you will never forget them.

OLAF. Yes, yes!

ALFHILD. There you heard my father's songs. I have grown up with them. In truth I have never understood them fully, either. To me they were treasures beyond price, indeed life itself. Now they mean little to me—a hint only of the glory that was to come. All of them contained a handsome knight; him I pictured as the most wonderful thing in all the land, the most wonderful thing as far as bird can fly, as far as cloud can travel. Olaf! It was you—I recognize you! Oh, you must tell me about your home, about the distant valley whence you have come. How rich and light it must be there! That is where all my birds must fly when the leaves fall; for when they return again, they have so many strange things to tell, so many marvels to sing about—how all plants sprout and blossom, all trees turn green, and how the great and glorious sun rises early and goes late to rest in time to listen to all the lovely songs and stories. But I understand little of all they tell me. You must explain these things to me, all those things my questioning heart craves knowledge of.

OLAF. Little can I do that. You asked about my home. My home? If I have had any other home than this I remember little of it. To me it is like some misty dream forgotten in the hour of waking. Yet, come! Far below is a village, where I seem to remember I lived before I met you; where I seem to remember my kinsmen live. Do you hear the urgent sound of the river? Let us follow it. On the ledge by the waterfall we can look down upon the village where I . . . once had my home. Come, come!

ALFHILD. But dare I . . . ?

OLAF. Trust me and follow. I shall protect you!

ALFHILD. I am ready. I know full well that I must follow you wherever you go, whether I will or no.

[*They go out, right.*]

CHORUS OF WEDDING GUESTS *and* LADY KIRSTEN'S RETINUE [*in the distance from the forest, left*].

So take good care, and free your soul
From the treacherous elves of the grove!

SCENE XI

[LADY KIRSTEN *and* HEMMING *enter from the left.*]

HEMMING. He was here. See. . . . Why, now he is gone!

LADY KIRSTEN. And he said he was waiting for his bride to come?

HEMMING. Yes, but whom he meant I could not rightly tell. For his speech was strange and wild. Ingeborg he did not mean, that is certain.

LADY KIRSTEN. Quiet, good Hemming! Be silent about what he said! You did well to tell me alone that he was here. You shall be richly rewarded for this, but first we must find him . . .

HEMMING [*looking out to the right*]. Look, look there in the moonlight on the hill by the river. . . . Yes, I do believe . . .

LADY KIRSTEN. Quiet, quiet, it is Olaf!

HEMMING. There are two. A woman stands beside him . . .

LADY KIRSTEN. Heavenly spirits!

HEMMING. He is pointing down to the village, as if . . . There they both go!

LADY KIRSTEN. Fetch Sir Arne and our people! We meet again here. I shall go and bring Olaf!

HEMMING. Dare you . . . ?

LADY KIRSTEN. Do as I say. But keep silent about what you have heard and seen. You can say that Olaf came up here hunting deer and bear, and that he lost his way in the mountains.

HEMMING. You may rely on me, Lady Kirsten!

[*Goes out left.*]

LADY KIRSTEN. Can this be true? Have evil spirits got him in their power? Ah, such things I can pretend to Arne of Guldvik, but I little believe it myself. And yet they say it often happened in bygone days. Yet I fancy it is elfin maids of flesh and blood that . . . There he goes down by the river. I must hurry! [*Goes out right.*]

CHORUS [*in the distance in the forest, left*].
With hymns of praise, and ringing of bells,
We wander abroad in the valleys!
Oh, Christian man, pay heed to our song,
And wake from your drowsy enchantment!

SCENE XII

[OLAF *and* ALFHILD *enter, right rear. Subsequently,* LADY KIRSTEN.]

ALFHILD. Please, you must tell me more, much more!
Your words fall upon my soul like dew.

You interpret the runes of my yearning heart
By your precious speech . . . !
Have you ever reclined by a mountain tarn,
So deep its depths could never be plumbed?
Have you seen reflected the stars of heaven,
Those eyes that know all you'll ever know,
That say what a thousand tongues might say.

. . .

In vain I have often tried to scoop
Those glittering mysteries with my hands,
Trying to grasp them, wanting them close;
But they clouded like eyes that fill with tears—
It was idle to search and seek . . . !

. . .

The same has been true of my soul till now!
So many a riddle I wanted to solve.
But they mocked me like stars in a mountain pool—
The harder I tried, the more hopeless it was!

OLAF. Am I not an insoluble riddle to myself?
Am I Olaf Liljekrans, the high-born knight,
So proud of his race, so proud of his line,
And scornful of love as the twittering of birds!
Yet I pluck from my memory thoughts like these!
Happy am I, which I well understand—
Though your prophecy's wrong: that my happiness craved
I should find the loveliest flower in the land.
This is happiness *now*!

ALFHILD.   I prophesied naught.
But . . . tell me some more of the life down below!

OLAF. Let life down below go its own sweet way.
My home is up here, my dearest, with you,
My loveliest wife! Oh, Alfhild, say!
Is it not as though some vaulted hall
Were constructed here in the green hillside?
And snowdrops scattered on every path!

There is feasting and laughter and joy in this place,
So much that it seems my heart must burst!
From the river there echoes that haunting song
That moves me to laughter but also to tears!
This magical song, this melody rare,
Has made me so happy, so joyful, so wild!

[*He takes her passionately in his arms.*]

I bid farewell to the village below!
Up *here* I shall make my marriage bed.
I bid farewell to the distant world—
And prepare to embrace my delightful bride!

ALFHILD [*draws back anxiously*].
   Olaf!

OLAF [*stops suddenly, as though seized by some vague and painful memory*].
      My bride! What is this I am saying!
   Do tell me . . . dear Alfhild . . . when first I came . . .
   Do you still remember the night we first met?
   What thing was I seeking? . . . What was my intent?
   To collect you and take you . . . to the village below?
   To bid you take part in a wedding down there?

ALFHILD. What's that? In a wedding! I don't understand . . .

OLAF. At Guldvik we plighted our troth, did we not?
   And three weeks from then our wedding-day set. . . .
   But I seem to recall—Oh, these feverish thoughts!
   I must put them entirely out of my mind!

CHORUS [*softly, and deep in the forest*].
         Olaf Liljekrans! Olaf Liljekrans!
         Why sleep you so long and so heavy?

ALFHILD. Hush, Olaf! Do you hear?

OLAF.   You heard it too?

ALFHILD. What is it?

OLAF.   A half-forgotten memory
   That sometimes calls when I come to this place!
   It bodes me ill—for it summons me below.

LADY KIRSTEN [*aside, as she enters from the rear, without being noticed by
    the others*].
    They are there! He speaks! Could I understand . . . !

                [*She approaches and listens.*]

OLAF [*with increasing vehemence*].
    Yes, yes, I come! But I'll not go alone!
    Fair ladies and knights I shall summon to this place,
    To acknowledge my bride and to greet her with song!
    My swiftest steed shall be saddled with gold,
    And minstrel and poet shall ride at the head;
    And they will be followed by steward and priest,
    And the whole of the village will be guests at the feast!
    Courteous pages shall lead in your horse,
    Beautiful flowers shall be strewn in your path;
    The peasant shall bow like a reed as you pass,
    And his wife drop a curtsy as she stands by the gate!
    And churchbells shall ring through the whole countryside:
    There goes Olaf Liljekrans home with his bride!

CHORUS OF WEDDING GUESTS [*quickly but softly in the forest, left*].
              Now, off we go
             To the wedding hall,
        And the foal runs light on the hill!
           With thundering hooves
            In the grass-green woods,
      Where the merry young men do ride!

LADY KIRSTEN [*aside, during the chorus*].
    Heaven be praised! As Hemming has said . . . !

ALFHILD [*jubilant*].
    They are coming! They are coming! I hear them already!
    How lovely it sounds! Look, Olaf! See there!

LADY KIRSTEN
    Olaf, my son!

    [*She hurries across to him, unseen by* ALFHILD, *who remains looking
    out to the left.*]

OLAF.   God save me! What is it?
    My mother!

LADY KIRSTEN. My poor distracted boy!
   At last you are saved from this evil web!
   Here comes Sir Arne with Ingeborg, your wife!

OLAF [*with a cry, as though suddenly wakening*].
   Ingeborg! You shatter my life with that name!
   Was my happiness naught but an empty delusion?
   Alas, that you bring me such sorrowful tidings!

   [*Despairingly.*]

   Oh, dearest mother! I was dreaming so sweetly.
   But now that you wake me—everything's gone!

SCENE XIII

[*As before.* ARNE. INGEBORG. HEMMING. WEDDING GUESTS *and* LADY
KIRSTEN'S RETINUE *from the left.*]

ARNE. Well met, Lady Kirsten! You have found him, I hear.

LADY KIRSTEN. Indeed I have found him . . . and now for home!

ARNE [*to* OLAF]. And no harm has befallen you?

OLAF [*absent-mindedly*]. Me! What do you mean!

LADY KIRSTEN [*interrupting*]. Indeed no, Sir Arne! He lost his way
   while hunting and . . .

INGEBORG [*pointing to* ALFHILD]. But this young woman . . . ?

LADY KIRSTEN. A poor child! She gave him shelter and lodging.

ARNE. But nobody lives up here.

LADY KIRSTEN. Some do! Many families are still living up in the
   mountains since the time of the plague.

ARNE. Then come, come! The horses are waiting on the hillside down
   below.

OLAF [*anguished, with a glance at* ALFHILD]. Mother! I cannot!

LADY KIRSTEN [*in a low resolute voice*]. You must! It will be to your
   eternal shame if . . .

ARNE. What does he mean?

LADY KIRSTEN. He is still sick and weary. It will pass. Come! [*With a significant look to* OLAF.] The young woman will come with us!

INGEBORG. You mean that she . . . ?

LADY KIRSTEN. She has nursed him faithfully. It is fitting that she should be rewarded for it.

ARNE. And tomorrow is the wedding feast!

LADY KIRSTEN. Tomorrow! This I solemnly swear!

ARNE. I have your word!

HEMMING [*in a quiet triumphant voice as he takes out the bracelet*]. And I have Ingeborg's red golden ring!

INGEBORG [*takes the ring from him and says unmoved*]. My ring! Well, well! So you have it, Hemming! Thank you, now I shall take care of it myself.

[HEMMING *stands a moment astounded and then slowly follows the rest, who all go out to the left, except* ALFHILD.]

SCENE XIV

[ALFHILD; *shortly afterwards* THORGEJR *from the rear.*]

ALFHILD [*has watched the foregoing scene with quiet and childlike astonishment, yet without reacting to the events; when all the others have left, she suddenly gives a start, as though waking up from a dream*].

They are gone! Was it true? Can I really believe . . . ?
Yes, yes! There they stood in the moonlight clear!
Down there on the hillside I see them again.
And I am the bride! I must join them at once!

[*She begins to hurry away, left.*]

THORGEJR [*in the background*].
Alfhild, my child! How do you come to be here?
I have told you before . . .

ALFHILD.   Oh father dear!
Now I must fly as free as the wind!
I cannot stay captive up here any longer.

THORGEJR [*approaching*].
  What has occurred?

ALFHILD [*jubilantly*].   He has come!

THORGEJR.   Who?

ALFHILD. The handsome knight! He will take me off home!
  I now understand all this restless desire
  That has weighed on my heart and my mind for so long.
  How often we've sat by the turbulent stream
  And you've sung of the princess bewitched in the hill.
  That princess, dear father—that princess is me!
  And the handsome young knight has defeated the troll!
  And now I am free, and I know what I want!
  I want to take part in the great game of life!
  His words were like song! I seemed to have wings!
  No power on earth holds me captive from now!

THORGEJR. Poor child! You want to go down to the village?
  It will shatter your peace of mind. Do stay!

ALFHILD. I must, dear father! Your finest song
  Would seem to me now like a misty haze.

THORGEJR. Then go, dear Alfhild, and dream your dreams!
  Your father will always watch over you.
  But be on your guard against cunning young men
  Whose tongues do but try to deceive you.

ALFHILD. Where Olaf goes, there I go too,
  Far in the bright and distant valley!
  There is his castle with its golden halls!
  I knew him at once from the songs you sang.
  He's the handsome knight, the gallant prince,
  And poor little Alfhild is his chosen bride.
  Poor? Oh, no! I'm a proud princess!
  And more than a princess! His sweetheart, too!

  [*The wedding choir is heard far down the hillside.*]

  Hear how he calls with trumpet and horn!
  Farewell now, forests and flowers and rocks!
  Farewell to my valley! You have grown too small.
  The world is calling with laughter and song.

Tomorrow I'll don my golden dress
And ride to the church as Olaf's bride!
Together we'll sit on the cushioned throne—
This is the moment my life begins!

[*She hurries out, left.* THORGEJR *watches her thoughtfully. The chorus dies away in the distance as the curtain falls.*]

ACT TWO

The central enclosure of LADY KIRSTEN's *estate. On the right of the audience can be seen the main building with a hatch-door in the gable; neither windows nor doors can be seen. Towards the back of the stage on the same side, a small stave church and a churchyard. On the left a storehouse and other outbuildings. On both sides in the foreground, simple stone benches. It is afternoon.*

SCENE I

[LADY KIRSTEN. *Servants and maids occupied with preparations for the wedding feast.*]

LADY KIRSTEN. Let there be no lack of food or drink. [*To herself.*] It has been hard, and greatly have I laboured to achieve this, but now I shall put on a feast that will set all tongues talking. [*To the servants.*] Make sure that the banquet table is . . . No, that I shall do myself. The wine is to be poured into the silver flagons, and the great drinking horns are to be filled with Italian cider; the ale is only for the servants, and likewise the home-brewed mead. . . . And listen, see to it that there are plenty of yellow candles in the church. The bridal pair do not go to the altar until late evening, and flaming torches are to light them on their way from the banquet hall. Go now, all of you, and see to the thing I have given each one of you to do. [*The people go.*] God knows this wedding is costing me more than I can well afford; but Ingeborg is bringing a good dowry with her, and moreover . . . Oh, Arne can surely be advised and guided as I think best, so long as he first . . . [*Looks out right.*] Here comes Olaf! If only I knew that he . . .

SCENE II

[LADY KIRSTEN. OLAF *comes out from the house dressed in his finery; he is pale and thoughtful.*]

OLAF [*to himself*]. Yesterday and today! Only one midsummer night lies between them, and yet to me it seems as though both autumn and winter had come over my soul since the time I was up there on the mountainside . . . with her, with Alfhild! [*Notices* LADY KIRSTEN.] Ah, my dear mother, are you here!

LADY KIRSTEN. Indeed I am, my son! And very glad to see you dressed in your gold and silks. Anybody looking at you can see who is the bridegroom tonight. I see you have rested.

OLAF. I have slept, but little rested. For all the while I dreamed.

LADY KIRSTEN. A bridegroom must dream—that is an ancient custom.

OLAF. My best dream is ended. Let us not think about it any more.

LADY KIRSTEN [*changing the subject*]. We shall have a gay time today, I think.

OLAF. Heaven does not seem pleased with my wedding day!

LADY KIRSTEN. How so?

OLAF. A storm is gathering. Do you not see the heavy clouds massing in the west?

LADY KIRSTEN. All the brighter the bridal torches will shine when you walk to the church tonight.

OLAF [*walks a few paces up and down, and finally halts in front of his mother and says*]. If I had taken a poor man's daughter, without wealth or family . . . tell me, mother, what would you have done?

LADY KIRSTEN [*looks at him sharply*]. Why do you ask?

OLAF. First answer me. What would you have done?

LADY KIRSTEN. Cursed you and gone to my grave of grief! But tell me, why do you ask?

OLAF. Oh, it was only a jest. I thought little of it.

LADY KIRSTEN. I should think so. For you have always held your family in respect and honour. But be now happy and glad. To-morrow Ingeborg will take her place in there as your wife, and then you will find both peace and happiness.

OLAF. Peace and happiness. Only one thing is lacking.

LADY KIRSTEN. What do you mean?

OLAF. The fairest flower which I was to pluck apart and scatter to the winds.

LADY KIRSTEN. That silly dream . . . think no more of it.

OLAF. Perhaps it would serve me best if I could do that.

LADY KIRSTEN. Your betrothed is sitting in her chamber with her maids. You have said little to her today. . . . Do you not want to go in?

OLAF [*in thought*]. Yes, yes! Where is she?

LADY KIRSTEN. In her chamber, as I said.

OLAF [*eagerly*]. She shall lack for nothing after today. I shall give her shoes with silver buckles; she shall wear brooches and rings. She shall put off the spray of withered flowers and I shall give her a golden necklace to wear!

LADY KIRSTEN. Of whom do you speak?

OLAF. Of Alfhild!

LADY KIRSTEN. I spoke of Ingeborg, your betrothed. Olaf! Olaf! You make me worried and anxious, you are so strange. I am almost tempted to believe she has bewitched you.

OLAF. She has! Yes, in truth, mother! I have been bewitched. I have been with the elfin maidens at their play. I was happy and gay as long as it lasted, but now . . . for long years to come I shall be burdened with sorrow and grief the moment I call it to mind.

LADY KIRSTEN. If she were a witch, she would be sure of fire and stake. But she is a sly and cunning woman who has lured you on with fine stories.

OLAF. She is as pure as the very mother of God!

LADY KIRSTEN. Perhaps, but beware! However it is, remember that tomorrow you are wed. It would be both a sin and a scandal if you paid any more heed to her.

OLAF. I know that well, mother! Full well!

LADY KIRSTEN. And Ingeborg, to whom you are betrothed and who loves you. . . . Yes, Olaf, loves you with all her heart. . . . The punishment of heaven would strike you if . . .

OLAF. True, true!

LADY KIRSTEN. I will not speak of our own circumstances. But you will be aware that Arne's daughter can provide help in many ways. Our family has gone sadly downhill, and if the harvest fails this year I should be little surprised if we were reduced to begging.

OLAF. I know that well enough!

LADY KIRSTEN. With Arne's money all this can be made good. You will win a place of honour among the King's men. Think carefully. If your promises to Alfhild are more than you can keep . . . And she gives me that impression, despite her silence . . . then you must speak to her. Tell her . . . Well, tell her what you will. She shall not leave here empty-handed. That you can freely promise. Look, here she comes! Olaf, my son! Think of your betrothed and of your family pride. Think of your old mother who would be brought to her grave of grief if . . . Be a man, Olaf! Now I must go in and see to the banquet table.

[*She goes into the house.*]

SCENE III

[OLAF *alone.*]

OLAF [*looks out, right*].
    She is as gay as the youthful roe,
    As it frolics beside the flanks of the hind;
    Soon she must wring her hands in woe,
    A victim of sorrow and grief!
    Soon I must shatter her simple trust,
    And wake her out of her dreams;
    And then—ah, then we must part, we two!
    Poor Alfhild! Yours is a bitter draught!

[*Brooding.*]

What was honour to me, what was power to me,
What was family to me up there with her!
To me it seemed that her eyes contained
A treasure beyond what the world could show!

Forgotten was all the trouble and strife!
But since I returned to this place anew
And sat at my ancestors' table again,
And stood face to face with my mother once more . . .

[*Breaks off.*]

I was born and bred to a noble line,
And Alfhild lives on the solitary hill—
For Olaf scarcely a suitable match.
I must tell her! No, no, this I cannot do!
And yet, tonight, she must be told
The cause of my most bitter sorrow!

SCENE IV

[OLAF. ALFHILD, *from the church.*]

ALFHILD [*hurries joyfully over to him*].
Olaf! Olaf! You have led me to the place
Where I walk among flowers instead of on sand.
This is in truth a delightful spot,
Where I can happily live and die!
So much I would ask, so little I know.
You must teach me about these mysterious things—
Is it always like summer and spring out here?

OLAF. Ah, Alfhild!

ALFHILD.   Don't tell me just yet!
You see that house with its spire and wing?
Thither I went this morning to play.
Outside it was noisy and merry and gay,
But within all was quiet—so quiet!
I stepped through the doorway, and saw a great hall,
And there all was peaceful and still;
By the dawn's gentle light, in the cool of the morn,
I saw menfolk and women on their knees.
But high, high above, a virgin stood,
Borne aloft by billowing clouds.
Her head was a blaze of crimson glory,
And shone like the heavens at break of day.

Her face was calm, her dress was blue,
And she held in her arms an elfin child,
And angels played about her feet
And all of them laughed when they looked at me
From their chariot of cloud above!

OLAF [*aside*].
Alas! I have done an unholy deed!
Must her joy be so rudely shattered!

ALFHILD. Oh, tell me, Olaf! Whose is that place?
Who are they who live in there?

OLAF. All those who are good and kind like you!
All those with the mind and heart of a child!
It's the church! God's house! It belongs to Him.

ALFHILD. The mighty Father! You do but jest!
His house is far beyond the stars,
There where the great white swans do fly
Beyond the range of mortal eye,
And only seen by a sleeping child!
The church, you said! So it's there we shall ride
Together in festal procession
As bride and bridegroom!

OLAF [*aside*]. The time is now come!
I dare not conceal it further!

ALFHILD. Each word of yours has burnt its way
Indelibly deep into my soul!
They fill my breast with joy and with song;
Wherever I roam, whether near or far,
They light my path at each step I take,
Like golden nails in the loft of night!
You said the whole world would be asked as our guests,
And minstrel and priest would ride at the head,
And noble knights would lead my horse,
And roses blossom on every path,
And every lily should bow like a reed,
And every flower acknowledge the bride!

OLAF. Did I say . . . ?

I11

ALFHILD.   Oh, surely you recall!
   You see how all is as you said!
   The linden trees beside the church,
   The roses bursting into bloom,
   And swaying as in some elfin dance.
   Never did the brilliant eye of heaven
   Shine so radiantly from the sky,
   Never so sweet the song of the birds,
   Singing to honour the bride and groom!
   To me you brought such sheer delight
   The whole wide world I could embrace!
   No straw upon the ground so mean
   That I could tread beneath my feet!
   No creature in the earth so poor
   But I could share its joys and sorrows!
   I hold in my breast all the glories of spring,
   Like the surging waves of the storm-tossed forest!

OLAF [*aside*]. Soon must the serpent tooth of sorrow
   Tear at this lovely woman's heart!

ALFHILD. Oh, glorious life!

> [*She kneels with hands outstretched.*]

                    Oh, Father who lives
   In distant heaven! Had I but the words,
   Had I the tongues of angels,
   I would full loud thy praises sing.
   But that I cannot. For Thou art too great.
   I can only bow down low before Thee.—
   Oh thanks, Thou ineffable! Honour and praise
   Be Thine for what I shall find down here.

> [*Rises.*]

   Yes, life is fair in Olaf's home,
   As fair as the journey to death's domain!

OLAF. You call it fair to be borne to the grave?

ALFHILD. I don't understand you. I wondered so long,
   And asked of my father what dying meant.
   He answered me by singing a song:

'When the child of man is sorely grieved
And longs to be cradled in slumber,
There comes an elf with wings of white
And frees its soul from care and trouble.

That little elf with wings of white
Prepares a bed so soft;
He weaves the sheets of lilies small
And pillows of roses red.

Upon the pillows he bears the child,
Holding it safe in his arms,
And carries it home to heaven above
In a carriage of golden clouds.

And this in truth I say to you:
There are children in heaven on high
Who sprinkle the pillows so rosy-red
With pearls both white and blue.

Then wakes the little child of man,
It wakes to heavenly bliss—
Though no one here on earth can know
Of the joy and the happiness there!'

OLAF. Better by far if your life had been lived
In peace and calm on the mountain side.
Your joy will snap like a withered reed,
Your faith destroyed . . .

ALFHILD.   As Olaf's wife
I'll be strong and brave like the tumbling falls!
You stand by my side; let come what will,
With you I shall laugh, with you I shall suffer.

[Listens.]

Hush, Olaf! Do you hear that mournful lament
That sounds like a song of deepest sorrow?

CHORUS OF PALLBEARERS [*softly, off-stage right*].
> This little child we carry
> With sorrow to the grave.
> Beneath the earth we bury
> What worms will soon devour.
> Our lot is hard and weary:
> With woeful songs and sighs
> To bear the tiny coffin
> Its final mournful way!

ALFHILD [*uncertain and anxious*].
> What is it, Olaf? What is it, I say?

OLAF. A child being borne to the home of death
> By its mother, and brothers and sisters five.

ALFHILD. To death! But where are the pillows red?
> The lily-white sheets? And the one who died?

OLAF. I see no pillows, neither red nor blue,
> Though I do see the blackened boards.
> There rests the corpse on shavings and straw.

ALFHILD. On shavings and straw?

OLAF.   Yes, that and no more!

ALFHILD. And where is the elf who holds the child,
> And drives it home in the carriage of clouds?

OLAF. I see but a mother with breaking heart,
> And the children who follow the corpse to the grave.

ALFHILD. And where are the pearls, both white and blue,
> Which the angels strew in the fields of heaven?

OLAF. I see but the tears the children shed
> As they stand and weep by the coffin.

ALFHILD. And where is the home, the place of delight,
> Where the dead can dream their dreams?

OLAF. See where they lower him down in the ground,
> And cover him over with earth!

ALFHILD [*quiet and pensive, after a pause*].
> Death was not thus in my father's song!

OLAF. In truth! For no one here below
Knows aught of that joy and happiness.—
Have you never heard of the elf-king's treasure,
That glows each night like shining gold;
But try to grasp it in your hand,
And gravel and straw is all you find?
Oh, hear me, Alfhild! 'Tis often so
That life itself turns out like this!
Don't come too close—it's so easily done—
You may find you have burnt your fingers.
In truth it may shine like the stars of heaven,
But only when seen from a distance.

[*He notices* LADY KIRSTEN *off-stage, right.*]

My mother. . . . She'll tell you. . . . Now I must go.
May the angels fill your heart with peace!

[*He goes towards the house, but is stopped by* LADY KIRSTEN. *The sky becomes overcast with dark clouds; the wind begins to howl in the tree-tops.* ALFHILD *stands deep in thought.*]

SCENE V

[*As before.* LADY KIRSTEN.]

LADY KIRSTEN [*in a low voice*]. Well, my son! You have told her, have you not . . . ?

OLAF. All I could bring myself to say, I have said. Now you tell her the rest. And then, mother, never never let me see her again. [*Casts a glance at* ALFHILD *and goes out past the house.*]

LADY KIRSTEN. This madness in him will soon burn itself out . . . [*As though suddenly struck by an idea.*] But if I . . . Ah, if that were possible, he would be cured, that I guarantee. But Alfhild . . . ? Yet, all the same, it must be tried!

ALFHILD [*to herself*].
So pain and woe is found here too!
Yet, even so, I shall never despair.
The world can never do me harm,
For Olaf is so good and kind!

LADY KIRSTEN [*approaches*]. It seems to me that sad thoughts weigh on your mind.

ALFHILD. Yes, caused by things I have only just learned.

LADY KIRSTEN. From Olaf?

ALFHILD. Yes, from Olaf! He has told me . . .

LADY KIRSTEN. I know, Alfhild! I know what he has said. [*Aside.*] He has mentioned his wedding to her, I imagine. [*Aloud.*] And it's taking place this very night.

ALFHILD. What is taking place?

LADY KIRSTEN. The wedding!

ALFHILD [*eagerly*]. Oh yes, I know!

LADY KIRSTEN. You know and yet take the news no harder than this?

ALFHILD. No, why should the news be hard?

LADY KIRSTEN [*aside*]. She is contemplating something, I see that clearly. [*Aloud.*] Well, so much the better for all of us. But tell me, when the wedding is over, what do you mean to do?

ALFHILD. I? I have little thought about that.

LADY KIRSTEN. I mean are you thinking of staying here, or are you going home?

ALFHILD [*looks at her in astonishment*]. I am thinking of staying!

LADY KIRSTEN [*aside*]. There we have it. She means to keep him in her snare even after he is married. Well, well, that's where we differ. [*Aloud.*] Alfhild! I wish you well, and if you care to put your trust in me . . .

ALFHILD. Yes, that I certainly do!

LADY KIRSTEN. Good! Then let me do what is best for your happiness. I shall look after things for you as best I know how. And if you agree, you shall go to the church this very night as a bride.

ALFHILD. Of course, I know that.

LADY KIRSTEN [*starting*]. You know that! Who told you?

ALFHILD. Olaf told me himself.

LADY KIRSTEN. Olaf! [*Aside.*] Has Olaf . . . ? He must in truth have had the same idea as me—to marry her off in order to rid himself of her! Or perhaps to . . . ? Well, no matter, once she is married off, and when Olaf himself is a married man, then . . . [*Aloud.*] Very good, Alfhild! If Olaf has told you of our plans for you, then there is no need for me to. . . . But hurry! Go into the storehouse. My own wedding dress is hanging there. That you shall wear!

ALFHILD [*with child-like joy*]. May I! Your own wedding dress!

LADY KIRSTEN. Do as I say. Go in and dress yourself as splendidly as you wish.

ALFHILD. And shall I also have a bridal crown?

LADY KIRSTEN. Certainly! A bridal crown and silver rings and a red golden bracelet. You will find plenty of those things in the boxes and chests.

ALFHILD. Silver rings and golden bracelet!

LADY KIRSTEN. Go, go, and make what haste you can.

ALFHILD. Oh, I shall not take long. [*Claps her hands.*] I shall have a bridal crown and a red golden bracelet. [*She hurries out left.*]

SCENE VI

[LADY KIRSTEN *alone.*]

LADY KIRSTEN. That cursed evil woman! To be so pleased and confident though she knows that Olaf is to marry another. Yet that serves my purpose; things will be easier than I thought. She looks as innocent as a child, and yet she can consent to take as a husband the first man I picked for her. And I who thought that she truly loved Olaf! If he still does not know what her true feelings are, he will soon learn. He shall know her for what she really is. He shall know how she has lured and bewitched him. And then . . . then she is no longer a danger to him. [*Smiling.*] Well, well! Olaf must have thought of the same solution as I did. I would never have thought him to be so kind. . . . But where shall we find the man who is willing to . . . ? Well, she is pretty, and we need not worry about a little silver and some land. Perhaps Olaf has already approached somebody? No, that is hardly conceivable! . . . Well, I shall look after that matter. I have men enough on the farm and . . . [*Looks out right.*] Hemming! I might try him! But he saw them together on the mountain yesterday. He must surely know that there is something between them. Nevertheless . . . he is a lowly servant, and poor besides. And weak of will. . . . We shall see, we shall see!

SCENE VII

[LADY KIRSTEN, HEMMING, *from the right.*]

HEMMING [*to himself*]. Nowhere is Ingeborg to be found. She will drive me to my grave, that is certain. Yesterday she was kind to me, and gave me her bracelet. But then she took it away from me again, and today she will hardly spare me so much as a passing glance.

LADY KIRSTEN [*softly, as she approaches*]. I must be a little cautious! [*Aloud.*] Ah, Hemming, so it's you? You prefer to be alone, I notice. You keep away from the maids and the servants. When I see that sort of thing, I know very well that it does not happen without good reason.

HEMMING. Why, my lady! What should . . . ?

LADY KIRSTEN. No indeed, Hemming! There is something you have on your mind. You are not very cheerful!

HEMMING [*disconcerted*]. Not cheerful? I?

LADY KIRSTEN [*smiling*]. There is a young and beautiful woman here today who appeals to you greatly.

HEMMING. By all the saints!

LADY KIRSTEN. And she in turn thinks well of you.

HEMMING. Of me? Who? I do not know who you mean.

LADY KIRSTEN. Ah, Hemming, don't say that! You need not be bashful with me. Ah yes, I see things clearly, believe me.

HEMMING [*aside*]. Dear heaven! She must have seen from Ingeborg that . . .

LADY KIRSTEN. I have observed that this wedding feast means little joy to you. You dislike this church occasion, because you would very much like to be there as bridegroom yourself, but you cannot see any way of doing that.

HEMMING [*in greatest agitation*]. Ah, Lady Kirsten! My noble lady! Do not be angry! Do not be angry!

LADY KIRSTEN [*surprised*]. I? Why should I be angry?

HEMMING [*continuing*]. I have struggled and battled against this fateful love for as long as I could. And I honestly believe she has too.

LADY KIRSTEN. She? Has she told you she likes you?

HEMMING. Yes, almost!

LADY KIRSTEN. Very well. So you have spoken to each other about it?

HEMMING. Yes. But only once—on only one single occasion, I swear to you!

LADY KIRSTEN. Once or ten times, it's all the same to me. . . . [*Aside.*] So they are already agreed. What a great stroke of fortune it was that I came across Hemming. Now I am not at all surprised that Alfhild was so ready to go to the altar. [*Aloud.*] Hemming! I am greatly indebted to you for finding my son again and for other services you have done me. Now I can make suitable return. I will help you all I can in this matter we have just been talking about.

HEMMING [*overcome with joy*]. You will! You will do that, Lady Kirsten! Oh, by God and the saints, I can scarcely believe it. [*Stops.*] But Lord Olaf, your son! What do you think he will say?

LADY KIRSTEN. He will place no stones in your path—I shall see to that.

HEMMING [*trustingly*]. Indeed that would also be in his best interests, for I know that in her heart she does not like him.

LADY KIRSTEN [*smiling*]. That I have noticed, Hemming!

HEMMING. You have! Ah, you are so clever, Lady Kirsten. And I thought I was the only one to have noticed it. [*Doubtfully.*] But do you think that Sir Arne will give his consent?

LADY KIRSTEN. Your master? I shall manage to talk him round—that will be all right.

HEMMING. You think so? Ah, but I am such a poor man!

LADY KIRSTEN. I shall see to that, if Sir Arne is not prepared to do so himself.

HEMMING. Thank you, thank you, Lady Kirsten! May heaven reward you for your kindness?

LADY KIRSTEN. But you will keep silent about the things we have been discussing!

HEMMING. That I promise!

LADY KIRSTEN. Then hold yourself in readiness. The guests will shortly gather out here. Do not stray too far away.

[*She goes over to the door of the out-house, and looks for* ALFHILD.]

HEMMING [*to himself*]. No! To me this seems like a strange and mocking dream. That Ingeborg and I . . . should win each other! Can it be true? I never dared think so high. . . . If I so much as dreamed about it at night, it seemed in the morning a most presumptuous deed. . . . Hm! Of course I well know Lady Kirsten is not going to all this trouble just for my sake. She has something in mind. What she wants to do is break the agreement with my lord Arne; and now that she has noticed Ingeborg likes me, she will use that as a pretext. Well, I have often warned my master about this, but he would never believe me.

ARNE [*calls, offstage left*]. Hemming! Hemming!

LADY KIRSTEN [*comes downstage*]. Your master is calling! Go now! I shall talk to him later. He will agree. Believe me, he shall follow his vassal to the church at the same time as he leads his daughter thither.

HEMMING. Thank you, thank you, Lady Kirsten! Truly, you do well for us all.

[*He goes out, left.*]

LADY KIRSTEN [*to herself*]. So young she is, and yet so cunning. She flirted with Hemming whilst at the same time making my son imagine that . . . Well, he will soon recognize her tricks. But first

I must get hold of Sir Arne. He is very fond of Hemming, and will not like to be parted from him. It also seemed as if Hemming feared that this might present an obstacle. But they could easily remain together even if Hemming gets married. —Hemming has a clearer view of things than I had imagined. What will Olaf say, he asked. So he must also have noticed that my son's heart is still with Alfhild. Well, let him. If he takes her, he will say nothing. And once Alfhild is married—I know Olaf. He has always set a high value on the honour and respect he enjoys from the men of the village, and for that reason he will probably. . . . Yes, it must and shall succeed.

[*She goes out, right.*]

SCENE VIII

[HEMMING *enters, left, with a bowl of ale concealed beneath his coat.* ARNE *follows him continuously, looking around.*]

ARNE. Anybody there?

HEMMING. No! Come along, master!

ARNE. But I thought I heard Lady Kirsten.

HEMMING. She's gone now. Come along!

ARNE [*sits on the bench, left*]. Pass me the bowl. Hemming! It is good that the wedding is to be tonight. Tomorrow I am going home.... Yes, indeed I am! I am not staying a day longer in Lady Kirsten's house.

HEMMING. Ah, master! Have you fallen foul of each other again?

ARNE. Don't you think it's enough that she and all her fine kinsmen look down on me. At supper they laughed and joked among themselves because I could not bring myself to eat all those ungodly foreign foods. And what were we given to drink? Sweet wine and cider that will lie on my stomach for a week. No, I'm all for my good old home-brewed ale. [*Drinks, then adds bitterly in a low voice.*] Three full barrels of this I sent the bitch, and what has she done? Thrown it to her servants! And I have to sneak off for a quick drink of it here, Hemming! Sneak a drink of my own ale in case they call me a boorish peasant with no taste for refined drinks.

HEMMING. Yes, master! I warned you.

ARNE. Ah . . . warned me! You are stupid, Hemming! Do you think I haven't noticed it myself! But wait, just wait! [*Angrily.*] To give my good refreshing ale to the servants as though it were not worthy to be served at the master's table. . . .

HEMMING. Yes, Lady Kirsten treats you shabbily, that is certain!

ARNE [*passes him the bowl*]. There! Sit down and drink. [HEMMING *sits.*] Listen, Hemming! I could wish we were back home.

HEMMING. Yes, I don't like being in this wedding house.

ARNE. No, my old room at Guldvik for me . . . when the two of us sat together of an evening playing draughts with a pot of ale between us. . . .

HEMMING. Whilst Lady Ingeborg sat at her loom and embroidered roses and all sorts of flowers in the linen. . . .

ARNE. And sang so delightfully that it seemed to me I became young and vigorous again. Yes, Hemming! When the wedding is over we'll continue with our old way of life again.

HEMMING. But then there'll be nobody to work the loom and sing delightful songs.

ARNE. No, that's true. Ingeborg will be gone. . . . That will be hard to bear. She is wild and self-willed, but I shall certainly miss her, and miss her greatly. [*Reflects.*] I suppose I could visit her here from time to time. . . . No, I won't! They laugh at me here. They whisper behind my back. . . . I see that well enough.

HEMMING. But if you wanted to, things could still be changed.

ARNE. Changed! You are stupid, Hemming! You are always talking about changing things. [*Hands him the bowl.*] There, drink! That will do you good. Changed? No, no, it shall never be changed! It was evil spirits that filled my head with the idea of marrying into Lady Kirsten's family. But now it is done. Her fine kinsfolk can behave as they like, but my own relatives shall not mock me. . . . I have given my word, and I shall keep it. [*Sadly.*] If only I could be sure that Olaf would be good to her.... I shall ask him to...[*Vehemently.*] He shall be, or else I shall take these old fists to him.

HEMMING. It would be well if you kept an eye on her, for Olaf does not care greatly for her, I rather think.

ARNE. So, you think so?

HEMMING. You recall Alfhild, the poor girl who came down from the mountain with us yesterday?

ARNE. Indeed I do. She is pretty!

HEMMING [*rises*]. Olaf thinks so too.

ARNE. What does that mean?

HEMMING. Olaf loves her! Many are the times he has visited her up there. . . . You haven't to believe all those things Lady Kirsten told you.

ARNE. And the things you tell me, I believe even less. You are angry with Ingeborg because she sometimes makes fun of you, and you can't bear to see her make this good match. Ah yes, I know you.

HEMMING. Oh, master, could you believe . . . ?

ARNE. You want me to believe that Olaf Liljekrans loves that beggar girl! A respected, high-born man like him! It's equivalent to somebody saying that my daughter Ingeborg had a fancy for you.

HEMMING [*embarrassed*]. For me . . . What makes you imagine . . . ?

ARNE. No, I don't imagine! But the one is as improbable as the other. Here! Drink! And have done with this nonsense! [*Rises.*] Here is Lady Kirsten with the guests. What's happening now?

HEMMING. Everybody is to assemble out here, and then follow the bride and bridegroom to the banquet table, and thence to the church.

ARNE. Ah, what a cursed custom! To the church at night! Is getting married a deed of darkness?

SCENE IX

[*As before.* LADY KIRSTEN, OLAF, INGEBORG, GUESTS, *together with servants and maids enter gradually from various sides.*]

LADY KIRSTEN [*to herself*]. I have not seen Olaf alone. But when I think about it, it is probably best if he knows nothing about it before it happens. [*Softly to* HEMMING, *who has been whispering to* INGEBORG.] Well, Hemming! What sort of mood do you think your master is in?

HEMMING [*in a low voice*]. Ah, Lady Kirsten! I have little hope unless you help.

LADY KIRSTEN. Ah, we shall manage.

[*She mingles with the guests.*]

INGEBORG [*to* HEMMING, *in a low voice*]. What do you mean? What is this joyful hope you speak of?

HEMMING. Ah, I daren't believe it myself. But Lady Kirsten means well by us. She will soon show you that . . .

INGEBORG. Hush! They are coming!

OLAF [*in a low voice*]. Tell me, mother! How are things with her?

LADY KIRSTEN. Well enough, as I knew they would be.

OLAF. Can she find comfort?

LADY KIRSTEN [*smiling*]. Seemingly. Just wait! You'll know for certain this very evening.

OLAF. What do you mean?

LADY KIRSTEN. I mean that she is a cunning witch. All her fine words have been lies and deceit.

OLAF. No, no, mother!

LADY KIRSTEN. That we shall now see! Alfhild is happy and gay, as far as I know.

OLAF. Well for me if she were!

LADY KIRSTEN [*in a loud and clear voice*]. Sir Arne of Guldvik! Now at last the hour is come which I believe we have all been waiting for.

HEMMING [*aside*]. Now things are starting!

LADY KIRSTEN. Soon the church will call down peace upon our children, and bind them together in a long and loving union.

HEMMING [*aside, startled*]. What's this?

LADY KIRSTEN. We have agreed the terms. But I think we should seal them once again by hand and mouth.

HEMMING [*as before*]. Heaven and earth! Does she mean to deceive me?

ARNE. It is not necessary. I stand by my word as an honourable man.

LADY KIRSTEN. I know that well, Sir Arne! But it is quickly done. First: there shall be an end to all dissension and enmity between our two families for all time; and nobody shall demand any recompense for damages and injuries caused to either side by our old disputes; they must be borne as best they can. This we promise, do we not?

ALL. This we promise!

[*General shaking of hands among the families of the bridal couple.*]

HEMMING [*in a low voice*]. Shame upon you, that you told me such cursed lies!

LADY KIRSTEN. Next one must declare—something we are all agreed upon—that the boundary line between Sir Arne's territory and mine shall be moved as far in upon his land as good and impartial men have agreed is just and proper.

ARNE. Yes, yes, so be it!

LADY KIRSTEN. This we promise, then?

THE GUESTS. This we promise!

[*Handclasps as before.*]

LADY KIRSTEN. Finally Lord Arne gives his daughter by way of dowry as much silver, linen and other household furnishings as were defined and listed at the betrothal feast, all of which are to be deposited in this house from the day Lady Ingeborg has moved into residence as my son's lawful wife, which is tonight. On this we are agreed?

THE GUESTS. This we promise and witness!

[*Handclasps.*]

LADY KIRSTEN. Then let the bride and bridegroom take each other's hand to go to the banquet table and thence to the church.

ARNE [*aside*]. Aha! Now Hemming will see whether Lady Kirsten is deceiving me.

HEMMING [*in a low voice*]. Oh, then all is lost for me. I was a fool to rely on her.

LADY KIRSTEN. But on this joyful day it behoves us to make happy as many as we can. And that is why I have a boon to ask of you, Sir Arne!

ARNE. Speak! I grant it gladly if I can.

HEMMING [*aside*]. What does she mean to do now?

LADY KIRSTEN. There is yet another young couple who would gladly be led to the altar this evening. They are both agreed, from what I hear. I shall take care of the bride, but you must assist the bridegroom. It is Hemming, your vassal, and Alfhild!

INGEBORG [*with a cry*]. Hemming!

OLAF [*similarly*]. Alfhild!

HEMMING. Ah, woe! Now I understand . . . !

THE GUESTS [*at the same time*]. Hemming and Alfhild! The mountain girl!

[*Laughter and whispering.*]

OLAF. Alfhild! You want to marry her off to . . . ! No, no! It shall not happen! Never! never!

LADY KIRSTEN. Be still, Olaf, my son! Be still! I beg you!

ARNE [*to himself*]. What is this! Yes, in truth, Hemming was right. There is something between Olaf and Alfhild. [*Whispers.*] Ah, Lady Kirsten! I see what you are after. Now I know why Olaf spent three days in the mountains. And now Hemming is to rid you of her. Ha, ha!

LADY KIRSTEN [*with forced composure*]. Sir Arne! How can you believe that?

ARNE [*in a low voice*]. Ah! I see that well enough! I rather believe I have adequate grounds for breaking the agreement.

LADY KIRSTEN [*softly and frightened*]. Break the agreement! I beg you! Will you shame us all?

[*They talk together in low voices.*]

HEMMING [*to* INGEBORG, *to whom he has been whispering*]. That's how things are, I swear. Lady Kirsten and I did not understand each other.

INGEBORG. Then say so! You must! I command you!

HEMMING. No, no, I dare not. She will realize I was thinking of you.

INGEBORG. Very well, then I shall. [*Aloud.*] Hemming shall not go to the altar with Alfhild. . . . He is too good to marry another man's wench.

OLAF [*with a cry*]. Infamy!

THE GUESTS. Wench!

ARNE [*to* INGEBORG]. What do you say?

LADY KIRSTEN. Heaven preserve us!

OLAF. I am cursed! She is disgraced!

INGEBORG. Yes, I speak the word, loud and clear. She is another man's wench! Let him contradict it who dares!

ARNE. Ingeborg! [*Aside.*] What is the matter with her?

LADY KIRSTEN [*in a low voice*]. So that's how it is! She . . . she is the one who loves Hemming! [*Quietly and firmly to* ARNE.] Do you still intend to break the agreement? You see yourself from your daughter's behaviour what cause I had to get Hemming married!

ARNE [*disconcerted*]. My daughter! Do you think she . . . ?

LADY KIRSTEN. Do not pretend! Ingeborg has a mind for your servant. I would say now that *I* have adequate grounds for breaking our agreement!

ARNE. Break, break . . . ! What are you thinking of! To do me this wrong!

LADY KIRSTEN [*mockingly*]. Otherwise you would do it yourself!

ARNE [*quickly*]. No, no. I have had second thoughts. It is best we both keep silent!

LADY KIRSTEN [*to herself*]. See! Now I have won! I know Olaf. A woman so scorned will have no attraction for him!

Kɪɪ

SCENE X

[*As before.* ALFHILD *emerges unnoticed from the out-house in a glittering bridal dress, with a crown on her flowing hair.*]

ARNE [*aside*]. This has been a cursed day for me. Oh, that Hemming is a cunning dog! He knew that Ingeborg had a liking for him, and that is why he did not like the idea of Olaf having her.

LADY KIRSTEN [*who has meanwhile regained her composure*]. And now to the banquet hall! Hemming we can think about later. —Olaf, take the bride by the hand!

ARNE [*brusquely, as he sees* INGEBORG *whispering to* HEMMING]. Where is the bride? Come along! Come along!

ALFHILD *and* INGEBORG [*simultaneously, each one seizing one of* OLAF'*s hands*]. Here I am!

THE GUESTS. What is this! She is taking Olaf?

[*General amazement.*]

LADY KIRSTEN [*aside*]. So he has taken it as far as that! [*Loudly to* ALFHILD.] You are mistaken! That is not your bridegroom!

ALFHILD. Yes it is! This is Olaf!

INGEBORG [*lets go his hand*]. So he has promised her . . . !

LADY KIRSTEN [*greatly agitated*]. Olaf is not your bridegroom, I tell you. Tell her yourself, my son!

[OLAF *remains silent. Lady Kirsten's kinsmen look at each other embarrassed. Arne's relatives step closer, frowning and threatening.*]

LADY KIRSTEN [*raising her voice*]. Olaf Liljekrans! Answer loud and clear! This can with justice be asked of you.

OLAF [*in despair, struggling with himself*]. Then be it as you wish, mother! Yes, by all the saints, I shall answer! Alfhild, you are mistaken! I am not your bridegroom. [*He points to* INGEBORG.] There . . . there stands my bride!

ALFHILD [*steps back as though petrified and stares at him*]. She! Your . . .

OLAF [*with rising anger*]. Alfhild! Leave this place! Go! Go deep into
the mountains again! That will be best for you. I was sick and
confused in my mind when I went up there! I remember little of
what I said to you! I do not know and I do not want to know!
Do you hear! I do not want to know! You can keep the golden
crown! Keep everything you are dressed in, all the silver and gold.
You shall have more, ten times more. . . . Well! Why are you
looking at me like that?

[ALFHILD *takes off the crown and the rest of the jewellery and puts them
at* OLAF'*s feet, staring at him all the while.*]

OLAF. Perhaps I let you think you were to be my bride tonight!
Perhaps you believed me! Perhaps you thought that Olaf Liljekrans
would marry a . . . What was it you called her? [*Stamps his foot.*]
Don't look at me like that, I tell you! I know you for what you are.
You have bewitched me! I forgot my family! I forgot my bride, my
betrothed who is standing there. [*He seizes* ALFHILD *roughly by the
arm.*] Look at her, Alfhild! Ha! ha! She is the one I love!

[ALFHILD *sinks to her knees and covers her face with her hands.*]

OLAF. Get up Alfhild! Get up, I say! If you grieve like this, I shall
strike you dead! . . . Why aren't you glad? Be wildly happy like
me! . . . And the rest of you! Why do you stand there in silence,
looking at one another? Laugh! Laugh, I say! So that the whole
house resounds with it! . . . Alfhild, why don't you answer? Haven't
I told you enough? Ha, ha! Then why don't you others tell her a
word or two! Have your say as well! Lady Kirsten wants to! Laugh
at her, mock her, trample her under your feet! [*With strident laughter.*]
Ha, ha, ha! Is she not Olaf's wench!

[ALFHILD *sinks to the ground so that she lies prostrate against the stone
bench, left. A flash of lightning illuminates the stage; thunder rolls. As
the rest of the scene progresses, the darkness and the storm increase.*]

OLAF. See! see! That's what I like! They are joining in up there, too!
Now I shall take my bride to the church! Come, Lady Ingeborg!
But first we will drink. . . . Yes, drink, drink! Bring the jug and
the horn. . . . No, in there! . . . Light the candles in the church!
Let the organ play music for dancing. . . . No mournful psalms. . . .
No, a dance! [*Thunder and lightning.*] Ha, ha! Heaven is inquiring
if Olaf Liljekrans is celebrating his wedding!

[*He rushes out, right.*]

ARNE. Christ save us! He has lost his reason!

LADY KIRSTEN. Oh, have no fear. It will soon pass. . . . I know him.

[*She draws* ARNE *away with her.*]

ARNE [*threateningly in a low voice to* HEMMING, *as he passes*]. Oh, Hemming, Hemming! You are a cunning dog!

[THE GUESTS *go out silently and upset, right; the servants go out, left.*]

INGEBORG [*holds* HEMMING *back*]. Hemming! I will not enter the church with Olaf Liljekrans.

HEMMING. Alas, what can prevent it?

INGEBORG. If it comes to the point, I shall say 'no'. . . 'No' at the very altar, in the sight of all!

HEMMING. Ingeborg!

INGEBORG. Keep my horse saddled and ready!

HEMMING. What! You will . . . !

INGEBORG. I will! Only now do I realize how much I love you . . . now that I am in danger of losing you. Go! Do as I say, and warn me when the time comes.

[*She goes out, right.*]

HEMMING. Yes, now I am strong. Now I dare do what is needed!

[*He goes out, left.*]

SCENE XI

[ALFHILD. *Later* HEMMING, INGEBORG, *and others at various times.*]

ALFHILD [*lies for some time motionless with her face hidden in her hands; eventually she half rises, looks around bewildered, gets up and says with quiet broken laughter*]:

The one falcon rests on the monarch's arm,
The other must suffer great need and distress!
One bird has feathers both scarlet and blue,
Another must manage with colourless grey!—

I have known the comfort that tears can bring
When the whole wide world is out of joint;
But now I am suffering grief so wild
I could almost laugh myself to death!

[*It is now quite dark. The windows of the church are lit up.* ALFHILD
*walks over to the house and listens as the following song is faintly heard
within.*]

CHORUS OF WEDDING GUESTS.
Hail and honour to both bride and groom,
Sitting in joy and gladness here.
So proud a knight is Olaf bold
And Ingeborg so fair a lady!

HEMMING [*stealing onstage during the song*]. The horse stands saddled!
Now, a secret sign to Ingeborg, and then away!

[*He goes out, right, behind the house.*]

ALFHILD. They drink to him from the silver cup.
The bride, enthroned, sits by his side;
The candles are lit on the altar piece,
And soon to the church they will ride!
They sit in there at the festive board
Laughing and joking among themselves!
And I, alone in the night and the storm,
Forlorn and abandoned by everyone.
Olaf! The tempest tears at my hair!
Olaf! I am lashed by the wind and rain!
Olaf! Olaf! Can you see me thus suffer
These nameless torments, this anguished fear!

[*Laughs.*]

Rain and storm are but trifling things,
Nothing compared with the stabbing pain
I feel within my breast!
My house, my father, my all I gave
To follow Olaf, my dearest heart!
He swore to me I should be his bride!
And I came—with love of God in my heart.
But he drove me from him, thrust me away,
And loud he laughed as I writhed in pain!

Like a dog I must sit at the door of the feast
In the storms of night. I must go! Must go!

[*She starts to go, but stops.*]

No, I haven't the strength. I cannot go!
Here I must stay and endure my pain!
No more than the meadow flower has strength
To uproot itself from its rightful soil!
I have taken root by Olaf's side,
Regardless of whether he is false or kind.

[*Pause. The* MENSERVANTS *appear with torches, left.*]

ALFHILD [*as though seized by some fearful foreboding*]. Where are you
going? Where? Where? What is to happen?

A SERVANT. Well, look here! It is Alfhild. She is still here.

ALFHILD. Oh, tell me! What is to happen? What is going on?

THE SERVANT. The wedding! Wouldn't you like to watch?

ALFHILD [*in feverish anxiety*]. The wedding! Oh, no, no! Wait! Just
until tomorrow! If the wedding is held, then all is lost! I know!

THE SERVANT. Wait! No, Alfhild! Neither the bride nor the groom
want that.

ANOTHER. Think again! If you were the bride yourself, you wouldn't
want to wait.

[*Laughter.*]

FIRST SERVANT. Now we are going down to the church gate to light
the way with the red bridal torches as the party leaves the house.

SECOND SERVANT. Come along with us, Alfhild! You can also carry a
torch!

SEVERAL. Yes, yes, you must! After all, it is Olaf's day of glory!

[*Laughter.*]

ALFHILD [*takes one of the torches*]. Yes, yes, I will! There I will stand, the
humblest of all. And when he sees me, when I beg him, when I
remind him of everything he promised me, swore to me . . . tell
me, don't you think he will be kind to me again! Do you think he
will? Oh, say yes, say yes! Say you think he will!

THE SERVANTS. Ha, ha, ha! Surely he will! Come along!

[*They go out, right, behind the house.*]

ALFHILD [*bursting into tears*].
Everyone mocks me—one and all!
So hard is not the mountain rock
That lets the moss grow freely there.
No kindness I find! I must perish and die!

[*Thunder and lightning.*]

Even heaven itself is cruel to me,
Pouring its anger upon my head.
Yet it sends no thunderbolt for him
And the cruel deceit of all that he said.

[*Organ music is heard from the church.*]

Oh hear! God's angel choir is singing,
Summoning Olaf before the altar!
I shall stand beside the door of the church
And grieve in my golden rags!

[*She swings the torch high.*]

No, no! I will not, God on high!
Tempt me no more, else Thee I'll deny!

[*She stops and listens to the organ music.*]

God's angels sing! From the dark of the grave
Their singing recalled the dead!
Oh, my heart is bursting with grief!

[*She kneels facing the church.*]

An end to this gentle music!
To end to your singing, so tender and sweet!
For it lures the groom to the altar!

[*Whispering, and in extreme fear.*]

Be still! Oh, be still! If just for a moment!
He is lulled in a sleep of forgetfulness!
Oh, wake him not, or else he will ride
Straight to the church—and I should die!

[*The organ sounds louder through the storm.* ALFHILD *leaps up, beside herself with despair.*]

All God's angels now forsake me,
And mock me in my anguish!
They summon him out—they hold him fast!
If I'm to be banished to blackest night,
In the bridal chamber at least there'll be light!

[*She throws the torch in through the hatch in the gable and falls to the ground.* HEMMING *and* INGEBORG *come hurriedly from behind the house.*]

HEMMING. The time has come! The horse stands saddled behind the storehouse.

INGEBORG. And all the servants are down by the churchdoor, are they not?

HEMMING. Yes, yes, do not be alarmed. And I have barred all the doors and shutters in the house with the great iron rings. Nobody can get out!

INGEBORG. Then away! Up to the valley Alfhild spoke of!

HEMMING. Yes, up there! No one will look for us there!

[*They hurry out, left.* ALFHILD *remains for some time lying motionless. Suddenly commotion and shouts are heard from the house; flames shoot out through the roof.*]

ALFHILD [*leaps up, confused*].
It burns! Aha! Now I remember!
I found it too dark—it filled me with fear!
Ha, Olaf! It was you who was laughing before;
Now it is Alfhild, so wild and so gay!
Within the house there is fear and alarm,
The bride is burning on the bridegroom's arm!

[*The servants run in without their torches, and stand as though turned to stone.* OLAF *appears up at the hatch which he tries desperately to widen.*]

OLAF. Alfhild! It's you! I was sure it was!
Gold and ermine you'll always wear,
If you'll but save me in my distress!

ALFHILD [*with wild laughter*].
Yes, I know now how you keep your word!
Now ride to church with the minstrel and priest!
Now hold your wedding—forget your wench!
Alfhild has honoured you as she knew best
And borne a torch at your wedding feast!

[*She rushes out at the rear. The servants rush to help; part of the roof
falls in.* OLAF *can be seen high up, surrounded by flames, as the curtain
falls.*]

ACT THREE

A valley, full of light and blossom and trees, surrounded by high, snow-capped mountains. In the middle distance a quiet mountain tarn; on the left a rocky cliff that falls abruptly into the water. On the same side nearer the foreground a very old log hut, almost completely overgrown. The sun shines red on the mountains; in the valley itself, the day has only half dawned. During the following scenes, the sun rises.

SCENE I

[ALFHILD *lies sleeping, half hidden among the bushes beside the house; soft music indicates her shifting dreams.* OLAF *comes down the hillside, right. He wears a coarse jacket over his wedding finery.*]

OLAF. It was here. I recognize the green here by the tarn. It was under that linden tree I dreamed my strange dream. There I stood on the mountain slope when Alfhild first came towards me. I held my betrothal ring to my bow-string and shot. That shot has been a magic shot—it struck the bowman himself.

Strange how, when I wander up here high above the village, it is as though a different air played about me, as if a livelier blood coursed through my veins, as if I had a different mind, a different way of thinking.

Where is she now?

I shall . . . I will find her again! She must return up here; there is no home for her out there in the cold, wide world. And I? Am I not also a homeless fugitive! Did I not become a stranger in my mother's house, a stranger among my own kinsmen, from the very first moment I met her?

Is she then a witch, possessing secret arts that . . . ?

My mother! Hm! I rather think it bodes me no good to let her determine my life. She insinuates thoughts into my heart that have no place there. No, no! I will find Alfhild again, and confess all the wrong I have done her, and then . . .

[*He stops and looks out, left.*]

[OLAF. ALFHILD, *still asleep.* THORGEJR *enters from behind the house, left.*]

OLAF. Well met, stranger!

THORGEJR. Thank you. I wish you the same. You are about early!

OLAF. Or late! Early in the morning, but late at night!

THORGEJR. You have your home down in the village, I suppose.

OLAF. My family belongs there. And you?

THORGEJR. Wherever one's heart is bound, there one has one's home. That is why I prefer to be up here. . . . My neighbours cause me no harm.

OLAF. That I have noticed.

THORGEJR. Then you have been up here before?

OLAF. This summer I chased a hind in here. But when I look closer, I see it is a royal child bewitched.

THORGEJR [*looks fixedly at him*]. To hunt that is dangerous!

OLAF. For the hunter? [THORGEJR *nods.*] Yes, I was sitting thinking the same thing myself. I do believe I was struck down by magic at that hunt.

THORGEJR. Farewell, and good luck!

OLAF. Shame on you! Wish a huntsman luck and he'll never come within range of his quarry.

THORGEJR. If the shot should hit the hunter himself, then the best luck he could have is to have no luck at all.

OLAF. You speak shrewdly.

THORGEJR. Well, there are many things to be learnt up here.

OLAF. Indeed! Here I learnt the best thing of all.

THORGEJR. Farewell! I shall take greetings from you to your kinsmen.

OLAF. Are you meaning to go down there?

THORGEJR. That was my intention. There are merry days down there, I am told. A mighty knight is celebrating his wedding. . . .

OLAF. Then you should have been there last night. By now the best of the fun is probably over.

THORGEJR. I fancy I'll still be there in time.

OLAF. Perhaps! But you should have been there last night. You've never seen so bright and warm a banquet hall.

THORGEJR. Very good for him who was in it.

OLAF. I know one who had to stand outside.

THORGEJR. Yes, yes, outside—that is the poor man's place.

OLAF. I know one who had to stand outside, and who still was better and worse off than those who were inside.

THORGEJR. I can see I must go down there. I shall play at the party. I shall collect my harp, and then . . .

OLAF. You are a minstrel?

THORGEJR. And not among the worst. Now I shall fetch my harp hidden beside the waterfall. You should hear its strings. With them I once sat on the edge of the bed and played the bride out of the festive house and over hill and dale— Have you never heard the song of little Ingrid? Anyone who could play the bride out of the bridegroom's arms can surely play the child back to her father again. Farewell! If you remain here we may meet again when I come down once more.

[*He goes out, right, to the tarn.*]

SCENE III

[OLAF. ALFHILD.]

OLAF. Ah, if that was . . . ! Surely there can be no doubt. Alfhild said herself that her father plucked the strings so cunningly that, once heard, it could never again be forgotten. He mentioned Lady Ingrid who disappeared on her wedding night many years ago—there was a young minstrel called Thorgejr who loved her, so the story went. Afterwards there were many strange stories about him. Sometimes

he stood in the middle of the village and played so beautifully that
everybody had to weep. But nobody knew where he lived. Alfhild—
yes, she is his child! She must have grown up here, here in this wild
valley which nobody has known of for many a year. And Ingrid
who disappeared . . . Did he not say . . . ? [*He notices* ALFHILD.]
Alfhild! There she is! She must have fled up here in her wedding
dress. Now you must wake her after the wedding night. My day of
glory was a sad day for you! You wanted to go out into life, you
said. You wanted to discover all the glory of the world. What a
weary journey you have had. But now all shall be well! She moves.
It is as if she twisted in fear and sadness. . . . When you wake, it shall
be to joy and gladness!

ALFHILD [*still half dreaming*].
  It burns! Oh, save him! He is inside!
  He must not die! He must find an escape!

[*She jumps up, terrified; the music stops.*]

  Where am I? I seem . . . to see him there!

[*Hurries across to him.*]

  Olaf Liljekrans! Preserve me from my dreams!

OLAF. Alfhild, be calm! And have no fear!

ALFHILD [*retreats, timid and fearful*].
  Do you mean to beguile me with tender endearments?
  With a smile on your lips, and evil in your heart,
  You'll never ensnare me with magic charm!

OLAF. Alfhild! Come to your senses again!
  For this is Olaf, your dearest heart!
  Much have you suffered; I have acted unkind;
  But deep in my heart I thought only of you!
  Blind and confused and weak I have been—
  And this has meant for you mortal hurt!
  Alfhild! Can you forgive what I've done?
  I swear I shall try to be worthy of you!
  The tears of sorrow I shall kiss from your cheek,
  Your path I shall smooth, and make easy your way,
  And temper the sorrow that saddens your soul,
  And heal all the wounds that burn in your heart!

ALFHILD [*gently and sadly*].
  I know you too well, and your cunning deceit.
  I am wiser now than I was, you know.
  You want to confuse me, trick me with words
  Into thinking it's you who oppresses my mind.
  You pretend that you were the one who taught
  Me that melting rapture, that anguished pain!
  Don't think to succeed! I know you too well,
  Though you come to me early, or come to me late.
  I know you too well. I can see on your brow
  The signs of deceit. So unlike the other!

OLAF. The other? Which other?

ALFHILD.   The one who is dead!
  On whose account I suffer this grief.
  You don't understand? You know there were two—
  Which is why I can never find peace of mind!
  The one gave all his love to me—
  The other deceived me as cruelly as you.
  One came to me on a late summer's eve,
  And roses blossomed within my heart.
  The other one lured me into the hills
  A place devoid of the summer sun!
  You are the evil, deceitful one!
  The other who came to me with love,
  The other who is always in my heart,
  I burned with fire!

[*She sinks down on a stone by the house, and breaks into tears.*]

OLAF. He has ravished your peace, and robbed you of rest.
  Why let him remain any more in your heart!

ALFHILD. Ah, if to my grave I were to sink,
  I do believe my grief would follow!
  I did not know—I swear to you
  I thought I cared for him but little.
  But now I see I must die of grief,
  And yet I cannot forget him!

[*Short pause.*]

Say, is there music in your breast?
Quite likely, for your voice sounds sweet,
Sweet—though blended with deceit.
If music is in your breast then go
And sing to all the village girls
The plaintive song of Alfhild! Thus:

> But yesterday I was a hind,
> And lived in the grass-green grove;
> When into the forest came many a man
> And chased me with falcon and hound.

> But yesterday I was a bird,
> And sat on the linden tree.
> They came and drove me from my perch,
> And harried me with stones.

> But yesterday I was a dove,
> A restless and untamed thing.
> They came with quivers, and came with bows,
> And shot arrows into my breast!

OLAF [*deeply moved*].
> Did I but lie below the hill,
> Enjoying eternal rest!
> Your every word is a bow of steel
> That drives an arrow in my breast!

ALFHILD [*jumps up with childish delight*].
That's how it should be! That is just right!
In truth you have music within your breast!
It must be sung thus! So that all may suppose
That you yourself are moved by my sorrow,
That your personal grief is just as great
As the one you portray in your plaintive song!

[*Stops and looks sadly at him.*]

Yet no—you shall not sing of these things,
For none will be moved by Alfhild's lament.
Whither I went, and whence I came
Are no concern of the people down there!
Sing rather of Olaf Liljekrans

Who joined the ranks of the elfin dance!
Sing of Alfhild and her woman's wiles
Who made him forget his promised bride.
Sing of all the sorrow and grief
When Olaf Liljekrans lay cold and dead!
Sing of all the anguish and woe
When they bore from the hall the three who died!
The one was Olaf, the other his bride!
The third his mother who died of grief!

OLAF. Yes, Olaf is dead! It is just as you say.
But to you I shall be as faithful a friend;
Wherever you go or wherever you stay,
I shall always be there by your side!
Though I suffer full sore for the wrongs I have done,
My punishment will be a sweet reward.
Comfort and solace will then be mine
If I can but share this place with you!
From early dawn to setting sun
I'll follow your steps like a faithful hound.
I'll express my remorse in such plaintive words
That you finally must admit it's real.
Each moment of joy that we know up here
I'll capture and store for your memory!
Each flower that blossoms shall speak of these things,
And the song of the cuckoo and swallow repeat!
And every tree in the verdant glade
Shall whisper these things in a thousand ways!

ALFHILD. Oh, stop! Would you try to deceive me anew!
Better by far if you fled from me now!
So fair is the falsehood of your words,
And the treacherous thoughts that live in your heart!
Why do you come here? What is it you seek?
Do you really pretend you remember this place?
How pleasant a spot this used to be—
But now a curse has laid it waste!
In the past, as I walked in the forest alone,
There were fragrant leaves on every branch!
The flowers bloomed and the birds all sang
When you held me close and called me your bride!

But the valley last night was swept by fire—
Trees and shrubs are scorched and burnt;
The straw is withered, the leaves are gone,
The flowers have turned to smouldering dust!
   I clearly see—in a single night
The world has grown old! As I stood forlorn,
Suffering torment and shame down there,
The golden hues of life turned pale,
Nothing survives but deceit and guile—
Olaf taught me this on my wedding day!
My father lied when he made me believe
The dead are borne to the angels' home.
And Olaf knew the harsher truth—
The dead are buried within the black earth.

[*She cries out in deepest pain.*]

Yes, I can witness you knew what you said—
For I have sunk deep down in the earth!

OLAF. Alfhild! Your words are unbearably sad!
   Oh God! Your heart so gentle and mild—
   Forgive me my wrongs, and forget all your woe!

ALFHILD [*showing signs of increasing frenzy*].
   Speak no more to me! See, Olaf, see!
   They carry a corpse away to the grave.
   But no mother I see, nor children five,
   Nor any pillows of red or of blue—
   Alfhild lies there on shavings and straw!
   I shall never ride in the carriage of heaven
   To wake in God the Father's arms.
   No mother have I whose heart will break,
   Nor any to mourn at the coffin's side.
   In the whole wide world, neither great nor small
   Will weep for me at the grave.
   No angels to scatter pearls of blue
   About my feet in the garden of heaven.
   And never shall I reach that place of delight
   Where the dead do dream their dreams!

OLAF. Alfhild!

Lıı

ALFHILD.   And now I sink below the ground!
And now they cover me with earth!
And here I must lie in my distress,
Must live and suffer though I am dead.
Must know that naught remains for me,
Yet cannot forget, nor fight myself free.
Must hear the man whom once I loved
Riding to church across my grave!
Must hear his cries in the leaping flames,
And know I cannot relieve his pain!
So tight this grief within my breast!
Forgotten by all God's angel host!
None can hear my sobbing prayer—
Shut on me the gates of life—
Oh, dig me up! Let me not lie here!

[*She hurries out, left.*]

OLAF. Alfhild! Alfhild! Dear Christ, what have I done?

[*He hurries after her.*]

SCENE IV

[INGEBORG *and* HEMMING *enter after a short pause, from the right.*]

INGEBORG. Well, here we are up here! How lovely and light and
peaceful it is!

HEMMING. Yes, we can live together very happily here!

INGEBORG. But mark well that you are my servant, and nothing more—
until my father has given his consent.

HEMMING. He'll never do that!

INGEBORG. Do not worry—we shall find a way. But now we must
think of choosing a cottage to live in.

HEMMING. There are plenty of them here. The valley is covered with
abandoned houses. Everything is still as it was when the last people
died in the great plague many years ago.

INGEBORG. I like it here! There's one of the old cottages over there.
We have water nearby, and the forest will surely have plenty of
game. You can fish and hunt. Yes, we will live a very pleasant life!

HEMMING. Yes, indeed, a very pleasant life! I shall fish and hunt, while you pick berries and see to the house.

INGEBORG. I? No, you must see to that!

HEMMING. Very well, as you will. Ah, we shall live a merry life! [*Stops and adds rather dejectedly.*] But now I remember. . . . I have neither bow nor fishing-rod with me.

INGEBORG [*with a similarly despondent expression*]. And it occurs to me there are no servants here to give me a hand.

HEMMING. That I'll gladly do!

INGEBORG. No, thanks all the same! . . . And all my good clothes. . . . I brought nothing with me but the wedding dress I am standing in.

HEMMING. That was not very thoughtful of you!

INGEBORG. True enough, Hemming! So one night you shall steal down to Guldvik and bring such clothes and other things that I need.

HEMMING. And be hanged as a thief!

INGEBORG. No, you must take care—I order you. [*Doubtfully.*] But what about when the long winter comes? No people up here, and never the sound of singing or dancing . . . Hemming! Should we stay here, or . . .

HEMMING. Where else could we go?

INGEBORG [*impatiently*]. But nobody can live here.

HEMMING. Of course they can.

INGEBORG. You can see for yourself they are all dead! Hemming! I think it would be best if I went back to my father.

HEMMING. Then what will become of me?

INGEBORG. You shall ride to the wars!

HEMMING. To the wars! And be killed!

INGEBORG. Certainly not! You shall perform some famous deed, and then you'll be knighted, and then my father will not stand against you.

HEMMING. Yes, but what if they do kill me?

INGEBORG. Well, we can always think about that. We might as well stay here today and tomorrow. The guests will sit that long at table enjoying the wedding feast. . . . If they do look for us, it will probably be in and around the village. We can feel safe up here. . . .

[*She stops and listens.*]

CHOIR [*in the distance, off-stage, right*].

> Away, away to find
> Alfhild, the evil one;
> For all our woe and sorrow,
> She must pay with her life!

HEMMING. Ingeborg! Ingeborg! They are after us!

INGEBORG. Where can we go?

HEMMING. How do I know. . . .

INGEBORG. Go into the cottage. Mend the door so that it can be locked from inside.

HEMMING. Yes, but . . .

INGEBORG. Do as I say! Meanwhile I'll go up the hillside and see if they are far away.

[*She goes out, right.*]

HEMMING. Very well! Just as long as they don't catch us!

[*He goes into the house.*]

SCENE V

[OLAF *comes out of the forest, left. Immediately afterwards* INGEBORG *from the right.*]

OLAF [*looks around him, and calls in a low voice*]. Alfhild! Alfhild! She's not to be seen anywhere! Like a bird she slipped from my sight in the forest, and I . . .

INGEBORG. They are close at hand and . . . [*Stops, startled.*] Olaf Liljekrans!

OLAF. Ingeborg!

HEMMING [*puts his head, unnoticed, out of the door and catches sight of* OLAF]. Sir Olaf! So! Now surely all is lost!

[*He hurriedly withdraws.*]

INGEBORG [*aside*]. He must have ridden on ahead.

OLAF [*aside*]. She must have come up with her father to look for me.

INGEBORG [*aside*]. But I won't go with him!

OLAF [*aside*]. I will not move from here!

INGEBORG [*aloud, as she approaches*]. Olaf Liljekrans. Now you have caught me. But you would be ill-advised to try and force me.

OLAF. That is far from being my intention!

INGEBORG. Why then have you come here along with my kinsfolk?

OLAF. Have I? On the contrary it is you who . . .

INGEBORG. You do not fool me that way. I have just seen the whole crowd. . . .

OLAF. Who? Who?

INGEBORG. My father and his relatives!

OLAF. Up here?

INGEBORG. Yes, close by!

OLAF. Then my mother is with them.

INGEBORG. Yes, she is indeed. But why should that alarm you?

OLAF. Because I am the one they are looking for!

INGEBORG. No, it's me!

OLAF [*astonished*]. You!

INGEBORG [*begins to understand*]. Or . . . wait a moment . . . Ha, ha, ha! What an idea! . . . Listen! Shall we two be honest with each other?

OLAF. Yes, that was my intention!

INGEBORG. Good. Then tell me what time you got up here?

OLAF. Last night!

INGEBORG. I too!

OLAF. You!

INGEBORG. Certainly! And you went away without anybody knowing?

OLAF. Yes!

INGEBORG. I too!

OLAF. Then tell me . . .

INGEBORG. Ssh! We have very little time! And you fled up here because you had little desire to go to the altar with me?

OLAF. How can you think . . . ?

INGEBORG. Ah, I can think it very well. Just speak out—we were going to be honest with each other.

OLAF. Very well. That *was* why . . .

INGEBORG. Good, good. I did the same!

OLAF. You, Ingeborg!

INGEBORG. And now you are not anxious to see anybody on your track?

OLAF. That I do not deny!

INGEBORG. I too! Ha, ha, ha! That's good. I fled from you, and you from me! We both fled up here, and now we meet just as our relatives are after us! Listen, Olaf Liljekrans! Let us promise not to betray each other!

OLAF. That is a promise.

INGEBORG. But now we must separate!

OLAF. I understand!

INGEBORG. For if they found us together . . .

OLAF. Then it would be more difficult for you to get free from me!

INGEBORG. Farewell. If ever I get married, you must come and be the bride's man.

OLAF. And if the same happens to me, you must come and do a similar service for me.

INGEBORG. Naturally! Farewell! Farewell! And do not think badly of me.

OLAF. Certainly not! I shall offer you my hand wherever we meet!

INGEBORG. I too! Wherever we meet . . . except before the altar!

[*She goes into the house.* OLAF *goes into the forest right, at the rear.*]

SCENE VI

[LADY KIRSTEN, ARNE OF GULDVIK, WEDDING GUESTS, FARMERS *and* SERVANTS *enter from the right.*]

LADY KIRSTEN. See, here we shall start the hunt. The party must spread out and look round the lake. . . . She will be brought out. . . . Then woe to her! There is no mercy or pity in my soul.

ARNE. What will you do?

LADY KIRSTEN. I shall pass sentence on her . . . at the very spot where she is found! Those crimes she has committed on my lands I have the power and authority to punish according to our laws and customs.

ARNE. How would that help? What is lost cannot be regained that way.

LADY KIRSTEN. No, but I shall be revenged on her, and that is no small matter. Revenge—I must have revenge if I am to bear and survive my loss and all the shame she has brought me. The storm last night ruined the entire year's crop. Not a single stalk stands undamaged in my fields. Yet up here, where she said herself that she lived, everything thrives and blossoms more richly than I have ever seen before! Is that not the workings of secret arts? She has tangled Olaf so completely in her devilish net that he fled last night from the village to follow her in the wildest of storms. She has burnt my house right down to the ground. All the doors and hatches she had barred from the outside. It was God's miracle that the servants brought help in time!

ARNE. Alas, God save us! I am afraid it might have cost two lives that I held very dear—Ingeborg and my man Hemming!

LADY KIRSTEN. Now, now, Sir Arne! You must not wholly despair yet. Ingeborg might well have got clear. All the rest of us escaped

without injury, despite the cursed tricks of that witch. . . . Ingeborg
has taken fright and panicked and gone rushing off somewhere.

ARNE. Well, well, let us suppose that of Ingeborg. But Hemming is
beyond recall, I'm sure!

LADY KIRSTEN. How so?

ARNE. Oh, he had become a sly and cunning devil recently! He let
himself be shut in and burnt just to be revenged on me. He knew
I can't manage for a single day without him. Oh, I know him!

LADY KIRSTEN. But however it is, we must capture Alfhild. She must
be tried, sentenced and executed. I have plenty of charges to bring
against her.

ARNE. And I can mention several more if necessary. She stole my
dapple-grey horse from its stable last night. This morning it was
gone, along with saddle and bridle.

LADY KIRSTEN [*aside*]. Ingeborg and Hemming gone! And his horse
gone, too. If I were in his place, I know what I would be thinking.
[*Aloud.*] Let us break up now and split into small groups. He who
first catches sight of Alfhild is to blow his trumpet or his horn.
The others listen for it and follow the sound to bring us together.

[*They go out at various points.*]

ARNE [*who remains behind alone*]. How shall I manage when I don't
know my way about here? [*Calls.*] Hemming! Hemming! [*Stops.*]
Ah yes, I forgot, he is . . . [*Shakes his head.*] Hm! hm! That was a
shameful thing he did.

[*He goes out, right.*]

SCENE VII

[ALFHILD *appears by the lake, left; she carries a little bundle.*]

ALFHILD. I have wept so much I can weep no more.
Now I must rest—I am weary to death!

[*She sinks down on a stone in the foreground.*]

First I shall bid my father farewell!
Then make my way to the barren peaks!
Down here I'd meet Olaf wherever I went;

To the heights I must go to harden my mind.
These doleful lessons I must try to forget,
And deaden my memory of bygone things.
 I who imagined that life was so rich!
All is illusion, nothing is truth;
All is deception and fraudulent lies;
Naught can be taken and held in the hand;
Naught may be looked at with clear-sighted eyes;
Nothing endures when we know it aright!

[*The sound of the lur is heard from the forest.*]

My mother's trinkets I'll take with me
And bury them safely below the ground!
I shall bury them deep by the birch-tree root,
That tree where Olaf and I once stood!

[*She opens the bundle and takes out a bridal crown and other ornaments.*]

This silver crown my mother once wore,
She who was also deceived by the world,
Putting her faith in the power of love!
Was her awakening also so rude?
Was it to mock that my father sang
Of the joys of love that gladden the heart?
How better if he had held his tongue.
His songs have robbed me of peace of mind.
His songs created a home in my breast
For the joys of life—now dashed to ruins!

[*The lur is heard again.*]

Silver indeed is a precious ore,
Which does not wither like autumn hay.
Though buried in the ground a thousand years,
It still would glitter, and never decay!
The joys of life are like autumn's hay,
Sorrow is silver, a precious ore!

[*Packs the trinkets into the bundle.*]

My father told of a magic treasure,
From which there dripped nine pearls each night;
But regardless of how many pearls were formed,

The treasure remained undiminished in size!
  My grief is like that magic treasure
From which shall drip by night and day
Not nine—but a thousand tiny pearls
And the treasure remain as it was!

[Plucks a flower and contemplates it sadly.]

You little flower! I used to believe
That you could enjoy this life.
I used to think that to you was given
A sense of life, a feeling of joy!—
But now the world instructs me better.
If I trample you down, you feel no pain.
I can pull you up without a qualm,
For you never knew that you were alive!
Yes, now the world has made me wise!
In the past I followed the clouds in flight,
Rode with them in my dreams through the sky,
And called them the heavenly swans!
In the past I believed that the leaves of the trees
Were spread so that I might walk in the shade;
I thought that the stones on the mountain were living,
But now I must sadly revise my faith.
Now I know better—only human kind
Can suffer from pain, can revel in joy.
No friend can I find among flowers and trees,
I must suffer my sorrow alone.

[Rises.]

Away then! Up among ice and snow—
Only the grave gives shelter here!

[Is about to go.]

SCENE VIII

[ALFHILD, LADY KIRSTEN, ARNE, WEDDING GUESTS, FARMERS *and* SERVANTS *come from different directions. Later* OLAF LILJEKRANS.]

LADY KIRSTEN. There she is! Stand still, Alfhild! Do not try to escape, or we will shoot you down.

ALFHILD. What do you want with me?

LADY KIRSTEN. That you will discover soon enough! [*Points to the bundle.*] What is that you are carrying?

ALFHILD. My mother's heirlooms!

LADY KIRSTEN. Give it here! Look! A silver crown! Indeed, Alfhild, if you are your mother's only daughter I am very much afraid that the bridal crown will no longer be needed in this family. [*To the* SERVANTS.] Bind her! There she stands and looks so innocent. But nobody knows what she is scheming.

[ALFHILD *is bound.*]

LADY KIRSTEN [*aloud, with suppressed passion*]. The court is in session. As you all know, I have legal right and authority to protect my properties, to pass judgement in accordance with the law of the land upon any person who does me an injury on my own lands. This is what you, Alfhild, have presumed to do. Therefore you now stand here as an accused person before your judge. Defend yourself if you can, but do not forget it is a matter of life and death.

ARNE. But listen, Lady Kirsten!

LADY KIRSTEN. Excuse me, Sir Arne! I am within my rights, and on them I insist. [*To* ALFHILD.] Step forward and answer me!

ALFHILD. Ask, and I shall answer!

LADY KIRSTEN. Many and grievous are the charges levelled against you. In the first place, I charge you with having deceived my son, Olaf Liljekrans, by your godless arts, so that his heart and mind turned against his betrothed to whom he had plighted his troth—so that he, sick in heart, at no time found peace in his home, but instead made his way up to this unknown valley where you had your home. Such things could not have come to pass by any normal means. You are therefore accused of witchcraft. Defend yourself if you can!

ALFHILD. I have little to say in answer to this. That strange power that drew Olaf up here, you call witchcraft. Perhaps you are right. But that power did not derive from the Evil One—every moment Olaf was here he was in the sight of God! Every thought I gave to Olaf must have been known to God's angels! And they had no cause to blush.

LADY KIRSTEN. Enough! enough! You add blasphemy to your misdeeds. Woe to you, Alfhild! Every word is weighed in the balance. Yet that is your concern! [*To the others.*] I call on you all to witness what she answered. [*Turns again to* ALFHILD.] I further accuse you of having again, last night and by the selfsame secret powers, lured Olaf up here, and of holding him hidden here!

ALFHILD. In that you are right. He is secretly hidden here!

LADY KIRSTEN. You admit it?

ALFHILD. Yes, but however powerful you are, you will never be able to release him. Perhaps it would be best for me if you could. But neither you nor the whole wide world have powers potent enough for that!

LADY KIRSTEN [*bursting out vehemently*]. Now you can be certain of death! Speak! Where have you got him.

ALFHILD [*presses her hands to her breast*]. In here—in my heart. If you can tear him out of it, you are a better witch than I!

LADY KIRSTEN. That answer means little! Speak! Where is he?

ALFHILD. I have answered!

LADY KIRSTEN [*choking back her anger*]. Very well!

ARNE [*to the others*]. If Hemming had been alive, he'd have got the truth out of her. He had grown very cunning of late.

LADY KIRSTEN. Now for the third charge against you. Last night you set fire to my house, and burned it to the ground. Perhaps human lives were lost—this we do not know yet. But however it is, it neither helps nor hinders your case. For your intention to burn us all to death is clear as day. Do you deny my charge of having burnt the house down last night?

ALFHILD. I do not deny it. I burnt your house down.

LADY KIRSTEN. And what extenuation for your actions do you claim? [*With bitter scorn.*] You cannot say that you acted over-hastily. From what I remember, you had plenty of opportunity for second thoughts. You stood outside. Nobody came near you. Nobody prevented you from considering things as calmly as you could wish. You cannot say that the revels had gone to your head, or that the wine made you heated and confused. For you were never inside. You stood outside, and it was cool enough there. There was a wind chill enough to keep you sober.

ALFHILD. Yes, I burnt your house down last night. But you and Olaf and all the rest of you out there have done me a greater wrong. To me the world was a great hall, which belonged to the Great Father. The blue heavens were its roof, the stars the lamps that shone from the ceiling. I lived there, happy and rich. But you—you cast a brand into the middle of the golden splendour. Now everything is withered and dead!

LADY KIRSTEN. Such talk will serve you little. Once again I ask you: where is my son, Olaf Liljekrans?

ALFHILD. I have answered!

LADY KIRSTEN. Then you have passed sentence upon yourself, and I shall confirm it.

[OLAF *appears on the rocky cliff among the trees, unnoticed by the others.*]

OLAF [*aside*]. Alfhild . . . ! God help me! What is this?

[*He withdraws unseen.*]

LADY KIRSTEN. As one guilty of witchcraft and arson, the law of the land condemns you to death. This sentence is herewith pronounced upon you, and will be carried out here and now.

ARNE. But listen, Lady Kirsten!

LADY KIRSTEN. Judgement has been passed. Alfhild shall die!

ALFHILD. Do as you please. I shall not seek to obstruct you. When Olaf denied his love, my life was finished—I will not live any longer!

LADY KIRSTEN. Take her to the top of the precipice there!

[*The two* SERVANTS *take* ALFHILD *up.*]

LADY KIRSTEN. For the last time, Alfhild! Give me back my son!

ALFHILD. I will answer no more!

LADY KIRSTEN. Be it as you will! [*To the* SERVANTS.] Push her over! No, wait! I have an idea! [*To* ALFHILD.] Standing there like that, you remind me that yesterday you appeared wearing a golden crown, thinking you were worthy to be the bride of Olaf Liljekrans. Now we shall see how much you are worth. There are a number of peasants and servants and other humble men present here— perhaps your life can still be saved! Yes, Alfhild! You stare at me— but so it is! I shall be merciful! [*She turns to the others.*] You all know the old custom, don't you, that when a woman stands condemned of a capital offence, as she does, she can be freed and her life saved if an honest man steps forward and proclaims her innocence and declares himself ready and willing to marry her. You know the custom?

ALL. Yes, yes!

ALFHILD [*bursting into tears*]. Oh, that I should have to be mocked— mocked so pitilessly in my last moments!

LADY KIRSTEN. Well then, Alfhild! You shall have the benefit of this custom. If even the humblest man in my service steps forward and declares himself willing to marry you, then you are free? [*She looks about her.*] Does anyone volunteer? [*All remain silent.*] Put the silver crown on her. That shall be part of the bargain. Perhaps this increases your value, Alfhild! [*The crown is placed upon* ALFHILD'*s head.*] For the second time I ask: Is anybody willing to save her? [*She looks around; all are silent.*] This is it, then. I fear your moments are numbered. Hear me well, you men up there. If at the third call nobody answers, then act on my signal and cast her into the lake! Now use your arts, Alfhild! See if you can conjure yourself out of death. [*In a loud voice.*] For the last time! There stands the witch and fire-raiser! Who will marry her and save her?

> [*She looks about her. All are silent.* LADY KIRSTEN *quickly raises her hand to give the signal. The* SERVANTS *seize* ALFHILD. *At the same moment* OLAF *rushes out on the ledge in full wedding apparel.*]

OLAF. I will marry her and save her!

> [*He pushes the* SERVANTS *aside and unties her.* ALFHILD *sinks with a cry on his breast. He puts his left arm round her, and raises his right arm in defiance.*]

ALL [*standing rooted and shouting*]. Olaf Liljekrans!

LADY KIRSTEN. Olaf Liljekrans, my son! What have you done. Disgraced yourself for ever!

OLAF. No, I am blotting out all the shame and disgrace which I brought on myself by the way I treated her! I shall atone for my wrongs, and in so doing bring happiness to myself! [*Leads* ALFHILD *forward.*] Yes, before you all I solemnly declare this young woman to be my bride! She is innocent of all she has been accused of. I alone have done wrong. [*Kneels before her.*] And at your feet I beg you to forgive and forget . . .

ALFHILD [*raises him up*]. Ah, Olaf! You have given me back all the glory of the world!

LADY KIRSTEN. You mean to marry her. Very well, then I am no longer mother to you!

OLAF. That gives me great sorrow, although it is a long time since you were any true mother to me. You used me only to buttress your own pride. I was weak and acquiesced. But now I have found strength and willpower. Now I stand firmly on my own feet and lay the foundations for building my own happiness!

LADY KIRSTEN. But don't you consider . . . ?

OLAF. There is nothing more to consider. I know what I want. Only now do I understand my strange dream. It was foretold that I should find the fairest flower, and that I should pluck it apart and scatter it to the winds. Oh, that is what has happened! A woman's heart is the fairest flower in the world; all its rich and golden petals I have torn apart and scattered to the winds. But be comforted, Alfhild! Many a seed has gone, too. Sorrow has nurtured them, and from them shall grow a rich life for us in the valley. For here we shall live and build!

ALFHILD. Oh, now I am as happy as in the first moment we met!

LADY KIRSTEN [*aside*]. Ingeborg is gone. . . . This rich valley belongs to Alfhild. Nobody else has any right to it. . . . [*Aloud.*] Well then, Olaf! I shall not stand in the way of your happiness. If you think you can find it in this fashion, well. . . . You have my consent!

OLAF. Thank you, mother! Thank you! Now I lack for nothing!

ALFHILD [*to* LADY KIRSTEN]. And you forgive me all my wrongs?

LADY KIRSTEN. Well, perhaps there was some wrong on my side as well. Let us say no more about it!

ARNE. But what about me? And my daughter, to whom Olaf had pledged . . . ? And yet . . . perhaps she is no longer alive!

OLAF. Indeed she is alive!

ARNE. She lives! Where is she? Where?

OLAF. That I cannot say. But what can be said is that the two of us have amicably broken the engagement.

LADY KIRSTEN. You see, Sir Arne, that I . . . !

ARNE. Yes, yes, my daughter shall not be forced upon anyone. Alfhild was destined to marry a knight. The same might well be true of Ingeborg. [*With dignity.*] Noble lords and gentle men! Hear me! It has come to my ears that among many of you I am taken for a man little practised in courtly manners and customs! It is said in the old chronicles that when a good King loses his daughter, he promises her hand and half his kingdom to the one who finds her again.—I shall do as the good old Kings did. He who finds Ingeborg shall have her hand and half my possessions as well. Is everyone agreed?

THE YOUNG MEN. Yes, yes!

SCENE IX

[*As before.* INGEBORG *hurries out from the house, drawing* HEMMING *after her.*]

INGEBORG. Here I am! Hemming has found me!

ALL [*astonished*]. Ingeborg and Hemming! Up here!

ARNE [*angrily*]. Ah, in that case . . .

INGEBORG [*throwing her arms about his neck*]. Oh, father, father! That will do you no good! You have given your word!

ARNE. It did not apply to him! I now see it all! He took you away himself!

INGEBORG. On the contrary, father! I was the one who took him away!

ARNE [*terrified*]. You mustn't say things like that! Are you mad?

INGEBORG [*in a low voice*]. Then say 'yes', right here on the spot! Or else I shall tell everybody that it was I who . . .

ARNE. Be silent! Of course I'll say 'yes'! [*He steps between them and looks sternly at* HEMMING.] So it was you who stole my dapple-grey horse with saddle and bridle?

HEMMING. Ah, Sir Arne . . . !

ARNE. Oh, Hemming! Hemming! You are a . . . [*Catches himself.*] Well, you are my daughter's betrothed. Let us leave it at that.

HEMMING *and* INGEBORG. Oh, thank you, thank you!

SCENE X

[*As before.* THORGEJR *with a harp in his hand has already mingled among the people during the foregoing.*]

THORGEJR. Aye, look now! Lots of people about in the valley today!

THE PEASANTS. Thorgejr the minstrel!

ALFHILD [*throws herself into his arms*]. My father!

ALL. Her father!

OLAF. Yes, old man! Lots of people and lots of merriment here today! And that is how it is going to be from now on. It is your daughter's wedding we are celebrating. Love has guided her choice of husband; love is what you sang to her about—you will not stand in our way!

THORGEJR. May all the good spirits watch over you!

ALFHILD. And you will remain with us?

THORGEJR. No, no, Alfhild!

> A minstrel has no settled home,
> He wanders far, he finds no rest!
> The man who has music in his breast
> Finds no home in the hills, no home by the coast.
> On the leafy slopes, on the meadow green
> He must sing and pluck the vibrating string.

Mii

He must watch the life that is secretly led
By the rushing stream, the savage fjord.
He must watch the life that beats in the breast,
And set the dreams of the people to words,
And clear their fermenting thoughts!

OLAF. But at times you must certainly visit us here!
We shall build a hall by the birch trees there.
Here, my Alfhild, your life is secured.
I and my love will always be near;
And never a tear shall dim your eyes!

ALFHILD. Now I can see that life is rich!
Rich as the fairest poem of my heart!
No sorrow was ever so black and drear
That was never relieved by a bright sunny morn!

[Kneels.]

God's angels small! You have guided my steps,
And given me solace and peace again!
You directed my path at the edge of the abyss,
And supported my feet that were feeble and weak!
Although my mind can scarce understand,
I can trust my heart to my dying day!
Yes, heavenly powers! You watch always!
The sun shines bright when the storm is past—
My love was saved from the fire of life.
Let come and happen now what may!
Now I am cheerful, now I am strong,
Ready for life and its varied demands!

[With a glance at OLAF.*]*

And when we in time . . .

[She breaks off and raises her hands high in the air.]

On angel arms
Home we shall ride in the carriage of heaven!

[The others have formed a group about her; the curtain falls.]

⟨ALFHILD *crossed out*⟩

'THE MOUNTAIN BIRD'

Romantic Opera
in
Three Acts
by
Henr. Ibsen

Christiania
1859

CHARACTERS

IVAR, a rich old farmer

INGEBORG, his daughter

SVEND, in his service

KNUT SKYTTE, a young farmer

THORGEJR, a minstrel

ALFHILD

Chorus of Wedding Guests

Chorus of Elfin People

The action takes place in a mountainous region some years after the Black Death

ACT ONE

SCENE ONE

A wild mountain valley shut in by steep rocky sides; a swift river rushes down from the snowfields in the background, and disappears into the scree, right. Birch trees cover the mountainside, left. The entire landscape glows in the red sunset; gradually dusk falls.

THORGEJR sits playing by the waterfall. ALFHILD lies pensively under the trees, left.

THORGEJR.

The song that echoes
In rushing waters—
The tune that rustles
Through mountain birches—
That sound so tempting
In leaf and branch—
Seems to require
A minstrel's reply!

[*The grassy mound opens; the elfin folk come out quietly and listen.*]

CHORUS OF ELFIN FOLK.

Hush! and hark!
Elfin folk
Gladly will a-dancing go!
Summer night
Falls a-right
To go tripping over the hill!

THORGEJR.

The song that echoes
etc. etc.

ALFHILD [*dreaming*].

The song that echoes
In rushing waters
Carries within it
A heavy lament.
That sound that rustles
In leaf and branch
Seems to require
Reply from the heart!

all
together

CHORUS OF ELFIN FOLK [*as they quietly approach*].
> Alfhild the comely!
> Softly, softly—
> Do not disturb her
> While she is dreaming!
> Hear the strings sobbing,
> Hear the falls singing!
> The hillside re-echoes
> As we step to our dancing!

all
together

[THORGEJR *plays*; ALFHILD *seems to listen in her dreams, while the* ELFIN FOLK *dance, and repeat:*]
> Hear the strings sobbing
> etc. etc.

CHORUS OF WEDDING GUESTS [*off-stage, right, in the distance*].
> Wake up, wake up, you Christian man!
> Why sleep you so long and so heavy!

CHORUS OF ELFIN FOLK.
> Ooh! Ooh!
> Fear and dread
> Fill the hearts of the elfin folk!
> Hurry! be quick!
> The mountain ridge—
> Hide you there, and you'll be safe!

[*They disappear.*]

all
together

CHORUS OF WEDDING GUESTS [*still off-stage, but nearer*].
> Wake up, wake up, you Christian man!
> Why sleep you so long and so heavy!

⟨ALFHILD [*springs up*].
> Ah, what is this? Along the valley
> A party of gentlefolk!
> Never before did I see such a thing.
> They're coming! Now where can I hide? *crossed out*⟩

[*She takes refuge in the hillside, left.* IVAR, INGEBORG, SVEND *and* WEDDING GUESTS *enter from the right.*]

CHORUS OF GUESTS.
> See where the mountain bare and steep
> Stands in the evening shadow!
> Darkness is falling! Soon it is night.
> See! Beyond the rocky peaks
> The gleam of ice and snow!

SVEND.	Master, were you to heed my words— Swift as the wind you would return. You recall—there is danger up here!
INGEBORG.	And legend says that the nixies' game Does craze all men who lose their way, And they never return again!
IVAR.	Stupid tales!
INGEBORG.	Turn back!
THE GUESTS.	Turn back!
SVEND.	Yes, back to the village!
INGEBORG.	Oh, come!
THE GUESTS.	Oh, come!
SVEND.	Deserted this valley for many a year. Him whom you seek you'll never find. Master—if you only knew. . . .
IVAR.	If I knew what?
THE GUESTS.	Say what it is!

SVEND.	If you but knew the smallest part
	Of what I myself have endured here!
	   I once was hunting reindeer
	   Within yon distant mountains,
	   When sounds came from a chasm
	   As though a woman were singing!

THE GUESTS.	Accursed this valley from that dark day When plague imposed its fatal mark On the last survivor!
SVEND.	I peeped beyond the hillside, I looked in the rushing waters. There sat she . . .

[*He points to the background where* THORGEJR *sits; all catch sight of him and withdraw to one side in astonishment.*]

THE GUESTS.	Thorgejr! Thorgejr!
SVEND.	So master! Now you can judge!

THE GUESTS [*whispering among themselves*].
                            Hulder's calls
                            Song of the falls,
                            He has learnt!

THORGEJR [*rises and steps forward*].
                            Quick! As one!
                            Across the hill!
                            If life you love!

SVEND *and* INGEBORG. See, he threatens!

THE WOMEN.   Woe that we did come so far!

THORGEJR.   The elfin folk's assembly rooms
                   Open wide their doors at night!
                   If you feel inclined for dancing,
                        I shall play!

IVAR.   Softly! softly!

INGEBORG *and* THE WOMEN.
                   I am almost numb with terror!

THE GUESTS.   Down to the village! Down, yes, down!
                   This is an accursed place!

THORGEJR.   Accursed, yes! You speak the truth!
                   Humankind has no place here!
                   Long ago were buried here
                   The last remaining man and woman!
                   The plague went sweeping through the land
                   From farm to farm; and people died.
                   Winter and spring have come and gone,
                   But still the valley lies deserted!

THE GUESTS.   Down to the village! etc.

THORGEJR [*to* IVAR].
                   Your daughter wears a golden crown!

IVAR [*raging*].   Tomorrow to the altar she should go
                   But the bridegroom is not to be found!

THORGEJR.   The hulder's hall has a gate so strong.
                   The woes of the world are there forgotten.
                   He who once has gone therein
                        Never returns
                   To the light of day, to the summer sun.

THE GUESTS.   He never returns
                      To the light of day, to the summer sun!

IVAR.   Strike him down! He bodes us ill!

INGEBORG *and* SVEND.
                      Softly! softly!

THE GUESTS.   Further, ever further onward,
                      Though we go with fearful hearts!
                      Knut Skytte! Knut Skytte!
                      The mountain door you watch in silence!
                      We call your name in the cool of the evening—
                      Tarry no more in the hulder's hall!

[THORGEJR *vanishes beside the river; the others go out, left; gradual transition to the following:*]

INVISIBLE CHOIR OF ELFIN FOLK.
                      He never returns
                      To the light of day . . . to the summer sun!

[ALFHILD *and* KNUT *appear up on the hillside, left.*]

ALFHILD.   Listen! In the distance . . . there!

KNUT.   Like the sound of horns and bells!
                      Seeking to release the victim
                      From the magic mountain.
                      Let them sing, and let them tempt me,
                      Let forgotten memories cluster
                          In my bosom,
                              There resounding.
                      Shut is the village there below me
                      There I'll never go!

ALFHILD.   Fair as the song of the lark in springtime
                      Is the way you compose your words.
                      Birds in the trees and leaves in the valley
                      Seem to be heeding, seem to be listening!
                      Truly your home is far, far away
                          Beyond the forest!
                      Truly you must be the fair young man
                      Renowned in song and legend—
                      He who was destined to meet my desire
                          In the lonely nights!

Rowan and cherry grew on the slopes,
And cloudberries ripe in the marsh.
I sheltered so snug in the lee of the hill,
A sister to creatures all.
The Old Man of the Waterfall sang in my sleep
The fairest of all his songs—
This meant that I lived both happy and warm,
Forgetting I was alone!

He sang of a people I never saw—
Of ladies and handsome men—
Of something I often brooded upon—
Of love. Do you know what I mean?
He sang of a valley I'd never known,
He called it the wide, wide world—
This caused me to be both early and late
Possessed of a secret despair!

KNUT.
I had my land, and I had my gold;
They gave me a loving bride.
But still my desire was dark and deep,
And I fled from bride and home.
In frenzy I wandered—till I found you,
My fairest of summer joys!
Knut Skytte's path will never now lead
To those Christian lands below!

ALFHILD [*in delight*].
He is found, he is found—
He who often
Lived within in the Old Man's songs.
He who seemed to
Me to beckon
Through the voice of
Thrush and starling;
He is found, he is found!
Now is Alfhild's springtime dawned!

KNUT.
She is found, she is found!
Fine and comely,
Summer-bright as meadow-flower!
Never will I
Miss my homeland,
If I but have
Her to fondle!
She is found, she is found!
Fairest springtime now has dawned!

ALFHILD.   He is found, he is found!
            He who often
            Lived within in the Old Man's songs
            etc. etc.
                                                    } all
KNUT.   She is found, she is found!   together
            Fine and comely,
            Summer bright as meadow-flower!
            etc. etc.

[INGEBORG *and* SVEND *have made their appearance up on the hillside, left, during the foregoing.*]

INGEBORG *and* SVEND.
            He is found, he is found!
            See, a woman
            Seems to hold him here bewitched.
                Doubtless he's been
                Sorely tempted,
                And has lost both
                Sense and reason!
            He is found, he is found!
            Saddest day for me has dawned!
                                                    } all
ALFHILD.   He is found, he is found!   together
            He who often
            Lived within in the Old Man's songs!
            etc. etc.

KNUT.   She is found, she is found!
            Fine and comely,
            Summer bright as meadow-flower!
            etc. etc.

[INGEBORG *and* SVEND *hurry out unseen again, left.*]

KNUT.   Snug in the hill I will build us a home,
            Here we will live our life together—
            Living as free as the reindeer wild
                Over the glacier's ridge!

ALFHILD.   No, beyond the ice-blue ridge,
            Far into life beyond I must go!
            Alfhild's vale is too narrow for me,
            In the vale of life one can play and sing!
                Into the world!
                Loyal and true

Come along and be my guide!
High on mountains
Twisting the footpaths—
There like the scudding
Clouds and the rushing
Rivers we'll make towards life!

KNUT. Yes, I'll come with you,
Hiding from no one
The treasure I won up here!
Hither shall hasten
Girls to attend you,
Servants shall follow
Singing your praises,
Alfhild, my fairest, in truth!

CHORUS OF GUESTS [*off-stage, left*].
He is found, he is found!
Now the great day has dawned!

KNUT [*as though coming to his senses*].
Woe is me!
My dream is ended!

ALFHILD [*overjoyed*].
See! Oh, see!
Oh, what delight!
Men and women at your call
Come here singing,
Dressed in their finery,
All in your honour,
To welcome your bride!

[IVAR, INGEBORG, SVEND *and* THE GUESTS *enter, left.* ALFHILD *stands somewhat apart, right, without being noticed and follows with great attention the following scene but without hearing what it is all about.*]

THE GUESTS. Now the bridegroom has been found
Where he stood as though bewitched!
Cares are over!
Music and dancing shall there be
Down at the house from early morn!

INGEBORG [*to* SVEND].
See how he stands with a heavy heart!

IVAR [*to* KNUT]. What has occurred?

KNUT [*aside*].   What shall I answer?

THE GUESTS.   You can clear these matters later.

[*To* KNUT.]

Homeward now, to keep your promise!

KNUT [*in a low, sad voice, with a glance at* ALFHILD].
                   Must I cause her so much anguish!

THE GUESTS.   Priest is waiting, the table is spread
                       For the wedding feast.
                   Short and easy the path to church.
                   Tomorrow we hear in the lofty nave
                       The sacred marriage vows!
                   Come, follow us! Away!

KNUT [*battling with himself*].
                   Yes, I'm coming. But . . . she comes too!

[*He points to* ALFHILD, *who approaches; all draw back fearfully.*]

THE GUESTS.   Ah, a woman! She's the woman
                   Who has turned his heart away
                   From his dear beloved!

IVAR.   Notwithstanding who she is,
                   She shall come along with us!

[*Aside to* KNUT.]

Whatever has happened, reveal it not.
See, your bride is near!

ALFHILD [*to* THORGEJR *who unnoticed has joined the group*].
                   He is found, he is found
                   He who lay like gleaming gold
                       In my stream of thought!

THE GUESTS.   She's the woman, she's the woman
                   Who has turned etc.

THORGEJR.   Then, alas, your flower will wither;   all
                   Frozen hard by icy winter   together
                   Is your secret dream!

IVAR *and* THE GUESTS.
                   To the village she must follow!
                   Not in church will it stay hidden
                   Who she really is!

KNUT.   Now, ah woe, will Alfhild follow!
                Not in church can it stay hidden
                Which one is the bride.

INGEBORG.   To the altar I'll not follow
                One who rather would stay hidden   } all
                Beside his heart's desire.   together

SVEND.   Fairest Ingeborg must follow
                Him as wife; while I keep hidden
                All the pain I feel!

[*The twilight has now reached its darkest point, and it gradually begins again to grow light. The* ELFIN FOLK *appear upon the hillside in the background.*]

ALFHILD.   He has come, he is found,
                    He who often
                Sang to me within your strings!
                    Worldly fortune
                    Draws me onward,
                    Through the sound of
                    Horn and bells!
                He has come, he is found!
                Now is Alfhild's springtime dawned!

KNUT.   Long bewitched and mind-bereft
                    Have I been.
                Shut myself away from living.
                    Light and peace was
                    In my bosom.
                    Now shall sorrow   } all
                    Wound me deeply.   together
                Skytte's carefree life is over.
                Saddest day for me is dawned.

INGEBORG *and* SVEND.
                He is found, he is found.
                    Here a woman
                Holds him in her magic power.
                    From tomorrow,
                    From tomorrow,
                    Fast shall I be
                    Bound to sorrow!
                Woe to me that he was found;
                Saddest day for me is dawned!

THORGEJR.   Now is dawned the day of trial!
            Here you've always
       Lived upon my songs and music.
          Now by leaving
          You shall suffer
          Worldly anguish,
          Worldly sorrow.
       But if the castle is burnt to rubble,
       Me you'll see in your hour of trouble!

IVAR *and* THE GUESTS.
       Now the bridegroom has been found!
          Long he listened
       To the witching strings up here.
           But tomorrow,
           Yes, tomorrow
           We forget our
           Fear and sorrow!
       Through the grove at the midnight hour
       To the village we make our way!

                                                       all
                                                 together

CHORUS OF ELFIN FOLK.
       Hail and farewell at this our parting!
          Where you're going,
       No power have we to follow you there!
          You are going
          Chasing fortune;
          All you'll find is
          Grief and sorrow.
       Soon your lovely dream will vanish.
       Visit us then in your hour of trouble!

[*The* ELFIN FOLK *wave flowers and twigs as* ALFHILD, *overjoyed, accompanies the departing group; they all leave, right, except* THORGEJR *who remains behind by the river, pensive.*]

⟨Change of scene *crossed out*⟩

ACT TWO

The enclosure at IVAR's *estate. The residential building is seen half up-stage,*
right; the storehouse and other buildings, left. In the background a thickly-
wooded hillside with a mountain ridge above. Evening is approaching. Eight
BRIDESMAIDS, *with* INGEBORG *in a wedding dress, come from the storehouse.*

THE MAIDS.   Now she is dressed in her brooches and crown.

                     [*Eight pages appear from the house with* KNUT SKYTTE.]

THE PAGES.   Now he is ready to fetch his wife.

CHORUS OF BOTH.

                  Today there is joy in this festive house!
                  Forgotten the pangs of yesterday's sorrows.

INGEBORG.   Worse are the sorrows that afflict me today!

KNUT.   Were I up there beyond ice and snow—
                     Far, far up there
                     Past the edge of the forest . . .

CHORUS.   Today there is joy etc.

                      [IVAR *and* SVEND *enter, right.*]

IVAR.   Is the table spread . . . ?

SVEND.   Yes, master, yes!

IVAR.   And the ale is foaming thick and well?

SVEND.   Yes, master, yes!

IVAR.   The way to church is long to ride.
                  Depart we must while still is night.
                  Torches of pine shall light our way.
                  From the wedding place to the holy house.

                  ⟨*The manuscript breaks off here abruptly.*⟩

OLAF LILJEKRANS: OPERA FRAGMENT

ACT ONE

A wild mountain valley, narrow and with steep rocky walls on both sides.
Left, a waterfall down the rock face. In the background a distant view down
to the village far below. It is dusk on a summer evening.
TORGEJR *stands by the waterfall, listening and looking down into the*
depths.

TORGEJR.
Who are they who ⟨come in a group together *crossed out and replaced by* climb
the green hillside *again crossed out and replaced by*⟩ climb the fir-clad hill?
Women and men in a thronging crowd!
Stay down below! The village is far!
Do not approach!
The sun's going down—
And the valley is mine and the sprite's.

LADY GURID'S FOLLOWERS [*distant and far below, left rear*].
Young Olaf! young Olaf! With song and with bells
We summon and call thee.

ARNE'S FOLLOWERS [*high up, right*].
Through the pass goes the ⟨march *crossed out*⟩ way
To the wedding place;
Over the highest heath
We take our way.

TORGEJR [*looks upward*].
There too! there too! By ⟨the glacier *crossed out*⟩ summit and peak,
⟨Forward *crossed out*⟩ Hither they swarm
Both men and women!
May avalanche crush you,
And landslide ⟨crush *crossed out*⟩ ravage you,
Till the Judgement Day!

LADY GUNHILD'S ⟨*sic*⟩ FOLLOWERS [*approaching*].
Young Olaf! young Olaf! Where art thou, bewitched?
Oh waken! oh, see!
We wander in woe!
Where wert thou, bewitched, these three long nights
And this fourth long day?

ARNE'S FOLLOWERS [*closer, at the same time*].
    Merry and gay
    The games we play
    Among the peaks and summits.
    By the glacier's edge
    We dance our way.
    Heigh ho! We leap the river!

TORGEJR [*looking both upwards and downwards*].
    May the glacier crush you!
    The river swallow you!
    May trolls and spirits
    Scare you away with shrieks and howls,
    Wherever you may set foot!
    The valley is mine and the sprite's.

[*He withdraws into a cleft by the waterfall.* PEIK *comes with his followers down the mountain side, right.*]

PEJK ⟨*sic*⟩.
    Well able are you to leap and hop
    ⟨I can manage no more; I have stiff legs *crossed out*⟩
    But I can manage no more;
    I am stiff in both limbs and joints.

ESPEN.
    Down here it goes.

PEJK.   Let us halt a while.

SEVERAL [*in low voices*].
    Let us go; it is eerie, and ⟨day's far gone *crossed out*⟩ night is near.

⟨INGEBO *crossed out*⟩ GERTRUD [*looks over and down*].
    See there, who comes . . . !

SEVERAL.   Who comes, who comes?

GERTRUD.
    Lady Gunhild with all her kith and kin.

PEJK AND HIS FOLLOWERS.
    Lady Gunhild!

[LADY GUNHILD AND HER RETINUE *come up from below, left.*]

GUNHILD.   Pejk of Botn, are you here?

PEJK. As you see! I always keep my word.
  Three days from today the wedding will be.
  But there's no way through from Botn to Borg.
  An avalanche carried away the road.
  Nor were there boats for as many as us.
  But I must and will uphold my word.

GUNHILD. You've crossed ⟨Bad Mountain *crossed out*⟩ Troll Mountain?

PEJK.   Straight over the top.

GUNHILD'S WOMEN.
  There, where even the day is haunted;
  There, where there's magic by night! Hu-hu!

PEJK. But I never expected to meet you here.

GUNHILD. You must let me explain . . .

PEJK.   A very great honour!
  Coming to meet me with maids and with men.
  I imagined you busy preparing the wedding.
  Imagined you baking, brewing and roasting—
  With your hands quite full, not a moment to spare . . .

GUNHILD. If only you knew ⟨what sorrow *crossed out*⟩ the grief that I bear.

PEJK. What sorrow?

GERTRUD.   Where is Olaf?

PEJK.   I do not see Olaf.

APPENDIX I

CATILINE: COMMENTARY

1. Dates of composition
2. Draft manuscripts
3. The revised play (1875)
4. Public reception

1. DATES OF COMPOSITION

The following account of the composition of *Catiline* supplements Ibsen's own version in the Preface to the Second Edition (translated above, pp. 109–12).

Ole Schulerud took the manuscript to Christiania in September 1849 and received a notice of rejection from the Christiania Theatre in December. Replying, on 5 January 1850, to Schulerud's news of '*Catiline*'s death sentence' Ibsen wrote:

'... It distresses me, but there is no point in losing heart. You are quite right that this apparent defeat should not in fact be considered as such. *Catiline* was after all only intended as a precursor of our agreed plans along these lines and may still fulfil its purpose just the same. I am entirely of your opinion that it is best to sell the play and I think that its rejection, to go by what they write from the theatre, will be beneficial rather than detrimental to us, because the reason it was not accepted does not seem to have been any lack of intrinsic quality. You will, of course, negotiate the sale of the play as you think best. I would only observe that it seems better to me to sell the publishing rights than to have it printed privately, as in the latter case we would have to pay out quite a tidy sum of money to cover printing costs and, moreover, would only gradually get anything back, whereas in the first case it would simply be a matter of receiving the honorarium—but this must be arranged according to circumstances.'

The same letter contains the unprinted preface to the first version (translated below, p. 580). The book was privately published on 12 April 1850 with the author's name given as Brynjolf Bjarme.

Encouraged by the promised success of new editions of *The League of Youth* and *Lady Inger of Østråt* Ibsen wrote, on 23 November 1874, to his Danish publisher, Frederik Hegel, about the possibilities of a revised edition of *Catiline*:

'But now I have another suggestion to submit to your consideration. Next year I am celebrating the 25th anniversary both of my matriculation and of my literary career. For it was in March [*sic*] 1850 that the three-act drama *Catiline* was published, the first book of mine to be printed. It is a work containing much that is good, side by side with much that is immature; in recent years critics have often emphasized that it was characteristic of me to have made my début with this play, and I myself am bound to agree with them because I feel now that it is closely related to my circumstances at the time and that it contains the germs of much that has come out in my later writings. So I had been thinking of giving an account of this and other things in a preface and at the same time of preparing a new, corrected edition of the book. The thoughts and ideas would not be touched, only the language; because, as Brandes has said somewhere, the verses are bad, this being due to the fact that my first hastily scribbled manuscript was used uncorrected when the book was printed.

'I for my part think that this poetic work will be received with a good deal of interest, and that those who possess my other works will also buy this one. The book is now only known to the public by repute; in its time some 60–100 copies at the most were in circulation and I myself was a witness when the remainder of the edition was sold as waste paper.

'I would like to hear your frank opinion about this suggestion. If you doubt whether it would be a good idea, please say so. If you do agree to it I would be most grateful if you would get me a copy of the book as soon as possible, because the whole thing will have to be written out for the printer in view of all the corrections and rewriting; and the new edition should, of course, preferably be published at the same time of year as the first. The borrowed copy shall be returned undamaged; I assume it will be possible to obtain one from one of the big libraries.'

Hegel immediately agreed to Ibsen's proposal. The revision was done in December 1874 and the following January. On 27 January Ibsen dispatched the manuscript to Hegel. Remaining copies of the first edition were withdrawn from sale and the second edition was published in March.

2. DRAFT MANUSCRIPTS

One almost complete draft manuscript and two fragmentary scenarios of *Catiline* have survived. These are all to be found in two notebooks, quarto, now in the University Library, Oslo.

(a) Scenarios

The two scenarios, here called I and II, were written in the first of the draft manuscript notebooks, on the last and last but one pages respectively. It is to be inferred that Scenario I is older than II because, *inter alia*, Furia is called Fulvia in the former. Moreover II is closer to the completed play than is the relevant section of I.

The scenarios, of which II is scored through, were probably written at about the same time as the play. It is even possible that the play was begun before the scenarios because the first scene of the completed play (Catiline's soliloquy) was originally lacking in the draft manuscript but is apparently envisaged in Scenario I.

SCENARIO I

Scenario

ACT ONE

1

The Appian Way near Rome

Catiline; conversation with the Allobroges. . . .

2

The Forum

Lentulus, Cethegus, etc. Allusion to the conspiracy. Decision to approach Catiline.

3

The Temple of Vesta

A vestal. Catiline and Curius enter unobserved, the former for a meeting with Fulvia. She enters; conversation between her and Catiline. Catiline is warned that Aurelia is coming; he flees. Fulvia wildly excited; the sacred flame goes out . . . people swarm in; she is led away . . . Curius resolves to rescue her. . . .

4

Catiline's house

Catiline and Aurelia conversing; he is agitated . . . she soothes him. An old man enters to beg for help in procuring his son's release from the debtors' prison. . . . Catiline gives him all he has left.

5

The subterranean cavern

Fulvia frantic and despairing . . . Curius rescues her. . . .

ACT TWO

I

Catiline's residence

Catiline alone, in a state of indecision. Cethegus has been with him and prepared him for a visit from the conspirators. . . . Aurelia enters; discovers the reason for his restlessness.

SCENARIO II

ACT TWO

A room in Catiline's house

Lentulus and Cethegus have told him of their friends' decision . . . and invited him to lead the enterprise . . . but he refuses and they leave. . . . Soliloquy. . . . Furia appears. . . . He gets worked up to fever-pitch and dashes off to where the conspirators are meeting. . . .

A tavern

The conspirators are gathered together. . . . L. & C. enter and report on the result of their mission and L. offers to lead the enterprise . . . which meets with approval. However, Catiline rushes in like a madman, offers to be leader, and all of them gladly join him. They talk of the conspiracy, and Cethegus goes to the Allobroges to get them to take part in it. . . .

A garden, with Catiline's house in the background

Curius is pacing up and down, guarding the entrance . . . Furia appears . . . animated conversation. . . . He declares his ardent love and she demands that he prove it by informing against the conspirators. . . . Conflict between love and duty . . . the former wins and he departs. . . . Furia alone . . . . The Allobroges come out of the house, discussing the conspiracy . . . she comes forward . . . warns them . . . they are frightened and decide to withdraw. . . . Catiline comes out of the house. . . . Soliloquy. Aurelia seeks him out and tries to persuade him to abandon the whole thing . . . in vain . . . and she decides to follow him. . . . She goes indoors. . . . Catiline alone. . . . She comes back, armed. . . . The conspirators assemble . . . Furia is among them . . . they all hurry away. . . .

(b) The draft text of the play

Each of the two notebooks in which it is written originally consisted of 16 leaves. Additional leaves, some loose, some stuck in, others (in the second book) sewn in, now give a total of 18 + 29 leaves, or 47 in all. The last leaf of the second notebook has been cut out and the manuscript ends with Aurelia's words: 'No, to the right, towards Elysium' (see p. 106). The author's final note is also missing. On the title page, which lacks the author's name, the manuscript is dated 1849 and the date 25/2–49 is written at the end of Act Two.

The manuscript, which differs only slightly from the 1850 book version, is generally written in a rapid hand with varying degrees of legibility. The script is Roman but some of the corrections and additions are in Gothic script. While most of the corrections were made immediately, some were made later, apparently not always in Ibsen's hand. The reason for inferring that many of the corrections were made immediately are: (*a*) the text following the correction conforms to the sense of the correction; (*b*) the evidence of rhyme. This was probably then the original manuscript, not a copy. However, it is possible that, sporadically at any rate, Ibsen had some sort of copy before him, perhaps on loose sheets of paper. This is suggested by the fact that lines 28–9 on p. 52 were written twice (and corrected) in the manuscript.

Three of the corrections in the manuscript may be mentioned here:

(i) The play originally began on page 3 of the manuscript with the scene between the Gaulish envoys, thus:

ACT ONE

View from the Appian Way—Rome in the background; it is evening. AMBIORIX, OLLOVICO, *with several attendants, enter from the right.* ⟨*Added later: without noticing* CATILINE.⟩

The words ACT ONE have been crossed out and transferred to page 2, where Catiline's soliloquy has been added, under the stage direction *A road near Rome.*

(ii) The scene headed *A colonnade in Rome* (see p. 42) was originally entitled *The Forum*, abandoned rather more than half-way through, and crossed out. A folded sheet was subsequently inserted, containing virtually the same text as that of 1850. The rejected text is also almost the same, as far as it goes, but some of the roles are differently apportioned. Of the five characters mentioned in the stage directions, the name of Cethegus has been crossed out and the part later to be played by him is taken by Statilius. In the approved manuscript insertion Gabinius is deleted from the stage directions in favour of Cethegus, who now assumes his definitive role.

(iii) On the first occurrence Furia is called Fulvia (see p. 45), but the letters *lv* are scored through.

The corrections in the manuscript are mostly insignificant. They show a tendency towards a more elevated style and a greater concreteness of expression. Defective metre is occasionally corrected.

(c) Draft text and 1850 book version

Although there are many differences of detail between the draft manuscript and the book of 1850, in all essentials they agree. They also coincide in those parts where the scenarios printed above diverge from the book.

The most interesting difference between draft and book concerns Lentulus. In the former Lentulus is 'moved' when Catiline tells him he has no intention of resigning (see p. 95). This is corrected to 'hypocritically', as in the 1850 version, but the next speech, in which Lentulus shows his duplicity, is lacking in the draft. A small change in Act II is in line with this clearer focusing of Lentulus' character. The draft lacks the bracketed words in the following line (see p. 73):

ALL [*except for* LENTULUS]. Yes, Catiline, yes, we will follow you!

Of the other differences, we may mention the following:

(i) List of characters: Aurelia is, in the draft, Aurelia Orestilla; Curius is not stated to be related to Catiline; Coeparius is crossed out; the gladiators and the phantom are not mentioned; the places of the action are not given.

(ii) 'An old man' in the draft's list of characters is also thus designated in the text. The books of 1850 and 1875 call him 'An old soldier' in the text, but erroneously retain the words 'An old man' in the list of characters.

While one must assume that Ibsen was responsible for the changes introduced into the 1850 version it is clear that the fair copy, made by C. L. Due, submitted to the printers was not entirely accurate, not even in the matter of dashes, as Ibsen claims—Due has added a goodly sprinkling of his own. Some verses which are correct in the draft are defective in the book. The printer must doubtless take his share of the blame. But it is uncertain whether one curious change (see p. 39) should be ascribed to copyist, printer, or to Ibsen: in Catiline's first soliloquy we have the line 'It is too late! I have no aim in life!' This translation depends on the Norwegian *forbi*, but in the draft the word was *fordi*, which gives better sense: 'It is because I have no aim in life!'

(d) The unpublished preface

A preface Ibsen wrote for the 1850 version was not printed. In a letter to Schulerud (5 January 1850) he wrote:

'I think *Catiline* needs to have a few prefatory remarks, and would like you to copy and add the following:

PREFACE

The present play was originally meant for the stage, but the management of the theatre did not find it suitable. Despite the fact that the author has cause to suppose that the main reasons for the play's rejection are not its intrinsic defects, it is nevertheless not without very natural misgivings that he offers his work to the public, from whom however he expects the leniency which an absolute beginner may reasonably demand.'

3. THE REVISED PLAY (1875)

The revised play, the manuscript of which is in the University Library, Oslo, is identical with its predecessor in plot and construction. Yet although the 1875 version follows that of 1850 closely, scene by scene, usually line by line, there are numerous differences throughout, which increase as the play progresses and are most extensive in the final pages. The illustrative extract given on pp. 113–25 above is, for example, longer than the corresponding section of the 1850 version. In fact some 100 lines in all have been added to Acts II and III.

The alterations made in 1875 are largely of a stylistic nature: the language is more mature and the vocabulary more varied; the frequent use of proper names in the vocative ('Oh Catiline', 'Aurelia dear', etc.) has been reduced; exclamations have often been removed; and overworked words ('eternal', 'evermore', etc.) are less prominent. Occasional infelicities have also been ironed out, as on p. 47: 'who must shamefacedly recall Rome's past' which is now replaced by 'who with no sense of shame recall Rome's past'.

A number of specific changes may be mentioned:

(*a*) In the list of characters 'A phantom' is now 'Sulla's ghost'.

(*b*) The opening scene is set on the Flaminian Way.

(*c*) In 1850 the name Tullia did treble duty. In 1875 Cethegus' mistress (p. 43) has become Livia; Furia's sister is Silvia (p. 49); the Tullia of legendary history (p. 67) retains her name.

(*d*) Furia is now literally immured in Act I: a newly bricked-up wall replaces the iron door.

(*e*) Curius' treachery is more convincingly motivated: Furia holds out to him the promise of her favours.

(*f*) The Allobroges' decision to join the rebellion, previously unexplained, now follows a rejection of their plea by the Senate.

(*g*) The finishing touches are given to the characterization of Lentulus: (i) his line (see p. 76) 'Yes, yes, we will follow you' is transferred to Statilius; (ii) Lentulus tells the gladiators to stab Catiline in the back; (iii) the stage direction 'hypocritically' (see p. 580 above) is omitted, presumably now considered superfluous.

The occasionally defective pentameters of the 1850 version (reproduced in our translation) were corrected for the 1875 version, but the intermittent passages in rhyme (here given in blank verse) were retained. Deviations from iambic pentameters (e.g. the seven-beat trochaic verses in Act III) are common to both versions.

One curious feature of the 1875 edition is that it agrees here and there, in minor details, with the original (i.e. not yet corrected) forms of the 1849 draft manuscript, although this was no longer in Ibsen's possession when he revised the play.

4. PUBLIC RECEPTION

A long and appreciative review of *Catiline* appeared on the day after publication in the handwritten *Samfundsbladet,* a students' magazine which Ibsen himself was later to edit. This review, together with other contemporary criticism, has been printed by Karl Haugholt in *Edda,* vol. lii, 1952. The reviewer, Paul Botten Hansen, soon to become one of Ibsen's closest friends, noted that this was the first serious play to be published by a Norwegian since Wergeland's *The Venetians* (1843). Botten Hansen discerned in *Catiline,* which made no concessions to fashion, a certain Shakespearean strength and earnestness. He thought that the author *ought* to gain recognition in the theatre, but believed that the play might fail because it lacked a 'national' [Norwegian] theme and, some might erroneously argue, was not suited to the times. While making several adverse comments (e.g. the treatment of minor characters, faulty metre) he particularly praised the author's conception of the tragedy as a consequence of Catiline's inner conflict.

On 16 May 1850 *Christiania-Posten* printed an anonymous and less enthusiastic front-page review. The author, F. L. Vibe, a classical scholar, was disturbed by the departure from historical fact: Catiline was a rogue, not a hero. But despite criticism in detail (e.g. Catiline's killing of Aurelia, by which he forfeits our interest), the review was not on the whole discouraging. Although Vibe objected to the excessive pathos and declamation he thought 'the author has a rare talent for rising to tragic heights and strength, he has a rare talent for letting passions emerge in all their intensity, and his language is of a purity we rarely find'. The play revealed unmistakable talent, although it was scarcely suited for the stage on account of the numerous changes of scene.

Catiline had created a not inconsiderable sensation in the literary world, according to 'A', the anonymous reviewer in *Morgenbladet,* 5 July 1850. The review combined in general the opinions of the preceding critics and concluded that this was the work of a beginner of no ordinary talent. Recommending it to all serious lovers of literature, 'A' hoped the author would write more plays and, if possible, try his hand in the more rewarding field of Norwegian history.

In October 1850 *Norsk Tidsskrift,* Norway's leading literary periodical, published a long review under the pseudonym Tø. The reviewer, Carl Müller, another classical scholar, while prepared to accept a playwright's free treatment of history, objected to the author's conception of Catiline, partly because a well-known historical person must not be tampered with in essentials, partly because the characterization was confused and contradictory. The author had made him 'feeble and without character', and 'his whole being is an indeterminate groping and longing for something he himself is not clear about'. Müller admitted that this was a hard-hitting attack but nevertheless had high hopes of the author, congratulating him in particular (with reservations) on the language and poetry of the play. This review was followed by an editorial postscript in which Professor M. J. Monrad dissociated himself from Müller's views. The weakness of the play lay in superficialities which could be overcome with experience (e.g. careless metre, diffuseness, rhetorical excess); the basic idea of the play was clear and beautiful, namely the contrast between the moral principle and the individual's yearning for independence.

On the whole, then, the critics were not as unfavourable as Ibsen suggests in the Preface to the Second Edition. He himself seems to have taken a more cheerful view in a petition to the King, on 10 March 1863, for an annual grant of 400 Speciedaler, i.e. 1600 crowns. *Catiline,* he wrote, had been 'the subject of very favourable criticism by a number of reviewers, particularly in Lange's *Tidsskrift for Videnskab og Literatur* [*Norsk Tidsskrift*]'.

The book sold badly: of the edition of 250 copies only some forty had sold within a year. Not all the remaining stock was turned into waste paper—some was in the hands of the agent and there were copies in the bookshops—but by 1875, when the first edition was withdrawn, there were still fifty-five unsold copies.

Replying on 28 January 1880 to a letter from Ludvig Josephson, Ibsen agreed to a performance at the New Theatre, Stockholm. The honorarium asked was 400 crowns, on condition that the performance took place not later than 31 December 1881. In fact this, the Scandinavian première, was given on 3 December 1881. In a letter to Josephson, dated 25 January 1882, in which he refused a requested reduction in the agreed honorarium, Ibsen wrote: 'From your last letter I learn that the Stockholm performance of *Catiline* was not the success both you and I had expected. I am quite fond of this drama and still think that it must have a not inconsiderable effect on the stage, given an absolutely first-class production.' When the Norwegian première came, in August 1935 at the New Theatre, Oslo, Stein Bügge, the producer, treated the play in twentieth-century terms: drunken Romans entered the stage to jazz music, clad in togas and top hats, and Catiline and the conspirators wore German steel helmets.

The first (partial) translation of *Catiline* was into English: *Translations from the Norse,* by a B.S.S. [Andrew Johnston], Gloucester, 1879 (or 1880?). This volume, printed for private circulation, contains, *inter alia,* a translation of Act One of the second version and a résumé of the remainder. The only other English translation, also of the second version, seems to be that by Anders Orbeck in *Early Plays by Henrik Ibsen* (New York, 1921). The play was staged on 27 January 1936 at the Croydon Repertory Theatre, where it ran for one week before being transferred on 18 February to the Royalty Theatre, London. Donald Wolfit played the title role and the production was again by Stein Bügge. In a review on 1 February 1936 the *Croydon Advertiser,* reiterating an introductory speech by the producer, found that there 'seems to be manifest a tendency towards softer emotional colours than those to which we are accustomed in his mature work'. The reviewer made no mention of audience reaction, but of the play itself wrote: 'In its mould *Catiline* derives directly from the Greek tragic drama, exemplified here and there in detailed imitation. . . . It is in the essential treatment of the theme that the classical conception is apparent. Nemesis broods over the action from the very first scene, as dominating an influence as in *Oedipus Tyrannus* and *Macbeth*, and the technical devices of the Greek school are exploited in other ways with telling effect. That stress should be laid on the postulate that man's fate is determined by the elements of his own personality is the natural outcome of a nineteenth-century genius expressed in Athenian terms and thence too arises that moving picture of the entirely human love of Aurelia for her self-contradictory husband.'

According to a letter of 23 February 1896, Ibsen had himself read through a German translation by Paul Herrmann which had been in the possession of Fischer, the publisher, for some eight to ten years. Assuming that Fischer had abandoned any intention of publishing, Ibsen had already given another publisher permission to issue a German translation. This was presumably the authorized translation by Hugo Greinz (1896). The translation in the Complete Works is by Christian Morgenstern (1903). A French version also appeared in 1903.

APPENDIX II

IBSEN IN CHRISTIANIA 1850–1851

A. 1. Academic aspirations (p. 585). 2. Drama and lyric poetry (p. 586). 3. Journalistic activities (p. 587). 4. Contributions to *Samfundsbladet* (p. 587). 5. Contributions to *Manden/Andhrimner* (p. 589). 6. *Norma* (p. 592).

B. Details of plays produced in Christiania 1850–51 (p. 594).

C. 1. 'Professor Welhaven on Paludan-Müller's mythological poems' (p. 599). 2. Review of Karl Gutzkow, *Zopf und Schwert* (p. 600).

A 1. Ibsen's prime purpose in coming to Christiania was to study for his matriculation examination, and then to go on to university. He enrolled at a well-known crammer's—'Heltberg's student factory', as it was affectionately known—for the shortest of its courses: three months, instead of the more usual two years. He sat the examination in August 1850, and the result was disappointing; the certificate reads:

Henrik Johan Ibsen

presented himself for the *Examen artium* in August 1850,
and on the basis of his individual subject marks, viz:

— Norwegian	Good
— Latin translation	Good
— Latin composition	Fairly good
— Latin (oral)	Satisfactory
— Greek	Fail
— Hebrew	—
— German	Very Good
— French	Good
— Religion	Good
— History	Good
— Geography	Good
— Arithmetic	Fail
— Geometry	Good

received the overall result: *non contemnendus.*

Faculty of Philosophy, 3 Sep. 1850
(signed) J. S. Welhaven
Dean.

Technically, therefore, he had passed the examination; and this gave him the right of being addressed as 'Student Ibsen'. In practice, however, it meant that if he wished to continue with his ambition of studying at the University, he would need to re-sit in Greek and Arithmetic; and this he was not prepared to do. His examination success also entitled him to membership of the Students' Union, however; and it was there that Ibsen saw his opportunities.

A 2. From the first, Ibsen had no intention of allowing his studies to interfere too greatly with his writing. Within a few days of his arrival in Christiania he began work on revising a drama he had drafted in Grimstad and provisionally entitled 'The Normans'; this was the play that eventually became *The Burial Mound*.

After completing this drama, he then seems to have turned immediately to work on 'The Grouse in Justedal', the drama out of which *Olaf Liljekrans* eventually grew. The manuscript of 'The Grouse in Justedal' stops abruptly in the middle of Act Two; it is not known whether Ibsen had worked out any of the play beyond this point in draft form.

He also continued to write poetry. His work in this genre during these eighteen months in Christiania can conveniently be grouped under three main heads:

(a) the group of six poems which he sent in the autumn of 1850 'To Miss Clara Ebbell', a friend of his Grimstad days who had recently been on a visit to Christiania; they comprised:

> Ungdomsdrømme (Youthful Dreams)
> Sonetter (Sonnets)
> Bjergmanden (The Miner)
> I Natten (In the Night)
> Fugl og Fuglefænger (Bird and Bird-catcher)
> Blandt Ruiner (Among Ruins)

(b) the poems (including, it might be remarked, two of the above) which Ibsen published in the periodicals *Samfundsbladet* and *Manden/Andhrimner* (see section A 5 below) between January and July 1851:

Manden	12 Jan.	Svanen (The Swan)
„	19 Jan.	Paa Akershuus (At Akershuus)
Samfundsbladet	25 Jan.	Naturens stemme (Nature's voice)
Manden	26 Jan.	Gutten i Blaabærmyren (The Boy in the Blueberry Patch)
„	16 Feb.	Fugl og Fuglefænger (Bird and Bird-catcher)
„	4 Mar.	Taaren (The Tear)
,	6 and 20 Apr.	En Løverdagsaften i Hardanger (A Saturday Evening in Hardanger)
	27 Apr.	Edderfuglen (The Eider Duck)

Manden	1 June	Bjergmanden (The Miner)
,,	29 June	Til mine Abonnenter! (To my subscribers!)
Andhrimner 6, 13 and 20 July		Helge Hundingsbane

(c) a few occasional poems:

9 June 1851	For Danmark (For Denmark)
10 June 1851	Paa Ladegaardsøen (On the Island of Ladegaard)— both the above written for the Dano-Norwegian Student Congress in Christiania.
15 Oct. 1851	Prologue for the Evening Concert of the Students' Union in aid of the Norwegian Theatre in Bergen (translated pp. 608–10).

A 3. In 1851 Ibsen was elected one of the editors of the handwritten periodical of the Students' Union, *Samfundsbladet*. During the first quarter of the year (18 Jan.–1 Mar.), six numbers of the periodical appeared, of which nos. 2, 4 and 6 contained items from Ibsen's hand; in the second quarter from 5 April to 3 May, four numbers appeared, no. 3 of which had an item by Ibsen. Thereafter the periodical ceased to appear.

The reason for Ibsen's diminishing interest in *Samfundsbladet* was clearly the counter-attraction of the new weekly which Paul Botten Hansen started with the help of his friends Ibsen and A. O. Vinje in January 1851. The original intention was that Ibsen's contributions to it should be mainly poems—an appeal on 5 March for subscribers included reference to 'Poems by Brynjolf Bjarme [i.e. Ibsen]'—but it was not long before Ibsen was also contributing dramatic criticism, political commentaries and other articles of general interest. The paper also included some of Ibsen's drawings. Originally the paper, which had no formal title, was known as *Manden (The Man)*, from the drawing of a man on its front page; this name persisted for the first two quarters of its publication. For the third quarter of the year, it changed its name to *Andhrimner*— the name of the cook to the gods in Valhalla. Contributions were unsigned (apart from the poems signed 'Brynjolf Bjarme'), but Ibsen's contributions have now been firmly identified—see Sigmund Skard, 'Forfatterskapet til "Andhrimner"', in *Festskrift til Halvdan Koht* (Oslo, 1933), pp. 295–310. Already by mid-summer the periodical was on the point of financial collapse; private subvention from the three associates did no more than delay its ultimate demise at the end of September 1851.

It is also known that at this time Ibsen contributed to the *Arbeider-Foreningernes Blad (Labour Unions' Newspaper)*, edited by his friend Theodor Abildgaard; it has so far proved impossible to determine which pieces are from Ibsen's hand.

A 4. Ibsen contributed the following to *Samfundsbladet*:

I, no. 2, 25 Jan. 1851: A brief note, signed 'Henrik Ibsen', disclaiming any part of the authorship of an article (by A. H. Isachsen, one of his fellow editors) which had appeared in the previous number.

I, no. 4, 15 Feb. 1851: 'Kortfattet Oversigt over Samfundets Historie' ('Brief Survey of the Students' Union's History'), unsigned. A perfunctory piece, intended to serve as the introduction to a fuller account of the history of the Students' Union. The author promises to scrutinize in a later number three stages in the development of the Union: (i) the Danish period; (ii) the Norwegian period; and (iii) the Scandinavian period. The article was never completed.

I, no. 4, 15 Feb. 1851: 'Om Samfundstheatret' ('On the Union Theatre'), unsigned. Ibsen notes with approval two successful productions by the Students' Union Theatre in the course of the winter, but regrets that the opportunity for mounting some public performance during Festival Week was apparently being neglected.

'. . . To put on productions within the four walls of the Union is all very well, and indeed circumstances have often made it necessary to limit oneself to this. But it is equally clear that public performances are to be preferred. It has recently been stated in the Union that it is from us that any Norwegian Theatre must emerge. Undeniably, these are fine words; and it would also be splendid if the first step could be taken along the road which would have to be followed in this respect. Because the idea that our public theatre should be recruited from among the students will remain but a pious hope as long as the much discussed demand for a Norwegian theatre remains as dubious as it is at present. The preparatory work is our concern; we are the ones who must accustom the people to hearing the Norwegian tongue from the stage. But the public of the capital city is not the people. To travel round the country preaching theatre reform is not practicable. Why not take the chance of scattering the good seed as widely as possible? Festival Week is admirably suited to this. . . .'

I, no. 6, 1 Mar. 1851: 'Asylet paa Grønland—Studentervaudeville i een Act' ('Asylum in Greenland'), signed 'H.I.' The student vaudeville 'Asylum in Greenland' had first been performed the previous year, on 27 Feb. 1850, and had on that occasion been sharply criticized in Samfundsbladet. When it was revived and played on 28 Feb. 1851, Ibsen wrote a re-appraisal of it, and used the occasion to examine the nature of such 'student comedies', comparing them with vaudeville and comedy proper [lystspil].

'. . . In the earlier criticism it was said that the play lacked action, and in particular that the students do nothing but drink punch. In one sense this is indeed so; but if we look at things more carefully it will become apparent that in fact they do infinitely more than that. There is something called individual effort; and unless one knows how to utilize this, unless one understands how to read between the lines, one will find every image superficial, without depth, without background. If one is confronted by a good but roughly executed woodcut, one feels no artistic enjoyment in staring at the intersecting cuts and lines. Enjoyment only begins when the beholder begins to contemplate that image which presents itself to his imagination, and which the sight of the woodcut has evoked. So it is in a play, and particularly in vaudeville, where the characters should not be executed in other than woodcut style. . . . In vaudeville the epic element is dominant, in that the situation influences the characters, and not vice-versa; but it is only through the epic element as medium that the idea can emerge and be made tangible in conflict with other ideas. Vaudeville therefore is the only form usable for 'student comedy'; comedy proper, the opposite of vaudeville, cannot be used because the lyric element is dominant in it. . . .'

II, no. 3, 19 Apr. 1851: 'On Samfundsbibliotheket' ('On the Union Library'), signed 'H.I.'

A brief article complaining of the selfish ways of certain borrowers and other irritating matters connected with the operation of the Library.

A 5. Ibsen contributed the following articles to *Manden/Andhrimner* between January and September 1851:

I, col. 30, 12 Jan. 1851: 'Theaterrevue'. A very brief dramatic notice of Holberg's *Den politiske Kandestøber* (*The Political Tinker*) and of the one-act vaudeville *En Nat i Roeskilde*, adapted by Hans Andersen from *Une chambre et deux lits* by Varin and Lefèbres, performed 5 Jan. 1851.

I, cols. 190-2, 23 Mar. 1851: 'Professor Welhaven om Paludan-Müllers mythologiske Digte' ('Prof. W. on P.-M.'s mythological poems').

Johan Sebastian Welhaven, himself a poet of the older generation and now Professor of Aesthetics at the University of Christiania, had currently been lecturing on Holberg and his Age. His remarks on the modern fashion of employing Greek myth in literature provoked Ibsen to disagreement (translated in section C, below).

II, cols. 28-32, 13 Apr. 1851: 'Theatret' ('The Theatre')—dramatic notice of Karl Gutzkow's *Zopf und Schwert*, performed 20 Mar. 1851; translated in section C, below.

II, cols. 79-80, 4 May 1851: 'Theatret' ('The Theatre')—dramatic notice of Rossini's opera *Wilhelm Tell*, performed 24 April; and of *La famille Rique-bourg* by A. E. Scribe and *Une Chaumière et son cœur* by A. E. Scribe and R. A. G. Alphonse, both performed 2 May.

After complimenting the leading players in *Wilhelm Tell* on their enthusiastic and sincere interpretation, Ibsen went on:

'It is nevertheless regrettable that this splendid musical composition should be linked to such a mediocre text as is in fact the case. The thing has been flung together out of some loose bits of Schiller's tragedy of the same name, without the librettist being able to impose any real unity or coherence upon the fragments.'

The works by Scribe Ibsen described as 'two old plays one might long ago have regarded as dead and buried', and added:

'*La famille Riquebourg* is one of those plays where that well known Frenchness of moral concept manifests itself, admittedly not in the same high degree as for example in *Un cas de conscience* [C. Lafont] or *Les brodequins de Lise* [Laurencin, Desverges and Vaëz], but strong enough to wound the ethical and consequently also the aesthetic susceptibilities of many of us. By giving the public a taste for plays like this, moreover, one will inevitably vitiate the sense for the national element [*det Nationale*], which necessarily must present itself in the theatre without the tawdry glitter with which French authors know how to deck out their works. . . . Everyday life has its poetry too; and if it *has* to be presented from its coarse and prosaic side, it must at all events be illuminated by the torch of irony.'

II, cols. 90-1, 11 May 1851: 'Theatret' ('The Theatre')—dramatic notice of *L'homme blasé*, by Duvert and Lauzanne, performed 8 May.

Ibsen suggests that the title of the play leads one to expect a 'character drama': one expects to see the concept of *ennui* manifested in a dramatic character, developing and finally leading the individual who is the incarnation of it to the point where the spectator feels that the dramatic conflict is complete, and from which, when he looks back, he has a rounded image. How, he asks, has the author fulfilled these requirements?

'. . . Naturally one sits there expecting this main trait in the hero's character to reveal itself through dramatic action. But the author thinks otherwise. Instead of involving the hero in actions, he starts him off telling the audience how *blasé* he is, how life has lost its sparkle, how all things strike him as endlessly grey. . . . How all this boredom originated, we never learn; the hero assures us he is bored, and we have to believe him. He has drained the beaker of happiness; his senses are dulled; he no longer feels any emotion. . . . At last one of his friends has an idea—he must get married. It is remarkable he hasn't thought of this himself before; it is not such a terribly remote idea. But that's the way the author wants it, and one has to accept it. Meanwhile, the marriage comes to nothing, and that's the end of the first act. Following this, the *blasé* young man gets to know a peasant girl, and soon he is head over heels in love. Unfortunately this takes place behind the curtain in the interval between the first and second acts; and we have to content ourselves with an account of what has taken place which the hero is kind enough to give us. Some of us might harbour certain doubts about the psychological plausibility of all this; but there it is, and there's nothing to be done about it. . . . When one further remembers that the whole thing is well larded with *double entendre* (which more often than not is *not* ambiguous) and with slapstick, etc., one gets a rough idea of the circumstances in which we make the acquaintance of this *homme blasé*. The fact that the audience gave it the bird must be regarded as a happy indication that there are nevertheless many among us who can distinguish the kernel from the shell. . . . Yet we can scarcely blame the management for accepting this play for production. The public complains that it gets served nothing but warmed-up dishes. Something new must be found, therefore. We ourselves produce nothing, nor do the Danes. Scribe has become stale. What is left? Nevertheless, now and again it's good to be able to see quite clearly what a play should *not* be like.'

II, cols. 97–100, 18 May 1851: 'Handlinger og Træk af Storthinget' ('Proceedings and features of Parliament')— an account of the debate on the law of usury, in which Ibsen comments in particular on the part played by A. B. Stabell in that debate (see Section A 6, below).

II, cols. 125–6, 25 May 1851: 'Theatret' ('The Theatre')—dramatic notice of Bellini's opera *Norma* (see Section A 6, below).

II, cols. 154–6, 8 June 1851: 'Natvig og Ironien' ('Natvig and Irony')—a satirical piece with a political content (see Section A 6, below).

II, cols. 159–60, 8 June 1851: 'Bidrag til Svineslægtens Karakteristik' ('Contribution towards the characterization of the pig family')—a short political article, occasioned by the debate on a proposal to establish a School of Agriculture.

II, cols. 182–6, 22 June 1851: 'Theatret' ('The Theatre')—dramatic notice of *Huldrens Hjem* (*The Hulder's Home*) by P. A. Jensen, performed 4 June.

After a long résumé of the plot, in which he mercilessly exposes the ridiculousness of it all, Ibsen concludes his notice as follows:

'Such is the general content of this nationalistic play *The Hulder's Home*. You don't need to go very deep into the thing to discover that the national element is only something stuck on, something which in no way bears on the essence of the play. As part of this tawdry nationalism we must reckon verse-making contests, folk dancing, swear words and dialect expressions which might well dazzle the impressionable but which expose themselves as empty and trivial to any critical scrutiny. . . . Our national dramatic literature is as backward as ever it was before the performance of *The Hulder's Home*. And it will never be any different until our authors deign to distinguish between the demands of reality and those of art, until they have sufficient taste to smooth off the rough edges of reality before, in the form of a work of literature, it is incorporated within the confines of art. Then they will also realize that the national element in art is in no way enhanced by the trivial copying of scenes from everyday life; they will see that the truly national author is the one who knows how to impart to his work those undertones which ring out to us from mountain and valley, from meadow and shore, and above all from our own inner souls.'

II, col. 190, 22 June 1851: 'Godtkjøbsartikler' ('Bargains')—a very brief topical paragraph.

II, cols. 191–2, 22 June 1851: 'Etpar Forslag' ('Some proposals')—a short political paragraph.

II, cols. 195–7, 29 June 1851: 'Handlinger og Traek af Storthinget' ('Proceedings and features of Parliament')—a political article.

III, cols. 27–9, 13 July 1851: 'Broderlandets servile Presse' ('Our brother country's servile press')—an attack on the attitude shown towards Norway by the Swedish newspaper Morgenbladet.

III, cols. 54–6, 27 July; cols. 92–4, 10 Aug.; cols. 106–12, 17 Aug.; and cols. 136–9, 31 Aug. 1851: 'Storthings Saga'—political commentary.

III, cols. 75–80, 3 Aug. 1851: 'Hattemagerfeiden paa Ringerike' ('Hatter's feud in Ringerike')—a satirical account of an episode in the activities of the Labour movement.

A 6. *Norma* was dashed off in haste at the end of May 1851 and published anonymously in *Manden* (*The Man*) in two consecutive instalments on 1 and 8 June 1851, II, cols. 137–43 and 156–60. A glance at some of Ibsen's journalistic contributions about this time to *Manden* (see section A 5, above) does much to define the political and cultural context out of which this modest exercise in political satire grew.

The thirteenth Storting of 1851 had had all the promise of being an effective and radical session. Already at its previous session in 1848 there had been talk among Opposition members of moving an Address to the King expressing 'no confidence' in the government, and suggesting radical reforms; both O. G. Ueland, the farmers' leader, and A. B. Stabell had been prominent among the reformists at this time. In 1851, the Opposition felt confident of its ability to move a new Address. However, the intervening three years since the previous Storting had seen a growing working-class influence in liberal politics; and the more conservatively-minded elements in the Opposition, with Stabell as their chief spokesman, moved over more and more to the Government side. The motion to present the Address was eventually lost by 59 votes to 45 on 3 April 1851. The political column of *Manden* on 6 April (contributed on this occasion by A. O. Vinje) suggested that Stabell's abandonment of the Address was like a father's desertion of his child.

Ibsen's political column of 18 May was a slashing attack on Stabell, who was the member for Akershus, a bank director, and the editor of the newspaper *Morgenbladet* which increasingly had given its support to the Government. Ibsen felt that Stabell's conduct—shaped, it was said, by his overwhelming desire to be made a Cabinet Minister—had been a betrayal of the cause of freedom:

'Stabell's conduct [wrote Ibsen] inevitably reminds me of that persevering English vicar who had determined to live and die as pastor of his village; under Henry VIII he therefore renounced catholicism, embraced it again under Mary, renounced it again under Elizabeth, and once more embraced it under King James, and thus in fact achieved his aim. So it is also with Herr Stabell; a portfolio is his "idea", for which he must fight like an honest man, and indeed suffer martyrdom if necessary.'

Apart from Stabell, this short article comments on the actions of a number of other members whose names also occur in *Norma*: O. G. Ueland (1799–1870), member for Stavanger for thirty-six years, the recognized leader of the farmers, whose attempts to find compromise solutions Ibsen found wholly distasteful; Th. Natvig (1803–90), a master mariner, newly elected in 1851, also representing Stavanger; U. A. Motzfeldt (1807–65), sometime professor of law and high court judge, and one of the leading figures on the government side; and A. T. Harris (1804–66), diocesan prefect from Tromsø.

Within a couple of days of the publication of the above political piece, Ibsen attended on 20 May a performance in Christiania of *Norma*, a tragic opera in two acts by Vincenzo Bellini, with libretto by Felice Romani, translated into Danish by Adam Oehlenschläger. The next issue of *Manden* printed a brief notice of the performance by Ibsen, in which he wrote:

'This splendid music-tragedy, as Oehlenschläger naïvely calls the work despite the fact that it is no tragedy, is fairly well known, so I shall not discuss it further here, particularly since *Morgenbladet* has reported the essentials of its plot. . . . Both [Madame Dahl and Miss Hansen] received tremendous and well-deserved applause, which should also have been awarded to the director, Mr Sperati; for it is obvious that without great effort and enthusiasm on his part it would have been impossible to achieve such astonishing results, given the meagre resources of our theatre. It is furthermore a sad demonstration of the low level of musical appreciation here in Christiania that neither at its first nor at its second performance did *Norma* succeed in getting a full house; it is also regrettable that the controlling body of the theatre did not on this occasion have the satisfaction of seeing their efforts properly appreciated; and we can only wish that this apathy on the part of the public will not have too deleterious an effect on the theatre's economy.'

The action in Bellini's opera concerns the relations between Severus, a Roman proconsul, Ariovist, a leading Druid, and his priestess daughter Norma, together with Adalgisa, a maiden in the sacred grove of Irminsul. Norma, whom Severus has seduced, has borne two sons in secrecy; when she learns that Severus has also seduced Adalgisa, she tries to incite her countrymen to revolt against this foreigner, and contemplates slaying her two sons to revenge herself on their father. When Severus is threatened with execution, however, she confesses her own guilt and duplicity, hands over her two sons into Ariovist's keeping, and accepts death alongside Severus who, moved by her magnanimity, is once more reconciled with her. Ibsen's *Norma* is then the transposition of this plot into contemporary political terms.

In the same issue of *Manden* which contained the second half of *Norma* there was another satirically political article, 'Natvig and Irony', in which Ibsen compares the debating chamber of the Storting to Mount Olympus, and the representatives to the gods:

> 'The chamber is actually for us what Olympus was for the Greeks; here the people have set up their gods, and from their elevated positions these gods, in majestic calm and untouched by the turbulence of the times, look down upon the world, which lies far below and sorely distant from them. The lowest seats in that temple are naturally occupied by the demi-gods, i.e. beings one half of whom is divine, and the other half non-divine; to these, as one knows, belongs Stabell; and this is why he is governmental on one side, and oppositional on the other.'

Schydtz (according to Ibsen) was Morpheus, as anybody who had read his speeches knew; Lerche was Medusa's head; Skjerkholdt Prometheus; but 'the raisin in the end of the sausage, Gigas among the pygmies', was Natvig, a veritable Jupiter.

The criticism which Ibsen wrote of *The Hulder's Home* (perf. 4 June) for the 22 June issue of *Manden* has only passing relevance to *Norma* (cf. the reference in the stage directions, Act III, sc. i, p. 197). It has greater relevance to *St John's Night*.

On 29 June, there appeared the second of Ibsen's pieces in the series 'Proceedings and features of Parliament' which commented on yet another proposal—this time from the Workers' Party—to present an Address to the King. This proposal was also defeated like the others, and Ibsen commented:

> 'The sword of Damocles has now hung threateningly by a horse-hair for a third time over the heads of the Counsellors of State; but the horse-hair was once again too tough to break; the threatening danger can now be regarded as diverted, and the Ministry now seems set, at least for the immediate future, to live in peace and quiet in its old age.'

The emphasis given in the prologue to the phrase 'until further notice' (p. 188) is connected with the announcement of 26 April 1851 that the Storting, which had to have royal permission to sit for more than three months, was to be allowed to remain in session 'until further notice'. The mention of 3 dalers a day (p. 198) refers to the allowance given to representatives while the Storting was in session.

B.   *Plays, etc. performed in Christiania between*
                         May 1850 and October 1851

Ibsen arrived in Christiania from Grimstad via Skien on about 28 April 1850, and left for Bergen some eighteen months later, on about 20 October 1851.

As the records of the Christiania Theatre make clear (see Øyvind Anker, 'Ibseniana og Bjørnsoniana fra Kristiania-Theatrene', in *Edda*, 56, 1956, pp. 111–60), Ibsen's first official contact with the theatre had already taken place the previous year. The records also confirm that after 9 December 1850 Ibsen enjoyed the concession of free entry to the theatre's productions:

1.   24 Dec. 1849.
Brynjolf Bjarme.
In returning the drama 'Catiline' submitted by you, the management regrets that it does not find this otherwise well-written play suitable for production in our theatre.

2. Hr. Brynjolf Bjarme. It is hereby reported that the play 'The Burial Mound' submitted by you has been accepted for production; we await the missing musical items.

3. [Notes to the effect that: the casting of 'The Burial Mound' took place on 5 August 1850; there were rehearsals 23, 24, and 25 September; the dress rehearsal took place at 10 a.m. on 26 September; and the first performance was at 6.30 p.m. the same day.]

4.   18 November 1850
Received by the management: 1. A letter dated 18 November from Brynjolf Bjarme in which it is requested that the honorarium for 'The Burial Mound' be remitted to Mr. [Student] O. Schulerud. (Resolved:) Brynjolf Bjarme be awarded 15 Speciedaler [60 crowns] for 'The Burial Mound'.

5.   9 December 1850
Mr. [Student] Ibsen is granted a free pass to the Parterre for the present season.

[Ibsen applied at the beginning of the next season, on 8 September 1851, for a renewal of his pass, and on 15 September the answer came that this had been granted 'until the end of the present year'. Ibsen however left Christiania for Bergen some time about 20 October 1851.]

The following plays, operas, vaudevilles, etc. were produced at the Christiania Theatre during those months Ibsen was in residence in the capital (see, in particular, Øyvind Anker, *Christiania Theaters Repertoire 1827–99*, Oslo, 1956):

2 May 1850 *Seer Jer i Speil (Nimmt ein Exempel d'ran)*, comedy in rhyming verse by Karl Töpfer.
            Fjeldeventyret, musical in four acts by H. A. Bjerregaard, also on 12 May, 29 July, 14 Aug. 1850.

5 May 1850 *Soldaterløier*, musical in one act by C. Hostrup, also on 7, 9, 23, 30 May, 29 July, 16 Aug. and 17 Sept. 1850.
            Et Reiseeventyr, vaudeville in one act by A. L. Arnesen, also on 12 May, 12 Sept. 1850, 10 April, 21 Aug., 4 Sept. 1851.

Til Sæters, one-act play by C. P. Riis, also on 7 May, 6 and 12 Aug., 26 and 29 Sept. 1850.

7 May 1850   *Den første Kjærlighed (Les premières amours, ou: Les souven rs d'enfance)*, comedy in one act by A. E. Scribe, also on 28 May, 1 Sept. 1850, 13 March, 9 June 1851.

9 May 1850   *Charlotte Corday*, three-act play by F. Ponsard, also on 26 May, 6 Aug., 12 and 27 Dec. 1850, 5 Feb. and 7 Sept. 1851.

16 May 1850   *Tonietta*, comedy in four acts by H. Hertz, also on 20 and 30 May, 22 July 1850.

23 May 1850   *Emilies Hjertebanken*, monologue by J. L. Heiberg.

     En Nat i Roeskilde (Une chambre et deux lits), vaudeville in one act by C. V. Varin and H. Lefèbres, adapted by Hans Andersen, also on 26 and 28 May, 22 July, 23 Aug., 8 and 12 Sept. 1850, 3, 5 and 19 Jan., 2 and 27 Feb., 30 March, 9 June, 7 and 10 Aug. 1851.

28 May 1850   *Slægtningerne*, vaudeville in one act by Henriette Nielsen, also on 2 Aug., 22 Sept., 11 Oct. and 27 Dec. 1850, 7 and 27 Feb., 10 Aug. 1851.

2 Aug. 1850   *Søstrene paa Kinnekullen*, drama in three acts by C. Hauch, also on 16 Aug. 1850 and 3 Jan. 1851.

8 Aug. 1850   *Elverhøi*, play in five acts by J. L. Heiberg, also on 2 March 1851.

12 Aug. 1850   *En Søndag paa Amager*, vaudeville in one act by Johanne L. Heiberg, also on 23 Aug., 18 Nov. and 1 Dec. 1850, 10 Aug. and 18 Sept. 1851.

18 Aug. 1850   *Gjenboerne*, comedy in three acts by C. Hostrup.

     En Kone som springer ud af Vinduet (Une femme, qui se jette par la fenêtre), comedy in one act by A. E. Scribe and G. Lemoine, also on 3 Sept. 1850, 27 Feb., 5 and 10 Oct. 1851.

23 Aug. 1850   *Den Usynlige paa Sprogø*, by Hans Andersen, also on 30 Aug. and 24 Nov. 1850.

25 Aug. 1850   *En Spurv i Tranedans*, comedy in four acts by C. Hostrup.

27 Aug. 1850   *Svend Dyrings Huus*, tragedy in four acts by H. Hertz.

30 Aug. 1850   *Debatten i Politievennen*, vaudeville in two acts by H. Hertz.

1 Sept. 1850   *To Aar efter Brylluppet (La seconde année)*, comedy in one act by A. E. Scribe and A. H. J. Mélesville, also 8 Sept. 1850.

3 Sept. 1850   *Frierens Besøg (La demoiselle à marier)*, comedy in one act by A. E. Scribe and A. H. J. Mélesville, also on 10 April 1851.

5 Sept. 1850   *Babiole og Jablot (Babiole et Jablot)* by A. E. Scribe and J. Xavier.

9 Sept. 1850   *Søvngjængersken (La sonnambula)*, opera in three acts by V. Bellini.

17 Sept. 1850   *Kong Renés Datter*, lyric drama in one act by H. Hertz, also on 1 Jan. and 18 Sept. 1851.

19 Sept. 1850   *Embedsiver (Un château de cartes)*, comedy in three acts by J. F. A. Bayard, also on 22 Sept. 1850.

     Intrigerne, vaudeville in one act by C. Hostrup.

26 Sept. 1850 *Lises Halvstøvler (Les brodequins de Lise)*, by Laurencin, Desverges
and G. Vaëz, also on 29 Sept. 1850.
Kjæmpehøien, by B. Bjarme [i.e. Henrik Ibsen], also on 29 Sept.
and 24 Oct. 1850.

3 Oct. 1850 *Den sorte Domino (Le domino noir)*, operetta in three acts by
A. E. Scribe, also on 6 Oct. 1850.

11 Oct. 1850 *Nei*, vaudeville in one act by J. L. Heiberg, also on 3 Nov. 1850
and 28 Aug. 1851.

13 Oct. 1850 *William og Emma*, vaudeville in one act by H. P. Holst, also on
31 Oct. 1850 and 7 Sept. 1851.

17 Oct. 1850 *Den Ærgjærrige (L'ambitieux)*, comedy in five acts by A. E.
Scribe, also on 20 Oct., 10 Nov. 1850 and 12 Jan. 1851.

24 Oct. 1850 *Djævelens Memoirer (Les mémoires du diable)*, drama in three acts
by E. Arago and P. Vermond, also on 17 Nov. 1850, 17 and
31 Aug., 21 Sept. 1851.

31 Oct. 1850 *En høiere Dannelsesanstalt*, vaudeville in two acts by P. Chievitz
and A. v. d. Recke, also on 3 Nov. and 8 Dec. 1850.

7 Nov. 1850 *Eventyr paa Fodreisen*, musical in four acts by C. Hostrup.

15 Nov. 1850 *Naar Kjærlighed kjølnes (Quand l'amour s'en va)*, vaudeville in one
act by Laurencin and St. Michel, also on 1 and 9 Jan., 2 Feb., 16
March, 7 and 31 Aug. 1851.
Kejserindens Fanger (Un changement de main), comedy in two
acts by J. F. A. Bayard, also on 16 Jan. 1851.

17 Nov. 1850 *Christen og Christine (Michel et Christine)*, by A. E. Scribe and
J. H. Dupin, also on 21 Nov. 1850.

21 Nov. 1850 *Ægtemanden paa Landet (Le mari à la campagne)*, comedy in three
acts by J. F. A. Bayard and A. J. de Vailly, also on 24 Nov. 1850.

28 Nov. 1850 *Christens Hjemkomst*, comedy in one act by A. E. Scribe and J. H.
Dupin (sequel to *Christen og Christine*), also on 1 Dec. 1850.
Familiekjærlighed, vaudeville in one act by J. Davidsen, also on
1 Dec. 1850.

5 Dec. 1850 *Badet i Dieppe (La calomnie)*, comedy in five acts by A. E. Scribe,
also on 15 Dec. 1850, 16 and 19 Oct. 1851.

8 Dec. 1850 *Abekatten*, vaudeville in one act by Johanne L. Heiberg, also on
12 Dec. 1850, 1 and 30 Jan., 5 and 16 Feb., 8 and 11 May,
9 June, 7 Aug., and 23 Oct. 1851.

19 Dec. 1850 *To Naboer*, vaudeville in one act by E. Bögh.
Chevalier de St. Georges, drama in three acts by Mélesville and
R. de Beauvoir, also on 22 Dec. 1850.

26 Dec. 1850 *Pak*, comedy in three acts by Th. Overskou, also on 29 Dec.
1850, 6 Feb., 9 March, and 30 Oct. 1851.

5 Jan. 1851 *Den politiske Kandestøber*, comedy in five acts by L. Holberg,
also on 9 and 19 Jan., 7 and 16 Feb. 1851.

16 Jan. 1851 *For evig (Toujours, ou: L'avenir d'une fille)*, comedy in two acts
by A. E. Scribe and A. F. Varner, also on 2 Feb. 1851.

21 Jan. 1851 *Den stumme i Portici* (*La muette de P.*), opera in five acts by
A. E. Scribe and G. Delavigne, also on 23 and 26 Jan. 1851.

30 Jan. 1851 *En Familiehemmelighed* (*Un cas de conscience*), drama in five acts
by C. Lafont, also on 28 Aug. 1851.

9 Feb. 1851 *Axel og Valborg*, tragedy in five acts by A. G. Oehlenschläger,
also on 18 Feb. and 6 March 1851.

10 Feb. 1851 *Ørkenens Søn* (*Der Sohn der Wildnis*), drama in five acts by
Friedrich Halm (Münch-Bellinghausen), also on 14 and 23
Feb., 6 April 1851.

25 Feb. 1851 *Gulddaasen*, comedy in five acts by O. C. Olufsen.

13 Mar. 1851 *Frieren og hans Ven* (*L'ami Grandet, ou: La coquette corrigée*),
comedy in three acts by M. Ancelot and A. de Comberousse,
also on 16 March 1851.

20 Mar. 1851 *Haarpidsk og Kaarde* (*Zopf und Schwert*), drama in five acts by K.
Gutzkow, also on 23 March and 18 May 1851.

30 Mar. 1851 *Don Cæsar de Bazan* (*Don César de Bazan*), comedy in five acts
by P. F. P. Dumanoir and E. A. P. Dennery, also on 3 and 21
April, 14 and 24 Aug., 2 Oct. 1851.

10 April 1851 *Valeur & Compagnie* (*Moiroud et Compagnie*), comedy in one act
by J. F. A. Bayard and Devorme [i.e. A. J. de Vailly], also on 17
Aug. and 21 Sept. 1851.

24 April 1851 *Wilhelm Tell*, opera in four acts by G. Rossini, also on 27 and 29
April, 4 and 14 May 1851.

2 May 1851 *En Hytte og hans Hjerte* (*Une Chaumière et son cœur*), comedy in
three acts by A. E. Scribe and R. A. G. Alphonse.
Familien Riquebourg (*La famille Riquebourg*), drama in one act by
A. E. Scribe.

8 May 1851 *En blasert Herre* (*L'homme blasé*), vaudeville in two acts by Duvert
and Lauzanne, also on 11 May 1851.

20 May 1851 *Norma*, opera by V. Bellini, also on 22, 27 and 29 May, 10 and
12 June 1851.

4 June 1851 *Huldrens Hjem*, play with music in three acts by P. A. Jensen,
also on 6 June 1851.

21 Aug. 1851 *Man kan hvad man vil* (*Vouloir, c'est pouvoir*), comedy in two acts
by M. Ancelot and A. de Comberousse.

23 Sept. 1851 *De Uadskillelige*, vaudeville in one act by J. L. Heiberg, also on
26 Oct. 1851.

25 Sept. 1851 *Dronning Marguerites Noveller* (*Les contes de la reine de Navarre*),
comedy in five acts by A. E. Scribe and Legouvé, also on 28
Sept and 12 Oct. 1851.

4 Oct. 1851 *Guldkorset* (*Catherine, ou: La croix d'or*), comedy in two acts by
Mélesville and Brazier.
For Alvor, vaudeville in two acts by P. Chievitz and A. v. d.
Recke, also on 9 Oct. 1851.

[15 Oct. 1851 Evening Concert organized by the Students' Union in aid of the
        Norwegian Theatre in Bergen.]
26 Oct. 1851 *Sparekassen*, comedy in three acts by H. Hertz.

C 1. 'Professor Welhaven on Paludan-Müller's mythological poems', in
Manden, I, cols. 190–2, 23 March 1851.

'In one of his recent lectures on Holberg and his Age, Professor Welhaven
discussed the unsuccessful imitations of Greek and Roman authors which
frequently appeared in the literature of that time, and which—despite their
reputation as examples of poetic spirit and taste—did not escape Holberg's
satirical lash, of which we have striking examples in his *Peder Paars*. In this
connection the professor expressed the view that this tendency among poets
to take their material from the ancient Greek gods as well as other mythological figures of antiquity is once again beginning to assert itself in a fashion
that threatens good taste and true poetry; and he added that the time is not
distant when men will once again see the error of wishing to reproduce
ancient mythical literature and will once again return to the true path. As
examples of such unsuccessful reproductions he quoted Paludan-Müller's
mythological poems, and prophesied the fate which would strike these works
even in our own age: to be regarded as equally tasteless as those *poemata*
which Holberg parodied so strikingly. Nevertheless, it seems to me that if
two concepts are to be classified in the same category, then they must
either be synonymous or else mutually contradictory. Between concepts of
different natures it is hardly the thing to set up any comparison—and the
point of similarity between these earlier poems and those of Paludan-Müller
is in no way proven.

'The professor has himself characterized those imitations of ancient models:
they were in essence pastoral poems of an epic-lyric kind, in which one or
several mythological figures appeared as the driving force for the development of the action; or else they were philosophical poems with a tendency
generally to make an ostentatious parade of the entire divine world in order
"to draw out some trivial truth or other". It is self-evident that productions
of this kind can only be condemned—they carried their own parody within
them. But it by no means follows from this that myth is unsuitable for use in
our own time as poetic material for an "intellectual poem".

'In myth the original content of the folk consciousness manifests itself as a
union of speculation and history; consequently, by reason of this content, it
can rightly claim to act as clothing for speculative tendencies, in that it
simultaneously functions as a justifiable category in the genre of epic, since
one element in its content is historical. Lyric poetry on the other hand, the
expression of subjectivism, cannot manifest itself in myth, in so far as the
latter is ideally conceived. But since the emergence of every myth lies outside
that point in time when the immediacy of the folk consciousness was still

absolute, so in every myth the beholder (the original beholder) will appear self-consciously cognizant of that which he beholds; subjectivity will come into its own, and lyricism will thereby appear as a necessary element in myth.

'The period of mythological poetry is of course finished in so far as the original producer is concerned; but since myth bears infinity within itself, its time will never be finished in the sense of denying people the right to place further stones upon the mythological foundations. Nobody voyages any longer like Columbus over the ocean to discover new land on the other side; but they do go to investigate the nature of something, the existence of which is given. So is it also with mythological literature. The idea which mythological patterns of thought—folk consciousness in its original form—once laid down at the base of its production must not be re-shaped; nor in reality can it ever be, for it is in itself the true, the objective. But to drag it forth from its ocean depths, to scrutinize it on the level of speculation, is not in any sense an affront to the sanctity of mythological literature, nor any interference with its fundamental nature—indeed it is rather a necessary stage in its continuing development. The agent of folk consciousness, producing in the form of myth, has vanished; and with him direct poetry in its original sense. Our writing is reflective (or, if you like, direct in the sense of a higher union of reflection and original immediacy); and it is thus that our poetic treatment of myth must emerge. But this emergence can only characterize itself by raising the symbolic veil in which the idea is shrouded. This liberated idea, emerging from the darkness, is the product by which the speculative work of literature is to be judged. If the result (the revealed idea) is only "some trivial truth or other", then the poet has pronounced his own sentence of condemnation; his endeavours have failed; for the idea cannot in itself be trivial—he has desired to "embrace Juno, and seized a cloud".

'As far as Paludan-Müller's poems are concerned, evidence is still lacking that the only poetic yield from, for example, *Amor and Psyche, Venus, Tithon*, etc. is merely "some trivial truth or other". Some critical proof of this assertion would therefore be greatly desirable; for, as the matter now stands, it seems that the professor has denounced not merely several of his own poems, e.g. *Sisyphus and Glaucus*, as well as J. L. Heiberg's *Psyche's Initiation*, etc., but also the whole age and its general cultural trends.'

C 2. Review of Karl Gutzkow, *Zopf und Schwert*, in *Manden*, II, cols. 28–32.

THE THEATRE
Haarpidsk og Kaarde
Play in 5 acts
by K. Gutzkow

13 April 1851

'Following a long period during which our theatrical repertory has been exclusively recruited from France and Copenhagen, a drama of the modern

German school has recently been performed. The public did not seem to find this alteration in its regular diet particularly to its taste. Far be it from me to seek the reason for this in the public's sense of discrimination; that would be greatly unfair. For God knows the public is anything but discriminating! The real reason is not difficult to find. When, year in and year out, one has grown accustomed as our theatregoers have to Scribe and Co.'s sugar-candy dramas, well spiced with suitable quantities of various poetry substitutes, it is only natural that the more solid German fare must strike even the ostrich stomachs of our public as somewhat indigestible.

'Between modern French and modern German there are significant differences. French drama (naturally we take the word "drama" here in its basic meaning of "viewed performance") requires the medium of actors to establish contact with life; only thus does it come to exist. Drama, as it emerges from the hand of a French author, is still incomplete; only when it is linked to reality by dramatic *performance* is the concept fully realized. For a Frenchman, modern drama can make no claim to be *read* as literature, any more than our own countrymen would recognize as verse anything that was not sung. The German playwright on the other hand writes his drama without particular regard to its performance. If in the form it leaves his hand it can be performed in the theatre, well enough; if not, it can be read, and as such he sees it fulfilling the demands of drama equally satisfactorily. For in Germany drama finds its *raison d'être* as reading literature as much as it does as dramatic literature.

'From this it also follows very naturally that the German, when he writes for the theatre, believes he has quite different things to attend to than when writing a dramatic work without this special aspect. But this conflict between his general conception of drama and those demands he has to satisfy on some isolated occasion manifests itself in his work and disrupts the unity without which art is an impossibility. In order—as he supposes—to achieve reality, he depicts his characters and situations *in extenso*; but this is precisely what defeats his purpose, for he thereby transgresses the limits of drama. The German play then stands to the French as a *tableau vivant* to a painting; in the former, figures present themselves in their natural contours and natural colours; in the latter, on the other hand, they only *appear* so to us—which is, however, the only right way. For in the realm of art, reality pure and simple has no place; illusion, on the contrary, *has*.

'This is not in any way to suggest that French drama has any advantage over German; for that depends on how far it too satisfies the demands it has set itself. Undifferentiated reality may well have no justification in art, but any work of art that does not bear reality *within* it is equally unwarranted; and this is the real weakness of French drama. Here the characters generally appear as pure abstractions; in order to achieve maximum contrast—the hobby-horse of French drama—they reveal themselves either as angels or as devils, seldom as people. Whereas if the German concerns himself with reality, which for the most part is not usually his field, he does so with a vengeance. He portrays not merely people but the most trivial, ordinary people such as we see and hear every day. But the ordinary person's character is by no means trivial from an artistic standpoint: as represented by art it is just as interesting as any other.

'As regards the play under review, it is genuinely German in its faults as in its merits. It is essentially a play of situation; for the situation develops, the characters do not. As a consequence the latter are somewhat loosely drawn, all except the King who is revealed in an almost plastic clarity. The plot of the play is briefly as follows: The exiled Crown Prince Frederick has despatched his friend the Prince of Bayreuth to the Court of Prussia to inquire into the circumstances in which his mother and sister are living. Already at the sight of the latter's portrait, which the Crown Prince possessed, he has fallen in love with her; and very soon she returns his love. Meanwhile, the Crown Prince of England has asked for her hand, and is supported by the ambitious and intriguing Prussian Queen. This proposed marriage founders, however; and the English ambassador, a good friend of the Prince of Bayreuth, takes up the latter's cause; various difficulties interpose themselves but are cleared aside, and the thing ends with a betrothal.

'The design is in large measure simple and natural, and based on a combination of sheer historical facts. Frederick I reveals himself to us very much as the stern and tough soldier we all know from history; but the severity and angularity of his character the author has managed to soften without offending truth too greatly. He presents him to us as a true father of his people, as a genuine representative of the true-hearted, traditionally German nature vis-à-vis the French tinsel culture from the time of Louis XIV which at that time was imposing itself everywhere in Europe, and also as a well-intentioned paterfamilias, who sincerely desires his people's good even though his methods are not of the happiest.

'I admit I have several times heard it remarked that in the play under discussion one does not get any really vivid picture of the spirit of that age, because the Russian Court was an abnormality. This objection actually means nothing. That abnormality manifested itself as a *contrast* to what was normal; and in consequence this normality is generally there in negative form, and as such is equally visible. The Queen is in sharp contrast to her husband; Princess Wilhelmina is a likeable young lady but nothing conspicuously more; the Prince of Bayreuth is a genuine example of the cavaliers of his age; and Sir Hotham is a complete Englishman, who is quite ready to help his friend but never loses sight of "commercial interests".

'Because of what was adduced above about German drama, the play lacks a certain unity, something to which the many changes of scene also contribute; yet it has many excellent individual touches, including especially the two conversation scenes with the English ambassador, the scene in the smoking party, excepting the "funeral oration" which is wholly undramatic, and finally the whole of the fifth act, against which my only complaint is that it is unnecessarily drawn out after the complications of the play have been solved.

'Conspicuous among the play's dramatic shortcomings is the drum beating on- and off-stage, along with the design of the scene in the first act where the King speaks outside whilst the Queen, the Princess and the Prince very conveniently each stick their heads out of their doors to listen just when his speech refers particularly to them; then there is also the scene when the Princess is declared under arrest—she makes a thunderous speech to the dragoons, but stops after every item in order to let her lady-in-waiting put a few words in, which is greatly unnatural. . . .

'. . . But now a little about our theatregoers' attitude to the play! Had it not been the fashion at the present moment to show hostility to the management and to the "Danish" players, this might have been a suitable opportunity to express one's appreciation to both without threat to one's aesthetic conscience. But no—one took good care not to do that! The play evoked practically no applause except at those points where the author goes in for a bit of burlesque, e.g. the entrance of the dragoons with the soup tureen and the woollen stockings, and the King's entrance without coat or trousers. And what, I wonder, at this last point did our naïve public cheer at? Not at all at the fact that the King of Prussia received the Prince of Bayreuth in his underpants, though that situation is nevertheless artistically comic; but at the sight of seeing Herr Jørgensen in that costume on the stage, for that was frightfully funny!!!

'In selecting this play, the management has clearly not satisfied the public's taste, or rather its tastelessness. But this is precisely why one should be doubly grateful to the management. And this is the public that demands a national theatre! In truth, if this and the remaining demands currently made of the theatre by the public were to be satisfied, then "Goodnight, ye Muses!" But on our prospects for a national theatre we shall go into more detail in a later article.'

APPENDIX III

THE BURIAL MOUND: COMMENTARY

1. The 1850 version
2. The 1854 version
3. Later developments

1. THE 1850 VERSION

The earliest work on the drama which was eventually given the title of *Kæmpehøjen* (*The Burial Mound*, or *The Warrior's Barrow* as it has sometimes been called in translation) belongs to the winter of 1849–50, before Ibsen left Grimstad for the capital Christiania. At this time he thought of calling it 'Normannerne' ('The Normans')—one is reminded that the 1850 version of *The Burial Mound* (though not the 1854 version) is set in Normandy. By this time he had completed *Catiline*, though it had not yet been published. On 5 January 1850, Ibsen wrote from Grimstad to his friend Ole Schulerud:

'Now a little about my literary activity. Of Olaf T., as I think I told you before, approximately the first act is ready; the little one-act play "The Normans" is revised, or more correctly is to be revised, which is what I am at present busy on; in its new form it will emerge as the embodiment of a more extensive idea than the one for which it was originally intended. Similarly I have completed a longish, perhaps somewhat overwrought work, entitled "Ball Memories", which owes its existence to my imagined love-affair last summer. But what in fact must be called my main piece of work since you left is a nationalistic Novelle which I have called "The Prisoner of Akershuus", which tells of the sad destiny of Christian Lofthuus.'

Of this earliest version, 'The Normans', no written record seems to have survived.

In April 1850 Ibsen arrived in Christiania to study for the university entrance examination. *Catiline* was published the same month. In the May he seems to have undertaken a revision of 'The Normans'; and at Whitsuntide, about 19 May, he completed the rewriting of it, and gave it the title of *The Burial Mound*. It was submitted to the management of the Christiania Theatre under the pseudonym of Brynjolf Bjarme, and accepted by them for production. It was played there on 26 September, 29 September, and 24 October 1850; reviews of it appeared in *Christiania-Posten*, no. 744, 1850, and *Krydseren*, no. 77, 1850.

Danish actors played the chief male parts: Chr. Jørgensen that of Bernhard, and A. Smidth that of Gandalf. Laura Svendsen (who later under her married name of Laura Gundersen became famous as an Ibsen actress) played the part of Blanka.

This version of 1850 was never printed. Ibsen's friend Old Schulerud, who had arranged for the private printing of *Catiline*, also made preliminary arrangements for *The Burial Mound* to be published in printed form. He signed a contract on 19 December 1850 with the same Christiania bookseller as had published *Catiline*:

'I, the undersigned, Bookseller Steensballe, herewith declare having concluded a contract with Herr Student Schulerud in respect of the purchase of Brynjolf Bjarme's manuscript of "The Burial Mound", a dramatic work in one act, and "The Golden Harp", an epic poem, on the following conditions:

'1) Steensballe to have the rights to print 1 (one) edition of 4–500 copies.
'2) Steensballe to pay for the rights of this 1st edition 25 (twenty-five) speciedaler,[1] of which 10 (ten) speciedaler are to be paid immediately, and the remainder when 250 (two hundred and fifty) copies have been sold.

Xania 19 December 1850.'

Some of this book was set, and proofs were produced; but the enterprise foundered, and none of the proof sheets seems to have survived. The present translation of the 1850 version is made from the version preserved in the prompt-book of the Christiania Theatre, and reprinted in *Samlede Verker*, Hundreårsutgave, I, pp. 253–78. This text was also published (not without error) by Martin B. Ruud in *Scandinavian Studies and Notes*, v, 1918–19, pp. 309–37.

2. THE 1854 VERSION

The later revision was probably undertaken in the second half of 1853, in fulfilment of the terms of Ibsen's understanding with the Bergen theatre that he would have one play of his ready every year for production on the anniversary of the founding of the theatre: 2 January. The revised *Burial Mound* was performed on 2 January 1854; it was a resounding failure. The part of Roderik was taken by A. Isachsen, Gandalf by H. Nielsen, Asgaut by Johannes Bruun, and Blanka by Fru Louise Bruun—the two latter players being the Herr and Fru Bruun who had accompanied Ibsen for part of the time on his study tour of Denmark and Germany earlier in 1852. A criticism of the play and its production was given in *Bergenske Blade*, no. 1, 1854. It was revived for one further performance in Bergen during Ibsen's time there—on 15 February 1856—but with no great success.

[1] One speciedaler was equal to four kroner; in modern terms, a krone is approximately equivalent to an English shilling.

The text of this version of the play exists in a number of forms:

(i) a prompt-book from the Bergen Theatre, *not* in Ibsen's own hand;
(ii) a number of individual acting parts, in the same hand as (i) above; on each of them Ibsen himself wrote the name of the actor or actress playing the part, together with his own signature, and dated them all 28 Dec. 1853.
(iii) in printed form in four successive numbers of *Bergenske Blade*, nos. 9–12, 29 Jan., 1 Feb., 5 Feb., and 8 Feb. 1854, reprinted in *Samlede Verker*, Hundreårsutgave, I, pp. 279–309.

The text of (iii) has been taken as the basis of the translation of the 1854 version in this present edition.

3. LATER DEVELOPMENTS

When the first collected German edition of his works was being prepared, Ibsen wrote on 20 June 1897 to Julius Elias, one of the editors: '*Das Hünengrab* was printed many years ago as a feuilleton in a Norwegian periodical, and I hope to be able to get you a copy of it.' When, on 7 September, he forwarded this copy, he is said (*S.V.* I, p. 250) to have remarked in his covering letter that after reading the youthful little work again he found considerable good in it, and that he was grateful to Elias for compelling him to include it in the collection. The translation, *Das Hünengrab*, was by Emma Klingenfeld and appeared in 1898.

At about the same time, however, he declared in a letter to Jacob Hegel (16 January 1898) that he could not agree to a reprinting of this play in its original language: 'The two youthful works by me which have been mentioned in German periodicals are the dramatic work *The Burial Mound* in one act, and *Olaf Liljekrans*, a play in three acts. Neither of these plays exists in the kind of revised form that would allow me to recommend their publication unaltered in the original language; they would first have to be thoroughly worked over. As the basis for a translation the old texts are of course perfectly adequate. If you wished these two plays to be included in the Popular Edition, it might best be in the form of a supplement.'

In England, the play was performed under the title of 'The Hero's Mound' by the Ibsen Club at the Clavier Hall on 30 May 1910. It was, however, not until 1921 that an English translation was published: by Anders Orbeck, in *Early Plays by Henrik Ibsen* (New York, 1921) under the title of *The Warrior's Barrow*.

APPENDIX IV

IBSEN AND THE BERGEN THEATRE 1851–1857

A. 1. Ole Bull and the Bergen Theatre (p. 607). 2. Terms of appointment (p. 617). 3. Public relations (p. 618). 4. Relations with Laading (1) (p. 622). 5. Preparations for a study tour (p. 625). 6. Hamburg (p. 629). 7. Copenhagen (p. 630). 8. Dresden (p. 637). 9. Relations with Laading (2) (p. 640). 10. Ibsen's production notes (p. 646). 11. Relations with management and actors (p. 651). 12. 'Society of 22 December' (p. 660). 13. On tour in Trondheim (p. 661). 14. Final months at the Bergen Theatre (p. 665).

B. Details of plays produced in Bergen 1851–57 (p. 669).

C. 'On the Heroic Ballad and its significance for Literature' (1857) (p. 672).

A 1. Down to the year 1850 there was—as William Archer put it ('Ibsen's Apprenticeship', *Fortnightly Review*, no. 75, Jan. 1904, pp. 25–35)—'not only no Norwegian drama, but no Norwegian theatre'. Gerhard Gran, in his biography of Ibsen, makes the same forceful point: 'Even in 1850 our theatre was still to all intents and purposes wholly and completely Danish: Danish plays, Danish translators, Danish actors, Danish direction' (*Henrik Ibsen: Liv og verker*, 1918, I, p. 132). Archer goes on: 'There was a playhouse in Christiania, but the actors were all Danes; and the scant theatrical entertainments of the smaller towns were supplied by companies of Danish strollers. The Danes were in every sense of the word foreigners. It is true that the language spoken by the Norwegian townspeople was, in vocabulary, practically identical with Danish; but the Danish pronunciation differed from the Norwegian far more than (for instance) the most marked American pronunciation differs from English. The separation of Norway from Denmark in 1814 had been followed by a notable development of Norwegian nationalism in poetry, in painting, and in music.'

One of the products of this remarkable upsurge of 'national romanticism', which reached a peak in the years 1845 to 1850, was the founding of what was hoped would be a genuinely *Norwegian* theatre in Bergen. Ole Bull, the internationally famous violinist and a native of Bergen, was among those who took the initiative. The official opening was held on 2 January 1850, when a comedy by Ludvig Holberg (also a Bergenser by birth, though ultimately perhaps a Dane by adoption) was performed.

As part of a fund-raising campaign, Ole Bull came to Christiania in the autumn of 1851 to participate in an evening concert in aid of the theatre. He was to play the violin; the 'Prologue' for the occasion had been written by the young Henrik Ibsen, author of two plays—one published but not yet performed, the other performed but not yet published—and a man known in certain literary and journalistic circles as having a ready and witty pen. The two men were introduced; and in his characteristically impetuous fashion, Bull offered Ibsen a post as 'dramatic author' at the new Norwegian Theatre in Bergen. (The whole history of the founding and development of the theatre is told in T. Blanc, *Norges første Nationale Scene*, Christiania, 1884; for a useful discussion in English of the nationalistic background to the enterprise, see B. W. Downs, *Ibsen: the intellectual background* (Cambridge, 1948), pp. 17 ff.)

The Prologue, which was spoken at the concert on the evening of 15 October 1851 by the actress Laura Svendsen (later Gundersen), was in rhyming iambic pentameters. The following prose translation of it gives some indication of the spirit and the ideas behind the enterprise:

'There once was a time we call the days of yore, and which if we should cast a backward glance and, staring, gaze into the distant blue, one might describe as rude; and yet it was abundant, bold, and rock-like. Nor did it lack for ornament—since poetry was respected as an honourable activity, and the skald found approbation from King and people.

'For here it was as it is everywhere: wherever life's abundance swells vigorously, wherever the people's soul is wild, tempestuous and bold, the force must be tempered or else it sickens, stifled. For indeed the warrior wrote a heroic poem, powerful in its images, upon his enemy's brow, a poem rich in heroism and strength, as he went raiding on distant Southern shores; he sang in Hafursfjord, at Stiklestad, by the coasts of Svolder and behind the walls of Dublin—a poem with a succession of beautiful lines! A duel between sword and shield!

'But see! He wrote with all too powerful a pen, and the melody he set to it was the one the people could not fully grasp, and therefore it passed to the skald. He takes up the harp—oh! how silent it grows as he strikes the powerful chords, chords which the warrior drew out with sword and shield. But the skald transposed things from major to minor key, and gave a gentler intonation; and in this the people's urges found reconciliation.

'But that was why the bold skald took his seat by the King's side, high in the banquet hall; there the sound of his harp was like the waterfall rushing through the valley in the silence of a summer night; and even though in that age life was like a rock-strewn slope where Thor had flung his thunderbolts, casting stone upon stone along the mountain side, the skald's song was the smiling flower that covers the moss and earth in the rocky clefts, and lovingly enwreaths the stony surfaces, and conceals in the spring-fresh leaves a sublime meaning traced in a picture script.

'But this heroic time sank into lethargy; and similarly the voice of the skald grew silent. He sank as the tendril falls with the trunk, to which it has attached its tender shoot. An awesome winter fell over the North; the noble skald sat silent, dedicated to death like one bewitched who has forgotten the word with which he can find release from his enchantment. And the spirit of the people was cowed, just as his was; they drew back in terror from anything deriving from the heroic strength and sense of freedom of the past; they no longer had, as they had before, an oak-wreath to cast in gratitude about their poet's temples. A hush fell on all things, as on the barren strand when the shipwreck's splinters are rocked back and forth by the waves, rolling soundlessly upon the white sand. No sound of birds twittering in the forest; for the spirit of the people slept its winter sleep in there, and all lay like a faded memory.

'Yet other times came, and other customs; and the people broke the bonds of their outward chains; but still they were not receptive to the harp of longing which resounded in the soul, only half able to understand the sound; but that slothful calm cannot prevail, and what the soul demands must be answered boldly, else it must sicken and perish. It demands a solution to the mysterious images which, drawn in runes, confront its gaze. But where is that which can interpret these runes? It is the miraculous power that was given to art!

'For art is like a harp's sounding-board, amplifying the strings of the people's soul, whereby its sounds, richly swelling, can powerfully echo and long vibrate. And that is why the spirit of art woke only when the inward strings of the people trembled. It broke the constraining narrow bands, and boldly raised itself to life and freedom. It presented to the glad gaze of the people fair images from valley and mountain. As to dear, familiar music, we listened to the telling of forgotten childhood tales; the rich and glorious images of the distant past rose up once more in fresh and vivid colours.

'Also roused within the people's dawning consciousness—like butterflies from the broken larvae—were melodies from forest and meadow; the deep hulder melody from the wooded slopes resounded in the ears of the people like an echo from our own inwardly vibrating strings.

'But the temple of art is still not built in all its full glory and splendour: one art stands homeless among our mountains, where yet its brothers found a home secure—that art which everywhere found native soil and sent out its deep roots among the people. For by it life is most truly interpreted, and presented sharply and most clearly to our gaze.

'Now it steps modestly forth among us and asks the people to grant it a home, a dear refuge by the mother heart, that all its joy and pain might be interpreted.

'Then it will settle down with its harp, like that Jewish maiden beside the river of Babel, and sing intimately for its aged mother of the vanished glory and splendour of the past. But not about the past alone it sings, nor moves alone within the home of memory; it will also describe to us the rich scene presented by the life and activity of the people. For art is like a harp's sounding-board, amplifying the strings of the people's soul, whereby its sounds, richly swelling, can echo powerfully and long vibrate.'

The original pattern on which the Bergen theatre was organized in its early days is clear from its Regulations drawn up in 1850. From these it can be seen that the overall policy of the theatre was decided by a management committee ('Bestyrelsen'), which nevertheless seems to have delegated certain responsibilities to an executive committee or 'Inspectorate' ('Inspectionen'); the chief officers of the Theatre were the Regisseur, the Instructeur and the Music Director, with terms of appointment as indicated in the Regulations below (taken from T. H. Blanc, *Norges første nationale Scene*, Christiania, 1884, pp. 383 ff.).

REGULATIONS

FOR THE NORWEGIAN THEATRE

(Bergen 1850)

Section One

General

1. Every member is required, on entering upon his engagement, to recognize these regulations as an integral part of his contract.
2. All comments, complaints, etc. directed to the management shall be made in writing.
3. All circulars, announcements, cast lists, etc. require a signed receipt from the members of the company; nobody may refuse to accept, even if he believes he has good reason to object. Such a person must immediately upon giving his signature make his protest in writing to the Regisseur for further action.
4. No member must forget the respect the artists owe each other. Any person who at rehearsal, at performance, or anywhere on the Theatre's premises is the cause of altercation, insinuation or accusation is to pay a fine in accordance with the conditions contained in the contract. Anyone causing a quarrel or fisticuffs must pay 3 speciedaler; anyone insulting any of the officers or officials of the Theatre must pay 5 speciedaler; officials of the Theatre pay double for their transgressions.

   If the quarrel concerns the affairs of the Theatre, the matter may be referred to the management to deal with.
5. Anyone who in conversation with any of the female members of the company permits himself expressions which offend feminine modesty must pay 5 speciedaler.
6. Offences in respect of the public are punished by a fine of half the monthly salary.

7. Refusal to carry out the stage arrangements drawn up by the Instructeur or Regisseur carries with it a fine of $\frac{1}{2}$ speciedaler. Other persons must not involve themselves in the matter, the penalty for so doing being 1 speciedaler. Continued refusal clearly resulting from malice or spite may be punished by the management with extra fines, or even with instant dismissal.

8. Anyone found in the Theatre in a state of intoxication must pay 1 speciedaler. If anyone arrives for rehearsal in such a condition he must pay $\frac{1}{4}$ of his monthly salary; and at dress rehearsal $\frac{1}{2}$ of it. If it occurs for the performance itself, the management may according to the circumstances punish with instant dismissal.

9. Bringing dogs into the Theatre carries a fine of 1 ort.

10. Smoking in the Theatre, even if it is indicated as part of an actor's role, is completely forbidden under penalty of 1 speciedaler.

11. Nobody is exempt from the requirement of taking extras' or non-speaking parts; for extras' parts, each person must familiarize himself with the necessary cue-words.

12. None of the Theatre's staff, technicians, etc, can or must be encouraged, let alone ordered, to carry out tasks which are not part of their proper functions.

13. Damage to vocal or acting parts, to wardrobe or scenery items, properties etc. is to be made good by the offending person.

14. The actors' assembly room must not be accessible during performance or rehearsal to anybody but those immediately concerned, and to the directors of the Theatre. If an unauthorized member of the Theatre is engaged on any task during the performance, he must leave immediately he has completed his business. No person must dress or undress there, nor must costumes or properties be put down there. Card games and similar games are not permitted in the Theatre building.

15. Strangers and other unauthorized persons cannot in any circumstances be permitted on-stage or back-stage or in any of the rooms in use by the Theatre. During rehearsals and performances, including intervals, nobody is to have access to the Theatre except those persons essential for the performance.

16. For watching the performance, the ladies are directed to the boxes on the right. For the men the Parterre is available.

17. In case of sickness, a medical certificate is required. Otherwise invalid. Fines as for non-attendance.

18. Any person spreading disparaging rumours about the Theatre, the company, the management or the repertory will—in so far as this can be proved —be fined $\frac{1}{8}$ of his monthly salary.

Section Two
Parts

1. On receiving his or her role, each person must sign an acknowledgement in the receipt book.
2. No part formally allocated by the Regisseur may be refused. Complaints must be made in writing to the 'Inspectorate'.
3. Nobody may regard himself as being in exclusive possession of a particular part, no matter how many times he has played it. Reallocation of parts may take place at any time.
4. Individual exchange of parts is not permitted, and is subject to a fine of 5 speciedaler.
5. For a main part in a full-length play, three weeks are allowed; for supporting and small parts as much time as the Instructeur thinks appropriate, but not more than 3 days per folded sheet (ark).
6. All so-called cutting is forbidden except by the Instructeur and the Regisseur.

Section Three
Rehearsals

1. Rehearsals as well as the Repertoire will as a rule be determined every Thursday for the coming week. Further announcements will be made on the notice-board or by circular.
2. The definitive time will be as by the Theatre clock.
3. At all rehearsals, without exception, there must be order, quiet and attention. Any disturbance brings a fine of 8 skillings.
4. At reading rehearsals, everybody engaged in the play must be present from beginning to end, under penalty of 24 skillings.
5. Each person must be perfectly familiar with his part *before* the reading rehearsal. Any person who leaves it till then to attempt to learn to read it, or in any other way makes too great a claim upon the patience of those present, will pay a fine of 24 skillings.
6. By the first reading rehearsal, each person must have all possible copying errors in his part corrected. The Regisseur or the Inspecteur is to supervise this, and also to ensure that all foreign words and names are correctly pronounced at the first rehearsal.
7. At all rehearsals in the Theatre, the start of the act is to be announced by the Regisseur ringing the bell; all the cast must then report, and all unauthorized persons must leave the stage.
8. Any person who either enters at the wrong point in the set or comes in too early or too late at his cue is fined 4 skillings. At the dress rehearsal the fine is doubled. At a performance proper the fine is 60 skillings.
9. Any person who by the dress rehearsal has failed to memorize his part perfectly is fined one quarter of his monthly salary.

Section Four
Performances

1. Both the music and the performance is to begin at the time announced. Any delay means a fine imposed on the offender in accordance with the circumstances (see table of fines).
2. Every member of the cast is to be completely prepared to begin at the Regisseur's first bell, subject to penalties in accordance with his contract.
3. The interval time is to be arranged according to contract.
4. Running and rushing from the dressing room up and down the steps of the Theatre whilst the curtain is up is entirely forbidden, unless wholly necessary tasks require this. The Instructeur and the Regisseur are exempt from this.
5. Eating or drinking of any kind during rehearsals and performances is forbidden, whether it be on-stage or back-stage, in the dressing rooms or the foyer. If a rehearsal or a performance lasts so long that people need refreshment, this must be sought outside the Theatre.
6. Gentlemen must not frequent the ladies' dressing rooms, nor the ladies the gentlemen's, during the performance.
7. In general nobody must extemporize, and in no circumstances in serious plays.
8. Nobody must on his own responsibility alter anything of the costumes once they have been accepted or approved, without the permission of the Regisseur.
9. Any person may be called on to make announcements. Refusal carries with it a fine of 1 speciedaler.
10. Only the Regisseur may give the order to begin a performance or an act. No other person apart from him may order the curtain to be raised.
11. Every order of the Regisseur during a performance must be observed, even if that order is in conflict with earlier agreements. If any person feels he has suffered injustice, a protest is to be made the following day to the 'Inspectorate'.
12. Only those with stage parts may remain by the entrance to the stage.
13. No person, regardless of whether his part is large or small, may show himself in or out of costume, among or in front of the public during the course of a performance. Offences carry a fine of 1 speciedaler.
14. All entry or exit from the Borggaard side is forbidden after 4 p.m., or within two hours of the beginning of a performance. It is not to be re-opened until one hour after the end of the performance.
15. No visiting is permitted before, during or after the performance.
16. In the case of offences for which no specific penalty is prescribed in these regulations, the penalty will be determined by the management.

Music director

1. As often as possible, the music director is to arrange the rehearsals of the vocal parts which the plays require. To avoid conflict, he is to confer with the Instructeur or Regisseur. Singing rehearsals must not disrupt text rehearsals.

2. He is to draw attention to any factors which in his opinion might present obstacles to the planned repertoire, or be detrimental to the productions, and make recommendations.

3. He is to provide all the music, whether performed on- or back-stage, requested by the Regisseur.

4. He is to keep a catalogue of all musical items. He is to deliver the singers' parts in good time to the Regisseur, who is then responsible for distributing them and collecting receipts for them.

5. The music director, like all the other members of the company, must obey the rules of the Theatre, and hold himself subject to the penalties contained therein regarding offences, misdemeanours, etc.

The Regisseur

1. The Regisseur is to follow strictly the procedures laid down for the Theatre, and see that they are complied with; he is to be accountable for fines, supervise costumes and scenery, act as the representative of the management and implement their decisions.

2. He is, as far as possible, to prevent anything happening that might interfere with the progress of rehearsals or performances, and to make in good time all necessary arrangements with the Instructeur and the management.

3. All disputes the settlement of which brook no delay he is to decide promptly as provided for in the regulations.

4. It is his responsibility to see to the casting, to the rehearsals and to the calling of them; absences through sickness are to be reported to him, and he will investigate their validity, and take what measures are necessary in the circumstances to prevent interruption. He is moreover to present to the management any complaints or objections from the members of the company, and to give advice and assistance to the Inspecteur.

5. He has to draw up and present estimates of the cost of scenery, costumes, properties, etc. which the various productions might require; and, once approved, to see to the acquisition, the maintenance and storage of these articles, at the theatre's expense and by its own personnel.

6. Underneath him, and at his disposal, stand all the functionaries in the Theatre's employ, e.g. the stage machinist [*Maskinmester*] (who is responsible for his own men), the lighting man [*Lampisten*], the wardrobe people, the property man [*Reqvisteur*], hairdresser [*Friseur*], tailor, messenger, chorus and supernumeraries, part and music copyists, and the like. If he

thinks it is necessary to have regulations for any of these branches, he is to draft them, present them to the management and have them approved. The members of the company are to obey him implicitly, but if he offends against any of the regulations that apply to him or generally, he shall be fined double the ordinary penalty.

7. He is not permitted to lend out any of the effects of the Theatre, be they costumes, books, or other things, without the approval of the management.

8. Any demonstrable ill-will or negligence on the part of the Regisseur, which has been or could be detrimental to the good of the Theatre, is punishable by the management by a fine of between one-quarter and one whole month's salary, according to the circumstances, or even by instant dismissal.

9. At the end of each month he is to present the cashier with a statement of fines, so that the fines can be deducted from salary. After this has been completed, he receives back from the cashier this statement, endorsed 'Presented'. Neglect to do this carries with it a fine totalling the sum of the fines.

10. He has the supervision of the library and the wardrobe, and keeps catalogues of these as well as of the cast lists.

11. He composes the play bills, despatches them in good time to the printer, corrects the proofs, delivers to the bill-poster and supervises the latter's obligations.

12. The Regisseur sees to all correspondence and writing matters (except part copying and music copying).

The Instructeur

1. The Instructeur is to provide guidance to the actors and actresses, by giving training and essential instruction, so that they may execute to the best of their ability the parts assigned to them; also, together with the Regisseur, to supervise everything relating to the *ensemble* and the arrangement of persons on the stage.

2. In this connection he is required to devote to the service of the Theatre at least five hours daily on those days when there is no performance; and on days when there is a performance or a dress rehearsal he is to be on duty for as long as the dramatic production requires, and on other occasions whenever and as often as the demands of the Theatre require.

3. He must under no pretext whatsoever disregard the times of duty given in 2 unless he has an illness, confirmed by medical certificate, of a kind which makes it impossible for him to attend.

4. The Instructeur is empowered to exclude any unauthorized person from the ordinary rehearsals, but is required to admit the members of the management and the 'Inspectorate' to same, unless special circumstances (which he must make known to the members) make it necessary or desirable for nobody to be present at a rehearsal unless concerned in it.

5. With reference to the choice of plays and the casting of them, any proposals or discussions must be made via the 'Inspectorate'.

6. He is required, by ways and means causing the minimum of expense to the Theatre, to keep up with the latest dramatic works to appear in Norway and Denmark, and to report to the 'Inspectorate' those which he considers suitable for production.

7. With reference to the times of rehearsal, he is always to confer with the Regisseur; similarly he must also share with the latter in determining the costumes, sets, properties and the like, relevant to the production of the play.

8. He must arrange in good time with the Regisseur for the acquisition of the necessary books and parts, and for their distribution.

9. If the Regisseur so request it, he must assist in the drafting of any notices that are to be published.

10. He has no direct authority over the employees of the Theatre, but may requisition their services only through the Regisseur and with his consent.

11. Anything coming to his notice which by its nature inhibits him in his work he is to report to the 'Inspectorate', to see if it can be removed by their action. If it is anything of greater magnitude, he must report it in writing to the management; they must also be informed in writing of any complaints he has about the members of the company which are not covered by the prescribed penalties; those which are so covered, however, he must duly report to the Regisseur.

12. In cases where the difficulty is such that immediate measures must be taken against any person employed by the Theatre, he is to request the intervention of the Regisseur in the matter. He himself has no executive or administrative authority apart from that which is necessary and appropriate for the sake of order and discipline within his own sphere of action.

13. He may not, without the approval of the 'Inspectorate', lend to any persons unconnected with the Theatre any books or other materials assigned to him.

14. Demonstrable ill-will or negligence on the part of the Instructeur, which has had or could have deleterious effects for the Theatre, may be punished by the management's inflicting a fine of between one-quarter and one whole month's salary, according to the circumstances, or if necessary by instant dismissal.

15. The Instructeur, like all the other employees of the theatre, must observe the regulations of the Theatre, and accept the penalties listed there for offences, misconduct, etc.

At its meeting on 1 June 1852 the management added the following supplementary paragraph:

Where any of the Instructeurs consider that any rehearsal has been unsatisfactory as a result of lack of industry on the part of any of the members of the company—which may be assumed to be the case if, after 1 or at most 2 rehearsals on stage, a play is still insufficiently memorized for the prompter merely to have to give the new starting words (puncta, together with the main section in the sentences)—this rehearsal will be cancelled and a new one arranged, and the offenders fined from 1 to 5 speciedaler. During summer sessions half this amount.

Schedule of Fines

The Theatre clock is the norm.

Offences	Ord. rehearsal	Dress rehearsal	Performance
up to 5 mins late	4β	8β	1 Spd.
up to 10 mins late	8β	16β	5 Spd.
up to 15 mins late	12β	24β	10 Spd.
up to 20 mins late	24β	48β	
up to 25 mins late	36β	72β	as determined
up to 30 mins late	48β	96β	by the
up to 60 mins late	96β	1 Spd.	management
over 60 mins late	1 Spd.	5 Spd.	

after which the rehearsal is cancelled.[1]

A 2. Apparently Ibsen was not immediately appointed to the post of Instructeur —which came later—but was first invited to assist the Theatre as 'dramatic author'. In the following months and years, the management gave repeated thought to the problem of how best to divide responsibilities among the various functionaries of the theatre, as is clear from sections A 4, 5, and 9 of this Appendix. A record of the original agreement between Ibsen and the management of the Bergen theatre appears in the Minute Book of the theatre for the years 1850–6:

6 November 1851. Present: the undersigned members of the management committee. The following item was discussed and resolved:

1. The management engages Herr Student Henrik Ibsen, who has declared his willingness to assist the Theatre as dramatic author, for which he is to receive a stipend of 20 speciedaler per month, calculated from 1 October of this year; this agreement to be binding in the first instance upon both parties for the current season.

Hr. Ibsen is moreover to attend the general management meetings to

---

[1] *Editor's note:* 120 skilling (β) = 5 ort = 1 speciedaler, used up to 1873 in Norway, and equivalent to 4 kroner in modern currency; one krone is, very approximately, equivalent to an English shilling.

assist with such information or guidance as may be required. In confirmation of this agreement, the Minutes for this session will be signed by Herr Ibsen.

Ole Bull
Nergaard
Hoff
D. C. Danielssen
Edv. Bull
Henr. Ibsen[1]

It is often asserted that it was part of Ibsen's contract with the Theatre that he should write one play a year for performance on 2 January, the anniversary of the founding of the Theatre. It can be seen that this condition does not appear in the original written agreement; nor was it included in any of the many written revisions made to the original terms of appointment (see pp. 624 and 640 below). Some such oral agreement seems very likely, however—excluding the first Foundation Day of Ibsen's tenure of office, where the notice was obviously too short—in view of the subsequent pattern of Ibsen's contributions to the Foundation Day celebrations:

2 Jan. 1852: Prologue on the Norwegian Theatre's Foundation Day
2 Jan. 1853: *St. John's Night*
2 Jan. 1854: *The Burial Mound*
2 Jan. 1855: *Lady Inger*
2 Jan. 1856: *The Feast at Solhoug*
2 Jan. 1857: *Olaf Liljekrans*

A 3. One of Ibsen's first official duties was to compose a Prologue, to be spoken on the occasion of an evening concert arranged for 17 November 1851 by the Theatre in aid of the Student Society's building fund—a return gesture following the students' concert on 15 October in Christiania to raise money for the Bergen Theatre. The original Prologue is in rhyming verse, in three eight-line stanzas; the following is a prose translation of it:

'We all build—in our different ways. One builds temples in praise of his Creator; another works on his own account, and builds himself a comfortable home, if he can. But if he has poor fortune and has to be content with a thatched cottage, there he sits industriously, as daylight fades, and builds delightful castles in the air.

---

[1] The source of this and of other communications between Ibsen and the Bergen Theatre mentioned in this Appendix is Anthon M. Wiesener, *Henrik Ibsen og 'Det Norske Theater' i Bergen 1851–1857, Skrifter utgivne af Bergens Historiske Forening*, no. 34, 1928.

'Ah, from the stage here we also build, as well as we with our youthful powers are able, with honest will and free endeavour, striving for the distant goal we all yearn for. True, we do not build a work which meets the outer eye, a visible image—yet we hope that he who looks closely will see that the work makes quiet progress.

'And this striving, this delight in building must arouse sympathy in our breast for all those who pull down things dilapidated, for all who build in the place of the old. Warmest of all, however, are the feelings we have for those who serve the things of the spirit with the energy of youth—and that is why we step forward on the boards and greet you this evening.'

The Prologue which he wrote soon after this for the anniversary of the Foundation Day on 2 January 1852 is in two sections: a fifty-one-line statement in unrhymed verse, followed by a Chorus of three eight-lined stanzas of rhyming verse; in prose translation it runs:

'Two years have slipped away since the first time the sounds of home [i.e. Norwegian language and pronunciation, instead of the usually prevailing Danish] were heard here from the stage. Uncertainty and doubt ran through the people at the thought of this young Norwegian art trying its infant wings, and in only a few hearts was hope not joined with fear. And how natural that it should be thus! We are all bound by the chains of custom, and are always fearful of breaking them. The old things we know; their faults and their merits are stamped so deep upon our minds that things can scarce be thought without them. So when a new-born thought appears and progresses along an unfamiliar path and bids the people follow it, we are fearful; and the masses do not listen to the call of the idea, but silently shake their heads and keep to the old things they know. But the time of people's doubt is over; the right of the idea is recognized by us all. But he is greatly mistaken who thinks that now the people have done all that they can, and that now art must manage on its own; for that time *will not* and *cannot* come. The people must also go forward with the art, for otherwise it will stand there like some foreign plant, whose powers nobody knows or understands. And is not our art still young and new? A child in swaddling clothes it must still be called— Alexander after all needed ten years to conquer the world, and he was a hero in reality, and we are only heroes and heroines on the stage sometimes; and that, alas, avails but little! For we also have a world to conquer, a world which is all too great and distant to be taken without effort. And what, then, was our young art from the start? A farmer's boy who left home, that quiet mountain village, where his father lived—and was placed right in the middle of life's hurly-burly. The images which met him here he was to present to the eyes of the people in the way that he himself conceived them; and who will be surprised if he sometimes failed and did not always comprehend what he saw? He was still young and inexperienced, and brought with him only an honest purpose; but this he will long preserve, and will work with this as well as he is able, cheerfully confident of the people's love.

Chorus

'A Spirit prevails in the bosom of the mountains, with healthy and vigorous powers; its beloved voice was heard at our cradle, and the people hearken to it. For the sound is gentle and homely and wild, like the stringed melody of a rippling forest stream. It brings to life, it evokes an echo in the breast of the people.

'And that is the Norwegian Spirit, the power of which time has not lulled into lethargy. The Norwegian Spirit which is allied with the elves in forest and valley. It accompanies us faithfully on mountain and on sea; it prevails by the hero's mossy grave; it explains and interprets to the world our quiet, unostentatious ways.

'It speaks to us through saga and song, and through the sounds of home; it pleasantly embodies our urges and desires, our longings which are reconciled in love; it has powerful roots in our memory; it strengthens our powers, it ennobles our blood. At home as also in distant places it is our guiding star.'

Both of the above Prologues might be thought of as exercises in public relations, as ways of using Ibsen's talents in the service of the Theatre until he could properly fulfil the terms of his appointment of 'assisting the Theatre as dramatic author'. During these early months, Ibsen also put his journalistic skills at the service of the Theatre; and in the November and December of 1851 he contributed a series of polemic articles in defence of the Theatre against the hostile criticism of a certain Poul Stub. 'A few remarks provoked by P. J. Stub's theatre articles' appeared in *Bergens Stiftstidende*, 30 November and 4 December; and 'Poul Stub as a dramatic critic' in the same paper on 18 and 21 December 1851. Poul Stub—who had incidentally helped in a small way to tutor Ibsen in the spring of 1850—began what was to be a series of dramatic notices in *Bergens Blade* with an article entitled 'A visit to the National Theatre', criticizing a performance of *Et Fjeldeventyr*. Ibsen accuses him of writing merely negative criticism, very largely limited to unhelpful remarks of disapproval concerning the acting, and of making no real attempt to interpret the play or communicate anything of its meaning. Ibsen prefaced his direct repudiation of Stub's remarks with some general remarks about the nature of art and the function of criticism:

'It is generally regarded as axiomatic that wherever artistic endeavour is to manifest itself, some critical activity must also be presumed, the task of which is to compare theory with practice—those productions to which the critic has directed his attention. If artistic development is left to itself, then either it will very slowly move in the direction which natural instinct indicates as the true one, or it will run the danger of losing its way on a path, the terminus of which sooner or later is the negation of art itself. This is why there must be criticism; for an absolute condition of it—something which is lacking in artistic activity pure and simple—is a conscious recognition of those fundamental principles upon which artistic activity is based. But it is not enough for the critic to have clarified for himself the concept of art in the abstract—he must also be aware of those demands which are made upon the special branch of art to which he has applied himself. Only from such a standpoint is it possible for the arbiter of art to fulfil his role and work for the benefit of art, and for its true and proper development. If the contrary is the case, then criticism must sink to being a useless and empty demonstration, a threshing about with everyday phrases, which might perhaps have some validity as general abstractions, but which nobody can be bothered to take to heart, because when they are applied to a concrete instance they proclaim their inner emptiness and pointlessness.

'This sure mark of dilettantism brings us all too soon to the gloomy realization that criticism among us is indeed in a very sorry state. For one comes across this abstract theorizing nearly everywhere, except in those cases where the critic makes it even worse by going to the other extreme and, instead of producing a well-grounded judgement, regales one with his own subjective opinions, to which anybody can of course oppose his own as equally justified: "This book is good", "Actor A. was excellent", "B. played badly"—thus run the formulas by which so many of our critics brew their small beer; whilst it seldom if ever occurs to them to inquire whether the idea and the artistic performance are commensurate or not. And yet in the last resort this is the sole task of criticism.

'But whilst this critical ineptitude manifests itself in all branches of art, it occurs in its most obvious nakedness where the talk is of dramatic performance; and this with good reason. For since dramatic art objectifies itself in both time and space, it thereby approaches closer to reality and manifests itself with greater visuality [*Anskuelighed*, cf. Ger. *Anschaulichkeit*] than, for example, music which finds its medium in *time*, or painting and sculpture which manifests itself in *space*. From this follows the fact that many a man who feels incompetent when it is a question of pronouncing on these last-mentioned arts nevertheless firmly believes he is well-placed as dramatic critic. He seizes his pen; and after he has referred in general terms to inelegant arm movements, wrong inflections, etc., he naïvely believes that some genuinely critical treatise has been produced. . . .'

Ibsen then went on to regret the fact that such critics not only mislead the general public, who are deceived by the critic's unwarranted display of authority, but also unsettle the dramatist.

Stub's reply was entitled 'Criticism of Ibsen's attempt at a Norwegian composition', a spiteful reference to their earlier tutor-pupil relationship; he accused Ibsen of 'absolute ignorance and immaturity', and added that he 'had taught the lad to write'. When Ibsen finally replied to this and several other articles Stub had written in the meantime—articles on the Theatre's productions of *La famille Riquebourg*, *Michel Perrin*, *Coliche* and *La Somnambule*—the tone of the exchanges was much more personally abusive, with Ibsen showing little inclination to make any large generalizations about art. It is worth remarking that, after this early exchange of polemic in Bergen, Ibsen refrained from any further journalistic activity—with the one exception of the extended letter he wrote to the press on 8 February 1857—during the whole of his residence in the city.

A 4. Ibsen's was, however, not the only nor even the senior appointment to be made to the Theatre on the production side. A Bergen man, thirty-eight years old and a university graduate called Herman Laading, had been appointed 'Artistic Instructeur' to the Theatre shortly before Ibsen came. It was always understood that, initially at least, he was the senior person—his salary in 1852 was apparently agreed at 500 speciedaler per annum, compared with Ibsen's starting salary of 20 speciedaler per month. Laading was a man with very real literary interests, and a considerable knowledge of drama; he was said to be a gifted teacher. The division of responsibilities between him and Ibsen was not always an easy matter either to agree or to define (see also A 9 below); and things were occasionally made rather difficult by their differences in temperament.

Peter Blytt, later one of the directors of the Theatre, has commented (*Minder fra den første norske Scene* (Bergen, 1907, pp. 9–19) on these differences as he saw them. Of Ibsen he wrote that there was not very much about him to betray the creative genius he later displayed:

'This quiet, taciturn, not particularly prepossessing yet modest young man, whose eyes generally had a somewhat veiled look which only rarely and then only momentarily brightened, rather gave the impression of being extremely reticent and shy by nature. Of him, one knew that he had a quick and richly-flowing poetic vein. . . . He went about his business quietly, almost soundlessly, in the wings at rehearsals. In his early days, he was not very familiar with the theatre, or rather the stage and its ways. Not infrequently he displayed a certain helplessness, and felt embarrassed when he had to make a direct approach to some individual actor, or more particularly actress, to rebuke or even correct them. The stage management [*Regie*] was assigned to him [see p. 643 below], and the production books [*Regiebøger*] were kept by him without his being in the strict sense of the word Regisseur. This subordinate function was carried out by another employee. Everything that Ibsen wrote in these records was accurate, punctilious, almost finicky.

'He seemed to me to be a man by nature withdrawn in upon himself, a man who found difficulty or reluctance in forming close or intimate or confidential relations with anybody. He seemed to prefer to walk alone, without attracting attention.

'This contemplative element in his make-up was obvious to everybody who came into close contact with him at this time. Clearly, then, many of his practical duties, as stage Arrangeur and related matters, were a considerable burden to him.

'On repeated occasions it became apparent that financial estimates and other calculations, things which were indissolubly linked with his appointment, were altogether beyond him. But nobody doubted his good will. Undemanding and retiring within this volatile and in many ways impassioned world of the theatre, he aroused nobody's displeasure. But now and then one fancied one could perhaps detect a certain indolence, a product probably of his quietly fermenting intellectual life.

'One quickly remarked in him a personality which was out of the ordinary. He was regarded with a certain shy veneration; and when, as was remarked above, he wandered noiselessly—or, as it was sometimes called by the company, 'padded about'—back-stage in his peculiar, capacious, and shabby greatcoat, he was respected, but aroused little fellow-feeling. . . . He did not often break into the rehearsals with instructions or directions; he delivered no lectures; but when he did intervene, his remarks were acute, illuminating and relevant. His directions were brief, clear, firm and helpful.'

As for Laading, he was (according to Peter Blytt) much more sociable in nature; and before returning to Bergen in 1850 to take over a school there he had mixed much in the higher levels of society in Christiania:

'He was a well-educated man with an easy elegant manner, well-spoken and polished. . . . His knowledge was extensive and comprehensive, an encyclopaedist. His thirst for knowledge made it difficult for him to devote all his powers to any single one of the branches of scholarship. Vocational study was not for him. He wanted to know about everything, and studied for studying's sake. There was scarcely any branch of human knowledge where he could not with good reason join in. During his time in Christiania he had at one time read law, then glanced at medicine, then made a sortie into the realms of theology; but in his blood he was an aesthete, and pretty certainly saw all branches of knowledge through the eyes of an aesthete. But at the same time this Protean nature had also a practical disposition. He was a useful carpenter, and by the standards of that age an accomplished sportsman, a clever fencer and an excellent shot with a pistol. Along with a wide reading in various languages, he was possessed of an unusually kind disposition. He was generous within his means—or rather, beyond his means. He was obliging, helpful, and always willing. Warm-blooded by nature, he was easily aroused; he could be violent, and angry to the point where sparks flew, but never ill-mannered. . . . He was and is in my eyes a gentleman, a complete gentleman, one of the old school as it is sometimes called, and in the best sense of the word.'

Nevertheless, the problem of dividing and defining the responsibilities of these two men was a difficult one. The management committee of the Theatre gave much thought to the question of how best to harness the talents of Ibsen and Laading in the interests of the Theatre, and in February 1852 decided that instead of having only one 'Instructeur', namely Laading, they would divide the post into two. On 10 February 1852 they sent the following letter to both men:

'Several circumstances—not the least among which is the consideration that in a theatre which is just beginning, and where the Instructeur is needed by everybody and for everything, it is an impossibility for *one* man to take over all the Instructeur's duties—have convinced the management of the necessity of dividing the post of Instructeur between two persons; particularly since in this way there will also be an opportunity of affording the Theatre's pupils—who so far have entirely lacked guidance—some necessary training and instruction. Such a division might conceivably be achieved in various ways: *either* the one Instructeur could have the task of studying the parts with the personnel, and the other deal with stage management; *or* the one could be assigned to the "instruction" of the actors and actresses, and the other to training and education. However, before the management takes a final decision, it would like to hear a statement of the opinions and proposals of the two gentlemen concerned in regard to this matter, which is therefore kindly requested as soon as possible.'

In preparation for the change in the terms of appointment, both Ibsen and Laading were apparently given three months' notice at the next board meeting on 12 February. It would be surprising if Laading had not felt offended; and it seems he expressed his feelings with some vigour in a personal letter to an individual member of the board, both about the manner in which he was given notice and about the proposed plan of action. The management's reply of 15 March to Laading was quite blunt on the latter point:

'Although we fully respect the suggestion you have made to us concerning the division of the task of instruction, we nevertheless feel obliged to express the view that the Theatre will indubitably benefit most from a division by which the theoretical part is separated from the practical, and where each of these specialities is in consequence assigned to a particular official. For this reason we have decided that there shall be such a division; and we felt that we should set the salary of each of the two functionaries in question at 300 speciedaler per annum. As we are of the opinion that, by taking over the theoretical side of the instruction, you will give greatest benefit to the Theatre, we take the liberty of asking you whether you are willing to accept such an appointment.'

In the end, Laading agreed to this general division of labour; and the whole question was fully discussed at the meeting of the board on 10 April 1852. The actual terms of reference were not finally formulated and approved until the end of August (see Section A 9 below); and partly perhaps to alleviate the situation in the meantime, and partly as one move in an enlightened policy of theatre management, it was proposed that Ibsen should undertake a three-month study tour in Denmark and Germany to gain experience by visiting a number of established theatres.

During the years that followed, and while Ibsen and Laading were colleagues together at the Bergen Theatre, relations between the two men were generally very good. Ibsen had much to be grateful to Laading for, though he was not always able to show it. It is also clear that in importance he stood very much in the shadow of Laading. A letter Ibsen wrote to Laading twenty or so years later, accompanying a presentation copy of the second edition of *Catiline*, conveys some impression of how things were at the time between them:

'Dresden, 10 March 1875

'Dear Mr Laading,

'In the hope that you still retain friendly memories of me, and begging to assure you that for my own part I always remember you with pleasure, and with high esteem and a sense of obligation, when I think back to that period of my own youthful immaturity when we were working together at the theatre, may I be permitted to send you the enclosed book which has come out in a new edition and with which I made my debut as an author twenty-five years ago.

'Yes, those years in Bergen were verily my apprentice years! At that time I found myself in a state of ferment which prevented me from attaching myself completely and openly to anyone. Nor had I any real understanding of myself; and this explains, though it does not excuse, a great deal of my tom-foolery and similar things. *You*, by contrast, were already a complete man, and that led to a certain gap between us. But you often showed a confidence in me that levelled out the difference, and I was grateful to you for that, without it being in my power to give proper expression to my feelings. . . .'

A 5. The arrangements for Ibsen's study-tour were embodied in a contract drawn up between the board of management and Ibsen:

'Between the undersigned, being the board of management for the Nor-wegian Theatre in Bergen, on the one side, and Student Hendrik Ibsen on the other side, there has been arranged the following

Contract:

1. The management agrees to pay Herr Ibsen a stipendium of 200 specie-daler from the Theatre's funds to permit him within a period of three months to visit certain theatres abroad, particularly in Copenhagen,

Berlin, Dresden and Hamburg, with the purpose of acquiring such knowledge and experience as will enable him to assume the position of Instructeur at the Theatre, which embraces not only the instruction of the actors and actresses, but also the management of everything pertaining to the equipment and properties of the stage, the costumes of the players, etc.

2. The tour shall be undertaken from mid-April until the end of July of this year, by which last-mentioned time Herr Ibsen shall have returned to Bergen.

3. Granted that Herr Ibsen has returned, he is pledged to assume such a post in the Theatre as was adduced in 1 above, and to remain in that same post, without rights of resignation, for a period of 5—five—years, and also in that time to follow the terms of appointment which will be drawn up by the management to that end, as well as any regulations the management may later communicate to him.

4. As long as Herr Ibsen occupies the above-mentioned post, in which he can at any time be given 3—three—months notice by the board of management, he will enjoy from Theatre funds an annual salary of 300—three hundred—speciedaler, which will be paid to him at the rate of 25 speciedaler monthly by the treasurer.

This contract exists in two copies, of which each of the parties retains one.

> Bergen, 13 April 1852
> Nergaard
> Edv. Bull
> D. C. Danielssen
> Henr. Ibsen'

The fortnightly boat from Hamburg—there were no direct boat connections between Bergen and Copenhagen at that time—was due to leave on 15 April. Ibsen was to be accompanied for at least part of his tour by Johannes and Louise Bruun, a young married couple who belonged to the company at the Theatre, and who had also been awarded travel grants; neither of them was yet twenty-one. Ibsen, who was to be in charge of the party, was just turned twenty-four. To assist him to get the most out of his journey, both for himself and for the Bruuns, the management wrote letters to J. L. Heiberg, the Danish writer and critic and Director of the Royal Theatre, Copenhagen, and to the well-known Norwegian painter, Professor J. C. Dahl in Dresden, soliciting their help:

(a)

[Undated]

'To Councillor of State J. L. Heiberg in Copenhagen. It is not without the fear of seeming importunate that we venture to address ourselves to you, Councillor, with these few lines; and only the great importance of the matter has given us courage to make this approach, which however bold it may seem can nevertheless be excused as sheer zealousness for the development of our youthful artistic enterprise. You may possibly know that an attempt has been made here in Bergen to form a National Theatre—and this has so far been successful enough for us at least to be able to say that a start has been made. But nobody knows better than you, Councillor, what a series of obstacles presents itself in the way of such an undertaking, and the quite exceptional difficulties that have to be overcome before the development of a national theatre appropriate to the age can come into being—and that, however favourable it is in some respects to live in an isolated place it is nevertheless all too certain that the difficulties of our enterprise increase in proportion to the distance we are from the rest of the civilized world.

'Like almost any new start, ours was also crude and imperfect; the elements from which the Theatre was to be created were more than usually intractable; and we had to go through a period in which everything had to be regarded as provisional, and in which everything hung suspended between the fear that the newly dawning idea might simply stagnate and the hope that our long cherished desires, our bold conception, might be realized. During this dark time, when even the emergent artists had but a vague sense of their sublime mission and had scarcely any idea of what was required, it was not too difficult to find teachers who could satisfy the most necessary requirements; and therefore we found it comparatively easy to manage with the resources over which our own poor country disposed. But it is a different matter now: nobody any longer doubts that it is possible to form a National Theatre; the dedicated young people of the Theatre are now for the most part conscious of how infinitely distant the goal is which they have set themselves; and our public naturally make much greater demands than mortal power can satisfy. We have thus taken a few steps forward; but it is precisely this progress, precisely the greater cultural maturity among our apprentice actors and actresses, that makes it necessary to seek out those countries where this art has already long had its home in order to try to learn in some small way from their achievement, even if only in small degree. With this in view we have awarded stipendia to two of our young players, Herr Bruun and his wife, as well as to Instructeur Herr Student Ibsen to enable them to spend a period of six weeks in Copenhagen informing themselves. We fully recognize the inadequacy of such a short stay, and we also realize all too well that without some firm direction such a trip would bring little or no artistic benefit. But in reaching this decision, we were fully confident that you, Herr Councillor, would vouchsafe our young theatre a modicum of attention, that you would render some help to our scholarship-holders, and that through your considerable influence they would have the opportunity of being attached to the Royal Theatre and doing what you might think most appropriate for their future development. . . .'

(b)

14 April 1852

'To Professor Dahl in Dresden.

'Convinced that you, Herr Professor, still remember the National Theatre which has now been formed in Bergen, and persuaded that your interest both for Bergen and for Norway is just as lively, just as warm and strong as it was before, we venture to address the following lines to you.

'You may possibly remember that at the time of your last visit to Bergen [Sept. 1850] a start had just been made on the formation of a Norwegian Theatre. You will also remember that you more than once helped to repel the heavy attacks made on us at that time; with your ardent support for the arts, with your genuine enthusiasm for assisting them in the beloved land of your birth, you encouraged us to work towards the goal we had set ourselves. You cannot have forgotten that you have enriched our theatre in a cultural sense by sending us a curtain, which in truth has aroused the admiration of everybody. And all this is a sure guarantee that also in the future you will feel the same concern and affection for our newly born dramatic art as you have always felt hitherto for the cultural institutions in this country. It will scarcely surprise you, Herr Professor, to hear that our efforts to form a National Theatre have been unappreciated and in part scorned; for nobody knows better than you how difficult it is to combat prejudices which have taken root in the people. Meanwhile we have defied every storm, however tempestuous it has been, and we now think we glimpse a coast which will provide us with a little more shelter. The theatre has made steady progress in an artistic as well as in a pecuniary sense; and we now see ourselves in a position to send out some of our young artists at the Theatre's expense. The bearer of this letter, Herr Student Ibsen, has a stipendium from the Theatre to take training abroad as a Stage Instructeur, and it is incumbent upon him to go to Copenhagen and thence to Dresden with the above purpose in mind. We have chosen Dresden principally because we relied on your readiness to give him all the assistance your great influence could achieve; and we venture to beg you to assist him to get the kind of access to the Schauspielhaus in Dresden that would reveal to him something of the inner life of the theatre. Altogether we beg you, Herr Professor, to grant a little time to Herr Student Ibsen so that he can unburden his heart to you, and in that way be so much more easily led in the right direction. . . .'

In addition to these two letters, the board also drew up a kind of aide-mémoire to assist Ibsen on his tour:

'Reminder List

for Herr Ibsen as guidance on his tour abroad in the service of the Theatre.

1. Herr Ibsen must be of as much assistance as possible to Herr Bruun and his wife in everything concerning their artistic training.

2. In Copenhagen he is immediately to apply to State Councillor Heiberg, and in Dresden to Professor Dahl, to obtain from them such assistance as they may be prepared to give him.

3. He is everywhere to seek information in the various theatres about matters of "instruction", stage management, costume and scenery—in brief about all things which either in an artistic or even merely technical respect can be of interest to our Theatre.

4. To seek out, mainly with Professor Dahl's help, in second-hand bookshops or elsewhere, useful and reasonably priced books on costume; and when the purchase has been made, to inform the board of management at once so that they can send money.

5. To investigate as soon as possible in Copenhagen whether some capable teacher of dancing would be willing to come up here [to Bergen] for a few months to give the members of the company instruction in dancing. If the possibility is confirmed, to inform the board of management without delay about the conditions, so that a decision can be taken.

6. He is to investigate whether it is possible to procure modern orchestral music at a reasonable price, whether or not used copies. In this case, too, he is to inform the management as soon as possible.

7. To find some reliable man in Copenhagen who would be ready and willing to take on the task of procuring for the Norwegian Theatre those plays, either in printed or in manuscript form, which in the course of the season are likely to be given a first performance on the stage (the Royal or the Casino), and which either he judges suitable for performance here or which are requested by the management—and in the case of vaudeville, together with the music, preferably the scores.

8. To inform the management once a month about his address and how things are progressing for him.

9. Not later than two months after his return to submit a detailed account of the entire journey and its achievement.'

A 6. The short time the party spent in Hamburg was not a particularly happy one. Ibsen found the prices in Germany so alarming that he feared his grant would not last (see below, Ibsen's letter of 16 May 1852). And Johannes Bruun, writing from Copenhagen on 25 April to the Theatre management, reported: 'We had very bad weather on the way to Hamburg, and had to lie-to for two nights on account of fog. We were so horribly bored in Hamburg that we wished for nothing so much as to get out of it. As for the expense, I imagine Ibsen will be telling you about that. . . . In Hamburg we went to the theatre and saw Der Sohn der Wildnitz; there was a Herr Baumeister [at that time 'Oberregisseur' at the Hamburg Stadt-theatre] whom we liked very much; but it was a remarkable way of acting. Gesture and speech and everything was so terribly forced.'

A 7. The party appears to have arrived in Copenhagen from Hamburg some time about the beginning of the fourth week of April. On 25 April Johannes Bruun reported back to Bergen from Copenhagen that they had been received with very great kindness at the Royal Theatre by Thomas Overskou, who had expressed considerable interest in the Bergen enterprise, had asked about many of the technical details, and had promised to help in any way he could. Bruun added wryly, however: 'We can see the performances free; but the rehearsals —these we are not allowed to see.'

An attempt to fill in some of the details of Ibsen's stay in Copenhagen has been made by Robert Neiiendam (*Mennesker bag masker*, Copenhagen, 1931, pp. 111–29: 'Henrik Ibsens første Besøg i Kjøbenhavn 1852'):

'One day in early spring, 15 April 1852, Ibsen left Bergen on the steamer for Hamburg on the way to Copenhagen—in those days the cheapest route— whose theatre served as the mother of all dramatic art in the two countries. . . . One of his first visits was to the Councillor of State, Dr. phil. J. L. Heiberg, the director of the Royal Theatre, a man of 60 who stood at the pinnacle of his power—the critics had not yet succeeded in embittering his existence. Heiberg was finished as a writer and creative spirit, but he was head of a great institution to which everybody in those art-conscious days attached great importance. . . . Since "Student" Ibsen had been commended to the director not only by the management of the Bergen Theatre but also by one of Heiberg's own literary associates, Mr. C. Hansson, Recorder of Bergen, the little taciturn Norwegian received a most fulsome reception. In his letter to Heiberg, Hansson called Ibsen "a bright and talented young man, with more than ordinary lyrical gifts", of whom he had become very fond because he "discovered in him the same enthusiastic admiration for you that had con- stituted one of the better emotions of my own youth".

'No wonder Heiberg immediately allowed Ibsen and his companions free entry to the theatre every evening; at the same time, however, he dissuaded him from attending rehearsals because nothing new of any great interest was being rehearsed so late in the season. The Norwegian visitors were invited to dinner at his home, where the hostess [Fru Johanne Heiberg] was the most celebrated actress of the age; and Thomas Overskou, the Instructeur, was given orders to act as cicerone in the labyrinths of the theatre.'

Neiiendam also suggests that it was in Copenhagen—and not, as is generally supposed, in Dresden—that Ibsen first became familiar with Hermann Hettner's influential little book *Das moderne Drama*:

'The visit also brought into his hands a work of dramatic criticism which greatly captivated him. It was the recently published *Das moderne Drama*, written by a young German literary and art historian called Hermann Hettner; it was a thought-provoking work, almost manifesto-like in charac- ter, which clarified for Ibsen much about the various forms of dramatic composition. In his very knowledgeable way, Hettner discussed historical tragedy, domestic drama, and comedy. In the last-mentioned category, intrigue found its rightful place; in drama, however, the essential thing was to present a spiritual conflict. In historical tragedy, character delineation was to be well-founded psychologically. The poet must not get too caught up in the historical events or in the historical trappings; there should be a confrontation of wills, a conflict of a kind that would appeal to contemporary man. . . . Professor Koht believes that Ibsen found this book in Dresden. Is this so certain? All his days Ibsen was an avid reader of newspapers; naturally he could not stay in Copenhagen without giving some attention to the leading paper of the day *Fædrelandet*, in which Hostrup, on the occasion of the production of his *Mester og Lærling*, was writing very interestingly about the human content of his musical play. Every day in that same paper there was a large advertisement drawing attention to a recently opened "Newspaper Salon" at the corner of Kjøbmagergade and Silkegade, where books and papers were available at an entry fee of eight skilling, "returnable upon payment for refreshments". Among the new publications, Hermann Hettner's book was given daily mention. The title alone must have been enough to catch Ibsen's attention.'

Some other details of their six weeks' stay are contained in the four letters of 25 April, 16 and 30 May, and 2 June 1852 (see below) in which Ibsen reported back to the management in Bergen.

(*a*)

'Copenhagen 25 April 1852

'I herewith have the pleasure of being able to inform the board of management that through Professor Heiberg we have been given admission to the theatre's performances; as far as the rehearsals are concerned, the Professor did not believe that we could get any special benefit from attending these, since there is nothing new being rehearsed at the moment.

'Both Heiberg and Herr Overskou have received us with the utmost goodwill; and it will be easy for me, with the latter's help, to get all the instruction about the internal organization of the theatre that I might need. Concerning the other duties included in my instructions, such as the provision of a dancing teacher for Bruun and his wife, etc., I have not managed to arrange that yet, but I hope it will be possible to do that in the course of the next week; and I shall then write to the management in more detail. My address is: Reverentsgaden 205, II.'

(*b*)

'Copenhagen 16 May 1852

'In my previous letter to the management I could only very briefly indicate what I had accomplished here of my instructions; this time I shall permit myself to be more detailed.

'As dancing teacher for H. Nielsen [another of the Bergen company who had subsequently joined the party in Copenhagen at his own expense] and for Bruun and his wife, I have engaged Herr Hoppe, a solo dancer with the Royal Ballet, who is regarded as the premier dancer in the ballet company, and who moreover—from what I had been able to ascertain in advance—has had the most experience of teaching. The main feature of the dancing lessons is the minuet, together with such other things as contribute towards elegant movements on stage, in respect of which Herr Hoppe is keeping very much in mind the instructional methods of the drama school here. He has drawn up a course of instruction of three weeks, with one hour's dancing daily, the fee for which for all three together has been fixed at 24 Rixdaler, or approximately 12 Norwegian Speciedaler, which cannot be regarded as expensive.

'With regard to the proposed engagement of a dancer for the rest of the acting company in Bergen, I should like to explain the following: I was only able to have a cursory talk with the ballet master Bournonville the evening before he left for Christiania almost immediately after my arrival here; at the end of this month the greater part of the ballet company is following him up there. The solo dancer Gade, who is remaining behind, will perhaps be not unwilling to come to Bergen; but the board of management would in that case have to give such guarantees as would allow him to undertake the journey without the fear of financial loss. After the discussions which the management will remember have taken place on this matter, I believe that you will not wish to agree to this; as far as I remember, you had supposed that the dancer in question would attempt to meet his travel expenses by offering private tuition, and would regard the Theatre's honorarium as being in respect only of the time he spent on the Theatre's company. But on such conditions it will be impossible to engage any dancer, unless by some kind of advance subscription it were possible to assure the person concerned of a definite and adequate honorarium for private tuition. The season for the ballet company begins again in August, and everybody must be back again by then. If the management thinks that the arrangement suggested here might possibly be implemented, and that the time left this year is not too short, may I ask to be informed as soon as possible? If not, Herr Hoppe has expressed a readiness—if agreement can be reached in good time—to come to Bergen next year with a section of the ballet company; he assumes that during the time the Theatre is not in use he would be able to take it over to present a certain number of subscription performances, for which advance arrangements would have to be made. In this way the Theatre company would be able to have a complete course in dancing. This last-named arrangement of things clearly has several attractive aspects; but a whole year would nevertheless have gone by, and it would clearly be preferable if the public were able to enjoy as soon as possible the benefits of the efforts which the management has made in this respect on behalf of the Theatre. If the management therefore believes that it might be able to give some reassuring guarantees for the dancer who might then be able to come to Bergen this year (e.g. by inviting subscriptions on a provisional basis for tuition in dancing), then as I mentioned before I beg to be informed.—

'Both H. Nielsen and Herr and Fru Bruun are finding great interest in their dancing tuition, and—which is the main thing—fully realize the necessity of it all. . . .

'With reference to the theatre's internal arrangements, I have been familiarized with them by Herr Overskou, as well as with the stage management side, the machinery, etc.— Books on costume are not to be obtained here, but Herr Overskou will inform me what editions there are of these things, and where they can be obtained. These I should be able to get in the course of my journey. To say anything precise about their cost is impossible, though I assume that 10–12 Speciedaler should be able to meet the needs of the Bergen Theatre. I have only bought one of the new plays, namely *For 10 Aar siden*, by Carl Bernard.[1] But to this expenditure head, too, it will be necessary to allocate a tidy little sum, since I shall probably find a considerable number of things in Germany that would be worth acquiring. With the help of an actor named Sichlau I am hoping to be able to get hold of a certain number of used musical scores. In this respect I am however in some uncertainty since I am more or less totally ignorant of what the theatre already possesses; and I might easily run the risk of involving it in a lot of unnecessary expense. If I could therefore be given some list of what Music I should *not* buy, it would be very agreeable.—

'As far as my travel grant is concerned, I have good reason to fear that it will not be adequate. During my stay in Hamburg I had a foretaste of what it means to travel in Germany. In the same way, Bruun would have been seriously embarrassed if he had not been able to call on the help of a travelling companion, Dr Hofmann, to continue his journey to Copenhagen. May I therefore be allowed to apply to the management for an advance on my salary in the sum of 48 Speciedaler, which together with the 12 Speciedaler I applied for on my departure—and which I hope the management have approved—can be deducted from my salary at the rate of 5 Speciedaler per month. If the management approves of this, I hope it will kindly take steps to let me have this money here, along with the fees for Herr Hoppe, and the amount you approve for the acquisition of books, scores, etc.

'Concerning the repertory, we have been very fortunate. We have seen *Hamlet*, along with several other Shakespearean plays, as well as Holberg— and also *La bataille des dames*, *En Søndag paa Amager*, *Slægtningerne*, and others. It is also obvious that we must acquaint ourselves with all things having any kind of artistic interest. The Danes have everywhere been especially polite and helpful to us; and far from showing any ill-feeling at the fact that we are attempting to liberate ourselves from their influence in our theatre, they are

[1] Actually it was written not by Carl Bernard but by his cousin Andreas Buntzen.

R11

merely astonished that this did not happen long ago. I have made the acquaintance of Hans Andersen; he strongly advises me to go on from Dresden to Vienna to see the Burgtheater; he may even be staying there at the same time and would assist me with guidance; if not, perhaps one might hope that this might be done with Professor Dahl's assistance.'

(c)

'Copenhagen, 30 May 1852

'. . . On this occasion I have little to report. The theatre's performances came to an end on Friday; yesterday our actors finished their dancing course. Herr Hoppe is particularly pleased with them, and he has special praise for Madame Bruun. . . . I cannot determine my departure from here before I have received an answer to my previous letter. On the other hand, Bruun has decided to leave by Wednesday's steamer, and therefore took his leave of Councillor Heiberg on Friday. Herr Overskou has promised to show me something of the theatre's machinery, etc.—something which was not possible during the season. In any case, the machinery of the Copenhagen Theatre is not of the best, and I hope in this respect to be able to draw much greater profit from the German theatres. I am sending home with Bruun a number of small things which the Theatre needs, along with a number of books. I fancied I might travel via Lübeck to Dresden, where with Professor Dahl's help I hope to draw up an appropriate plan for the rest of the tour. . . .'

(d)

'Copenhagen, 2 June 1852

'To the Management of the Norwegian Theatre.

'I am forwarding with Herr Bruun a number of books, together with a number of receipts for various things I have paid for on behalf of the Theatre as listed below:

2 copies of *For ti Aar siden* @ 3 ℔ 8β each	1 Rd	1 ℔	–β
1 copy of *Statsmand og Borger* [i.e. *Bertrand et Raton*]		2	4
1 ditto of *Medbeilerne* [i.e. Sheridan's *The Rivals*]		2	4
5 ditto of *Kvindens Vaaben* [i.e. *La bataille des dames*] @ 28β	1 Rd	2	12
Enclosed bill from Bing and Son	3 Rd	–	–
1 copy of *Billedgalleri*	1 Rd	3	–
Enclosed bill from Herr Hoppe	24 Rd	–	–
	31 Rd	5 ℔	4β

for which amount I shall take payment from the sum which the board of management might decide to put at my disposition.[1]

'I propose that *For ti Aar siden* be taken into the repertoire, in which case I had imagined the following casting:

Capt Rømer	Herr H. Nielsen
Grethe	Mme Bruun
Frahm	Herr Isachsen
Ehlers	Herr Bruun
Brandt	Herr Pram
Stoltenberg	Herr Bucher
Hanne	Miss Johannessen

'I have acquired Høedt's translation of *La bataille des dames* (*Kvindens Vaaben*), as the one our theatre possesses is bad, and as such should not be used.

'As far as *The Rivals* and *Bertrand et Raton* are concerned, it is not my firm intention to suggest that these plays be taken into the repertoire for the time being. In the course of the winter they have been given here to much applause, and are therefore submitted for the management's consideration.

'The *Billedgalleri* [a volume of costume illustrations], forwarded herewith, I have bought even though the theatre will not find constant use for it, or at least not before we have got to the point of presenting big plays in which masquerades etc. are included. (If *Scheik Hassan* should be produced, then we have in *Billedgalleri* the necessary guidance as far as costumes are concerned.)

'As the season is finished here now, and as I am in many respects clear about the advantages I have gained, there are many things I could say about it at this point; as however such remarks will very naturally find their place in the account I am to give after my return, I shall not for the present say anything about it. Only one remark I cannot refrain from making: namely, that the procedure whereby the actors are expected to know their parts before the rehearsals on stage begin is closely followed here. Herr Overskou has repeatedly declared "that he has had thirty years experience of the fact that any part which is not understood by the time of the last reading-rehearsal will never be understood, and that the necessity for this increases in proportion to the actors' lack of training".

'Last week the students played at the Hoftheater before the King; Herr Bruun and I were invited to be present. I have had an invitation from Fru Heiberg to a dinner party on Friday; Herr Bruun and his wife were there on Sunday.

'I am, now that the season is over, quite anxious to leave, and I am simply now waiting for the management's reply to my letter of the 16th.

[1] *Editor's note:* 96 skilling (β) = 6 mark ,($\mathrm{\mathbb{Rd}}$) = 1 Rixdaler, currency used in Denmark up to 1875, and equivalent to 2 kroner in modern currency.

Herr Hoppe is leaving today, and he tells me that if the management are ready to agree to his proposal to come to Bergen next year, the agreement must be signed at least three months before the end of the season.'

A letter from the board of management to Ibsen, written on 21 May and before Ibsen's letter of 16 May had come into their hands, does no more than express its concern over the fact that proper arrangements for Herr Nielsen to attend the theatre had apparently not been made. It was not until 28 May that the management in Bergen received Ibsen's letter of 16 May, and it hastened to reply by return:

'28 May 1852

'To Herr Instructeur Ibsen.

'The board of management has today received your letter of 16th inst. and hastens to send you a few lines by the post leaving today. The management expresses its thanks to you for the trouble it now learns you went to to get dancing tuition for our visiting actors, but thinks it best to postpone until next year the matter of engaging a dancing instructor for the rest of the company. Our thanks are all the warmer following the fears we had for a moment that we might be disappointed in our expectations of you; we no longer have any doubt that you will continue to do all you can to meet our reasonable requests. As far as the fee for dancing tuition is concerned, mentioned in your letter, there must be some misunderstanding on your part; it has of course never been our intention to make any further money available to our grant-holders for their stay in Copenhagen above the 200 Speciedaler already authorized, which we regard as perfectly adequate to meet necessary expenses, tuition included, especially when admission to the theatre is free.

'The management unfortunately cannot refrain from expressing its displeasure at your not having arranged for H. Nielsen to be given free admission to the Royal Theatre, for there appears to be no reason for this omission in your letter. As regards the orchestra music mentioned in your letter, the management will get in touch with Herr Sichlau later if it decides it wishes to have any. Books of costume have recently been acquired from Paris, along with a number of other theatre items. Finally the management regrets that it cannot accede to your request for an advance of 48 Speciedaler on your salary; not only are the theatre funds inadequate to bear such a large deficit, for nearly everybody in the company has got something similar, but we are also unable to accept that you need the sum mentioned so long as your journey is not extended further than originally decided. The management had certainly hoped that you might have visited Vienna for a short time; but, as was said to you at the time, the plan had to be abandoned for compelling reasons. We rather believe that it would be much more profitable for you to stay for a longish time at a place like Dresden, instead of rushing about from one place to another without being able to establish any close acquaintance with the theatre, which is of course the main purpose of your journey. As far as the size of the stipendium is concerned, we can assure you with complete confidence that nowhere else in this country or perhaps even abroad does one find larger stipends awarded to artists and scholars, and indeed generally they are much smaller; and that the cost of accommodation is known from our own earlier visits to be very cheap. If then against all expectation you are not able to manage on 200 Speciedaler, we might very well feel inclined to say that your budgeting has not been very sensible.'

It is not easy to determine which plays Ibsen saw performed during his stay in Copenhagen. The plays which were in the repertory of the Royal Theatre during April and May 1852 are known; it is also known that, certainly in their early days in the city, the members of the party were very assiduous in their attendance at the theatre—Johannes Bruun's first letter back to the Bergen management stated that they had been to the theatre every evening up to then, and listed six works they had seen. Ibsen himself never gave any detailed account of his attendances at the theatre; although he did mention a number of authors and titles, some of which he expressly claimed to have seen in production (marked * below), others of which he mentions as texts he has acquired or sought (marked ** below). A full list must necessarily include some conjectural items; there are, however, some grounds for believing that in the course of his stay in Copenhagen (lasting about six and a half weeks), Ibsen might well have seen the following plays produced:

Ludvig Holberg, *Pernilles korte Frøkenstand; Barselstuen; Henrik og Pernille; Den Vægelsindede* / William Shakespeare, *Hamlet; King Lear; Romeo and Juliet; As You Like It* / A. E. Scribe, *La bataille des dames;***[1] *Bertrand et Raton*** / H. Hertz, *Scheik Hassan; Kong Renés Datter; Stedbørnene* / J. L. Heiberg, *Nei; Recensenten og Dyret* / Johanne L. Heiberg, *Abekatten; En Søndag paa Amager** / Chr. Hauch, *Æren tabt og vunden* / A. Buntzen, *For ti aar siden*** / Oehlenschläger, *Hakon Jarl* / Hostrup, *Soldaterløjer* / Sheridan, *The Rivals*** / A. F. Hartnak, *Den bevægende Tid* / Henriette Nielsen, *Slægtningerne** / Bayard and de Vailly, *Le mari à la campagne.*

A 8. Seemingly, Ibsen wrote only one letter by way of report back to the management from Dresden. It was in large part a reply to the board's letter of 28 May and is disappointing in the paucity of its detail referring to his stay in Dresden:

'Dresden, 24 June 1852

'To the Management of the Norwegian Theatre.

'I herewith report to the board of management that I left Copenhagen on Sunday 6 inst., and arrived here the following Wednesday. The reason for my not writing to the board before now is that I was unfortunate enough on

---

[1] Known and referred to by Ibsen by two different Dano-Norwegian titles: *Naar Damer fører Krig* and *Kvindens Vaaben.*

my arrival here to find Professor Dahl not at home; he had in fact left for the country, and it was not until the 16th I was able to speak to him.

'He has now arranged for me to have access to the inner affairs of the theatre, which I am sure will be of great benefit to me, for everything is in excellent condition. On the other hand I must myself pay for admission to the performances in the theatre; the repertoire is admittedly very good, but so far I have only seen one play which we can use, and which I shall therefore bring back with me.

'From the board's letter I see that the Theatre has acquired some books on costume from Paris; if that had not been so, I would have recommended a few excellent works which I have come across, namely Bonnard's *Costumes* from the 13th and the five subsequent centuries, together with a *Collection of Spanish folk costumes*, which has been recently published here.

'From the board's last letter I also discover that it was not the board's intention to provide fees from the theatre's funds for dancing tuition— nothing was said to me about this when I left, and all I was asked to do was find a dancing teacher for the actors; and as the board further expressed the desirability of getting another teacher for the actors in Bergen, I assumed that the principle implicit here was that dancing instruction for the company was to be met from theatre funds. In any event, this principle must surely apply in H. Nielsen's case; he is after all travelling at his own expense, and it would hardly have done to impose an extra expense on him, especially as the Theatre will find adequate recompense for the leave granted him in the education his journey must otherwise be regarded as having given him. And in respect of Bruun, I believe that he had enough left from his travel grant to meet the expenses of his return journey, but nothing more. I could thus do nothing other than pay up.

'For all these circumstances I hope that the board will agree to recompense me for my outlay.

'In connection with my application for an advance, which is not granted, the board remarks that I must not have budgeted properly if the stipendium is not proving adequate. I would be unhappy if the board were to continue to hold to that opinion, so I shall permit myself to draw attention to the following: the journey from Bergen to Copenhagen took approximately 40 Speciedaler. I have thought it essential to acquire a fair number of books, and could really do with many more, if I had the necessary money. Furthermore I have to pay my own admission to the theatre here, and it is obvious that I must visit it regularly; for it would be of very little use to me to find out about the stage machinery, and about matters of scenery, etc., if I cannot at the same time see the way these things are applied. Moreover, the grant must now last not three but three and a half months; finally, Herr Neergaard might remember that, when on my departure I received 60 Speciedaler from him, I requested that 20 Speciedaler of this ought to be regarded as an advance, since that amount would go on certain outfitting items and would thus not be available during my tour; to this Herr Neergaard replied that that might in time be done if it became apparent that the stipendium was insufficient.

'I am convinced that this latter is the case; I hope therefore that the board will in any case allow me the 20 Speciedaler mentioned above, or else I shall be compelled to try to catch a casual ship at Hamburg, and thereby perhaps lose much of the time I desperately need if I am going to get anything done for the Theatre before the start of the season. I have enough of my stipendium left to cover my accommodation and board here; and with the above 20 Speciedaler together with payment for my expenditure in Copenhagen as calculated, I shall be able to meet the travelling expenses of my return journey, but no more. In the hope that the board will be able to accede to my request, I sign myself

Respectfully
Henr. Ibsen

PS. My address is: C/o Surgeon Fröitzh, Töpfergasse 13, III. May I also request that the board inform me when the steamer leaves Hamburg at the end of July for Bergen, so that I can organize my departure from here. There is no information to be obtained here about this.'

In the end, the management relented somewhat in the matter of the finances of his trip, and sent him the following letter:

'To
Herr Instructeur Ibsen.

'On behalf of the board I am to inform you that it has approved an advance to you of 30 Speciedaler on your salary for August and September, which together with the sum for dancing tuition in Copenhagen amounts to 42 Speciedaler, which are herewith forwarded to you by bill of exchange drawn upon Altona. If you should be in financial embarrassment already in Dresden, the best thing is to apply immediately to a finance house in Dresden to get the bill cashed; alternatively, you can yourself apply to Mathieson and Co., Altona. The steamer leaves Hamburg 15 and 29 July, so that you must determine the date of your departure from Dresden yourself. It would be most desirable if the Theatre could acquire the Bonnard works on Costume which you mention, but we are apprehensive about the expense and must therefore request you to tell us the price—or, if this is not too high for you to meet, to acquire them without further ado.'

Ibsen therefore arrived in Dresden on 9 June; if on his return he caught the 29 July steamer from Hamburg—which is likely, since his return to Bergen was reported to the board of management at its meeting on 5 August—he probably had to leave Dresden about 26 or 27 July. He would then have been in the city for about six and a half weeks. The art galleries of the city clearly made a deep impression on him; and in the sonnet cycle 'In the Picture

Gallery', first published in September 1859, as well as in the poem 'In the Gallery', probably written some time in the period 1869–70, he mentions by name the following artists and pictures represented in the Dresden galleries: Correggio's 'Holy Night', Raphael's 'Sistine Madonna', Jan van Mieris, and Murillo's 'Madonna'. It is less easy than in the case of Copenhagen to determine which plays he probably saw performed. This time he had to pay for admission; and even though Dresden was a relatively inexpensive place to live—many years later, in 1869, when Ibsen was once again resident in Dresden, he wrote to his publisher that Dresden was 'a very agreeable place, and very cheap to live in'—this doubtless had a certain inhibiting effect on his theatregoing. It has been established (by Roderick Rudler, in *Edda*, lxvi, 1966, pp. 236–45) that among the plays performed during Ibsen's time in Dresden were probably the following: Shakespeare's *Midsummer Night's Dream*, *Hamlet*, and *Richard III*; Scribe's *Les contes de la reine de Navarre*; Lessing's *Emilia Galotti*; Goethe's *Egmont*; Schiller's *Kabale und Liebe*; Roderich Bendix's *Doctor Wespe*, *Das Gefängnis*, *Die Eifersüchtigen*, *Der Vetter*, and *Der alte Magister*; Charlotte Birch-Pfeiffer's *Dorf und Stadt*, and *Mutter und Sohn*; Hackländer's *Der gemeine Agent*; Karl Töpfer's *Der beste Ton*; Eduard Devrient's *Die Gunst des Augenblickes*; Carl Holtei's *Lorbeerbaum und Bettelstab*; Ernst Raupauch's *Die Schlichhändler*; and the Danish dramatist Henrik Hertz's *König Renés Tochter*.

Although Ibsen probably did not see the Dresden theatre's leading actor, Emil Devrient, who was away in London at the time, he did nevertheless see the Polish-born Borguwil Dawison who was substituting for Devrient, probably in *Hamlet*, *Richard III* and *Emilia Galotti*.

After Ibsen's return, the board of management then on 24 August sent letters of appreciation to both Heiberg and Dahl.

A 9. After Ibsen's return from Dresden, and with the approach of the new season, it became a matter of some urgency to determine and define the respective duties of Laading and Ibsen in the Theatre. It was to continue to be a matter of dispute and revision for the next three years at least. At an extraordinary meeting of the board on 30 August 1852, the following terms of appointment were agreed:

Terms of appointment
of the two Instructeurs at the Norwegian Theatre

1. The *Role-Instructeur* is required to be present at the Theatre every day between 9 and 12 o'clock in the forenoon to direct the reading rehearsals, and to utilize any remaining time for the special study of parts and for the general instruction of the members of the company, all in as far as this can be done without hindrance to the plays which are being dealt with by the Stage-Instructeur. Equally, it is part of his duties to study parts with beginners during the same hours.

With reference to the reading rehearsals he is to be particularly attentive to the following:

(i) To remove all obstacles to a rapid and satisfactory stage rehearsal, both in regard to language and to explanation of vocabulary.

(ii) To give the players such historical explanation as is necessary, and to ensure a correct interpretation of their roles.

(iii) To see that diction is correct.

(iv) To ensure that the players memorize their parts carefully and accurately enough for them to appear at the first stage rehearsal without books or papers.

2. The *Stage-Instructeur* is required to be present in the Theatre for as many hours daily, holidays included, as are required for a thorough and careful 'instruction' on stage for each play to render it suitable for public presentation by the date the management has determined. When he is satisfied that the players have been adequately prepared, he is then to continue the instruction from the point reached at the last reading rehearsal; furthermore he is to draw up draft lists of stage rehearsals, and may return the performers for further reading rehearsals if he finds it necessary.

It is further incumbent upon the Stage-Instructeur:

(i) To organize the scenic arrangements, including the costumes and scenery of each play, and to direct its general staging (groupings, entrances, exits in certain postures, etc.).

(ii) To scrutinize the mime and the gestures of each individual player, to ensure that all bodily movements are appropriate to the words and the nature of the part.

(iii) To achieve the necessary interplay, and to define for each of the players his contribution to the general action of the play in accord with the changing situation.

3. Before any new play goes into production, the two Instructeurs are to confer with each other to seek agreement concerning the interpretation of the various characters; and where no agreement can be reached, it is to be put before the management for a decision.

4. Before the management casts the parts in a play, the Instructeurs must furthermore confer to see if they can agree on a proposed cast list, which is then to be submitted jointly; where differences of opinion arise, the Instructeurs are to send individual proposals.

5. In so far as the Role-Instructeur desires it, the last stage-rehearsal before the dress-rehearsal shall be held between 9 and 12 o'clock in the forenoon and in his presence; it is moreover self-evident that he is free to attend stage rehearsals in order that—within the limits of his function—he may supervise the observance of the prescriptions he has given to the players.

6. The Role-Instructeur will see to the requisitioning of new plays and to all correspondence connected with this, together with the copying of

parts, in so far this latter is not by regulation one of the duties of the Regisseur.

7. Differences of opinion arising between the Instructeurs concerning the execution of their respective functions which cannot be reconciled by agreement between them are to be decided by that member of the board of management [Danielssen] appointed by it for this purpose; both Instructeurs are to be bound by his decision.

8. If within the limits of the Instructeurs' functions any matter should arise in which the Instructeur concerned does not regard himself as competent to act on his own responsibility, and where a decision is to be reached without delay, he will apply to the responsible member of the board referred to in 7, who will take the necessary decision which the Instructeur concerned will then implement.

9. The Instructeurs are furthermore to follow any such alterations or additions to these present terms of appointment as the management may determine.

30 August 1852.

At the same meeting it was decided to appoint Laading as Role-Instructeur from 1 September at an annual salary of 300 Speciedaler; and, following the earlier contract, to appoint Ibsen as Stage-Instructeur from 16 August, also at an annual salary of 300 Speciedaler. Following these decisions, the management then sent a circular letter to all members of the company on 7 September:

'With two people now sharing the task of Instruction, it is possible to allocate some time to the general education of the actors and actresses of the company. Herr Instructeur Laading will therefore probably be able to devote those forenoon hours which are not given over to reading rehearsals, i.e. 2–3 mornings a week, to instruction in languages, aesthetics, history, geography, etc. All with special reference to the standpoint of the members of the group.

'It must be obvious to everybody that knowledge acquired from the study of individual roles can only be fragmentary and deficient, and consequently incapable of reaching that level of education without which no position in society can in the long run be sustained; for in these days it is education which differentiates the classes and gives individuality to a person— and how delighted we would be to see the personnel of the Norwegian Theatre occupy a most worthy place both in matters of education as well as in morals and talent.

'But such courses will—where one's earlier youthful education has taken a different direction—demand great mental effort and stamina, as well as the recognition that one is not here to work merely for the fickle applause of the day.

'In thus encouraging everybody to take advantage of all courses which the Instructeur can provide, a reminder must nevertheless be given that it is by individual effort that the goal can best be brought nearer, and that honest endeavour in this direction will give the Norwegian Theatre a proper foundation. And just as we have felt occasioned to draw attention to this, so we similarly cannot refrain from once again informing the company that in allocating the few incentives the Theatre has at its disposal, attention will primarily be given to the industry and endeavour which the members have displayed during their instruction.'

There are no grounds for supposing that the two men did not loyally attempt to make the system work. Laading was still the senior of the two, both in age and experience of the theatre; he also had other official duties in the Norwegian Theatre, and was on close and friendly terms with the individual board members. Ibsen seems to have accepted this situation, though as time went on he seems to have suffered more and more from it—as was later shown in his letter of 23 July 1857 to the management, in which he complains of never having had a free hand in the theatre, and of finding his way very often blocked (see p. 668 below). Particularly when it came to the interpretation of plays and parts, it was inevitable that in many instances the two men would disagree; and Laading very naturally was unwilling to deliver his reading of the play entirely over to Ibsen at the point where stage rehearsals were to begin. Within a few months of trying to operate the system Laading found the situation intolerable, and on 30 November 1852 wrote to the management asking to be allowed to resign. In its reply, the management asked Laading to reconsider his decision, and to remain loyal to the enterprise; and in admitting that the planned division of responsibilities had shown itself to be 'less than appropriate', it suggested using the rest of the winter season for gathering further experience and eventually drafting a new solution acceptable to both Instructeurs and to the management. In consequence of this letter, Laading remained at his post; and presumably the matter was discussed further among the three parties.

The revision of duties which was eventually carried out the following summer added considerably to the responsibilities which Ibsen had to bear, increased somewhat the duties and probably substantially enhanced the status of Laading, but apparently left untouched the very unsatisfactory frontier between the Role-Instructeur and the Stage-Instructeur. Essentially what happened in Ibsen's case was that he was given a large extra element of stage management to do, some details of which can be gathered from the letter the management sent him on 5 May 1853:

'Instructeur Ibsen.

'During the past season, the theatre management has carefully observed your efforts in the post to which you were assigned, and still cherishes the hope of seeing you develop those talents which we, by our earlier faith in you, showed we were sure you possessed. We have therefore assigned to you those *Regie* functions which do not clash with your duties as Stage-Instructeur, and wish therefore to direct your attention to the following: You are to attend each stage rehearsal as Arrangeur, Regisseur and as far as possible Instructeur. As far as the duties of Arrangeur are concerned, you are to inform the scene painter and the stage foreman in good time of your opinions about the stage setting; and a final decision about the scenery must be taken before the second stage-rehearsal. At the first stage-rehearsal draft proposals for the sets are to be ready, which are not to be deviated from after the second stage rehearsal.

'As far as *Regie* is concerned, you are to ensure that order is observed in the rehearsals and to determine penalties. You will draw up *Regie* lists and lists of properties, as well as scrutinizing and supplementing the older ones, and see to advertisements and the copying of parts. You are Regisseur on stage during performances, and as such will pay regard to curtain, lighting, heating, and sets etc., as well as determining who is to give signals, see to announcements, etc. in so far as you do not do these things yourself. You will inform Herr P. Nielsen and Herr Losting in good time of your proposals for costumes. You will draw up and if need be amend rehearsal lists, though always after consultation with the other Instructeurs [!] where time allows. You will confer regularly with Instructeurs Rojahn and Laading concerning the repertoire and casting, and seek to be prepared for unexpected eventualities. You will undertake all other *Regie* business not explicitly assigned to any other official. During general rehearsals you will note speech and acting, and especially interplay, and also that nobody by inadequate memorizing speaks another's part. Apart from the penalties you yourself decree, you are also to apply the penalties reported to you by the other Instructeurs and the Wardrobe Inspecteur.'

The reasons for this very considerable transfer of duties were probably fairly complex. On the one hand, it may well be (as Wiesener suggests) that the previous Regisseur, Herr Nielsen, found his stage-management duties interfering too much with his acting, and therefore welcomed the reduction in the scope of his responsibilities to include only the rehearsal rooms, singing room, and foyers—he still retained supervision of the wardrobe, the library, and the fabric of the theatre. On the other hand, it may have been in the management's mind so to occupy Ibsen's attention with (admittedly important) practical details that he should have less time and perhaps less inclination to argue about matters of dramatic interpretation.

Laading for his part found a new emphasis placed on his duties as Inspecteur. Yet another letter of resignation had come in from him to the Theatre, sometime in the middle of June; this time it was a difference of opinion relating to his duties as Inspecteur. Once again the Theatre was reluctant to lose him, and negotiations were begun to re-draft Laading's terms of reference as Inspecteur:

Terms of appointment
for the Inspecteur of the Norwegian Theatre in Bergen

1. The Inspecteur fills the position normally occupied by an artistic director. He confers directly with the board of management, and is their authorized representative vis-à-vis the Theatre.

2. As such he proposes the repertoire, and conducts the necessary correspondence in connection with it; makes nominations for the casting of approved plays after discussions about this with the music director and the Instructeurs; determines, attends, and if necessary takes a hand in the rehearsals, as well as taking any immediate measures which circumstances, or any defection by the personnel, or any managerial decisions might make necessary. He undertakes to make such casting changes as are necessary to maintain the repertoire, and supervises all the Theatre's actors and actresses. To this end he will determine penalties in accordance with the regulations.

3. He will see to it that all the Theatre's apparatus is used appropriately; and as a consequence of this he will ensure that all the Theatre's employees carry out their duties, and will impose such penalties as the regulations may require.

4. In the above-mentioned fields he is to take decisions (which are then to be reported to the board at the next meeting) in such a way that he is bound by any decisions taken or opinions expressed earlier by the board in similar circumstances; this authority is suspended when the board or one or more members of it are present, either before or at the same time as he is, and to his knowledge are informed of the matter in question; they will then take the decision, in which instance he acts then merely as expert consultant.

5. All applications addressed to the management from the actors proper or from actors and pupils reporting to our Theatre will be passed to him, of which he will then give an account. All employees of the theatre will pass their reports and proposals to him for forwarding with endorsements and comments along with his own proposals to the chairman of the board in time for its next meeting.

6. He is required to assist the board with any advice the latter requests in dealing with matters reaching it from outside.

This post, under the conditions defined here, was offered to Laading on 22 August 1853, to take effect from 16 September at a supplementary salary of 5 Speciedaler a month; he accepted three days later. It is clear from his duties that, however modest his responsibilities as Instructeur were, as Inspecteur he exercised considerable control over the artistic and organizational aspects of the Theatre's activities.

The arrangements so made seem to have run for two whole seasons before the management, in the summer of 1855, attempted another revision. On 25 June, the board wrote to both Ibsen and Laading with a suggested alteration that meant in effect that, as far as their duties as Instructeurs were concerned, they should exchange; moreover the revised salaries which were suggested apparently represented for both of them a reduction in total emoluments. Ibsen cautiously asked for further information and clarification before committing himself:

'Bergen, 27 June 1855

'To the Management of the Norwegian Theatre.

'Before I can regard myself as being in a position to answer the letter from the board of management of 25 inst. I am compelled to ask for further details about the proposed change in the positions of Instructeur. It appears from the management's letter that what is in view is: an exchange of those functions as Instructeur at present allocated to Herr Laading and to me. As however there are at the moment quite a number of other functions we both as Instructeurs have to do which in your view are not applicable to the office of Instructeur, I am uncertain which of them the management has taken as the basis of the proposed alteration—the practice prevailing for us up to now, or the inherent relationship of the different duties. The latter indubitably seems to me to be the most appropriate; the entire business of Instruction can then be assigned to one person, and the business of *Regie*, together with such other things as can naturally be combined with it, given to the other. As far as the reduction in salary is concerned, I shall not express any opinion until I have had further information from the management.'

Laading, in his reply the next day, turned the proposal down out of hand— he did not feel qualified to take over stage-rehearsals, despite his expressed willingness three years earlier to do his best in that particular appointment. Although the management tried to pursue the matter, nothing ever came of this proposal.

A 10. A measure of scholarly research has already been done on the manuscript production notes (*Regiebøger*) which Ibsen kept during his tenure of office at the Bergen Theatre, and which are now preserved in the University Library in Bergen; though it is also clear that, with still closer scrutiny, these records could be made to reveal a good deal more information about Ibsen's theatrical apprenticeship. The following brief account is based on a study of this manuscript material.

The *Regiebøger* for 1852 to 1857 inclusive contain production notes for the plays listed below. The works themselves are identified in these production notes by their Dano–Norwegian title, very occasionally with a note of the author or translator; the original titles and the dates of performance, where these could be determined, have been added to the tables below from other sources.

Plays in the Bergen Theatre's Regiebøger *1852–7*

Author	Dano–Norwegian title	Original title	First performed in Bergen
	1852 [sic]		
Dumanoir and d'Ennery	*Don Cæsar de Bazan*	*Don César de Bazan*	29 Dec. 52
K. Töpfer	*Den gode Tone*	*Der beste Ton*	18 Nov. 53
Enevold de Falsen	*Dragedukken*	*Dragedukken*	6 Oct. 52
J. F. A. Bayard	*Den hemmelige Lidenskab*	*Pas de fumée sans feu*	20 Oct. 52
A. Buntzen	*For ti Aar siden*	*For ti Aar siden*	27 Oct. 52
C. Hauch	*Æren tabt og vunden*	*Æren tabt og vunden*	9 Jan. 53
A. Duval	*Henrik den Femtes Ungdom*	*La jeunesse d'Henri V*	21 Nov. 52
J. L. Heiberg	*De Uadskillelige*	*De Uadskillelige*	10 Dec. 52
L. Holberg	*Jacob von Tyboe*	*Jacob von Tyboe*	7 Feb. 53
A. L. Arnesen	*Et Reiseeventyr*	*Et Reiseeventyr*	16 Feb. 53
A. E. Scribe	*Den unge Gudmoder*	*La marraine*	25 Feb. 53
	1853–4		
P. Henri Murger	*Den Gamle*	*Le bonhomme jadis*	28 May 53
J. L. Heiberg	*Kong Salomon og Jørgen Hattemager*	*Kong Salomon og Jørgen Hattemager*	24 Jul. 53
Bayard and Devorme	*Valeur & Comp.*	*Moiroud et Compagnie*	31 Jul. 53
H. Hertz	*Indkvarteringen*	*Indkvarteringen*	7 Aug. 53
J. Nestroy	*Lykkens Omveie*	*Der Zerrissene*	18 Dec. 53
Moreau	*Richard Savage*	*Richard Savage*	5 Mar. 54
M. Ancelot	*Et Ægteskab ved Hoffet*	*Comtesse de Chamilly*	4 Jan. 54
Th. Overskou	*Pak!*	*Pak!*	15 Oct. 53
Ernst Raupach	*Rafaele*	*Rafaele*	4 Dec. 53
J. F. A. Bayard	*Embedsiver*	*Un château de cartes*	16 Oct. 53
?	*En fattig Piges Dagbog*	?	27 Nov. 53
Laurencin and Marc-Michel	*Naar Kjærlighed køjlnes*	*Quand l'amour s'en va*	12 Oct. 53
Théaulon, Deforges and Jaime	*Dagen før Slaget ved Marengo*	*Carmagnole, ou: Les français sont des farceurs*	26 Oct. 53
N. Fournier	*Skuespillerinden*	*L'interprète*[?]	4 Nov. 53
Erik Bøgh	*Huldrebakken*	*Huldrebakken*	30 Nov. 53
Th. Overskou	*Kunstnerliv*	*Kunstnerliv*	11 Dec. 53
Roderich Benedix	*Hvor hun kan lyve!*	*Die Lügnerin*	14 Dec. 53
H. Hertz	*Scheik Hassan*	*Scheik Hassan*	12 Feb. 54
E. Souvestre	*En Bonde i vore Dage*	*Un paysan d'aujourd'hui*	3 Feb. 54
Duvert and Lauzanne	*Et enfoldigt Pigebarn*	*Renaudin de Caen*[1]	17 Feb. 54
A. E. Scribe	*Den unge Hovmesterinde*	*La tutrice*[?]	26 Feb. 54
A. E. Scribe	*Adrienne Lecouvreur*	*Adrienne Lecouvreur*	19 Mar. 54
E. Arago and P. Vermond	*Djævelens Memoirer*[2]	*Mémoires du Diable*	2 Apr. 54
A. E. Scribe	*Statsmand og Borger*[2] (Act III only)	*Bertrand et Raton, ou: L'art de conspirer*	[14 Oct. 57]

[1] Itself an adaptation of Calderon's *Casa con dos puertos mala es de guardar.*
[2] Not in Ibsen's hand.

Author	Dano–Norwegian title	Original title	First performed in Bergen
	1855–56 [sic]		
J. C. Hostrup	*Mester og Lærling*	*Mester og Lærling*	4 Oct. 54
A. E. Scribe	*Dronning Marguerites Noveller*	*Les Contes de la Reine de Navarre*	20 Oct. 54
J. C. Hostrup	*Den Tredie*	*Den Tredie*	20 Sept. 54
L. Feldmann	*Min Elskedes Portræt*	*Das Portrait der Geliebten*	30 Mar. 55
A. E. Scribe	*De Uafhængige*	*Les Indépendants*	11 Oct. 54
M. Ancelot and Dumanoir	*Et keiserligt Indfald*	?	12 Nov. 54
A. E. Scribe	*Min Lykkestjerne*	*Mon Etoile*	21 Mar. 55
C. Hostrup	*Drøm og Daad*	*Drøm og Daad*	9 Apr. 55
Magdalene Thoresen	*Herr Money*	*Herr Money*	?
W. Shakespeare	*Livet i Skoven*	*As You Like It*	30 Sept. 55
F. B. Hoffmann	*Skatten, eller: Staa ikke paa Lur*	*Le trésor supposé, ou: Le danger d'écouter aux portes*	7 Oct. 55
A. E. Scribe	*Halvdelen Hver*	*La part du diable*	4 Nov. 55
Mélesville and Xavier	*Hoffnarren imod sin Villie*	*Le buffon du prince*	11 Nov. 55
Bayard and Théaulon	*Debutantindens Fader*	*Le père de la débutante*	2 Dec.. 55
S. Mosenthal	*En Landsbyhistorie*	*Der Sonnenwendhof*	21 Nov. 56
Barbier, Guillard and Decourcelle	*Den sidste Nat*	*Le bal du prisonnier*	12 Nov. 56
Oehlenschläger	*Væringerne i Miklagard*	*Væringener i Miklagard*	30 Nov. 56
H. Ibsen	*Olaf Liljekrans*	*Olaf Liljekrans*	2 Jan. 57
A. E. Scribe	*Statsmand og Borger*[1] (Acts I and II only)	*Bertrand et Raton, ou: L'art de conspirer*	14 Oct. 57
	1857		
E. Augier and Jules Sandeau	*Herr Poiriers Svigersøn*	*Le gendre de M. Poirier*	3 May 57
Octave Feuillet	*I Alderdommen*	*Le village*	1 June 57
Laurencin and Lubize	*Ikke en Smule jaloux*[1]	*Pas jaloux*	28 Aug. 57
A. E. Scribe	*En Lænke*[1]	*Une chaîne*	30 Aug. 57
A. E. Scribe	*Lazarilla*[1]	*La chanteuse voilée*	10 May 57
Soulié and Badon	*Et Eventyr under Carl den 9de*[1]	*Une aventure sous Charles IX*	?
M. J. Bouchardy	*Ringeren i St. Paul*[1]	*Le sonneur de St. Paul*	6 Sept. 57
Thomas Morton	*Den hjemkomne Nabob*[1]	*A cure for the heart-ache*	26 Dec. 58
Mélesville	*Zampa* [*Marmorbruden*][1]	*Zampa, ou: La fiancée de marbre*	?
Bayard	*Dronningen paa 16 Aar*[1]	*La reine de seize ans*	8 Oct. 57
Mélesville and Dumanois	*Gamle Minder*[1]	*Les vieux péchés*	21 Oct. 57
D'Epagny and Dupin	*Dominique*[1]	*Dominique, ou: Le possédé*	1 Nov. 57
Chr. Monsen	*Gudbrandsdølerne*[1]	*Gudbrandsdølerne*	14 Jan. 58

[1] Not in Ibsen's hand.

Proposals for the 1852–3 season, beginning in the autumn, were discussed by the board as early as 10 April, for which meeting both Ibsen and Laading had made suggestions. Although it is unlikely that the definitive programme was drawn up as early as this—and indeed room was eventually found for one or two recommendations Ibsen made from his visit to Copenhagen and Dresden—it can be assumed that Ibsen had good warning about a number of likely titles, and was in a position to begin his study of them, as Stage-Instructeur, pretty promptly on his return to Bergen from abroad. Indeed, there is no reason why he could not have begun even while still abroad, though there appears to be no positive evidence to support this supposition.

It is however clear from the manuscript of the *Regiebog* for 1852 that Ibsen gave systematic scrutiny to the eleven plays listed there. The analyses run serially, in the sense that in a number of instances he began his notes for a new play on a page already containing notes from the previous one. The diagrammatic representation of the characters' movements on stage in *Den gode Tone*, for example, follow straight on from the end of the notes for *Don Cæsar de Bazan*, which had occupied only half a page; indeed this arrangement occurs in all the plays up to and including *Æren tabt og vunden*, and also in the case of *Den unge Gudmoder*. The handwriting is in general carefully formed throughout, and bears all the signs of careful and leisurely preparation, with the exception of *Et Reiseeventyr*, which is not titled, and where of the work's forty-three scenes the first fifteen have entries in Ibsen's hand and the remaining twenty-eight are in a different hand.

Apart from this last-mentioned irregularity, the evidence of the handwriting suggests that this batch of plays was studied in one relatively unbroken and uniform operation. This conclusion is further supported by the fact that the general pattern of note-making for these eleven plays is unchanged throughout, whereas for the later plays a number of modifications were introduced. The entries are made with the longer side of the sheet running horizontally; a normal page then takes the form of being divided vertically into two, each half consisting of a narrower column on the left headed (or later simply intended for) 'Cues', and the remainder used for written entries, headed by act and scene number, of the entrances, positions, groupings, movement, and exits of the characters. At the beginning of the notes for each play, however, and for the beginning of each subsequent act, there is a half-page plan drawing (some of them partly coloured) of the stage, showing the position of the wings and side shutters, curtains, prompt box and built sets (e.g. the steps and façade of an inn) or stage furniture (tables and chairs, etc.). Superimposed on this, using dotted lines which are identified and plotted either by letters and indices (a, a′, a″ . . . b, b′ . . . etc.) in the case of the main characters, or by arabic numerals (1, 2, 3 . . . etc.) for crowd players, are details of the characters' entrances, movements, positions, and exits. The identifying letters and numbers are used for cross-references to the notes.

It is worth remarking at this point that 'left' and 'right' correspond to the

S 11

modern English practice of 'stage-left' and 'stage-right', i.e. as determined by an actor facing the audience, and not as in Ibsen's later practice where 'left' and 'right' mean 'as viewed from the audience'.

It should also be admitted that whereas these diagrams are very detailed for the earlier plays, they become progressively less detailed. After *Dragedukken* the dotted lines virtually disappear and the positions of the characters are shown statically by letters; and for the last two plays in the list of eleven, the details on the diagrams are only rudimentary.

In the actual programme for the autumn, not all the plays on this list were performed, nor does their order in the *Regiebog* correspond to the sequence of performances. The first play to be produced under Ibsen's 'Instruction' was *Dragedukken* on 6 October 1852, and with the performance of *Den unge Gudmoder* on 25 February 1853, ten of the eleven plays listed had reached the theatre. Töpfer's *Den gode Tone* was not performed until November 1853.

For the plays shown under 1853, the pattern of note-making was changed. Entries were still made with the sheet held horizontally; but diagrams disappear, except for a startlingly detailed diagram (including elaborate dotted line movements) for Ancelot's *Comtesse de Chamilly* (*Et Ægteskab ved Hoffet*), and one or two thumbnail sketches for Nestroy's *Der Zerrissene* (*Lykkens Omveie*). Now the page is ruled vertically into five columns of unequal width, of which the first is the narrowest and the third generally the widest, headed 'Scene', 'Scenarium', 'Positions', 'Properties' [*Reqvisiter*], and 'Remarks'. The entries for the last two plays are not in Ibsen's hand; that for *Mémoires du diable* (*Djævelens Memoirer*) is not unlike the hand that added to the notes for *Et Reiseeventyr* in 1852 (see above); the notes for Act III of *Bertrand et Raton* (*Statsmand og Borger*) are in a different hand both from Ibsen's and from that used for *Mémoires du diable*, but which is found again in the notes for Acts I and II of *Bertrand et Raton* in the 1855–6 series.

For the plays in the 1855–6 and the 1857 *Regiebøger*, the format of the note-keeping was once again changed. Now there are double-page entries, still with the longer side of the sheets horizontal, with seven columns: 'Scene', 'Entrance', 'Position', 'Exit', 'Remarks', 'Properties', and 'For use by'. As time passes some of the entries become very laconic, even cryptic, and are mostly limited to the more obvious comings and goings on-stage. (A translation of Ibsen's notes for Act I of his own *Olaf Liljekrans* based on this pattern of note making is given on pp. 708–9.) In the 1857 *Regiebog*, only the first two plays have notes in Ibsen's handwriting; the remaining eleven entries are probably by the same hand that wrote the notes to *Mémoires du diable* in the 1853–4 collection.

It is also remarkable that of Ibsen's own plays produced during these years in Bergen, the only one for which there is any entry in these *Regiebøger* is *Olaf Liljekrans*.

A 11. The board of management was not always persuaded that Ibsen was performing his duties with the necessary zeal and efficiency; in the summer of 1853, shortly after the first major redistribution of responsibilities, the management felt constrained to write to Ibsen (in a most contorted Norwegian, incidentally) drawing attention to certain deficiencies in the way he was carrying out his duties:

'30 July 1853

'To
Instructeur Ibsen.

'At various times the management has been aware that a number of matters within your province have in part been postponed and eventually forgotten, or else have in part not always been executed in the way the Theatre regards as desirable. In particular one might draw attention to mistakes or inaccuracies in announcements, incomplete *Regie* lists, the all too summary treatment of sets and scenery, etc.; it would moreover also be to the benefit of both parties if you could display greater effectiveness on stage both as Regisseur and as Instructeur. Nevertheless, the board of management still feels that this neglect of duty derives more from a lack of routine organization than from any lack either of efficiency or of determination to carry out your appointment; and in regretting the necessity of having to urge you to bestir yourself to make up for these and similar complaints, it wishes briefly to indicate the method and the means wherewith this might be achieved. That the Stage-Instructeur must have gone through in advance the plays being produced is something so obvious that one would not have drawn your attention to it if one were not persuaded—and wanted to indicate the fact—that going through the plays thus is the only way to achieve full and complete lists, both of stage-management and of other arrangements. Sustained attention of this kind to the plays being dealt with by the Theatre would surely of necessity be accompanied by a deeper understanding of them in production; and as these are generally the ones scheduled soon for performance, this would help you to avoid all manner of mistakes; and it is this alone which can put you in a position to use the Theatre's properties and equipment in the most efficient way for the plays in question.

'In this last respect, one must remind you that you must yourself ensure a tasteful arrangement and deployment of the properties which have been assembled—properties which as far as possible you must seek to acquire or to borrow from places known to you, both so that you can supervise any purchases and also because you are responsible for ensuring that things are returned properly. In respect of such purchases, as well as of any objects specifically requested by you as stage properties, you must follow a course of the strictest economy—naturally within the limits of what is required by the circumstances—for it is your responsibility to confirm that the bills are in accord with what you have ordered, and that they have been drawn up with the greatest possible care and economy; however, you do not possess the power to authorize payment of them, since this is a matter for the board of management alone.'

Ibsen replied within a few days:

'Bergen, 4 August 1853.

'In reply to the letter of 30 ult. from the board of management, I have only to state the following:

'From the time I was made responsible for *Regie* [5 May], I have had the following *Regie* lists to compile:

1. *Den Gamle.*
2. *Kong Salomon og Jørgen Hattemager.*
3. *Valeur & Comp.*
4. *Indkvartering.*

'These four Regie lists are naturally open to inspection if demanded; and it will be seen from them that the informer concerned has been less than well informed. There are no inaccuracies in those *Regie* lists compiled by me.

'As far as [Scribe's and Xavier's] *Babiole og Jablot* and [F. von Holbein's] *Efterskriften* are concerned, these plays were arranged by translator and author, whose properties [*Reqvisit*] lists are available in the theatre from the time the plays were performed by the Danes. For the remaining plays performed since I was handed the task of *Regie*, the lists were compiled by Mayson and Nielsen. Repeated performances of these plays have over a a long period of time given opportunities for correcting what must have been incomplete or inaccurate items in these lists from the very start.

'As far as the accusation of "summary treatment of sets and scenery" is concerned, I would have been very grateful to the board of management if this reproach had been couched less "summarily"; for I might then have been in a position to make good in some respects one thing which I indeed no less than the board consider especially important. Meanwhile as long as I continue to be kept in uncertainty about the improvements which are regarded as desirable in this matter, it is not easy for me to approach the problem any differently from before. That there is a great deal which one might wish different in the scenic arrangement of sets, etc., is not open to doubt; but whether the board would approve the expenditure necessary to supplement what the Theatre lacks is another question. That I shall seek in the meantime to make the most effective use of the materials I have at my disposal is something I have always supposed was self-evident.

'Finally I am very ready to admit that my arrangements as Regisseur still do not in all respects work as smoothly as one would desire; I imagined it would be obvious to anybody familiar with the theatre that what a Regisseur chiefly requires is a routine; and I know full well that I have not found it possible to achieve this in sufficiently high degree by acting as Regisseur for 4–5 productions.

Respectfully

Henr. Ibsen

'PS. The above reply would have been handed in last Thursday, if by a misunderstanding I had not assumed that because of the absence of Herr Steen and Herr Wille no meeting would be held, as a result of which a fair copy of the above lines was not quite completed for the beginning of the meeting. 11 August 1853.'

The board was not impressed by Ibsen's reply, and wrote back:

'To

Herr Instructeur Ibsen

'Your communication of 4 inst. was received by the board on the 11th; it does not find itself occasioned to retract any of the complaints made in its letter to you of 30 July, nor to regard as superfluous the instructions contained in it as to how to remedy these.'

Reading between the lines of this exchange one finds some reinforcement for the view which Peter Blytt expressed (see above, p. 622) that Ibsen was not the kind of person who found it easy to issue orders to others, nor did he take any pleasure in it. Letters to the management of 3 November, 5 and 21 December 1853, 4 November 1854 and 19 August 1856 throw some light on the kind of difficulties Ibsen faced in attempting to keep discipline in the company.

(a)

'3 Nov. 1853

'To the Management of the
   Norwegian Theatre!

'At the rehearsal yesterday afternoon of *Den gode Tone*, Herr Isachsen quite blandly permitted himself to babble his lines in a way that rendered the rehearsal practically useless for his fellow players, namely Mme Hundevadt and H. Nielsen, both of whom have new and substantial parts to learn in the play without any expectation of very many rehearsals. On inquiring of him the reason for this conduct, I was given the answer that he did not feel justified in rehearsing any differently, and that he "was greatly astonished that the theatre did not show him the consideration of releasing him from rehearsals" at this time when his wedding was approaching. I do not know the extent of the obligation which the management feels it owes to the theatre's "indispensable artists"—but for my own part I venture to suppose that I have never undermined these obligations by holding the above-mentioned rehearsals. At the rehearsal this morning Herr Isachsen did not attend at all, of which he gave me provisional warning already yesterday evening, adding that he was naturally willing to pay the statutory fine for being absent. Since I now learn that the officers of the theatre cannot directly apply the letter of the law against the artist in question, and also as the fine would merely apply to the one matter of being absent from rehearsal, but would in no sense provide any protection against the poison of insubordination which Herr Isachsen seems to have given himself the task of spreading within the theatre, I must herewith request the management to take a hand as soon as possible.

'Nor must I refrain from remarking: Isachsen's scenes in *Den gode Tone* can be run through in twenty minutes; and during the preliminary rehearsals of *Feltgiftermaalet* he had ample opportunity to learn his lines. The enclosed rehearsal programme for the week is moreover a natural consequence of the benefit performance, which over the past eight days took all the unoccupied hours. Isachsen is of course aware of this; so it is therefore with the benefit performance in mind that Herr Isachsen is suggesting that insufficient consideration is being shown him by the theatre. Herr Isachsen has set up a very significant yardstick for his demands—and as in this instance the fault for this allegedly inconsiderate treatment is seemingly to be sought in me, by my assigning him to the rehearsals in question on the rehearsal programme, I must herewith request the management to investigate the matter as soon as possible.'

(b)

'5 Dec. 1853

'To the management of the
Norwegian Theatre!

'In answer to the communication overleaf, the following may be remarked:
    a. The rehearsal programme for Friday, 25 November was originally as follows

        9.15 a.m. *Keiserindens Fanger* (Sc:f: Miss Jensen)
          a.m.   (Reading rehearsal)

    b. As far as the reading rehearsal is concerned, therefore, *nothing* on the programme was changed; there was simply the addition of which play was to be read, and at what time. This was all entered on the programme immediately after Rosendahl's acceptance of the proffered engagement was communicated to me, or approximately 6.15, during the rehearsal of Act II of *En fattig Piges Dagbog*, which can be confirmed by Herr Laading, who took over the surveillance on stage whilst I prepared *Kunstnerliv* for reading, distributed the parts of the play and collected the signatures of the cast. Herr Isachsen was the only one who was not present, as he was not included in the play which was being rehearsed.

'At the conclusion of the evening rehearsal (approaching 7 p.m.) the theatre messenger was not there, which is why I requested Mme Isachsen to pass on to her husband the information that *Kunstnerliv* was scheduled for rehearsal for 11 a.m. the following morning—which she promised to do. It will be remembered that Rosendahl's acceptance of the management's offer was the crucial factor in determining the casting of the play in question, which is the reason for Isachsen not having had the play to read through. Mme Isachsen was therefore asked similarly if she would take her husband's part with her, so that he could take steps to familiarize himself in advance with what was necessary. The original rehearsal programme referred to above is enclosed.'

(c)

'Bergen 21 Dec. 1853

'To the management of the
Norwegian Theatre!

'As a result of a communication the management received last week, it will be aware that Herr Isachsen has taken the liberty of writing in the Theatre book his criticism of certain organizational arrangements. To this criticism I felt justified in adding a comment; and in consequence of my comment—which his own words seemed in the most natural way possible to invite—Herr Isachsen apparently feels insulted. He has therefore once more seized his pen, and this time he has produced a literary abortion which I herewith enclose for the scrutiny of the management.

'As the management is presumably not unaware, Isachsen's style is peculiar in that one generally has to read between the lines if one wishes to form any kind of positive estimate of the writer's sense and logicality. This characteristic is in no way contradicted by the enclosed abortion; and as I attempt to the best of my ability to interpret the accusation against me contained in it, the management must kindly forgive me if, by force of necessity, I have to be somewhat prolix.

'To judge from his phrases, Isachsen seems to want to make me responsible in my duties for sustaining the feeble-minded "in this, that and the other respect". Ah, the things that the instinct for self-preservation can lead a man to demand as right and proper, when one is blinded by egoism to the degree Isachsen is! I must honestly admit that I have never been aware of such responsibilities; on the contrary, I have always thought that instead of "sustaining" I rather had to attempt, as far as it was in my power, to *break down* those obstacles that get in the way of artistic progress and development, among which—despite Isachsen's apparent protest—I count feebleness of mind "in this, that and the other respect". And even if one were to leave artistic development out of consideration, Isachsen's own conduct towards the theatre yields sufficient evidence of how dangerous it is to "sustain" the mentally feeble no matter how this feebleness manifests itself—either as blind and unjustified self-confidence, boundless faith in one's indispensability, or any other way and in any other respect.

'Yet, doubtless what Isachsen *thought* was not as stupid as what he *wrote*— he obviously meant the opposite. Clearly and often enough previously, Isachsen has announced that the "instruction" the theatre manages to provide is not adequate for him; and when he now claims that the feeble-minded in the company are not being "sustained" as they require, I cannot see other than that these two complaints are identical, the only difference being that in the instance in question he has used a different and more naïve form. As far as the other members of the company are concerned, I have reason to believe that in this case they are for once less modest than Herr Isachsen and will therefore protest at being placed under the heading of "feeble-minded", where he looks like having to stand alone. Moreover, Isachsen has frequently and unanimously insisted on his right to be placed under a rubric of his own; and I feel certain that at least this time one can with a good conscience allow him that with perfect right.

'If then, as a result of what is set down above, I have been so fortunate as to find the right interpretation of the passage cited, I feel that a point of departure is then vouchsafed to which I have to attach my remarks. These I shall permit myself to present in the form of an explanation of the following three factors:

pro primo:) Which among Isachsen's mental weaknesses are the most significant?

pro secundo:) How ought these weaknesses best be treated?

And finally I shall

pro tertio:) prove that at the moment Isachsen is and must be unreceptive to any "instruction" from without.

'The answer to the first point, a more detailed indication of the inner difficulties which prevent him from developing artistically, is so obvious that I need not detain myself. I shall therefore limit myself to mentioning his remarkable superficiality, his dull and deficient sense of his art, and his immodest opinion of his own relation to it. The evidence that Isachsen actually suffers from these weaknesses I think I can justifiably pass over—if desired, evidence would not be lacking.

'Taking for granted that this is how things are with Isachsen, I now ask with what right he reproaches *me* for the fact that his deficiencies are not given adequate attention? If, instead of thinking that he gets help from the aesthetic crumbs he has snapped up here and there in his early days and only half digested, Isachsen would recognize how weak his foundations actually are—furthermore if instead of "working on" the classics Isachsen would use his many leisure hours to "work on" himself, by studying properly and similar intellectual dredging work—his mind could still become a navigable channel for wholesome and sensible ideas. But before that happens, before Isachsen begins his cure himself by recognizing the dubiousness of his present attitude, I cannot see that any outside influence would be particularly fruitful for him. Isachsen's resistance to constructive criticism is moreover not insubstantially increased by the fact that he thinks he sees in the management's actions etc. confirmation of his own opinion of the superior place he occupies vis-à-vis the rest of the company. Far be it from me to concur with Isachsen's interpretation of the management's actions. But it strikes me that anybody, even if he lacks medical training, must recognize the danger of treating such a patient with substances which feed instead of suppress the sickness—but I cannot deny that Isachsen's smugness makes the misunderstanding on his part readily explicable; and that this misunderstanding will be difficult to remove until the management have drawn Isachsen's attention to it in clear and precise terms. But it is not only in his relations with the theatre that egoism and superficial thinking lead Isachsen to draw false conclusions; the same holds also for his relations with the public. If one inquires in which roles Isachsen has had curtain-calls or pronounced applause, one finds that it is virtually exclusively in those cases which either sustain themselves or in which Isachsen has had the opportunity to copy from successful models—yet it never occurs to him to ascribe the happy result to anybody but himself.

'As a contribution to the characterization of Isachsen, may I adduce a trait that emerges from the production of *Rafaele*. When the play was given its first performance, Isachsen played his part with so much "power" that, according to his and the newspaper's account, three women had to be carried out of the theatre (mischievous people assert it was the three Graces who felt pained)—he was applauded, given curtain-calls and was greatly pleased with himself and the public. On the Wednesday a cold compelled him considerably to moderate his "powerful performance"; applause was more meagre; his curtain-call somewhat uncertain; and yet there is scarcely any competent man, having attended both, who has not admitted that Isachsen's second performance satisfied the demands of art, taste and beauty in a much higher degree. But Isachsen himself, misled by the less brilliant result, considered the performance unsuccessful, threw the blame on his indisposition and—delivered himself of the comforting assurance that when the play was given its next performance he would certainly give the part its original power.

'But if Isachsen, as an actor, finds his satisfaction in attracting some momentary applause from the public, by no matter what means; if he feels his aesthetic conscience satisfied by seeing himself mentioned with approval in some amiable dramatic notice; and if furthermore the fulfilment of the universal demands of art is a matter of such subordinate importance to him, then it is my opinion that the inauthenticity of Isachsen's view of his art is adequately demonstrated. And as he is moreover unshakable in his views, he has shut himself off from all outside influence; and I conclude from this what I was at pains to demonstrate above, namely: that at the present moment Isachsen is and must be unreceptive to any "instruction" from without.

'With this I might very well finish; but from what was said above one other thing emerges, which I cannot deny myself the pleasure of mentioning in passing: Isachsen proposes that my immediate and most solemn duty is to employ my best cultural talents in the service of the Theatre—and the truth of this is admitted. But if Isachsen is to be consistent, he would also have to acknowledge that the same applies to every intellect in the pay of the Theatre, including himself. And as the Theatre can thus lay claim upon his abilities in so far as these latter can be developed in conditions of natural progress, and yet he nevertheless resists this progress, so it is obvious that in consequence of his own words he is cheating the Theatre, in that he is neglecting his responsibilities to the same.

'As far as the remaining rude remarks of his are concerned, I consider I can ignore them. The tirade about public opinion I do not understand; the public knows absolutely nothing of my written remarks in the so-called "waste-paper" books. The tirade is therefore, as I said, meaningless—unless Isachsen, naïvely enough, is wanting to say that what is known to him of the domestic affairs of the Theatre is *eo ipso* public knowledge—an admission the truth of which I have too much experience of for it to occur to me to contradict.

'And with this I place the matter in the hands of the management; I am not petitioning for any measures to be taken against Isachsen, but hope to see made explicit in the freely-taken decision of the management on which side right may be supposed to lie.

Faithfully
Henr: Ibsen'

(*d*)

'4 Nov. 1854

'To the Management of
   the Norwegian Theatre.

'I have received a complaint from Controlleur Jacobsen that the actor Johansen attacked him in coarse language during the last performance because he (Jacobsen) had denied an unauthorized person access to the theatre. In this instance I must request that Johansen be summoned before the assembled board of management to be given a serious reprimand; since the kind of order desired in the theatre will be difficult to maintain if this matter is allowed to pass without comment.

Faithfully
Henr: Ibsen'

(e)

'Bergen 19 Aug. 1856

'Mr Baars!

'Today I received a note signed by you, which apparently was drafted by decision of the entire board. When I learn from this note that the Over-kontrolleur (!) has made a complaint about me, and that the board has made a pronouncement without my (the accused) having been asked for an account, I simply discover in this a new attempt on your part to introduce into the Theatre a form of justice which I do not respect, even though it is prescribed by that corporation which I, by reason of my contractual obligations, am required to regard as an authority in artistic matters and all things related to them. I must therefore regard your note simply as a private communication, and it is as such that I hereby answer it.

'The matter is as follows: Last Sunday evening during the performance, the actor Hestenæs approached me in the foyer with a complaint that a policeman who had been put there on duty had turned him out of the Royal Box, which was practically empty and where he had sat to watch the performance because his dress did not permit him to show himself in the stalls.

'As, according to Hestenæs' own words, it had been greatly insulting for him to be hauled up and turned out in the middle of a performance and in full view, by a policeman with baton and in full uniform, he (Hestenæs) urged me to get for him the recompense the matter demanded, which in his view was best achieved by his being set in possession of the empty seat from which he had been turned out. I therefore accompanied him up to the balcony, asked the man on duty to let him pass, and promised the latter to talk to Kooter about the matter; for the latter was the man referred to me as the one who had ordered his removal. When I approached Kooter, I discovered that he had acted on a management decision which rescinded a practice prevailing in the Theatre long before my time by which the actors not on stage may have access (without ticket) wherever there is room among the audience.

'This is the matter as far as it concerns me. You see therefore that I have in no sense, as your communication suggests, interfered with the board's opportunity to show its "authority"; on the contrary, the whole thing appears as though ideas about the board's authority have caused you to forget a board's duties. For you would otherwise realize that when the board takes a decision like the one in question here, a decision the application of which in practice must necessarily be extremely offensive to those affected by it— it is your prime duty as a board to have this decision communicated. Admittedly your "authority" as a board would then appear less conspicuous than when, as happened, it is asserted by the action of policemen, but the demands of humanity and good organization in any case call for this, and these are not insignificant aspects.

'You will therefore see that I have committed no offence, and that I have not made any untimely encroachment upon the activities of the board; the board's decision in question was in no way communicated to me or to any other relevant person; and that consequently I acted in good faith in that I followed a convention sanctioned for years by practice is something that anybody must admit. And if the board in future is going to continue its business in the way indicated by this first step, then I too intend to continue as I began. The board can dismiss me, and this I would have to accept—but unjustified reprimands I will not accept. And I shall prove my contention that the reprimand is unjustified—unless: either you can establish that that decision was communicated to me, or you declare that in future all conventions in the theatre are abolished and only the strict letter of the law prevails.

'But the first of these you cannot do—and you will hardly want to do the second; for those who would be worst affected if the so-called Theatre Regulations were given practical validity, would in truth be the board and the theatre's functionaries. And to claim that the Regulations shall prevail only when it is convenient for the management, and not otherwise—that can surely not be your intention. That the members cf the company only have access to the stalls is a regulation that has always only existed on paper; it is dictated by a limited view of things, by which the actors are thought of as visiting the theatre with the same object as the public. But that is not how it is in reality: the actor, who at best can see only *one* play monthly from the audience, has a quite different purpose and need in mind; and indeed the Theatre is not the least beneficiary of such a free entry once every month.

'In conclusion, therefore, I must request you—if the Theatre Regulations are to be taken as operative—to repeal Section 1, para. 16, so that the members of the company, for the sake of their art, can make the best use of their freedom on performance evenings.

'The many additions and amendments which the reintroduction of the Regulations will demand, the consequences of which will presumably be quite clear to the board, are awaited with great anticipation.

Respectfully
Henr: Ibsen.'

A 12. In the autumn of 1855 Ibsen was elected to membership of the 'Society of 22 December'. This was a society established by a group of Bergen citizens on 22 December 1845, with a 'literary and social' emphasis; fortnightly—sometimes weekly—meetings would be held during the winter months, at which generally lectures or readings were given, or newly published books discussed; subscriptions were taken out for certain literary periodicals. Ibsen was proposed for membership by the chairman, Peter Blytt, who the previous year had joined the board of management of the Theatre and there made the closer acquaintance of Ibsen. Within a few weeks of his election, on 27 November 1855, Ibsen read a paper to the Society entitled: 'W. Shakespeare and his influence upon Scandinavian literature'. The text of this paper has apparently not survived; nor is there anything in the records of the Society but a laconic entry confirming that the lecture had in fact been given.

For the tenth and eleventh anniversary celebrations on 22 December 1855 and 1856, Ibsen wrote occasional poems (reprinted by Francis Bull, 'Fra Ibsens og Bjørnsons ungdomsaar i Bergen', *Edda*, v, 1919, pp. 161–2).

The Society's minutes for the meeting of 2 February 1857 include the entry: 'Instructeur Ibsen gave a lecture on the Norwegian heroic ballad. He has promised to draft an account of this to be included in the Minutes.' Doubtless this lecture was substantially the same as the essay 'On the Heroic Ballad and its significance for Literature', which Ibsen published in the *Illustreret Nyhedsblad*, nos. 19 and 20, 10 and 17 May 1857 (translated below, pp. 672–84).

A 13. In the early spring of 1856 the company undertook a tour to Trondheim where according to T. Blanc (*Norges første nationale Scene*, p. 209) the company gave thirty-three performances in the months of March, April, and May, together with a benefit performance for the players on 1 June. Ibsen did not remain with the company for the whole of its tour; in the course of March, however, he sent three fairly detailed reports, before eventually at the end of the month requesting permission to return to Bergen.

(*a*)

'Trondhjem, 6 March 1856

'To the management of the
Norwegian Theatre in Bergen

'I have the pleasure to report to the management that we all arrived here on Sunday afternoon, safe and well. In the course of Monday and Tuesday we obtained the permission of the diocese to give performances, orchestra musicians were engaged, largely on the existing terms, also singers, supporting players, properties, and the like; subscription lists were made out and are now circulating round the town. Agreement has been reached on favourable terms about the supply and the improvement of the necessary sets, and Alsing has declared his readiness to apply more than the sum stipulated (100 Speciedaler) to this purpose—which will assist us greatly. Yesterday (Wednesday) we performed *Embedsiver* [*Un château de cartes*, by J. F. A. Bayard] and *Abekatten* ["The Monkey", by Johanne Luise Heiberg]. Madame Isachsen is still hoarse, and I therefore gave her part in the former play to Miss Jensen, who distinguished herself. When Madame Isachsen can be called upon is uncertain, so I have passed her part in *Indkvartering* ["Lodging", by H. Hertz] to Miss Guldbrandsen. "Caprice" in *Rataplan* [by Sewrin and Vincentini] had to be taken over by Miss Jensen. Unfortunately *Ude og Hjemme* [*Le mari à la campagne*, by Bayard and de Vailly] cannot be played without Madame Isachsen; if her indisposition continues, the performance of that play must be postponed—but I hope that will not be necessary. The takings from yesterday's performance were 122 Specie-daler, which must be thought quite good, especially considering the shocking weather conditions as well as the choice of play. *Embedsiver* has a bad reputation here; it was twice performed very badly by Danes—and booed off. *Abekatten* has been played here innumerable times. I was admittedly already aware of these facts on Monday, but saw no reason to depart from the planned repertoire. Both plays were received with loud and continuous applause; the audience was in a good mood—interest in the theatre is great.

'The Theatre's seal (stamp) was left behind in Bergen; could it please be sent by the first steamer? This oversight caused us a certain amount of trouble; nevertheless we have now made satisfactory arrangements for the sale of tickets. We might well have brought tickets with us from Bergen; we are not too well supplied here, for most of the sets are defective—nevertheless we shall manage. Tomorrow we play *De Deporterede* ["The Deportees", by H. Hertz] and *Cousine Lotte* [by C. M. Wengel]. Approximate cost of gas lighting is estimated at 3 Speciedaler per performance, rehearsals included. The conduct of the company, both on the journey and while here, has been exemplary. All are well lodged. The freight costs for the Theatre's effects were 12 Speciedaler. Access to the first class was possible without extra charge. The takings have provisionally been deposited in the Bank of Norway.

Respectfully
Henr: Ibsen'

(*b*)

'Trondhjem, 14 March 1856

'To the management of the Norwegian
  Theatre in Bergen

Friday, 7th.	*De Deporterede* and *Cousine Lotte*	69 Sp.	54 β
Sunday, 9th.	*Nei* [by J. L. Heiberg], *Indkvartering*, and		
	Ja [by J. L. Heiberg]	148 Sp.	108 β
Wednesday, 12th	*Scheik Hassan* [by H. Hertz] and *Rataplan*	128 Sp.	36 β
(1st subscription)			
Half of the subscriptions which have now come in			
amount to		349 Sp.	80 β
Takings at the first performance (Wed. 5th)		121 Sp.	6 β
Total		817 Sp.	44 β

The takings were deposited in the Bank of Norway (per folio); we could perhaps remit a proportion, but I thought it would be sensible to wait for the outcome of the first two performances after the week's pause to avoid any embarrassments about paying wages, etc. to 1 April. May I please ask for a copy of the lease arranged with the Trondhjem Theatre; as the theatre here is let annually (and presumably calculated from the day the contract is concluded), it seems reasonable to me that the sums received from letting the theatre in the meantime should be deducted from the rent our Theatre has to pay. Perhaps that is what Alsing intends; but as I do not know the details of the contents of the contract, I have refrained from mentioning this matter to him.

'Madame Isachsen is still indisposed, and in the event of her not being available till Easter Monday I have arranged for the following reserve programme:

Monday, 24th	*Skomageren og Grevinden* [*Riquiqui*, by St. Georges and de Leuven]
Wednesday, 26th	*Livet i Skoven* [*As You Like It*, by Shakespeare]: 2nd subscription performance.
Friday, 28th	*Charlotte Corday* [by F. Ponsard] (Marie = Miss Jensen); *Soldaterløier* ["Soldier's fun", by C. Hostrup].
Saturday, 30th	*Gildet paa Solhoug* ["The Feast at Solhoug", by Ibsen]; and:

I hope, however, she will be better again by then; meanwhile I have arranged for Miss Sørensen to prepare the role of "Josseline" in *Min Lykkestjerne* [*Mon Etoile*, by Scribe], and that of the Queen in *Halvdelen hver* [from *La part du diable*, by Scribe]. *Gildet paa Solhoug* cannot be performed unless the sets and decor are sent from Bergen; and I request that Larsen (Schjøll's assistant) be instructed *without delay* to dismantle and pack the scenery for the first (and third) act, together with the house for the second—all of which must of course be removed from the wooden framework, and must reach here on the next steamer. I have obtained the assistance *gratis* of nine singers by approaching a local choir group, with not inconsiderable saving.

'The company is working well together, and energetically, and behaving well in every respet. We are presenting *Eventyr paa Fodreisen* ["Adventure on a walking tour", by C. Hostrup].

Respectfully,
Henr. Ibsen.'

(c)

'Trondhjem, 20 March 1856

'To the management of the
    Norwegian Theatre.

'Although I really have nothing to report this time, I think I ought to draw the attention of the management to an arrangement which may possibly prove to be necessary. Madame Isachsen's hoarseness looks like lasting some time (she is pregnant, and they say that in that condition the voice takes a long time to come back) and to keep her out of the repertoire for any length of time will be impracticable; those plays in which she can be replaced will be exhausted in the course of one month. I therefore propose that the management considers whether it might not be sensible to send Miss Siewers up here. If so, it ought to be at once, because she could probably be of most use to us in the immediate future. In my earlier letter I mentioned that *Skomageren og Grevinden* would be performed on Easter Monday if Madame I. was not recovered. In the meantime I have had second thoughts, and *En ital. Straahat* [*Un chapeau de paille d'Italie*, by Marc Michel and Labiche] will be given after all. I have asked Miss Jensen to study Madame Isachsen's role in the event of the latter not being able to appear (she is actually a little better than last week); Isachsen will play not only his own part but also Miss Jensen's (chambermaid with the Baroness, which is changed to a man-servant); and Hansen, apart from his own role, also plays the Corporal in Act V. The takings at Friday's performance (*Eventyr paa Fodreisen*) amounted to 91 Speciedaler and a few skilling. The play was a huge success; it has also been suggested from many quarters that it should also be performed for those who have taken subscription tickets. I do not know if the management has received my letter of 14th inst; if not, I must repeat my request that Larsen be instructed to pack and send the scenery for *Gildet paa Solhoug*, along with the painted house for Act II. The play is down for performance on 2 April. All is well. I was pleased to receive the management's letter.

Respectfully
Henr: Ibsen'

(*d*)

'Trondhjem, 31 March, 1856

'To the management of the
  Norwegian Theatre in Bergen.

'Despite the fact that theatre business during our stay in Trondhjem only takes up a small part of my time, nevertheless the small daily interruptions prevent me from finding the undisturbed calm I need to devote myself to a work which it is essential I complete as soon as possible. May I therefore request the approval of the management to my returning to Bergen by the next boat.

Respectfully,
Henr: Ibsen'

The 'work' that Ibsen was intent on finishing may well have been *Olaf Lilje-krans*, of course, which was eventually produced in Bergen on 2 January 1857. There may have been other personal and more compelling reasons for his return, however. In the January of that year he had met the nineteen-year-old Suzannah Thoresen at the house of her father and her stepmother, Magdalene. He met her again shortly afterwards at a ball arranged by the Bergen Philharmonic Society, and subsequently he sent her a poem, entitled 'To the Only One' and dated January 1856, which served as a kind of proposal of marriage. Whilst in Trondheim he wrote her another poem, entitled 'To Susannah [sic] Thoresen', which was apparently enclosed in a letter he sent her in March 1856 (cf. *Efterladte Skrifter*, III, 338). Laading, who remained behind in charge of things in Trondheim, wrote in a letter to Bergen on 24 April: 'Regards to Ibsen, whose departure has left people rather busy here and there—whether that departure was for the sake of the nine muses, or for *one* of the muses.' A little over two years later, on 18 June 1858, Ibsen and Suzannah Thoresen were married.

Two performances of *The Feast at Solhoug* were given in Trondheim, on 2 April and 25 May, both well attended. On 26 May 1856, Laading reported: '*The Feast at Solhoug* was a success. . . . After the performance, we gathered at the theatre and drank Ibsen's health from the takings. After the dessert we drank to Ibsen and his betrothed. H. Nielsen was charged with taking the congratulations of the entire company to Ibsen and his beloved.'

A 14. After the completion of *Olaf Liljekrans* (first performed 2 January 1857), and the reading of his paper on the heroic ballad to the 'Society of 22 December' in the February, Ibsen apparently turned without delay to his next play. By 28 April 1857, in a postscript to a letter to his friend Botten Hansen, Ibsen was able to report that he was already working on a new play which would be different in both tone and content from his previous works. This doubtless was *The Vikings at Helgeland*, the first two acts of which Ibsen had apparently completed by the early autumn of that year, and the whole of which seems to have been ready before the year was out (cf. Hans Midbøe, *Streiflys over Ibsen*, p. 143).

Ibsen's five-year contract with the theatre—his study-visit to Copenhagen and Dresden in 1852 having been conditional upon his signing up for five years —expired in April 1857. His contract was renewed for a further year until April 1858, but he may well have had the terms of his appointment changed at this point. The *Regie* book for 1857 shows production notes in Ibsen's own hand for only three new plays: his own *Olaf Liljekrans* on 2 January; a production of *Le gendre de M. Poirier* by Augier and Sandeau on 3 May; and of Octave Feuillet's *Le village* on 1 June.

On 17 April he sent Botten Hansen the text of his paper on the heroic ballad in the hope that it might be considered suitable for publication in *Illustreret Nyhedsblad*, which was edited by Botten Hansen; with the article he sent an accompanying letter:

'Bergen, 17 April 1857

'My dear old friend!

'First of all I send you warmest greetings, and secondly a few notes on the heroic ballad in the hope of having them published in your periodical. If you should be willing to use my article, may I ask you to print it in as large sections as possible, and above all to divide it at the most appropriate points, as well as making sure that spelling and punctuation are as they should be—as you will see, I have had the fair copy of the manuscript made by somebody else, and I have only checked it cursorily.

'I have often thought of writing to you, but I have always put it off. I once thought of sending you some travel articles, but nothing came of that either. This summer, however, I intend going on a long walking tour, and I might be able to send you something you can use.

'About things here I can think of nothing of interest to tell you, except that last year I got engaged to the daughter of Dean Thoresen here in Bergen (her stepmother is the authoress of *Et Vidne* ["A Witness"] and a number of other things you have at some time or another discussed in *Nyhedsbladet*).

'My warmest thanks for your notice of *The Feast at Solhoug*; I sent my new play *Olaf Liljekrans* to the Christiania Theatre a few months ago, but Borgaard is not one to be hurried. He would not accept my best play, *Lady Inger*, unless there were considerable changes—something which I could not agree to; about New Year I sent it to Christian Tønsberg with the suggestion that he might publish it, which he could not do at the present time, however. As it means a great deal to me to get this, my best play, published, I want to ask you if you will take the matter in hand and do what you can for me. The play is still with Tønsberg. Read it through and—get me a publisher. I'm not worried about terms—I'm quite prepared to do without payment if you can only get it into print—I'm sure that if you were kind enough to act for me, something could be done. It occurred to me it might be published in aid of the Students' Union building fund—I'd be very happy to preface the play with a little prologue dedicated to Young Scandinavia. Dear friend! See if you can help me—I give you an absolutely free hand with *Lady Inger*—bully some publisher until he gives in!!

'It would be nice if you could drop me a line soon! Let me know how things are with you and with our friends over there! Best wishes for now.

Affectionately
Henr: Ibsen'

Botten Hansen was quick to accept the article on the heroic ballad, and also suggested printing the play in instalments in his paper. Ibsen wrote a second letter before the month was out:

'Bergen 28 April 1857

'My dear friend!

'Today a few lines only, in order to catch the post. If you like, call my article: "On the Heroic Ballad and its Significance for Literature". I cannot quickly think of any other title that defines the content more precisely. "A Note on . . . etc." might not be too bad, for I could have found enough for ten such articles on this subject. But since the expression is rather "Ole Vig-ish" and plebeian—let's not have it!

'Your suggestion of printing *Lady Inger* in *Nyhedsbladet*, and then issuing it as an independent publication I think is quite splendid. There wouldn't be enough space in two numbers to take the play, however; surely the best thing would be *to print* ONE *act per number*. I am confident that the separate off-print will be handsome and tasteful, and I authorize you to deal with all aspects of the matter as though it were your own property, and in particular to get hold of the manuscript sent previously to Herr Tønsberg, for which purpose I enclose a further letter.

'*Olaf Liljekrans* I should also very much like to see published in the same fashion as soon as it has been performed at the Christiania Theatre; but I still haven't heard a word from Borgaard about this. I feel greatly inclined to take him up publicly about his reluctance to produce *Lady Inger* in its present form. According to his own letter he considers the play is "poetic", full of good character delineation and powerful dramatic elements—yet nevertheless—well, you'll understand his motives when you read the play.

'About fees, etc., please arrange everything as you think fit; anything you decide will be acceptable to me. One other thing: at a number of points in *Lady Inger* I have called the lady's late husband "Lord High Steward Henrik Gyldenløve", although as I later discovered he was called "Niels Henriksen Gyldenløve"—but as there are two other Niels's in the play in addition to him, I would ask you please to call him simply "Lord High Steward Gyldenløve" (without any first name). I should be specially grateful if you could send me a few words to tell me your opinion of the play when you have read it.

'If you run into O. Schulerud, do give him my regards. Abilgaard—how are things with him? You aren't thinking of taking a trip to this part of the world, are you? Believe me, it would be a journey well worth the trouble. Marvellous country! Quite unique!

'Best wishes for now. I know I can rely on you doing whatever is best for me.

Affectionately
Henr: Ibsen

PS. I am already busy on a new play; it will in content and tone be somewhat different from my earlier ones.'

Ibsen was granted leave from the theatre from 9 July until the end of August.

He left for Christiania. A fortnight later he wrote a letter from Christiania to the Theatre management in Bergen which revealed what was afoot:

'Christiania, 23 July 1857

'To the management of the
   Norwegian Theatre in Bergen

'On my arrival in Christiania I saw a report in the papers which has probably now reached Bergen, and which I would therefore like to correct. It claims that the management of the Norwegian Theatre here have been negotiating for me to take over the post of artistic director at the Norwegian Theatre, from which Cronberg has resigned.

'The facts are as follows: Shortly before my departure, G. Krohn received a letter from Lieut. Lund, who as head of the Norwegian Theatre was making inquiries as to whether he knew of anybody in Bergen who might be willing to take on the above job. Krohn passed on to me the contents of the letter (which was quite confidential), and I said that if I could be released from my contract with the Bergen Theatre, and if the people in Christiania offered acceptable terms, I might not be disinclined to accept the offer. This was the gist of Krohn's reply; and the very day of my departure from Bergen I received an offer from Lieut. Lund, writing on behalf of the management, asking me to accept the appointment at an annual salary of 600 Speciedaler, with the prospect of a gratuity and an increase in salary as soon as the theatre could manage it.

'The reason I did not mention anything to the management in Bergen was solely due to the uncertainty with which I regarded the matter. I had to assure myself on the spot of the theatre's circumstances, prospects, etc. This I have now done; and I have come to the view that the Christiania Theatre is as securely established as Bergen's, and that something might be accomplished here. I need not emphasize the advantages for me of living in the capital; they are decisive; and however painful it would be for me to leave Bergen and the Bergen Theatre, I wonder whether it would not be indefensible of me to renounce the opportunity now offered of securing for myself a reasonably rewarding appointment. I speak of salary and prospects, but I am in truth being neither selfish nor ungrateful. I shall never forget what I owe the Bergen Theatre; but I also have a duty to myself; the conditions at the Bergen Theatre I have long found oppressive; every avenue where I might have achieved something has been blocked; I have never had a free hand, and every day I felt weighed down by the thought that I was working without really achieving anything. In now applying to the management with an inquiry as to whether, and when, I might be released from my obligations in Bergen, in the event of my reaching agreement with the Christiania Theatre, I regard this as an application not merely to my superiors but also to sympathetic advisers who will not draw back from looking at the matter from what is for me the most important point of view.

'If I should be released from my contract, I would naturally be ready to pay back my last month's salary which has already been paid. It is also obvious that, all other things being equal, I should prefer to remain in Bergen, with whose Theatre I feel I have grown up; but the Theatre there can surely not develop any more than it has already; and it can therefore come as no surprise to the management that I feel compelled to seize this opportunity for a more assured future. I eagerly await your answer.

Respectfully
Henr: Ibsen

PS. My address is: c/o Schulerud, Hassels Gaard, The Market Place.'

Laading replied on behalf of the Theatre management:

'4 August 1857

'Herr Instructeur Ibsen
Christiania.

'In answer to your letter of 23rd ult. requesting release from your contract with this theatre, I have the honour to inform you on behalf of the Theatre that the management is willing to accede to your request. They do not wish to oppose your wish to accept the post offered to you, even though they regret that your request arrives at a time when, as you must realize, a reduction in the number of Instructeurs must have serious consequences, now that the repertoire is thoroughly disrupted following the resignation of Bruun, the actor. What counted most for the management were the advantages that would follow for you in your new post in the capital city.

'You are therefore herewith released from your contractual obligations to the Bergen Theatre; with all best wishes in your work for the theatre which of course has the same objectives as our own.

Laading.'

Ibsen's new contract with the Norwegian Theatre in Christiania was signed on 11 August 1857.

B.

Plays produced at the Bergen Theatre
October 1851–August 1857

In the 1851–2 season, thirty-six new plays were added to the repertory; in 1852–3, a further thirty-eight; in 1853–4, a further twenty-six; in 1854–5, a further twenty-three; in 1855–6, a further fourteen; and in 1856–7, a further twenty. In addition to these, some thirty or so plays which had been given their first performance in the theatre before October 1851 were later revived (see, chiefly, T. H. Blanc, *Norges første nationale Scene*, Christiania, 1884). Wherever possible, the titles of the plays have been given in the original language; where it has not proved possible to identify the original, the play is shown with its translated Norwegian title within square brackets.

1. Plays first performed before October 1851 and subsequently revived:

Ancelot, M. L. V., *Clémence* / Ancelot and Decomberousse, *Vouloir, c'est pouvoir* / Bayard, *Un changement de main* / Bayard and Vanderburgh, *Le gamin de Paris* / Blom, *Tordenskjold* / Dubois and Chazet, *Marton et Frontin* / Dumas père, *Le mari de la veuve*; *Les demoiselles de St. Cyr*; *Mademoiselle de Belle-Isle* / Heiberg, *Supplikanten*; *Aprilsnarrene* / Holberg, *Julestuen*; *Jeppe paa Bjerget*; *Henrik og Pernille* / Hostrup, *Gjenboerne*; *Intrigerne* / Lafontaine, *Le veau perdu* / de Leuven, Deforges and Dumanoir, *Sous clé* / Mélesville, *Le précepteur dans l'embarras* / Mélesville and Brazier, *Catherine* / Nielsen, Henrietta, *Slægtningerne* / Overskou, *Hvilken er den rette?* / Rowley, *A new wonder, a woman never vext* / Riis, *Til Sæters* / Schneider, *Der reisende Student* / Scribe, *Les premières amours* / Scribe and Duport, *Le Quaker et la danseuse* / Scribe, Dupin and Dumersan, *La pension bourgeoise* / Scribe and Lemoine, *Une femme, qui se jette par la fenêtre* / Scribe and Varner, *Toujours* / Sewrin and Vincentini, *Rataplan*.

2. Plays first performed in the season 8 Oct. 1851–22 Aug. 1852:

Ancelot and Decomberousse, *L'ami Grandet* / Bjerregaard, *Fjeldeventyret* / Bøgh, *Narret April*; *Tre for Een*; *Den graa Paletot*; *To Naboer* / Calderón, *El alcade de Zalamea* / Castelli, [*En Mand paa Kast*] / Davidsen, *Familie-Kjær-lighed* / Delavigne, *Don Juan d'Autriche* / Dumanoir and Bayard, *Indiana et Charlemagne* / Dumanoir and Lafargue, *L'Homme qui a vécu*[?] / Duport and Foucher, *Coliche* / Fournier, *Mademoiselle de Bois-Robert*[?] / Garrick and Colman, *The jealous wife* / Hansson, *Den første Jøde* / Hauch, *Søstrene paa Kinnekullen* / Heiberg, Johanne, *En Søndag paa Amager* / Hertz, *Tonietta* / Holberg, *Den politiske Kandestøber* / Hostrup, *Soldaterløier* / Laurencin, Desvergers and Vaêz, *Les brodequins de Lise* / Mélesville, *Chevalier de Grignan* / Mélesville and Duveyrier, *Michel Perrin, ou: L'espion sans le savoir*; *Clifford, le voleur* / Ponsard, *Charlotte Corday* / Riis, *Julegjæsten* / Scribe, *Malvina*; *La famille Riquebourg*; *Les surprises*; *La protégée sans le savoir* / Scribe and Delavigne, *La Somnambule* / Scribe and Duport, *La tutrice* / Scribe and Legouvé, *La bataille des dames* / Scribe and Varner, *Les deux maris* / Oehlenschläger, *Axel og Valborg*.

3. Plays first performed in the season 6 Oct. 1852–14 Aug. 1853:

Andersen, Hans, *Fuglen i Pæretræet* / Arnesen, *Et Reiseeventyr* / Bayard, *Pas de fumée sans feu* / Bayard and Biéville, *Si Dieu le veut* / Bayard and Devorme, *Moiroud et Compagnie* / Bayard and Savage, *Le gant et l'éventail* / Bøgh, *Herr Grylle og haus Viser* / Dumanoir and d'Ennery, *Don César de Bazan* / Dumas père, *Catherine Howard* / Duval, *La jeunesse d'Henri V*/Falsen, *Dragedukken* /

Gutzkow, *Zopf und Schwert* / Hauch, *Æren tabt og vunden* / Heiberg, *For ti aar siden*; *De Uadskillelige*; *Recensenten og Dyret*; *Ja!*; *Kong Salomon og Jørgen Hattemager* / Hertz, *Kong Renés datter*; *Indkvartering* / Holbein, F. von [*Efterskriften*] / Holberg, *Jacob von Thyboe* / Ibsen, *Sankthansnatten* / Jensen, *Huldrens Hjem* / de Leuven and Brunswick, *Le mariage au tambour* / Mélesville and de Beauvoir, *Chevalier de St. Georges* / Moreau, *Marie* / Murger, *Le bonhomme jadis* / Olsen, *Anna Kolbjørnsdatter* / Overskou, *Misforstaaelse paa Misforstaaelse* / Sandeau, *Mademoiselle de la Seiglière* / Scribe, *L'ambitieux* / Scribe, Locroy and Chabot de Bouin, *La marraine* / Scribe and Varner, *Le plus beau jour de la vie* / Scribe and Xavier, *Babiole et Jablot* / Tegnér, *Frithjofs Saga* (extracts) / Thoresen, Magdalene, *Kongedatterens Bøn*; *Et Vidne*.

4. Plays first performed in the season 5 Oct. 1853–20 Sept 1854:

Ancelot, *La Comtesse de Chamilly* / Arago and Vermond, *Mémoires du Diable* / Barrière and Lorin, *Le piano de Berthe* / Bayard, *Un château de cartes* / Benedix, *Die Lügnerin* / Bøgh, Jomfruen; *Huldrebakken* / Demerson and Angely, [*Fjorten dage efter Sigt*] / Duvert and Lauzanne, *Renaudin de Caen* / Fournier, *L'interprète* [?] / Hertz, *Scheik Hassan* / Hostrup, *Den Tredie* / Ibsen, *Kjæmpehøjen* / Jolin, *En komedi* / Laurencin and Marc-Michel, *Quand l'amour s'en va* / Moreau, *Richard Savage* / Nestroy, *Der Zerrissene* / Overskou, *Kunstnerliv*; *Pak!* / Raupach, *Rafaele* / Scribe, *Adrienne Lecouvreur*; *La tutrice* [?] / Souvestre, *Un paysan d'aujourd'hui* / Théaulon, Desforges and Jaime, *Carmagnole* / Töpfer, *Der beste Ton* / Anon., [*En fattig Piges Dagbog*] (from the English).

5. Plays first performed in the season 4 Oct. 1854–19 Aug. 1855:

Anicet and Dumanoir, *La savonnette impériale* / Armand and Théaulon, *Les jolis soldats* / Bayard and Biéville, *Un fils de famille* / Bayard and de Vailly, *Le mari à la campagne* / Birch-Pfeiffer, Charlotte, *Die Günstlinge* / Dumas père, *La fille du régent* / Feldmann, *Das Portrait der Geliebten* / Heiberg, *Elverhøi* / Hertz, *De deporterede* / Hostrup, *Mester og Lærling*; *Drøm og Daad* / Ibsen, *Fru Inger til Østerraad* / Isachsen, *Dobbeltgjængeren* / Mallefille, *Le cœur et la dot* / Marc-Michel and Labiche, *Un chapeau de paille d'Italie* / Munch, *En Aften paa Giske* / Overskou, *Et Mageskifte* / Recke, *Han skyder sin Kone* / Scribe, *Les contes de la reine de Navarre*; *Mon étoile*; *Les indépendants* / St. Georges and de Leuven, *Riquiqui* / Thoresen, Magdalene, *Herr Money* / Wengel, *Kusine Lotte*.

6. Plays first performed in the season 30 Sept. 1855–24 Aug. 1856:

Bayard and Théaulon, *Le père de la débutante* / Fournier and Meyer, *Chassécroisé* [?] / François and Fournier, *Une présentation* / Hertz, *Svend Dyrings Huus* / Hoffman, F. B., *Le trésor supposé* / Hostrup, *Eventyr paa Fodreisen* / Ibsen, *Gildet paa Solhoug* / Mélesville and Xavier, *Le bouffon du prince* / Munch, *Donna Clara* / Nestroy [*Talismanen*] / Scribe, *La part du diable* / Souvestre, *Henri Hamelin* / Shakespeare, *As You Like It* / Wergeland, *Søkadetterne iland*.

7. Plays first performed in the season 1 Oct. 1856–6 Sept. 1857:

Augier and Sandeau, *Le gendre de M. Poirier* / Barbier, Guillard and Decourcelles, *Le bal du prisonnier* / Bouchardy, *Le sonneur de St. Paul* / Buckstone, John, *A rough diamond* / Feuillet, *Le village* / Holberg, *Erasmus Montanus*; *Den Stundesløse* / Ibsen, *Olaf Liljekrans* / Laurencin and Lubize, *Pas jaloux* / Legouvé, *Par droit de conquête* / Mosenthal, *Der Sonnenwendhof* / Nestroy, *Einen Jux will er sich machen* / Scribe, *Une chaîne*; *Le verre d'eau* / Scribe and Brulay, *Le gastronome sans argent* / Scribe and Delavigne, *Le Diplomate* / Scribe and de Leuven, *La chanteuse voilée* / Wolff, *Preciosa* / Oehlenschläger, *Væringerne i Miklagard*.

C. 'On the Heroic Ballad and its Significance for Literature' (1857).

Of the art of past ages, almost the only surviving thing that consistently enjoyed a lively and vigorous existence in the consciousness of the people [Folket] throughout all the vagaries of time is the heroic ballad. The heroic ballad has passed from generation to generation through the centuries by means of an oral tradition, admittedly with some gradual distortion, as one can well imagine in the circumstances, but with its basic tones preserved. The ordinary people, who here as elsewhere have stood apart from any direct influence from literature proper, found in folk poetry a satisfying medium for expressing their own inner life; in it they have a form which manifests the spiritual content of this life and makes it accessible to everybody. The heroic ballad was not composed by any one individual; it is the sum of the poetic forces of the entire people, the fruit of its poetic talent.

That objectivity which represents a basic element in the character of the heroic ballad and which provides a kind of yardstick for the people's demands in this respect is possibly the reason why the majority of people have so far remained untouched by the greater part of our national literature. Literary subjectivity has no significance for the people; they do not care about the poet, only about his work in so far as they recognize in this a peculiar aspect of their own personality. The people do not resemble the theatregoers of our own day, who visit the theatre only when offered the opportunity of being titillated by some novel situation or excited by some novel intrigue. If the new is to appeal to the people, it must also in a certain sense be old; it must not be invented, but rediscovered [ikke *opfindes* men *genfindes*]; it must not appear as something strange and incongruous in the conceptual range inherited by the people from their ancestors, and in which our national strength mainly resides; it must not be presented like some foreign utensil whose use is unfamiliar and which is inappropriate for the familiar routine; it must be reproduced like some old family piece which we had forgotten but which we remember as soon as we set eyes upon it, because all kinds of memories are linked with it—memories which, so to speak, lay within us fermenting quietly and uncertainly until the poet came along and put words to them.

Naturally this is not to imply that the poet should never take some initiative *vis-à-vis* the people—quite the reverse. He must provide an arena for its desire for independent activity; he must draw his raw material from the people itself, and then he can make of it what he will. The desire for individual poetic activity is indeed characteristic of all the Germanic peoples; this is the reason why only very few art forms are truly 'popular' among these peoples, whilst the remaining art forms have with the advance of civilization become the property of the educated classes alone, forms which even today strike ordinary folk as being alien and dead. It was different with the Greeks and Romans, and it is still different with the Latin races, the Italians, the Spanish, and the French. None of these nations possesses a folk poetry corresponding to our heroic ballad. These Southern peoples did not make poetry themselves; they had their poets and minstrels. The Southerner had artists to glorify him and his past; the Northerner glorified himself. The Southerner had songs sung about him; the Northerner was both poet and singer himself. Ariosto, Tasso, Cervantes, Calderón, etc. stood above their compatriots and in a sense also above their age; the poetry of the North on the other hand emerged as the natural fruit of the abundance of the age. It became the expression of what was richest and best in the inner soul of the people—and it is here that the great distinction lies. It was as if, in the case of the Southern poets, the whole of the nation's poetic power was concentrated in them; and in relation to them the people were consumers, an audience, and not collaborators. In this passive attitude to art among the peoples of the South is also found the reason why the visual arts predominate there: the sculptor and the painter offer, so to speak, a complete and tangible manifestation of the idea that preoccupied them, something requiring for its interpretation scrutiny rather than personal activity from the beholder. The same applies in large measure to the art of drama. Neither of these art forms has in any real sense become native to us. The Northerner is not altogether at ease within these bounds, where he cannot let his fancy build further upon what is given. He does not want to see the phantoms of his own imagination, his own ideas and concepts, fully incarnate, made flesh and blood by another's hand. All he wants are the outlines of the design, to which he will put the finishing touches, according to his own desires. He does not, as the Southerner does, want the artist to point to his work and indicate where the centre lies—he wants to seek the centre himself, not along any prescribed path but along the radius which the individualistic nuance of his people signifies as being the most direct.

Connected with the way this ballad poetry springs directly from the people itself is also the readiness with which we make it our own. For us the ballads are not something merely given, not something simply acquired from without; they are structures to which each one of us feels he has carried a stone; we all of us individually feel some spark of the spirit that animates the whole. Unlike troubadour poetry, the ballad is not an independent and restricted aspect of the national scene it belongs to. It is an essential ingredient of all aspects of popular life; it has cast its peculiar light over them all, grown into them, and thus retained its vigour for a much longer time by comparison with the other kind which grew feebler as the conditions and circumstances which had given it life themselves faded.

There is, however, something strange about this, as there is about any product deriving directly from the poetic impulses of the people. It seems as though oral transmission was alone able to allow it free development and the chance of continued youthful existence among the people. It seems as though the rigidified written form was unsuited to what it had so say, as though it set barriers against those improvisations and revisions that the ballad needs in order to be transmitted youthful and fresh from generation to generation. If the ballad takes book form, it immediately ceases to that extent to live on the tongues of the people, and presents itself to us in a very different light. In print, the ballad looks old and grey, indeed old-fashioned, if you will; on the lips of people, age does not concern it. The living word is to it what the Ydun apple was to the Aesir worshippers—it not only nourishes, it renews and rejuvenates.

Nevertheless, it is fortunate that these written records are being made, and it would be well if more were put in hand whilst there is still time. The people's season of poetic productivity can now be regarded as more or less over; and if the summer is finished, then a harvest of dry growth is better than nothing at all. With the rise in the level of civilization, those national peculiarities which are the prerequisite of all folk poetry diminish. Moreover, to produce poetry the people requires a strong and vigorous and urgent age, rich in events and in distinguished personalities, rich in men in whom some or other of its peculiarities have realized themselves. For just as the people draws its poetry from itself, in the same way it can in the last resort only produce poetry about itself—it sings only when it bears within itself more than it can absorb, more than it requires for its daily needs. The present age and the prevailing state of affairs can no longer satisfy all these conditions for a vigorous folk poetry; and consequently the heroic ballad cannot but cease to be the property of the people in the same sense as before. The need to go on producing it, the impulse towards it, is no longer operative, and ballad poetry is thereby cut off at the root. Its individual products may well be preserved in the memory; but this only makes it like a bunch of flowers in a pot of water, remaining apparently fresh for a while but with its vital fibres cut and further propagation impossible. Ballad poetry was once the fruit of the poetic abundance of the people; henceforth it can only be an object of study.

But as with all things that carry within them an element of culture, so it is with the ballad—it does not die with death. As folk poetry in any real sense it has virtually ceased to exist, yet it does hold within it the potential of some new and higher existence. The time will come when our national literature will turn to ballad poetry as to an inexhaustible gold-mine: refined, restored to its original purity and elevated by art, it will once again take root in the people. A beginning has already been made with the sagas: Oehlenschläger's

genius sensed the need for some national foundation for his country's literature, and it is on this principle that the whole of his work is based. That
Oehlenschläger turned to the sagas and not to the heroic ballads naturally
followed from the state of things as they were when he started writing: the
significance of the sagas had already been recognized; considerable research had
been undertaken in this field; Saxo's work was widely known in translation;
and the sagas were better suited than the heroic ballads to combat prevailing
tastes. Admittedly the latter were available to the public in the editions of
Anders Vedel and Peder Syv, in which Sandvig and Nyerup had already
published a few items in 1780 and 1784. But some stylistic reform like that of
Oehlenschläger's was needed to bring out the true significance of ballad poetry,
and elevate it beyond the state of being a merely 'pleasant past-time'; moreover, its peculiar poetic quality only became evident after the Romantic
School had developed in Germany and had begun to exert influence on the
cultural consciousness of Scandinavia—something which did not occur until
after Oehlenschläger had made his debut. Admittedly in his first creative
period he took material for a couple of his best dramatic works—*Axel and
Valborg* and *Hagbart and Signe*—from the heroic ballads, but he seems to have
attached little importance to the different treatment required by the heroic
ballad from that by the saga. These two tragedies are certainly masterpieces,
but are works very different in kind from the respective ballads. That these
works nevertheless are what they are is in part due of course to the genius of
the poet, but also to the fact that the heroic ballad lends itself to dramatic
treatment far more readily than the saga does. The saga is a great, cold epic,
closed and complete within itself, essentially objective, and remote from all
lyricism. It is in this cold, epic light that the saga age stands for us; it is in their
magnificent sculptural beauty that its figures parade before us. Only thus and
not otherwise can we, *must* we conceive the saga age; for every period is
reflected for posterity through the composition of those traditions by which
it becomes known.

If then the poet is to create a dramatic work from this epic material, he must
necessarily introduce a foreign element into this given material: he must
introduce a lyrical element; because, as is well known, drama is a higher
compound of lyric and epic. But this causes him to distort the original relationship between the material and the beholder. Events which had impressed us
by their abstract sculptural beauty of form are now presented to us by the
poet as a painting, with colours, with light and shade. We cannot come to
terms with a content which we had become accustomed to through a completely different medium. By being given dramatic treatment, the saga age is
brought into a closer relationship with reality; but that is exactly what must
not happen. A statue does not gain by being given hair, eyes, and natural
colouring.

The inevitable distortion that follows from this left not inconsiderable
traces upon Oehlenschläger's dramatic work. (The question of how much this

might have been avoided if the poet had chosen a different and more appropriate form of language need not detain us here.) A *Hakon Jarl* in prose from Oehlenschläger's pen might well have been quite as poetic as one in verse. At least it will in time become apparent that the iambic pentamenter is far from being the most appropriate metre for dealing with Scandinavian themes from the past. This poetic metre is altogether foreign to our national rhythms; yet it is only through some national *form* that national *themes* can fully realize themselves.

The saga is, as remarked above, completely epic; in the heroic ballad on the other hand there are lyric elements present, admittedly in a different form from drama, but present nevertheless—and the dramatist who draws his material from the ballads does not have to subject his material to the kind of transformation necessary when it is drawn from the saga. This represents a very considerable advantage, permitting the poet to give in his work a more accurate and more intimate reflection of the period and of the events he is dealing with; and he is thereby enabled (if he is otherwise capable) to present his heroes to the beholder in the way in which they are already familiar from folk poetry direct. To this must be added that the flexible ballad metre allows many liberties of considerable importance for dramatic dialogue. There can therefore be little doubt that sooner or later this poetic source will be diligently exploited by future poets, building further on the foundations laid down by Oehlenschläger. That his achievements can only be regarded as a foundation for future works is obvious enough—something which in no way diminishes his reputation; for it is of course a characteristic of all things good and beautiful that they are not complete and limited in themselves, but contain within them the seeds of a higher perfection. National literature in the North began with the saga, and now it is the turn of the heroic ballad; Oehlenschläger's treatment of the saga offers variations by a musician of genius on a folk theme; the dramatic treatment of the ballad can be folk melody itself, artistically treated and artistically executed.

Although the recording in written form of the sagas falls within the Christian era in Scandinavia, its poetry is nevertheless essentially heathen; for this reason saga material will lend itself much more readily to treatment in ancient Greek style than in what is called the modern Christian style. This is doubtless the reason why Oehlenschläger's *Death of Balder* was more successful than any of his other dramatic works. Where I have used the term 'saga' above, I ought to remark here that I understand by it not merely the historical accounts but also the mythic stories and songs. In contrast to these, the heroic ballad must be regarded as essentially Christian. Admittedly it has heathen elements in it, but these are present on a quite different and higher level than in the mythic stories, and it is by virtue of this that the poetic offshoot of Christianity, romanticism, manifests its influence on the ballad. The Aesir worshippers, who did not know the power of faith where reason fails, constructed a world for themselves in which no rational laws were valid. In this world therefore everything—but consequently also nothing—was supernatural; and this was their solution, for in this way they were able to reconcile faith with reason. The romantic philosophy on the other hand takes a different path, venerating Shakespeare's phrase that 'there are more things in heaven and earth than are dreamt of in your philosophy'. This allows rational things a right and a validity; but alongside it, above it, and through it goes the mystery, the inexplicable, the Christian if you like, for Christianity is of course itself a mystery. It preaches faith in those things 'beyond all understanding'. It is in this that the mythic tales differ fundamentally from the heroic ballad; the former is to the latter as the fable is to the fairy tale. The fable does not know the miraculous, the fairy tale is rooted in it.

This world, at once natural and supernatural, is the one which the heroic ballad exposes to us. In many of the ballads it is the heroes and the events of the Aesir doctrine which form the actual content, but always in a more modern guise, always under a more or less explicitly Christian form. Tor and his battles with the Tursers, Sigurd Fafnersbane and his exploits, the saga of Tyrfing etc. are all recognizable enough under their medieval dress and names; from being gods and saga heroes, the characters have descended to being warriors and mortal knights; but one is surely in error if one seeks the reason for this transformation either in the religious feelings of the people or in any political or ecclesiastical pressure on the part of those in power. The myths presumably continued to live among the people long after the introduction of Christianity; and it is doubtful whether the understanding of Christianity was clear and pure enough to kill faith in the ancestral gods. The many apparent points of contact between the old and new doctrines rather make it probable that both persisted for a long time alongside each other, and that Christian doctrines in the first instance probably served more as a civilizing power than actually as a religion. Either the priests, the advocates of the new doctrine, had not grasped the situation with sufficient clarity, or else they were unable to tear themselves free from the traditions they had inherited; but instead of proclaiming the merely imaginary nature of the existence of the Aesir, instead of declaring their annihilation along with the faith that abandoned them, they presented them as evil, hostile powers, dangerous to the new teaching and to its true believers. No wonder therefore that the old spirits were long-lived, for they had a good footing. St. Olaf might well summon them in stone to a day of judgement—they nevertheless continued to live in the consciousness and faith of the people, and there they have continued to live until our own days.

It is therefore not the case that these myths took form as we know them in the ballad as a result of external pressure. External influence might perhaps have subdued or even destroyed this spiritual heritage from our ancestors; no force would have been powerful enough to compel the people to give them an altered form. A people cannot be *forced* to write and to sing in puzzles and in obscure circumlocutions, the right meaning of which might very soon be lost. An oppressive censorship might perhaps influence the press for a time, but never a people.

No, what led the people into the ways of the ballad was not some external circumstance, but the stimulation of its own unconscious artistic sense. Not the religious but the aesthetic sense, which never misleads a nation in the way it can a single individual. The people did not clothe its mythical heroes in medieval finery because through Christianity it had lost the true sense of the Asa faith, its spirit and its nature—but surely because the romantic conception of art, entering the consciousness of the people through Christianity, did not permit any continuation of poetic activity in the ancient heathen style. That was why the material had to be transformed; this was why it had to be made amenable as material for the new art form.

Now just a few words about the lyricism of the heroic ballad. Apart from the fact that it is present in the ballad's narrative in much the same strange way as metal is present in a metallic salt, it is also found as a special element separate from the other constituents of the ballad—in the refrain. The refrain is for the heroic ballad what the prelude is for a piece of music—it determines the mood in which the work is to be received. But *that* lyric is not subjective in its nature; it is not rooted in the individual peculiarity of the poet. The poet does not communicate to the listener any of his own individual riches; he simply wakes to conscious life what lay dreaming and fermenting within the people itself. His poetic talent consists essentially in his clear vision of what the people wish to see expressed, and in a certain ability to give that expression a form in which the people can most easily recognize what is said as belonging to them.

From what I have said it will presumably be clear that I have not really involved myself in any contradiction here—though I earlier referred to the heroic ballad as something written by the people itself, and I now distinguish between the people and the poet. The situation is the same as with the saga: this, too, naturally owed its first written form to some individual; but this written form, the form in which it has reached us, was in the closest accord with the mind of the people. In the case of the heroic ballad, however, there is that long period of time in which it lived fresh on the lips of the people and was never written down, and therefore it is not so easy as with the saga to determine what was in the original composition and what later periods have added or taken away. One thing is nevertheless certain: that ballad poetry, even in the distorted form in which it is now found, reveals a pure and firm art form; that a correct metre can generally be obtained by a somewhat different arrangement of the words; and that, as Professor Petersen has shown in his Danish History of Literature, the same is the case with the rhymes.

The strongest evidence of cultural kinship among the separate branches of the great Germanic race is found in the heroic ballads. The Scandinavian, the German, the English and the Scottish ballad poetry show the same basic similarities, even though these take on different shades of colour among the different peoples, depending on local conditions and the various fates suffered here and there at various times by the ballad. In Germany, the ballads seem to have become the property of a privileged class early; wandering minstrels turned it into an art product [Kunstpoesie], heard only in castles, whilst the unemancipated classes, the citizens and peasants, toiled in silence for their daily bread, cowed and suppressed and—as it seems—robbed of their impulse and their ability to sing. As times changed there was, however, a reversion; it seems as if the ballad once again descended from the castles to the lowlier homes of the people, as if they again took possession of their inheritance, as if the ballad once again became a really national possession, though only at second hand. Doubtless much the same took place in Denmark and Sweden, but not in Norway. The Norwegian, unlike his brother Scandinavians, has never acknowledged a sharply defined caste system; peasant and knight never denoted opposites for us, but simply two alternative forms of reality. Together with the remote situation of the country, the comparative lack of contact between the people and the outside world, and finally the appropriately heroic landscape and its influence on the character of the people, these provided good reasons why the Norwegian heroic ballad was able to keep its ancient stamp, whilst for example the Danish and Swedish ballads have in many respects lost something of the original language and tone, and thereby seem to belong to a relatively much more recent period.

Just as the *basic tone* in the whole of Germanic ballad poetry is the same, so also the *content* is largely taken from closely related imaginative sources. In Scandinavian ballad poetry we find again—in more or less recognizable figures—heroes from the German national epic *Nibelungenlied*, as well as from the *Rolandslied*, etc. Chivalry, the taking and avenging of women, battles with dragons and serpents, journeys to the home of the trolls which was thought to be far up in the North, fights with trolls and dwarfs who lived in mountains and hills and possessed infinite treasure—this and much more seems in particular to have provided folk poetry with its themes; purely historical persons and events are much more rarely treated, and in the Norwegian ballads virtually never.

The heroic ballads in the form we now have them have a strongly marked medieval character; and our historians seem for that reason to agree in placing the period of authorship of these ballads between the end of the saga period and the Reformation. There seems to be similar agreement about the reasons for the spread of the same (or at least similar) ballads among the various Germanic peoples. This is said to be attributable to translations from one language to another. But none of these explanations seems to me to have the ring of inner probability.

If the heroic ballads replaced scaldic poetry in *time*, there must surely also have been some taking over of its *spirit* and its *content*. But a greater contrast can hardly be imagined. Scaldic poetry as it had taken shape in its last days, i.e. immediately before the emergence of the heroic ballad, had sunk to something completely empty and formal, a shell without a kernel. What mattered for the scald was not poetic talent but merely a capacity for storing up all the conventional and traditional turns of phrase, expressions and images. His poetry was only a ghost from the past, an empty shell for a spirit that had long ago passed away, which nobody any longer believed in, and nobody any longer understood. They had something similar in France in their imitations of antique tragedy; and what happened *there* to it also happened *here* to scaldic poetry. Both forms of art to some extent found a kind of acceptance within individual circles of the community; but neither of them was in a position to grow deep and intimately within the people, to become familiar with its way of thought. Scaldic poetry was an artificial fabrication, ballad poetry a vigorous living fruit; the scaldic poem was *manufactured*, the heroic ballad *composed*.

Of the stiff formalities which formed a *conditio sine qua non* of scaldic poetry, there are no traces to be found in the heroic ballad. Admittedly the latter also has its expressions and images that look to the past, but nobody need be in any doubt that these things do not derive from scaldic poems. There is no trace of lyricism to be found in scaldic poetry. The events referred to in it are not calculated to achieve their effect by their method of presentation, which was in general always the same. What concerned the scald seems exclusively to have been to offer, in the prescribed elegant and orderly fashion, his adulation of this or that warrior, whose glorification was to be served by the poem, and whose generosity—one may remark—was often what mainly inspired him.

And is the fresh and living blossom of the ballad to have grown from this arid tree? Never! It would in any case have been a transplant without any comparable example. No vigorous folk poetry can ever stem from an uninspired and artificial literature. It is much more probable to suppose that both forms of art existed side by side in prehistoric times; and the period of the ballad's transformation, the transition into the romantic form in which we now know it, coincides with the last days of scaldic poetry—in other words with the period which (doubtless erroneously) one assumes as the first childhood of ballad poetry. For there can scarcely be any doubt that the ballad has not come down to us in its original form. Much internal evidence in the ballads points to close kinship with the Edda poems, which are of course not available either in their original form. The intimate connection between the ballads and the mythical themes makes it probable that the entire pagan doctrine, far back in time, was given expression and given currency among the people in age-old songs, which somehow formed the skeleton for our heroic ballads. At the introduction of Christianity, at the consequent transition of poetry to romantic forms, along with the shifting manifestation of the spirit of the age in successive periods, this ancient form of song underwent various transformations until they finally emerged as 'heroic ballads' at the Reformation, after which they are subject to no particular influence. The same may very well be the case with the so-called 'historical ballads'; they too might very well be in essence merely a new version of older mythical songs. All this is palpable enough in the Norwegian ballads; any more detailed evidence would be superfluous at this point, and I shall therefore merely refer to Landstad's collection, where confirmation may be found for what is asserted here.

If it may be assumed that ballad poetry in some form or another has lived on the lips of the people since prehistoric times, it in no way weakens that assumption that there is nowhere any mention in the sagas of the existence of such poetry. Scaldic poetry, which developed simultaneously with the earlier (heathen) ballad poetry was an artificial poetry; ballad poetry proper on the other hand was folk poetry; that the men of the sagas paid attention to the former and overlooked the latter need surprise nobody who realizes that much the same thing has happened in much more recent times and almost to our own day. Nor must it be forgotten that ballad poetry, with its then doubtless wholly heathen content, could not decently appeal to the learned and enlightened man of the sagas, even though the people took pleasure in it. It naturally escaped the attention of the scribe that the *saga* was also heathen in its *poetic* qualities; after all, the theme had nothing to do with the glorification of the mythical heroes, as in the ballads; and to use the scaldic songs as points of reference would disturb his conscience even less, for although these were also heathen in both form and content, the difference was that whilst the heathen gods continued to live a healthy and inspired existence in the ballads, in the scaldic poetry everything had by then already sunk to mere formulas and empty phrases which could give offence to nobody. This applies particularly to the later scaldic poetry; as far as the earlier and better poetry is concerned, it naturally enjoyed a certain esteem as an artistic product in the learned world of that time, which outweighed other considerations.

If it is then the case that the heroic ballads are to be regarded as a later form of the mythical poems of ancient times, then we need have no recourse to speculation about translations to explain the spread of the same songs throughout all the Germanic tribes. Such an explanation is forced enough, and in many respects wholly inadequate to throw light on the phenomenon. Above all, it is most unlikely that any form of poetry that succeeded as well as the ballad did in rooting itself in the inmost life of the people should not have germinated at that same place, but been transplanted there from foreign soil. In what period of the past, for example, might the Norwegians have felt an urge to glorify—via Danish, Swedish or German songs—events which in no way affected their own lives, or to sing the praises of men whom they knew only from hostile encounters? Contact in those days between the tribes was scarcely of a kind to encourage cultural exchanges. To this is added the fact that what are called translations deserve the name only in a very special sense; rather they are alternative mutually independent treatments of the same material. Apart from the improbability that a rich oral literature, drawing its vitality direct from the creative impulses of the people, should wish to draw sustenance from translations—it must also be remembered that the historical ballads are in general not translated, and even where they are, it is doubtful

U11

how far these translations were at all popular. In Norway, where the written versions were taken down directly, there are no translated ballads; among the Danish and the Swedish they may in fact be found; but as these collections were largely derived from older written volumes of ballads, this furnishes no certain evidence for supposing that these translations were in any real sense current among the people itself. Rather they seem to derive from a relatively earlier period—which also seems to be indicated by the language—when ballad poetry in Denmark and Sweden was found in the hands of the nobility and had thus ceased to be nourished by the people. The so-called Euphemia ballads, translated here in Norway from French about the year 1300, and found in manuscript in both Swedish and Danish, in no way weaken this assertion; partly because these poems do not belong to genuine ballad poetry, and partly because it may be assumed with some certainty that they were not widely current among the people but were at best known among some of the nobility, who took up Queen Euphemia's idea of introducing troubadour poetry in the North—an idea which was nevertheless stifled at birth.

It seems improbable to me, for all these reasons, to assume that the spread of the ballad was based on translations; a more probable explanation lies closer to hand. If it is admitted that the earliest origins of the ballads is to be sought in the mythical period, then there is nothing to prevent us from going as far back as possible, i.e. to a period that pre-dates the migration of the Germanic tribes into Europe, to a time (in other words) when this great ethnic group formed a unified whole.

The imaginative framework within which the heroic ballad has its being seems to argue in high degree for such an assumption. On the great plains at the foot of the Urals, the Teutonic peoples lived as a powerful and warlike tribe; the Chudic people, who populated the hills in the regions stretching northwards to the White Sea—and whose brothers, the Finns, migrated to the Scandinavian highlands—were the Teutons' natural enemies, who were fought and subjected, and who therefore had to defend themselves by cunning as best they could. This tribe are the dwarfs of the original ballads, living among the mountains and possessing the knowledge of how to work metals into weapons or works of art. The dwarfs are described as small, cunning and malevolent; all this fits well the Finns or the Chudes; and their dwellings among the Urals could well give them the reputation of being creatures who understood the secret arts of deriving wealth from stone—an art our forefathers did not understand but which the testimony of history accords to the Chudic tribe. After the migrations in the North, one cannot imagine any notions being formed about hidden treasure in the mountains, for up here mountains are rather thought of as the home of barren poverty. Nor are those ballad descriptions of journeys to the home of the trolls appropriate to the case of a people who are themselves settled in the North: for one thing, the original inhabitants (the trolls and the dwarfs of the ballads) continued to populate the Norwegian highlands as far as the southernmost limits well down the ages, so one could hardly talk of seeking them in the *North*, which is what always happens; and for another, a hardy people familiar with our own climate and conditions would hardly be so greatly affected by the difficulties and dangers of a journey to the North as is seen to be the case in the heroic ballads. This home of the trolls in the Far North is described as icy cold and enveloped in eternal darkness; but as those journeys which were really undertaken from the South of Norway doubtless were only undertaken in summer, it can be seen that the description cannot have been directly derived from experience, but rather from dark legends which are in part misinterpreted, and in part embellished and elaborated. Admittedly, there is mention that the journeys to 'Trollebotn' were by water; but one might just as well suppose here a voyage along the great rivers of Russia as one could a sea voyage along the Norwegian coast; and one must also always remember that our ballads reveal all kinds of accretions which are clearly the work of a later period. The journeys to Bjarmeland can scarcely have given rise to these notions, either; for again at other places there is talk of enormous 'iron forests' that had to be traversed, which brings to mind the conifer forests of Northern Russia, which were not known to our forefathers during their time in the East, but which they had to pass in their migration to the North and which might strike them as 'iron forests'. It is also remarkable that the entire fauna of the ballads point to a more southerly latitude. With the exception of the wolf, there is as far as I know no mention of the North's wild animals, whilst the serpent or the dragon (even if one regards this as stemming from the mythological Midgard serpent) inevitably direct one's thoughts to the gigantic primeval creatures still to be found in Eastern Russia, which were surely even more prevalent then and which first gave our forefathers the notion of those fabulous monsters which the ballads have since made so popular. It is furthermore worth noting that although after their migration to the North the Teutons became a sea-faring nation, the greater part of whose heroic deeds were performed at sea, the heroic ballads tell us absolutely nothing about *sea battles* or any achievement or happenings *aboard ship*; this is counterbalanced by accounts of fighting on land, which is almost always on horseback, despite its being well known that this method of battle was alien to our forefathers. Here too we are moved to think of the East; that the terrain there did not permit *sea* warfare is obvious, whilst it is highly probable that the Teutons at that time were a horsed people, just as is the case today with the tribes who inhabit those regions.

Let us not object that the world of the heroic ballad is merely a fictional world that has nothing to do with reality. The poetry of the people is equally its philosophy; it is the form in which it expresses its sense of the spirit's existence in concrete fashion; like all artistic production, it naturally seeks a point of departure in real life, in history, in first-hand experience and in the natural environment. There can be little doubt, for example, that the myths about Thor and his battles with the Jotuns are symbols of primitive Germanic strength and its conflicts with foreign opponents. A people must to some extent always have a history before it can create for itself a religion, and such was the case with our forefathers. The glorification in poetry of the exploits of the earliest tribes, their attempts to penetrate to the North etc., have provided the stuff of the mythical poems, and these in their turn of the heroic ballads.

Evidence placing the origins of the Germanic ballads at the time of the Eastern settlement—which is only really touched on here—could be infinitely augmented if it were my intention to provide exhaustive proof of this matter. It is not; I only wished to enter a protest against the assertion that the spread of the ballad was by translation, an assertion that would deny our rightful claim to a large and essential part of the cultural heritage of our forefathers. There have been attempts to deny us the honour for the so-called Icelandic saga literature, but our scholars have defended our rights in this respect. Might it not also be worth taking the same trouble about the ballads? Will none of our historians respond to the challenge and speak out with authority in this matter? If these few lines were to hasten this, I would consider this to be reward enough and more—irrespective of whether the ideas I have put forward are themselves favourably or unfavourably received.

APPENDIX V

ST. JOHN'S NIGHT

1. Genesis of the work
2. Manuscripts
3. Public reception

1. GENESIS OF THE WORK

Although in his early career Ibsen evinced no great eagerness to see *St. John's Night* in print, he was nevertheless quite ready to claim the authorship of it. In a letter of 15 June 1858 to a member of the management committee of the Theatre, he lists the plays he had written for the Bergen Theatre, and explicitly includes '*St. John's Night*, play in three acts'. In his letter of application to the Government for an annual grant, written on 10 March 1863, he refers to his study tour:

'In the summer of 1852 I undertook at the theatre's expense a tour to Copenhagen and several big German towns, principally with the task of studying art and literature, and from that tour I brought back with me a new play in three acts, entitled *St. John's Night*, which was subsequently produced but which is still unpublished.'

Robert Neiiendam (*Mennesker bag Masker* (Copenhagen, 1931), pp. 125 f.) believes that J. C. Hostrup's *Mester og Lærling* (*Master and Apprentice*), which had its première at the Casino Theatre, Copenhagen, during Ibsen's visit to the city in 1852, and about which its author wrote very illuminatingly in the Copenhagen press at the time, might have left its impression on *St. John's Night*:

'*Master and Apprentice* ... raised attention and stimulated some polemics, and its peculiar mixture of romanticism and realism must have interested Ibsen very considerably, for he went to call upon Hostrup at home at Fredriksberg to talk about the play, which also came to be performed up in Bergen [4 Oct. 1854]. But Ibsen's actual motive for seeking a talk was doubtless the "eventyrkomedie" *St. John's Night*, which he was wrestling with in his "elegant" room on Laksegade, and which was to be performed on his return. ... It might well be supposed that the goblins and little people who set things in action in *St. John's Night* between the students and the susceptible girls came into existence under the influence of Hostrup's amiable muse.'

St. John's Night received further passing mention in Ibsen's correspondence in 1876, when in the December of that year he wrote to Alfred von Wolzogen, who had recently translated *Brand* into German: 'As regards the three plays mentioned by Catherine Ray [translator of *Emperor and Galilean* into English], I can only say that *Norma* is merely a political satire in dramatic form, and is without any great significance. *St. John's Night* and O[*laf*] L[*iljekrans*] have not been printed, and it is doubtful if they ever will be.'

When in 1887 Henrik Jæger interviewed Ibsen in connection with a biography of the dramatist he was writing, the information he elicited (but did not in the end use in his book) was much more explicit. The notes which Jæger kept of their conversation (reprinted in Hans Midbøe, *Streiflys over Ibsen*, Oslo, 1960, pp. 141 ff.) contain the following note:

'*St. John's Night* was written during Ibsen's first journey abroad; he had agreed with a student at that time, called Bernhoft, that they should collaborate in writing a play. As is known, Bernhoft had tried his hand at drama. Ibsen made a draft of *St. John's Night* and sent it to B., but got the reply that he (B.) had begun a course of study which had taken his thoughts away from such things, and that he would rather forget that he had ever had anything to do with the theatre or literature or any such vanities.
    Oral account, Fredrikshavn (2 Sept 87).'

Ultimately Ibsen disowned the play. In reply to Julius Elias, the editor of the projected German collected edition of his works, who had innocently inquired about the possibility of including *Sancthansnatten* in the edition, Ibsen replied irritably on 19 Sept. 1897:

'For the last time I hereby categorically declare that I neither will nor *can* allow the play *St. John's Night* to be included in the collected edition of *my* works. The play is a miserable product, which actually does not come from *my* hand. It is constructed upon a rough, botched-up sketch which I at one time received from a fellow student, re-drafted and set my name to, but which I now cannot possibly acknowledge as mine. I must therefore earnestly request you and Dr Schlenther not to insist any further on publishing this wretched thing. Far from casting any light on the rest of my work, it stands completely apart from and unrelated to it. For many years now I have therefore regarded it as unwritten and non-existent.'

Publication had therefore to wait until the appearance of the three volumes of posthumous papers, *Efterladte Skrifter*, in 1909. (It is, however, not a little strange that Julius Elias, who edited these volumes along with Halvdan Koht, made absolutely no mention there of this peremptory letter which he had personally received from Ibsen only twelve years before.)

2. MANUSCRIPTS

1. No complete manuscript of the play from Ibsen's own hand, either draft version or fair copy, has been preserved. The following versions and fragments have, however, survived:

(*a*) A manuscript prompt copy *A*, containing a number of alterations and additions in Ibsen's own hand; some of his entries were made directly on to the original copy, others were written out on separate pieces of paper and stuck over the passages in the manuscript which they were meant to replace (see 2. 3 below). This prompt copy is now in the Bergen Theatre Museum.

(*b*) A manuscript copy *B*, now in Bergen Public Library, which contains some (but not all) of Ibsen's alterations to *A*, but which also has a number of alterations not included in *A*. The names of the actors and actresses playing the main parts were entered on the page containing the list of characters:

Mrs. Berg	Miss Wiese
Jørgen	Mr. Pram (or Prom)
Juliane	Mrs. Hundevadt
Anne	Mrs. Bruun
Berg	Mr. P. Neilsen
Birk	Mr. Isachsen
Poulsen	Mr. Bruun
Goblin	Mr. (or Miss) Johannessen

This manuscript does *not* carry any emendations in Ibsen's own hand.

(*c*) A further (poor) manuscript copy *C*, 112 leaves, apparently taken from *B*, now in the University Library, Oslo.

(*d*) 12 acting parts *D*, the texts of which are substantially the same as in *B* above; the separate parts are marked both with the name of the character and also (in the case of the eight principal players) with the name of the individual actor or actress playing the part; these names correspond with the casting as given in *B*.

(*e*) A fragment (one torn leaf) in Ibsen's own hand, containing the text of Act II, scene 1; this fragment is in the University Library, Oslo. The differences between this version and those in *A* and *B* are slight, being for the most part minor matters of orthography or punctuation only. For 'INVISIBLE ELVES', both *A* and *B* have 'CHORUS OF INVISIBLE ELVES'.

2. The basis selected for the present translation is the text of manuscript *A*, as amended by Ibsen himself; the following points should, however, be noted:

(*a*) Manuscript *A* originally used the form ANNA throughout; at a number of places this was changed on the manuscript to ANNE; manuscript *B* originally had ANNA in the first six scenes and this was subsequently altered to ANNE; and in the remainder of the play, the form ANNE was written from the first; in manuscript *D*, ANNE is the form used throughout. This seems to suggest that on second thoughts Ibsen himself preferred the form ANNE.

(*b*) All three manuscripts *A*, *B*, and *D* have the form PAULSEN, except for those additional passages inserted in *A* in Ibsen's own hand where the spelling is POULSEN; this latter is the form adopted for this present translation, as seeming to reflect Ibsen's own considered view.

(*c*) The four lines of verse spoken by the Goblin at the end of Act II, together with the associated stage-directions, are missing from *A*, but are to be found in both *B* and *D*.

3. On several separate occasions the alterations which Ibsen wanted to make to the original manuscript *A* were substantial enough to persuade him to write the new formulation as a separate piece of paper and stick it over the original passage. The inserted passages were:

(*a*) Act I, scene 5 (pp. 213–14)

> . . . Christiania. He is the one who founded the Society for the Restitution of Old Norse.
>
> MRS. BERG. Really! Is it a sort of temperance society?
>
> BIRK. Well . . . no. I don't think you could call it temperate, exactly. . . .
>
> JØRGEN. No, you see . . . it is a society for. . . . Well, you see, it's rather difficult to explain before the society has got its programme drawn up.
>
> BIRK. Yes, that is the real difficulty.
>
> JØRGEN. Nonsense. It's a piece of cake for Poulsen. . . . He said so himself. 'You see, Jørgen,' he said to me once . . . because he and I are on Christian-name terms. We many a time go about arm in arm smoking our cigars, . . . don't we, Birk?

which in the original manuscript A, as well as in B and D ran simply

> . . . Christiania. He and I are on Christian-name terms. We often go about arm in arm, smoking our cigars, don't we, Birk?

(*b*) Act I, scene 7 (pp. 216–17)

> JULIANE [*to* JØRGEN]. Gracious me, what interesting ideas he has!
>
> BIRK [*aside*]. What! She too!
>
> JØRGEN. Ah, but they haven't the right ring. No, you should hear him when he propounds them in the old dialect tongue [i.e. Nynorsk]!
>
> JULIANE. But can anybody understand it?
>
> JØRGEN. Good gracious, no! That is precisely what one is to learn.

which in the original manuscript A, and (in all essentials) in B and D ran simply

JULIANE [*softly to* JØRGEN]. Gracious me, what interesting ideas he has!

JØRGEN [*similarly*]. Yes, I think he has.

BIRK [*aside*]. What! She too!

(c) Act I, scene 8 (p. 220)

> ... is a bath of rejuvenation in which man may drown all his dispirited-
> ness. . . . Dispiritedness. . . . Low in spirits! That's a good word . . .
> he shall . . .

which in the original manuscript A, as well as in B and D, ran

> ... is a bath of immediacy, which. . . . Bath of immediacy! That's a
> good expression! . . . He shall . . .

(d) Act I, scene 14 (p. 228)

> POULSEN. You haven't? Really? But I have tried to clothe my ideas in as
> popular a form as possible.

which in the original manuscript A, as well as in B and D, ran

> PAULSEN. You haven't? Really? Well, I know well enough I don't express
> myself popularly. But this is in fact one of my principles, and I'll tell you
> the reason why. You see, my thoughts, my ideas are not popular ones . . .
> To this I testify, but now it has become my adopted language: Beauty
> before everything. But what is beauty? The congruence of content and
> form— And if my thoughts are not popular, how . . .

(e) Act I, scene 14 (pp. 229–30)

> ... more clearly. Well, you see. . . . There was once a time when I was
> still a child. . . .

> JULIANE. Yes, that's understandable, but . . .

> POULSEN. And a highly intelligent child, from what I'm told. I grew up
> under the purest nationalistic influences. . . . My father was a country
> shopkeeper, you see. . . . And so you can easily comprehend how my
> breast became a sounding board for all the popular sentiments I have
> received in my childhood. But then life's conflicts began. I went to
> Christiania, became a student and began, like the others, to go in for
> aesthetics and criticism and all that unpatriotic nonsense. God knows
> what would have happened to me if I hadn't had my eyes opened in
> time. Poulsen, I said to myself, if you continue thus, then you deliver
> your national Self a mortal wound. You must make an end of it! The
> which I did and bade farewell to town, aesthetics and art and went on a
> hiking trip to Drammen. I thus rediscovered my original Self and fell
> in love. . . .

JULIANE. In Drammen?

POULSEN. No, on the way, of course. In those delightful, fresh pine forests.
I chose the most national creature that ever existed. Can you guess

which in the original manuscript A and in B ran

. . . more clearly. But first . . . Miss Kvist! I shall teach you what love is!

JULIANE. I beg your pardon . . .

PAULSEN. Yes, it is said in few words! . . . Love is the desire for love! . . .
That is my own idea, my incontestable possession. . . . But in order that
my desire might be eternal, to be certain of not being loved in return,
I had to love hopelessly . . .

JULIANE. Yes, of course!

PAULSEN. But of course my love had to be in the folk tradition . . .

JULIANE. Indeed it had. . . . Are you not a cultured person!

PAULSEN. Yes, yes, I mean. . . . I chose the most national thing we have. Can
you guess

*Parts of the above passage, together with the immediately following lines, are
different again (and probably earlier) in D:*

PAULSEN. Yes, it is said in few words! Love is the desire for love! That is
my own idea, my incontestable possession. . . . Love is the desire for
requited love, for only when we love do we desire to be loved in return;
but as soon as the object of our desire has been achieved, our desire must
cease . . . ergo, love must cease as soon as it is requited. . . . But in order
that my love should be eternal, to be certain of not being loved in return,
I had to love hopelessly. . . .

JULIANE. Yes, of course.

PAULSEN. Therefore I couldn't love a human being. . . . [*Whispers.*] Can
you guess who I loved?

JULIANE. If it wasn't a human being, then it would have to be some animal
or other. . . . A dog, for instance, or . . .

PAULSEN. No, no, I tell you. . . . No dog! . . . It was . . . the *hulder*!

(*f*) Act I, scene 14 (pp. 230–1)

I can't tell you how I suffered. Aestheticism and nationalism fought a life
and death struggle in my breast. . . . But I may as well tell you at once
that on this occasion . . . culture triumphed over nature.

which in the original manuscript A and in B and D ran simply

You will well understand that, with my aesthetic principles, I could no longer continue to feel for her.

(*g*) Act I, scene 14 (p. 231)

But I could never escape the reproachful voice that reminded me that I had renounced my love from paltry prejudice. I did my best to revive my nationalist zeal; I started wearing a sheath knife and began to spell phonetically. . . . The world was deceived by it . . . but I knew it was no use. Do you know what is stirring in me now? It's rather like what the Germans call 'Weltschmerz'.

which in the original manuscript A and in B and C ran

I had to adopt a negative standpoint towards humanity. I began by laying down my soul in dramatic criticism and in articles in the provincial press, as mentioned. . . . I went steadily on along that negative path. Little by little there took root in me something dark, something devilish . . . dæmonic, I should have said. . . . Something indeed . . . let me call it contempt for humanity, something Byronic. From this is derived that schism, that disharmony which one notes in my being; on the surface I am cold, if not to say ice-cold; but here within it burns. . . . Believe me, it burns.

3. PUBLIC RECEPTION

T. Blanc (*Norges første nationale Scene*, Christiania, 1884, pp. 149–50) reported: 'The play was no success. Just as its content in general is somewhat confused and foggy, so also its ideas and action must presumably also have struck the public as unclear; at the fall of the curtain people probably felt a trifle confused at the curious blend of romanticism and realism which they were offered. Meanwhile the theatre had done all it could to stage the play nicely and in keeping with the poetic nature of its plot; new scenery was painted, and this was described as particularly well done. . . . For the first performance [on 2 Jan. 1853] the house was sold out, and many were turned away without tickets; but already by the second performance, on 5 January, the many empty rows of seats showed that the play had not met the taste of the public. *Stiftstidende* had no compunction about describing it as "a less than successful play, though it possesses a number of nice individual touches". After these two performances it was taken out of the repertoire.'

In England the play was presented on 1 May 1921 by the Pax Robertson salon at the Chelsea Theatre.

APPENDIX VI

LADY INGER: COMMENTARY

1. Dates of composition
2. Draft manuscripts
3. The revised play (1874)
4. Public reception

1. DATES OF COMPOSITION

Lady Inger was written in the summer of 1854. Peter Blytt relates (*Minder fra den første norske Scene i Bergen*) how, several weeks after his appointment as chairman of the directors at the Bergen Theatre on 9 September 1854, Ibsen came to him with a note-book under his arm. 'It immediately struck me that he looked even more self-conscious that day than usual. After a few confused prefatory remarks he handed me the book saying it was a manuscript sent to him by a friend in Christiania, a historical drama or, if preferred, a tragedy, which the author in question, who wished to remain anonymous, wanted to have performed on the Bergen stage, if it were considered worth accepting.' The play was immediately accepted and Ibsen admitted he was the author during the rehearsals for the first performance, which took place on 2 January 1855.

The play was not printed until three years after it was written. In a letter to Paul Botten Hansen on 17 April 1857 Ibsen wrote: 'I sent it about New Year to Christian Tønsberg [the publisher of *The Feast at Solhoug*] with the suggestion that he might publish it, which he could not do at the present time, however. As it means a great deal to me to get this, my best play, published, I want to ask you if you will take the matter in hand and do what you can for me. The play is still with Tønsberg. Read it through and—get me a publisher. I'm not worried about terms—I'm quite prepared to do without payment if you can only get it into print—I'm sure that if you were kind enough to act for me, something could be done. It occurred to me it might be published in aid of the Students' Union building fund—I'd be very happy to preface the play with a little prologue dedicated to Young Scandinavia. Dear friend! See if you can help me—I give you an absolutely free hand with *Lady Inger*—bully some publisher until he gives in!!' Then on 28 April he wrote, again to Botten Hansen: 'Your suggestion of printing *Lady Inger* in *Nyhedsbladet*, and then issuing it as an independent publication I think is quite splendid. There wouldn't be enough space in two numbers to take the play, however; surely the best thing would be *to print* ONE *act per* number. I am confident that the separate off-print will be handsome and tasteful, and I authorize you to deal with all aspects of the matter as though it were your own property, and in particular to get hold of the manuscript sent previously to Herr Tønsberg, for which purpose I enclose a further letter.' And later in the same letter: 'About fees, etc., please arrange everything as you think fit; anything you decide will be acceptable to me. One other thing: at a number of points in *Lady Inger* I have called the lady's late husband "Lord High Steward Henrik Gyldenløve", although as I later discovered he was called "Niels Henriksen Gyldenløve"—but as there are two other Niels's in the play in addition to him, I would ask you please to call him simply "Lord High Steward Gyldenløve" (without any first name).' The play was printed in five hundred copies of *Illustreret Nyhedsblad* from 31 May to 23 August 1857. Several hundred offprints, also printed on newspaper, were published on 5 November 1857.

Ibsen's intention to revise the play was mentioned in a letter to J. H. Thoresen, his brother-in-law, as early as 26 June 1871. The new edition was clearly to be undertaken with an eye to production at the Royal Theatre, Copenhagen, a point repeated in several letters during the following years. He planned to start work on the revision after completing *Emperor Julian* (i.e. *Emperor and Galilean*) by Christmas, he hoped. Meanwhile, in the autumn of 1871, J. H. Jensen, the former proprietor of *Illustreret Nyhedsblad* wrote to Ibsen announcing his intention of reprinting *Lady Inger* (1st edition) and *The Vikings at Helgeland.* The ensuing dispute is summarized in *The Oxford Ibsen,* vol. II, p. 345. Work on the revised version started much later than foreseen. On 30 June 1872 Ibsen wrote to his friend Michael Birkeland asking for a copy of the first edition, with a request to keep it dark (because of Jensen). In February 1873 he asked Hegel, his Danish publisher, to procure him a copy, and a similar request went to Ludvig Daae on 27 May. On 25 June he wrote to his wife that he now had one. But although he wrote to Hegel on 8 August that he was about to start work, there was a further delay and not until 23 May 1874 did he report to Hegel that he was now working on it daily. On 27 June he wrote to Hegel: 'I can deliver the manuscript of *Lady Inger* as soon as the beginning of August. In its present form I put this play high among my works and do not doubt that it will be performed at the Royal Theatre [Copenhagen], for whose personnel it is admirably suited.' The final instalment of the manuscript was dispatched on 22 October 1874 and the book appeared at the end of the year in an edition of 4,000 copies which was already nearly fully subscribed before publication.

Some years later the interest shown in the preface to the second edition of *Catiline* made Ibsen toy with the idea of writing a short book on similar lines about the background to other works. In the section on *Lady Inger* and *The Vikings* he would, for example, tell of his period in Bergen. Although this suggestion, made in a letter to Hegel on 31 May 1880, did not meet with Hegel's approval, Ibsen did in fact do some work on this project, and could even give Olaf Skavlan (letter of 12 November 1881) the title: From Skien to Rome. The idea was subsequently dropped.

2. DRAFT MANUSCRIPTS

There are apparently no draft manuscripts of *Lady Inger*. There is, however, a prompter's manuscript of the first version in the Teatermuseum at Bergen. This copy contains a number of corrections, nearly all of them in Ibsen's own hand. The corrections, which were incorporated in the printed text, are comparatively unimportant, consisting mainly of interpolated actor's instructions. The most interesting change covers, on two inserted leaves, the passage from p. 328 above ('LADY INGER: Listen Olaf Skaktavl! . . .') to p. 330 ('. . . to this very hour'), which was originally all assigned to Lady Inger, including, in slightly modified wording, the lines now spoken by Nils Lykke and Olaf Skaktavl. The same manuscript also has a number of pencilled deletions, some of them made by Ibsen. These are occasionally substantial, e.g. the whole of Lady Inger's opening soliloquy in Act V.

3. THE REVISED PLAY (1874)

The revised version of *Lady Inger*, of which the manuscript is in the University Library, Oslo, is substantially the same as the first. As a drama and in its language it represents a marked improvement. The principal changes are:

(a) Østeraad is spelt Østråt.
(b) New styles in the cast list, including: Lady Inger Ottisdaughter Rømer, widow of Lord Steward Nils Gyldenløve; Councillor of State Nils Lykke, a Danish knight; Lord Jens Bjelke, a Swedish commander.
(c) There is no division into scenes.
(d) Less frequent use is made of asides.
(e) Greater attention is generally, but not consistently, paid to stage directions. Thus (see p. 273 above):

> LADY INGER GYLDENLØVE *enters hastily from the hall without taking notice of the others; she goes straight to the window, draws back the curtain, and stares out for a while, as if looking for someone along the road; then she turns and goes slowly back into the hall.*

(f) Modes of address are more formal.
(g) The language is more polished and the dialogue livelier. Occasional lapses of taste have been eliminated, e.g. the reference to the hungry wolf (see p. 279 above). Longer speeches have been broken up and some soliloquies compressed (e.g. the opening scene of Act V).
(h) Some disparaging references to the Danes have been modified, presumably with an eye to a Copenhagen performance.
(i) Jens Bjelke, now a Swede, uses sporadic Swedicisms.
(j) Attempts are made to achieve greater credibility. Thus Eline's knowledge of the secret exits from Østråt is mentioned as early as Act II.

(*k*) The blunder about Lucia's burial in the ground (pp. 270 and 284) is corrected.

(*l*) The date of the action is specified by Olaf Skaktavl, who has instructions to meet the stranger at Østråt on the third evening after Martinmas.

(*m*) At the end of Act I (see *The Times*' review, p. 696 below) Olaf Skaktavl makes an anonymous entrance:

[*A strongly-built* STRANGER *with grizzled hair and beard has entered from the Great Hall. He is wearing a torn lamb-skin tunic and carries rusty weapons.*]

THE STRANGER [*stops at the door, and says in a low voice*]: Greetings to you, Lady Inger Gyldenløve!

LADY INGER [*turns with a scream*]. Ah, the Lord protect me! [*She falls back in the chair. The* STRANGER *stares at her, motionless and leaning on his sword.*]

4. PUBLIC RECEPTION

Lady Inger was first performed on 2 January 1855 at the Norwegian Theatre in Bergen. The play was a failure and was taken off after a second performance two days later. It was acted in Trondheim in 1857, but in the same year Borgaard, head of the Christiania Theatre, refused it. In a letter to Botten Hansen of 17 April (see above, p. 692) Ibsen wrote: 'He [Borgaard] would not accept my best play, *Lady Inger*, unless there were considerable changes—something which I could not agree to.' And in the letter of 28 April (see above, p. 692) he said: 'I feel greatly inclined to take him up publicly about his reluctance to produce *Lady Inger* in its present form. According to his own letter he considers the play is "poetic", full of good character delineation and powerful dramatic elements—yet nevertheless—well, you'll understand his motives when you read the play.' On 11 and 13 April 1859 Ibsen himself staged the play at the Christiania Norwegian Theatre (not to be confused with the Christiania Theatre), again with no success. In 1863 Clemens Petersen, the Danish literary critic, suggested he should try the Royal Theatre at Copenhagen, an idea Ibsen readily fell in with. But it was not accepted. The theatre found it 'not without talent and inventiveness', but 'not stageworthy'. In Sweden, on the other hand, *Lady Inger* was performed in the provinces in the early 1860s, e.g. at Östersund on 3 July 1863.

The second version fared better. Admittedly it was again rejected by the Royal Theatre, Copenhagen, for which it was primarily intended, and had to wait until 1895 for its Copenhagen première at the Dagmar Theatre. But it was immediately accepted by the Christiania Theatre. Ibsen wrote on 4 January 1875 to the Swedish producer Ludvig Josephson, at that time head of the Christiania Theatre, suggesting a cast list and expressing his confidence that the play would keep its place in the repertoire for a long time. The first performance was on 20 March at Ibsen's request, and, according to Halvorsen (*Norsk*

Forfatter-Lexikon) it was in the repertoire of that theatre until 18 December 1882, receiving 18 performances in all. In 1884 it was acted at the People's Theatre in Christiania. The Royal Dramatic Theatre in Stockholm gave a performance on 27 October 1877, and in 1880 it was acted in Helsinki at the Swedish Theatre.

In Germany a translation by Emma Klingenfeld, paid for by the author, was published in December 1876 (dated 1877) and was reprinted in the Complete Works in 1898. The play was apparently accepted for performance at Meiningen and Munich (Ibsen's letter to Hegel on 15 September 1876), but the German première was in fact at the National Theatre, Berlin, on 13 December 1878. It was revived ten years later at the People's Theatre, Berlin.

The first version of *Lady Inger* has not hitherto been translated into English. The second version, by Charles Archer, was published in 1890 in William Archer's *Ibsen's Prose Dramas*. In a review on 23 August 1890 the *Athenæum* noted that it had 'striking characters and situations' but preferred the other plays in the volume—*The Vikings at Helgeland* and *The Pretenders*. On 28 and 29 January 1906 *Lady Inger* was performed by the Stage Society at the Scala Theatre, London. The title role was played by Edyth Olive, Eline by Alice Crawford, Nils Lykke by Henry Ainley, Olaf Skaktavl by Alfred Brydone, and Nils Stensson by Harcourt Williams. The audiences were puzzled, according to William Archer, and *The Times* (30 January 1906) was moved to the following outburst:

'The Stage Society may be supposed to have produced this play chiefly for the encouragement and warning of young dramatists. "Do not despair," it says in effect. "Come and see what Ibsen was doing 50 years ago, when he was already 27; writing huge, historical, romantical tragedies, crammed full of stage tricks, and quite void of that mastery of the stage which he acquired when he had learned the tricks—and thrown them all away. See how this tragedy of his lacks one of the chief essentials of a tragedy, a good strong backbone of a plot, and yet how stuffed with 'plot' it is, tangled political intrigue which even the commentators cannot explain lucidly; and which leaves the plain man in the theatre, who is not well up in the history of Norway, Sweden, and Denmark in the early 16th century, utterly bewildered. See how Ibsen was satisfied still with the old machinery—these mysterious strangers who arrive one after another at Lady Inger's manor-house, and all mistake each other for somebody else. See the traditional villain—the spy, the schemer, the gallant whom no woman can resist—worming his absurd path through all this jumble of intrigue. See him win the love of the woman who has vowed since childhood to hate him—and then think of the scene between Richard and the Lady Anne. Notice that unblushing trick by which a good 'curtain' is secured for the first act; a distraught woman is on her knees, shrieking to the spirits of her ancestors whom she sees about her, and in the doorway appears a strange and awful figure. It is really only Olaf Skaktavl the outlaw, in his skins and his armour, but the author got his 'curtain'; half the audience thought it was a ghost. Notice one or two other things—the uncertainty which is the 'plot' and which the 'sub-plot'; the long soliloquies and explanations which leave nothing explained; the inspissated gloom; the author's respectable determination to have a 'mad scene' at any cost; the language. . . . Note these things, remember what Ibsen became later and then go home and work hard. . . ."

'It remains to say that the interesting, bewildering, depressing piece was beautifully produced by Mr. Herbert Garman and well acted by all. Most of the work fell to Miss Edyth Olive, our only tragedy queen, and she did it with just that combination of the heroic and the human that fits her so well for these parts. Mr. Ainley (in a beard) did his best with Nils Lykke, and Miss Alice Crawford was very good as Elina.'

A second English translation, by R. Farquharson Sharp, appeared in 1915. Other translations include Russian (1896) and French (1903). The play has since been acted, on 26 March 1947, at the Gateway Theatre, London, with Molly Veness as Lady Inger, and Olave March as Eline.

APPENDIX VII

THE FEAST AT SOLHOUG: COMMENTARY

1. Dates of composition
2. Draft manuscripts
3. The second edition (1883)
4. Public reception

1. DATES OF COMPOSITION

The Feast at Solhoug was written in the summer of 1855 and first performed at the Norwegian Theatre in Bergen on 2 January 1856. Six days after the first performance at the Christiania Theatre it was published by Chr. Tønsberg on 19 March 1856, being the first book to bear Ibsen's name on the title page.

In later years Ibsen did not think highly of the play and in a letter to his friend Peter Hansen on 28 October 1870 he referred to it as 'a study which I now disown'. When he eventually suggested a revised edition to Hegel he had even forgotten that Hegel himself had made such a proposal some years previously (letters of 21 February and 15 March 1883). In the first of these two letters to Hegel Ibsen gives reasons for his revived interest: 'This play has so far been completely misinterpreted by the critics and is no doubt known only to very few. In his new book about me Dr. Valfrid Vasenius, university lecturer in Helsingfors, has now given a correct and exhaustive exposition of the play as he got it from me in Munich some years ago. This book has been received with great interest, at any rate in Sweden and Finland. I thought therefore that the play might now be published with a preface, like *Catiline*. The book has, I suppose, not been on the market for many years and the play is quite short; in all it will scarcely amount to 120 pages.' The words 'completely misinterpreted' presumably refer to the accusations of plagiarism which had been levelled at the play, and Francis Bull (Centenary Edition, vol. III) was probably right to infer that Ibsen, who was always reluctant to admit that he had been influenced by other writers, was now mainly concerned with the proposed preface. Ibsen, however, writing at the time (12 June 1883) to Georg Brandes, explicitly denied this: 'That I haven't previously told you anything about the genesis of *The Feast at Solhaug* now strikes me too as strange; but I have never ascribed much significance to the matter. As, however, the new edition of this youthful work required a preface I found it a suitable occasion to indicate the real situation.' The revision of the play took little time. Half the manuscript was sent off on 15 March, the remainder of the play on 30 March, and the preface on 6 April. The book was published on 10 May 1883.

2. DRAFT MANUSCRIPTS

Ibsen seems to have left behind no draft manuscripts or preliminary notes having relevance to this play.

3. THE SECOND EDITION (1883)

The second edition of *The Feast at Solhoug* (now spelt *Solhaug*) is preceded by a Preface, translated above, pp. 369–74. The manuscript fair copy of the play is in the University Library, Oslo. Although the plot was virtually untouched, numerous, yet almost without exception slight, changes were made in the text. Apart from spelling and punctuation, the most frequent alterations are perhaps to be found in the stage directions, which are now more frequent and precise. The prose text shows more changes than the verse passages. One underlying principle was the elimination of obscurities and infelicities; another was the substitution of modern, and therefore more colloquial, words for the not infrequent obsolete or obsolescent words of the first edition. Long speeches are occasionally broken up with interpolations by another character.

The following more important changes may be mentioned:

(a) The action takes place in the fourteenth century. 'At the beginning' is omitted.
(b) There is no division into scenes.
(c) Margit, having poured the poison into the goblet, tells Bengt to drink no more that night.
(d) Knut kills Bengt in self-defence.
(e) Margit leaves the stage immediately after her words: 'your contract is hallowed and safe in God's care'. Her departure is followed by the sunrise (cf. p. 425).

As an example of the 'elimination of obscurities and infelicities' we may cite Bengt's speech beginning 'Have her? . . . Yes, since . . .' (p. 419). The reference here to summer and winter does not make good sense. Bengt was of course tipsy at the time, but Ibsen, in 1856, had no such subtleties of characterization in mind, for in 1883 he removed the seasonal confusion: 'we will go visiting each other and we will sit indoors the whole day long.'

On one occasion the text of the second edition has been used for our translation to make good a printer's error in the first edition: the line 'MANY [*shouting*]. Hear, hear!' (p. 412) originally lacked the first two words.

Note. All the verse of both plays is rhymed. In this translation rhyme has only been used for the songs. Thus Margit's verse passage (p. 378, ll. 1–8) is here unrhymed because it is, in the first edition, printed in normal type and not in the small type always used for the songs. In the second edition it is explicitly referred to as a song and would therefore need to be in rhyme.

4. PUBLIC RECEPTION

The Feast at Solhoug was Ibsen's first success in the theatre, though it apparently fell short of complete triumph. After the first night, Ibsen wrote to the actress who had played the part of Signe: 'Please accept my warmest thanks for your fine and poetic playing in my drama which was performed this evening. This young woman with her childlike mind, forcibly thrown into that dark conflict, you presented with such dignity, with such moving and sensitive force that you stood there in reality as the one who held the light over the dark image you were placed beside; and even if it did not illumine it strongly enough for the audience to find its way on to the right path, the fault was certainly not in the clear and fair image you presented. —Once again please accept sincerest thanks from your respectful, Henrik Ibsen.'

The Bergen production of 2 January 1856 was repeated five times, the last being before Prince Napoleon, nephew of Napoleon I, on 24 August 1856. The Prince, who was given a manuscript copy of the play, made an unkept promise to have the play translated and performed in France. The play was staged at Trondheim in the spring; and on 13 March, equally successfully, the first of six performances was given at the Christiania Theatre. The play's popularity may perhaps be gauged by the fact that it was parodied by Olaf Skavlan in *The Feast at Marrahaug* in 1857. *The Feast at Solhoug* was the first play of Ibsen to be performed outside Norway: it was acted at the Royal Dramatic Theatre in Stockholm on 4 November 1857 and at the Casino Theatre in Copenhagen in 1861. There was a noteworthy revival at the Christiania Theatre on 6 December 1897 where the play was performed 36 times within one year. Some seven composers have written incidental music and provided music for the songs, Ibsen's preferred version apparently being that by the Dane Lange-Müller (letter to H. Schrøder on 5 November 1897). In 1893 the Swede Wilhelm Stenhammar turned it into an opera.

The first German translation, by Emma Klingenfeld, appeared in 1888 and this was followed in the 1890s by performances in Munich and Vienna. The Vienna Burgtheater production of 21 November 1891, with music by Hugo Wolf, was taken off after four performances. Christian Morgenstern provided the translation for the Complete Works (1898). In England, where the play has never been performed, the translation of the 1883 version by William Archer and Mary Morison was published in 1908. Other translations include Russian (1896) and French (1904).

Although *The Feast at Solhoug* appealed to theatregoers, the book sold badly. The publisher Tønsberg declined *Lady Inger* the following year, and the edition was not exhausted for some fifteen years. Nor was the play well received by a number of critics. Although Bjørnson and Botten Hansen were favourable, the accusation of plagiarism levelled at Ibsen by other Norwegian critics (e.g. Hartvig Lassen in *Aftenbladet*) still rankled after more than a quarter of a century. In Denmark too the play was considered an imitation, by Georg Brandes, *inter alios*. Nor can Bjørnson's support have been entirely encouraging. In two further articles in *Morgenbladet* in addition to that referred to by Ibsen in the Preface to the Second Edition (see above, p. 369), Bjørnson saw the strength of the play in its lyrical rather than its dramatic qualities. (For a fuller account of the work's reception in Scandinavia, see Åse Hiorth Lervik, '*Gildet på Solhaug* og samtidens kritikk', in *Edda*, lxix, 1969, pp. 40–6.)

APPENDIX VIII

OLAF LILJEKRANS: COMMENTARY

1. Versions and dates of composition
2. Manuscripts
3. Production and public reception

1. VERSIONS AND DATES OF COMPOSITION

Four times Ibsen attempted the folk-tale theme of the man placed between a fey or elfin maid and a girl he is under family pressure to marry: once in 1850, once in 1856–7, once in 1859–61, and finally some time probably in the late 1870s. On three of these occasions, however, the work remained a fragment, and only the drama *Olaf Liljekrans*, first performed in Bergen in January 1857, was carried through to completion.

The earliest attempt was the drama called 'The Grouse in Justedal', a work which immediately by the place-name of its title established a connection with one of the folk tales in the collection *Norske Folk-sagn*, made by Andreas Faye, the second edition of which was published in 1844. This story tells of a young girl from the farm of 'Birkehaug'—the groom's father in Ibsen's fragment is given the name of Bengt af Birkehoug—in the valley of Justedal who is the sole survivor in that valley of the Black Death, and who in consequence has become a fey creature. If, as seems probable, Ibsen started work on this drama after completing the first version of *The Burial Mound*, this would place it some time in the second half of 1850. In form it is for the most part in unrhymed iambic pentameters, though there are also one or two rhyming passages and some prose dialogue.

For the title of his second attempt on this theme, 'Olaf Liljekrans', Ibsen went to the collection of folksongs, *Norske Folkeviser*, which had been published by M. B. Landstad in 1852–3. (Ibsen makes the kind of reference to this publication that suggests easy familiarity in his article on 'The Heroic Ballad and its Significance for Literature'; see Appendix IV, p. 681). Most of the work on this new play doubtless belongs to the year 1856, and it was performed in Bergen under Ibsen's own direction on 2 and 4 January 1857. This was in all essentials a new play, and not a continuation or revision of 'The Grouse in Justedal'; the one tenuous link, apart from the general theme of the play and its setting in the years following the Black Death, is in the nature of the fey girl, who retains the name of Alfhild. The play was not published in its original Norwegian until forty-five years later.

Ibsen's first attempt to write an opera libretto based on *Olaf Liljekrans* was apparently—taking the evidence of the title page of the manuscript—begun in Christiania in 1859; its title was originally 'Alfhild', and this was subsequently changed to 'The Mountain Bird'. On 18 July 1861 Ibsen sent the following letter to the composer M. A. Udbye in Trondheim:

'I take the liberty of enclosing the opening scenes of an opera libretto and to inquire how far you would be willing to compose the music. As your name enjoys a better reputation as a composer than any other in this country, I would regard it as an honour and a double guarantee for the success of the work if you were to agree to take it on. I greatly look forward to receiving a few lines from you concerning this matter. The remainder of the manuscript can be sent shortly.'

A note by Udbye dated 25 Dec. 1882 (reprinted in Ibsen's *Efterladte Skrifter* III, p. 379) on the back of the manuscript Ibsen sent to him runs as follows:

'The foregoing fragment of a one act [*sic*] opera libretto by Henr. Ibsen was sent to me by the author accompanied by the letter of 18 July 1861. I declared myself willing to start on the work as soon as I received the continuation; this however did not arrive and still has not arrived. Getting on for a year after I had received the manuscript, Isachsen the actor came to this town with greetings from Ibsen and an inquiry as to how far I had got with the work. —At the Choral Festival in Bergen in 1863 I had a brief opportunity to ask Ibsen, who was present, when I could expect the continuation of it. From what he said, it appeared he had come to the conclusion that the subject he had chosen was not suitable for an opera—which, judging from the beginning of the text I had received, I felt obliged to say I greatly regretted.'

Finally, towards the end of 1876, Ibsen once again was taken with the idea that *Olaf Liljekrans* might be suitable for adaptation as an opera libretto. It was about this time that he wrote to Alfred van Wolzogen: '*St. John's Night* and O.L. have not been published, and it is doubtful if they ever will be. The latter piece I may be able to make something of as an opera libretto.' On 20 June 1877 Ibsen took the step of writing to someone at the Bergen Theatre about his plans for an opera:

'Permit me please to ask you to do me a favour. It is my intention to convert my old play *Olaf Liljekrans* into an opera libretto for Grieg, and therefore I very much want to borrow the copy of the play lodged in the Theatre library. May I ask you to see to this for me? And may I ask that the cost of postage be deducted from future honoraria? But I beg that the matter be kept secret so that it does not get into the newspapers.'

A further (but chronologically not altogether reliable) commentary is provided on this by John Paulsen (*Samliv med Ibsen*, 2nd collection, 1913, p. 16), who in company with Grieg visited Ibsen in Gossensass in the late summer of 1876:

'Grieg, who constantly dreamed of writing a lyric opera, was on the hunt for a good libretto.

'About his youthful work, the lyric-romantic, folksong-inspired *Olaf Liljekrans*, Ibsen once remarked to me that if nothing else it was at any rate suitable for—an opera libretto. At one time he had in fact attempted to re-write it as such. He called his new work "The Mountain Bird", and urged the composer Udbye in Trondheim to set it to music; but the scheme foundered for some unknown reason.

'I told Grieg this; and Grieg now approached Ibsen, who drew his attention to his old drama. But *Olaf Liljekrans* could not tempt Grieg. He was after something new and fresh, something that could inspire him—and he doubtless cherished the secret hope that Ibsen would write something or other specially for him.

'But Ibsen was at that time too taken up with his new play [*Pillars of Society*]. He dared not get caught up in such an enterprise which would only distract him.

'He contented himself with giving good advice.'

2. MANUSCRIPTS

A. 'THE GROUSE IN JUSTEDAL'

The manuscript consists of 30 leaves, in two gatherings of 16 and 14, quarto; the fragment (translated above, pp. 427–58) fills the first 49 sides only, with Act One running from side 3 to side 33, and Act Two—which is incomplete —from 33 to 49. It bears some signs of having been written by Ibsen as a fair copy, though there are a number of minor corrections and emendations, and the name of the minstrel changes from Harald to Knud during the course of Act One. It is dated 1850 on the title page, which also has in its top right-hand corner a small pen-and-ink drawing of a church tower. The manuscript is in the University Library, Oslo.

B. *OLAF LILJEKRANS*

None of Ibsen's original manuscripts of *Olaf Liljekrans* appears to have survived. The basis of the present translation is one of the two longhand transcripts of the play which have been preserved, both of them in the same hand (believed to be one of the actors, Andreas Isachsen, of the Bergen company): one of these (Transcript A—used for this present translation) is of 144 leaves, the other (Transcript B) is of 141 leaves. Apart from two points of some substance, they differ from each other only in inessentials; the two substantial points are:

(i) In Transcript B, the name of the minstrel is not THORGEJR but THORGJERD; Transcript A also had THORGJERD originally, but this was subsequently altered throughout to THORGEJR.

(ii) Transcript B has six extra lines, subsequently crossed out, which are altogether lacking in A; they come after the line: 'A sense of life, a feeling of joy!' (p. 546, line 10), and are as follows:

> And I had thought that you were my friend,
> Who smiled whenever I sat by you;
> And I had thought that your eye did weep
> In summer time at the setting sun—
> And I had thought that you did unfold
> When dawn approached, to thank your God!

Both transcripts are in the University Library, Oslo.

C. 'THE MOUNTAIN BIRD'

The manuscript, now in the University Library, Oslo, consists of eight folded sheets, quarto, arranged in two gatherings of eight leaves each; the last nine sides of the second gathering are blank. It is dated 1859 on the title page. The handwriting of Act One is carefully formed and contains few alterations; the fragment of Act Two, which begins one-third of the way down side 23 and follows immediately upon Act One, is in a less carefully formed hand, and may well have been written some time later than Act One.

D. UNTITLED FRAGMENT OF AN OPERA LIBRETTO

One single, folded sheet, quarto, undated but numbered '1', of an opera libretto based on *Olaf Liljekrans* has survived. Some of the spellings suggest that it is unlikely that it was written before 1870, the year in which Ibsen adopted certain new spelling conventions; and the style of the handwriting itself further suggests that it was written after the completion of *Emperor and Galilean* in 1873. Indeed the resemblance to the handwriting of the manuscript of *Pillars of Society* (1877) and *A Doll's House* (1879) is probably closest, though Ibsen's hand in the late 1870s and in the 1880s did not change greatly. It has also been suggested (by Francis Bull, *Centenary Edition*, XIX, pp. 25–26) that the use of the word 'handling' (Act) in this manuscript, rather than the word 'akt', tends to place it somewhere in the period 1873–8; this same scholar reports, however, that the evidence of the kind of paper used for this draft does not very happily support this supposition. The handwriting is carefully formed; but the presence of a number of corrections, together with the experimental changes in the characters' names—Fru Gurid to Fru Gunhild, Arne to Pejk, Ingeborg to Gertrud—so characteristic of Ibsen's *draft* manuscripts, seems to argue against the acceptance of this manuscript as a fair copy.

The version translated in this volume is as it was before the corrections were made on it; subsequent alterations to the draft are shown as editorial insertions. It is not known—though one imagines it is unlikely—whether the work ever progressed beyond these first four sides. The manuscript is now in the University Library, Oslo.

Changes in the characters' names over the four documents are as shown in the following table:

	Grouse in Justedal (1850)	Olaf Liljekrans (1857)	Mountain Bird (1859)	Opera (late 1870s?)
Bridegroom	Bjørn	Olaf Liljekrans	Knut Skytte	[Olaf]
Groom's parent	Bengt af Bjerkehoug	Kirsten Liljekrans	—	Fru Gurid/ Fru Gunhild
Betrothed	Mereta	Ingeborg	Ingeborg	Ingeborg/ Gertrud
Betrothed's parent	—	Arne	Ivar	Arne/Pejk
Elfin girl	Alfhild	Alfhild	Alfhild	?
Peasant youth	Einar	Hemming	Svend	Espen
Minstrel	Harald/Knud	Thorgjerd/ Thorgejr	Thorgejr	Torgejr

3. PRODUCTION AND PUBLIC RECEPTION

For the first performance of *Olaf Liljekrans* on 2 Jan. 1857, with music by G. Schediwy, Ibsen served not only as producer but also apparently as costume designer. The *Regiebog* for this year contains skeleton production notes for the play, written in Ibsen's own hand. A sample extract is given on pp. 708–9.

A number of costume designs—at least eight—executed by Ibsen himself in his Bergen period have also survived in the form of water-colour sketches; they all pretty clearly relate to *Olaf Liljekrans*. A full account, including six black-and-white reproductions, is to be found in Otto Lous Mohr, *Henrik Ibsen som maler* (Oslo, 1953), pp. 37 ff. They show a number of characters in peasant national costume; and Mohr comments that the strong colours, the stances of the figures, the arrangements of the costumes and the splendour of the jewellery are reproduced with the greatest care and with considerable technical facility:

'Arne Eggen has shown [article in *Oslo Illustrerte*, no. 21, 1928] that six of these costume pictures represent the chief characters in Ibsen's youthful romantic drama *Olaf Liljekrans*. Eggen identifies five of the roles as: Olaf

Liljekrans himself, in two versions, one of them more a preliminary sketch; his mother Kirsten Liljekrans; Ingeborg and Alfhild, both in splendid wedding dresses with bridal crowns; and Arne of Guldrik, Ingeborg's father.

'. . . The list can now be supplemented with yet another water-colour from the same series. It is reproduced by Poul Reumert in his *Masker og Mennesker*. . . . And yet another costume drawing has found its way to the Theatre History Museum at Chrsitiansborg in Denmark. . . . It is possible that it shows the child of nature, the "mountain maid" Alfhild, in her everyday dress.'

Eggen claimed that the drawings illustrated not merely the characters in general, but how they might have appeared in the big dramatic scene of the play, the wedding scene in Act II:

'The old woman [Lady Kirsten], with her arms crossed, with her worn, hard-bitten face, with the severe and scornful look in her eyes . . . such desperation and such rage must Ibsen have wanted to depict. . . .

'The young woman [Ingeborg] with the blonde Norwegian look, infinitely tender and pure in expression, with embarrassed grief in the features of her face, with her deep, fathomless, trusting eyes. . . .

'And who is the young lad [Olaf] standing in an attitude that is caught in quite masterly fashion? He looks as though he wants to advance and retreat. At one and the same time. He wrinkles his brow. His eyes stare, bewildered. . . . He faces a fearful choice.'

The play was given two performances. The public's expectation was high after the comparative success of *The Feast at Solhoug* the year before, but the new play was no great triumph:

'Already by mid-afternoon all the tickets had been sold, and the demand for tickets was so great—according to *Bergensposten*—that only the more robust were able to force their way through to the box-office under the not very happy arrangements they had at that time for selling tickets. The author was called for, but . . . for most people the play was a disappointment. . . .

'Neither the play itself nor its performance was discussed in *Bergensposten*; *Bergens Tidende* on the other hand (a new publication, which, however, had only a brief life) contains a quite long and in part rather sarcastic account of the form and content of the play, which the reviewer finds long-drawn-out and overdone, even though he was attracted by "the beautiful versification and the often wonderfully fine poetic images".' (T. Blanc, *Norges første nationale Scene* (Christiania, 1884), pp. 213 f.)

One correspondent in the Christiania *Aftenbladet*, writing from Bergen and signing himself 'n–s', complained that one performance was not enough to make sense of this very confused play; Ibsen wrote a sharp rejoinder which was published on 13 Feb. 1857:

'Olaf Liljekrans' Play in 3 Acts

Act I	Entrance	Characters	Exit	Remarks	Sc	Properties	For use by:
Sc 1.	—	Thorgjerd/Choruses off-stage, l. and r.	Thorgjerd rear	Set: from prompt book.	1	Some birch branches with leaves	Stage./Trees./
2.	Arne, Hemming and 2nd Chorus from r.	Arne, Hemming and 2nd Chorus		Lighting: /ditto./			Arne's men
3.	Lady Kirsten and 1st Chorus from l.	As above. Lady Kirsten and 1st Chorus					Lady Kirsten's men
4.	Ingeborg and bridesmaids from r.	As above. Ingeborg and bridesmaids	Thorgjerd, to l.		4	Knives Axes	
5.	Thorgjerd from rear	As above. Thorgjerd	All off r. and l.				
6.	—	As above except Thorgjerd	Ingeborg, l.				
7.	—	Ingeborg and Hemming	Olaf r.		7	A bracelet of gold	Ingeborg
8.	Olaf, from rear	Hemming and Olaf	Hemming l.	8th scene: Moon rises	8	Some wild flowers	Olaf Liljekrans
9.	Olaf, from r.	Olaf/alone			9	Some wild flowers	Off-stage, r.

No.	Alfhild, from rear	Olaf. Alfhild	Both off, r.	N.B. Chorus off-stage		A garland of birch leaves	Alfhild
10.			Both off, r.	N.B. Chorus off-stage, l. for p. 89	10	A garland of birch leaves	Hemming
11.	Lady Kirsten and Hemming: from l.	Lady Kirsten and Hemming	Hemming l. Lady Kirsten, r. foreground	N.B. Chorus off-stage, l. for p. 93			
12.	Olaf and Alfhild, from r./later Lady Kirsten, from r.	Olaf and Alfhild /later/Lady Kirsten	All except Alfhild off, l.	N.B. Chorus off-stage, l. for p. 98	13	Ingeborg's bracelet	
13.	Arne, Hemming, Ingeborg, 1st and 2nd Chorus, from l.	As above. Arne, Hemming, Ingeborg, the Choruses Alfhild. Thorgjerd	Alfhild off, l.	N.B. Chorus off-stage, l. for p. 100			
14.	Thorgjerd, from rear		Alfhild, l.	N.B. Chorus off-stage, l. for p. 110			

'To Herr n–s of Bergen.

'In a letter contributed to *Aftenbladet* (no. 22) you have among a number of other things given yourself the pleasure of commenting on my new play in the following terms:

'"Since I have spoken so much about the theatre I may as well say a little about the new play that was performed last week; but I have only seen it once, and that is not enough to make sense of all the muddle to be found in it. Nor would the judgement I would then find myself passing be particularly favourable to the author, who in contrast to the rich poetic source he possesses seems to lack knowledge both of the world and of human nature. Therefore more about this when it is next performed."

'Starting a feud with an anonymous correspondent is generally a useless undertaking; but as your above remarks contain, in sum as it were, all the irresponsibility and petulance with which nearly everybody these days capable of using a pen thinks himself competent publicly to dismiss any product in the field of literature or art, I cannot for the sake of the principle involved let your words go entirely without comment.'

He then goes on to demand some fuller explanation of these brief dismissive phrases, challenging the anonymous correspondent to produce evidence for his assertions. His letter was left unanswered.

Ibsen made no attempt to have his play published in book form. The question of publication did not arise again until June 1897 when Julius Elias and Paul Schlenther sent Ibsen a detailed plan for a collected edition of his works in German translation. At first Ibsen was reluctant to have *Olaf Liljekrans* included; his reply of 20 June 1897 showed that he was not prepared to accept *St. John's Night* or *Olaf Liljekrans* in the edition: 'The two other plays I wrote in my youth I have never wanted to publish and I do not wish them translated', he wrote. When the German editors demurred, however, he eventually gave in over *Olaf Liljekrans*, and on 1 September sent them the manuscript with the suggestion that Emma Klingenfeld should do the translation. But he refused to compromise on *St. John's Night*.

It was not until 1902, in the supplementary volume to the first collected edition of his works in Norwegian, that *Olaf Liljekrans* was published in its original language.

On 18 June 1911 there was a performance in English of this play at the Rehearsal Theatre, London, by the Ibsen Club; Valentine Penna played Olaf, and Pax Robertson played Alfhild. An English translation was published in 1921 in *Early Plays by Henrik Ibsen*, translated Anders Orbeck, New York, pp. 127–238.

SELECT BIBLIOGRAPHY

IBSEN 1850–1857

1. *General*

Paul Botten Hansen, 'Henrik Ibsen', in *Illustreret Nyhedsblad*, 19 July 1863.
Herleiv Dahl, *Bergmannen og byggmesteren: Henrik Ibsen som lyriker* (Oslo, 1958).
Brian Downs, *Ibsen: The intellectual background* (Cambridge, 1946).
Chr. Due, *Erindringer fra Henrik Ibsens ungdomsaar* (Copenhagen, 1909).
Chr. Due, 'Ibsen's early youth', in *The Critic* (N.Y.), xlix, 1906, pp. 33–40.
Gerhard Gran, *Henrik Ibsen, liv og verker* I–II (Christiania, 1918).
J. B. Halvorsen, *Norsk Forfatter-Lexikon 1814–1880*, vol. iii (Christiania, 1892):
    'Ibsen'.
Bergliot Ibsen, *De tre* (Oslo, 1948)—translated by Gerik Schjelderup as *The Three Ibsens* (London, 1951).
Henrik Ibsen, *Efterladte Skrifter*, I–III (Christiania, 1909).
Henrik Ibsen, *Samlede Verker*, 21 vols., ed Bull, Koht and Seip (Oslo, 1928–57).
Henrik Jæger, *Henrik Ibsen 1828–1888: Et literært livsbillede* (Copenhagen, 1888).
Theodore Jorgenson, *Henrik Ibsen: A study in art and personality* (Northfield, Minn., 1945).
Erik Kihlman, *Ur Ibsen dramatikens idéhistoria* (Helsingfors, 1921).
Halvdan Koht, 'Shakespeare and Ibsen', in *Journal of English and Germanic Philology*, xliv, 1, 1945, pp. 79–86.
Halvdan Koht, *Henrik Ibsen: Eit diktarliv*, 2 vols. (Oslo, 1928)—translated as *The Life of Ibsen* I–II (London, 1931). Second revised and augmented Norwegian edition, Oslo, 1954.
Michael Meyer, *Henrik Ibsen: The making of a dramatist 1828–1864* (London, 1967).
Fredrik Paasche, 'Ibsen og nationalromantikken', in *Samtiden*, xx, 1909, pp. 511–20, 645–57.
Emil Reich, *Henrik Ibsens Dramen*, 14th ed. (Berlin, 1925), pp. 1–39.
D. A. Seip, 'Henrik Ibsen og K. Knudsen', in *Edda*, i, 1914, pp. 145–63.
P. F. D. Tennant, *Ibsen's dramatic technique* (Cambridge, 1948).
Valfrid Vasenius, *Henrik Ibsen: Ett skaldeporträtt* (Stockholm, 1882).
Roman Woerner, *Henrik Ibsen*, 2 vols. (Munich, 1900, 1910).
A. E. Zucker, *Ibsen: the Master Builder* (London, 1930).

2. *Catiline*

A. R. Anderson, 'Ibsen and the classical world', in *The Classical Journal*, xi, 1916, pp. 216–25.

H. Anker, 'Catilina: Ibsens dramatiske prolog', in Edda, lvi, 1956, pp. 41–90.

S. Bretteville-Jensen, 'Lys og mørke i Catilina', in Edda, lxvi, 1966, pp. 225–35.

S. Bretteville-Jensen, 'Blomstersymbolikken i Catilina', in Ibsen-Årbok 1967 (Oslo, 1967), pp. 61–71.

A. H. Ebbestad, 'Catilina—Cinq-Mars, bisp Nikolas—Richelieu', in Ibsen-Årbok 1955–56 (Skien, 1956), pp. 186–97.

J. Faaland, Henrik Ibsen og antikken (Oslo, 1943).

Pavel Frænkl, Ibsens vei til drama (Oslo, 1955).

K. Haugholt, 'Samtidens kritikk av Ibsens Catilina', in Edda, lii, 1952, pp. 74–94.

R. Iversen, 'Henrik Ibsen som purist i Catilina, 1875', in Edda, xxx, 1930, pp. 96–100.

A. H. Lervik, 'Ibsens verskunst i Catilina', in Edda, lxiii, 1963, pp. 269–86.

H. Meyer-Benfey, 'Ibsen in seinem ersten Drama', in Germanisch-romanische Monatsschrift, xvii–xx, 1932, pp. 267–77.

O. Myre, 'Henrik Ibsen och Catilina', in Bokvännen, v, 3, 1950, pp. 72–7.

J. C. Pearce, 'Hegelian ideas in three tragedies by Ibsen: Catilina, Kongsemnerne, Kejser og Galilæer', in Scandinavian Studies, xxxiv, 1962, pp. 245–57.

E. Skard, 'Kjeldone til Ibsens Catilina', in Edda, xxi, 1924, pp. 70–90.

T. T. Stenberg, 'Ibsen's Catilina and Goethe's Iphigenie auf Tauris', in Modern Language Notes, xxxix, 1924, pp. 329–36.

A. Thuesen, 'Om førsteutgaven av Ibsens Catilina', in Morgenbladet, no. 80, 11 March 1922.

A. Thuesen, Henrik Ibsens 'Catilina': Et hundreårsminne (Oslo, 1950)—reprinted from Morgenbladet, no. 84, 12 April 1950.

R. Sokolowsky, 'Henrik Ibsens Römerdramen', in Euphorion, ix, 1902, pp. 593–608.

H. B. G. Speck, Katilina im Drama der Weltliteratur (Leipzig, 1906)—pp. 67–71: 'Henrik Ibsen'.

3. Ibsen in Christiania 1850–1

Ø. Anker, 'Ibseniana og Bjørnsoniana fra Kristiania teatrenes arkiver', in Edda, lvi, 1956, pp. 111–61.

Ø. Anker, Christiania theaters repertoire 1827–1899 (Oslo, 1956).

H. Jæger, Norske Forfattere (Copenhagen, 1883)—pp. 160–207: 'Fra Henrik Ibsens Rusaar'.

Halvdan Koht, Henrik Ibsen i 'Manden' (Det Norske Videnskaps-Akademi i Oslo, II, Hist. Filos. Klasse, 1928), no. 1.

P. G. La Chesnais, 'Norma, ou les amours d'un politicien', in La Revue Européenne, 1928, pp. 337–56.

Sigmund Skard, 'Forfatterskapet til Andhrimner', in Festskrift til Halvdan Koht (Oslo, 1933), pp. 295–310.

4. *The Burial Mound*

M. B. Ruud, 'Ibsen's *Kjæmpehøien*' in *Scandinavian Studies and Notes*, v, 1918–19, pp. 309–37.

A. M. Sturtevant, '*Kjæmpehøien* and its relation to Ibsen's romantic works', in *Journal of English and Germanic Philology*, xii, 1913, pp. 407–24.

5. *Ibsen in Bergen 1851–7*

William Archer, 'Ibsen's Apprenticeship', in *Fortnightly Review*, lxxv, Jan. 1904, pp. 25–35.

S. Arestad, 'Ibsen and Shakespeare: A study in influence', in *Scandinavian Studies*, xix, 3, pp. 89–104.

Harald Beyer, 'En samtale mellem Henrik Ibsen og Peter Blytt', in *Nordisk Tidskrift*, v, 1929, pp. 497–504.

T. H. Blanc, *Norges første nationale Scene* (Christiania, 1884).

T. H. Blanc, *Christiania theaters historie 1827–1899* (Christiania, 1899).

Peter Blytt, *Minder fra den første norske Scene i Bergen i 1850-Aarene* (Bergen, 1907).

Gran Bøgh, *Henrik Ibsen på Ole Bulls Teater. Tekst til to tegninger* (Bergen, 1949), 16 pp.

Francis Bull, 'Fra Ibsens og Bjørnsons ungdomsaar i Bergen', in *Edda*, x, 1919, pp. 159–64 ['Foreningen af 22 December'].

Marie Bull, *Minder fra Bergens første nationale Scene* (Bergen, 1905).

Herleiv Dahl, 'Ibsen og Johanne Louise Heiberg', in *Ibsen-Årbok, 1954* (Skien, 1954), pp. 95–108.

Marcus Grønvold, *Fra Ulrikken til Alperne* (Oslo, 1925).

S. Johannessen, 'Ibsen's Theater a Museum', in *American Scandinavian Review*, xxvii, 4, 1939, pp. 313–16.

Erik Kihlman, 'Ibsen och det franske dramaet', *Festskrift til Yrjö Hirn* (Helsinki, 1930), pp. 217–40.

F. Kummer, *Dresden und seine Theaterwelt* (Dresden, 1938).

Hans Midbøe, *Streiflys over Ibsen* (Oslo, 1960).

Otto Lous Mohr, *Henrik Ibsen som maler* (Oslo, 1953)—also in English: *Henrik Ibsen as a painter*.

Oskar Mosfjeld, 'Ibsen og J. L. Heiberg', in *Ibsen-Årbok 1954* (Skien, 1954), pp. 82–94.

Robert Neiiendam, *Mennesker bag masker* (Copenhagen, 1931).

Roderick Rudler, 'Myten om den hapløse teatermann Henrik Ibsen', in *Aftenposten*, 30 March 1960.

Roderick Rudler, 'Scenebilledkunsten i Norge for 100 år siden', in *Kunst og Kultur*, xxxiv, 1961.

Roderick Rudler, 'Ibsens første teater opplevelser', in *Ibsen-Årbok 1960–62* (Skien, 1962), pp. 7–35.

Roderick Rudler, 'Ibsens debut som sceneinstruktør, in *Ibsen Årbok 1960–62* (Skien, 1962), pp. 46–81.

Roderick Rudler, 'Ibsen som teaterstipendiat i Danmark', in *Nordisk Tidskrift*, xxxvi, 1961, pp. 369–85.

A. M. Wiesener, *Henrik Ibsen og 'Det norske theater' i Bergen, 1851–57* (Bergen, 1928).

Z. Zini, 'Il noviziato teatrale di Henrik Ibsen, gli anni di Bergen, 1851–57', in *La Cultura* (Rome), xii, 1933, pp. 861–84.

6. *St. John's Night*

J. Lescoffier, '*La nuit de Saint-Jean*, une œuvre inédite de Henrik Ibsen', in *Revue Germanique*, i, 1905, pp. 298–306.

A. M. Sturtevant, 'Ibsen's *Sankthansnatten*', in *Journal of English and Germanic Philology*, xiv, 1915, pp. 357–74.

H. Wiers-Jenssen, 'Ibsens *Sankthansnatten*' in *Aftenposten*, no. 655, 24 Dec. 1912.

7. *Lady Inger*

O. Brahm, *Kritische Schriften*, I (Berlin, 1915)—pp. 224 ff.

O. Dalgard, 'Studiar over *Fru Inger til Østeraad*', in *Edda*, xxx, 1930, pp. 1–47.

F. Engelstad, '*Fru Inger til Østrât* jubilerer' in *Morgenbladet*, 4 Jan. 1955.

H. Freihow, 'Fragment frå Ibsenstudium: *Fru Inger til Østrât*', in *Syn og Segn*, 1928, pp. 713–45.

Y. Hauge, '*Fru Inger til Østrât*—en nederlagets skikkelse', in *Morgenbladet*, 17 Feb. 1961.

F. Helveg, 'Om æmnet i H. Ibsens drama: *Fru Inger til Østrât*', in *Nordisk månedsskrift for folkelig og kristelig oplysning*, i, 1875, pp. 63–72.

R. Iversen, 'Trumpeterstråle og Jens Bjelke', in *Nysvenska Studier*, x, 1930, pp. 66–9.

G. Krog, '*Fru Inger til Østraat*', in *Nylænde*, xvi, 1902, pp. 89–93.

A. Thuesen, 'Om førsteutgaven av Ibsens *Fru Inger til Østeraad*', in *Morgenbladet*, no. 319, 13 Oct. 1923.

O. Vindenes, 'Sproget i *Fru Inger til Østeraad*', in *Acta Philologica Scandinavica*, xi, 1936–37, pp. 201–49.

8. *The Feast at Solhoug*

S. Bødtker, *Kristiania-premierer gjennem 30 aar*, I–II (Christiania, 1923–4)—I, pp. 41–3: 'Gildet paa Solhaug'.

Francis Bull, 'To franske beretninger om opførelsen av *Gildet paa Solhoug*, 1856', in *Edda*, xxxi, 1931, pp. 106–8.

J. Jansen, '*Gildet paa Solhaug* som historisk skuespill', *Ibsen Årbok, 1964* (Skien, 1964), pp. 98–113.

A. H. Lervik, '*Gildet på Solhaug* og samtidens kritikk', in *Edda*, lxix, 1969, pp. 40–6.

F. Paasche, *Gildet paa Solhaug* (Smaaskrifter fra det litteraturhistoriske seminar, v, Christiania, 1908).

R. Rudler, 'Ibsen som turnéleder', in *Edda*, 3, 1970, pp. 163–8.

A. Thuesen, 'Om førsteutgaven av Ibsens *Gildet paa Solhoug*', in *Morgenbladet*, no. 47, 10 Feb. 1923.

Raymond Williams, *Drama in Performance* (London, 1954)—pp. 75–84: '*Hamlet* and *The Feast at Solhoug*'.

9. Olaf Liljekrans

Arne Eggen, '*Olaf Liljekrans*', in *Oslo Illustrerte*, xxi, 23 May 1928.

Henrik Jæger, '*Olaf Liljekrans*', in *Nyt Tidsskrift*, vi, 1887, pp. 76–103.

Otto Lous Mohr, *Henrik Ibsen som maler* (Oslo, 1953).

Fredrik Paasche, '*Olaf Liljekrans*; et bidrag til studiet av Ibsens forhold til vore viser og sagn', in *Maal og Minne*, 1909, pp. 142–61.

P. R. Sollied, 'Fjeldfuglen', in *Ibsen-Årbok 1954* (Skien, 1954), pp. 154–72.

A. M. Sturtevant, '*Olaf Liljekrans* and Ibsen's literary development', in *Scandinavian Studies and Notes*, v, 1918–19, pp. 110–32.